The Encyclopedia of
Tibetan Symbols and Motifs

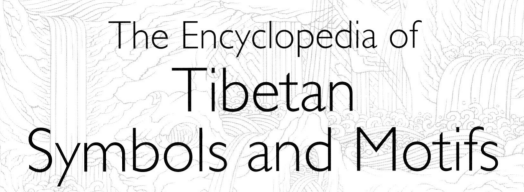

The Encyclopedia of
Tibetan
Symbols and Motifs

Text and Illlustrations by

Robert Beer

Serindia Publications
Chicago and London

ISBN 1 932476 10 5

Published by
Serindia Publications, Inc.
PO Box 10335
Chicago, IL 60610
www.serindia.com

Fourth Impression 2004

British Library Cataloguing-in Publication Data
A catalogue record for this book is available from the British Library.

Typeset by Toby Matthews
Printed in China through Midas Printing (Asia) Ltd.

Contents

List of Plates   IX

Acknowledgements   XI

Introduction   XII

Chapter 1: Landscape Elements   3

ROCK FORMATIONS   4

SIMULACRA IN LANDSCAPE   11

WATER   13

FIRE (FLAMES)   17

AIR (CLOUDS)   24

SKY   31

RAINBOWS   31

AURA LINES   34

Chapter 2: Flowers and Trees   37

THE LOTUS   37

LOTUS SEATS OR THRONES   38

FLOWERS, FLOWER BUDS, AND LEAVES   41

TREES, LEAVES, AND FRUIT ROUNDELS   48

Chapter 3: Animals   59

ANIMALS MYTHOLOGICAL AND REAL   59

THE WINDHORSE AND THE FOUR SUPERNATURAL ANIMAL

GUARDIANS OF THE FOUR DIRECTIONS   60

    The horse   60

    The windhorse   60

    The supernatural animals of the four directions   62

THE DRAGON   63

GARUDA   65

THE MAKARA   68

THE FACE OF MAJESTY   69

THE NAGA   70

    Nagas and the civilisations of the Indus Valley   72

THE THREE VICTORIOUS CREATURES OF HARMONY   73

DOMESTIC AND WILD ANIMALS   75

    Animal heads   77

TIGER, LEOPARD, SNOW-LION AND HORSE 78

THE ELEPHANT 80

DEER 83

BIRDS 85

THE SIX-ORNAMENT THRONE OF ENLIGHTENMENT 88

THE ANIMAL THRONES OF THE FIVE BUDDHAS 90

THE FIVE BUDDHA FAMILIES – COLOURS, ORIGINS, AND CONTRADICTIONS 92

Chapter 4: Narrative Subjects 95

THE FOUR FRIENDS OR HARMONIOUS BROTHERS 95

THE SIX SYMBOLS OF LONG LIFE 95

DIAGRAM OF SHAMATHA MEDITATION PRACTICE OR 99
   'TRANQUIL ABIDING'

Chapter 5: Cosmology 103

MOUNT MERU 103

THE VEDIC LEGEND OF THE CHURNING OF THE OCEAN 109

THE MANDALA OFFERING 110

THE TIBETAN ASTROLOGICAL DIAGRAM 115

   The legend of the golden tortoise diagram 115

THE 'ALL-POWERFUL TEN' INTERLOCKING SYLLABLES 123

THE STUPA 127

   The symbolism of the stupa 128

   The proportions of the stupa 130

   The eight great stupas 133

THE CHANNEL-WHEEL SYSTEMS 135

   The Hindu Kundalini Yoga chakra system 137

   The Buddhist channel-wheel system 140

     Sexuality, conception, and birth 140

     The death process 141

     The generation and completion stages of Highest Yoga Tantra 141

     The Kalachakra channel-wheel system 145

     The numerical symbolism of the channels and channel-wheels 146

Chapter 6: Mudras 149

Chapter 7: The Chakravartin and his Seven Precious Possessions 160

THE SEVEN POSSESSIONS OF THE CHAKRAVARTIN 162

   The precious wheel 162

   The precious jewel 162

   The precious queen 162

   The precious minister 163

   The precious elephant 163

   The precious horse 163

   The precious general 163

THE SEVEN SECONDARY POSSESSIONS OF THE CHAKRAVARTIN 163

   The sword 163

   The naga skin 164

   The royal house 164

   The robes 164

The royal gardens   164

The throne   164

The boots   165

Chapter 8: Auspicious Symbols   171

THE EIGHT AUSPICIOUS SYMBOLS   171

The lotus   173

The endless knot   173

The golden fishes   176

The parasol   176

The victory banner   180

The golden treasure vase   181

The white conch shell   183

The wheel   185

THE EIGHT AUSPICIOUS SUBSTANCES   187

The mirror   188

The medicine   188

Curds or yoghurt   188

Durva grass   189

The bilva fruit   189

The right-spiralling conch   190

The vermilion powder   190

Mustard seed   190

THE FIVE OFFERINGS OF SENSORY ENJOYMENT   194

The mirror   194

Musical instruments   198

Perfume and incense offering   201

Fruit and food offerings   201

The silk cloth   202

Chapter 9: Various Peaceful Offerings, Jewels, and Ritual Implements   205

THE THREE JEWELS   205

THE SEVEN WATER BOWL OFFERINGS   205

JEWELS   208

GZI STONES OR BEADS   212

THE ROSARY   215

Rudraksha beads   216

HAND-HELD PLANT ATTRIBUTES   217

ASSORTED RITUAL IMPLEMENTS   219

THE POSSESSIONS OF AN ORDAINED MONK   226

MONASTIC AND CEREMONIAL MUSICAL INSTRUMENTS   228

Chapter 10: The Wheel of Sharp Weapons   233

THE VAJRA   233

The iconography and symbolism of the five-pointed vajra   235

THE CROSSED VAJRA   239

THE BELL   243

The iconography and symbolism of the bell   243

THE RITUAL DAGGER   245

The iconography and symbolism of the phurba   247

THE HINDU KAPALIKAS, PADMASAMBHAVA, AND THE BUDDHIST
    MAHASIDDHAS — 249
THE EIGHT GREAT CHARNEL GROUNDS — 250
THE HINDU RITE OF CREMATION — 252
THE TANTRIC STAFF — 252
  The iconography of the khatvanga — 253
  The khatvanga: outer symbolism — 254
  The khatvanga: inner symbolism — 254
  The khatvanga: secret symbolism — 254
THE HAND DRUM — 258
THE THIGHBONE TRUMPET — 259
THE CURVED KNIFE OR CHOPPER — 261
THE SKULL OR SKULL-CUP — 263

HAND-HELD WEAPONS AND THE RITUAL IMPLEMENTS OF SPECIFIC DEITIES — 267
ARCHERY — 267
THE BOW — 268
THE ARROW — 270
  The flower attributes of the bow and arrow, hook and noose — 274
THE SWORD — 276
  The scorpion and the scorpion-hilted sword — 277
THE TRIDENT-PIKE, CADUCEUS, DART, AND OTHER BLADED WEAPONS — 280
THE SPEAR, LANCE, JAVELIN, HARPOON, AND PIKE — 282
THE TRIDENT — 285
THE CLUB — 287
THE SNARE, NOOSE OR LASSO — 294
THE IRON CHAIN — 295
THE SHIELD — 298
THE DISCUS — 298
THE AXE — 300
THE ELEPHANT GOAD OR IRON HOOK — 302
MISCELLANEOUS RITUAL IMPLEMENTS AND WEAPONS — 302

Chapter 11: Wrathful Offerings, Tormas, and Ritual Fire Hearths — 311
DISMEMBERED BODY PARTS AND OTHER WRATHFUL ATTRIBUTES — 311
FLAYED SKIN FRIEZES OF WRATHFUL OFFERING ASSEMBLIES — 313
THE EIGHT ATTIRES OF THE CHARNEL GROUNDS — 315
THE SIX BONE ORNAMENTS AND THE FIVE-SKULL CROWN — 318
RITUAL OFFERING CAKES AND THREAD CROSSES — 320
THE WRATHFUL OFFERING OF THE FIVE SENSES — 325
THE INNER OFFERING — 327
  The visualised generation of the inner offering
    according to the Chakrasamvara Tantra — 327
  The symbolism of the inner offering — 330
  The possible origins of the inner offering substances — 331
AN ASSEMBLY OF WEAPONS AND WRATHFUL OFFERINGS — 333
THE RITUAL FIRE OFFERING — 335

Chapter 12: Geometric Borders, Patterns, Designs, and Motifs — 343

SELECT BIBLIOGRAPHY — 375

List of Plates

PLATE   PAGE

The Eight auspicious symbols   II

Chapter 1: Landscape Elements

1 Landscape elements   2
2 Rock formations   5
3 Rock formations   6
4 *Vajra*-rock promontories, rock stacks and Mt Meru   7
5 *Vajra*-rock promontories and cliff faces   8
6 Various landscape elements   9
7 Foliage around rock formations   10
8 Simulacra forms in landscape   12
9 Stylistic representations of water   14
10 Turbulent water   15
11 Waterfalls   16
12 Flame formations   18
13 Flame formations   19
14 Flame formations, haloes and aureoles   20
15 Flame aureoles and haloes   21
16 Symmetrical flame aureoles as 'mountains of fire'   22
17 *Makara*-tail aureoles as 'rosaries of light'   23
18 Cumulus and cirrus cloud formations   25
19 Cumulus, cloud streets and mare's-tail clouds   26
20 Mare's-tail and swirling cirrus clouds   27
21 Cloud formations, horizontal cloudbanks and cloud streets   28
22 Cloud formations in mountainous landscapes   29
23 Cloud thrones   30
24 Rainbow phenomena   33
25 Shading of flames and clouds   35

Chapter 2: Flowers and Trees

26 Lotuses and water lilies   36
27 Lotus thrones   39
28 Lotus thrones and their shading   40
29 The shading of flowers, buds and leaves   42
30 Stylised peony and chrysanthemum blossoms   43
31 Flowers, buds and leaves   44
32 Compostion of flowers, buds, fruit and leaves   45
33 Flower buds   46
34 Leaves   47
35 Various trees (willow, mango, aloewood, etc.)   51
36 Various trees (fig, peach, sandalwood, etc.)   52
37 Various trees (cypress, fig, peony, bamboo, etc.)   53
38 Various trees (palm, banana, plantain, peony, etc.)   54
39 Various trees (mango, sandalwood, fig, pine, etc)   55
40 Entwining trees, leaf and flower roundels   56
41 Stylised leaf and fruit clusters   57

Chapter 3: Animals

42 The windhorse and the 4 supernatural creatures   61
43 Dragons   64
44 The *garuda*   67
45 The *makara*   68
46 *Kirtimukha*, the face of glory   69
47 The *nagas*   72
48 The three victorious creatures of harmony   74
49 Various domestic and wild animals   76
50 Animal heads   77
51 Tiger, leopard, snow-lion and horse   79
52 Elephants   81
53 Deer   84
54 Birds   86
55 Water birds   87
56 The six-ornament throne of enlightenment   89

Chapter 4: Narrative Illustrations

57 The four friends   94
58 Shou-lao (symbols of longevity) & the Four Friends   97
59 The six symbols of longevity (in Tibetan style)   98
60 Diagram of *shamatha* meditation practice   101

Chapter 5: Cosmology

61 Cosmology of Mt Meru   102
62 The Mt Meru mandala offering   112
63 The thirty-seven heaps of the mandala offering   114
64 The Tibetan astrological diagram   117
65 Astrological symbols   119
66 The all-powerful syllables of the Kalachakra   125
67 Variations of Kalachakra's all-powerful syllables   126
68 The eight great stupas   131
69 Construction grid of the enlightenment stupa   132
70 The Buddha image and the stupa   134
71 The Hindu Kundalini-yoga chakra system   137
72 The Buddhist channel-wheel system   143

Chapter 6: *Mudras*

73 *Mudras* made by combining both hands   151
74 Single hand *mudras*   155
75 Hands holding ritual implements   157
76 Footprints, handprints and foot postures   159

Chapter 7: The Chakravartin and his Seven Precious Possessions

77 The seven precious possessions   166
78 The seven precious possessions   167
79 The seven secondary possessions and insignias   168
80 Jewel heaps and the seven insignia   169

Chapter 8: Auspicious Symbols

81 The eight auspicious symbols   172
82 The eight auspicious symbols   174
83 Variations on the eight auspicious symbols   175
84 The parasol or umbrella   177
85 The victory banner   179

PLATE		PAGE
86	Treasure vases, pennants, banners and flags	182
87	The conch shell	184
88	The golden wheel	186
89	The wheel and deer emblem	187
90	The eight auspicious substances	191
91	Offering bowls with eight auspicious substances	193
92	The peaceful offering of the five senses	195
93	Offering of sight – the mirror	197
94	Offering of sound – musical instruments	199
95	Offerings of touch – taste and smell	203

Chapter 9: Various Peaceful Offerings, Jewels and Ritual Implements

96	The seven offering bowls	204
97	Alms bowls, offering bowls and vases	207
98	Jewels and gemstones	211
99	*Gzi* stones	214
100	The Buddhist rosary	216
101	*Rudrakasha* beads	217
102	Plant and grain attributes	218
103	Ritual vases and assorted ritual implements	220
104	Assorted ritual implements	225
105	The possessions of an ordained monk	227
106	Monastic and ceremonial musical instruments	228
107	Peaceful offerings and ritual objects	230

Chapter 10: The Wheel of Sharp Weapons

108	The nine-pronged *vajra*	232
109	The various forms of the *vajra*	237
110	*Vajras*, crossed-*vajras* and *vajra*-chains	238
111	The *vishvavajra*	241
112	The *vishvavajra*	242
113	The ritual bell	245
114	The ritual dagger	248
115	The *khatvanga* or tantric staff	255
116	The *khatvanga* or tantric staff	257
117	The hand drum and the thigh-bone trumpet	260
118	The curved-knife and chopper	262
119	The skull-cup	265
120	The bow	269
121	Arrows, divination arrows and mirrors	273
122	Flower bows and arrows	275
123	Various swords	279
124	The trident pike, caduceus, dart, water-knife etc.	281
125	The spear or lance	283
126	The trident	286
127	Tally-sticks, clubs, skull-topped clubs, etc.	289
128	Maces, clubs, forked-sticks, ploughs, etc.	291

PLATE		PAGE
129	Skeletons and skeleton-clubs, etc.	293
130	Snares and iron chains	297
131	The shield, discus or *chakra*, etc.	299
132	Axes, iron hooks and elephant goads	301
133	Miscellaneous ritual implements and weapons	304
134	The five magical weapons of Palden Lhamo, etc.	307

Chapter 11: Wrathful Offerings, Tormas, and Ritual Fire Hearths

135	Dismembered body parts, etc.	312
136	Flayed skin friezes, carrion birds, corpses etc.	314
137	Tiger and leopardskin *dhotis*, etc.	317
138	Skulls and skull offerings	319
139	Thread crosses, tormas, ransom offerings	323
140	The wrathful offering of the five senses	326
141	The inner offering	328
142	An assembly of weapons and wrathful offerings	334
143	Designs for the *homa* fire hearths	337
144	Designs for the *homa* fire hearths	339
145	A variation of the square hearth design	340

Chapter 12: Geometric Borders, Patterns, Designs and Motifs

146	Composite Chinese pictograph	342
147	Meander and endless knot designs	344
148	Geometric border designs	345
149	Borders of interlocking chains, knots, etc.	347
150	Repeating knot and swastika patterns and borders	348
151	Repeating swastika borders and patterns	349
152	Endlessly repeating swastika patterns	350
153	Repeating swastika patterns	351
154	Knots and border designs	352
155	Swastika and endless knot borders	354
156	Endless knots	355
157	Endless knots	356
158	Knots, *jui'i* symbols and syllables	357
159	Chinese *shou* or longevity symbols	359
160	Various Chinese symbols and trigrams	360
161	Armour and chain-mail designs	362
162	Border designs and linear brocade patterns	364
163	Geometric border designs	365
164	Brocade pattern designs	366
165	*Makara*-tail scrolls and crests	367
166	Repeating lotus or peony flower designs	369
167	Repeating *vajra* and lotus designs	370
168	Repeating *vajra* and bell upon lotus designs	371
169	Repeating sword and book upon a lotus	372

Note on Transliteration

Many Sanskrit and Tibetan terms are given in the text; italics are used for both (though not for proper names, or certain words which have passed into general English use, e.g. dharma, mandala). Unless otherwise indicated, italicised words are Sanskrit. Tibetan terms appear in brackets, transliterated according to the Wylie system. Sometimes the pronounciation of Tibetan words or names of deities is also given, e.g. Troma Nagmo (Tib. Khro ma nag mo). Where both

the Sanskrit and Tibetan are given, Sanskrit (Skt.) is given first, and Tibetan (Tib.) follows. Diacritical marks have been omitted from the Sanskrit, and the transliteration has been adjusted accordingly: *ri* is used for *ṛ*, *ch* for *c*, and *sh* for *ś* and *ṣ*. Apologies are offered to Sanskrit scholars. With a text of this length, and with the frequent appearance of both Sanskrit and Tibetan, it is very difficult to keep within the bounds of consistency, and inconsistencies will undoubtedly remain.

Acknowledgements

To the countless anonymous artists of Tibet who revealed
the sublimity of divine form.
To the lineages of Mahasiddhas who revealed the bliss of
great immaculate nakedness.
For He who has no name,
And She who cannot be named.

My deepest gratitude is expressed to the many Tibetan lamas who have inspired me through the examples of being
who they are, in particular H.H. The Dalai Lama, Khamtrul
Rinpoche, Apo Rinpoche, Karmapa, Dilgo Khentse Rinpoche, Zenga Rinpoche, Tokden, Dorzong and Choegyal
Rinpoche, and the Tokdens of Tashi Jong. From the Indian
traditions the lives and teachings of Ramana Maharishi and
the incredible Sai Baba of Shirdi have always remained closest to my heart, as have the many saints, sadhus, beggars
and liars of India who taught me things that I needed to
know. Within the Sufi tradition thanks are expressed to Kabir
and Jalaal'uddin Rumi for writing the language of love and
clarity, and to all of those who have had the courage to live
within its light.

For artistic inspiration my gratitude is expressed to the
late John Miles, Khamtrul Rinpoche, Jampa from Lhasa,
Oleshe from Sola Khumbu; and to the living artists Sherab-
palden Beru, Siddhimuni, Udaya and Dinesh, Lalman,
Chewang and Cho Tsering, and in particular to my close
friend and artistic-brother Phuntsog Phrengwa and his wife
Dawa of Sikkim.

I would like to thank Ani Tenzin Palmo who gave me
the courage to finish this work, and my *vajra*-sister and lifelong friend, Ani Jampa – who true to form always arrives at
the beginnings and ends of things.

My deepest thanks are to my dear wife Helen, who endured so many things through and for me with a strength

that belonged to the gods. To my joyful daughters Carrina
and Rosia, who already as budding teenagers are 'wiser than
the horses of instruction'. To Christina Svane and a vow made
beneath the stars of Gyantse. To Liz Specterman, the most
honest and generous friend I have ever known. And to Gill
Farrer-Halls for being here now.

For spiritual and philosophical source material I would
like to thank Karma Phuntsog, Thubten Jinpa, Gyurme
Dorje, Thubten Chodron, Lati Rinpoche, Geshe Tenpa
Dargey, Serkong Rinpoche and many others for their unpublished works; and Martin Willson, Edward Henning,
Martin Boord, Petri the Alchemist, Martin Brauen and
David Snellgrove for their translations and published
works. And especially to my close friend Robert Svoboda
and his lineage of Ayurvedic, alchemical and Indian tantric
transmissions.

For material support I would like to thank Jane Reed,
Noel Forster and the committee of the Harold Hyam Wingate
Foundation in London for funding me and enabling this
project to be realised; and for practical encouragement to
David and Dorothy Ford, Evan Dvorsek, Sean Jones, John
and Anne Driver, Hugh Clift, Pete Fry, Phuntsog and Riga
Wangyal and the staff of Tibet Foundation in London, and
to the staff of Wisdom Books, London.

Thanks are due to Noel Cobb, Linda Baer, Stuart Hamill,
Edie Irwin, Dave Wade, Stephen and Martine Bachelor,
Louise Dubois, Christine Daniels; and to Toby Matthews who
helped in the last stages of designing this book.

And last but not least I would like to thank my publisher
Anthony Aris of Serindia Publications and his wife Marie
Laure, who have always been close friends, but who have
had to suffer with patience, kindness, humour and dignity
the many broken deadlines and vicissitudes of this erratic
human being.

Introduction

Spiritual Window Shopping

These spiritual window shoppers, who idly ask.
"How much is that?" – "Oh, I was only looking".
They handle a hundred items, and put them down again,
shadows with no capital.
What is spent is love, and two eyes wet with weeping.
But these walk into a shop, and their whole lives pass suddenly,
in that moment, in that shop.
"Where did you go?" – "Nowhere".
"What did you have to eat?" – "Nothing much".
Even if you don't know what you want, buy something,
to be part of the exchanging flow.
Start a huge foolish project, like Noah.
It makes absolutely no difference what people think of you.

Jalaal'uddin Rumi (translated by Coleman Barks)

Like Noah, I began a huge foolish project. Ark building has never been easy, especially when you have to do it alone, and when the summer days are long and the seasons appear to be in order. When questioned by consensus reality as to why one has undertaken such a seemingly endless task, Noah knew well the only answer. Vision is sometimes a terrible thing.

Ideas are easy to come by, they spring effortlessly out of the vacuity of the mind and cost nothing. When they are held and projected onto one's self or others they become a project. When the project is enacted it becomes the work, and when the work is completed it appears to be self-existent. Creation is the process of form manifesting from emptiness, where that which arises from the mind comes into existence. Yet the distance between conception and realisation may be enormous, as vast as the distance between stars.

The drawings contained within this book took almost eight years to complete, and form part of a larger series of drawings that span eighteen years of my life. One has to be very careful about what one chooses to trade one's life for, and there were many times when I doubted my own sanity in having undertaken this work. For me the price was high, it wasn't bought cheaply. There was no short cut, no-one to assist, and no-one to refer to. Solitude and despair are close emotional companions, and for me there was much despair in the process. Solitude and joy are close spiritual companions, and simultaneously there were prolonged periods of inspiration, intuition and ecstatic love. Both states – of the most intense visionary luminosity and its absence – are difficult to live with, and always cause insomnia. Like pearls of joy and despair, the necklace of creativity was strung on the continuous thread of perseverance. I was driven by the strength of passion, the work came through me, not of me, like the clear piercing thread of tradition.

Having spent the last thirty years painting, drawing and studying Tibetan art, I am invariably asked the same group of questions:- "How long have you been doing this? How did you first get interested? Where did you learn? How do you manage to make a living? Are you a Buddhist, and do you practice meditation? What does it all mean?"

The first of these questions is easily answered above in a few words, and the last question is perhaps partially answered in the long text of this book. As to the second question, personal history is something that tends to become erased as one focuses upon the aspiration of the present moment. It is inevitably too long a story, and it is only another lifetime. Ultimately anyone's life story is a mythology of dreamlike experiences in time, they have a beginning and an end, but the colour in between is modal. It was my destiny to become involved in Tibetan art, in retrospect I can modally see that the entire universe conspired to make it so. There are meetings, omens, events in each individual's life that clearly point towards the direction in which one's destiny unfolds. We have a choice, we can either follow or ignore them.

But for me personally one specific experience that occurred in time marked a distinct point of change, where there really was no choice. In 1969 and at the age of twenty-one I had already developed an understanding of both Eastern and Western esoteric traditions, and was already painting oriental style imagery. In the autumn of that year I underwent a full blown 'Kundalini crisis' and was catapulted into another reality. This was the end of life as I had previously known it. I spent a large part of the next decade trying to survive the psychic onslaught that spontaneously arises when one loses that seemingly solid sense of self-identity called 'me'. For several years it was relentless, with every aspect of the personality continually disintegrating. There is no language to describe this reality, and the threshold of fear that it evoked was far beyond any existential state of being that I could previously have conceived of. To me, at this point in time, the wrathful deities of Tibetan art were the closest mirror to my internal process. The destruction that these deities inflicted upon the ego was exactly what I was undergoing in my 'divided self'. They automatically became a vehicle of self-expression. The decision to begin to paint them was not academic or philosophical, it was instinctive, intuitive and primordial. This is a short mythology of 'how it all began', the rest is internal.

The answer to the third question – "Where did you learn?" – is that I am essentially self taught. As a child growing up after the second world war my prized possession was a sketch book entitled 'Tanks and How to Draw Them'. From repeatedly copying these drawings until they had been committed to memory the qualities of patience, a sense of perspective, and a meticulous attention to detail began to develop. At sixteen and living 'on the road' I applied to enter art college, but was refused admission because I was red-green colour blind. At this point destiny conspired to introduce me to my first and greatest artistic mentor, John F.B. Miles. John's best friend had committed suicide the week before we met, and I looked just like him. Thus was our destiny sealed. Without doubt, John was the greatest living artist that I ever met. With a passion that transcended insanity, he lived, loved and died for art, leaving behind an as yet unrecognised legacy of the most potent visionary art. The inspirational reality we shared was extreme. John was far larger than life, and he knew it. Until his death in 1997 at the age of 52, we remained the closest of artistic allies.

In 1970 I travelled to India and spent the next five years living there, with a year in Nepal. At Dharamsala in the Himalayan foothills, I lived initially for a year in the same compound as the artist Jampa from Lhasa, painter to H.H. the Dalai Lama. From Jampa's sketches I first learned the iconographical rudiments of the Central Tibetan style. But these were mere preliminaries that I would have to penetrate to a far deeper extent in later years. It wasn't what Jampa did that impressed me, it was who he was. In the early hours of the morning, whilst dogs barked at the moon, ours were the only windows illuminated in the whole valley. Jampa died from cancer and overwork in 1987, but his beaming smile and glowing heart live on with the bodhisattvas.

In Nepal I studied the iconographical grid structures (Tib: *thig tshad*) of the major deities, as compiled by the yogin artist, Gomchen Oleshe of Sola Khumbu. Although I never actually met Oleshe his artistic precision essentially defined my style, and with his death in the late '70's I felt that I had to take on his artistic baton and continue the drawings that he had begun. My last year in India was spent living in the Tibetan Craft Community of Tashi Jong in the Kangra valley. Here I was adopted by my main Tibetan teacher, Khamtrul Rinpoche, and worked for him for a year creating an extensive series of small paintings known as *tsakali*, and used for initiations. Khamtrul Rinpoche was the personification of what many people conceive of as a 'Tibetan Master', except he was the genuine article, and as always truth was far more vivid than fiction. A master of all the Tibetan arts – thangka painting, sculpture, sacred dance, architecture, etc. – Rinpoche was first and foremost a highly realised being, an embodiment of wisdom and compassion. Although Rinpoche had few Western students, amongst them were four ordained nuns; Ani Jampa, Ani Tenzing Palmo, Ani Lodro Palmo, and Ani Zimba. The very existence of these four spiritual ladies has always been of the greatest inspiration to me, and although they wouldn't like to hear me say it, to me they have the purest realisation of all Western dharma practitioners. Khamtrul Rinpoche died in 1980, but his immaculate presence and impeccable activity continue to blossom in my awareness and memory.

In 1976 and back in England I began incorporating airbrush technique into Tibetan imagery. To some this innovation was untraditional, but since these images were primarily created for book illustrations, their purpose was to inspire. In 1980 I began this 'huge foolish project' of iconographical drawings, and this is when the real work of learning actually began. Working with a friend and Tibetan translator, Edward Henning, we set out to produce a work entitled, 'The Deities of the Karma Kagyu Tradition'. From Edward's translations of deity practices (Skt. *sadhanas*) and art commentaries, we began to illustrate and explain the descriptive symbolism of around seventy of the major deities. After two year's work with no funding this project had to be shelved. This pattern of working on various projects without financial recompense or funding was to repeat itself over the next twelve years. Which leads into the fourth question – "How do you manage to make a living?" – The answer is simple – "With great difficulty."

Working independently as a committed artist often carries the stigma of financial struggle. This is amplified a hundredfold within the field of Tibetan Buddhism, where the main emphasis is often on fund raising, and undertaken for the benefit of all sentient beings and the cause of the holy dharma. Although the motivation may be pure its application is often hazardous, resulting in the repetitive strain injuries of exhaustion and poverty to an individual upon whom it is continuously projected. An endless stream of well-intentioned requests for paintings, drawings, logos, designs and information led me to understand the plight of the fruit-laden tree which consistently receives the stones of the passers-by. Eventually it felt like I was being continually asked for glass trinkets, whilst inside diamonds were crystallising. It took me a long time to realise that I should do what I knew I had to do and not what others thought I should do. In 1991 I applied for and received a two year scholarship from the Harold Hyam Wingate Foundation in London, which marked a distinct change in my material destiny and enabled me to bring this work to fruition.

The final question – "Are you a Buddhist, and do you practise meditation?" – is perhaps best answered by silence. Things change, thoughts and appearances incessantly arise and fade, sometimes one is wise, sometimes one is foolish. Essentially one is a human being and aspires to open the human heart to its own infinity, and to accept every affliction of fate as a wound rather than an insult. Geshe Wangchen once said, "Dharma practice is not about sitting quietly on one's bottom somewhere in a corner. It's about living one's life to the full. It's about having the courage to make mistakes and the wisdom to learn from them."

The drawings illustrated in this book attempt to cover the whole spectrum of Tibetan Buddhist symbols and attributes. Many of the individual images I have based upon the finest representational examples found in Tibetan art, yet each of them – being drawn by the same hand – has undergone some degree of stylistic innovation. Much thought went into the layout and design of these illustrations, which are drawn as full compositions rather than assembled collages. The majority of the plates are reproduced in the same size as the originals, but some of the more complex compositions in the first half of the book were drawn slightly larger and reduced to scale. All of the illustrations were drawn with a fine brush and Chinese ink onto art paper, a technical drawing pen was only used for straight lines and circles. Each of the plates took between fifty and two hundred hours to draw. The original drawings have more 'life' than the illustrated reproductions, as the tonal gray or 'soft' lines of the original come out black in mechanical reproduction and some dimension is lost. The 'life' embodied in the originals emanates a peace and stillness which I was never able to attain, and looking at them now is like reading one's diaries from previous years.

The oriental technique of drawing with a line brush rather than a pen is a skill that is virtually unknown in the world of contemporary western art, and I have only come across a few western artists who understand the processes involved. The 'perfect brush' is the Tibetan artist's most important tool, and traditionally each individual artist would make his own brushes from selected hairs. Some people claim that oriental artists use one-hair brushes or the single eyelash of a camel. But this is a myth, the single hair of any animal is not porous and is incapable of holding colour or ink; the liquid pigment is only held within the brush by the surface tension created between a converging group of hairs. Tibetan artists use the hairs of a wild cat, marmot or sable for their brushes, and Indian miniature painters use the curved hairs of a squirrel. The brush that I used for these drawings was of sable hair, which had been broken down to a fraction of its original thickness by previously being used as a shading brush for painting. By the time the brush had been broken down to around thirty hairs at its tip it would become incapable of retaining enough ink to create even a short line. Consequently I would have to load the brush with ink many times to create a long curved or continuous line. To pick up a line exactly where you left off and continue it in precisely the same curve requires much skill and long periods of breath retention. A pen cannot be used successfully for Tibetan art; it is too rigid, picks up the minute vibrations of the hand which the brush's flexibility absorbs, and gives an even thickness of line. The line-weight of a brushstroke is controlled by pressure, creating a thicker line at its curved centre and thinner lines at its tapering ends. Although the proverb says – 'It's a poor workman who blames his tools' – the fluidity of a perfect brush is a delight to use, whilst the stubbornness of a bad brush is extremely frustrating.

In contrast to the many years spent drawing the illustrations, the text for this book was written over a much shorter period. To complicate things, destiny – as it always has in my life – threw a hand of wild cards into the equation, and every distraction that possibly could have arisen during this period inevitably did, usually with relentless complexity.

The text of this book is not an academic work or a thesis. I have no credentials and no lineage of transmission from which to feel the security of traditional descent. The text 'just came into existence' in the same way that the drawings had come into existence, and essentially represents my own understanding of Buddhist symbolism at this time. Most of this information has arisen from four converging avenues of investigation. The first is the intellectual aspect of having read a large amount of often obscure literature on the traditions, history and development of Hinduism and Buddhism. The second is the visual aspect of having studied many thousands of Tibetan thangkas. The third is the intuitive aspect of repeatedly drawing these symbols, where the visually impressed images 'reveal their nature' in the same way that an explorer begins to map unidentified areas through his expanding familiarity with the terra incognito in which he finds himself. The fourth is the spiritual aspect of understanding what these symbols really mean as pure expressions of the Buddhist teachings.

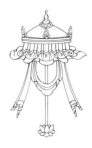

The rich assembly of Tibetan Buddhist symbols are purely an encapsulation of the manifold qualities of the enlightened Buddha-mind, manifesting as the absolute realisation of wisdom and compassion. Like a perfectly cut and many-faceted jewel that refracts a myriad rays of light throughout the universe, the nature of the light is one, although its aspects of illumination appear to be many. Most of the symbols that arise in Tibetan art are of Indian Buddhist origin, and many of these symbols already existed in ancient India prior to the advent of Buddhism itself. I have tried to explain the origin of these ancient symbols and their incorporation into Mahayana and Vajrayana Buddhism, along with the various esoteric levels of symbolic interpretation placed upon them.

The indisputable Indian origin of most of these symbols inevitably poses the question – "What is it that distinguishes Tibetan Buddhism from early Indian Buddhism?" In his book *The Jewel in the Lotus* (Wisdom Publications. London. 1987), Stephen Bachelor writes, "In their presentation of Buddhism, then, the Tibetans did not diverge greatly from their Indian forerunners in terms of doctrinal content but in the ways in which they organised this content into systematic stages leading to enlightenment. It is the logic of the Buddhist path which is Tibetan, not the individual doctrines or insights which are arranged in the light of this logic. What gives Tibetan Buddhism its own peculiar flavour, therefore, is not any uniquely Tibetan ingredient, but the way in which these common Buddhist ingredients have been blended together in the Tibetan mind." As a westerner practising Tibetan art another cultural ingredient has inevitably been added to this unique blending.

Vajrayana Buddhism is one of the most complex of all metaphysical systems known to man, and to try to explain its symbolic content with clarity and simplicity is certainly not an easy task. There are now believed to be more than two thousand extant Tantric Buddhist texts, which makes the Vajrayana the most voluminous of all the Buddhist traditions in its textual source material. Although none of the Vajrayana deities are illustrated or described in this work, the conceptual setting in which they arise – their landscape environment and thrones, their gestures, ornaments, attire, attributes and offerings – are all explained in detail. In essence what is presented in this work resembles a certain kind of thangka known as 'an assembly of offerings' (Tib. *rgyan tshogs*) where the whole spectrum of peaceful and wrathful attributes and offerings to the deities are represented, but the images of the deities themselves are absent.

Starting with landscape elements, flora, fauna and narrative subjects, the first four chapters begin to introduce the reader to the background composition of a Buddhist thangka. A section at the end of Chapter Three introduces the conceptual framework of the Five Buddha Families, an understanding of which is vital to the mandala principle on which the foundations of Vajrayana Buddhism rests. Chapter Five concerns cosmology, and the last section on the Buddhist channel-wheel systems – where the tantric theories of human conception, embryonic development, maturation, the death process and rebirth are explained in relationship to the 'generation and completion stages' of the profound 'Highest Yoga Tantra' systems – essentially forms the key to an understanding of the deep inner symbolism of Vajrayana Buddhism. The complexity of this subject – which is in practice only fully understood through experiential realisation rather than intellectual comprehension – is extremely difficult to convey, and I have tried to explain it in as clear and simple a manner as possible to enable the reader to have at least some insight into the incredible beauty, richness and sophistication of these Vajrayana practices.

Chapters Six to Nine describe hand gestures known as *mudra*s; the possessions of the *chakravartin* or 'universal monarch'; and the various groups of auspicious symbols, offerings and ritual implements that are generally associated with peaceful deities.

Chapter Ten, on ritual implements and weapons, is the longest chapter of this book and is divided into three sections. The first section describes the four important ritual objects of the *vajra*, crossed-*vajra*, ritual bell and dagger. The second section describes the tantric yogin and yogini attributes of the tantric-staff, hand drum, thigh-bone trumpet, curved-knife and skull-cup. The third section describes the array of hand-held weapons, beginning with the bow and arrow, and ending with certain obscure or magical weapons of specific deities.

The main part of Chapter Eleven describes the charnel-ground attributes, attires, ornaments and symbolic offerings associated with wrathful deities. The following section covers in some detail the visualisation practices, symbolic meanings and possible sources of origin of the extremely esoteric 'inner offering'. This chapter concludes with the various hearth designs employed in the sacred fire rituals or *homa*. The final chapter of this book consists of twenty-four full page drawings of various border patterns, designs and motifs.

Throughout the text I have used the traditional English terms found in many of the 'classical' translations of the Buddhist scriptures to describe the various listings of enlightened qualities. These terms – such as wisdom and method (or skilful means); the six perfections of generosity, morality, patience, effort, concentration and wisdom; the four 'immeasurables' of compassion, love, sympathetic joy and equanimity – are all 'relative' with no verbally definable 'absolute'. Their meanings are essentially inspirational, and continually deepen in interpretation to accord with the Buddhist practitioner's emotional, mental, psychological, philosophical and spiritual capacities. Their 'absolute' meaning exists only within the enlightened mind, where they spontaneously manifest as the innate radiance of the Buddhas' infinite clarity and boundless love.

Most probably this book cannot be assimilated in its entirety in a single reading. Readers with little knowledge of Buddhism may find much of it complex and dense – reflecting perhaps the commonly held perception that Tibetan Buddhism is ritually complicated, too colourful a subject to be readily accessible to the western mind. It is hoped that, for those who persevere in their personal study of Buddhism, the incredible depth of the symbolic meanings discussed here may increasingly clarify over the course of time. The most excellent reference source for concise explanations of Buddhist terminology employed within my text is to be found within the 'Glossary of Key Tibetan, Buddhist and Sanskrit Terms' in *A Handbook of Tibetan Culture* (Rider and Shambhala. London and Boston. 1993), compiled by Thubten Jinpa and Gyurme Dorje. I am also greatly indebted to Martin Willson for allowing me to use his 'General Index and Glossary' (compiled for a forthcoming volume on a collection of *tsakali* paintings), which has been of invaluable assistance in my writing of this book.

When I first began studying thangka painting in India during the early '70's textual information and visual reference material were not easily obtainable. The language barrier was a great obstacle as few Tibetans spoke English, and many competent refugee scholars and artists were forced to work as manual labourers on Indian road crews in order to earn a livelihood. Over the last three decades Tibetan Buddhism – with its infinite gradations of penetrative insight into the layers of self-centred 'human conditioning' that veils our essential nature – has had a potent impact upon the existential intelligence and inquisition of the western psyche. Many books have now been published on Tibetan Buddhism and culture. In the field of Tibetan art there are now quite a few beautifully illustrated books on Tibetan thangkas with full-page colour reproductions. Although I have many of these books in my own private collection and have spent many hours 'absorbing the essence' of the finest and most favoured of these images, the text that accompanies these illustrations is often disappointing.

The trend amongst western scholars and dealers in Tibetan art has been to approach the subject from the conventions of art history and criticism – where the provenance, identification, dating, style and cultural influences are discussed, along with an often unnecessary verbal description of the painting – but very little is written about its iconography, symbolism or real meaning within a purely Buddhist context. Often these thangkas are incorrectly identified, and where the deity's often highly specific attributes are listed many errors and omissions may occur. Deity identification is essentially of little value without an understanding of the qualities of the deity, and these qualities have everything to do with the Buddhist teachings, yet little to do with art history. 'Naming the names' is perhaps akin to trainspotting, or to knowing the names of everyone in a crowded room and something of their dress sense or style – but unless one goes beyond the superficial and gets to know these people in their full and unique individuality, they will always remain strangers. Pablo Picasso once said, "There is no such thing as ancient or modern art. There is only good and bad art." A Tibetan artist would readily

agree with this statement, knowing that a thangka is good when it is iconographically correct and painted with patience and devotion, and bad when it contains iconographical errors and is poorly painted.

Vajrayana Buddhism is little understood in the West, yet there is hope for the future. The transmission of the teachings is still in its infancy, but many seeds of wisdom and compassion have germinated, taken root and begun to blossom into maturity. Tantra is even more misunderstood, often being equated in the Western World with hedonistic sexuality and the dynamics of interpersonal relationships. One of the meanings of the word tantra is 'weaving', and one of the meanings of the word *sutra* is 'thread'. This implies that the 'expansion' (Skt. *tan*) of weaving depends upon the establishment of a continuous thread. Without a deep and firm grounding of the Buddha's spoken discourses or *sutra* teachings as the 'thread', one may easily end up weaving a veil of illusions as insubstantial as the fabled 'Emperor's new clothes'.

It must be emphasised again that the understanding presented in this book is my own understanding at this time of my life, and is in no respect a 'definitive truth'. In many sections of the texts I have thrown caution to the wind and gone out on a limb in introducing certain controversial theories. In all humility I accept full responsibility for these theories, which are based upon an extensive network of tangential information which is only briefly alluded to in the text. At the worst these tangents may be ridiculed, at their best they may inspire further research.

The possession of an extensive knowledge of Vajrayana Buddhism is commonly held in awe by a newcomer to the Tibetan teachings. Yet the difference between an accumulation of knowledge and the development of wisdom may be enormous – 'there are the learners and there are the learned; memory maketh the one, philosophy the other'. Knowledge is communicable, wisdom is not. The content of this book represents a body of knowledge that can lead to the development of wisdom. Yet paradoxically, although it has been my destiny to live within and explore this knowledge, I am strangely detached from it. Much speech leads inevitably to silence, and when I repeatedly penetrate to the depths of these symbols and the truths that they point to, I feel that in front of all this divine beauty I really understand nothing.

Robert Beer

Oxford
Midsummer's Night 1999

Too much good luck no less than misery
May kill a man condemned to mortal pain,
If, lost to hope and chilled in every vein,
A sudden pardon comes to set him free.

Beauteous art, which, brought with us from heaven,
Will conquer nature; so divine a power
Belongs to him who strives with every nerve.
If I was made for art, from childhood given
A prey for burning beauty to devour,
I blame the mistress I was born to serve.

Attributed to Michelangelo (1475–1564).

Plate I: Landscape Elements

Chapter One
Landscape Elements

The drawings on Plates 1 to 24 illustrate examples of the five great elements: earth, water, fire, air, and space, as they are represented in the landscape of Tibetan art. The element earth is depicted by rock formations, caves, meadows, mountains, and simulacra in landscape; water by lakes, rivers, and waterfalls; fire by flame motifs and aureole flames; air by cloud formations; space by sky, aura lines, and rainbows.

Plate 1 depicts an abstract composition of these landscape elements, with turbulent water in the foreground; rock formations, water, trees, and waterfalls in the middle ground; clouds and mountain peaks in the far ground; and the sun, moon, stars, and entwining rainbows in the sky. Although such an abstract and dense composition would never be compounded within the spacious landscape of Tibean art, all of the individual elements are drawn in a conventional Sino-Tibetan style.

Anatomically earth represents the skeletal body of nature, water its life veins, fire its warmth and complexion, air its breath, and space its consciousness. As pure symbols earth is represented by a yellow square, water by a white circle, fire by a red triangle, air by a green semi-circle or crescent, and space by a dissolving blue drop (Tib. *thig le*). Three-dimensionally the elements are represented by a yellow cube (earth), a white sphere (water), a red conical pyramid (fire), a green hemisphere (air), and an ethereal dissolving drop or vanishing point (space). Esoterically earth is represented by the yellow Sanskrit syllable *Lam*, water by the white syllable *Vam*, fire by the red syllable *Ram*, air by the green syllable *Yam*, and space by the blue syllable *Ham*.

There are few rules that govern the painting of landscapes. Other than the fact that the landscape should be beautiful, pleasing, inspiring, and in accord with its compositional subject, the artist is given free rein to express his vision.

The simplest rendition of a landscape may consist only of a tonally shaded background, from green at the bottom through to the deep blue of the sky at the top. This gives the impression that the deities in the composition float in space. Mandalas, too, may be painted against such a gradated background, and above a low horizon; this creates the impression of the mandala appearing in the clear space of the sky.

A common rendition of a landscape usually places the horizon roughly in the centre of the painting, with a subtly gradated sky ornamented with cloud formations rising to a deep blue at the top. The lower foreground consists of sloping green meadows or hills, often with grassy tufts along their ridges, and lakes, low clouds, rocks, flowers, and offerings strategically placed amidst the shaded meadows. The hills on the horizon are sharply defined against the paleness of the low sky; clouds and snow peaks may rise behind the hilly meadows.

Paintings depicting biographical subjects, such as events in the lives of lamas or yogins, will usually have recognisable sites or buildings painted in a stylised form. In the case of wandering ascetics, who travelled widely through the Himalayan areas, these representations could be purely imaginative as the artist would rarely have visited or recorded these places. The very fact of the artist's geographical confinement within the Tibetan plateau gave Tibetan art its unique and specific visionary quality. In a landscape dominated by vast empty spaces, under a deep azure cloudscaped sky, with the contrasting terrain of deep valleys and high mountain peaks, with lakes, waterfalls, cliff and rock outcrops, the soul of the landscape itself became the essence of the artist's inner vision.

As breathtakingly majestic as the external world appeared, it was still but a pale reflection of the internally visualised worlds of the deities' paradise realms. Descriptions of dimensions which were permeated with rainbow light, iridescent colour, divine perfume, and heavenly music, only served to heighten the perceptions of an artist's visionary reality. Here, in a landscape which was lit up from within, perspective, scale and shadow lost their logical solidity. A distant mountain peak possessed the same clarity and importance as a foreground flower. Nothing was hinted at or alluded to: everything in a composition existed in a state of independent 'Is-ness' and the same meticulous detail and clarity was applied to each component. Yet the whole is always more than the sum of its parts.

Visualised descriptions amplify nature's creations by enhancing the intensity of colours. Objects appear as self-illuminated and composed of the five precious substances of gold, silver, coral, pearl and gemstones. Gemstone comparisons include emerald, beryl, crystal, diamond, sapphire, lapis lazuli, amber, turquoise, and ruby. "A glint of red appears in the rock face, and suddenly the whole cliff is lit up with ruby" (Rumi).

The most finely painted thangkas display much of these other worldly qualities, the whole composition possessing a highly integrated structure and sublime grace. Such works are described as 'divinely inspired'; they radiate an innate tranquility where the deities' qualities shine through. In this respect they may also be classified as the 'self-consecrated' works of a divine artist, yet in reality they are essentially a product of much time, patience, and attention to detail.

Paintings of the Sixteen Arhats made in the 'Chinese style' are prime examples of such visionary works. The choreography of movement and of spatial relationships between the figures, landscape, flowers, trees, wildlife, and offerings, exhibit a fluent vocabulary in the language of line. The colours are exquisitely shaded, rocks glow with an inner warmth, a flower radiates an inner purity, an image of divine grace has been captured and held in a stolen or frozen moment of time.

Wrathful forms similarly exhibit such refined qualities. The dynamic movement of a wrathful deity's body is echoed in its flowing hair and the twisting mass of flames which engulfs its form. Mountains, clouds, rocks, and water may be more angular, billowing, convulsed or turbulent, yet their expression reveals an equally infused grace. Whether dynamic or static, visions of the divine are infinite, reflecting that pure, still moment of 'seeing'.

ROCK FORMATIONS

The depiction of rock formations and landscape elements in Tibetan painting reveals a strong influence from Chinese art. During the fifteenth century an artist named Menla Dondrup from Eastern Tibet developed a painting style known as the Menri, which emphasised a far more realistic treatment of landscape than the previously ornate styles from Nepal, Kashmir, central and Western Tibet. During the sixteenth century three further styles developed in Eastern Tibet, known as the Mensar or 'New Menri', the Khyenri, and the Karma Gadri. Each of these styles incorporated elements of Chinese Ming style painting with its spaciousness and natural depiction of landscape elements. From the late seventeenth century cultural ties with China brought a stronger parallel between Eastern Tibetan and Chinese artistic influences.

Under these influences landscape composition moved from a static ornate tranquility into a dynamic vehicle of poetic expression, through the medium of line and form. The most potent representation of this dynamism is found in the depiction of rock formations, outcrops, and cliff faces. The most favoured colour scheme for shading these rocks was with blue and green. Azurite blue and malachite green, the two mineral pigments derived from natural stone deposits, were symbiotically suited to rock shading. Each of these mineral pigments produced three colour grades in their grinding process – a light, middle, and dark hue. Rocks were predominantly shaded in dark blue tones on their extremities, fading to a light blue or green tone in their interior. The rock outlines and inner striations would be defined in a dark indigo outline, using bold, angular, and tapering brushstrokes. Individual striations could be shaded with colour dyes, or alternated blue and green, to produce a jewel-like glowing texture. Brown, ochre, or grey rock-shading could complement the blue-green shading of rock areas to create a spectrum of various hues, the hard edges of the rocks seeming to solidify as they emerged from their amorphous light interiors. The outline brushstrokes of the rock striations revealed the bold thrusting tectonic movements within the rock faces. Gold highlight lines, running parallel and inside of the dark indigo outlines, gave the rocks a luminosity, enhancing their appearance as precious stones.

Plates 2 and 3
Illustrated here are examples of rock formations drawn mainly in the Karma Gadri style. Fantastic rock shapes have always held a fascination for the human imagination, their sculptural forms evoking mythological legends or episodes in local folklore. Ornamental rocks are a feature of oriental gardens, such as Japanese Zen gardens or miniature bonsai tree arrangements.

Natural spiral structures in rocks, such as those which resemble the twist of a conch shell and especially those which spiral to the right, are regarded as being highly auspicious. Caves that bear a resemblance to the opening or lip of a conch shell, or the marks of some other auspicious sign, are regarded as highly sacred. The sanctuary of a cave's orifice symbolised the womb of earth, and the presence of a freshwater source nearby rendered it fertile. The location and naming of caves by their natural signs, historical or legendary occupants, and their affiliation with local animal or spirit entities, were usually firmly established. Many caves were famous, particularly those associated with great masters such as Guru Rinpoche, Yeshe Tsogyel, or Milarepa, and became places of pilgrimage. Sometimes paintings of rock orifices or fissures reveal hidden treasures in their interiors, such as texts, vases or jewels;

Plate 2: Rock formations

Plate 3: Rock formations

Plate 4: *Vajra*-rock promontorics, rock stacks and Mt Meru

Plate 5: *Vajra*-rock promontories and cliff faces

Plate 6: Various landscape elements

Plate 7: Foliage around rock formations

these often allude to the 'concealed treasure' traditions (Tib. *gter ma*) of Tibetan Buddhism.

The interior lines in the drawings are the rock striations, which would be both shaded and outlined in gold and dark indigo. The tops of cliff or mountain buttresses could be capped with snow or grass turf.

Plates 4 and 5

These drawings illustrate examples of '*vajra*-rock' formations. These are the rocky islands or promontories on which rest deities and their lotus seats. Wrathful deities in particular are usually depicted on *vajra*-rock islands or cliffs. The visualisation practice (*sadhana*) of Vajrakilaya describes the *vajra*-rock as the seat of all wrathful deities, composed of all kinds of precious substances. In the *sadhanas* of wrathful deities such as Vajrakilaya, Mahakala, and Ekajati, the triangular *vajra*-rock – shaped like the wrathful element of fire – arises as the 'reality source' (Skt. *dharmodaya*; Tib. *chos 'byung*) from the syllable *E*, which arises out of emptiness (see page 348). The syllable *E* forms the first letter of the Sanskrit word *Evam*, which appears in the opening stanza of many early Buddhist scriptures: "*Evam* [thus], have I heard". The *dharmodaya* emerges from the syllable *E* in the empty expanse of space as a vast inverted pyramid – like the triangular blade of a ritual dagger (Tib. *phur bu*) or the tapering expanse of Mt Meru – indicating the pinning down and stabilising of the earth element.

At the top of Plate 4 are representations of Mt Meru, the axis-mundi of the universe. Below on either side are protruding cliff buttresses. The complex *vajra*-rock at the bottom has many orifices with springs from which water pours. Water often surrounds these *vajra*-rock formations, creating an island.

In the upper area of Plate 5 are examples of snow or grass-covered hills with tapering cliffs. The sharply pointed mountain ranges in the upper background are characteristic of wrathful-deity landscapes. The irregularly formed island rocks in the lower half are typical of the elevated rock formations on which siddhas, arhats, guardian kings, peaceful, and wrathful forms may appear. Occasionally the top surface of such rocks may be painted in a light tone with cloud-shaped marbling decoration; this indicates that the rock is formed of an opaque or translucent precious mineral, such as crystal, agate, ruby, or turquoise.

Plate 6

Illustrated in these drawings are some specific aspects of landscape illustration. At the top of the left-hand column a mythical white snow-lion makes an auspicious appearance amongst snow-capped peaks. Below this are two representations of Mt Himavat, the personification of the Himalayan mountain ranges. The four snow-melt rivers which emanate from the snow peaks are symbolic of the four rivers which spiral around Mt Meru. Below this are a glacial

crevasse on the left, and Mt Kailash on the right. Four great rivers which encompass the Indian subcontinent emanate from the Kailash and Lake Manasarovar region. The striations on its southern face form the arms of a natural swastika. Mt Kailash in western Tibet is sacred to both Hindus and Buddhists, who consider it the abode of Shiva and Chakrasamvara respectively. Since Chakrasamvara tramples on the Hindu god Shiva, any site or shrine sacred to Shiva is also sacred to Chakrasamvara. Below this are three examples of auspiciously spiralling conch-shaped rocks, and below this again are interpenetrated horizontal and vertical rock formations. At the bottom is a fourfold triangular *vajra*-rock on which very wrathful forms, such as Mahakala, stand.

At the top of the right-hand column are sharply pointed mountain peaks which make up the encircling horizon in certain wrathful images, where they form an impenetrable 'iron-wall' of razor-sharp spikes. Below this are a square-topped rock pile with conch-like formations, and a protruding cliff face with multiple buttresses. Below are two hill escarpments with examples of tufted vegetation along their ridges. In the bottom three rows are examples of conifer tree plantations growing along hilltops.

Plate 7

This page of drawings illustrates some examples of the plants, flowers and shrubs that grow around rock formations. Foliated rocks are commonly placed in the foreground of thangkas, particularly in the lower corners, to create vitality, beauty and perspective in the composition. These small rock outcrops are most expressively painted in the Karma Gadri style, with curving or angulated striations. Leaves usually emerge from behind the rock edges, giving the illusion of depth to the meadows in the foreground. Vibrant flowers may also be depicted amongst the foliage, adding grace, harmony, and light to the composition. Where these rock formations appear in the low or mid horizon their bases are usually flat or merge into the meadows. Rolling clouds along low foreground hills are also a favourite embellishment. Small mosses or lichens are sometimes placed along rock edges or cave entrances; these may be depicted as a single, triple, or multiple cluster of dots.

SIMULACRA IN LANDSCAPE

Many of Tibet's sacred sites are geomantic power places endowed with strange landscape, rock, and cave formations. Siddhas who practised at such often remote places would leave evidence of their miraculous accomplishments: imprints of their hands, feet, or ritual objects can be found impressed into rocks or cave walls. Often these imprints appear as if they were virtually fused into the rock whilst it was in a plastic state. There are a large number of such sacred places scattered throughout Tibet and the Himalayan foothills. Many of these sacred sites are attributed to Guru Rinpoche and his consort Yeshe Tsogyel, who performed

Plate 8: Simulacra forms in landscape

miraculous acts across these regions. Caves, grottoes, hot springs, oracle lakes, hidden valleys, and places with fantastic natural geological anomalies are often identified with miraculous activities. 'Self-generating' images also occur at such places.

At Parping, in the Kathmandu valley, are several caves which bear miraculous handprints, bodyprints, and the imprints of Guru Rinpoche's ritual implements. Also to be seen here are a self-manifesting rock image of Ganesh, and two small images of Tara which emerge in clear relief from the rock formation. These Taras appear in reverse as mirror images, their clarity of detail changing perceptibly over the years. At a temple set in a surreal landscape nearby, a large right-spiralling conch shell thrusts itself from a small rock formation. The strange rock formation behind this knuckled white conch is hollow, and the conch can be blown easily. Mt Kailash in western Tibet is endowed with a large number of impressed footprints (Tib. *zhabs rjes*), handprints, and other miraculous signs. In certain areas of this mountain it almost appears as if every other rock is impregnated with some enigmatic quality or simulacra, the surrounding cliffs assuming the forms of temples, forts, or deities. Such imprints have also been left in the Western World. At a site in Scotland clear footprints of the Sixteenth Gyalwa Karmapa have been left on a boulder. These imprints did not manifest immediately but appeared slowly, year by year, on a rock where he had been light-heartedly requested to leave such a sign.

Plate 8

Illustrated here are some examples of simulacra forms which occasionally appear in paintings, especially those depicting the life stories of various siddhas. At the top is a cloud formation which is copied from a thangka depicting the wrathful mandala palace of the goddess Palden Lhamo. The billowing clouds assume the form of caricature spirit faces, representing the ethereal presences which emanate from her domain. In the central cloud are two specific cloud faces, the *kirtimukha* or 'face of majesty' above, and the *simhamukha* or 'lion face' below. On either side dragons descend from the clouds causing a storm of hail, lightning and thunderbolts.

Below this are illustrated three auspicious cloud formations of a parasol and two conch shells. Cloud simulacra of auspicious symbols, or 'seed-syllables' in Tibetan script, are familiar occurrences in miraculous Buddhist legends. Across the middle row are knot, cloth, and flower simulacra in rock formations. Below these, on the lower left, are three examples of conch-shaped rock formations. The conch-shaped rock is considered a highly auspicious natural geomantic sign; monasteries, stupas, and temples are often established in the vicinity of this natural phenomena. Next are a self-manifested *vajra*, *vajra* and bell, bell, ritual dagger and banner, all formed or fashioned from rock. In the lower left corner are two animal-head rock formations, from which emanate springs or rivers. These originate in the sources of the four great rivers – the Sutlej, Indus, Brahmaputra, and Karnali – which arise in the Mt Kailash area. The sources of these four rivers were believed to issue from rock formations resembling the heads of an elephant, lion, horse, and peacock respectively. At Gangotri, the source of the River Ganges in northern India, the river emerges from a glacial outcrop known as Gomukh – the 'cow's head'. This glacial formation, which collapsed several decades ago, took on the simulacra of a cow's head. To the right of these rock faces are the two syllables *Hum* and *A* fashioned out of folded rock. Syllabic rock simulacra are preserved at several temples in Tibet. They usually take the form of the *mani mantra Om Mani Padme Hum*, and are composed of two very distinct minerals, such as white quartz in a black granite stone. In the bottom right is a bear-like creature which represents the mineral magnetite, magnetic iron oxide. Since magnetite attracts other ferrous-based ores, the creature is depicted in the act of devouring rocks. The mysterious properties of magnetic iron, especially meteorite iron, have always been regarded as a magical phenomena.

WATER

Pure water is said to possess eight qualities: it is clear, cool, healing, soothing, odourless, delicious, light, and soft. Rivers, streams, waterfalls, and lakes invariably occur within a landscape composition. The simplest form of representing water consists in painting downward-pointing triangular lakes or pools, which are formed by the intersection of two sloping hills. Such lakes are usually shaded in several horizontal layers, from dark blue at the base into middle blue at the top. These layers display waves, eddies, and small wave crests along their tops. The linear shading of these small waves is from dark blue into light; white highlights may be emphasised on the wave tops. The deep blue of these lakes naturally accords with the reflection of the sky on its calm, mirror-like surface.

Shallower moving waters, such as streams and waterfalls, are usually painted in a lighter blue tonality. Fast-moving streams, descending through mountainous terrain, are often formed of a series of small arcs with light wave crests at their tops. Rivers exhibit a slower motion, often with long wave-formations interrupted by swirling eddies and crests where the river bed is shallower. Waterfalls consist of slightly curving parallel lines, which descend like a curtain from the precipice above, their parallel lines straightening as they fall vertically. At the base of a waterfall is usually a seething mass of wave crests.

Turbulent waters, with long, twisting, or spiralling wave motions and complex wave crests, are extremely difficult to draw. Their colour shading requires much patience. The depiction of turbulent water in Tibetan art is quite realistic. Minute observation of the natural movement of water descending or cascading reveals a complex interplay of changing forms. Wave crests are thrown up by the force of the water and curve into scythe-like shapes, which fall back upon themselves by their own weight and loss of momentum. Little

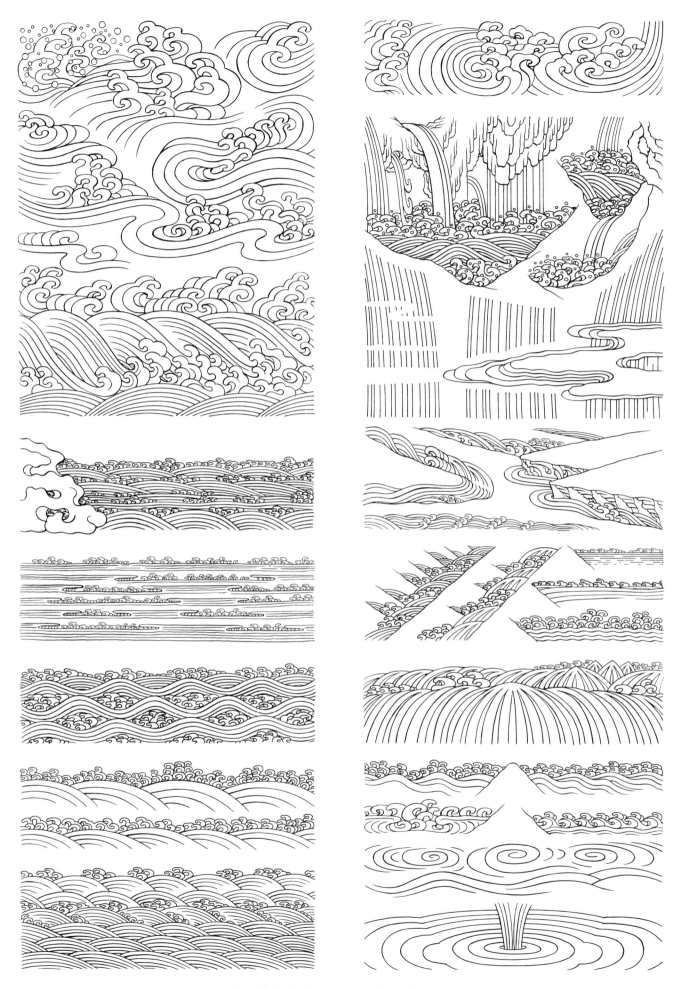

Plate 9: Stylistic representations of water

Plate 10: Turbulent water

Plate 11: Waterfalls

spheres of water are thrown out by these crests, which for an instant appear to hang in space. The subtle shapes of wave crests amidst long gracefully-curving wave lines can be very expressive: one can almost feel the pull of the currents in the water. Wave crests which fall to the left are far easier to draw than those which fall to the right. The tip of each wave crest is usually white; as it recedes deeper into the wave its shading becomes darker. In the painting of turbulent water each individual wave form is usually shaded separately, making the whole process very time consuming.

Plate 9

Illustrated here are various stylistic representations of water. At the top of the left-hand column are details of turbulent water, showing the long curving waves ending in wave crests. Below this are various methods of depicting horizontal wave formations.

A whirpool created by the impact of a descending waterfall is shown at the top of the right-hand column. Below this are details of the seething water at the base of waterfalls. Below this, curtains of mist drift across the faces of waterfalls. The waterfall on the left shows empty spaces across its descending parallel lines; in Chinese art this technique of illustrating empty cloudbanks in front of a waterfall is known as 'cloud bridge'. Below the waterfalls are rivers and tumbling mountain streams. Below again is a horizontally stepped waterfall or weir, its cascading overflow creating a central dome effect. Underneath are two more wave crest formations. At the bottom are whirlpool eddies, and ripples emanating around a lotus stem.

Plate 10

This drawing depicts extremely turbulent water. Billowing wave crests are massed above the larger wave lines, the crests appearing like clawed hands and fingers. The wave formation near the centre is an extremely graceful passage of movements, with its eddies and whirlpools forming very subtle curves. The billowing band of repetitive waves just above the bottom centre shows the counter formation of waves against the wind. The complex serpent-like waves at the bottom cast out a multitude of water globules and bubbles. Such detailed methods of illustrating turbulent water were influenced by Chinese Ming artists, who excelled at evocative landscape painting styles.

Plate 11

Illustrated here is a complex abstract composition depicting waterfalls cascading through rock formations. This brush drawing was one of the most time-consuming images produced for this book, having taken at least a hundred hours to draw.

FIRE (FLAMES)

The billowing mass of flames that surrounds wrathful deities is described as a 'blaze of awareness fire'. The wisdom-energy of wrathful forms blazes like the sun's inexhaustible fire. The sun, as a symbol of pure wisdom, is consumed with fire, yet is not itself consumed. Its eternal fire is inexhaustible. Like the sun, wrathful forms abide in the ultimate emptiness as the immovable sphere of *dharmadhatu* (Skt. *chos dbyings*), the expanse of absolute reality of the enlightened Buddha mind. The wrath of these deities is not ordinary anger, but wisdom-anger manifesting in its most indestructible or *vajra* nature, with the capacity of terrifying all evil spirits such as *maras* and *rudras*.

The twisting and blazing fiery aureole of wrathful forms is also described as *kalagni*, meaning 'the fire of time'; *kalagni* is literally the 'fire at the end of time', the ultimate conflagration of the universe at the end of this aeon. Each *kalpa*, or cosmic cycle of the universe, is believed to end in a penultimate destruction by flood, wind, or fire. Kalagni is also identified astrologically as the 'tenth' planet. Its yellow disc is the uppermost of the four planetary discs on which the deity Kalachakra stands, the three other discs being a black Rahu disc (eclipse planet), a red sun disc, and a white moon disc. In the inner yoga practices of the *Kalachakra Tantra*, *kalagni* is identified with the central channel below the navel centre, and Rahu with the central channel above. The internal fire below the navel centre, awakened in the yoga of 'inner heat', is known as *chandali* (Tib. *gtum mo*), meaning the 'fierce woman'.

Like water, flames are also depicted in a realistic manner in Tibetan art, the twisting tongues of fire rising to a point and reddening at their tips as they cool. Aureole flames can be drawn with much grace and expression of movement, the flames curling to one side and leaping out at the other. This transverse movement of the flames usually enhances the dynamic body posture of the wrathful deity at its centre. The flames may also emanate from the deity's heart, with the tongues of fire reaching out towards the ten directions. Inverted horseshoe-shaped auras of flames can also encircle wrathful forms, but are more common with semi-wrathful or tutelary deities (Tib. *yi dam*), such as Hevajra, Kalachakra, or Chakrasamvara.

In the painting of flames a base of minium orange is usually applied, then each individual flame is shaded with vermilion or red towards its tip. U-shaped folds occur where several flame-tips emanate from the same bank of flames; the tear-shaped centres of these folds are painted in a dark tone to give body to the flame mass. The curling roots of the flames are also shaded into red, as are the inner areas of the U-folds. The outlines of the flames are decorated with matt gold lines, which enhances their luminosity and fiery quality. Thangkas painted on a black background either have vermilion-shaded flames with a gold outline, or gold-shaded flames with a gold outline.

Certain deities, such as Palden Lhamo, are encircled by a mass of wind rather than flames. Wind is coloured and shaded in green, this being the colour of the element air.

Plate 12: Flame formations

Wind is very much like fire in shape and formation, but it has thicker billows than fire and less slender tongues. Consequently it is usually painted with more density and less complexity than flames. Amongst the swirling green winds there usually appear friction sparks, like the lightning produced by crashing thunderclouds. These sparks, often described as radiating in all directions, are painted as small tongues of bright red fire which sporadically lick around the edges of the green winds. On less wrathful forms the element of air may be represented by cumulus cloudbanks outlined with blue and indigo. Flames may also circle around the edge of haloes, such as in paintings of the four guardian kings; the circle of flames usually envelops an inner halo of green, representing the element air. Without air fire would not exist, as wind gives life to fire. The great 'wind at the end of time' causes the *kalagni* fire to blaze ferociously.

Flames also emanate from wrathful offerings, the hot hells, and cremation ground scenes. The sacred fire (*dhuni* or *agnikund*), often kept perpetually alight by ascetics who practise fire rituals, is believed to 'speak' with six or eight voices, the crackling, roaring, snapping flames revealing the prophetic voice of the fire god, Agni.

Plates 12 and 13
Illustrated in these two drawings are examples of flame formations. Sparks are illustrated in the lower left and centre

of Plate 13, where they appear as thin tapering tongues of fire. Flames are not difficult to draw and shade. As with clouds, the curving base lines of flames should always have a rounded edge and not come to a sharp point. Flames gracefully drawn with long slender tips are believed to increase the wisdom of the artist, a belief inspired by the sharp, flaming tip of Manjushri's sword. A stylistic innovation, present in both my flame and cloud drawings, is the addition of an inner crescent-shaped line to the 'U-shapes' in flames, and the 'comma-shapes' in clouds. These inner lines are never illustrated in painting, as the colour contrast between the dark nucleus of the flame or cloud interior and its lighter surrounding areas creates the requisite harmony and depth. I habitually use these inner crescent lines in drawing, as I find they increase perspective, gravity, and complexity, giving a sharper definition to flame and cloud designs.

Plate 14
Illustrated in this drawing is a composition of various flame elements. At the top centre are double-outline flames. These are time-consuming to shade, as their thin outer bands are vermilion-shaded whilst their inner areas are red-shaded, the duo-tone shading blending together at their tips. Their visual effects are both elegant and complex. Across the centre of Plate 14 are examples of the aureole flames which encircle semi-wrathful deities. In the lower area are long

Plate 13: Flame formations

Plate 14: Flame formations, haloes and aureoles

Plate 15: Flame aureoles and haloes

Plate 16: Symmetrical flame aureoles as 'mountains of fire'

serpent-like flames, which are commonly painted around wrathful offerings. In the bottom centre are circulating halo flames.

Plate 15

Shown here are examples of flaming aureole and halo designs. At the top are two complex masses of 'blazing awareness fires', symbolic of the *kalagni* aspect of extremely wrathful forms. At the centre are two inverted horseshoe-shaped flame aureoles, which predominantly surround semi-wrathful deities. Usually the broad inner area of the aura is painted dark blue, or sometimes dark maroon, depending on the textual description (*sadhana*) and colour of the deity depicted. Radiating gold aura lines emanate from the deity's heart centre, terminating just inside of the outer flame aureole. Illustrated here are two rare methods of decorating the inner aura. The drawing on the left shows small, golden, serpent-like tongues of flame radiating from the deity's central or '*brahma* axis': these represent tiny wisdom flames emanating from the pores of the deity's skin. The symmetrical golden dot pattern on the right represents emanating sparks of wisdom. At the bottom are various examples of the flaming haloes which surround the heads of certain

protective deities (*dharmapalas*) or guardian kings. Interspersed throughout these illustrations are individual examples of flame motifs.

Plate 16

Shown here is a detail of a symmetrical flame aureole on the right and left sides. These aureoles often consist of repeat pattern flame sections. They are quite difficult to draw, especially as their sections frequently taper progressively from the apex to the base. Back-tracing or a pinhole pounce (stencil) are commonly used to create symmetry between the two sides. At the top centre is a detail of a complex flame aureole, showing how the two symmetrical sides meet in a single 'S-shaped' flame crest at their apex. The two lower central drawings illustrate the meeting of two continuous, yet separated, flame friezes at their apex.

Plate 17

Illustrated in this drawing are some complex examples of highly ornate flame aureoles, known as '*makara*-tail' designs. The *makara* or crocodile is a mythological sea-monster with

Plate 17: *Makara*-tail aureoles as 'rosaries of light'

an elaborate scrolling tail. These *makara*-tail patterns invariably consist of angled segments which form a repetitive design around the aureole. Commonly there are between eight and twelve segments on each side of the aureole of a standing deity. For seated deities the number is usually between five and eight. There are several methods of colouring the segments. One method consists of shading the *makara*-tail segments with vermilion against an inner background of dark red, as if they were flames. The vermilion can be shaded evenly from a darker tone on the aura's inside to a lighter tone on the periphery. This can be simply achieved by applying a light shading over the whole aureole, whilst ensuring that the original drawing can still be seen through the shading (see Plate 25). The inner background areas can then be painted in dark red, the design lines outlined, and finally filigree gold lines applied decoratively over the vermilion. A more common and lavish method consists in painting the *makara*-tails in pure gold against a vermilion or red background. The gold is then outlined in vermilion and finally skilfully burnished with filigree lines, which follow the curves of the *makara*-tail designs.

Since the aureole represents the wisdom energy of the deity it is frequently specified with deities of the Highest Yoga Tantras (*anuttarayoga tantra*), such as Kalachakra or Chakrasamvara, that the segments are coloured to represent the wisdoms of the Buddha Families. In the case of Kalachakra, each of the Five Buddha wisdoms is represented, the ascending colour sequence of the segments being yellow, white, green, red and blue. In other tantric traditions the central deity itself may embody one of the Five Buddha wisdoms, resulting in only four colours being depicted in the aureole segments.

The same system of coloured wisdom-fire energies is also employed in mandalas. The outer protective circle of most mandalas, known as the 'mountain of fire' (Tib. *me ri*), consists of a similar series of coloured angular fire segments. According to the description of the mandala they can either incline towards the right or left in a clockwise or anticlockwise motion, and usually twenty-four or thirty-two segments are counted. In a four-colour 'mountain of fire' circle the sequence is usually yellow, blue, red, and green. The separate colour segments in both the deity's aureole and mandala circle are shaded in a darker colour tone on their inside, fading to a light tone at their periphery. The deity's aureole is outlined in a darker-tone colour, whilst the mandala is commonly outlined against a very dark background. Inner gold lines are finally painted, which follow the curves of the *makara*-tail swirls.

AIR (CLOUDS)

Tibet is a high altitude mountainous plateau with most of its land over 12,000 feet above sea level. With such rarified air and thin atmosphere, the sky appears a very deep azure blue, and the sun blazes with a searing white intensity. The clarity of distant vision and the sharp contrast of light and shadow light up the landscape, lending much magical enchantment to the view. Colours are very intense in such a light, haloes may appear around the sun, a distant mountain range appears in pristine detail, the proverbial silver lining of clouds may suddenly refract all the colours of the rainbow.

All forms of magical cloud formations are to be found in Tibetan art. They are never heavy or sombre, but always full of light, colour, form, and movement. Clouds wreathe themselves around the high peaks, veiling them in mystery. The convection caused by dramatic mountain rifts results in rapid air currents producing an ever changing cloudscape. Lenticular wave clouds (Altocumulus lenticularis), formed by the wave motion of rising and falling air pockets over mountainous terrain, create strange flying saucer or lens-shaped cloud patterns. Wispy streaks of cirrus clouds create 'mare's tail' streamers, and banks of long stratocumulus clouds produce perspective lines or 'streets' of receding clouds.

Great skill is employed in the depiction of clouds in thangka painting. Cumulus cloudbanks are drawn with a series of stylised arcs which render each cloud as a separate and clearly defined object. Symmetrical cumulus clouds spiral outwards from several focuses, producing a series of levels within each cloud. These focuses are painted as dark 'commas' or 'nipples' within the central spirals of the clouds. This 'nipple', as it is described in Chinese art, is shaped like half of a *yin yang* symbol, and represents the vortex or 'seed essence', which nourishes the cloud and renders it fertile with life-giving rain. Symmetrical cumulus clouds with two or three commas are very common in Tibetan art; they are known as *simhamukha* or 'lion-faced' clouds because of their resemblance to lion heads.

Clouds are usually shaded from a white base-colour at the top to a slightly toned colour at the base. Many colour schemes are used in the depiction of clouds, and their shading as three-dimensional integrated forms can be highly complex (see Plate 25). Flat-based cumulus clouds rest upon a horizontal beam of cloud, which is also shaded along its length. Truncated mare's tails twist away below a cumulus cloudbank, giving the illusion of the cloud moving across the sky. The clearly defined edges of clouds contrast sharply with the dark background of sky or landscape in which the clouds float.

A technique of hard-edge outlining applied to certain clouds involves painting one or more narrow bands of colour (usually light blue or pink) around the cloud's edge. An outer outline of a darker colour – such as indigo – is then applied, often with a serrated edge. Gold is also used within the outlining of some clouds. Gold clouds, depicted on black or vermilion background canvases, are shaded outwards from their interiors using a gold wash technique. The cloud outlines are then painted in thin gold line.

In the wrathful landscape illustration of the 'eight great cemeteries' which are depicted around mandalas, eight specific storm clouds are listed. In the *Vajrabhairava Tantra* these clouds are known as: the proclaiming, the moving, the wrathful, the great proclaiming, the stable, the filling, the effortful, and the furious. Their inner symbolism represents the white drops of *bodhichitta* which descend from the crown centre in the head.

In very finely painted thangkas the choreographic movement of clouds can resemble a divine ballet of the heavens. Dragons and gods, who glide through the clouds, entwine in the passage of clouds across the skies. The delicacy of the shading of clouds, sky, flowers, water, and rock formations are often the most time-consuming aspects of thangka painting. A fine thangka, which took a year to paint, will inevitably display such exquisite shading.

Plate 18

Shown here are complex cumulus cloud formations. At the top are truncated mare's tail cumulus clouds; the ends of their tails can either blend subtly into the sky background or be sharply truncated. Below these are a row of upward-billowing clouds (known meteorologically as Altocumulus castellanus, as they resemble castle walls). In the centre are a stack of cumulus clouds bearing rainwater above their spiral 'nipple' centres. In the lower area are examples of drifting cumulus and cumulonimbus clouds.

Plate 19

Depicted here are mainly dense banks of cumulus clouds interspersed with drifting mare's tail designs. Mare's tail clouds resemble the body and swirling serpent tail of *nagas*. In the upper right corner and mid lower left are examples of Chinese-style 'hook' clouds, which take the form of ghostly drifting mists. The flat-based stratocumulus clouds, illustrated on each side of the middle section, are clouds which are pulled or drawn out by the wind. Their horizontal bases are usually shaded to resemble a rainbow. At the bottom cumulus clouds drift amongst mountain ranges.

Plate 20

Depicted here are examples of swirling clouds and elongated mare's tail cumulus clouds. The linear passages of some of the swirling cloud movements are similar to the drapery billows on the floating silk scarfs of deities. Their integrated cloud components are refined to produce an evocative grace.

Plate 21

Illustrated in this drawing are examples of horizontal cloudbanks. The upper half of the drawing shows a variety

Plate 18: Cumulus and cirrus cloud formations

Plate 19: Cumulus clouds, cloud streets and mare's tail clouds

Plate 20: Mare's tail and swirling cirrus clouds

Plate 21: Cloud formations, horizontal cloudbanks and cloud streets

Plate 22: Cloud formations around mountainous landscapes

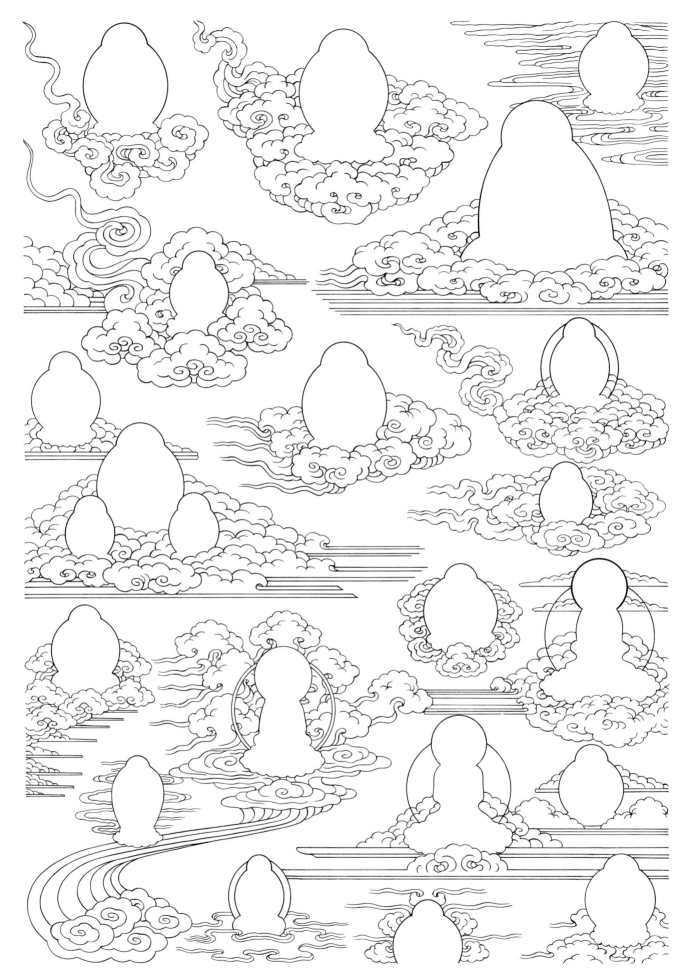

Plate 23: Cloud thrones

of flat-based stratocumulus and cirrostratus clouds, with receding 'streets' of horizontal cloudbanks. The lower half includes various examples of Chinese-style 'hook' mists. Cirrocumulus or 'mackerel sky' patterns are shown on either side with elongated holes. Above the mountain peak on the right are formations of lenticular wave clouds, shaped like long French loaves or fishes. These surreal cloud formations are very rare, and only occur in the lee of mountain valleys. At the bottom cirrostratus and stratocumulus clouds wreathe among the mountains.

Plate 22

Shown here is a complex composition of all the main cloud forms swirling and penetrating mountain landscapes. Because of the high vantage point of Tibetan uplands or mountain passes, clouds often appear below the visible horizon, and one can essentially look down on them.

Plate 23

Depicted here are examples of the 'cloud thrones' on which deities, lamas, or gurus appear, seated and floating in the heavens. These celestial thrones are borne aloft by billowing cloudbanks. The outline of the figures' aureoles are shown in all the main cloud throne arrangements.

SKY

The distant planes of the blue sky and green landscape foreground are always the first areas to be coloured in thangka painting. The sky is usually gradated from a very light blue at the horizon to a deep blue at the top. The smoothest gradations are produced by fine wet-shading, where the colours imperceptibly blend from light to dark tonalities. Line shading is also commonly used to create the sky gradation. Here a series of short darker thin lines are applied from the top downwards, the lines becoming more widely spaced and progressively paler as they descend towards the horizon. Literally thousands of these short thin parallel lines are applied to create the most subtle effect, and much time is required in their rendition. Certain thangkas have skies painted in other colours such as ochre, or with a pale green or light yellow horizon blending into the deeper blues in the upper area. Occasionally two levels of sky are painted with a horizontal bank of cloud dividing them. This system is used in paintings of 'assembly fields' where the paradise realms of Maitreya and Amitabha are placed at the top.

The pure clarity of the sky is metaphorically an illustration of Buddha Mind. Clouds may come and go across the heavens, like the transitory thoughts or delusions which appear to obscure the mind's true nature, yet the nature of the sky remains unchanged. Like the mirror, which is always unaffected by the appearances which arise in it, the sky is clear, transparent, infinite, and immaculate.

RAINBOWS

The rainbow is eternity's expression of momentary delight. It cannot but be auspicious, even if it portends the demise of a great master. For such a master – now merged into the 'clear light' (Skt. *prabhasvara*; Tib. *'od gsal*) of the death process where the most subtle level of mind is experienced as pristine inner radiance (see page 141) – there is no sense of 'leaving behind', the notion of self and others having been transcended. For the 'others', the disciples or students, there is inevitably a great sense of loss and grief. Yet the miracle of the master's departing rainbow will always remain as a great source of strength and inspiration for the devotees.

The vaulting arc of the rainbow is known as 'Indra's bow' (Indrachapa or Indradhanus), one of the weapons of the ancient Vedic sky god, Indra. Natural rainbows are created by the prismatic effect of sunlight on raindrops, reflecting and refracting the sun's rays into spectrums in each individual water drop. The seven colours of the rainbow – red, orange, yellow, green, blue, indigo and violet – naturally blend from red on the outside to violet on the inside. When a double rainbow occurs, the order of colours in the second rainbow is reversed. On rare occasions a similar rainbow effect is created by the moon's light at night, producing a silver 'moonbow' on the opposite side of the sky. A circular rainbow, known as a 'glory', can sometimes be seen from high vantage points, such as hazy mountain summits, forming an aureole halo ring of rainbow light.

In Tibetan art the rainbow takes on a more supernatural manifestation. Since light, colour, dimension, form. and emptiness are the five aspects of visualisation, spectral light becomes its natural essence. The divine forms of deities manifest and dissolve into emptiness, just as a rainbow appears and vanishes into the sky. Rainbows in Tibetan art arise from sacred places or objects, expanding outwards as they twist and interweave with other rainbows or horizontal cloudbanks. They originate from a point and eventually dissolve into space, like winding rivers of light. Multiple strands of rainbows take on the appearance of a horse's tail, rarely following their natural form as arcs. They are coloured in a red, orange, yellow, green, blue sequence, often with alternating straight and wavelike threads of gold line running through each colour.

A well known miraculous phenomena in the Tibetan tradition is the taking of the 'rainbow body' (Tib. *'ja' lus*) at the time of death. This miraculous sign of realisation is known as the 'body of light'. When a great master has attained the realisation of Mahamudra or Dzogchen, the world is no longer perceived as a conceptual concrete dimension. Since all appearances have transformed into the ultimate nature of reality itself – as the fully enlightened 'body' of the Buddha (Skt. *dharmakaya*; Tib. *chos sku*), permeating space with a luminous transparency, there is no solidity or separation. When the notion of an individual self has dissolved, leaving no residue of an intermediary 'I' between unmanifest consciousness and the appearance of a physical universe as light, the physical body is likewise perceived as merely an appearance of light. Such a master will leave instructions that his body should remain undisturbed for a period of days after his death. During this period rainbows emanate from the place where his body rests, as his consciousness remains absorbed in the state of 'clear light'. When the miraculous rainbows have ceased all that remains of the master's bodily form are his clothes, his hair, his fingernails and toenails.

Rainbow phenomena are often witnessed at the cremation ceremonies of highly realised lamas, along with other miraculous sky-signs such as the appearance of eagles, or clouds which take on the colour of rainbows or the forms of auspicious symbols. The lama's cremation ashes are afterwards sifted for relics such as small pieces of bone which bear the images of stupas, deities, or mantras, small coloured stones or jewels, and unburned organs or bones such as the heart or skull.

Transubstantiation is not a phenomenon confined to the Tibetan plateau alone. The Old Testament prophet Elijah ascended to heaven in a chariot of fire borne on the winds of a storm. As an immortal Elijah remains ever present. It is his task to announce the coming of the Messiah, and a goblet of wine is always left for him at the Jewish Pesach or Passover. The Biblical stories of the prophets Elisha and Ezekiel abound with legends of transmutation and resurrection. Likewise the resurrected Jesus ascended to heaven on the third day. The Catholic Church has a rich tradition of the incorruptible relics or preservation of the bodies of several saints. The Indian traditions are full of legends of the miraculous absorption at death (*mahasamadhi*) of its myriad saints. Kabir, the fifteenth-century Indian mystic and poet, transformed his body into a bed of flowers, whilst his Hindu and Muslim devotees were disputing over disposal by cremation or burial. The Indian siddhas Nandanar and Manikavasagar both dissolved their bodies into blazing light. At Virupaksha Cave on Mt Arunachala in south India a sackcloth *lingam* is formed of the compacted ashes of the saint Virupaksha. As burial on this sacred mountain is not permitted, Virupaksha took 'fire absorption' (*agnisamadhi*), dissolving his meditating form into sacred ash (*vibhuti*). Ramana Maharishi, the great Indian sage of Arunachala, said of this occurrence, "When the mind melts away and blazes forth as light, the body is consumed in that process". In the Indian tradition the strange phenomena of 'spontaneous human combustion' (*agnisamadhi*), in which a person immolates from within the body leaving only ashes and often unscorched clothing, is explained as the result of a potent karmic imprint that occurred in a previous life.

Tibetan folklore ascribes various omens to the appearance of rainbows. At the end of every rainbow is believed to be a wish-fulfilling jewel. A moonbow at night is believed to be an ominous sign. A white rainbow augers the death of a yogin. A rainbow around the sun is usually caused by ice crystals, but in Tibet it is seen as an omen of the birth or death of a great teacher.

Plate 24

Illustrated here are various examples of rainbow phenomena. In the central circle is a specific form of the Buddha,

seated in the meditation posture of Amitabha and manifesting in a rainbow body, which radiates as a swirling sphere of rainbow-coloured light. At his heart is the syllable *Hum*, from which the rainbow emanates. Each segment of the radiating circle rotates clockwise in a progressive spectrum of colour. A three, five, or six-colour sequence may be used, a simple three-colour scheme being red, yellow, and blue. A five-colour scheme would rotate through red, orange, yellow, green, and blue. Indigo could be added as the sixth colour. Thin gold radiating lines are painted as embellishments in each individual section. In painted depictions of rainbow-form emanations, the rainbow-circle dominates the composition, the deity's bodily form appearing almost as a faint, yet defined, silhouette behind the rainbow.

One of the most frequently painted forms of a rainbow-body emanation is that of Guru Rinpoche. When Guru Rinpoche is represented as manifesting on the *dharmakaya*, *sambhogakaya*, and *nirmanakaya* levels simultaneously, then three rainbow sources emanate from his crown, throat and heart centres respectively. These three rainbow-spirals merge together very subtly to produce a harmonious triple whirlpool of blended rainbow-waves.

The outer rainbow-circle on the drawing encloses a number of motifs. At the top and bottom straight rainbows interpenetrate rainbow-arcs creating a woven effect. On either side multiple suns emanate on rainbow-arcs. The miraculous appearance of several suns in the sky simultaneously fortells a major event, such as the birth of a highly realised being. The spheres of rainbow light positioned around the outer circle are 'seminal points', known as *bindu* (Tib. *thig le*). The three upper spheres manifest the syllable *A*, the three lower spheres contain variations of the spinning 'wheel of joy' (Tib. *dga' 'khyil*).

In the upper area various rainbows twist and entwine. On the left, mare's tail clouds are borne aloft by rainbow tails. In the upper left and right are two rainbow thrones on which deities sit.

At the top centre is a rainbow throne with a rainbow emanating from the heart centre of the deity within. Rainbow thrones, which emanate from the hearts of gurus or lamas, usually terminate in a small image of the tutelary deity (Tib. *yi dam*) of that particular lama. In the mid centre the moon and sun are encircled by rainbow aureoles. Across the bottom from left to right are illustrated:

A treasure vase emanating rainbow light.

An example of a rainbow body (Tib. *'ja' lus*), which pours out of the apertures of a lama's robes.

The Buddha's cremation casket, which manifests rainbows from within the funeral pyre.

The hair and nails, which alone remain after the attainment of the rainbow body

At the centre, rainbows emanate from within a cremation stupa (high lamas are cremated in specially constructed stupas; the stupa's conical spire is often shortened or omitted to form a chimney flue for the flames).

Plate 24: Rainbow phenomena

On the right are three manifestations of rainbow bodies; the central image depicts a legendary episode where two masters took the rainbow body together.

Behind are a rainbow manifesting from a triple gem, and a series of 'drops' (Tib. *thig le*) strung along rainbows like pearls.

AURA LINES

The aureole designs on Plate 17 also depict the extremities of the radiating aura lines which emanate from a deity's heart. These fine curving gold lines are applied over the deity's inner aura, which is usually coloured dark blue, or occasionally dark red. These fine gold lines alternate between straight and waving. They represent the natural radiance of wisdom and compassion from the deity's body. Just as the sun, glimpsed through a gap in a tree's foliage, casts a radiating network of rays into a shimmering moiré pattern, so are the deity's wisdom and compassion rays made manifest. On some early thangkas the extremities of the aura lines terminate in a curved-over hook on the straight rays, and a small round lotus on the waved rays. The hook represents the 'binding of awareness' or wisdom; and the lotus, compassion or method. If all of the rays terminate in small hooks it represents the deity's ability to hook and draw all sentient beings to its heart.

In the Indian alchemical tradition the deep blue aura of divinities is known as the 'mercurial body' or body of immortality. The beautiful ethereal blue of this aura emanates as the pure consciousness of the deity abiding in the transcendent state of pure compassion and spiritual incorruptibility. The fine gold lines which radiate from the heart of the deity represent the 72,000 purified psychic nerves (Skt. *nadi*) of the deity's subtle or *vajra* body (see page 145).

When Buddhas or bodhisattvas appear in each of the six realms of existence, their wisdom and compassion light-rays emanate from the different psychic centres of their bodies. Very rarely this scheme of assigning radiation aura lines to different focii is depicted in paintings of the 'wheel of life', where the Buddhas of the six realms are represented. When Buddha manifests in the god realm his light rays emanate from the crown centre; in the *asura* realm from the throat centre; in the human realm from the heart centre; in the animal realm from the navel centre; in the hungry ghost realm from the sexual centre; and in the hell realms from the soles of the feet.

Because all Buddhas and bodhisattvas manifest for us in the human realm, then the light rays always emanate from their hearts. An exception to this rule is in the depiction of certain *dakinis*, such as Vajrayogini, where the practice of inner heat (Tib. *gtum mo*) is emphasised; here the light rays may emanate from just below the navel centre.

Each of the six realms of existence have their ultimate origin within the central channel of the subtle body. When dreams arise in the dream state they are caused by the movement of psychic winds around the location of the channel-wheel centres or *chakras*. When these psychic winds carry consciousness up towards the opthalmic centre and crown of the head, dreams of the god, paradise and *asura* realms occur; one ascends or flies in the dream. When the winds radiate outwards from around the heart centre, then dreams of the human realm occur. When the winds descend near the navel and sexual centres, or pass down through the anus, then dreams of the animal realm, spirit realm, and the nightmares of the hell realms occur. One descends into the falling dreams of the three lower realms. A similar process happens during the experiences of the intermediate state (Tib. *bar do*) at the time of death, where the Five Buddhas, the peaceful knowledge-holders, and the wrathful Heruka deities emanate from the heart, throat, and crown centres within the central channel.

Plate 25

This illustration shows examples of the tonal shading of flames and clouds. The twisting tongues and swirling scrolls of the flames in the upper half of the illustration are shaded in progressively darker tones at their extremities, with contrasting lighter shading in their central areas. The tips of the flames are shaded to a deep vermilion or red against their base colour of minium orange. The techniques of shading the U-shaped folds are shown in the upper and lower left and on the centre right of the illustration.

The lower half of this plate depicts the tonal shading of clouds, with the cloud edges shaded from white into their densest colour tones at their centres. The clouds emerging above the hill on the top left of the illustration are simply shaded in monotone towards their centres, whilst those above the hill on the right are also shaded around their central spirals. The horizontally based cloud-streets below are likewise gradated from their edges to their centres or bases, with the horizontal cloud bases of the cloud-streets appearing at the left also shaded. In the bottom area are examples of the more complex shading applied to dense and continuous cloud formations, such as mare's tail and cumulus clouds.

Plate 25: Shading of flames and clouds

26: Lotuses and water lilies

Chapter Two
Flowers and Trees

THE LOTUS
(Skt. *padma, kamala*; Tib. *pad ma chu skyes*)

The lotus is the symbol of absolute purity; it grows from the dark watery mire but is untainted or unstained by it. As the seed of the lotus grows from the water and not from the earth's soil, it is a symbol of divine or spontaneous generation. The lotus seat or throne on which most deities sit or stand symbolises their innate purity; they manifest into cyclic existence, yet they are completely free from its defilements, emotional hindrances, and obscurations.

The lotus opens and closes with the sun. In ancient Egypt the sun was conceived as rising from an eastern lotus at dawn, and setting into a western lotus at sunset. Similarly Surya, the Vedic sun god of India, holds a lotus blossom in each of his hands representing the sun's path across the heavens. Brahma, the Vedic god of creation, was born from a golden lotus which grew from the navel of Vishnu – lotus-born from an umbilical womb. Padmasambhava, the 'Lotus-Born' tantric master who introduced Vajrayana Buddhism into Tibet, was likewise divinely born from a lotus which miraculously blossomed from Dhanakosha Lake in the western Indian land of Uddiyana.

Birth from a lotus implies immaculate conception and that the being born is innately divine and uncontaminated by karmic faults. Thus the lotus, as divine womb, becomes a potent sexual metaphor. *Padma* or *kamala*, meaning lotus in Sanskrit, is a synonym for the female vagina – it is soft and open. *Vajra* is a synonym for the male penis – it is hard and penetrative. The union of *vajra* and lotus is a sexual metaphor for the union of form and emptiness, compassion and wisdom, blissfully uniting in divine embrace. The inner symbolism of sexual union refers to the psychic winds entering and ascending the central channel of the subtle body, and piercing the 'lotuses' of each channel-wheel and causing them to open.

The alluring, wide-open eyes of goddesses and *dakinis* are described as being like lotuses. The most beautiful of female consorts are known as *padmini*; they possess lotus-like fragrance, eyes, breasts, navel, and vagina.

Throughout Egypt, India, Persia, Tibet, China, and Central Asia the lotus was adopted as a sacred symbol. The blue lotus (*Nymphaea caerulea*) was especially venerated in Egypt, its fragrant perfume and aromatic oil essence exuding the scent of divinity. The Indian blue lotus or water lily (Skt. *utpala, nilabja,* or *nilakamala*), is held by deities such as Green Tara, where it represents the deity's purity and compassion. The Tibetan equivalent of the Sanskrit term *utpala* (Tib. *ut pa la*) most commonly refers to the blue lotus, but it is also used to refer to a variety of coloured lotuses. The white lotus (Skt. *pundarika, kumuda*; Tib. *pad ma dkar po*) or edible lotus (*Nymphaea esculenta*) is held by deities such as White Tara, its sixteen or one hundred petals symbolising her purity and the perfection of all her qualities. The red or pink lotus (*Nelembium speciosum*), known as the *kamala* (Tib. *pad ma dmar po*), is the most commonly depicted of hand-held lotuses and lotus seats. The yellow *utpala* lotus is actually not a water lotus or lily; it grows as a small alpine flower throughout Tibet. The black or 'night lotus' is a dark indigo species of the *nilakamala* or blue lotus. In Tibetan iconography the colours assigned to lotuses are white, golden, red, blue, and black.

The lotus in all its colour variations and stylistic forms is one of the most common sacred symbols in Tibetan art. As a symbol of purity, perfection, compassion, and renunciation it is without parallel. Amitabha, the red Buddha of the west, is Lord of the Lotus or Padma family; his fiery red sunset colour and lotus emblem represent the transmutation of passion into compassion or discriminating awareness.

Plate 26

Depicted in this drawing are examples of lotuses and water lilies. Many innovative liberties are taken by artists in their portrayal of heavenly lotuses. The central section illustrates typical stylisations of lotus blossoms which arise from water. Here hybrid multifoliate leaves, derived from the peony and chrysanthemum, replace the circular leaves of the true lotus.

On either side of the drawing are illustrations of fully-opened lotuses, lotus buds, and leaves. Lotus leaves are circular; veined from their centre, they often have splits, and usually float like discs on the water's surface. Yet stylised leaves are often depicted rising on stems above the water, with convoluted or folded forms.

The dark seedpods, illustrated on the middle right, contain circular seeds which float on the water until they find a place to root. Lotus seeds are used to make rosaries (*mala*).

LOTUS SEATS OR THRONES

Some examples of the lotus seats or thrones on which deities sit or stand are depicted in Plates 26 and 27. Viewed from above, the lotus base forms a circular mandala of petals; within this the pericarp or lotus heart rests as a slightly domed green disc. Above this are placed discs of the sun and moon. Seen from the front the lotus seat appears as a slightly curved frieze, with the sun and moon discs forming a cigar shape due to foreshortening.

The lotus symbolises purity and renunciation; the sun disc, ultimate *bodhichitta*; and the moon disc, relative or conventional *bodhichitta*. The Sanskrit term *bodhichitta* (Tib. *byang chub kyi sems*) means 'the mind of enlightenment', which is the foundation of the Mahayana path. Conventional *bodhichitta* refers to the altruistic resolve to attain enlightenment for the benefit of all beings, and ultimate *bodhichitta* refers to the enlightened wisdom which directly realises emptiness through the perfection of this altruistic aspiration. Within the tantras *bodhichitta* also refers to a subtle physiological essence which permeates the body as white male and red female 'drops' of seminal fluids (see page 145).

The lotus also represents the fruition of the Hinayana and Mahayana as renunciation and stainlessness, and the sandwiched union of the sun and moon discs represents the Vajrayana as symbols of conjunct wisdom and compassion. These two discs are described as being fashioned of sun crystal and moon crystal, or 'precious water crystal' and 'cooling water crystal'. The sun disc is like a fiery lens which ripens the 'sprout' of enlightenment; the moon disc, like a frosted crystal lens which cools with its white rays of compassion.

In general an upper white moon disc, either alone or placed above a sun disc, is assigned to peaceful deities, where the 'father tantra' aspect of compassion or skilful means is emphasised. A gold or red sun disc is usually assigned to active or wrathful deities, where the 'mother tantra' aspect of wisdom or emptiness is emphasised. Certain

traditions assert that when the moon disc is uppermost then the petals of the lotus point upwards, since the moon's nocturnal influence is to partially open the lotus; and when the sun disc is uppermost then the fully-opened petals point downwards. Another tradition asserts that upward-facing lotuses are assigned to peaceful forms, and lotuses with downward-facing petals, to wrathful forms. As a general rule this is somewhat applicable, yet the complexity of Vajrayana imagery rarely accomodates rules of generality. When a major meditational deity (Tib. *yi dam*) appears with its retinue or with other deities placed in the cardinal and intercardinal directions, it is described as being 'in mandala'. Deities such as Vajrasattva, Vajradhara, or Guhyasamaja when depicted in mandala are represented on either single or double multicoloured lotuses with upward-pointing petals. Certain deities have specific lotus descriptions in their *sadhanas*. White Tara, for example, sits on a simple white *utpala* lotus. Deities such as Green Tara, who sit in the *lalitasana* posture of 'royal ease' with one leg pendant over the lotus seat, are depicted with a small lotus cushion or pedestal to support the foot.

The number of petals on a lotus seat mirrors the number of petals which arise on the internal 'lotuses' of the *chakras*: four, eight, sixteen, twenty-four, thirty-two, sixty-four, and one thousand. Although descriptions allude to the deity's seat as the eight-petalled lotus of the heart *chakra*, lotus seats are most commonly illustrated with sixteen petals. On seated figures usually five full petals are shown at the front, with two or four turning petals on each end. With standing figures, where often the legs are spread and consequently the sun and moon discs elongated, seven or nine full petals are usually depicted, with again two or four turning petals at the edges.

The simplest form of lotus depiction is the downward-pointing monochromatic lotus. These are usually shaded with pink, either as individual petals shaded from their centres outwards, or as a simple continuous band of shading from the top downwards, with their individual petals outlined in a dark red line. Monochromatic lotuses are commonly painted on the small figures which surround a central image.

Multicoloured lotuses represent the wisdom aspects of the Five Enlightened Buddha Families. Generally four colours are depicted on the lotus petals – red, blue, orange, and green – but white may be applied to the inner lotus petals behind the main petals. The petal colours of a multicoloured lotus alternate. The double central petal is usually painted red on its inside and blue on its outside. On either side of the central petal are double petals coloured orange on their inside and green on their outside. The next two petals on either side would be red and blue again. These colours can interchange, with the central petal being red and green, or orange and green. The inner petals are shaded from their centres to give them form; their central curving creases are also delicately shaded. The outer blue and green petals are shaded with indigo, either from their inner or outer edges. A second row of petal tips appear behind the main petals; these are usually softly shaded from a white base to a red, orange, yellow, green or blue tip. Upward-pointing

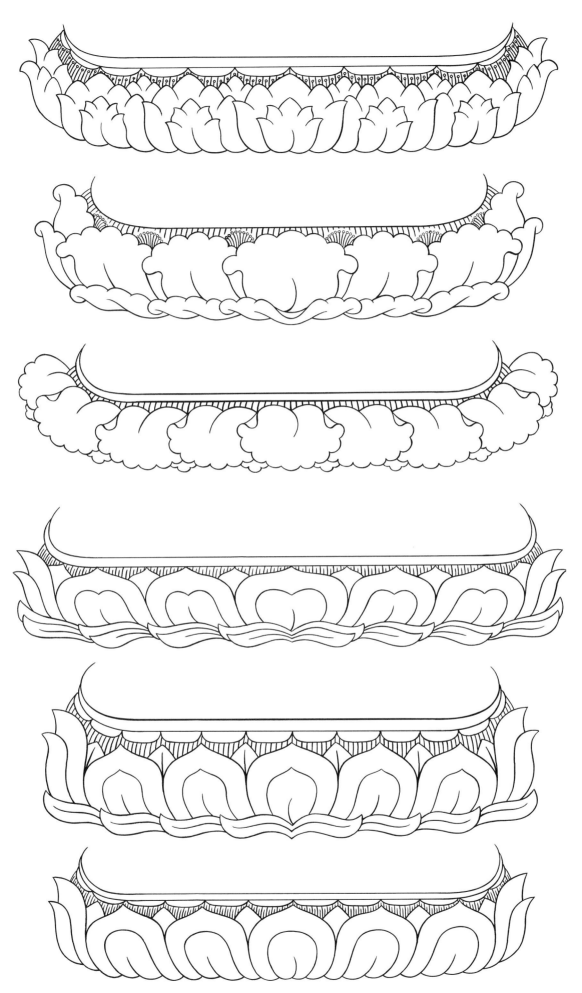

Plate 27: Lotus thrones

Plate 28: Lotus thrones and their shading

multicoloured lotuses often have a symmetrical row of leaves at their base, which are painted in an alternating green and blue sequence. Surrounding all of the outer and inner petals is a thin band of gold, ornamented with small 'cloud' or 'vine' scrolls at the sides and top. Simpler multicoloured lotuses are outlined with a plain gold line. The double multicoloured lotus (*vishvapadma*) has two rows of double petals; the main petals face upwards and the smaller lower petals face downwards.

The pericarp of the lotus, which rises behind the lotus petals, is usually painted in green with many parallel stamens painted in dark vertical lines. Lighter tonal lines of white or gold are usually painted between these stamen lines. The pericarp is frequently divided into sections, with the bow-shaped bulges of its seed-head appearing under the sun or moon discs.

Elaborate lotus thrones with multicoloured or multi-petalled lotus designs are very difficult to draw symmetrically. Techniques of back-tracing or pinhole charcoal pouncing – using a pinhole stencil – are used to draw them precisely. The thousand-petalled lotus is particularly hard to draw. The delicate shading of the lotus petals also requires much time and patience.

Plate 27
From the top downwards are illustrated:

A simple double-petalled multicolour lotus design.
A monochromatic lotus with curved over petals and lower petal formation.
A monochromatic lotus with downward-facing petals.
An upward-pointing, wide-base, multicoloured lotus, on which standing figures are depicted.
A multicoloured lotus with lower leaves on which seated figures are depicted.
A simple upward-facing multicoloured lotus.

Plate 28
The upper half of this illustration depicts three examples of multicoloured lotus thrones with their respective shading techniques depicted below. From the top downwards are drawn:

A simple, downward-facing, multicoloured lotus, on which standing deities may be depicted.
A more complex form of the above, with gold cloud or leaf-scroll ornamentation around the petals.
An upward-pointing multicoloured lotus, ornamented with cloud-scrolls on its petals and lower leaves.

The shading applied to the first lotus throne alternates between a red and orange sequence on its inner petals, which are shaded darker at their bulbous centres. The outer petals are gradually shaded towards their centres in a blue

and green sequence. The small base petals behind are shaded darker towards their centres, and may be shaded in any colour of the artist's choice. The second lotus throne shows the alternating red and orange sequence of the inner petals shaded towards their edges, with the blue and green sequence of the outer petals similarly shaded. The gold cloud or leaf-scroll ornamentation is shown around the outer edges of the petals. The third lotus throne at the bottom is shaded in the same manner of the petals on the previous lotus, but with alternating green and blue horizontally shaded leaves at its base. Ornamental golden cloud or leaf-scrolls are depicted around each petal and lower leaf, and the bulges on the central dais or pericarp and its vertical stamen lines are shown.

FLOWERS, FLOWER BUDS, AND LEAVES

Flowers (Skt. *pushpa*; Tib. *me tog*) are a universal symbol of love, compassion, and beauty. They are open, giving of their glory and fragrance, they attract and nourish bees to produce the nectar of honey. Essentially they are the sexual organs of plants and their short season of love produces an abundance of fruit which sustains the cycle of nature. Flowers abound in Tibetan art. As symbols of the paradise realms they surround deities and blossom profusely in the landscape.

Chinese art distinguishes four flowers to represent the seasons: the peony for spring, the lotus for summer, the chrysanthemum for autumn, and the plum blossom for winter. Tibetan art employs stylisations of these four flower forms, which are essentially modelled on the peony and chrysanthemum. Various hybrid forms of leaves and flowers are thus combined, more as flowers of the imagination than as true botanical representations. Other popular flowers which inspire visionary creation are: the five varieties of lotus, the flax lily, the daisy, magnolia, hollyhock, jasmine, poppy, gardenia, wild rose, saffron crocus, peach, plum, and pomegranate flower, and species of exotic Indian flowers such as the wild orchid, *ashoka*, coral, white and yellow *champaka* or frangipani. Small Tibetan alpine flowers, such as the blue Himalayan poppy, safflower, and 'flower of Tara', are also painted as meadow flowers.

Certain deities have affiliations with specific flowers. The goddess Vajravarahi, for example, wears a neck garland of red *karavira* (oleander) flowers, which in ancient India adorned the corpse of a person slain by a king. Flowers of the white *champaka* or *naga* (nagakesara) tree are an attribute of Maitreya. The delicate flowers of the *udumbara* or glomerous fig tree, and the blue *utpala* lotus, are attributes of many deities such as Tara and Avalokiteshvara. Poisonous flowers, such as datura, wolfsbane, aconite, and the flowers of the Upas or 'poison tree' (Skt. *vishavriksha*) – whose sap is used to poison arrow-tips – may be presented as flower offerings to certain wrathful deities.

Hand-held lotuses are usually described as having eight or sixteen petals, and are painted in a naturalistic form. The pink lotus (*padma*) is the most common hand-held lotus, but the red lotus (*kamala*), the white lotus (*pundarika*), or blue

Plate 29: The shading of flowers, buds and leaves

lotus (*utpala*), may be specified. Hand-held lotuses are supported by a single, leafed stem held between the fingers of a deity or lama. This single stem branches into three just below the lotus base. The central stem bears the fully opened lotus, the right stem carries a fruit with discarded leaves, and the left stem bears an unopened bud. These three stems represent the Buddhas of the three times: the fruit of the past (Dipankara), the open blossom of the present (Shakyamuni), and the potential bud of the future (Maitreya).

In painting, white usually forms the base colour of flowers, although a light blue, pink, or yellow undercoat may also be applied. Blue flowers are often shaded with indigo dye, pink flowers with lac dye or red sandalwood, and yellow flowers with saffron, wild yellow rose, or yellow *utpala* dyes. The use of plant and flower petal dyes is appropriate in the shading of flowers. Each individual petal on the flower is shaded separately, progressively blending the deeper tones from the petal's centre to the white outer edges. Shading around the central crease of each petal is also sharply delineated in light and dark shading. After shading, white highlights are applied to the central creases of petals, and the white petal edges are retouched with white to give a clear and sharp definition.

Meticulous gradations on the shading of flowers, clouds, water, rocks, and sky are invariably the hallmark of a finely painted thangka. The most delicate shading of these components take long periods of time to accomplish. A painted flower is believed to be perfect if it has received a hundred shading applications. As the visionary poet William Blake observed, "A little flower is the product of ages, and eternity is in love with the products of time".

Plate 29
Illustrated are examples of tonal shading applied to flowers, buds, and leaves. The upper three illustrations show round peony or chrysanthemum blossoms. The lower three illustrations depict two angular flower blossoms to the left and right, and the middle one depicts three buds.

Plate 30
Illustrated are examples of fully opened flower blossoms. Flowers are usually depicted with a dense central heart surrounded by a circle of fully opened petals. Often there is a gap in the petals at the flower's base where the stem appears. Usually petals are drawn with rounded edges like clouds, or with many points like leaves. The various flowers illustrated here are mainly modelled on peony and chrysanthemum designs.

Plate 30: Stylised peony and chrysanthemum flower blossoms

Plate 31: Flowers, buds and leaves

Plate 32: Compostion of lotuses, flowers, buds, fruit and leaves

Plate 33: Flower buds

Plate 34: Leaves

Plate 31

This drawing shows a composition of foliated flowers, buds and leaves. The flower arrangements in the upper area are typical of those placed behind the auras of deities. Buds and leaves are illustrated in the two bottom rows.

Plate 32

Depicted here is an abstract composition of lotuses, flowers, buds, leaves, and fruit.

Plate 33

Illustrated here are many divergent methods of drawing buds and budding flowers. Buds are a symbol of potential, of growth, of the future. The compact grace of their forms and bulbous weight emphasises the subtle curves of the stems which bear them. As with flowers their base colour is white, which is then delicately shaded in blue, pink, mauve, red, orange, or yellow. The shading emphasises their roundness and the compactness of their folded secret petal interiors. When the heart of the bud is revealed through a gap in the petals, a darker colour tone indicates its density. In buds this is often represented as a small, dark, jewel-shaped recess. Buds are rarely outlined, their sharp, shaded edges contrast strongly with the background tones of sky, rocks, leaves, or ground. Occasionally gold highlights are applied to buds.

The stem of the bud is often crowned by a darker seed box where the base of the petals join. The casings which enclose buds before they burst open are frequently shown; these are usually painted in a darker tone of red, blue, violet, or green. The small petals that begin to unfold around the bud's base are shaded like flower petals. In early Tibetan art flowers, buds, and leaves were highly stylised and ornate, and the employment of conch-like spirals in these ornate floral designs was common. Two examples of buds with spiral centres are shown in the lower left. To the right of these is a convoluted 'vulva' shaped design.

Plate 34

Illustrated in this drawing are many of the leaf forms that appear in Tibetan painting, although their scale may vary. Leaves are usually painted in medium or dark malachite green on their upper front surfaces, with a light green on their under or folded surfaces. Their upper surfaces are usually shaded across half the leaf with a gradated indigo dye, blending from the central stem to the upper or lower edges. This creates the effect of a natural indentation along the leaf's central stem. Ribbed veins may also be painted in dark indigo lines, which gives texture to the leaf. These veins either emanate from the central stem like ribs, or run parallel to the central stem. Gold line is applied along the central

stem and all around the outer edges of the leaf, which gives it life and luminosity. Often gold is wash-shaded into the green at the tips, which produces in it a bright lustre. Finally the central stem and edges are outlined in dark indigo line, which gives it definition. The stems that support leaves and flowers are usually painted in a lighter green, which blends into the leaf's base. Stems are also outlined in gold and a lighter indigo. Leaves may also be painted in a variety of green tones by adding yellow to the green pigment, or over-glazing with a yellow dye. Blue leaves may also alternate with the greens.

The top three rows of the drawing show a variety of mainly single foliate leaves with veins, such as are found on a wide variety of Indian trees. The middle five rows depict the multi-foliate leaves which surround open peony-chrysanthemum style flower heads, typically those around a deity's aura. The more convoluted of these leaf designs are common in Eastern Tibetan painting, having been influenced by Chinese art. Stylisations of such multi-foliate leaves in both Chinese and Tibetan art are derived from the shapes of chrysanthemum and peony leaves, their lilting graceful forms echoing their delicate movement.

The bottom two rows illustrate long composite leaves, and varieties with serrated edges. These particularly occur as decorative shrubbery around rock outcrops. In the bottom row are several stylised leaf tendrils, which are more evocative of crests or floral patterns.

TREES, LEAVES, AND FRUIT ROUNDELS

Many ancient cultures worshipped trees as manifestations or abodes of the divine. The Druids devised a sacred 'tree alphabet', and the Egyptian, Christian, Hebrew, Kabbalist, Zoroastrian, and Taoist traditions based many of their mystical teachings around the central 'tree of life'. From the dualistic 'tree of knowledge' in Genesis, to Islam's 'tree of blessings', the great 'world tree' was seen to ascend like a pillar from earth to heaven.

In ancient India the sacred qualities of trees were recognised long before the advent of Buddhism. Shrines were built at the bases of certain trees to honour the tree spirits – the *nagas*, *yakshas*, and *yakshinis* which inhabited them. In every Indian village the shade of a large central tree provides a focus or meeting place, where people and animals can find respite from the heat of the blazing sun. The bodhi tree, which is sacred to both Vishnu and the Buddha, is also known as the *ashvattha* tree – meaning the tree under which horses stand.

The universal motif of a great 'world tree' ascending from a sacred mountain finds its expression in Buddhist cosmology as the famous 'wish-fulfilling tree'. The Chitraratha Grove, the central of the five great paradise gardens of the god Indra, is described as having an arboretum of heavenly trees with *parijata*, the 'wish-fulfilling tree', at its centre. These celestial trees change their appearance in each season, are laden with beautiful blossoms and fruit, radiate divine perfumes, and are as brilliant as precious jewels.

Parijata, the 'wish-fulfilling tree', is identified as the beautiful Indian coral tree which was produced at the 'churning of the ocean' (see page 109). Yet in Tibetan art it is usually painted in the form of a white magnolia or *champaka* tree, with its trunk and roots in the jealous god (*asura*) realm, and its fruit- and flower-laden branches in the god realm. The *asuras* and gods continually wage war over the possession of this tree, the ambitious *asuras* always being jealous of the delicious fruit and fragrant flowers which the gods enjoy. For this reason the *asuras* are known as the 'jealous gods', and their eternal battle against the gods is depicted in paintings of the 'wheel of life'. The central wish-fulfilling tree grows from the top of Mt Meru, with its axial trunk being the central pillar of the universe. Our world system is placed on the southern side of Mt Meru, on the great 'continent' known as Jambudvipa, the 'land of the rose-apple tree' (*Eugenia jambolana*).

Five of the Six Universal Buddhas (Skt. Manushi Buddhas) of the previous epochs preceding Shakyamuni are believed to have attained enlightenment under different trees. The Buddhas and their trees of enlightenment are as follows:

1. Vipashyin, who attained enlightenment under the red-flowered *ashoka* tree (*Saraca indica*).
2. Shikhin, who attained enlightenment whilst sitting before a *pundarika* or edible white lotus tree.
3. Vishvabhu, who attained enlightenment under the *sal* or *sala* tree (*Vatica robusta, Shorea robusta*).
4. Krakuchandra, who attained enlightenment under the *shirisha* tree (*Acacia sirissa*).
5. Kanakamuni, who attained enlightenment under the glomerous fig tree or *udumbara* (*Ficus glomerata*).
6. Kashyapa, who attained enlightenment under the banyan tree (*Ficus indica*), a very well known tree across tropical Asia. The banyan puts down many aerial roots which grow into separate trunks; its labyrinth of roots often forms a virtual forest of intertwined trunks and branches. Maitreya, the Buddha of the next era, is destined to attain enlightenment under the white flower canopy of the *naga* or *champaka* tree (*Michelia champaka*). One of Maitreya's attributes is a sprig of the *naga* tree.

Shakyamuni, the Buddha of the present era, attained enlightenment under the famous bodhi tree at Bodh Gaya. The bodhi tree (Skt. *ashvattha*) is also known as the pippala or 'religious fig' tree (*Ficus religiosa*). Shakyamuni symbolically described the bodhi tree as his 'permanent abode', and the 'cult' of the bodhi tree was firmly enshrined in early Buddhism. Cuttings and seeds from the original bodhi tree were planted in all the regions to which Buddhism spread. Early representations of Shakyamuni Buddha depict not his human form, but that of a bodhi tree ascending from a throne. The bodhi tree has pointed heart-shaped leaves, and early figurative representations of the Buddha often represent his halo in a heart-shaped bodhi leaf design.

When Shakyamuni Buddha was conceived, his mother, Mayadevi, retired to a grove of *ashoka* trees in the royal gardens of Lumbini. The tall slender *ashoka* tree is a very common tree in India. It has long fluted leaves which hang downwards, and produces an abundance of bright orange or red flowers in April and May. *Ashoka* means 'without grief or sadness'. As a symbol of love it is sacred to Kama, the god of love. The tree is believed to be so sensitive in nature that it bursts into blossom when touched by a beautiful or virtuous woman.

Mayadevi gave birth to the Buddha ten months later from the right side of her body, whilst holding on to the branch of a flowering tree in the Lumbini gardens. In the Burmese Buddhist tradition this tree is believed to have been the red flowering *ashoka* tree, whilst certain other traditions favour the *sal* tree. The *sal* tree (*Shorea robusta*) is a teak-like hardwood tree, which yields dammar resin – from which wood varnish is manufactured. Since the *ashoka* tree has a tall cedar-like trunk and does not produce lower branches, the tree underneath which Shakyamuni was born is more likely to have been a *sal* tree.

Shakyamuni first practised meditation under the rose-apple or *jambu* tree. He attained realisation at Bodh Gaya (Vajrasana) under the canopy of the sacred pippala or bodhi tree, and he passed into Parinirvana between the trunks of two *sal* trees at Kushinagara.

Two other trees which were popular in early Buddhism are the *champavidala* (*Bauhinia variegata*), which appears on early Buddhist carvings, and the rare white coral tree (*Erythrina indica alba*), which graced the courtyards of monasteries or viharas. The common red coral tree (*Erythrina indica*), with its bright scarlet flowers, is one of the most beautiful of India's trees. The tree is a natural haven for all kinds of birds, and it is virtually alive with birdsong through all the seasons. It is one of the trees which grows in Indra's paradise gardens, and its three-stemmed leaf symbolises the Hindu trinity of Brahma, Vishnu, and Shiva.

In the Hindu tradition specific trees and plants are considered sacred to certain deities. The banyan, pippala, and *neem* trees, along with the sacred basil or *tulsi* bush, are sacred to Vishnu. The *bilva* or wood-apple and the *rudraksha* tree are both sacred to Shiva. In the Shaivite tantric tradition any wood which produces a white sap is sacred to Shiva, and any wood which produces a red sap is sacred to his consort Parvati. The white sap symbolises the semen of Shiva, and the red sap Parvati's menstrual blood.

Myrobalam, the healing panacea derived from the fruit of the cherry-plum tree (*Terminalia chebula*), is sacred to both the Hindu 'Lord of Physicians', Dhanvantari, and to the Buddhist 'Lord of Physicians', the Medicine Buddha. Some other flowering trees which share a common symbolism in both the Hindu and Buddhist traditions are listed below.

The 'flame of the forest' tree (*Butea monosperma*), whose Latin name means 'one-seeded', produces a lavish display of bright orange flowers in March and April, with few early leaves to obscure their flame-like effect. The tree is believed to have originated from an amrita-laden feather that fell from Garuda's plumage. Its wood is used for making sacred utensils, the staff of a brahmin, and for sacred fires. Three of its large oval leaves are pinned together with thorns to produce the eating plates used in temple feasts; here they again symbolise the trinity of Brahma, Vishnu, and Shiva. The rare white 'flame of the forest' tree has very specific sacred qualities which are 'tapped' in Hindu tantric rituals.

Four separate species of Indian trees which produce highly scented flowers are commonly known as the *champa* or *champaka* tree. The first of these is the frangipani (*Plumeria acutifolia*) also known as the 'temple tree', pagoda tree, or white *champa* tree – which has beautiful yellow and white waxy flowers that are extracted to produce perfumes and incense. The second is the scented frangipani (*Plumeria rubra*) – also known as the nosegay frangipani or jasmine tree – which has yellow and white flowers tinged with pink. As the scented frangipani exudes its fragrance mostly at night, its perfume is known 'night queen'. The third variety of *champa* tree is the yellow *champa* (*Michelia champaka*), which belongs to the magnolia family. Its fragrant yellow flowers are used both for perfume and cloth dyes. The fourth variety of champa is the *nagchampa* (*Mesua ferrea*) or *nagkesar*, meaning 'snake hair'. The white flowers of the *nagkesar* are an attribute of the bodhisattva Maitreya, and they are used to produce the famous Indian incense known as *nagchampa*.

The gardenia (*Gardenia resinifera*), the white jasmine, the yellow silk-cotton tree (*Cochlospermum religiosum*), and the *gul mohur* (*Delonix regia*) or peacock-rose tree, are all commonly grown to decorate temple grounds and provide flowers for deity offerings. In India the red hibiscus flower is sacred to the goddess Kali.

The indigenous magic traditions of India embodied in their lore beliefs that potent properties were instilled in plants at particular astrological configurations. Talismans and ritual objects fashioned at midnight under a particular lunar or stellar influence, and in a haunted place such as a crossroad or cemetery, could be used for magical rites of subjugation or destruction. Ritual daggers (Tib. *phur bu*), for example, carved from the heart wood of acacia or from acacia thorns, or forged from meteoric iron, were thus astrologically and geomantically empowered. Different woods are prescribed for the four tantric rituals or activities (*karmas*): for pacifying rites sappy wood should be used; for enriching rites the woods of the *shrivriksha* or *shirisha* are employed; *khadira* (acacia) is used for subduing; and the metal iron for destructive rites.

Eight species of trees are listed in the landscape description of the eight great cemeteries of early Indian Buddhist texts. These are: *nagkesar* (east); *karaya* (south-east); mango tree (south); *bataki* (south-west); banana tree (west); *arjuna* (north-west); bodhi tree (north); and walnut tree (north-east). Other Indian trees which are specified by name are: *shami, madhuka, tinduka, karnikara, badara, devadaru*, and *shishum*. A great problem in identifying Indian trees from their original Sanskrit names arises in the vast number of names (Sanskrit and colloquial) these trees are given.

Buddhist deities such as Mahakala and Khadiravani Tara are associated with specific trees. Six-armed Mahakala, whose abode is the Cool Sandalwood Grove (Sitavana) at Rajghir – one of the eight great cemeteries, is described as having a sandalwood tree (Tib. *tsan dan*) supporting his back. Khadiravani Tara (Tara of the Khadira Forest) is described with *khadira* trees (*Acacia catechu*) surrounding her, along with other fragrant trees, such as the nutmeg, sandalwood, and frangipani. 'Refuge' or 'assembly tree' thangkas depict a vast assembly of deities grouped in rows to form the heart or jewel shape of a giant tree. The thick golden trunk of this tree arises from a lake, and symbolically divides into three or five branches at its foliage base. A tree such as this is mythologically described as emerging from the centre of Lake Manasarovar in western Tibet.

Trees in Tibetan art are highly stylised, often bearing little resemblance to their true botanical appearance. As in Indra's Chitraratha Grove they take on the qualities of heavenly trees of paradise. Leaf clusters or roundels are a common way of depicting foliage, particularly of trees belonging to the fig family, peach, mango, magnolia, and evergreen trees. Other trees, such as the cherry blossom, citrus, pomegranate, myrobalam, fir, and pine, usually have more realistically painted individual leaves.

A simple way of painting leaf clusters is to outline in dark indigo each individual leaf against a solid green background. An inner gold outline and central stem enhances the tree's beauty. The most satisfying results, however, are obtained by shading each leaf, roundel or cluster separately. The Chinese-style depiction of trees is very graceful and aesthetically expressive, the subtle movements in its composition often reveal the hand and eye of a master artist.

The drawings on Plates 35 to 40 are abstract compositions depicting a variety of identifiable and stylised trees.

Plate 35

In the upper left corner are the hanging branches of the weeping willow tree. The willow is a symbol of gentleness, its pliant branches are used for basket-weaving, and willow stems are used in the ritual sprinkling of consecrated water.

On the upper right are shown two trees with auspicious intermingling branches: the mango tree with its fruit centred in a large leaf cluster, and behind a stylised fruit tree with dense leaf clusters. At the centre of each leaf cluster are three small round fruits from which the leaves emanate. Fruit trees with an upward-pointing triangle of three small fruits are common in Tibetan tree illustration. Hanging below the mango fruits are the leafy fronds of the aloewood or eaglewood tree, which is also known as the incense tree.

On the left side below the willow branches, are examples of fir or pine trees showing several different pine-needle designs. The evergreen pine is a symbol of longevity, and amber is obtained from its fossilised resin.

On the right side, below the mango tree, is an entwining flowering tree with a double trunk. This stylised tree with trifoliate, peony-like leaves bears a resemblance to the silk-cotton tree or rhododendron.

Plate 35: Various trees (willow, mango, aloewood, fir, rhododendron, banana, bamboos and grasses)

Plate 36: Various trees (fig, peach, sandalwood, cypress, gardenia, mulberry, oak, banana, vine, wish-fulfilling tree)

Plate 37: Various trees (cypress, fig, peony, bamboo, banana, plantain etc)

Plate 38: Various trees (palm, banana, plantain, peony, persimmon, etc)

At the bottom, emerging from behind the rock, are the large, long, convoluted leaves of the banana plant. One of the meanings of the word 'banana' is finger, and the fruit grows in clusters known as 'hands'. Appearing above the banana leaves are three pink banana flowers. These large tulip-like flowers actually hang downwards from the upper foliage of the banana plant, the bananas growing upwards from their long stems. Sprouting from the left-hand corner on long slender stems are heads of knotgrass. Within the rock formation are some species of bamboo to the left, and tubers of cane sugar to the right.

Plate 36

In the upper left is a stylised example of a fig tree with large composite clusters bearing fruit, flower and seed simultaneously, and symbolising the three times of past, present, and future. On the upper left, two birds of paradise perch and peck in a peach tree. On the upper right are peach trees, with sandalwood and cypress trees growing behind them. A small pine-needle branch is to the left of these peach trees. Below this and in the upper centre, is a flowering peony or gardenia bush. To the lower right of this is a dense mulberry bush, the leaves of which are used in the cultivation of silkworms. On the mid-left side are leaves and branches of the Chinese oak tree, a symbol of

majesty and strength. Its acorns are used medicinally, and its leaves provide nourishment for the wild uncultivated silkworm. In the lower left corner, banana plant or plantain leaves curve from behind a rock outcrop. In the lower right corner a twisting floral vine winds around the trunk of a peach tree.

In the bottom centre are two drawings of the wish-fulfilling tree, also known as the *kalpataru* or *kalpavriksha*. Indra is said to have five such wish-fulfilling trees growing in his paradise groves. This miraculous tree was believed to bear spontaneously an abundant supply of any kind of fruit that one desired. The contemporary Indian saint, Sathya Sai Baba, miraculously endowed a tamarind tree near his ashram with the status of a *kalpataru* tree, from which any desired species of fruit would instantaneously appear, whether in or out of season. The Tibetan wish-fulfilling tree is decorated with silk scarfs and golden, jewelled pendants, which hang in strands from its foliage.

Plate 37

At the top are many stylised pear-shaped leaf clusters of cedar-like trees such as the cypress, *ashoka*, or evergreen bushes, where the leaf cluster itself forms a leaf shape. Below and to the left, is the auspicious entwining of a sacred fig tree with a

54

Plate 39: Various trees (mango, sandalwood, fig, pine, etc)

flowering peony-style tree. Behind their trunks are star-shaped bamboo leaves. In the lower left corner split banana leaves mingle with plantain leaves and small shrubs. In the lower right is an elaborate flowering bush with lotus or peony-style flowers. Profusely flowering bushes of this kind can represent stylised hybrids of the peony, gardenia, rhododendron, azalea, or chrysanthemum blossoms. In the mid right is a triple fruited cluster with long overlapping leaflets. In the background are several trees with detailed leaf formations.

Plate 38

On the left hand side the waving fronds of a palm tree rise behind banana or plantain leaves. In the centre are peony blossoms and buds, which are depicted against a dense small leafed tree. In the upper right is a fruit-laden persimmon tree (*Diospyros kaki*), an evergreen bearing yellow or orange fruits which look like tomatoes. At the bottom right are long sword-like leaves, similar to the iris or sweetflag.

Plate 39

In the upper left a sprouting creeper entwines with the branches of a mango tree. Highly stylised fruit, flower, seed, and leaf roundels dominate the four fig trees in the upper

right corner. At the centre are three sandalwood trees, with the stylised appearance of drooping 'yaktail' foliage. Sandalwood is defined by the colour of its fragrant wood into two species: white and red sandalwood. Fragrant red sandalwood produces a red dye which is used in thangka painting. Because of its fragrant and auspicious quality red sandalwood has always been highly esteemed in the East. Sacred images are carved from it, and it furnishes the wood for many ritual implements and weapons. On the lower left is a fig tree, and on the lower right a spring blossom tree with flowers of the prunus or citrus families. In the bottom centre is a Chinese pine with a twisted trunk. In Chinese art the trunk of the pine or peach tree, both symbols of longevity, are sometimes calligraphically twisted to form the character '*shou*', the Chinese symbol of longevity.

Plate 40

Interlocking trees, small trees, and leaf roundels are illustrated here. In the upper area are drawings of stylised trees entwined by the 'wish-fulfilling vine' (*kalpalata* or *kalpavalli*). Like *kalpavriksha*, the wish-fulfilling tree, this legendary vine or creeper is ever blossoming with leaf, flower, and fruit. The depiction of trees embraced by vines is an auspicious configuration, representing the union of male and female

Plate 40: Entwining trees, leaf and flower roundels

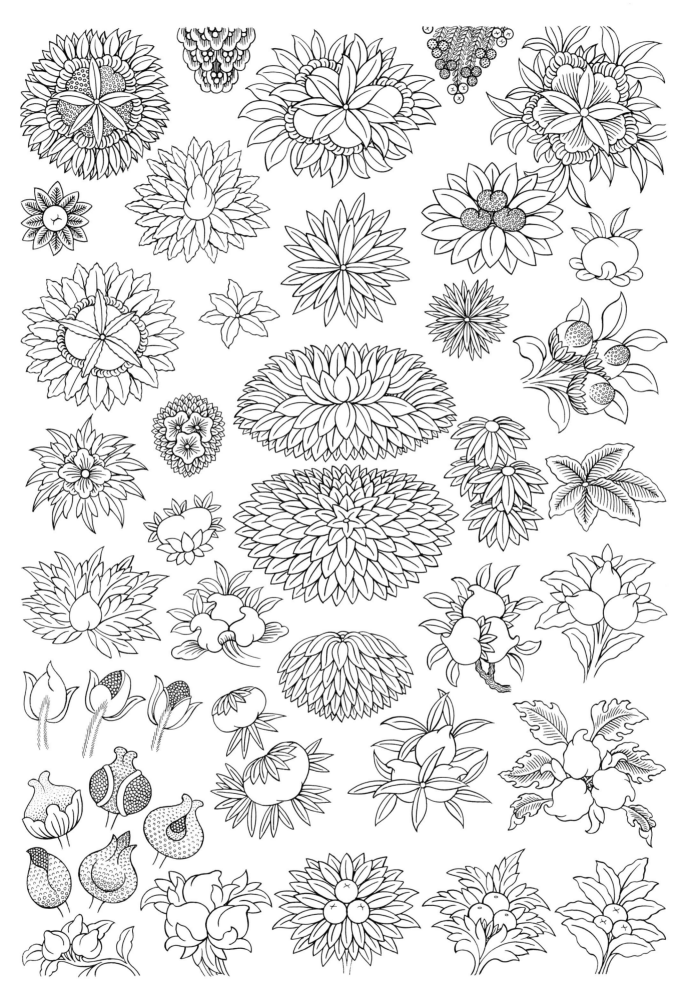

Plate 41: Stylised leaf and fruit clusters

as method and wisdom. Trees with an entwining vine motif are commonly depicted in Tibetan art.

In the central area are stylised examples of small bushy trees; a sandalwood tree is on the far right. The two small flowering trees are *ashoka* trees, whose vivid red flowers are one of the attributes of the goddess Marichi.

In the lower area are complex examples of leaf, fruit, flower, and seed roundels. Beneath these are leaflet style clusters of mosses, with beard-like hanging tendrils. In the lower centre are three sugar cane tubers. Along the bottom are rock foliage, flowers, and mosses. At the bottom centre are three stylised juniper trees. Juniper produces a very fragrant odour when burned. In Tibet it is widely used as an incense (Tib. *bsang*). Juniper is burned in large urn-shaped incense burners (Tib. *bsang khung*) which are commonly constructed on the flat roofs of Tibetan houses or in the courtyards of monasteries or temples. Cedar wood also produces a fragrant incense, and its branches are often used as kindling for powdered incense.

Plate 41

Some complex examples of leaf and fruit clusters are depicted here. In the top row are ornate fig-style clusters displaying leaf, flower, fruit and seed simultaneously. Above these are two bunches of hanging berries or grapes. Along the central axis are complex radiating leaf clusters, which are commonly depicted as the foliage of wish-fulfilling trees. On either side of these are various examples of leaf, flower, and fruit compositions.

In the lower area are stylised examples of fruit. Fruits are usually painted in a triangular group of three, representing the Three Jewels of Buddha, dharma, and sangha. The fruit of the 'tree of plenty' symbolises abundance, maturity, and ripeness. Plums, apples, oranges, apricots, and persimmons are depicted as round fruits; peaches and guavas, as oval fruits; mangoes, lemons, and figs, as pear-shaped fruit; and *bilva* fruit, pomegranate and myrobalam, as bulbous formations.

The pomegranate is illustrated on the lower left. Its bright red colour and bursting seeds are symbols of happiness, passion, and fertility. The peaches, illustrated in the lower left corner, are symbols of longevity and immortality. The citron or lemon (*jambhara*), depicted third up from the bottom right corner, is a symbol of prosperity and is held by some wealth deities, such as Jambhala. In Chinese Buddhism these three fruits – the pomegranate, peach and citron – are known as the 'three fruits of blessings', symbolising happiness, longevity, and wealth.

The *bilva* or *bel* fruit (Bengal quince or wood-apple), is depicted in the second row above the bottom right. The *bilva* and the peach are probably the most common offerings placed before deities. They usually appear in a triple fruit formation connected by one branch, symbolising the three jewels and the united fruition of the 'three vehicles'.

Chapter Three
Animals

ANIMALS MYTHOLOGICAL AND REAL

As Mark Twain humourously reasoned, Noah's ark must have been quite immense, dwarfing even the Titanic in its capacity to accommodate the millions of species of animals, birds and insects that populated the globe, there being ten thousand species of roundworm alone. The flies were Noah's biggest problem.

In an even more remote beginning than Noah's eventual arrival on dry land, the agriculturalist Cain slew his nomadic brother, Abel. Ancestral hunter-gatherers were displaced by settlers; the cultivation of land gave credence to the notion of ownership. Private property gave birth to security, protection, and greed, and greed to the sense of power – a ravenous mental hunger which swallows whole cultures and rainforests in its search for an imagined satisfaction. The meek may inherit the earth but never its mineral rights – as John Paul Getty once prophesised. Jesus's parable of the lilies of the field and the birds of the air was doomed forever to fall on deaf ears, as somewhere along the line civilised man lost sight of the simple wisdom that even a millionaire can only eat a bellyful. Animals and their natural habitat have always been the losers in mankind's eternal war of acquisition.

The ancient world teemed with wildlife. Populations were smaller then; mankind's needs and desires, fewer. Yet even as Shakyamuni Buddha walked the jungle pathways of forested India, the elephant was nearing the brink of extinction in nearby China. Species extinction is not only a modern phenomena; the dodo had many distant ancestors – unknown, uncatalogued, unidentified.

In days of yore there was certainly a far deeper instinctive rapport between man and the animal realm. Vedic Hinduism held a deep respect for the sanctity of animal life, even though blood sacrifice was a scriptural necessity. Within the Hindu theological framework Shakyamuni Buddha is popularly recognised as the ninth of Vishnu's ten incarnations (*avataras*), whose divine mission was to delude the demons and dispel the ritual of animal sacrifice. Buddhism, with its karmic conclusion that everything that lives is holy, had an enormous impact on the preservation of the natural world. Weaving legends of the Buddha's previous lives, the *Jataka* tales revealed a deep compassion for animal welfare.

India was the cradle of vegetarianism. Tibet, paradoxically, was not. Tibet's sparse agricultural landscape ensured that animal products were a necessary part of the national diet. Yet respect for the slaughtered was of the highest order: the skulls of yaks and sheep were inscribed with mantras and placed high amidst carved *mani*-stone cairns as an act of prayer for the auspicious future rebirth of the slain. The hunt of the wild yak was a challenge to life and limb, where cowardice and not slaughter was the real transgression.

An enormous variety of actual, mythical, magical, and hybrid animals are to be found in Tibetan art. The mounts (*vahanas*) or animal vehicles of the deities, particularly wrathful protective deities, create an elaborate pantheon in themselves. Ferocious deities often possess vast retinues of animal-headed gods, local gods, demons, spirits, emissaries, and animal messengers. Virtually every common species of animal, bird, and reptile is adopted as the mount of one of these deities. When colour variations and zoological mutations are included, the pantheon becomes seemingly endless, ranging from a vixen or black bear cub to a seven-headed iron wolf, a nine-headed turquoise dragon, or a meteoric scorpion with nine eyes, stings and claws. Sitatapatra, one of the most complex Vajrayana goddesses, tramples on a thousand specified animals and minor gods. There are also creatures with magical powers that can render themselves invisible, read the hearts of all beings, and speak in the tongues of men.

The most important mythological Buddhist animals are described and illustrated here. These comprise the windhorse, dragon, garuda, *makara*, *naga*, unicorn, magical deer, the *feng huang* or Chinese phoenix, the *kirtimukha*, and the three victorious creatures of harmony. Other Indian mythological animals which occur rarely in early Buddhist art include the griffin, chimaera, *virali*, *sardul*, and *yali*. These hybrid creatures, mostly formed from the various unions of the horse, elephant, lion, eagle, serpent, boar, ram, and deer, are usually grouped under the name of *vyala*.

Many of these mythical creatures occur in the mythologies of the whole of the pan-Asian and European continents, their ancient origins and meanings shrouded in the mists of antiquity of vanished civilisations. Any symbolic or adopted representational meanings that a succeeding culture implants upon them inevitably leads to dilution. It is remarkable that the highly developed cultures of India and China were able to maintain an almost consistent artistic and iconographic tradition over millenia. The *kirtimukha*, for example, due to its pre-eminence in Newari art is believed by some to have originated in the Pala art of India. Yet its Chinese equivalent, the 'monster mask', can be found on excavated Chinese bronze vessels dating back to the sixteenth century BC.

When these images are transposed to foreign cultures a process of change may occur and the imagery may develop. Roman coins, bearing Caesar's profile, were minted in various parts of the Roman Empire, and Caesar's image became progressively more unrecognisable the further the mint was stationed from Rome. By way of contrast, the first listing of the twelve Chinese astrological animals and the twelve ornaments of the imperial emperor's robes are believed to have originated in the Shun dynasty, *circa* 2250 BC; both animals and ornaments remained unchanged until the present culture adopted the 'foreign' iconoclastic culture of communism.

THE WINDHORSE AND THE FOUR SUPERNATURAL ANIMAL GUARDIANS OF THE FOUR DIRECTIONS

The Horse (Tib. rta)

Before the development of the steam and internal combustion engines, the horse was universally relied upon as the swiftest means of transport. To pre-industrial man the qualities of a horse were esteemed as much as those of the modern motor car. Native American Indians recognised the steam train of the prairies as an 'iron horse', and the capacity of all motorised engines is still measured in horsepower. Communities were separated by vast distances and difficult terrain and depended upon equestrian livestock which possessed endurance, strength, swiftness, and obedience.

Competitive horse-racing developed thoroughbred strains which were light, fast, and beautifully elegant, and just as enlightened beings were endowed with the thirty-two major signs of divinity, so were horses assigned the thirty-two marks of perfection.

The 'pearl' of the horse's eye is the chief of these thirty-two signs. The eye should be round with a pure white colour, the pupil bean-shaped and of a deep colour, the iris should have a hue of five colours. The mane should consist of ten thousand soft hairs, and the upraised tail should flow like a comet. The ears should be shaped like a willow leaf, the tongue slender, pink, and clean like a two-edged sword, the gums a light colour, and the incisor and molar teeth spaced firmly apart. The neck, forehead, breast, bones, skull, sinews, legs, knees, and fetlocks all bear similar signs of distinction. A particular mystique is also accorded to the colour marks of the forehead, hoofs, and body of a perfect thoroughbred steed, which though possibly highly strung is never disturbed by sudden sounds or startling sights.

The Windhorse (Tib. rlung rta)

Wind is the natural element of the horse. As it gallops across the plain the wind arises to meet it, its long tail and mane flowing freely as it speeds through the stillness of the air, creating wind. The Chinese Manchu ponytail is said to have originated in honour of the flowing tails of the horses that served them. Both the wind and the horse are natural vehicles of movement, the horse carrying material form and the wind ethereal form. Prayers are carried on the wind, and in Tibet the prayer flag is known as the windhorse (Tib. *rlung rta*).

Prayer flags consist of auspicious mantras, designs, syllables, and prayers which are woodblock-printed onto squares of cotton cloth in each of the Five Buddha colours. Most frequently they display the windhorse at the centre with the four supernatural creatures at each corner along with auspicious mantras. Also commonly printed on prayer flags are the images of Padmasambhava; the three great bodhisattvas – Manjushri, Avalokiteshvara, and Vajrapani; the trinity of longevity – Amitayus, Ushnishavijaya, and White Tara; and the syllables of the Kalachakra mantra.

The prayer flag is believed to have originated in the constant struggle of the *asuras* against the gods. Weary of this relentless aggression the gods petitioned the Buddha to intervene, sending as their representative the goddess Gyaltsen Tsemo. Buddha responded with the recitation of a prayer which the gods then printed on their battle-flags; by virtue of this prayer the gods were victorious and peace once again prevailed. The great Indian pandit Atisha, who arrived in Western Tibet in 1042, is believed to have introduced the Indian Buddhist practice of printing prayer flags into Tibet. Prayer flags are strung in a five-colour sequence across high auspicious places, such as temples, stupas, rooftops, mountain passes and bridges. Tibetan new year (Tib. *lo gsar*) is the most auspicious time for renewing faded prayer flags, the winds of the previous year having borne the prayers across many lands. Their flapping and cracking in the prayer-laden wind is reminiscent of the clatter of horses hoofs.

Plate 42: The windhorse and the four supernatural creatures (garuda, dragon, tiger, snow-lion)

The windhorse gallops towards the left at the centre of the prayer flag. His saddled back carries the auspicious faceted jewel or wish-fulfilling gem of the *chakravartin* or 'universal monarch', radiating peace, prosperity, and harmony wherever it travels. The riderless horse speeds like the wind across the heavens, its strength inexhaustible, its hoofs like wings of the four winds. Tibet's epic hero, Gesar of Ling, is sometimes depicted on prayer flags riding his heavenly white steed Kyango Karkar through the billowing clouds.

The Tibetan medical and astrological systems define four categories of personal health and harmony: life energy (Tib. *srog*); health (Tib. *lus*); personal power (Tib. *dbang thang*); and success (Tib. *rlung rta*). The windhorse itself symbolises the combination of these four categories as the positive personal energy, which eliminates all hindrances caused by illness, misfortune, demonic, and planetary influences. The energy of wind equates with the unimpeded movement of vital airs through the channels (*nadi*) of the subtle body, creating a potent current of movement on which the mind, as windhorse, can ride. This divinely creative force corresponds to what William Blake called 'the body of imagination', whose nature is energy and whose energy is eternal delight.

Invocation of the windhorse is performed with a 'smoke puja' on the mornings of the waxing moon when juniper incense (Tib. *bsang*) is burned to purify the psychic channels and pacify the spirits of the locality.

The Supernatural Animals of the Four Directions

The four animals – garuda, dragon, lion, and tiger – that surround the windhorse in the directional corners have their origin in the ancient Chinese astrological and geomantic tradition. In ancient China the four cardinal directions were equated with the four seasons: the rising sun of the east symbolised spring; the midday sun of the south, summer; the setting sun of the west, autumn; and the sunless regions of the north, winter. To each of these directions were assigned one of the four 'supernatural' or 'spiritually-endowed' creatures. The blue dragon symbolised the eastern quarter; the red bird of the sun or phoenix, the southern quarter; the white tiger, the western quarter; and the tortoise or 'dark warrior', the northern quarter. The four colours of these animals correspond to the Chinese geomantic mandala design of the four quadrants of heaven, with blue in the east, red in the south, white in the west, black in the north, and the yellow of earth at the centre. In *feng shui* (literally 'wind and water') the four animals represent geomantic qualities or characteristics of the landscape. These four creatures with their different characteristics originally symbolised the four quadrant animals of the ancient Chinese zodiac. At a later time their number was increased to encompass all twelve animals of the Chinese zodiacal cycle, three of which still remain – the dragon, bird, and tiger.

In Chinese geomantic symbolism the opposition of dragon and tiger is a familiar motif. An old tiger gazes wistfully upwards towards a young dragon, symbolising both the polarity and unity of the *yin* and *yang* principles. The tiger, as lord of terrestrial creatures, represents the dark feminine *yin* principle of even numbers, and the dragon, as lord of celestial creatures, represents the light male *yang* principle of uneven numbers. As emblems of the life force the dragon of spring represents birth; the red bird of summer, youth; the white tiger of autumn, old age; and the 'black warrior', death. In Buddhist symbolism the four guardian animals symbolise overcoming of the four great fears of birth, disease, old age, and death.

The Tibetan tradition adopted and retained three of these four animals: the turquoise dragon, red garuda bird, and yellow striped tiger. The tortoise or 'black warrior' – a national emblem of China, was replaced by the white snow-lion – a national emblem of Tibet. This arrangement of colours – blue, red, yellow, and white – with the green windhorse at the centre, corresponds to the Buddhist mandala arrangement, with Amoghasiddhi representing the green element of air at the centre.

Plate 42

Here the windhorse is depicted bearing the wish-fulfilling jewel at the centre, and the four supernatural guardian animals in the four corners. The Chinese orientated their world axis on a north–south alignment, whilst the Tibetans adopted the east–west alignment of Buddhist India. In the Tibetan scheme illustrated the red garuda is in the west; the turquoise dragon in the south; the yellow striped tiger in the east; and the white snow-lion in the north. Another tradition ascribes the snow-lion to the east; the dragon to the south; the tiger to the west; and the garuda to the north. Often the orientations of these animals are changed, with either the positions of the garuda and dragon being reversed or those of the tiger and snow-lion. As the garuda and dragon are both airborne creatures they should appear at the top; the tiger and snow-lion, being terrestial creatures, should be positioned at the bottom.

Geomantically these four auspicious 'spiritually-endowed' creatures represent the harmonious configuration of native earth spirits (Tib. *gnyan*) in the Tibetan landscape. The red bird or garuda describes an area of red rock situated to the west; the turquoise dragon represents an area of greenery, pasture, streams, and a river laying in the south; the yellow tiger describes an incline of light earth or rock towards the east; and the tortoise or snow-lion represents a mountain situated towards the north. If these four earth spirits or 'earth pillars' are in their correct directions they indicate the perfect landscape setting in which to construct a monastery, stupa or temple. Milarepa's prophetic dream about a great mountain surrounded by four directional pillars, on which stood four creatures – a snow-lion, tiger, eagle, and vulture – symbolises these four supernatural creatures. Marpa's interpretation of the mountain as the Kagyupa teachings, and the four creatures as his four great disciples, foretold of the stability and unbroken transmission of his lineage of Mahamudra teachings.

THE DRAGON (Skt. *vritra*; Tib. '*brug*; Ch. *lung*)

The monotheistic religious traditions of the Middle East and Europe have portrayed the dragon as a ferocious satanic monster, a guardian of hidden treasure, an abductor of children and a seducer of virgins. St Michael and St George are the archetypal knights who destroyed the controlling primal power of the dragon, slaying that which was evil and releasing that which was pure – in the form of childlike innocence, a maiden's chastity, or sacred treasure.

The oriental dragon is viewed in a far more positive light: it represents the strong male *yang* principle of heaven, change, energy, and creativity. The basic image of the Chinese dragon first appeared in unearthed carvings from the neolithic period, dating back to around the fifth millenium BC. As such the dragon is one of mankind's earliest representational symbols. The dragon is believed to have served originally as a tribal totem, combining the head of a pig with the body of the snake, and the mane of the horse. In this aspect it is recorded that the Yellow Emperor Huang Di took the cloud as his symbol, the Fiery Emperor Yan Di took fire as his symbol, Emperor Gong Gang took water as his symbol, Emperor Da Hao took the dragon as his symbol, and Emperor Shao Hao took the phoenix as his symbol. Each of these dynasties were of different tribal origins yet their symbols are found to this day as emblems on Imperial insignia and brocade designs.

The dragon and phoenix, which represented the Emperor and Empress of China as the union of heaven (dragon) and earth (phoenix), are believed by archaeologists to have their origin in the pig and pheasant. Fossil remains of dinosaurs found in China, and very commonly in the Gobi desert, are more likely to have provided the inspiration for the dragon's gigantic serpentine form.

The earliest written description of the dragon occurs in the *I Ching* (Book of Changes), where its elusive or hidden creative nature is hinted at. The dragon is believed to be a 'shape-shifter' with the ability to transmute its form at will. It can render itself invisible, decrease to the size of a silkworm, or expand its body to fill the skies. At the spring equinox it ascends into the sky, where it remains until the autumn equinox when it descends into a deep pool, encasing itself in the mud until the next spring. As one of the four supernatural animals of Buddhism the azure or turquoise dragon represents the light-increasing power of springtime and the easterly direction of the sunrise.

Like the Indian *naga*, the legendary dragon of China has always had a strong association with weather prognostication; in particular it is linked to billowing thunderclouds and electric storms. Forked lightning emanates from its claws and fiery ball-lightning blazes from its mouth. Its voice is the roll of thunder, sheet lightning its restless writhing amidst the dark storm clouds, and torrential rain the downpour from its glistening scales. The four jewels it grasps in its claws produce dew and a downpour of rain when it clenches them tightly. The shell of a tortoise was used for weather divination and a jade dragon was prayed to in times of drought. A waterspout was known as a 'living dragon',

and a tornado or whirlwind, as a 'hanging dragon', while tidal waves and submarine earthquakes were viewed as the anger of one of the four dragons of the oceans. Chinese annals record several instances of famous dragon painters who were requested to paint dragons in times of drought – usually on the four walls of a special hall erected next to a 'dragon pool'. The painted dragons were so realistically painted that they are said to have become living creatures, destroying the walls of the hall in a fury of thunder and rain as they dived into the dragon pool. Dragon painting became a major art form in medieval China, particularly during the period of the Five Dynasties (AD 907–60) and Sang Dynasty (AD 960–1279), when individual schools of both dragon and fish painting evolved.

There are more than seventy different Chinese characters for writing the word dragon. It is said to occur in nine distinct sub-species: the celestial, spiritual, winged, coiled, horned, snouted, yellow, water, and treasure-guarding dragons. The typical dragon is said to possess three sections and nine likenesses. The three sections are its head to forelegs, forelegs to waist, and waist to tail. The nine likenesses are as follows: it has a head like a camel; horns like a deer; eyes like those of a demon, rabbit, or prawn; a snake-like neck; fish scales; the belly of a giant clam or frog; ears like a cow; the forelegs and footpads of a tiger; and claws of an eagle. Along its back it has a ridge of eighty-one dorsal fins like a monitor lizard, and its coiled and flowing hair resembles a horse's mane. Carp-like whiskers appear above its upper lip, the eyebrows flare upwards, a small beard hangs from the chin, it has wild staring eyes, wrinkled creases above its frowning snout, a flank of small pointed dorsal fins adorns its jaw, knees, and tail, it has the cylindrical horns of a deer, and tongues of lightning-flame emanate along the front of its legs. It writhes in a billow of clouds with its claws grasping the four wish-fulfilling jewels of the four limbs of magical attainments.

As an imperial emblem of the Chinese Emperor the celestial or palace dragon was represented with five claws. Ministers of the Emperor wore an insignia of a four-clawed dragon, and those of lower rank wore a three-clawed dragon. The elitism of the Imperial five-clawed dragon became mandatory in the Yuan Dynasty (1271–1368), when the Emperor issued a proclamation forbidding the depiction or wearing of the dragon by the common people. Officially only five claws constituted the true dragon; those with four claws were known as pythons.

The magical number nine has a numerological affinity with the dragon. It has nine varieties, nine likenesses, eighty-one dorsal scales, and the *yang* or heavenly lines of the *I Ching* formed by the number nine. Likewise the Chinese Emperor wore nine dragons on his brocade robe, eight of which were embroidered on the exterior with one 'hidden dragon' on the inside of his robes. Yet there are only three main species of dragons: the powerful horned *lung*, the deaf thunder dragon of the skies whose roar and movement produce thunder and lightning; the hornless *li* of the ocean; and the scaled *chiao* which dwells in mountain lakes and caves.

A separate emblem that accompanies the dragon is the mystical flaming pearl or 'night-shining pearl', which is

Plate 43: Dragons

depicted as a small red or white sphere surrounded by flames. Legend relates that a certain Chinese minister of state healed a wounded serpent, who was in actuality the son of the dragon king. In return for this act of kindness the serpent disgorged a brilliant pearl from its mouth and presented it to the minister, who in turn gave it to the Emperor. In the Emperor's palace it shone with such brilliance that 'night became as day'. Historically the Qianlong Emperor (1735–96) wore a rare freshwater pearl from the Songhua river as the crowning ornament on his helmet.

In China it was believed that pearls were formed from the mouth of the ocean dragon, whilst in India it was believed that they were produced by the fire of the sun. It was an Indian belief that pearls protected against harm from fire. A pair of Chinese dragons are often represented as fighting for possession of the flaming pearl, or chasing the elusive pearl across the skies. Momentary contact of the dragon with the flaming pearl produces the lightning flash which illuminates the darkness of the black clouds, revealing the brilliant zigzag form of the dragon as white lightning and the rolling roar of his voice as the crashing of thunder. The flaming pearl is in essence the egg of potentiality which is fertilised by the dragon. As a polarity symbol it is the negative point or seed-essence which comes into contact with a positive charge during an electrical storm. Its rapid movement across the skies is traced in the flicker of lightning and its forked ascent and descent to earth. One form of lightning is actually known as 'pearl lightning', where the fork tip explodes into a multitude of small white spheres. The flaming pearl has been identified as ball lightning, the sun, the moon, the essence of dragon seed, and 'the pearl of great price' as the Buddhist wish-fulfilling gem.

In the Hindu tradition the dragon is not specifically identified; its qualities are fully expressed in the indigenous Indian *naga*. Perhaps the dragon's closest counterpart arises in the Vedic legend of the sky serpent Vritra, the demon of rain and drought, against whom Indra wages a continual campaign in order to provide rain. Another Vedic legend concerns Meghanada, the 'roarer of the thunderclouds', who was the son of the demon Ravana and once overcame Indra by becoming invisible. The Sanskrit term *megha* meaning 'thunder' is also used loosely to refer to the dragon. The Japanese adopted the form of the Chinese dragon, which became known as Ryu-Jin, 'king of the seas'.

In Buddhism the dragon is the vehicle of Vairochana, the white Buddha of the centre or east. The blue turquoise dragon is the vehicle of many protective deities, aquatic or storm gods, and guardians of treasure – where it is closely identified with the *naga* serpent.

The Tibetan term for the dragon (Tib. *'brug*) refers to the sound of thunder. The Buddhist kingdom of Bhutan is known as Druk Yul meaning 'the land of the thunder dragon', and its inhabitants are known as Drukpas – named after the Drukpa Kagyu lineage established by Tsangpa Gyare, who had witnessed nine dragons ascending from the ground into the sky over the site of Ralung where he established the monastery of Ralung (*circa* 1180 AD). The ascent of a dragon or group of dragons is always an auspicious

sign. Even in the last decade there have been several reported sightings of dragons in Tibet, one of which is reputed to have been filmed on video camera. The dragon is not seen as a purely mythological creature in China or Tibet. Its appearance was too frequently recorded throughout history to have been assigned to the mythological or extinct species of animals.

Plate 43
Illustrated in this drawing are seven Tibetan and Chinese style dragons. In the upper right a four-clawed dragon descends from the clouds grasping jewels in its claws. In the upper left a five-clawed dragon splays its talon-like claws. Across the mid centre three dragons writhe, clasping jewels in their claws. Lightning, fireballs, and hailstones descend from the dragon on the left. In the lower left is a water dragon with a *makara*-like trunk and head. At the lower right the head and forelegs of a four-clawed dragon emerge dynamically from the clouds. Placed between the dragons are six examples of flaming pearls, appearing as a disc, jewel, and spiralling conch-like sphere. The scales of the dragons are painted in two different methods, either as reptilian scales or as rows of variably sized circles or ellipses. These methods are applied to all the amphibians, fish and reptiles depicted in Tibetan art: turtles, tortoises, fish, frogs, lizards, snakes, *nagas*, *makaras*, and dragons. In the lower left corner are two examples of dragon feet, showing the soft tiger-like soles and the scaled talons of the eagle or hawk. At the bottom centre I have included a small arched section of a scaled dragon's body with one scale pointing backwards in the opposite direction. In European chivalric mythology this is the one vulnerable point on a dragon's body where a knight must thrust his lance to slay the dragon.

GARUDA (Tib. *khyung, mkha' lding*)

Garuda 'the devourer' is the mythical 'Lord of Birds' in both the Hindu and Buddhist traditions. In the Hindu Puranic legends Garuda is the son of Kashyapa and Vinata, who after five hundred years' incubation hatched fully-grown from an egg, which his mother Vinata delivered at his 'first birth'. As soon as he emerged from the egg his vast terrifying form filled the skies, the hurricane from his beating wings shook the earth, and the unbearable luminosity emanating from his golden body caused even the gods to mistake him for Agni, the god of fire.

Garuda's mother Vinata had an argument with her sister Kadru concerning the colour of the tail of the horse, Uchaishravas, which emerged from the churning of the primal ocean. Kadru was the mother of the serpents and, as an act of vengeance, she held Vinata to ransom in her serpent-pit prison. In order to free his mother Garuda stormed the heaven of Indra and stole the sacred *amrita* as payment for the ransom. Through subterfuge Garuda was able to liberate his mother, but during the transaction a few drops of *amrita* fell from his beak onto some *kusha* grass. The serpents licked the grass and its sharp edges caused their tongues to become forked. The gods, with great difficulty, regained the *amrita* from Garuda's beak. Such was his power that even Indra's mighty *vajra* was broken on Garuda's body. Only Vishnu was capable of subduing him and, binding him by oath, Vishnu took Garuda as his vehicle and granted him the boon of immortality.

There were many variations of the legends of Garuda contained in the *Vishnu Puranas* and *Garuda Puranas*, yet many of these texts are now lost. In later mythology, Krishna, as the eighth incarnation of Vishnu, takes Garuda as his mount to subdue the great *naga* serpent Kaliya.

Garuda has always been the sworn enemy of snakes and *nagas*. The archetypal legend of the enmity that exists between birds of prey and serpents occurs across a wide spectrum of transcultural mythologies. Such birds include the Sumerian and Greek eagle, the poison-transmuting peacock of Persia and India, the Chinese *peng-niao*, and the gigantic snake-eating *simurgh* or *rukh* of Sinbad's adventures in *Arabian Nights*. Marco Polo recorded that the *rukh* (from Madagascar) was large enough to lift an elephant in its talons, its outspread wings measuring sixteen paces. Both snake and bird are 'twice-born' from an egg, and the image of a bird of prey seizing a snake in its talons was probably a common sight to a falconer. Garuda is also known as Suparna (beautiful wings), Garutman (the solar bird), Sarparati (enemy of serpents), and Khageshvara or Pakshiraj (lord of birds). The female bird is known as a Garudi.

Originally the Indian Garuda, the 'chief of feathered creatures', was represented as a great bird. Later his form assumed that of a 'bird-man' – a creature half eagle and half man, combining a human body with a bird's head, talons, beak, and wings. Zoomorphic variations of the garuda's artistic representation diffused throughout India, Nepal, Sri Lanka, Burma, Thailand, and South East Asia. In Bali his animalistic image assumed great popularity. Garuda is commonly evoked to ward off snakes, snakebites, and all manner of animal, vegetable, and mineral poisonings. In China the garuda is identified with the god of thunder, who carries a hammer and chisel representing the roar of thunder and flashes of lightning.

In Tibet the Indian garuda became assimilated with the Bon *khading* (Tib. *mkha' lding*), the golden 'horned eagle', king of birds, and the Bon bird of fire. The white *khading* is identified with the swan, the king of water birds. In Tibetan, two words are used for the transfigured Indian garuda (Tib. *khyung* and *mkha' lding*).

Tibetan iconography depicts Garuda with the upper torso and arms of a man, the head, beak and legs of a bird, and large wings which unfold from his back, shoulders, or forearms. Below the waist his feathered thighs terminate in ostrich-like lower legs, with large clawed feet ending in sharp talons. His back is feathered, with long tail feathers which reach to the level of his feet. His curved beak is like that of an eagle, falcon or owl and, like his talons, has a *vajra* nature comparable to indestructible meteorite iron. No *naga* serpent is able to survive his iron grip or bite.

His wings and eyes are commonly golden, the hair on his head blazes upwards, and his eyebrows twist like fire. Between his sharp horns, a head protuberance conceals a *naga*-jewel in his skull. This jewel, stolen from the king of the *nagas*, is sometimes represented as a head ornament placed above the sun and moon on his crown. An alternative legend relates how he took this jewel from Mt Meru and, having secretly swallowed it, vomited it back into existence. The vomit of an eagle is a Tibetan folk remedy for poisoning. The jewel is more likely to be a *naga*-king treasure which grants the possessor the power, or *siddhi*, of having control over all snakes.

In his sharp beak Garuda devours a *naga* king. Textual sources usually describe Garuda as biting on the head of a serpent whilst holding its tail in his hands. However Garuda is usually illustrated with a long snake held between both hands and biting into it in the middle. He is also described as wearing the eight great *nagas* as ornaments. One binds his hair, two others serve as earrings, two as bracelets, two as anklets, and one as a belt or necklace.

Garuda appears in many forms according to different traditions and lineages, perhaps assuming greatest prominence in the Dzogchen transmissions of the Nyingma and Bon traditions. He is commonly the vehicle of Amoghasiddhi – the green Buddha of the north, and crowns the apex of the Buddhas' enlightenment thrones. In the Nyingma tradition he personifies certain wrathful forms of Padmasambhava, and in the hidden treasure (Tib. *gter ma*) tradition he is often known as a guardian of treasures. He is also strongly associated with Vajrapani and Hayagriva; a triple *sadhana* of Vajrapani, Hayagriva, and Garuda is specified in removing obstacles and illnesses, especially *naga*-related afflictions such as kidney failure, plague, and cancer. In this triple *sadhana* of Vajrapani, garudas are visualised in various forms at many different points in the body.

A group of five garudas commonly represent the wisdoms, elements, and qualities of the Five Buddha Families: a yellow garuda stands for earth, a white for water, a red for fire, a black for air, and a blue or multicoloured for space. The multicoloured garuda is yellow from the waist downwards (earth), white from the hips to navel (water), red from the navel to throat (fire), black from the chin to forehead (air), and blue or green on his crown (wisdom). The wings of the multicoloured garuda have feathers of five colours, which symbolises the element of space scintillating rainbow light rays in all directions. Sometimes the ends of the wing feathers are *vajra*-tipped. The yellow or golden garuda is probably the most frequently represented form; he has a yellow jewel-body that blazes like fire; he spreads his golden wings and tramples on the eight great *nagas*. The garuda can have two or three eyes, which are usually golden. The auspicious crest of jewel, sun, and moon on his crown symbolises the union of the solar and lunar winds dissolving into the fire of the subtle body's central channel. His two wings represent the union of method and wisdom. His form symbolises the transmutation of poison into *amrita*. His emergence fully-fledged from the egg symbolises the birth of great spontaneous awareness.

Plate 44: The garuda

Plate 44

Five garudas are illustrated here, three of which are airborne and two of which strut dynamically on the ground. Four of the garudas devour serpents in their *vajra*-beaks, whilst the fifth has transmuted the body of the serpent into a string of jewels with a yaktail tassle for the serpent's head.

THE MAKARA (Tib. *chu srin*)

The Sanskrit word *makara* (and the Tibetan *chu srin*) refer to a water or sea-monster. Mythological sea-serpents or monsters occur in the symbolism of the collective unconscious of many ancient cultures. The *makara* is the vehicle of the river goddess Ganga, and by association has sometimes been identified with the freshwater dolphins that inhabit the river Ganges. Varuna, the god of water and the ocean, also has a *makara* as his vehicle. The tenth 'sign' or *rasi* of the Indian zodiac is the *makara*, which corresponds with Capricorn the sea-goat in the Western zodiac. The *makara* is also an emblem of Kama, the Indian god of love and desire. Kama is also known as Makara-Ketana, the *makara* being a symbol of his sensual energy. Kama has also been identified with Aphrodite or Venus, the Greek or Roman goddess of love, who was born of the sea and whose principal attributes are the scallop shell and the dolphin.

The *makara* is an ancient Indian symbol formed of a number of animals which together possess the nature of a crocodile. The *makara* has the lower jaw of a crocodile, the trunk of an elephant, the upper tusk and ears of a wild boar, the wide staring eyes of a monkey, the scales and flexible body of a fish, and the extended tail feathers of a peacock. This composite creature personifies the ferocious nature of the crocodile. In its stylistic evolution to its present form the *makara* has gained a lion's forepaws, a horse's mane, the facial gills and tendrils of a fish on its jaw and trunk, and the horns of the deer or dragon. From its once feathered fish-tail there now emerges a complex spiralling endless-knot pattern known as a '*makara*-tail' design.

Crocodile heads and skins were worn during ancient warfare to instil fear in the opponents. Vestiges of animal headdress survive in the armour depicted on warriors in Tibetan art, such as the four great Guardian Kings – particularly Virudhaka, the blue Guardian King of the south, who wears a *makara* or crocodile helmet. Ancient battle-standards frequently bore the skin of a crocodile, tiger, wolf, or bull. The *makaradhvaja* or crocodile-headed banner, such as is carried by Rahula, was originally the battle standard of Rudra or Shiva. It also formed the battle standard of the hosts of Mara, who attacked Buddha under the bodhi tree in the hours before his enlightenment. Militarily the term *makara* also refers to a specific battle formation of troops, which take the shape of a *makara* during battlefield manoeuvres.

The *makara*, as an ancient Indian symbol of power, was adopted by early Buddhism. It is commonly found on early south Indian temples and occurs on the earliest cave pillars at Ajanta, which date back to the second century. The *makara* motif assumed wide usage in Vajrayana Buddhism. The prongs of the *vajra*, the triangular blade of the ritual dagger (Tib. *phur bu*), and a host of other weapons and ritual objects emerge from the decorative mouths of *makaras*. Here the symbolic meaning of firmness and unshakeability are implied, as the crocodile proverbially will not release its jaws until its prey is dead. On temple roofs *makaras* form the corner projections from which rainwater descends. A *makara* head, frequently with a virile ram's head emerging from its mouth, may form the spout of a water source or spring. *Makaras*, along with *nagas* and the garuda, form the arching upper *torana* of gateways, doorways, and the surrounding throne of enlightened beings. Many variations of *torana* designs are found throughout Tibet, India, and especially Nepal, where it developed as a highly favoured motif amongst Newari craftsmen. The *makara* as guardian of gateways is echoed in the *vajra* prongs, which encircle the four gateways of the two-dimensional mandala.

Plate 45: The *makara*

Plate 45

Shown here are examples of *makara* motifs. On the left is a typical *makara* with a long scrolling tail. Like the dragon he is horned, bearded, whiskered, and has a horse's mane. The swirls of his tail form extremely intricate designs when the *makara* is placed on either side of an upper *torana*. In the centre is a *makara* with a short fish-tail, arching his head backwards. On the right is a roof gable or cornice detail, where the *makara* forms a decorative guardian water animal to protect from rain, hail, thunderstorms, and lightning bolts. At the top, from left to right, are a *makara* headdress, a *makara* headdress such as is worn by Virudhaka, and a *makara*-faced shoe. At the bottom is a typical *makara* weapon-head from a curved knife (Tib. *gri gug*). Further illustrations of the *makara* are found in Plate 48.

THE FACE OF MAJESTY (Skt. *kirtimukha*)

The *kirtimukha*, or face of majesty, fame, or glory, is commonly known as the 'monster mask' or 'the creature without a name'. In China it is known as *T'ao t'ieh*, or 'monster of greed', a hideous creature which was believed to have actually existed. Chinese cooking vessels were often ornamented with the 'beast of greed' as a caution against rapacity and indulgence. This ancient symbol is found, as guardian of doorways, across the whole of China, the Indian subcontinent, and South East Asia. The *kirtimukha* image is extremely popular amongst Newari craftsmen of the Kathmandu valley, its sculpted form frequently crowning doorways and appearing over *torana* archways.

The 'monster of greed' has its origin in a Shaivite legend from the *Skandha Purana*. Jalandhara, a demon created from the blaze of Shiva's third eye, assumes great power and desires an incestuous relationship with his adopted mother Parvati – the consort of Shiva. Jalandhara persuades his demonic friend Rahu to demand Parvati's favour. In an infernal rage, Shiva creates from the blaze of his third eye another horrific demon, which rushes to devour Rahu. Terrified, Rahu begs for mercy and Shiva accepts his repentance. Ravenously hungry and deprived of its prey, the demon turns upon itself, and devours its own body until only the head remains. Pleased with this manifestation of his supreme power, Shiva names him *kirtimukha* – 'the face of glory' – and bids him remain for all eternity as a guardian to the threshold of his door.

In Tibetan art the *kirtimukha* forms an heraldic device on armour, helmets, shields, and weapons of war. A connected frieze of *kirtimukha* faces, forming a continuous net of jewels, is often painted across the upper beams of temple walls. Tasselled hanging banners (Tib. *ka 'phan*), which decorated temple pillars, are often crowned with a dome-shaped image of the *kirtimukha* face. Architecturally they form a familiar motif on lintels, archways, and pillar cornices, echoing their incorporation into three-dimensional mandala palaces. As door handles or knockers, often festooned with white scarves (Tib. *kha btags*), they commonly occur on temple doors. A frieze of six, or eight, *kirtimukha* faces, bearing nets of jewels in their mouths, circulates around the upper section of the ritual hand bell (Skt. *ghanta*; Tib. *dril bu*).

Variations on the *kirtimukha* include the *simhamukha* (lion head), *garudamukha*, *kalamukha* (the devouring head of time; Rahu), *shankhamukha* (the conch, or alligator head), and the *kalamakara* (the *makara* which devours time). The lion head, as a symbol of Shakyamuni, is also fashioned into temple door handles, and may easily be mistaken for the *kirtimukha*. The association between Rahu and *kirtimukha* as disembodied and voracious heads is quite apparent.

Plate 46

Depicted here are several variations of the *kirtimukha* face with nets of jewels hanging from their mouths. The *kirtimukha* is

Plate 46: *Kirtimukha*, the face of glory

represented as a ferocious animal head, usually without a lower jaw. His face bears a strong resemblance to both the lion and dragon, with curling horns, mane, and snout. He may also have dragon whiskers, and like Garuda may have a head protuberance crowned by a sun and moon crest. Usually he holds two braceleted human hands to his mouth, whilst devouring a golden *makara*-tailed crest bar, or a net of pearls and jewels. He may also be shown swallowing a single large jewel, which fills his mouth. Only his hands and head are illustrated.

THE NAGA (Tib. *klu*)

The *nagas* are the serpent spirits that inhabit the underworld. They have their origin in the ancient snake cults of India, which probably date back to the Indus valley civilisation and were assimilated into Buddhism at an early date. In the Hindu Puranic legends *nagas* were the offspring of Kadru, the sister of Vinata who gave birth to Garuda. Both the *nagas* and Garuda shared a common father, Kashyapa, but due to the treachery of Kadru they became mortal enemies. Kadru gave birth to a thousand many-headed snakes which populated the region below the earth known as Patala. This subterranean realm is rich in treasures, with beautiful palaces ruled over by three great *naga* kings named Sesha, Vasuki, and Takshaka, who figure prominently in several Puranic legends. In Buddhist iconography these three *nagarajas* or *naga* kings are usually identified as Nanda, Varuna, and Upananda.

Historically, the Nagas were an ancient Indian race, of whom little is known other than the strong serpent-cult legacy that they appear to have left on Indian culture. Snake-lore, and its magical traditions of snake-charming and snake-catching are still widely practised by itinerant sadhus and fakirs across the Hindu and Muslim lands. The minor *siddhi* of controlling snakes through the force of willpower or 'snake-consciousness' is said to be quite easy to attain. Various traditions rely on written charms, talismans, and amulets to empower the snake-handler's will. The legendary stone or 'pearl' obtained from the head of an old king-cobra is probably the most potent of these talismans. A vast number of people still die from snakebite in India every year, and it is not difficult to understand the fear and veneration these reptiles inspired in rural Indian village life.

The Buddhist *nagas* inherited much of their early Indian symbolism. They dwell in the underworlds below land and sea, especially in the aquatic realms of rivers, lakes, wells, and oceans. In Buddhist cosmology they are assigned to the lowest level of Mt Meru, with their garuda enemies placed on the level above. *Nagas* are the underworld guardians of treasures and concealed teachings, and can manifest in serpent, half-serpent, or human forms. Nagarjuna, the great first or second-century south Indian Buddhist philosopher, received the *Prajnaparamita Sutra* (Sutra on the Perfection of Wisdom) from the undersea palace of a *naga* king and revealed it to mankind. This sutra, in both its abridged and expanded version, was originally entrusted to the guardianship of the *nagas* by Shakyamuni Buddha.

Nagas can have a beneficial, neutral, or hostile influence on human beings. Like their Chinese dragon equivalents, the *nagas* are responsible for controlling the weather, causing droughts by withholding rain when they are offended, and releasing rain when they are propitiated. Pollution of their environment, or disrespectful acts – such as smoking tobacco, and urinating or washing soiled clothing in a *naga*-inhabited stream – can result in illnesses or *naga* afflictions. Leprosy, cancer, kidney problems, and skin ailments are all viewed as potentially *naga*-related diseases.

In 1974 a new ring road was being built around Kathmandu city. At the foot of Swayambhu hill, just outside the city and within the ring road perimeter, there was a swift stream where everyone would wash their clothes, myself included. On the far bank of this stream two large snakes, about seven feet long, could regularly be seen basking in the sun. One day, as the road construction neared Swayambhu, these two snakes disappeared. The local people were extremely upset, believing that as these *nagas* had left, some dreadful calamity would soon occur. A few weeks later the stream began to dry up, doubtlessly due to some water diversion caused by the ring road construction. Whether viewed superstitiously or scientifically, the outcome was the same; it is all a question of belief.

Lake Yamdrok Tso in Central Tibet is believed to be the 'life energy' lake of the country, an abode of great *naga* kings. There is an ancient belief that when this lake dries up the whole population of Tibet will perish. At the present time the Chinese government is constructing a huge hydroelectric scheme at Yamdrok Tso, with a long drainage tunnel descending into the Tsangpo River many miles below. By slowly draining the lake it is estimated that this turbo-tunnel will provide enough electricity to supply the whole of Central Tibet. Perhaps the endless sands of the deserts of time will also eventually pour through the hourglass of this tunnel.

In the Tibetan tradition there are eight classes of spirits or demons that inhabit and interact with the human realm. Various listings are given for these eight classes of spirits, but three were probably most prominent from an early date: the *nagas* (Tib. *klu*) inhabit the underworld and aquatic regions; the 'lords of the soil' (Tib. *sa bdag*) inhabit the earth; and the 'earth spirits' (Tib. *gnyan*) occupy all places upon the earth.

Nagas are divided into a fivefold caste division based on the Hindu caste system or social order. In the east are the white *kshatriya* or warrior caste, in the south the yellow *vaishya* or merchant caste, in the west the red *brahmin* or priestly caste, in the north the green *shudra* or labourer caste, and at the centre the blue-black *chandali* outcastes or 'untouchables'. This colour placement corresponds with the traditional directions of the Five Buddha mandala with the blue-black Akshobhya at the centre.

These five castes of *nagas* with their respective colours are important in the iconography of wrathful Heruka deities such as Vajrapani, Vajrakila, Hayagriva, and Garuda. Here they form one of the 'eight attires of the charnel ground', known as the 'revolting snake ornaments' (see page 315).

These consist of pairs or clusters of ferocious, writhing, coiling and hissing snakes, which are worn as body ornaments on these wrathful forms. At the crown of a wrathful deity's head are the coiling, white snakes of the warrior (*kshatriya*) or royal caste, which wreathe around the half-*vajra* at the crown. The spherical hub of this half-*vajra* conceals the seal or image of the parent Buddha or 'Lord' of that deity's particular Buddha Family. Clusters of yellow snakes of the merchant (*vaishya*) caste hang as earrings, or from them. The deity's necklace is fashioned from a wreath of red snakes of the priest (*brahmin*) or 'twice-born' caste. As a sash or chest garland the deity wears an entwining bunch of long green or blue snakes of the commoner (*shudra*) or labourer caste. This chest garland was originally derived from the sacred thread of the brahmins. As bracelets, armlets, and anklets the wrathful deity wears encircling wreaths of small black snakes, representing the outcastes or untouchables (*chandalis*).

These snake ornaments represent the 'eight great *nagas*' or *naga* kings (*nagarajas*), and their symbolism conceals a multitude of meanings. Collectively the snake ornaments symbolise the rejection or destruction of anger, their writhing the 'turning away' of enemies, and their entwined coiling the bliss of the deity and his consort's sexual embrace. As the 'eight great *nagas*' they symbolise control over the eight *naga* realms, control over all eight classes of spirits, elimination of the eight mundane obsessions, and attainment of the eight great *siddhis* or psychic powers. The eight mundane obsessions are: praise and blame, pleasure and pain, loss and gain, infamy and fame.

The eight great *nagas* appear in the wrathful landscape of the eight great cemeteries or charnel grounds. Here they are depicted arising, waist upwards, from the waters of the eight great rivers or lakes, with hands folded in supplication (*namaskar*) *mudra*, holding a precious *naga*-jewel between their palms. The lakes symbolise compassion or 'conventional *bodhichitta*', the *nagas* symbolise the six or ten great perfections (*paramitas*), and the jewels symbolise the four modes of gathering disciples.

The names and listings of the eight great *naga* kings vary according to different deity *sadhanas* or traditions. One such list assigns Vasuki and Shankhapala as the yellow *vaishya* snake ornaments at the crown, Nanda and Upananda as the red *brahmin* earrings, Padma and Varuna as the white *kshatriya* armlets and anklets, with Suparna and Kulika forming the black *shudra* necklace. Another listing names Ananta, Padma, Vasuki, Takshaka, Mahapadma, Karkotaka, Shankhapala, and Kulika, or Anavatapa. The *Kalachakra Tantra* adds two more *naga* kings, Jaya and Vijaya, to complete a list of ten. Garuda, as the mortal enemy of snakes, is always described as wearing these eight great *naga* kings as ornaments, whilst he bites the head of another venomous *naga* king with his beak.

Pictorially these *nagas* are rarely painted in their specific colours as body ornaments. Usually a single small snake is placed around the *vajra* at the crown, another long snake forms the chest garland or sash, whilst small snakes are depicted coiling around the bracelets, armlets, and anklets.

Rarely are the snake earrings depicted, and commonly all of these *naga* ornaments are either painted green, blue or black. Sometimes these *nagas* are described as having small silver bells hanging from their necks, which tinkle with the overwhelming tremble of the wrathful deity's powerful energy or vibration. The eight *naga* kings, in an entwined serpent form and painted in their correct colours, are often illustrated under the feet of certain wrathful deities who perform the activity of 'crushing the eight great *nagas*'. A hundred, a thousand, or a hundred thousand *nagas* may also be described as being trampled underfoot.

The *Kalachakra Tantra* describes the *naga* as a ferocious serpent thus, "The enraged lord of hooded snakes has the colour of blue-black eye ointment. He writhes and hisses, displaying his hood and revealing his curved fangs and two tongues. He is wrathful and cruel, as swift as the wind when he strikes and bites."

In their half-human form *nagas* are depicted with a human body above the waist, and with a long serpent's tail which is usually half-submerged in water. They wear ornaments of gold, coral, and pearl, with a long silk scarf draped over their shoulders. The female *naga* is known as a *nagi* or *nagini*, and she is depicted with firm round breasts. The sexual organs of the male and female are never represented; as in snakes these are situated on the back of their tails. The *nagas* may appear in a peaceful form, holding a *naga*-jewel, vase of *amrita*, or a concealed text (Tib. *gter ma*). Or they may appear in a wrathful form, brandishing snakes and weapons. Ocean *nagas* may hold a pearl or a branch of coral. They may also be hybrid spirits, having an allegiance with another class of being, such as a lake spirit or a *naga rakshasa*, appearing as a wrathful demon with a *naga*'s tail.

Nagas usually have a canopy or hood of one, three, five, seven, eight, or nine small serpents above their head, which are variably coloured. These may represent the *nagas*' activities or castes, or the seven other *naga* kings accompanying them – which are rooted into a single union along the spine. A single *naga* head above may also represent Kundalini Shakti. The canopy of snake heads has its Hindu parallel in the forms of Shiva and Vishnu. Shiva wears similar snake ornaments to the wrathful Buddhist deities, and is frequently crowned with a five or seven-hooded canopy of cobras. Vishnu, who sleeps on the coils of the thousand-headed serpent Ananta, is also commonly crowned with a hood of seven serpents. Buddha is likewise believed to have been protected by the coils and hood of Ananta as he sat under the bodhi tree. Several other Buddhist deities, such as Nageshvararaja, Ratnachuda, and Nagarjuna, also wear a hood of five or seven snakes.

Plate 47

At the top left is a detail of Garuda and two *nagas* from Plate 56. These two young *nagas*, a male and female, hold the long *naga*-king serpent which Garuda devours. On the upper right is a typical representation of a peaceful *naga* king holding a jewel between its palms; this is the form in which the

Plate 47: The *nagas*

eight great *nagas* of the charnel grounds are represented. At the bottom left is the head of Nagarjuna, with a canopy of seven entwined serpents crowning his head, symbolising his control over the *naga* realms. In the bottom centre, a *naga* crowned with a single serpent presents the text of the *Prajnaparamita Sutra* to Nagarjuna. In the corners are drawings of *nagas* in serpent form. Snakes are often described as 'ox-headed' in Tibetan art, with the bovine-like head of a python or viper. Small horns or ears are also commonly depicted on the back of a snake's head.

Nagas and the Civilisations of the Indus Valley

The cosmology, domains, activities, qualities, and castes of the *nagas* define them as inhabiting a realm of existence and social structure approaching the complexity of the human realm. The same is true of all of the eight classes of spirits or demons. The incredible complexity and iconographical definition of these legions of spirit deities with their retinues simply staggers the human imagination. Although these iconographic elements are predominantly of Indian or Indian Buddhist origin, there are specific peculiarities which define their iconographical residue as being

of Tibetan or Central Asian origin. To postulate that this residue is purely of Bon origin is not an adequate explanation, as, like Buddhism, the Bon tradition is itself a 'foreign import' into Tibet.

Although the Bon tradition preceded Buddhism, and developed in the western Tibetan land of Zhang Zhung located to the west of the Kailash-Manasarovar region, it is said by the Bonpos to have originated in remote antiquity in the land of Tajik (Tib. rTag gzig), which lay to the west of Zhang Zhung. The term Tajik probably derives from the Persian name given to the Arabs who settled on the west coast of India during the early eighth century, although earlier Chinese sources identify Tajik (Ch. Ta hsia) with the Tajiki-speaking tribes of Bactria (Afghanistan), who later found autonomy in the area of Russian Turkestan now known as Tajikistan. Khyung Lung, the ancient capital of Zhang Zhung, is located on the upper reaches of the Indus valley, whose watershed is the Kailash area. All along the westward course of the Indus valley were the lands of Ladakh, Kashmir, Hunza, Gilgit, Uddiyana, and Swat – an area rich in archaeological remains. On the lower reaches of the Indus valley lay the ancient Harappan city of Mohenjo-Daro (*circa* 2500 BC). Amongst the artifacts unearthed there are clay seals which appear to indicate that the prototypes of the Hindu mother goddess and Shiva possibly originated here. Objects of solidified mercury have also been unearthed at Mohenjo-Daro, revealing that a sophisticated alchemical tradition existed at this time. Conjecturally one may conclude that the rudiments of Shaivism, alchemy, and tantra possibly had their origin in this pre-Vedic civilisation.

To the north of Zhang Zhung lay the early Buddhist Central Asian lands of Khotan, Yarkand, Turfan, and Kashgar. The kingdom of Ladakh or 'little Tibet' lay to the west, and beyond this the kingdom of Kashmir with its early tantric traditions of Kashmiri Shaivism and Vajrayana Buddhism. Beyond again lay the Swat valley, a great centre of Gandhara Buddhist culture and art, which is commonly identified with the tantric kingdom of Uddiyana – the birthplace of Padmasambhava.

The Kailash-Manasarovar area has been one of the most important Hindu pilgrimage routes since time immemorial. As Mt Kailash is regarded as the abode of Lord Shiva, it was especially important as a Shaivite pilgrimage centre. Kailash was also sacred to the Jains, with their parallel tantric lineages. Into this melting pot of the three great Indian tantric traditions – Buddhist, Hindu, and Jain – were poured other streams of non-tantric origin. From Persia and Central Asia came streams of both dualistic and gnostic thought, such as the Manichean, Zorastrian, and Nestorian Christian traditions. Foremost amongst the non-dual influences was the Indian Samkhya system of Vedantic philosophy known as Advaita-Vedanta. Advaita stressed the direct realisation of one's innate or 'unborn' nature through self-enquiry, and placed no importance or reliance upon hierarchies of gods and demons, visualisations, rituals or yogic practices. To its practitioners yoga itself was dualistic, implying in its very name the concept of 'union'. The Advaita philosophy has a profound similarity to the Tibetan Buddhist and Bon systems of Dzogchen. Their parallel traditions are far closer to a common jugular vein than they are to the divided hemispheres of the sectarian brain, which advances its own philosophical system of non-duality as the highest or only authentic tradition, to the detriment of all other philosophical schools of thought.

In Indian hagiographies many great saints are reputed to have attained realisation in the Kailash-Manasarovar area; this 'presence' cannot have failed to make a major impact on the indigenous religions – in later years predominantly Buddhism, in the middle years predominantly Bon, and in the early years the 'religion with no name'.

Pure Buddhist philosophy can easily be viewed as a science in the modern world, whether one takes it on an emotional, mental, psychological, philosophical, or spiritual level. At every level it can be accommodated to make 'perfect sense'. The world of demons, demi-gods, spirits, and ethereal beings is quite alien to the 'rational' Western intelligence, and the trend in the transmission of Tibetan Buddhism to the West has been to discard all that is theologically 'animistic' in favour of a pure and simple truth which can be analysed, applied, philosophised, and debated. Yet to the vast majority of Tibetans the world of

spirits and ethereal beings was as real as our own. To see a god on every mountain, a *naga* in every lake, a blessing or curse on every prevailing wind, was to see 'second nature' as second nature. When the spirits in all their 'eight classes' are forgotten, neglected, or chased away by the concensus reality of uniformity and technological communication, they become conspicuous in their absence: the more wrathful amongst them take root in the human psyche, manifesting geographically as inner-city 'no-go' areas or accident 'black spots'; the more benign, withdraw from the world of men and depart to the pristine sanctuary of the wilderness. When the *nagas* leave, pollution comes. It's all a question of belief. Although through the science of 'rational' or 'pure' Buddhism we may seek the simple truth, our external world remains as stressfully complex as ever. The truth, as Oscar Wilde so humorously stated, is rarely simple, and never pure.

THE THREE VICTORIOUS CREATURES OF HARMONY

This group of three hybrid creatures, formed by the union of pairs of traditionally hostile animals, appears to be of purely Tibetan origin. However they probably first appeared in early Indian Buddhism as the decoration motifs on the victory banner, fashioned from a hanging triple valance of silk cloth. Their images are found on thangkas, furniture, astrological or divinatory diagrams, auspicious offering compositions, victory banners, and most especially on prayer flags (Tib. *rlung rta*). They are known as the 'eight-limbed lion', the 'fish with hair', and the '*makara*-snail'. Collectively they represent the harmonious union of opposites.

The eight-limbed or garuda-lion is created from the interbreeding of the lion with its traditional competitor, the garuda bird. Its eight limbs are formed by having claws both on its foot-pads and knees, although usually only its foot claws are pictorially represented. As the garuda is the lord of the skies and the lion is lord of the earth, the garuda-lion unifies heaven and earth in victory. Its body, limbs, mane, and tail are those of a lion, whilst its head and wings are those of the garuda. This creature can easily be identified with its mythological Western equivalent, the griffin or gryphon. The griffin has the body of a lion, with the head, wings, and talons of an eagle. The historian Herodotus wrote that griffins lived on high Indian mountains, where they dug for gold with their sharp talons. The talons of a griffin were believed to change colour in the presence of poisons, and could only be acquired by holy men.

The 'fish with hair' is born from the union of a fish with its traditional enemy, the otter. Its body and limbs are that of an otter, but its head, gills, and sometimes its tail, are those of a fish. Like the otter its body is covered in brown, grey, or black hair. The scales of the fish's neck may dissolve into the otter's fur, or an abrupt demarcation may be formed at the forelegs.

The '*makara*-snail' is born from the union of the *makara* (Tib. *chu srin*) – a 'water monster' usually equated with the

Plate 48: The three victorius creatures of harmony (garuda-lion, fish-otter, *makara*-snail)

crocodile – and its traditional prey, the conch or water snail. The *makara*-snail is probably derived from the hermit crab which destroys the conch mollusc and takes up residence in its shell. Land hermit-crabs are also found in streams throughout the Himalayan foothills. The *makara* as 'water monster' is represented in its usual form with scales, horns, tusks, mane, upturned snout, and usually with its two legs protruding from the mouth of the conch shell. Often the *makara*'s fabulously swirling tail emerges from the tip of the conch shell.

Plate 48

Illustrated here are various combinations of the three victorious creatures of harmony. At the top are two examples of the garuda-lion. In the second and third row are five drawings of the fish-otter, showing the various ways in which the scales, gills, fins, and tails of the fish may be integrated with the body of the otter. Four examples of the *makara*-snail are illustrated below. The dynamic and highly detailed torso of the *makara* seems to thrust itself fearlessly from the conch shell, its swirling tail bursting from the shell's tip. To the right of these is another garuda-lion. In the bottom row are three further examples of these six traditional enemies blending into the three harmonious creatures.

DOMESTIC AND WILD ANIMALS

Plate 49

Illustrated in this drawing is a composition of domestic and wild animals. In the top row are the three animals – a black pig, a red cockerel, and a green snake – that symbolise the 'three poisons' of ignorance, desire, and aversion. These three creatures form the central hub of the didactic 'wheel of life' painting (Skt. *bhavachakra*; Tib. *srid pa'i 'khor lo*), which illustrates how the three poisons of ignorance, desire, and aversion give rise to the whole karmic phenomenology of the six realms of cyclic existence. The black colour of the pig symbolises the darkness of primordial ignorance or confusion. According to the *I Ching*, pigs and fishes are believed to be the most difficult animals to influence. The red cockerel is proverbially a symbol of lust or attachment, with an insatiable appetite for the fulfilment of its desires and a territorial male aggression that will tolerate no rivalry. The green snake symbolises the aversion, hatred, or anger which arises from attachment, the unpredictable instinct to strike out at any moment. In the upper right the three animals are depicted as vomiting out, chasing and biting each others' tails. The root cause of the primal ignorance of the pig gives rise to attachment, which in turn gives rise to aversion, which in turn creates further ignorance.

Below are shown a group of reptiles and insects. On the left (below pig) is a lotus-shaped pattern found on the underside of a female divinatory tortoise. Below this a section

of tortoise shell is being used in the Chinese divination method. Small holes are bored into the tortoise shell at the intersections of its geometric hexagons. A metal needle is then heated to a red-hot temperature and inserted into one of these holes. A divinatory pattern is determined by the way in which the intersecting hexagon lines of the shell crack. To the right are shown two other tortoises. The female at the top has an upper shell which resembles heaped lotuses, whilst the male below has an upper shell which resembles the stacked steps of a stupa.

The 'five poisonous creatures' – lizard, toad, centipede or spider, scorpion, and snake – represent the five poisons of ignorance, desire, hatred, jealousy, and pride. In certain Asian folk medicine traditions a homeopathic remedy is prepared from a compound of these animal poisons. Bear bile, centipede or scorpion poison, and snake venom are mulled in the stomach acid of a snake. The noxious paste derived is then applied as a salve for gangrene or festering wounds. The five poisons derived from venoms are described as being used to poison the tips of weapons, such as arrowheads and ritual daggers (Tib. *phur bu*); once the poison entered the bloodstream the death of the victim was certain.

Below the tortoise is a domestic goat with silk ribbons tied around its neck. Domestic livestock destined for slaughter are frequently bought from a butcher, adorned with silk ribbons and set free. Usually the purpose of this ritual was to save the life of a sick person by an act of ransoming a life for a life. In the modern international world many Buddhists perform compassionate acts of merit by purchasing and freeing large numbers of small creatures or fish from the live-food markets of South East Asia. To the right of the domestic goat is the wild goat of the Tibetan highlands.

Below the scorpion and snakes are two golden-haired tigers. Two Tibetan mastiffs are depicted to the left of and below the uppermost tiger. These extremely large mastiffs serve as watchdogs for Tibetan homes or nomad encampments, where they guard against thieves or predators. Their ferocious appearance is exaggerated by a bright red felt or wool neck-collar, which protects the dog's throat from attack by wolves or other dogs. At the centre right are two wolves. Wolves and jackals are frequently depicted devouring corpses in cremation ground imagery. The jackal is depicted in a similar manner to the wolf, only it is smaller and usually has brown fur whilst the wolf has grey. At the centre left are two Bactrian camels with double humps, the vehicles of the deserts of Mongolia and Central Asia.

The next row shows three examples of the yak, the versatile beast of burden of the Tibetan highlands. The meat, milk, butter and dried cheese of the yak form an essential part of Tibet's national diet, whilst its dried dung provides fuel for cooking fires. Its hair is spun into rope or wool, its leathery skin is used for tents, bags and coracles, and its long soft tail was traditionally exported for fly whisks. Skulls of slaughtered yaks are often carved with mantras and placed upon *mani*-walls of carved prayer stones. The native wild yak can be a large and fierce animal. The Swedish explorer Sven Hedin tells of killing a wild male yak which

Plate 49: Various domestic and wild animals

measured over ten feet in length and took eleven bullets to kill. In the second row from the bottom are: a buffalo on the left, a cow and calf at the centre, and another yak on the right. The buffalo is the vehicle of the Dharmaraja Yama (Tib. gShin rje), the 'Lord of Death'. In the bottom row are four elephants following their leader, their trunks and tails forming an 'elephant chain' symbolising cooperation.

Animals as vehicles, messengers, emissaries and animal-headed deities form a vast pantheon in Vajrayana imagery. In wrathful offering thangkas (Tib. *rgyan thogs*), which depict the attributes of deities such as Palden Lhamo, Begtse, Yama, Yamari, or the various forms of Mahakala, often as many as a hundred animal and bird forms are represented. A black raven, black dog, black wolf, and a black man form the simplest messenger retinue of one form of Mahakala. Other forms of Mahakala are described as having a retinue of 'a hundred thousand black-ones', or a host of ferocious animals.

Animal Heads

Plate 50

In the upper left corner are two boar or sow heads with upward protruding tusks. In the Hindu pantheon the boar manifestation or Varaha Avatara (boar incarnation) is the third of the ten incarnations of Vishnu. In Shaivism the boar's face was assigned as the southern face of Shiva,

which looked towards his right. In Buddhism the female sow's face (*varahi*) is an attribute of the goddess Vajravarahi, where the sow's head appears as a small protuberance above the right ear of the goddess. The symbolism of Vajravarahi's human and sow face represents the union of absolute and relative truth.

Second from the left in the top row is a wolf's head which adorns a victory banner in warfare. Next are the heads of three birds of prey. In the upper right corner are examples of horses' heads such as appear above the head of the deity Hayagriva – 'the horse-necked'. In certain *sadhanas* a single or triple horse-head adorns Hayagriva. A small Hayagriva horse-head surmounted by a half-*vajra* appears in the lower middle left. To the right of the boar's head in the second row appear the heads of a buffalo and lion. In the bottom left corner are the heads of two stags or Tibetan elks with many pointed tines on their antlers. The deer or stag is the vehicle of a number of gods and goddesses, particularly those associated with the wind, such as Vayu – the god of the wind. At the bottom centre and bottom right are the heads of two goats displaying horns which entwine around each other. This peculiarity is specific to the vehicle of the deity Dorje Legpa in his manifestation as 'the dark blacksmith', wielding a fiery bellows and a foundry hammer. The entwined horns symbolise the binding together of relative and absolute truths, samsara and nirvana, or phenomena and emptiness. The goat is primarily the vehicle of the fire god, Agni. Between the two goat heads is an elephant's head.

Plate 50: Animal heads

TIGER, LEOPARD, SNOW-LION, AND HORSE

Plate 51

At the top are two tigers (Skt. *vyaghra*; Tib. *stag*). The tiger is not a native animal of Tibet, but the Bengal tiger of India and the long-haired tiger of neighbouring China ensured its frequent appearance in Tibetan imagery. In China, which does not have native lions, the tiger is endowed with all the majestic qualities attributed to the Indian lion. The Chinese tiger is a symbol of strength, fearlessness, and military prowess. Tigers' skins were worn in battle, and the Buddhist victory banner (Skt. *dhvaja*; Tib. *rgyal mtshan*) is frequently adorned with a tiger skin. A full tiger skin often formed the seat or *asana* of certain deities, yogins, siddhas, oracles, and great teachers. This has its origin in the Hindu tradition, where Shiva killed the tiger of desire and used its skin as his meditation seat, symbolising his transcendence over desire.

The rifles of the British Raj decimated the population of the Bengal tiger, its luxuriant pelt becoming a fireside carpet and its regal head a snarling stuffed trophy. As a substitute for the scarcity of genuine tiger pelts and as an act of conservation, tigerskin rug designs began to be woven as Tibetan carpets during the nineteenth century. Stylistic interpretation of the tiger's stripes in Tibetan art often depicted a whirling spiral of stripes on the tiger's breast or back.

In China the tiger was believed to bear the natural simulacra of the Chinese character for 'king' on its forehead. As king of terrestial creatures symbolising royal power, authority, and strength, the medicinal properties of the various parts of the tiger's anatomy were held in high esteem in the Chinese medical tradition. Similarly in the Tibetan medical tradition tigers' bones are believed to cure bone disorders, a tiger's tooth or whiskers are used to cure toothache, and the ashes of its skin, bones, claws, and internal organs are prescribed as remedies for a variety of bodily ailments. In Buddhist folklore, a tiger's bone is believed to bring rain when thrown into a dragon well or *naga* pool. The tiger's claw is believed to be an extremely potent talisman for the generation of personal power.

Tigerskin loincloths (*dhoti*) are worn by wrathful male Heruka deities, and leopardskin skirts are worn by their female consorts. Here the symbolism represents freedom from anger, the tiger skin symbolising the transmuted '*vajra*-anger' of the wrathful deity. Tigers are the mounts or vehicles of many deities, particularly those of a wrathful or warlike nature, where the riding of a wild tiger symbolises fearlessness and an indomitable will. Sometimes the tiger mount may be specifically described as a male tiger, white tiger, yellow tiger with multicoloured stripes, pregnant tigress, or a lactating mother tigress. A commonly painted image often found on the walls of Gelugpa monasteries is that of the 'Mongol leading the tiger', where a Mongolian lama or dignitary leads a tamed tiger on a chain. The Mongol symbolises the bodhisattva Avalokiteshvara,

the chain Vajrapani, and the tiger Manjushri. Its more sectarian symbolism is the supremacy of the Gelugpa school, symbolised by the Mongol, over the older 'red hat' sects, symbolised by the tiger.

On the left of the second row is the spotted leopard (Tib. *gzig*). The natural habitat of the leopard is the forest, where the dappled effect of sunlight on the foliage of trees blends with the camouflage of the leopard's spotted skin. In contrast to the tiger's phallic stripes, the spots of the leopard resemble eyes or female vaginas, hence the leopard skin is more commonly worn by *dakinis* or wrathful goddesses as a skirt or apron. The leopard skin is also used as an *asana* or meditational seat; it also adorns victory banners, and is frequently used as the material for a bow case or arrow quiver. The skin of the rare white snow leopard is used as a warm fur lining for hats or garments. Leopards, along with lions, tigers, and wild cats, are commonly included in the retinues of animal messengers of wrathful deities.

Drawings of the white snow-lion appear in the second and third rows. The white snow-lion with a turquoise mane is the presiding local deity (Tib. *gnyan*) of Tibet's snow mountain ranges. Hence the snow-lion is the national animal symbol of Tibet; it adorns Tibet's national flag, its government seals of office, its coins, banknotes, and stamps, and forms the insignia of His Holiness the Dalai Lama. The lion, as king of all beasts, is the symbol of Shakyamuni Buddha – who is also known as Shakyasimha (Tib. Sakya senge), the 'Lion of the Shakya clan'. The lion is therefore one of the prime symbols of Buddhism itself, with the eight lions of the eight directions supporting Shakyamuni's throne of enlightenment.

The lion as sacred, solar, or regal symbol permeated many ancient cultures spanning westward from Egypt to the Greek and Roman empires of Europe, and eastward from Egypt into Mesopotamia, Assyria, and Persia. The lion of Indian Buddhism found its cultural representation in Tibetan art as the mythological snow-lion, which inhabited the formidable snow mountains of Tibet. Like Buddhism itself, which 'leaped' over the Himalayas from India, the white snow-lion with its turquoise mane is a magical animal which is auspiciously sighted making playful leaps from one mountain peak to another. Snow-lions often appear in the harmonious pairing of a male and female; when symmetrically depicted the male is to the left and the female to the right.

Snow-lions are often illustrated playing with a ball in the manner of cats or kittens. A Chinese legend relates that lionesses produce milk from their paws, and that by leaving hollow balls for the lions to play with, some of this milk would pass into the balls. In Tibetan art the ball is usually painted as a three-coloured 'wheel of pleasure' (Tib. *dga' 'khyil*) made from brocade. It frequently has coloured silk streamers attached, which emphasise its use as a cat's plaything. The ball is similar to the flaming pearl which dragons compete to possess; it is also sometimes equated with the precious jewel or the disc of the sun. Chinese stone images of the guardian male lion often show one of his forepaws resting on the ball, whilst the lioness may guard her

Plate 51: Tiger, leopard, snow-lion and horse

cubs. Small oriental long-haired dogs, such as the Pekinese and Lhasa Apso or Tibetan terrier are alternatively known as 'lion-dogs', since their beard, mane, tail, and shaggy coat resemble the snow-lion. The docile nature of the snow-lion is occasionally illustrated in painting by a mendicant carrying a snow-lion cub in his arms, whilst the lion and lioness follow after tamely.

Tibet's great yogin, Milarepa, once had a prophetic dream which included the snow-lion. His guru Marpa interpreted it thus, "The lion pressing on the top of the pillar shows the yogin's lion-like nature. His luxuriant mane show how he is adorned with the mystical teachings. The lion's four paws represent the four 'great immeasurables' (love, compassion, equanimity, and sympathetic joy). The lion's eyes turned towards heaven show the yogin's renunciation of samsaric life. The lion's roaming free over the mountain peaks show that the yogin has gained the realm of absolute freedom."

By way of contrast, the *Kalachakra Tantra* gives a description of the ferocious Indian lion, "The enraged lion roars with a distorted face. His red eyes are like early dawn, he bares his teeth and his tongue protrudes like a sword. His tail twitches and his long mane sways. With his strong curved claws he desires to kill, and he wards away the forehead of the crazed elephant."

Tibet's national emblem depicts two snow-lions holding aloft a flaming precious gem, *dharmachakra*, or the Three Jewels. On Tibetan coins, banknotes, and postage stamps a pair of snow-lions hold aloft a tray of jewels or playfully leap with a ball; a single snow-lion may also be shown in a mountain landscape. The snow-lion dance, where two men dress in the 'stage-horse' outfit of a snow-lion and leap to the crashing of cymbals or drums, is a much loved spectacle amongst the Tibetan people.

Snow-lions are frequently portrayed on wood carvings and their image is painted or woven on all manner of secular and religious objects. Yet iconographically their most important function is to serve as the vehicles or throne supports for enlightened beings. The snow-lion is painted in pure white with a turquoise mane, tail, facial, and limb hairs, and with comma-shaped tufts of hair which adorn the front of its legs. Another form of white or pale-blue lion is depicted with vermilion or brown hair.

In the second row from the bottom are shown from left to right: a wild Tibetan pony, a saddled, white precious horse, and a wild Tibetan ass (Tib. *khyang*), an extremely graceful animal with a gait like that of an antelope. Its bodily form is very similar to a zebra, but its brown fur resembles that of a deer.

In the bottom row from left to right are a mythological *sharabha*, a horse, and a pair of antelopes. The *sharabha* represented here is a hybrid creature with the head and horns of a goat, the mane of a lion, and the body and legs of a horse – symbolising the determination, strength, and speed of this magical creature. In Hindu mythology the *sharabha* is the wrathful animal form which Shiva took in order to subdue the 'man-lion' Narasimha – the fourth of Vishnu's ten incarnations.

THE ELEPHANT
(Skt. *gaja, hastin*; Tib. *glang chen*)

The elephant 'as large as a snow mountain' is usually painted white in the 'colour of the moon' in Tibetan art. In artistic representation it is often drawn proportionally smaller than its actual size. The rare white albino elephant was highly venerated as a royal or temple elephant in India, Sri Lanka, Burma, and Thailand. The proverbial 'white elephant' derives its title from the fact that albino elephants were reputedly difficult to control, and much care and expense was involved in their keeping. Elephantine 'pearls' were believed to form in the forehead or temples of the rare albino. Only two main species of elephants survive into the present time – the African and Indian species. The African elephant has large ears which resemble the shape of the continent of Africa; the Indian elephant has smaller ears which resemble the outline of the Indian subcontinent.

The word elephant has its etymology in the first letter of the Hebrew alphabet, Aleph – meaning an ox. In Sanskrit the elephant is known as *gaja* or *hastin* – which means 'possessing a hand' (*hasta*) – referring to the versatility of the elephant's dextrous trunk and its creation from the hand of Brahma. An Indian dance posture, adopted by Shiva as Nataraja – 'Lord of the Dance', places one arm horizontally across the chest with the hand held downwards to resemble the elephant's trunk. This posture is known as *gajahasta mudra*, meaning 'elephant-hand'. A hand *mudra* formed by pointing the middle finger outwards to resemble an elephant's trunk, whilst curving the other four fingers inwards to resemble an elephant's legs, is known as *hastiratna mudra* ('elephant-jewel'), and is used in invocations to the 'seven precious gems of the *chakravartin*'.

The domestication or taming of the naturally wild Indian elephant dates back to remote antiquity. Clay images of ridden elephants have been unearthed in excavations of ancient Harappan civilisation sites (*circa* 2500 BC), such as Mohenjo-Daro in the Indus valley. Images of a domesticated horned elephant have been recently unearthed from the Harappan site of Kalibangan in Rajasthan. Images of tamed elephants are also found in ancient Egyptian relief carvings, and occur in Chinese historical records dating back to before the first millenium BC. The once populous Chinese elephant of the Yangtse valley became extinct around the fourth century BC. Once abounding throughout all the lands of western Asia the extinction of the elephant was noted by Alexander the Great, who first encountered elephants on the threshold of the Indian subcontinent in the fourth century BC. Eastwards from the Indus river and downwards into South East Asia the native elephant population remained widespread, until the advent of gunpowder curtailed its military importance and the greed of ivory hunters forced it to its present-day brink of extinction.

In ancient warfare the elephant formed one of the 'four limbs' (*chaturanga*) of the Indian military system, which was divided into elephants, horses, chariots, and infantry. The elephant of war was highly trained to be able to withstand the clamour of battle, the thrusting of lances, and the savage

Plate 52: Elephants

onslaught of hand-held weapons. Perfect obedience, and the ability to stand its ground amidst the bloodthirsty frenzy of the battlefield, were prerequisites of the valiant war elephant. Armour, bells, tassles, conch earrings, harnesses, and a coarse blanket would equip the elephant's battlewear. On its back would ride six or seven warriors bearing hooks, swords, lances, clubs, bows and arrows. A contingent of foot soldiers would guard its flanks and protect against attack from the rear. Due to its sheer physical might the elephant destroyed much that was in its path; it could ford rivers, blaze trails or clear pathways, and batter against doorways and fortifications. As such it became the unstoppable 're-mover of obstacles', an appellation that the elephant-headed god Ganesha acquired. In warfare the main defence against elephants entailed the deployment of iron spikes which studded vulnerable doors and walls, or the use of sharp iron staves, which were anchored into the ground before the defensive battlefront.

The *Kalachakra Tantra* gives a description of the wild elephant, "The great blue elephant thunders like a dragon. His eyes are tawny and his temples full of aromatic rutting musk. He uproots and smashes trees, binding with his trunk and chopping with his long tusks."

Wrathful deities often wear the blood-stained skin of a freshly killed elephant stretched across their backs, which is sometimes referred to as 'Indra's skin'. The qualities of wrathful forms which are comparable to the wild elephant are revealed in their symbolic activities of bellowing, crushing, tearing, trampling, and uprooting. The symbolism of the flayed elephant skin refers to the deity 'having torn the elephant of ignorance assunder'. The elephant, human, and tiger skins which adorn wrathful forms symbolise the destruction of the three poisons of ignorance, desire, and anger respectively.

Ganesha, whose head had been decapitated by the gaze of the planet Saturn (Sani), was the first son of Shiva. In place of his original head he received the head of Airavata, the white bull-elephant who was the mount of Indra. Etymologically the name Airavata comes from the Sanskrit '*iravat*', meaning 'produced from water', referring to Airavata's emerging from the churning of the ocean in the creation myth (see page 109). Queen Maya, the mother of Shakyamuni Buddha, dreamed that a white bull-elephant entered her womb at the moment of conception. She gave birth to the Buddha in the royal gardens of Lumbini, which were said to resemble Indra's paradise grove known as Chitraratha. Maya's dream of the white elephant entering her womb perhaps indicates that the child destined to become the Buddha was originally perceived as an emanation of Indra. Indra and Brahma – the two great gods of the heavens – appeared to the Buddha at the precise moment of his enlightenment requesting him to remain in this world for the liberation of all beings.

The precious white elephant is the vehicle of many Vajrayana Buddhist deities. In particular the elephant is identified with Akshobhya, the blue Buddha of the east or centre. Eight elephants support Akshobhya's throne, equating him with the continent of India itself as the centre of the universe, also supported by eight elephants. Akshobhya means 'the immutable' or 'unshakeable', and the elephant symbolises his *vajra*-like unchangeable and immovable nature. Thangkas illustrating the life of Buddha invariably depict the episode of his subjugation of the wild bull-elephant. Devadatta, the cousin of the Buddha, through jealousy caused a schism to arise in the sangha. As Devadatta's pride increased he attempted to murder the Buddha. One of his schemes involved loosing a rampaging elephant into the Buddha's path, but as it approached the elephant perceived the radiant compassion of the Buddha, and coming to its senses it knelt down meekly at his feet. The elephant is one of the seven possessions of the *chakravartin*. It is both the most gentle and powerful of creatures, representing the endurance, self-control, patience, gentleness, and power of the Buddha.

An elephant can live as long as a hundred years. A fifty or sixty-year old bull-elephant was considered the most appropriate age for warfare, as a great degree of experience and maturity ensured full obedience and steadfastness. After sixty years the last of the elephant's twenty-four replaceable molar teeth wear away and the animal's health begins to decline. The treasured ivory tusks of the elephant are actually frontal teeth, which can grow to an enormous length of ten feet. A large pair of such tusks are displayed in the shrine room of Nyenri monastery at Mt Kailash, close to the Hidden Elephant Cave of Padmasambhava.

Plate 52

At the centre is the 'precious elephant', adorned with an elephant's saddle blanket and a jewelled harness bearing hanging tassles and bells. On his back is the wish-fulfilling gem, and in his trunk he bears aloft a mandala offering of the universe. His head and rump are adorned with single jewels, set in a head ornament and a golden wheel on his rear.

To his right is the head of Airavata, the six-tusked white vehicle of the god Indra. In his trunk he wields a sharp-pointed *chakra*, a weapon he uses as a flail to destroy the enemy. His six tusks are a magical symbol of power, formed from a triple row of teeth – a symbol of immortality – which represent his 'six perfections'. Airavata, in this form, is depicted in the 'wheel of life' painting leading the army of the gods into battle against the *asuras*. Indra, mounted on Airavata, wears the full armour of a warrior and wields his mighty *vajra* in his right hand whilst he holds a rope snare in his left. His 'secret weapon', the 'jewelled net of Indra', symbolises interdependence, and is like the stars of the night sky which he can cast to infinity.

Examples of elephants as depicted in thangka painting fill the rest of this page. The elephant is usually painted with long pointed tusks, and five nail-capped toes are spread across the front of his circular feet. The elephant was rarely seen by Tibetan artists and its representation tended to degenerate to a variable stylistic form through copying.

Two elephant steering hooks or goads (Skt. *ankusha*; Tib. *lcags kyu*) and a rope noose (Skt. *pasha*; Tib. *zhags pa*) are illustrated in the drawing. The sharp point of the goad symbolises penetrating awareness or clear understanding, and the rope, mindful recollection or memory. The goad is used by the mahout or elephant driver to control the creature, and the rope to tether or bind it.

The spotted elephant drawing at the bottom centre shows the sensitive spots on an elephant's body where the mahout inserts the point of the goad to convey various commands to the elephant's instinct or intelligence. These *marma* or 'sensitive points' on an elephant's skin, which were originally identified in remote antiquity, are believed to have been one of the possible sources of origin for the Chinese system of acupuncture.

DEER (Skt. *mriga*; Tib. *sha ba*)

Deer are commonly painted in the foreground landscape of peaceful thangkas depicting Buddhas, bodhisattvas, arhats, and Indian and Tibetan Buddhist masters. Their prime symbolic meaning here refers to the first teaching which Buddha gave in the Deer Park (*mrigadawa*) at Sarnath near Varanasi, where he set in motion the 'first turning of the wheel of dharma'. Deer are by nature extremely shy creatures, and their peaceful presence in a landscape represents a pure realm where fear is unknown.

In Tibetan art they usually appear in couples, a male and female, which indicates harmony, happiness, and fidelity. In this form a male and female deer rest on either side of the golden *dharmachakra* or 'wheel of dharma' (see Plate 89), which crowns the roof or gateway of Buddhist monasteries and temples. In China the deer is a symbol of longevity, and is believed to be the only animal which can locate the sacred fungus of immortality. The tips of its horns are believed to contain the essence of this fungus, and medicinal pills compounded from the horns are believed to confer longevity, health, and vitality. As a symbol of potency and longevity the horns of the deer are incorporated into several mythological hybrid animals, such as the dragon, *makara*, *kirtimukha*, and garuda.

Deer or antelope skins serve as meditation seats or *asanas* for Buddhist practitioners. Yogins such as Milarepa, Rechungpa or Thangtong Gyalpo are usually shown seated on a deerskin mat. As an *asana* the deer skin is believed to enhance the solitary tranquility and awareness required by the ascetic, the pure or *sattvic* energy or *shakti* of the deer being absorbed by the practitioner. In wrathful deity practice a tigerskin *asana* is more commonly used, denoting *rajas* or dynamic energy.

Avalokiteshvara, the bodhisattva of compassion, wears the turquoise-green skin of a magical deer, known as a *krishnasara*, draped over his left shoulder as a symbol of love (*maitri*). This magical deer is an extremely evolved creature which renders itself visible only to the pure in heart. As an emanation of the bodhisattva it is able to discern the thoughts of men and speak in their language. The soft compassionate eyes of the deer, particularly the gazelle, mirror the meaning of Avalokiteshvara's name – 'he who gazes compassionately over all the realms'. Tibetan tradition tells of a species of deer which was so compassionate that it could

easily be trapped by hunters. The hunters would simply begin to stage a mock fight amongst themselves and the deer would come to help resolve the conflict, unknowingly offering themselves as easy targets for the hunters. In peaceful thangkas deer are frequently counterbalanced by a pair of cranes; both are auspicious creatures personifying harmony, faithfulness, peace and longevity.

Plate 53

In the upper left corner is the mythical Tibetan unicorn, a species of single-horned deer (Tib. *bse ru*, which actually means rhinoceros). The phallic horn of the powerful rhinoceros is highly valued in Chinese medicine as a potent male tonic or aphrodisiac for increasing virility. In China the unicorn is known as the *chi-lin* or 'dragon horse'. The male possesses a single central horn and has the general appearance of a stag, but again is a hybrid creature composed of various animal similarities. The *chi-lin* is akin to the magical deer in its auspicious qualities, only manifesting in the presence of great teachers such as Confucius.

To the right of the unicorn is the small hornless musk deer. The musk deer only grows to a height of around twenty inches, and has long protruding upper canine teeth. Musk perfume is obtained from a small egg-shaped sac on the male's abdomen, or it is gathered from rocks where the deer leaves a trail of its scent. The musk manifests as a brown viscous fluid which dries into a highly perfumed powder. A second musk deer is drawn underneath, and a third appears just to the left of the centre of the page.

In the upper right corner are a group of four gazelles and antelopes. The left pair, with long, curving, transversely-ringed horns, are Tibetan gazelles. The right pair, with long backward-pointing ringed horns, are Tibetan antelopes.

The native species of Indian deer include the fallow, hog, red, blackbuck, musk, spotted or Chital, Nilgai, Barasingha, Sika, Kashmir, Sambar, Indian gazelle and black-tailed deer. The Tibetan native species include the Tibetan gazelle, elk and antelope, Hodgson's antelope, musk deer, spotted and roe deer. The saiga antelope, with a strange bulbous nose adapted for cold or rarified air, is also found on the Tibetan plateau. The Tibetan gazelle is an extremely graceful creature, and like wild asses a herd of gazelles will run in a long waving single file when startled. The horns of the gazelle are transversely ringed and are often present in both sexes. The proverbially poetic eyes of the gazelle are very soft and lustrous. (Zoologically, deer, antelope and gazelles are classified by their family species: deer include any animal of the *Cervidae* family, such as roe, fallow, red or spotted deer; antelopes are of the *Bovidae* family, with upward and backward-pointing horns; gazelles are of the *Gazella* family, which is akin to the wild goat.)

Prior to the Chinese invasion the land of Tibet was a veritable Garden of Eden for wildlife, its creatures showing little fear of man. Now few wild animals remain.

This page of drawings depicts the many variations in posture and movement which deer assume in Tibetan art.

Plate 53: Deer

Stags are usually depicted with five or six-pointed horns; a 'six-pointer' is an attribute of a strong mature stag. Six or ten-pointed antlers represent the six or ten great perfections (*paramita*) of a bodhisattva. Deer renew their horns each year, the horns are covered in a 'velvet' fur which soon erodes. The horns of a young buck stag form a single point or 'tine'. Older stags have more numerous tines which are zoologically categorised by maturity as: brow, bay, bez, royal and crown. At the bottom of the drawing two young stags engage in horned combat. Above them two female does 'sniff the air'.

BIRDS

Plate 54

Illustrated here are some of the countryside birds which grace landscape compositions. In the top row are a group of green Indian parrots. The parrot along with the myna bird symbolises translation, as both birds can mimic the phonetic sounds of human languages. A pair of parrots symbolises love, affection and fidelity. A black and yellow myna bird is drawn below the two parrots in the upper left corner. Birds of prey including a falcon, sparrow-hawk, buzzard or kite are drawn below the parrots on the right. The 'clever falcon' is a bird of prey messenger unleashed by the goddess Ekajati. On the far right below the falcon and corner parrot are two cuckoos. The cuckoo is a messenger of summer and a favourite bird in Tibetan folklore and parables – due to its selfish habit of forcing its offspring to dominate the nests of smaller birds. In the upper area above the peacock and raven are depicted various small and exotic birds such as a finch, tit, koel, weaver-bird, swallow, bird of paradise, and kingfisher. The raven near the left centre and the crow beneath are birds of portent in Tibetan folk culture. A tradition of omen interpretation is based on the 'language of ravens', determined by the direction and time of day in which a raven caws; other omens relate to its behaviour, vocalisations, or place of nesting. As predictive birds they are also divided into the four Indian castes of *brahmin*, *kshatriya*, *vaishya* and *shudra*, with the low caste *shudras* being the carrion and refuse eaters. The dark 'outcaste' and predatory birds of the 'twilight realms', such as ravens, crows, vultures, hawks, falcons and owls, form an extensive retinue of aerial messengers or emissaries for the dark wrathful forms of deities such as Mahakala. Ravens and crows are also messengers of the planetary gods Rahu and Sani (Saturn). As Saturday is Saturn's day, it is considered beneficial to feed raw meat to these birds on this day in order to placate the possible malevolent influences of these powerful planets. To the right of the raven is the hoopoe bird, its upper wings marked with a double trigram of *yang* lines, representing the first hexagram of creative energy in the Chinese divinatory system of the *I Ching*.

To the left of the centre is the most beautiful, famous and symbolic bird of Indian art and culture, the peacock (*mayura*). The vibrant peacock-blue and golden hues of its iridescent plumage and trailing tail or 'train' have endowed the peacock with many mystical qualities. As an emblem of romantic love and beauty the peacock features potently in Indian miniature painting, particularly in the dalliance of Krishna, Radha, and the Gopis. Its plaintive cry of longing and the ritual courtship of its magnificent tail display, which takes place before the fertile rainy season, have defined the peacock as a prophet of the monsoon. In Buddhism the peacock supports the throne of Amitabha, the red Buddha of the west, whose qualities include passion (lotus), love, vital fluids, evening twilight, summer and fire. The peacock throne is an emblem of the royal Shahs of Persia and the Indian Maurya dynasty. As a solar emblem the peacock is identified with both the Chinese phoenix and Indian garuda. Like the garuda the peacock is the mortal enemy of snakes, especially cobras, which peacocks kill with their claws. Its main symbolism is, however, the transmutation of poison into *amrita* or nectar. When Lord Shiva consumed the poison (*kalakuta*) which emerged at the churning of the ocean, it lodged in his throat causing his neck to turn blue: from this incident Shiva aquired the epithet *nilakantha* – the 'blue-throated one'. The transmutation of poison or venom by the peacock is believed to produce the electric-blue of its throat plumage and the wisdom 'eyes' of its tail feathers. An Indian folk tradition asserts that the eggshells of peahens or other fowl placed in the corners of a room will rid a house of scorpion or snake infestation. In Vajrayana symbolism a bundle of peacock feathers is used as a sprinkler for the consecrated water (*amrita*) contained in the blessing flask (Tib. *bum pa*). In specific tantric rituals individual feathers are used as fan, mirror, and parasol adornments; as the flights of darts; as the lower garment of certain deities associated with the low caste Indian Shabari tribe; and as the peacock-feather parasol which surmounts the goddess Palden Lhamo – symbolising her wisdom activities and the transmutation of all evils or poisons. A second flying peacock is drawn near the lower left corner.

Above this flying peacock and at the centre right are two vultures. The vulture is commonly depicted consuming corpses in wrathful charnel-ground imagery. Vultures are the main 'invited guests' for the great feast of dismembered corpses which occurs in the Tibetan funeral practice of 'sky-burial'. Based, again, on the fourfold Indian caste system these vultures have a certain hierarchical 'pecking order' for such delectable morsels as the eyes, tongue, liver, or heart of a human body. The falcon-like bearded vulture or lammergeir, which is frequently mistaken for an eagle, is very commonly seen in the Himalayan foothills or mountain fastnesses of Tibet. The feathers of birds of prey, such as the eagle, hawk, falcon, owl, or vulture, are specifically employed in a multitude of tantric offerings; they also form the steering feathers for divinatory arrows.

A long-billed snipe is drawn below the feet of the peacock. In early summer the snipe makes a strange boomerang-like drumming sound from its wing vibrations as it dives from the sky. On the lower mid-right edge are two graceful white birds of paradise, a shy bird rarely glimpsed

Plate 54: Birds

Plate 55: Water birds

in the western Himalayas. At the bottom centre are three examples of bird wing movements in flight.

Below the peacock's tail in the left corner are two graceful golden pheasants, with long tail feathers and head crests. Below the pheasants is a partridge with long speckled tail feathers. To the right of the golden pheasants are three detailed drawings of the Chinese phoenix or *feng-huang*, the most beautiful and gentlest of birds, with the sweetest of songs and so compassionate that it will not even eat grass.

The ancient Chinese phoenix is a mythological bird endowed with all the magical qualities of auspiciousness, longevity, resurrection, the solar and alchemical fire. Its transcultural symbolism is common to all the great civilisations, from Egypt to China. The alchemical phoenix, which immolates itself in fire after five hundred years and is resurrected from the ashes, is an androgyne bird not born from an egg. The name *'feng-huang'* indicates an androgynous bird composed of male (*feng*) and female (*huang*). It is a hybrid 'sun-bird' with twelve 'likenesses' and twelve or thirteen tail feathers, symbolising either the solar or lunar months. During the Chinese Ming dynasty (1368–1644) and Qing dynasty (1644–1912) the phoenix was accorded the highest rank as an insignia for civil officials. The 'pecking order' of these birds is: phoenix, golden pheasant, peacock, wild goose, silver pheasant, egret, mandarin duck, quail, and paradise flycatcher. These insignia appear as embroidered brocade squares on imperial robes. All nine birds resemble the phoenix in their stylistic designs.

The dragon and phoenix, two of the 'four supernatural animals', are symbols of the Emperor and Empress of China. In Chinese art the dragon and tiger are twin symbols of wrath, and the pheonix and deer twin symbols of peace. This motif entered Tibetan art in the peaceful combination of the deer and crane (phoenix).

Not illustrated here are the group of eight birds – vulture, owl, raven, parrot, hawk, kite, myna bird, and swan – that are trampled under the eight left feet of the deity Yamantaka. These eight birds are the mounts of the eight great Lords of Death (Tib. gShin rje). Under Yamantaka's right feet are eight kinds of animals: man, buffalo, bull, donkey, camel, dog, sheep, and fox – the messengers of the Lords of Death.

Plate 55

This drawing illustrates cranes and water birds. At the top are three examples of cranes in flight, their long wing feathers and trailing legs forming graceful lines of movement. At the left of the second row a diving crane, drawn from a Chinese painting, forms a graceful arc with its wings and indrawn neck.

The remainder of this illustrated page shows examples of water birds. In the centre of the second row a white goose spreads wide its wings, whilst a white snow goose with black wing tips struts to its right. Above is a goose in flight. In the centre row from left to right are a white egret which laps the surface of the water with its beak; in the centre a bar-headed goose turns its head backwards; and on the right a walking

crane twists its head upwards. Below this crane are three drawings of the grey heron, with its characteristic black headcrest. To the left of the herons are a goose, an egret, and a demoiselle crane standing like a heron in shallow water. On the far left is the lower half of a duck as it submerges its head under the water.

At the bottom of the page are drawings of swans, geese, and ducks gliding in the water. In the middle, one duck chases another, and in the bottom row a mother duck follows her ducklings. In thangkas such water bird images are commonly painted adorning the surface of ponds and lakes.

The swan (Skt. *hamsa*; Tib. *ngang pa*) and the goose (Skt. *karanda*; Tib. *so bya*), are often compounded in Hindu and Buddhist iconography under the general name of *hamsa*. The *hamsa* is the vehicle of both the creator god Brahma, and his consort Sarasvati – the goddess of wisdom. The swan is believed to be capable of separating milk which has been mixed with water, which symbolises discriminating wisdom. In the Indian Hatha Yoga tradition the word *hamsa* refers to the life force (*prana*) of the individual ego (*jiva*), where the outward breath makes the sound *'ham'*, and the inward breath the sound *'sa'*. With repetition the breath sounds become *'so-ham'* meaning 'I am He', where the individual self or ego (I) dissolves into the the formless absolute (He). Great Indian yogins are frequently referred to as *paramahamsa*, meaning 'supreme swan'. The white swan is also identified with the white garuda of Tibet (Tib. *mkha' lding*), as king of the water birds. The Brahmanic swan or goose motif was widely deployed in early Buddhist art, particularly as a roundel frieze which decorated stone carvings, or the borders on painted brocade designs.

Many migratory water birds sojourn for the summer months on Tibet's turquoise lakes, and the angelic *gandharvas* and *apsaras* of the celestial god realms are believed to be capable of transmuting themselves into swans and geese. It is quite possible that many of our neighbourhood feathered friends make instinctive annual pilgrimages to those fabled holy lands.

THE SIX-ORNAMENT THRONE OF ENLIGHTENMENT (Skt. *torana*)

The arched back-support (Tib. *rgyab yol*) which surrounds both painted and three-dimensional images of enlightened beings is commonly known as a *torana.* In Sanskrit the term *torana* means an arch or arched doorway, and the elaborate attention to detail displayed in its painted and sculptural form reveals the conceptual majesty in which enlightened beings are perceived. In Buddhist art the enlightenment *torana* probably developed with the advent of Mahayana Buddhism during the early Gupta period (*circa* fourth century AD), although certain established Indian elements of the *torana* probably predated this. In the early Mahayana Buddhist cave viharas of Ajanta and Ellora the representation of the mythological animal-*torana* had already achieved a precise definition. During the Pala-Sena period of artistic development in Eastern India (Bengal) between the eighth

Plate 56: The six-ornament throne of enlightenment

and twelfth centuries AD, the *torana* assumed pre-eminence as an artistic motif. With the demise of Vajrayana Buddhism in India under the iconoclastic hammer of Islam, many artisans of the fallen Pala-Sena dynasties took refuge in Nepal. Pala art influences subsequently established a firm foothold amongst the Newari painters and metal-casters of the Kathmandu valley; the natural Newar genius excelled in replication. Supply and demand for Vajrayana artifacts, both to the indigenous Newar Buddhists and to the proliferating patronage of Buddhism in Tibet, ensured a continuity and development of late Pala art. In Nepal the *torana* reached its zenith of artistic brilliance and innovation, evidence of which abounds in the stone and wood carvings of the Kathmandu valley, and in the decoration of Tibetan temples created by Newar craftsmen, such as the exquisite stupa of Gyantse. In Kashmir a similar artistic renaissance arose, with Kashmiri craftsmen creating inspiring masterpieces in the temples of Western Tibet, Kashmir, Ladakh, and the Zanskar, Kinnaur, and Spiti valleys of northwest India.

Plate 56

Shakyamuni Buddha is drawn in his customary *vajra*-posture with his right hand making the 'earth-touching' *mudra*. To his lower left and right are his two main disciples, Shariputra and Maudgalyayana, each holding the begging bowl and metal staff (*khakkhara*) of a Buddhist mendicant. Shakyamuni is seated on a moon disc placed above a multicoloured lotus which rests on a lion throne. An ornate square pedestal base forms the lion throne, which is supported on each of its four sides by a pair of lions.

Behind Buddha's radiant halo and jewelled aureole (*prabhamandala*) is displayed the intricate *torana* or back-support of the six ornaments (Tib. *rgyan drug rgyab yol*).

On either side of the base of the lotus throne are two white elephants who stand in obeisance before the Buddha, offering in their trunks a butter lamp and incense. On the brocade patterned blankets that cover the elephants' backs stand two blue or white lions. Above the lions stand two composite animals which resemble an antelope in appearance. This hybrid creature may take on several different forms according to different traditions. Represented here is a *sharabha* with the head of a goat, the horns of a deer, the mane of a lion, the body of a horse and the talons of an eagle. The *sharabha* may also be represented with the body of a horse, the head and feet of a lion, and the horns of a ram – symbolising the combined speed, strength and perseverance of this hybrid creature. Alternatively a hybrid winged-unicorn (*sharal*) or griffin (lion-eagle) may be represented, or, as in the early Gupta art, a hybrid known as a *sardul* – formed from the union of a lion and horse.

On the back of the *sharabha* sit two young gods or *devas*, whose hands support an entwined jewel crossbeam draped with silk brocade. The *devas* may also be represented as holding the crossbeam up with one hand, whilst blowing a white conch shell with the other. Alternatively these two human forms may be represented by two dwarfs (*vamana*). In Indian

art dwarfs are commonly sculpted onto pillared crossbeam supports, such as are again found in the early art of Ajanta. The dwarf is a symbol of colossal strength in a diminutive stature, and since all of the above animals symbolise strength, speed, and power, the dwarf is their human equivalent. The dwarf, Vamana, is also the fifth of Vishnu's ten incarnations.

Above the crossbeam, which is fashioned of precious stones and capped with an entwined jewel at either end, is the upper arc of the *torana*. Two *makaras* with upturned heads face outwards above the crossbeam, their fabulous 'feathered' tails forming the '*makara*-tail' design of intricate scrolling spiral roundels. On the *makara*-tails rest two young *naga* serpents, with human upper bodies and serpent tails from their waists downwards; five or seven small serpents form a canopy above their heads. At the very top stands the golden garuda, its talons gripping the tails of the *nagas*. With arms outstretched he devours a long snake which the *nagas* hold up for him. The distant background of the throne is ornamented with flowers, leaves, fruit, rainbow-coloured clouds, and strings of pearls and precious jewels.

These six creatures represent the 'six perfections' (*paramitas*) of the enlightened mind. The perfection of wisdom (*prajna*) is represented by the two lions at the base; the perfection of concentration (*dhyana*) by the two elephants; the perfection of effort (*virya*) by the two dwarfs or *devas* on the *sharabha* antelopes; the perfection of patience (*kshanti*) by the two *makaras*; the perfection of morality (*sila*) by the two *nagas*; and the perfection of generosity (*dana*) by the garuda. These six creatures are also symbolically named: *gurana, sarana, bharana, surana, varana,* and *karuna*.

Other symbolic interpretations placed upon the back-support throne include the 'four ways of gathering disciples'; 'the seven hindrances to be eliminated'; and the 'ten powers of a bodhisattva' – power over longevity, mind, necessities, karma, birth, imagination, resolution, miracles, knowledge, and presentation. However its obviously deeper and more accurate symbolic meaning appears to have been lost over the centuries. The motif of the lion on the elephant's back is known as the *gajasimha* (elephant-lion), combining the strength of these two lords of creatures. In Newar art dragons may also be included in the lower *torana*, sometimes entwined around a jewelled pillar which supports the crossbeam. A *kirtimukha* face consuming the snake may also displace the garuda at the *torana*'s apex. The crossbeam divides the *torana* into two distinct sections, with the three upper creatures of *makara, naga,* and garuda symbolising the watery, underground and heavenly realms, and the lower portion possibly symbolising the Buddha's conception (elephant), enlightenment (lion), ascent to Tushita heaven (*deva*), and reconciliation of the faction in the sangha (crossbeam).

THE ANIMAL THRONES OF THE FIVE BUDDHAS

At the central core of the tenets of Vajrayana Buddhism is the principle of the Five Enlightened Buddha Families, more commonly but erroneously known as the Five Dhyani

Buddhas. The conceptual assembly of the Five Buddha Families was first revealed in the *Manjushrimulakalpa* and the *Guhyasamaja Tantra*, probably dating from around the sixth or seventh century AD.

The Five Buddha Families form the basis of the geometric mandala, taking the central point and the four cardinal directions as the embodied emanations of their perfected qualities. The mandala's axis of orientation followed the sun's path, with east at the bottom (facing the viewer), and west at the top.

The Five Buddhas represent the purified manifestation of the five aggregates, elements, wisdoms, senses, and sensory perceptions. The five aggregates or 'heaps' (*skandha*) comprise the components of all sentient beings, namely: form (body); feeling (sensation); perception (discrimination); motivation (conditioning); and consciousness. Each of the Five Buddhas was assigned a direction, a consort, a progeny of bodhisattvas and deities, a colour, an animal throne, a specific *mudra*, and a symbolic emblem or attribute. To this list were added a vast array of pentad qualities, such as: the five tastes, sounds, precious substances, times of the day, internal and external elements, and the five seasons (spring, summer, rainy season, autumn, and winter). Essentially the Five Buddhas represent the transmutation of the five poisons or delusions (ignorance, desire, anger, jealousy, and pride), into the five transcendent wisdoms (all-encompassing, discriminating, mirror-like, all-accomplishing, and equaniminous).

Iconographically the Five Buddhas are represented on different animal thrones. In different tantric traditions the placement of the Five Buddhas in their respective directions and their specific animal thrones is open to some variation; the position of Vairochana and Akshobhya being interchangeable between the centre and the eastern direction;

the dragon throne of Vairochana being interchangeable with a lion throne; and the lion throne of Ratnasambhava being interchangeable with a horse throne. In the earliest tantras, such as the *Guhyasamaja* and *Hevajra Tantras*, a very precise geographical configuration is revealed in the directional placement and animal thrones of the Five Buddhas. In the later *Kalachakra Tantra* (*circa* tenth century AD) the colours, directions and qualities of the Five Buddha Families assume radically different arrangements.

At the centre is blue Akshobhya, Lord of the Vajra Family, representing the element of space, the aggregate of consciousness, the delusion of anger, and the all-encompassing wisdom of space. Akshobhya's emblem is the *vajra*, and he is supported on an elephant throne. In ancient India it was the exclusive privilege of a king to be carried on an elephant. Thus the throne of an Indian king is specifically the elephant. The elephant is the insignia of India, symbolising royalty and supremacy; eight or sixteen elephants supported the physical universe, and at the centre of this universe were India's Buddhist heartlands. The elephant represents the heartlands of Buddhist India, Vajrasana or Bodh Gaya to be more precise, as this was the cradle of Buddhism.

To the south is yellow Ratnasambhava, Lord of the Ratna (jewel) Family, representing the element of earth, the aggregate of feeling, the delusion of pride, and the wisdom of equanimity of earth. Ratnasambhava's emblem is the jewel, and he is supported on a lion throne. The lion represents Sri Lanka or Ceylon, which lay to the south of India. Its ancient name was Singhala, literally meaning 'the country of the lions'; its lion throne was the throne of its kings.

To the west is red Amitabha, Lord of the Padma (lotus) Family, representing the element of fire, the aggregate of perception, the delusion of attachment, and the discriminating wisdom of fire. Amitabha's emblem is the lotus, and

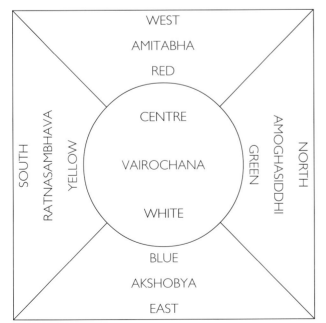

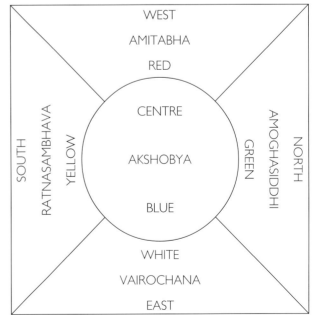

The Five Buddha mandala. The diagram on the left shows Vairochana positioned at the centre of the mandala and Akshobya in the east. The diagram on the right shows Akshobya at the centre and Vairochana in the east.

he is supported on a peacock throne. The peacock represents Persia or Iran, its fabled and legendary 'peacock throne' surviving until the recent deposition of the Shah of Iran.

To the north is green Amoghasiddhi, Lord of the Karma (activity) Family, representing the element of air, the aggregate of compositional factors, the delusion of jealousy, and the all-accomplishing wisdom of air. Amoghasiddhi's emblem is the crossed *vajra* or sword, and he is supported on a garuda throne. The garuda was associated with the Himalayan ranges to the north, and specifically with the ancient Bon legends of the 'horned eagle' of Tibet (Tib. *mkha' lding*).

To the east is white Vairochana, Lord of the Tathagata (Buddha) Family, representing the element water, the aggregate of form, the delusion of ignorance, and the mirror-like wisdom of water. Vairochana's emblem is the wheel, and he is supported on a dragon throne. To the east of India lay the vast land of China, with its ancient dragon throne of the imperial emperors, which also survived until the advent of Chinese communism – with its emblems of the red star and Chairman Mao's little red book.

THE FIVE BUDDHA FAMILIES – COLOURS, ORIGINS, AND CONTRADICTIONS

The above listing of the attributes and qualities of the Five Buddha Families may appear to be definitive. However, several inconsistencies should be clarified.

The central and eastern positions of Akshobhya and Vairochana are frequently interchanged. Most of the *yoga tantras* (the third of the four classes of tantra), for example, have the peaceful white form of Vairochana at their centre, whilst many of the *anuttarayoga tantras* (the highest of the four classes of tantra), such as the tantras of the semi-wrathful *yidam* deities Chakrasamvara, Hevajra, Guhyasamaja, Kalachakra, etc., have blue Akshobhya at their centre. This interchange has led to some ambiguity in their assigned qualities, particularly in identifying the aggregates of form and consciousness, the delusions of ignorance and anger, and all-encompassing wisdom and mirror-like wisdom – these three variants can be ascribed to either Akshobhya or Vairochana. Logical deduction should however identify both all-accomplishing wisdom and the aggregate of consciousness with the formless and infinite blue space element of Akshobhya; and mirror-like wisdom and the aggregate of form with the reflective white water element of Vairochana.

Similarly one can logically deduce that blue Akshobhya is associated with the delusion of anger, and white Vairochana with the delusion of ignorance. Each of the coloured directional faces of deities is associated specifically with one of the delusions, elements and directions. The white face of a multi-headed deity symbolises the transmutation of ignorance; the blue or black face, that of anger; the red face, that of passion, attachment or desire; the yellow face, that of pride; and the green face, that of envy or jealousy. We have similar figures of speech in our proverbial comparisons of turning 'black with anger'; blushing 'red with embarassment or lust'; becoming 'green with envy'; 'yellow with swollen pride'; a 'blank with ignorance'.

Each of the Five Buddhas is the 'Lord of a Family' (*kula*), consisting of a female consort and bodhisattvas as 'spiritual sons' or *sambhogakaya* offspring. Blue Akshobhya, as Lord of the Vajra Family, has as his female consort the goddess Mamaki 'she who can extinguish hatred', and as his bodhisattva the wrathful blue Vajrapani. From Akshobhya descend a large pantheon of blue wrathful deities, who are described as bearing the seal or image of Akshobhya on the crown of their heads. Heruka, Hevajra, Yamari, Vajrakila, Buddhakapala and Mahamaya, for example, are all emanations of Akshobhya.

White Vairochana, as Lord of the Tathagata (Buddha) Family, has Lochana, 'she who can extinguish ignorance', as his consort, and Akashagarbha or Samantabhadra as his bodhisattva. From Vairochana descend many major goddesses, such as: Ushnishavijaya, Marichi, Sitatapatra, and Vajravarahi.

Yellow Ratnasambhava, as Lord of the Ratna (jewel) Family, has as his consort Vajradhatvishvari 'she who can extinguish pride', and Ratnapani or Kshitigarbha as his bodhisattva. From Ratnasambhava descend the wealth god Jambhala, and goddesses such as Vasudhara, and certain forms of Tara.

Red Amitabha, as Lord of the Padma (lotus) Family, has as his consort Pandara, 'she who can extinguish desire', and Padmapani or Avalokiteshvara as his bodhisattva. From Amitabha descend the many forms of Avalokiteshvara, and deities such as Hayagriva, Kurukulla, Mahabala, and Bhrikuti.

Green Amoghasiddhi, as Lord of the Karma (activity) Family, has Green Tara as his consort and Vishvapani as his bodhisattva. From Amoghasiddhi descend goddesses such as Khadiravani Tara, Arya Tara, Sita Tara, Mahamayuri, and Parnashabari.

Again, a coherent principle of emanations or the lineal descent of deities, as listed above, may appear to be definitive and neatly categorised. However, a far more intricate pattern of the Buddha Families emerges when we look into their historical origins.

Originally there were only three Buddha Families: those of Ignorance (Tathagata), of Desire (Padma), and of Anger (Vajra). These correspond to the three primal poisons of ignorance, desire, and aversion, so succinctly symbolised by the pig, cockerel, and snake depicted at the central hub of the early 'wheel of life' painting. This trinity were symbolically related to the trinities of the 'three gates' (body, speech, and mind); the three directions (zenith, centre, and nadir); the three psychic centres (crown, throat, and heart); and to the Hindu trinity of Brahma, Vishnu, and Shiva (representing creation, preservation, and destruction).

A significant vestige of the three original Buddha Families survives in the importance placed on the three great bodhisattvas, Manjushri, Avalokiteshvara, and Vajrapani, who are known collectively as the 'Lords of the Three Families' – although they are bodhisattvas and not Buddhas. Red-yellow Manjushri, whose sword of wisdom cuts through the veil of ignorance, is the Lord of the Tathagata (Buddha) Family of ignorance or delusion. White Avalokiteshvara, whose lotus represents the transmutation of passion into compassion, is the Lord of the Padma (lotus) Family of desire or attachment. Black-blue Vajrapani, whose wrathful demeanour represents the transmutation of hatred into power or energy, is the Lord of the Vajra Family of aversion and anger.

Buddhism has always developed systems for categorising phenomena, qualities and attributes. Early Mahayana Buddhism developed a threefold division which consisted of the two Hinayana or 'lesser vehicle' paths of the *shravakas* (devoted listeners) and *pratyekabuddhas* (solitary realisers), and the third 'greater path vehicle' of the bodhisattvas or enlightened 'spiritual heroes' – the Mahayana. These correspond to the 'three scopes' or aspirations of individuals on a graduated path of lesser, middle, and great scope of mental capacity or spiritual aspiration. A similar categorisation is applied to the Lords of the Three Families (*kulas*), by defining the Vajra family as the smaller scope, the Lotus family as the middle scope, and the Tathagata family as the highest scope. This spiritual hierarchy is illustrated by depicting Manjushri above

Avalokiteshvara and Vajrapani, where the three bodhisattvas form a trinity of the Buddha's qualities of wisdom, compassion, and power.

Early Vajrayana Buddhism expanded this original group of three into four, five, and finally six, by placing Vajradhara or Vajrasattva above the central position as the sixth 'overlord' of all Five Buddha Families. The addition of the other two poisons of pride and jealousy created a fivefold system of a centre with four cardinal directions.

The principle of the Five Buddha Families finds its clearest expression in the layout of the geometrical mandala. In Nepal they also assumed vivid expression in their sculptural representation at the four cardinal directions of the stupa, with the fifth Buddha (Vairochana or Akshobhya) of the stupa's centre usually placed in the north-east intercardinal direction.

The development of the Three Buddha Families into the Five Buddha Families may still retain some semblance of cohesion. However, the complexity is again compounded when we discover that there was not only one original group of Five Buddhas, but several!

Plate 57: The four friends

Chapter Four
Narrative Illustrations

THE FOUR FRIENDS OR HARMONIOUS BROTHERS

The familiar Tibetan motif of 'the four friends' – an elephant, monkey, hare, and partridge forming an acrobatic pyramid beneath a tree – has its origin in the *Tittira Jataka* legend of one of the Buddha's previous lives. In the *Tittira* fable however, only three animals are mentioned – the elephant, monkey, and partridge. This moral tale illustrates that age must be respected above learning, greatness, or noble birth.

The parable relates how Shariputra, one of the Buddha's eldest disciples, was unable to find lodging in the town of Vaisali, as the younger disciples had hurried ahead to selfishly secure all available accomodation for themselves. Early the next morning Buddha learned that Shariputra had passed the night alone beneath a tree. In response to the self-cherishing attitude which prevailed amongst the younger sangha, Buddha related the *Tittira Jataka* parable of the 'honouring of age'.

"Once, beneath a great banyan tree in the Himalayan foothills, there lived three friends – a partridge, a monkey, and an elephant. Their mutual respect had diminished, and in order to determine who was the most senior they began to discuss the age of the banyan tree beneath which they dwelt. The elephant spoke first, telling of how when he was but a baby the banyan tree was only a small bush. The monkey then related how in his infancy the tree was merely a shrub. Then the partridge spoke, telling of how he had once swallowed the original seed, and how this mighty tree had actually sprouted from his droppings. The partridge was then honoured as the eldest, senior in rank to the monkey and the elephant. Once again harmony prevailed in the animal kingdom."

Buddha decreed that henceforth age would confer priority amongst the sangha. He revealed that in this previous existence his disciple Maudgalyayana had been the elephant, Shariputra the Elder had been the monkey, whilst Buddha himself had been the partridge. The hare was later included in this legend, and identified with the Buddha's eldest disciple, Ananda. The hare was second in seniority, as he had first seen the tree when it was a leafless sapling.

These four herbivorous animals represent the four terrestrial habitats of sky (partridge), tree (monkey), ground (elephant), and underground (hare). Sometimes the bird is identified as a grouse, and the banyan tree is usually illustrated as a fruit tree. A variation of the story has them standing on each other's backs in order to reach the fruit. Here the implied moral is cooperation. Occasionally the animals are illustrated on both sides of the tree: on one side separated into their respective habitats, and on the other side united in harmonious cooperation.

The German town of Bremen adapted this motif, drawn from the *Tittira Jataka* legend of animal cooperation, as an heraldic device for the city's coat of arms. A similar motif appears in the 'Musicians of Bremen' fairytale composed by the brothers Grimm, but here the four animals are an ass, a dog, a cat, and a cockerel.

Plate 57 and the narrow illustration on Plate 58 depict two drawings of the four friends.

THE SIX SYMBOLS OF LONG LIFE
(Tib. *tshe ring drug skor*)

The six symbols or signs of longevity (Tib. *tshe ring drug skor*) are of Chinese origin, and appear as secular rather than religious images in Tibetan art. They are frequently carved on wooden panels and furniture, or painted as wall panels and decorative motifs on porcelain chinaware. The six longevity symbols are: the old man of long life, and the tree, rock, water, birds, and deer of longevity.

The old man is Shou-lao, the Chinese god of longevity, who was originally a star-god of the southern hemisphere represented by the bright star Canopus in the southern constellation of Argo (in Greek mythology the ship of Jason and the Argonauts). Since Canopus is most prominently visible low on the horizon in March and April, Shou-lao came to represent springtime, renewal, peace, and longevity.

Shou-lao is often accompanied by his two star-god companions, Fu-hsing – the god of happiness, and Tsai-chen – the god of wealth. These three auspicious gods of longevity, happiness and wealth are symbolised by the 'three sacred fruits' of peach, pomegranate, and citron. Shou-lao was said to have been born from a peach, and in Chinese decorative art the peach tree of immortality is sometimes illustrated with its trunk twisted to form the character 'Shou', meaning longevity. Designs of the *shou* symbol of longevity are illustrated on Plates 159 and 160. Shou-lao is represented as a contented old man with a large prominent forehead, white hair, long white eyebrows and beard. In Buddhism the old man represents a contemplative sage who manifests the qualities of Amitayus – the deity of longevity.

The tree of longevity underneath which the old man sits is usually represented as a fruit-laden peach tree. The divine peach tree of the Chinese gods yielded the fruit of eternal life. Imbued with the eight medicinal qualities it blossomed and ripened over an immense period of time. The transitory nature of the peach blossom heralded the onset of spring and the marriage season; the development of these blossoms into ripe peaches symbolised fidelity and longevity. The medicinal properties of the peach tree are renowned in Chinese medicine, and the kernel of the peach is often carved into a talisman to protect children from untimely death. The pine tree is also a symbol of longevity, and is grouped with the bamboo and the plum as one of the 'three friends of winter' in Chinese symbolism. The evergreen pine is commonly represented with the deer and crane as triple symbols of longevity.

The immutable rock of longevity is an auspiciously shaped rock whose geomantic properties are believed to be beneficial to mankind. The rock usually takes the form of a *vajra* or conch-shaped rock whose fissures and striations turn towards the right. An area which is in close proximity to such an empowered rock formation is considered highly auspicious in the geomantic siting of monasteries, temples, stupas, retreat caves, and habitations.

The water of longevity possesses the eight qualities of pure water, and essentially pours forth as the nectar of immortality which is contained in the flask held by the long-life deity Amitayus. The water springs from the rock of longevity nourishing the tree, which in turn nourishes the man, deer and cranes. Water is the source of the fountain of life; it descends from the heavens giving life to the whole of organic creation. Dew drops, which appear to have descended immaculately from heaven each morning, contain the essence of flowers and plants believed to confer immortality. Water which springs from an empowered rock or from an auspicious formation of jade, was similarly viewed as a fountain of perpetual youth.

The cranes of longevity are a very popular motif in Chinese art. Birds were described as being 'twice-born' – once as an egg and again when the egg hatches. Cranes are believed to live to an advanced age, especially the black crane, which is said to survive on water alone. The stork is also a longevity symbol, and like the crane is believed to have only one mate in its lifetime. A pair of cranes or storks symbolise happiness, fidelity, and longevity. Cranes are believed to ferry the souls of the dead to the 'western heavens', just as the stork in Western folklore is said to ferry the souls of the newly born. Deer, cranes, and pine trees began to appear frequently in Tibetan art from the eighteenth century onwards as cultural motifs were assimilated from Chinese painting and patronage. A single crane symbolises the harmonious, timeless contentment of the recluse. In Chinese art cranes are commonly depicted with pine trees as double symbols of immortality.

The deer is the vehicle of Shou-lao, and he is usually represented riding on a stag with mature antlers. Deer were believed to live to a great age and were credited with the ability of being the only creatures capable of locating the *ling-chih* or 'plant of immortality'. This divine plant is a cultivated fungus which grows on the roots and lower trunk of certain trees and is consumed as a tonic. The deer is often depicted with a piece of this fungus in his mouth. Chinese legends describe the 'Islands of the Immortals' which were located in the eastern ocean. Here the immortals consumed the divine food of the *ling-chih*, and drank from the eternal waters of the jade fountain.

Plate 58

Drawn in the Chinese style, Shou-lao is shown with an enlarged domed head, long beard, and drooping eyebrows. In his hands he holds the curved dragon-headed wooden staff of spiritual power. Such a naturally created simulacra of a divine creature is common in the walking-staffs and crooks of many cultures. Walking-sticks are often crowned with a horn, bone, ivory or wood talisman of a specific totem animal, the serpent-staff of Moses being one such example. From the neck of the staff hangs a double gourd or distillation flask. In Taoism the double gourd is a symbol of the alchemist, the upper part of the gourd containing the red cinnabar and the lower part the silver mercury. The alchemical elixir of immortality is produced from the amalgam of their distillation. In both the Taoist and Indian alchemical traditions the 'marriage' of cinnabar and mercury provides a sexual metaphor for the union of menstrual blood and semen which creates life. This is in turn a metaphor for the inner-yoga union of the solar and lunar channel-winds dissolving into the central channel to produce the immortality of enlightenment.

The deer of longevity rests behind Shao-lao bearing mature five-tined antlers, and a pair of cranes stand in the water before him. Behind his back is the peach-laden tree

Plate 58: Shou-lao, the six symbols of longevity (in Chinese style) and the four friends

Plate 59: The six symbols of longevity (in Tibetan style)

of longevity with a white silk scarf auspiciously draped over a branch as a symbol of a Buddhist arhat. The churning water of long life cascades from a spring in the conch-shaped rock formation in the background. Above Shoulao's head flies the bat of longevity, one of the 'five bats' of Chinese symbolism which confer auspicious blessings: longevity, health, honesty, wealth, and a late death from natural causes. Placed before him is a bowl of peaches – the fruits of immortality.

To the right of this illustration is a narrow design depicting 'the four friends' – the elephant, monkey, hare, and partridge which cooperate in reaching the fruit of the tree of life. The partridge holds this fruit in his right claw.

Plate 59

This illustration of the six symbols of longevity is drawn in the Tibetan style and based on an original drawing by the contemporary Tibetan artist Tsering Wangchub of Tashijong.

The old man of long life holds a rosary in his left hand and feeds a piece of the plant of immortality to the stag at his feet. The fruit tree, cranes, conch-shaped rock, and cascading water of longevity complete the auspicious landscape that surrounds him. A bowl of peaches is placed before him, sometimes medicinal balls or precious pills of longevity are depicted in this bowl. The image symbolises the natural harmony of the recluse, who untroubled by the cares of the world lives a long life of contentment, peace and natural wealth.

DIAGRAM OF SHAMATHA MEDITATION PRACTICE OR 'TRANQUIL ABIDING'
(Tib. *zhi gnas*)

Primary consciousness itself is pure, yet habitual tendencies gathered over countless lifetimes have ensnared the mind in the fifty-one secondary mental consciousnesses. These habitual thought processes, which can be positive, neutral or negative, cause the mind to dwell continually in a state of unfocused distraction. The practice of *shamatha* meditation develops the ability to focus the mind in single-pointed equipoise or perfect concentration, and is a prerequisite for the development of *vipashyana* or analytical insight meditation.

The Tibetan word for *shamatha* meditation (Tib. *zhi gnas*) means 'calm' (Tib. *zhi*) 'abiding' (Tib. *gnas*), or 'dwelling in peace'. *Shamatha* should ideally be practised in a secluded retreat situation, adopting the 'seven point meditation posture of Vairochana', with the legs crossed in '*vajrasana*' or reversed full lotus posture, the spine straight, right hand resting lightly on the left palm in the *dhyana mudra* of meditative absorption, neck slightly bent, eyes focused along the line of the nose, mouth relaxed, and the tongue held lightly against the upper palate. The object of concentration is usually the image of the Buddha or a deity. Formless concentration usually takes the breath as the object of contemplation.

The illustration of the development of mental tranquility (Plate 60) is often painted as a fresco on monastery walls.

This mnemonic diagram depicts the nine progressive stages of mental development (Tib. *sems gnas dgu*), which are obtained through the 'six powers' of study, contemplation, memory, comprehension, diligence, and perfection.

Plate 60

Beginning at the start of the path in the lower right, the diagram shows a monk chasing, binding, leading, and subduing an elephant whose colour progresses from black to white. The elephant represents the mind, and its black colour the gross aspect of 'sinking' or mental dullness. The monkey represents distraction or mental agitation; and its black colour, 'scattering'. The hare represents the more subtle aspect of sinking or mental torpor. The hooked goad and lasso which the monk wields represent clear understanding and mindful recollection. The progressively diminishing flame, which occurs at intervals along the path, represents the decreasing degree of effort needed to cultivate understanding and recollection. The five sense objects of cloth, fruit, perfume, cymbals, and a mirror represent the five sensual sources of distraction.

At the end of the path single-pointed concentration is attained, and the 'purified elephant' of the mind is now completely submissive. The flying monk represents bodily bliss; and his riding of the elephant, mental bliss. Riding the elephant back triumphantly across the rainbow, wielding the flaming sword of perfect insight having attained the flame of clear understanding and mindfulness, represents the uprooting of samsara by the unity of *shamatha* and *vipashyana* which directly realises emptiness (*shunyata).*

Key to the nine stages of tranquil abiding (*shamatha*):

1. The first stage is attained through the power of study or hearing.
2. The monk fixes his mind on the object of concentration.
3. The lasso represents mindfulness or recollection.
4. The hooked elephant goad represents clear understanding.
5. The flame, which progressively diminishes along the path, represents the degree of effort needed to develop both recollection and understanding.
6. The elephant represents mind; its complete black colour represents the gross form of mental dullness or sinking.
7. The monkey represents mental agitation; its black colour represents distraction or scattering. The monkey at first runs wildly, leading the elephant.
8. The second stage is attained through the power of concentration.
9. This is achieved by lengthening the periods of concentration on the object.
10. The five senses of touch (cloth), taste (fruit), smell (perfumed conch), sound (cymbals), and sight (mirror), are the objects of distraction.
11. Beginning at their heads, the elephant and monkey begin to turn white. This shows the continuous progress in fixing and holding the object of concentration.

12. The third and fourth stages are attained through the power of memory or recollection.
13. The monk lassoes the elephant, fixing the wandering mind on the object.
14. The hare, which now appears on the elephant's back, represents the subtle aspect of sinking, or mental torpor. Here one is able to differentiate between the gross and subtle aspects of sinking.
15. The elephant, monkey, and hare look back; showing that having recognised these mental distractions, the mind turns back to the object of contemplation.
16. The meditator holds a clear and detailed conception of the object.
17. Attainment of the fifth and sixth stages of meditative absorption through the power of clear comprehension.
18. The monkey now follows the elephant; the arising of distraction diminishes.
19. Even the arising of virtuous thoughts must be perceived as a distraction from the object of concentration.
20. The monk hooks the elephant with his goad; the mind is stopped from wandering by clear understanding.
21. The mind is controlled.
22. The hare disappears and the mind is pacified.
23. The seventh and eighth stages are attained through the power of energetic perseverance.
24. The monkey leaves the elephant and now squats behind the monk in complete submission. However there are still slight traces of black; this shows that even the subtlest sinking and scattering may continue to arise. Should they begin to arise they can be eliminated with the slightest effort.
25. The monkey disappears and the elephant becomes completely white. The mind can now remain continually in absorption on the object of concentration.
26. Single-pointedness of mind.
27. The ninth stage of mental absorption is attained through the power of perfection.
28. Perfect equanimity. The path has ended and the elephant is at rest. From the heart of the meditating monk emanates a rainbow.

29. The monk flies alone; bodily bliss.
30. The monk rides the elephant; attainment of *shamatha*.
31. Riding the elephant across the rainbow; mental bliss.
32. The monk wields the flaming sword of perfect insight, and rides triumphantly back along the rainbow; samsara's root is destroyed by the union of *shamatha* and *vipashyana* (sword), with emptiness (*shunyata*) as the object of contemplation.
33. Control of the flame of supreme mindfulness and understanding represents the ability to examine the sublime meaning of *shunyata*: the knowledge of the ultimate reality of all phenomena.

The upper part of the illustration, where the rainbow emanates from the monk's heart, represents the tenth and eleventh stages of transcendental mental absorption. The tenth stage of bodily and mental bliss is symbolised by the flying monk and the monk riding the elephant. The eleventh stage is represented by the monk riding the elephant back across the rainbow. From the monk's heart emanate two dark rainbows, which the monk is just about to cut assunder with his flaming sword of wisdom. These two rainbows represent karmic hindrances and mental illusion (*klesha-varana*), and the obscurations of the instincts of mental distortion (*jneyavarana*).

A somewhat simpler but similar symbolic sequence for the attainment of meditative tranquility is found in the 'ten oxherding pictographs' of Zen Buddhism. Here the ox replaces the elephant, and in some Zen traditions the colour of the ox changes from black to white as the ox is glimpsed, found, herded, ridden, and finally forgotten. The ten oxherding images illustrate the search for the ox; seeing its footprints; catching the ox; herding it; riding the ox back home; forgetting it; forgetting the man who subdued it; returning to the place from which he started from; and appearing in the marketplace to teach and transform.

Plate 60: Diagram of *shamatha* meditation practice, depicting the nine stages of mental development

Plate 61: Cosmology of Mt Meru according to the Abhidharmakosha and Kalachakra systems

Chapter Five
Cosmology

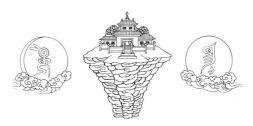

This chapter on Buddhist cosmology describes the conceptual outer macrocosm of the physical universe, the inner microcosm of the human 'subtle body', and their interdependent relationships. It begins with the cosmological plan of Mt Meru and its surrounding universe, and then recounts the Vedic Hindu legend of the creation myth known as 'the churning of the ocean'. The second section describes the mandala offering, where the visualised form of the universe is presented as a ritual offering. The third section deals with the Sino-Tibetan astrological system and its intricate symbolism. The fourth section describes the 'all-powerful ten' syllables of the Kalachakra mantra and their symbolic interrelationship with both the external universe and the visualised internal microcosm of the subtle body. The fifth section describes the monumental stupa and its architectural forms and symbolism as a reliquary representing the 'receptacle of Buddha mind'. The sixth and final section describes the internal microcosm of the subtle body – the *chakra* and channel-wheel systems – according to the Hindu model of Kundalini Yoga and various descriptions from Buddhist Highest Yoga Tantra.

MOUNT MERU (Tib. *Ri rab*)

Buddhist cosmology is based on two main conceptual systems of the structure of the universe. One is derived from the early *Abhidharmakosha*, composed by the Indian Buddhist master Vasubandhu (*circa* fourth century AD), and the other from the later *Kalachakra Tantra*.

The *Kalachakra Tantra* is of a much later Indian origin and was only introduced into Tibet in AD 1024. It is said to have been revealed to King Suchandra (Tib. Zla ba bzang po) by Shakyamuni Buddha in the mythical kingdom of Shambhala, 'the land held by Shiva'. The *Kalachakra Tantra* gives a very detailed description of the cosmos and its dimensional measurements; however elements of this system appear to have been adopted from the complex cosmology of the earlier Jain tantras.

The *Abhidharmakosha* postulates that the entire physical universe or 'great universe' consists of a thousand million world systems or 'small universes', of which our world system is but one. The creation of our world system began with an inward movement of four strong directional winds, produced by collective karma, which converged in the voidness of space. The impact of these four winds caused clouds to form, which released an incessant torrent of rain. Lightning and the storm force increase of wind drawn into this embryonic maelstrom caused the surface of the space-suspended rainwater to be churned. This churning produced yellow foam which began to solidify into the element of earth, and to sink below the surface of the water. As the earth element compacted, its atomic density caused various precious and common elements to come into existence and coagulate below the surface of the disc of water. At the very centre of this cosmic ocean emerged the great central mountain of our universe, Mt Meru, with four directional faces composed of the most precious elements derived from the solidified foam: crystal, lapis lazuli or sapphire, ruby, and gold. Surrounding Mt Meru there next arose seven concentric rings of golden mountains, each separated by an inner sea formed of rainwater and diminishing progressively in height as they ranged outward from Mt Meru. Surrounding these seven rings of mountains is a vast circular saltwater ocean, bounded on its outer circumference by a fence or ring of iron mountains. Within this great saltwater ocean there finally arose the four directional continents, which surround Mt Meru as islands in the middle of the salt ocean.

Each of these four continents is accompanied by two sub-continents positioned on either side, which bear the same shape and colour as their main continents but are each half its size or surface area. This schematic plan of the central four-sided and four-tiered Mt Meru, surrounded by an inner ocean, seven golden mountain rings – each with an inner ocean, an outer salt ocean in which the four continents and eight subcontinents are placed, and finally bounded by an outer ring of iron mountains, is the basic plan of our small universe according to the early Buddhist *Abhidharmakosha* model.

The measurements of Mt Meru and its surrounding mountains, oceans and continents are extremely vast, with precise, though different, dimensions given both in the *Abhidharma* and *Kalachakra* systems. The unit of measure is known as a *yojana* or league, equalling approximately four-and-a-half miles in the *Abhidharma* system, and nine miles in the *Kalachakra* system. As an example, in the *Kalachakra* system the upper surface of Mt Meru from east to west and north to south measures 50,000 *yojanas* or leagues across – equivalent to 450,000 miles. The seven concentric rings of surrounding gold mountains – which may be pictorially depicted in either a circular or square formation – diminish by half their preceding height and half their distances of separation as they proceed outwards. With a square formation of seven diminishing mountain ranges with Mt Meru at its centre, the illusion is created of a structural pyramid that echoes the ancient Asiatic model of the divine city, with its central citadel placed on the summit of a hill enclosed by seven defensive walls ascending around its slopes. It also echoes the structure of the great Egyptian pyramid of Giza (*circa* 2560 BC), the oldest and only extant of the eight wonders of the ancient world.

The metaphysical concept of the continuous creation of the cosmos as form manifesting from emptiness finds its expression in the progressive atomic concentration of the elements – from space to wind (clouds), to fire (lightning), water, and the solidification of earth. These five elements permeate the whole cosmological structure of Buddhism, from the outer macrocosm or mandala of the external universe to the inner microcosm or mandala of the individual form, and the secret body mandala of the movement of winds through the subtle channels.

As the axial centre of the universe Mt Meru represents, within the human body, both the spine and central channel. Iconographically it is represented by the central vertical or 'brahma-line' that runs through the centre of deity thangka compositions, and which is intersected by a second horizontal *brahma*-line in the construction of mandalas.

In the *Abhidharmakosha* cosmos, Mt Meru emerges from its surrounding ocean in the form of a slightly tapering, inverted pyramid, which has four lower tiers or terraces at its water-level base. The eastern face of Mt Meru is formed of white crystal, its southern face is the blue of lapis lazuli or sapphire, its western face is of red ruby, and its northern face is formed of pure gold. The sky, oceans, and continents in each of the four quadrants surrounding Mt Meru reflect the colour of its directional face. Our world system is situated on the main southern continent known as Jambudvipa – the 'island of the rose-apple tree', which is characterised by the blue sky and sea reflected from the southern lapis lazuli face of Mt Meru.

Mt Meru is also known as Sumeru in the Indian traditions, where it parallels Mt Olympus, the Greek mountain of the gods. Sumeru is located at the centre of the earth and capped by Swarga, the paradise of Indra. Its mythological description with four encircling rivers have frequently identified it with Mt Kailash as the source of the four great rivers which arise from its high watershed on the western Tibetan plateau.

Buddhist cosmology places its celestial hierarchies in perspective by assigning the entire formation of Mt Meru to the demi-gods and gods. Human beings are not the centre of the universe, and the human domain is humbly located on one of the surrounding continents in the outer salt sea.

The lowest of Meru's four tiers is inhabited by *nagas*, the second tier by garudas, the third tier by *rakshasas* and *danava* demons, and the fourth tier by the hosts of treasure-guarding *yakshas*.

The highest of the four tiers of Mt Meru above the visible water-line is inhabited by the four great guardian kings of the four directions and the hosts of demi-gods that comprise their retinues. These four 'earth-dwelling' guardian kings reign over the first celestial realm of Mt Meru and live in beautiful jewelled palaces in a landscape that is described as soft, smooth and striped. Flowers grow in profusion, and smooth roads of golden sand lead up to their palace steps. Although the inhabitants of these realms generally live in happiness and leisure some misery is experienced, and calamities like war do occur.

White Dhritirashtra is the guardian king of the east, who plays a lute and rules over the *gandharvas* or celestial musicians, and the *pishachas* or flesh-eating spirits. Blue Virudhaka is the guardian king of the south, who unsheaths a long sword and rules over the *kumbhandas* or large-testicled dwarf demons, and the *pretas* or hungry ghosts. Red Virupaksha is the guardian king of the west who holds a small stupa and a snake, and rules over the hooded *naga* serpents and the *putana dakinis* or poisonous female spirits. Yellow Vaishravana is the guardian king of the north who holds a banner of victory and a jewel-vomiting mongoose, and rules over the *yakshas*, who manifest as large-bellied dwarf spirit guardians of terrestial treasures, and the *rakshasas* or goblin-spirits.

The four guardian kings are sometimes placed on a fifth tier or even on the summit of Mt Meru, where from their first celestial realm they look out over the four directional quarters. The placement of these demi-gods on the tiers of Mt Meru is subject to slight traditional variations, and even the conceptual structure of Meru's cosmology cannot be taken as fixed. In fact the mountain itself is hollow, with a vast blazing syllable *Hum* at its central core. Below its summit and at the root level of the wish-fulfilling tree, which rises from its centre, dwell the jealous gods or *asuras*, who wage constant war with the gods over possession of this divine tree.

On the summit of Mt Meru is the palace of Indra, with the great wish-fulfilling tree of Indra's Chitraratha Grove at its centre and the four other divine gardens of Indra placed in the cardinal directions. This second celestial realm, presided over by Indra, is known as the 'heaven of the thirty-three gods' (Trayastrimsa), on account of the thirty-two other earth-dwelling gods which accompany Indra.

Above this, the third celestial realm comprises of the four heavens of the sky-dwelling gods. The first of these four heavens is that of Yama, known as the 'heaven of no dispute'. The second is Tushita, the 'heaven of contentment', where resides the bodhisattva Maitreya who is destined to become the Buddha of the next aeon. The third is Nirmanarati, or the 'heaven of delightful manifestation'. The fourth is Paranirmitavasavartin, or the 'heaven of delight in the illusory manifestation of phenomena'.

The two heavens of earth-dwelling gods (the four guardian kings and the heaven of thirty-three) and the four levels of sky-dwelling gods, comprise six heavens, and are known as the heavens of the form gods of the realm of desire (*kamaloka*).

Above these six heavens of the *kamaloka* arise the eighteen higher heavens of the gods of the desireless realms of pure form, known as *rupaloka*, although in certain descriptions their number is listed as seventeen. The gods of these heavens have transcended desire and possess divinely luminous etheric forms of the most sublime beauty. They are completely absorbed into the four levels of meditative absorption known as the 'four *samadhis*' (*chatur-dhyani-bhumi*), which are qualified by progressively refined states of awareness or purified consciousness. The first, second, and third of these four *samadhi* levels each consist of three ascending heavens, making a total of nine. The fourth level of pure form *samadhi* comprises of another nine ascending heavens, making a total of eighteen in all. The highest of these eighteen pure form heavens is known as Akanishtha, or the 'unexcelled', which is the heaven of the 'non-returners' (*anagamin*) on the very brink of arhatship.

Above these eighteen heavens of pure form are the four highest heavens of the formless realms, known as *arupaloka*. Beings in these realms have no corporeal form at all, but are still subject to traces of self-identification and therefore still bound by the laws of causation. The first of these four formless heavens is known as the 'heaven of limitless space' (*akashanantyayatana*). The second is the 'heaven of pure consciousness' (*vijnananantyayatana*). The third is the 'heaven of nothingness' (*akinchayayatana*), and the fourth the 'heaven of neither consciousness nor non-consciousness' (*naivashanjnanasamjna-ayatana*). Beyond these four formless realms is the state of enlightened Buddhahood, in which no trace of manifested self-identity exists and the flame of karmic causation has been entirely extinguished.

These realms of heavens which arise above Mt Meru are conceptually described in various Buddhist texts such as Vasubandhu's *Abhidharmakosha* and Buddhaghosa's *Vishuddhimagga*. The lifespans of the ascending god realms are of a progressively vast duration, culminating in the near-eternal existence of the gods of the highest formless realm, who live for a period of 80,000 'great *kalpas*' or creation-destruction cycles of the universe.

With the arising of any minor *samadhi* or state of bliss – whether induced by personal power, mystical experience, spiritual pride, or even psychedelic drugs – spiritually-orientated modern man may easily come to believe he has attained enlightenment. This delusion is infinitely more pronounced for a god of the highest formless realm who abides in the ultimate *samadhi* of tranquility whilst universes rise and fall. Yet causation has its own momentum and destiny turns with the exhaustion of previous good karma. The last seven days in the life of a falling god of the form realms is said to exceed the whole suffering of a human lifetime, even though the karmic transmigration may only be to a lower level of the heavens. For the first time aversion begins to arise towards the god's formerly beloved companions, his flower garlands wilt, perspiration and body odour begin to occur, his clothing begins to smell and his appearance rapidly changes from great beauty to ugliness. The signs of imminent death manifest as desertion by his companions, the tinkling of his decorative bells no longer sounds sweet, his wide-open lotus eyes begin to blink, and the brilliant radiance of his body light dims. Sun and moonlight do not exist in the *deva* realms; instead the radiance from the gods' bodies lights up the whole visible landscape and no shadows are perceived. As the *deva* is about to die he can forsee the realm of his next rebirth, and when it is in a lower realm he experiences much suffering at his future prospect. Yet for the *devas* there is ascent as well as descent amidst the celestial realms, and from the highest formless realms bodhisattvas can arise with the comparative sublimity of galaxies coming into existence.

Picture-postcards from the god realms are rare, yet to a highly realised being or bodhisattva who can 'see' through all realms of existence, the *devas* – who at their dream-like conclusion are as transcient and ephemeral as Prospero's speech – are just as real as beings of flesh and blood. Evidence of the form gods' presence seeps through the hairline of distinction that divides heaven and earth by the divine intercession of physically manifested (*nirmanakaya*) siddhas. Rainbow phenomena, flower-petal showers, boon-granted visions, rains of jewels, manifestation of sacred ash (*vibhuti*) and divinely tasting nectar (*amrita*), the production, apport and transmutation of miraculous material objects, may all be accomplished by the siddha who can traverse and command these realms.

Conceptually it is not easy to comprehend or visualise these realms of purified consciousness which hover on the very brink of the absolute cessation of conceptualisation itself. The problem lies purely in the illusory perception that consciousness is created from bodily manifestation in general, and by the brain specifically. Reversal of this mode of conception brings us closer to the truth. Consciousness persists as the underlying strata throughout the waking, dream, and deep sleep states. The 'I' thought arises at the moment of waking, and individuation immediately arises as the mind, which is nothing but a bundle of thoughts – gross, subtle, or extremely subtle – but thoughts none the less.

Because the waking mind arises the world arises, with its infinite illusions of a concrete and separate reality. In the waking state of consciousness, the physical reality of the external world appears to arise with an impeccable logic and conviction, yet it is merely a karmic projection onto the screen of pure consciousness, like the reflections in a mirror, or a white cinema screen which remains unblemished and completely unaffected by the endless epics, tragedies, comedies, and fantasies projected onto it. Karma is not some nescient storehouse where a being other than ourselves – or even our 'higher self' – deposits and dispenses blessings or curses of positive or negative destiny. Karma is what we are living in at this very moment – its variable fruits of sweetness or bitterness, the tang on our tongues: it is the sum total of our experience. Sowing and reaping, as cause and result, arise simultaneously as a myriad strands spanning the past, present, and future through beginningless time. In the dream state different identities of mind and an endless series of phenomenal worldscapes are projected; time compresses or expands in a seemingly convincing reality where anything may happen. To a clinical observer several minutes of 'real' time pass in the rapid-eye-movements of the dreamer, whilst for the dreamer a long sequence of entirely separate events may have arisen. Yet, whatever physical form or appearance one may assume in the dream, throughout all the phantasmagoria of dream reality the sense of 'I' remains absolute.

The Chinese sage Chuang Tzu once dreamed he was a butterfly and posed the question, "Did Chuang Tzu dream he was a butterfly, or is the butterfly still dreaming he is Chuang Tzu?" In the state of deep sleep the 'I' thought, the mind, and the world do not arise, as individuation or projection returns to its source as unmanifested consciousness. There is no screen, no projector, no cinema hall, no movie, no audience, spectators or witnesses – there is seemingly nothing at all. Yet consciousness persists, the heart and breath continue, one is definitely alive and says, on waking, that 'I' have slept soundly or peacefully. The ancient Greeks believed that sleep was produced by noxious fumes created by the food one had eaten during the day. The state of deep sleep remains almost as enigmatic today as it was to the ancient Greeks. Even though it is a state in which we spend a third of our lives, it cannot be subjectively analysed as there is 'no one' there to investigate its nature.

Each day we pass through three states of consciousness: awakeness, with a seemingly permanent mind which self-identifies with the body as being incarnate as a separate entity in an infinite universe; dreaming, with a multitude of personalities, emotions, and mindframes in an illusory infinity of visionary environments; and deep sleep, where there is no experience, no world, no individuation, no thing and no mind. Like a thread through pearls, consciousness persists through all three states, which are comparable to the three 'bodies' (kaya) of the Buddha – the nirmanakaya, sambhogakaya, and dharmakaya (see page 142). The psychic winds which accumulate in the head, throat and heart cause these three states to arise.

Karma creates all experiential reality, and karma is fuelled by the three primary poisons of ignorance, desire,

and aversion. Enlightenment is the total elimination or cessation of karma, the 'putting out of the flame' implied in the word 'nirvana'. The word enlightenment does not imply a breakthrough into a state of light or illumination; its meaning is to purify or 'to make the load lighter' by removing the 'weight' of karmas. The state of enlightenment is our essential Buddha nature, it is not something to be attained in the future; if so it could equally be lost again. Like a beautiful diamond encased in mud, ignorance veils our essential Buddha nature. To 'attain' or reveal this essential nature all that is required is to remove the ignorance. This is not an easy thing to accomplish; deep karmic impressions and conceptual thought compounds the difficulty by projecting it to a remote future date, or even onto another being who is going to do it for us.

"Sentient beings are unenlightened Buddhas, and Buddhas are enlightened sentient beings. Each man must work out his own salvation", the Buddha declared. This poses the ultimate question, "What is the primal cause of karma and ignorance?" On this topic the Buddha was almost silent, revealing the futility of any conceptual or verbal explanation. As the Buddha declared, "Suppose, Malunkyaputta, a man were wounded by an arrow thickly smeared with poison, and his companions brought a surgeon to treat him. The man would say: 'I will not let the surgeon pull out the arrow until I know the name and clan of the man who wounded me; whether the bow that wounded me was a longbow or a crossbow; whether the arrow that wounded me was hoof-tipped or curved or barbed.' All this would still not be known to that man and meanwhile he would die. So too, Malunkyaputta, if anyone should say: 'I will not lead the noble life under the Buddha until the Buddha declares to me whether the world is eternal or not eternal, finite or infinite; whether the soul is the same as or different from the body; whether or not an awakened one continues or ceases to exist after death', that would still remain undeclared by the Buddha and meanwhile that person would die." (From the Chulamalunkya Sutra cited in Nanamoli Thera and Bikku Bodhi.)

Similarly, Padmasambhava once asked his Burmese guru Shri Singha, "What is the difference between Buddhas and non-Buddhas?" To which Shri Singha replied, "Even though one seeks to discern a difference, there is no difference. Therefore be free of doubt concerning external things. To overcome internal doubt employ perfect divine wisdom. No one has yet discovered the primary or secondary cause. I myself have not been able to do so; and you likewise, Lotus-Born One, shall fail in this."

In the cosmological system of the Kalachakra Tantra the structural arrangement of Mt Meru and its surroundings is quite different from that in the earlier Abhidharmakosha model. The Kalachakra's Mt Meru forms a conical pyramid with an umbrella-shaped hemisphere of twelve interlocking planetary wind-wheels arching down from its summit. These twelve wind-wheels or planetary tracks, coloured in six pairs according to the six colours of the Kalachakra elemental system, represent the zodiac houses or the equinoctial orbits (gola) of the sun in each of the twelve months of the year. Aries and Virgo are white, Pisces and Libra are red, Taurus and Leo are yellow, Aquarius and Scorpio are black, Cancer and Gemini are blue, and Sagittarius and Capricorn are green. Meru's four faces and continents are coloured: blue-black in the east (circular continents); red in the south (triangular continents); silver or white in the north (half-moon continents); and gold in the west (square continents). In the *Kalachakra* system Mt Meru is surrounded by six concentric rings of mountains and lakes, and the outer salt sea rests on progressively larger and telescoping discs of earth, water, fire, and air suspended in space.

In the *Abhidharmakosha* cosmology the supporting base of the universe which arises within space is represented by an immense crossed *vajra* (*vishvavajra*), symbolising the four directional winds of the air element. Upon this rests the disc of the outer ocean, bounded by its circular *vajra*-iron walls which enclose the lights of the sun, moon, planets, and stars within our small universe. A thousand million such small 'island' universes manifest across the infinite expanse of space, constituting the great universe.

The *Abhidharmakosha*'s Mt Meru rises 80,000 leagues or *yojanas* above the surface of the inner ocean; an equal distance is ascribed to its lower submarine depths below the inner ocean's surface, and the width of the inner ocean between Meru's base and the first circular ring of mountains is also equivalent to 80,000 leagues. Positioned either above or just below the summit of Mt Meru, and midway between Meru and its surrounding continents, are the discs of the sun and moon. The sun is positioned in the north-east and the moon in the south-west (an alternative system, derived from the mandala offering cosmology, places the sun in the east and the moon in the west). The wind-wheels and the houses or palaces of the planets and stars spin eternally in a clockwise sidereal motion across the all-encompassing dome of the sky, their harmonic interrelations and transitory configurations creating the karmic patterns as cause and effect, or free will and destiny, of all that is born in time.

According to the *Abhidharmakosha*, each peak of the seven rings or squares of golden mountains surrounding Mt Meru is crowned by a city of the gods with a golden central palace. On the lower slopes, and in ocean caves along the shoreline, dwell various tribes of *asuras*. These seven rings of mountains, which progressively diminish in height as they encircle outwards, are known respectively as: Yugandhara, Ishadhara, Khadiraka, Sudarshana, Ashvakama, Vinataka, and Nimindhara. Between each of these mountain rings are the seven swirling freshwater lakes known as *sitas*, which diminish by half their width as they progress outwards between the seven mountain rings. The water of these lakes possesses the eight qualities of pure water, and are the abode of great *naga* kings with their precious mineral and jewel wealths.

In the *Kalachakra* cosmology the outer encircling mountain ring which encompasses the great salt ocean is known as the *vajra*-mountain ring, and the six inner mountain rings expanding outwards from Mt Meru beyond the inner freshwater ocean are known as Nilabha, Mandara, Nisata, Manikara, Drona, and Sita. The six inner lakes between the

mountains are composed of molasses, ghee, yoghurt, milk, water, and wine. The seventh outer lake is the great salt ocean in which the four continents and eight subcontinents arise.

The *Kalachakra Tantra* ascribes Mt Meru's circular cross-section to the indestructible *vajra*-like seed or disc (*bindu*) of the void nature of the element space. In the east is the half-circle of the wind element, in the south the triangle of the fire element, in the north the circular full-moon orb of the water element, and in the west the golden square of the earth element. The directional placement of the five elements forms the geometric base of the mandala of the deity Kalachakra, symbolising the Five Buddhas, the five emptinesses, and the five wisdoms. The directional arrangement of the elements occur in a differing sequence in the Kalachakra mandala, and in depictions of the Kalachakra cosmological system. The blue-black full-moon circles of the eastern continents are placed to the front of the Mt Meru mandala, the red triangles of the southern continents are placed to the left, the yellow squares of the western continents are placed behind or above, and the silver or white semi-circles of the northern continents are placed to the right.

In the *Abhidharma* cosmology the eastern pot-shaped or semi-circular white continent is known as Purvavideha (Tib. *shar lus 'phags po*), meaning 'vast land'. Its diameter is 9,000 leagues, and its inhabitants have moon-shaped faces and are twice as tall as human beings, with a lifespan of three hundred years. The land, sea and sky of Purvavideha are white, with a mountainous landscape composed of precious jewels. Although this realm is very peaceful the dharma is not taught or practised here. To the left and right of the main continent are the two smaller subcontinents of Videha (Tib. *lus 'phags*), and Deha (Tib. *lus*).

The blue southern continent is known as Jambudvipa (Tib. '*dzam bu gling*), meaning the 'land of the rose-apple or *jambu* fruit'. The name Jambudvipa is derived from the sound '*jambu*' which is said to have arisen as the rose-apple fruits fell into the water. These fruits were consumed by the *nagas*, whose excrement turned into the fabled gold of the Jambu river. Jambudvipa is characterised by an abundance of wish-fulfilling trees, which symbolise the earth's plenitude. Jambudvipa is 7,000 leagues in diameter and has the trapezoid shape of an axe-head or vase, derived from the shoulder blade or scapula of a sheep which is used in oracular divination. Jambudvipa is the continent on which our human realm is located, with Bodh Gaya at its centre; the eight great hell realms are located at various descending depths below Bodh Gaya, representing the comparative extremities of torment experienced deep in these underworlds. In the *Kalachakra* cosmology these eight hell realms are divided into four pairs and are situated in the telescopic discs of wind, fire, water, and earth below the lower earth base. The oceans and sky of Jambudvipa reflect the lapis lazuli southern face of Mt Meru, and the mountain's sheer immensity fills and chromatically coincides with the hemisphere of the visible sky. Its human inhabitants have trapezoid or pear-shaped faces and live for up to a hundred years. The dualism of the human realm yields the fruits of pleasure and pain; yet it is a fortunate realm in which the Buddhas manifest and the dharma is revealed. The main continent of Jambudvipa is accompanied by its two smaller satellite subcontinents of Aparachamara (Tib. *rnga yab gzhan*) to the left, and Chamara (Tib. *rnga yab*) to its right.

A melacholic Tibetan legend relates how mankind came to inhabit Jambudvipa. It forms a poignant counterpart to the 'fall' in the Book of Genesis.

Originally the land of Jambudvipa was empty, there were no humans, animals or vegetation. Due to karma, certain of the gods from Mt Meru came to our world, and because of their divine power Jambudvipa became a paradise. Their light illumined the darkness of the world, and with divinely manifested food the gods happily lived out their long years. Then one day one of the gods tasted a creamy substance which manifested from the earth, and found it to be very tasty. Soon all of the gods had given up their divine sustenance in favour of the food of earth. Because of this their divine powers diminished until they were living in complete darkness. Then the sun, moon, and stars came into existence, due to the gods' previous good karma. With the advent of external light vegetation began to grow from the earth, and the gods – having exhausted their supply of earth food – began to eat a corn-like vegetable. Each day they ate one vegetable from their own plant, and the next day it would grow again. Then one day one of the gods found two vegetables on his plant and ate them both. On the next day there were none, so this god stole from his neighbour. Thus did theft come into the world, and soon the gods were working to plant more food as a precaution against hunger and theft. As they stole and planted they began to think strange thoughts. One of the gods found his genitals disturbing, so he tore them off and became a woman. This female god was attracted to the male gods and soon bore children, who bore more children, until the world of the gods began to be populated with people. With so many people and a scarcity of food, humankind began to live as families and clans, with a need for shelter and sustenance. Soon theft, strife and war became endemic, as harmony disintegrated into greed and selfishness. Then one day people grew weary of their enmity, and gathering together they elected a king. The king taught his subjects how to build houses and grow their own food. Thus, according to legend, did divinity descend into the lot of man.
(Adapted from Norbu and Turnbull.)

The red western continent is known as Aparagodaniya (Tib. *nub ba glang spyod*), meaning 'wealth of cattle'. It is 8,000 leagues in diameter and has the circular shape of the sun. Its inhabitants are four times taller than human beings, have round sun-like faces, and live for a lifespan of five hundred years. The sky, earth, and sea reflect the ruby-red face of Mt Meru, and the land is rich in prime cattle, which provide milk, butter, yoghurt, cheese, and meat to its physically robust inhabitants. Aparagodaniya is accompanied by the subcontinents of Uttaramantrina (Tib. *lam mchog 'gro*) to its left, and Satha (Tib. *g.yo ldan*) to its right.

The gold northern continent is known as Uttarakuru (Tib. *byang sgra mi snyan*), meaning the 'northern race of Kuru'. It is the largest of the four continents being 10,000 leagues in diameter, and is shaped like the golden four-cornered square of the element earth. Its inhabitants are eight times taller than human beings, have square horse-like faces, and live for up to a thousand years. Uttarakuru is a land of great abundance, with uncultivated harvests of huskless rice spontaneously manifesting. Labour, clothing and shelter are unecessary in this pleasant paradise, yet like the falling gods of the form realms its inhabitants experience great suffering and deprivation during the last seven days of their lives. The sky, sea, and earth reflect the golden, or sometimes emerald, northern face of Mt Meru. Uttarakuru is accompanied by its two subcontinents of Kaurava (Tib. *sgra mi snyan gyi zla*) to its left, and Kurava (Tib. *sgra mi snyan*) to its right.

Pictorial representations of Mt Meru and its surrounding universe display elements of considerable innovation in their depiction. There is also a Bon version of Mt Meru which closely mirrors its *Abhidharmakosha* model. An elaborate series of paintings depicting the evolutionary stages of the *Kalachakra* cosmology is painted on the external walls of Paro Dzong and Punakha Dzong temples in western Bhutan. Another series illustrating the *Vaidurya Karpo*, an astrological treatise composed by Desi Sangye Gyatso – the regent of the fifth Dalai Lama, occurs as an independent series of paintings, several of which are housed in the Mentsikhang or Tibetan Medical Centre at Lhasa.

Plate 61

Illustrated in this drawing are five examples of the cosmology of Mt Meru. On the upper left an *Abhidharmakosha* model of the small universe shows Mt Meru with a square cross-section rising into the cloud-capped god realms above. Indra's beautiful city of Sudarshana can be seen at its summit, surrounded by his Chitraratha Grove of wish-fulfilling trees. Seven square lakes and mountain ranges enclose Mt Meru's base, which ascends in four tiers. The eastern continent of Purvavideha, represented by a half-moon or semi-circular island, accompanied by its two subcontinents of Deha and Videha, are placed at the lower right. The outer enclosing ring of *vajra*-mountains is drawn in a circular saw-like band of flames.

In the upper right *Abhidharmakosha* cosmos drawing, the southern continent of Jambudvipa, with its two subcontinents of Chamara and Aparachamara, are placed to the front of Mt Meru. The full moon is placed to the left or southwest of Mt Meru, and the sun to the right or north-east. Meru's four lower tiers and square upper faces are embellished with strings of hanging jewels. Above Indra's palace and paradise grove ascends an expanding series of cloud-streets representing the god realms. The continents, mountains, and lakes are arranged in an irregular pattern around Meru's base.

At the middle left a circular *Abhidharmakosha* cosmological system is drawn. Mt Meru is opened out or 'exploded' to reveal three sides of its faces and tiers. Cloud-streets, depicting the four desire realms and seventeen desireless realms of the gods, ascend above Indra's palace. The four highest formless realms are not depicted since they are without substance. The seven rings of mountains and lakes circle between the inner freshwater and outer salt oceans, and the southern continent of Jambudvipa with its two satellite subcontinents are placed to the front of Mt Meru.

At the middle right is an illustration of the *Kalachakra* cosmological system. Here a wind mandala of cosmic clouds supports the circular earth and ocean base of the universe. The continents are placed in a mirror-image sequence to that of the *Abhidharmakosha*, with the southern continent of Jambudvipa to the front. Only three rings of mountains and lakes are drawn to represent the actual sixfold scheme of the *Kalachakra* system. The cylindrical pyramid face of Mt Meru is depicted as a tapering rock stack. The moon and sun are placed to the left and right of Meru's summit. Above Indra's palace and the heavens of the thirty-three gods ascend the three cloud-borne realms of the form and formless gods.

At the bottom is a horizontal drawing of the *Abhidharma* cosmos in half-section, redrawn from a painting by the contemporary Tibetan lama and artist Ala Rigta. The *vajra*-mountain ring can be seen in the corners, with wind, earth, and water mandalas superimposed above. Again Jambudvipa is to the front of Mt Meru, with the moon and sun at Meru's left and right. The four lower tiers are drawn with the rainbow enhaloed palaces of the demi-gods on each of their levels. In a circular rainbow on the central face of Mt Meru is the palace of the blue guardian king of the south, Virudhaka. Above Mt Meru's summit Indra's palace and sacred groves are enclosed by a rainbow; from its upper arc ascend radiating rainbows which indicate the realms of the gods.

THE VEDIC LEGEND OF THE CHURNING OF THE OCEAN

The ancient Indian legend of the churning of the ocean, as briefly related here, is derived from the *Vishnu Purana*. The *Puranas* are early Indian texts which relate the legends of particular Hindu gods, and transmit through legend the earlier Vedic rituals which were primarily concerned with sacrifice. The *Vishnu Purana* contains its own creation myth that tells of the search for *amrita*, the nectar of immortality, which has its earlier origin in the Vedic sacrifice of the juice derived from *soma* (*Asclepias acida*), the sacred plant or vine. The legend of the churning of the ocean was absorbed into early Indian Buddhism and faithfully translated into Tibetan Buddhism. In the Tibetan medical tradition this legend is extremely important, as it describes how *amrita*, the divine physician, and many medicinal plants and poisons, came into existence. The myth also reveals the origin of such ancient symbols as the divinatory tortoise, the serpent Vasuki, the precious elephant and horse, the wish-fulfilling tree, jewel, and cow, myrobalam and *kusha* grass, the cosmic mountain and the principal Hindu deities, all of which were absorbed into later Buddhist symbolism.

The gods, having grown weary of their interminable enmity with the demons or anti-gods (*asuras*), approached Vishnu for the boon of immortality. Vishnu counselled the gods to seek cooperation with the *asuras* to churn the great ocean together, which would reveal the gems, herbs, and nectar of immortality (*amrita*) hidden within its depths. With the help of the creator god Brahma, and the great serpent Vasuki, they were able to uproot the vast mountain Mandara to use as a churning stick. From the depths of the ocean Vishnu manifested himself as the supreme tortoise, which rose to the surface. On his upper shell was placed Mt Mandara, which Brahma stabilised by pressing on from above. The great serpent Vasuki wound himself around Mt Mandara as a churning rope, and at either end of the serpent the gods and *asuras* pulled back and forth, pivoting the mountain and churning the ocean.

This churning caused chaos in the ocean, as gradually the water was churned into milk, and then clarified butter (*ghee*). The first things to emerge from the ocean were the thousand-rayed sun and the cool moon (*soma*), which Shiva took as ornaments for his diadem. Next arose the white horse Uchaishravas, and the precious six-tusked white elephant Airavata; these Indra took as his mounts. Then arose the wish-fulfilling tree Kalpavriksha (or Parijata), and the brilliant red gemstone Kaustubha; the gods claimed the tree, and Vishnu claimed the gemstone as his breast ornament. Next to emerge was the goddess Lakshmi (Shri), the 'fortunate one', whom Vishnu took as his wife. Next emerged the intoxicating goddess of wine, Sura. The gods were able to drink her wine without ill effects, but the *asuras* were not able to hold their alcohol. From Sura is derived the word 'asura', meaning 'those unable to consume wine' or 'those without the goddess of wine'.

As they continued their vigorous churning there next arose the wrathful fiery form of Halahala (Kalakuta), the embodiment of poison incarnate. Terrified by the ferocious manifestation of Halahala the gods swooned and Brahma, rousing the gods from their swoon, succeeded in subduing Halahala by uttering the long syllable *Hum,* which caused Halahala's body to explode into pieces. The *naga* serpent spirits claimed the essence of his poison as their own, whilst from the scattered fragments of his body arose all manner of poisonous creatures and plants. Another variation of this legend tells how Shiva manifested as mantra in order to subdue Halahala, but the poison remained in his throat, causing it to turn blue. Nilakantha – the blue-throated one – is one of the epithets for Shiva.

Next to arise was Surabhi, the 'wish-fulfilling white cow', whose abundance of dairy products grants all desires. Finally there emerged Dhanvantari – the physician of the gods – bearing in his hands the vase full of *amrita*, the nectar of immortality. Dhanvantari is attributed with revealing the medical science of Ayurveda, which subsequently became the root of the four tantras (Tib. *rgyud bzhi*) of the Tibetan medical system.

The *asuras*, reverting to their inherent characteristics, fought to obtain full possession of the *amrita*. But Vishnu, assuming the illusory form of the enchanting goddess

Mohini, beguiled the *asuras* and served the *amrita* only to the gods. Rahu, one of the *asuras*, noticed this enchantment, and assuming the guise of a god began to drink the *amrita* also. The sun and moon, witnessing Rahu's deceit informed Vishnu – who hurled his fiery discus (*chakra*) at Rahu, severing his head just as the *amrita* reached his throat. Rahu's body fell to earth causing great earthquakes, and his head – assuming again its normal raven form – flew into the skies, enraged at the treachery of the sun and moon. Rahu, the 'lord of eclipses', is forever doomed to chase the sun and moon across the skies, causing eclipses. But as soon as his dark shadow has swallowed them they re-emerge from his throat. A later legend relates that it was Garuda – the 'golden sun bird' and mount of Vishnu, who stole the *amrita* in his beak, bearing it aloft into the skies. Garuda was subdued by the sky god Indra, and forced to return the *amrita*. A few drops that spilled from Garuda's beak fell to the ground, landing on fields of *kusha* grass where they propagated medicinal plants such as myrobalam and garlic.

The gods' struggle to regain the *amrita* from the *asuras* is said to have taken twelve days, and the four drops that spilled from the pot (*kumbha*) of *amrita* fell to the ground near the Indian cities of Allahabad, Haridwar, Nasik, and Ujjain. At each of these four cities the great religious festival known as the Kumbha Mela is held every three years in rotation, with a larger festival taking place every twelve years (derived from the concept that one day for the gods is equivalent to one human year).

Infuriated by the gods' total possession of the *amrita*, the *asuras* engaged in an even mightier war against them. But since the gods had consumed the *amrita* their only mortal weakness was decapitation, whilst the *asuras* were vulnerable in every part of their bodies. The *asuras* were eventually vanquished into the earth and ocean, whilst the triumphant gods returned to their heavens. This battle is illustrated in paintings of the 'wheel of life', where the gods and *asuras* wage war over the wish-fulfilling tree, *kalpavriksha*. Indra leads the army of the gods, wielding his *vajra* and *chakra*, and riding his six-tusked elephant, Airavata. The *kalpavriksha* is usually identified as the Indian coral tree, but is commonly depicted as a magnolia-like tree. The gods dwell near its canopy and can freely partake of its fruit and flowers, whilst the jealous *asuras* live at the level of its roots and can never fulfil their desires.

Mt Mandara is a sacred hill, of no great height, in the Indian state of Bihar. The legend of the churning of the ocean makes it sacred to Hindus, Buddhists, and Jains, all of whom erected temples there. It features as one of the eight mountains represented in the mandala of the 'eight great cremation grounds'.

Exoterically the legend of the churning of the ocean represents embryonic creation out of chaos, where the elements of water (tortoise), earth (elephant), wind (horse), and fire (Halahala) arise from the primal ocean.

Esoterically, the churning of the ocean symbolises the Hindu yogic practices of *khechari mudra* and Kundalini Yoga.

In the practice of *khechari mudra* the frenum under the tongue is gradually severed, and the tongue stretched and lengthened until it can reach to the point between the eyebrows. The tongue (Mt Mandara) is then swallowed backwards and pressed upwards to 'churn' the cranial cavity above the soft palate. Eventually a channel is formed, which causes *amrita* or *soma* to descend from the crown of the head and flood the yogin's body with bliss. Indian fakirs use the practice of swallowing the tongue and pressing upon the carotid arteries in the neck to induce a state of catalepsy, or suspended animation. The fakir can then be buried underground or immersed in water for prolonged periods. When waking consciousness returns the fakir is impervious to pain for a short period, and there is no flow of blood if the body is pierced. It is a tantric dictum that a man's body possesses two boneless organs which must be controlled – the penis and the tongue, or for a woman the clitoris and the mouth.

In Kundalini Yoga Mt Mandara represents the central channel (*sushumna*). The serpent Vasuki, coiled around Mt Mandara, represents the goddess Kundalini – who is depicted resting upon the back of a tortoise. The act of churning (purification) causes the primal waters to change to milk (spiritual nourishment), butter (ritual practice), wine (divine intoxication), poison (ego annihilation), and *amrita* (transmutation, realisation and immortality). The initial emergence of the sun and moon represent the two subsidiary channels (*nadi*) of *pingala* (*surya* – solar) and *ida* (*chandra* – lunar), which ascend to the right and left of the central channel. All of the other forms that arise from the ocean represent the ascending *chakras*, culminating in the arising of *amrita* at the crown centre – where the goddess Kundalini unites with her lord, Shiva.

THE MANDALA OFFERING
(Skt. *mandala*; Tib. *dkyil 'khor, mandal*)

The offering of a mandala, representing the entire form and wealth of the purified universe to one's lama, guru, or meditational deity (Tib. *yi dam*), is the highest ritual expression of devotion in the Tibetan Buddhist tradition. In essence the mandala offering of the universe is the ultimate act of giving or surrender to the 'outer' manifesting guru or deity, who is inseparable from one's innate Buddha nature – one empties one's 'self' of self and only the 'one' remains. Form is emptiness, and emptiness is form – there is no separation.

The representational 'grain mandala', comprising of a visualised offering of Mt Meru and its surrounding universe, forms the physical manifestation of this ritual offering. In the preliminary practices (Tib. s*ngon 'gro*) of Vajrayana Buddhism, the mandala offering forms one of the four essential practices or *bhumis* – each of a hundred thousand prostrations, Vajrasattva mantras, mandala offerings, and Guru Yoga. The prostrations essentially purify the defilements of body, the Vajrasattva practice purifies the defilements of speech and mind, the mandala offering accumulates the merits of the six perfections, and Guru Yoga transmits the blessings of the Vajrayana lineages descending from Vajradhara, the 'primordial' or *dharmakaya* embodiment in which pure Buddha nature manifests to reveal the tantric Buddhist transmissions. The six perfections (*paramitas*) arise as the 'two accumulations' of merit or skilful means, and wisdom or insight. The five perfections of generosity, morality, patience, effort, and meditation constitute the accumulation of merit, and the sixth perfection of wisdom is self-constituted. The perfection of meditative concentration is the only one of these six perfections that implies an act of solitary withdrawal, the other five being of an integrated or communal nature. So when a person proclaims, "I have no time to practise" they are probably not perceiving the *buddhadharma* correctly. Panoramic awareness has no shutters or doors which open and close during the hours of meditation or practice. There are no walls, the 'view' is ever present in its pristine clarity, and no distinction is made between daily life and practice as concepts of samsara and nirvana, or 'ape and essence'. The true yardstick of one's practice is how one emanates the awareness of all six perfections in daily life.

The Tibetan term for mandala (*dkyil 'khor*) means 'that which circles ('*khor*) about a centre (*dkyil*)'; its inner meaning is 'absorbing the essence'. The grain mandala is traditionally offered to one's lama when a request has been made for teachings or an initiation – where the entire offering of the universe symbolises the most appropriate payment for the preciousness of the teachings. Once in a desolate Indian landscape the Mahasiddha Tilopa requested a mandala offering from his disciple Naropa, and there being no readily available materials with which to construct a grain mandala, Naropa urinated on the sand and formed an offering of a wet-sand mandala. On another occassion Naropa used his blood, head, and limbs to create a mandala offering for his guru. Tilopa was delighted with these spontaneous offerings. There are no inhibitions or hindrances in the heart purified by the fires of intense longing and devotion.

Traditionally a grain mandala is usually constructed on a circular base, which commonly measures between eight and twelve inches in diameter. The base may also be square, or more rarely semi-circular or triangular, representing one of the four activities or *karmas* of pacifying (circular), enriching (square), subjugating (gibbous or semi-circular), and destroying (triangular). The base may be fashioned of a material such as wood, stone, ceramic, slate, or metal, although embellished gold, silver, copper or bronze bases are more appropriate to the preciousness of the offering mandala. Modern mandala sets consist of a smooth, raised, precious-metal base with repoussé designs of the four continents and eight subcontinents, the great salt ocean, the *vajra*-mountain ring, the 'four wealths', and the inner mountain rings – inscribed in correct sequence on the outer ring of its raised circular base. A series of three or four progressively smaller open rings form the retaining rings for the grain mandala's stacked ascension. These metal rings are engraved with repoussé designs of the main mandala offerings on their sides. These include the seven insignia of the *chakravartin* and the treasure vase on the largest and lower ring; the eight offering goddesses on the second ring; and the sun, moon, precious umbrella, and victory banner on

the third ring. Mounds of grain are piled within these progressively ascending rings, and above the grain heap of the upper ring is placed an eight-spoked golden wheel (*dharmachakra*), fashioned in repoussé metal relief with a lower lotus base, which symbolises the crowning glory of Mt Meru itself.

A grain mandala composed from such a set of base, rings, and *dharmachakra* is commonly placed on a Buddhist altar – often with small rectangular painted images (Tib. *tsak li*) of the mandala's components mounted upon sticks and placed within the ascending stages of the grain rings. 'Grain' refers to the particle substances used to create the various mounds representing the constituents of the universe. Small precious stones, pearls, or jewels, form the most auspicious offering to accumulate the merit of wealth. Powdered medicinal herbs or pills accumulate the merit of healing. Small stones, shells, or granular mineral powders may also be used, but grain in the form of barley, pulses, or rice are most commonly used. The rice should be cleansed of foreign particles and washed in saffron water to give to the uncooked grains an auspicious golden tinge.

In actual performance of the mandala offering, the mandala base – which is usually circular and of a bronze or gold plating to represent the element of earth – is firstly washed in saffron-scented water. The practitioner then holds the base in his left hand, sprinkles a little rice over its surface, which he then wipes several times with his right forearm or wrist in a circular motion. At the same time he visualises wind, water, and earth mandalas arising above one another within the mandala base. The clockwise circling of the base with the forearm symbolises the cleansing of impurities and the drawing inward of virtues into the world mandala. Then three anticlockwise circlings are made with the forearm, representing the blessings of body, speech, and mind. All of the activities involved in arranging, offering, and dissolving the mandala are accompanied by visualisations, prayers, and mantras. The axis of orientation of the mandala follows the traditional Indian system of an east–west alignment. East is usually placed on the side facing away from the practitioner in an offering mandala, where it faces towards the blessings of the assembly of deities or 'merit field'. In the mandala offering of request, east is usually placed towards the practitioner.

The ring finger of the right hand is then dipped in perfumed or saffron-scented water and circled around the edge of the mandala base – whilst visualising the outer *vajra*-mountain ring arising like an adamantine fence. Grains of rice are then sprinkled over the surface of the base and visualised as an expanse of jewels and flowers permeating the entire expanse of the universe. An outer circle of rice grains is made around the edge of the mandala base to represent the enclosing *vajra*-mountain ring. Having established and purified the base of the mandala, the laying out of grain heaps symbolising Mt Meru, its surrounding environment, and offerings, begins. The most extensive construction of the mandala consists of thirty-seven grain heaps, although traditions of twenty-five, twenty-three, seven, and six heaps as a 'short mandala' offering are also common. The layout

Plate 62: The Mt Meru mandala offering

of the thirty-seven heaps, with their numerical order, directions, Sanskrit, and Tibetan names, are illustrated and listed on Plate 63.

At the centre of the mandala the syllable *Hum* is visualised, which characterises the inner essence or composition of samsara. As a large handful of grain is poured onto the centre the *Hum* transforms into the great world mountain of Meru, with its four faces, four tiers, submerged base, and its total pantheon of celestial beings ascending from its water base to the highest of the formless god realms. Medium sized piles of grain are next placed in each of the four cardinal directions (east, south, west, and north), representing the four main continents. Eight smaller heaps of grain are then placed to the right and left of these four continents in the same directional rotation, symbolising the eight subcontinents. Then midway between Mt Meru and each of the main continents are placed four mounds of grain representing the wealths of these four continents. In the east the wealth of Purvavideha is represented by a mountain of precious jewels; in the south our world continent of Jambudvipa is represented by a grove of wish-fulfilling trees; in the west Aparagodaniya is represented by a wish-granting cow, whose urine and dung are of liquid and solid gold; in the north Uttarakuru is represented by uncultivated crops, which spontaneously regenerate within the day that they are harvested. Inside the boundary of these four great 'wealths' are placed grain mounds symbolising the seven precious jewels of the *chakravartin*. To the east, south, west, and north are placed the precious wheel, jewel, queen, and minister. In the south-east, south-west, and north-west intercardinal directions are placed the three remaining *chakravartin* jewels of the precious elephant, horse, and general. In the last intercardinal corner of the north-east is placed the precious golden vase of treasures. Inside this circular or square sequence of *chakravartin* and vase mounds are then placed grain heaps to represent the eight offering goddesses. These goddesses are extremely beautiful and, attired in jewel garlands and silks, they assume graceful dance postures, whilst holding their specific offerings in their two hands. In the east is the offering goddess of beauty; in the south is the goddess offering garlands; in the west, the goddess of song; in the north, the goddess of dance; in the south-east, the goddess offering flowers; in the south-west, the goddess offering incense; in the north-west, the goddess offering light; and in the north-east, the goddess offering perfume. Finally in each of the four intercardinal corners and on a level with the four outer wealths are placed grain mounds representing the sun in the north-east, the moon in the south-west, the precious jewelled parasol in the north-west, and the banner of total victory in the south-east. Alternatively the sun, moon, parasol, and banner may also be placed in the east, west, south, and north respectively. This completes the thirty-seven offerings of the 'long mandala'. The twenty-five heap offering mandala omits the eight offering goddesses and includes the four wealths within the main continent heaps. The twenty-three heap mandala further omits either the parasol and banner, or the earth mandala base and *vajra*-mountain ring, according to different traditions.

After the grain mandala has been constructed and offered, the mandala base is tilted and the grain is poured into a cloth. When it is poured towards the practitioner it accumulates blessings, and when poured away it removes hindrances. A hundred thousand such mandala offerings are made as part of the preliminary practices (Tib. s*ngon 'gro*).

The symbolism of the mandala offering occurs on four levels: the outer mandala is the physical universe as samsara; the inner mandala is the body, speech, and mind of all sentient beings who inhabit this universe; the secret mandala is composed of the 84,000 thoughts which arise as 'mind'; and the inner secret mandala is innate self-revealed wisdom.

Plate 62

This drawing illustrates representations of the Mt Meru offering mandala. In the upper left is a geometric plan of the thirty-seven heap mandala with black spots corresponding to the numbered key on Plate 63. Here west is placed at the bottom, with east at the top. In the top centre are two numbered circles depicting the 'short mandala' of seven heaps to the left, and that of six heaps to the right. The seven-heaped mandala has Mt Meru at the centre (1), and the four main continents placed in the cardinal directions (2–5). The sun (6) is placed in the north-east, and the moon (7) in the south-west. The six-heaped 'practice mandala' represents the 'Buddha palace', with the guru at the centre (1), the meditational deity (Tib. *yi dam*) at the bottom (2), the protective deities in the four intercardinal directions (3), and the Three Jewels of Buddha (4), dharma (5), and sangha (6) placed in the north, east, and south. In the upper right corner are the four shapes of mandala bases, corresponding to the four tantric activities or *karmas* of pacifying (circular: 1), enriching (square: 2), magnetising or subjugating (half-moon: 3), and of destructive activity (triangle: 4). These also represent the four main continents: the western circle of red Aparagodaniya (1), the northern square of gold Uttarakuru (2), the eastern half-moon of white Purvavideha (3), and the southern triangle or trapezoid of blue Jambudvipa (4).

Below the triangle in the upper right corner is a three-dimensional drawing of Mt Meru, showing its four lower tiers and upper ascent as an inverted four-sided pyramid. To the left of this is the simple earth element representation of Mt Meru as a four-tiered base. To the central left is a sand or powdered mineral mandala base or tray, above which is placed a tripod supporting another metal mandala base representing Mt Meru. Left again is a bowl of medicinal pills used in the construction of a healing mandala. Other bowls and bags containing precious jewels, pills, grains, stones, and shells are depicted around the drawing.

Below the upper left corner are a group of five mandala offering drawings. On the left is a stacked grain mandala consisting of a base, three retaining rings, and a *dharmachakra* pinnacle. To the right are two precious jewel mandala offerings. At the centre is another stacked grain mandala. The fifth bowl to the right illustrates the lower tiers of Mt Meru with Indra's palace above. At the centre left is a triangular

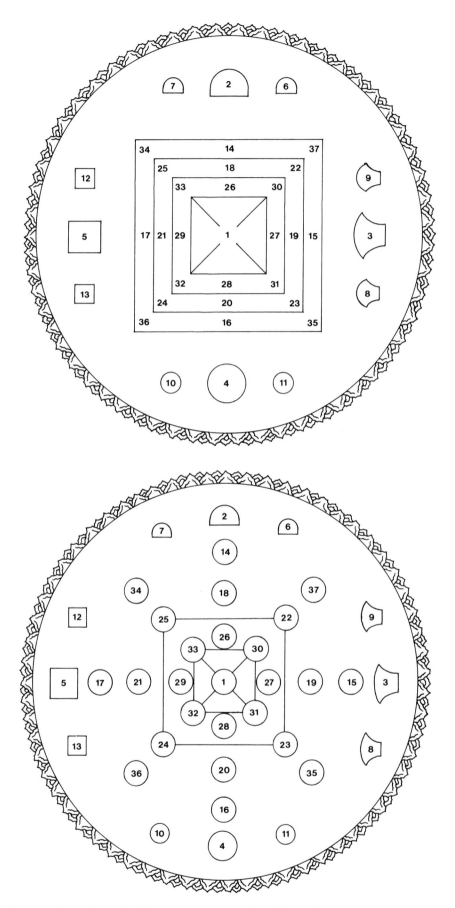

Plate 63: The diagrams above show the placement sequence of grain heaps for the thirty-seven offerings of the 'long mandala'. The diagram at the top depicts a square formation sequence for the grain heaps, and the diagram at the bottom shows a circular heap formation

four-tiered mandala employed in violent or destructive activity, which rests upon a low altar table.

Below this section are two drawings of hands forming the mandala *mudra* of Mt Meru. The two ring fingers placed back-to-back and pointing upwards represent Mt Meru; the remaining four fingers of each hand are interlocked to symbolise the four continents surrounding Mt Meru. The drawing on the left has a rosary coiled within the interlocking fingers to symbolise the six or seven encircling mountains and lakes. At the centre right Lama Serlingpa, the guru of Atisha, holds a jewel grain mandala with both hands. At the bottom right Khedrub Je, the disciple of Tsongkhapa, offers a mandala to his guru. The white silk scarf on which Khedrub Je presents the mandala illustrates the purity of his offering. Traditionally a cloth is also worn over the mouth to prevent defilements when a mandala or other sacred treasure is offered to a high incarnate lama (Tib. *sprul sku*). In the lower left corner are three further depictions of grain and jewel mandalas, two of which have tied silk scarfs on their carrying handles.

Plate 63

1. Mt Meru (Tib. *ri'i rgyal po ri rab*)
2. Purvavideha – the eastern continent (Tib. *shar lus 'phags po*)
3. Jambudvipa – the southern continent (Tib. *'dzam bu gling*)
4. Aparagodaniya – the western continent (Tib. *nub ba glang spyod*)
5. Uttarakuru – the northern continent (Tib. *byang sgra mi snyan*)
6. Deha – south of eastern continent (Tib. *lus*)
7. Videha – north of eastern continent (Tib. *lus 'phags*)
8. Chamara – west of southern continent (Tib. *rnga yab*)
9. Aparachamara – east of southern continent (Tib. *rnga yab gzhan*)
10. Satha – north of western continent (Tib. *g.yo ldan*)
11. Uttaramantrina – south of western continent (Tib. *lam mchog 'gro*)
12. Kurava – east of northern continent (Tib. *sgra mi snyan*)
13. Kaurava – west of northern continent (Tib. *sgra mi snyan gyi zla*)
14. Jewel mountain (Tib. *rin po che'i ri wo*)
15. Wish-granting tree (Tib. *dpag bsam gyi shing*)
16. Wish-fulfilling cow (Tib. *'dod 'jo'i ba*)
17. Uncultivated harvest (Tib. *ma rmos pa'i lo thog*)
18. Precious wheel (Tib. *'khor lo rin po che*)
19. Precious jewel (Tib. *nor bu rin po che*)
20. Precious queen (Tib. *btsun mo rin po che*)
21. Precious minister (Tib. *blon po rin po che*)
22. Precious elephant (Tib. *glang po rin po che*)
23. Precious horse (Tib. *rta mchog rin po che*)
24. Precious general (Tib. *dmag dpon rin po che*)
25. Vase of inexhaustible treasure (Tib. *gter chen po'i bum pa*)
26. Goddess of beauty (Tib. *sgeg pa ma*)
27. Goddess of garlands (Tib. *'phreng ba ma*)
28. Goddess of song (Tib. *glu ma*)
29. Goddess of dance (Tib. *gar ma*)
30. Goddess of flowers (Tib. *me tog ma*)
31. Goddess of incense (Tib. *bdug spos ma*)
32. Goddess of light (Tib. *snang gsal ma*)
33. Goddess of perfume (Tib. *dri chab ma*)
34. Sun (Tib. *nyi ma*)
35. Moon (Tib. *zla ba*)
36. Precious parasol (Tib. *rin po che'i gdugs*)
37. Victory banner (Tib. *phyogs las rnam par rgyal ba'i rgyal mtshan*)

THE TIBETAN ASTROLOGICAL DIAGRAM
(Tib. *srid pa'i ho, 'byung rtsis gab rtse*)

There is a Tibetan proverb which states that the Tibetans received their religion or dharma (Tib. *chos*) from India and their astrology (Tib. *rtsis*) from China. Although elements of Shaivite astrological tantras, such as the *Shiva Sarodhya Tantra,* had certainly been introduced into Bon Tibet from India at an early date, the dynastic marriage of the Buddhist king Songtsen Gampo to the Chinese princess Wen cheng (Kongjo) in the mid-seventh century heralded the arrival of the Chinese astrological system. Wen cheng is believed to have brought astrological and medical treatises with her from China. Amongst these texts was the astrological 'tortoise diagram', which one of Songtsen Gampo's ministers translated into Tibetan and recomposed. Padmasambhava designed several new protection circles and talisman seals which were incorporated into the diagram. Padmasambhava is said to have previously mastered Indian astrology under the guidance of a guru in Benaras, and Chinese astrology from a master at Wu T'ai Shan, the five-peaked mountain of Manjushri in China.

In AD 1024, the profound and extensive astrological system of the *Kalachakra Tantra* was introduced into Tibet, and three years later in 1027 its astrological cycle of sixty years was officially established. The *Kalachakra* system essentially synthesises the principles of Indian and Chinese astrology. The Indian system is known as 'white' astrology (Tib. *dkar rtsis*), and the Chinese system as 'black' astrology (Tib. *nag rtsis*) – so named because the Indians wore white clothing, whilst the Chinese predominantly wore black. The Tibetan astrological chart in its present form, as illustrated in Plate 64, is said to have originated in the old monastery of Mindroling.

The Legend of the Golden Tortoise Diagram (Tib. Rus sbal)

Manjushri, the bodhisattva of wisdom, originally taught the 84,000 astrological treatises to mankind, but people became so preoccupied with their esoteric doctrines that they neglected to practise the *buddhadharma*. So Manjushri reabsorbed all of the teachings into his head, symbolically concealing them as a 'hidden mind treasure' (Tib. *gter ma*), represented by the five-peaked mountain of Wu T'ai Shan in China: its five peaks symbolise the five protuberances (*ushnisha*) which adorn Manjushri's head. Bereft of the wisdom of these astrological teachings, mankind was plunged into the darkness of ignorance, and chaos ensued. Manjushri was divinely petitioned to reinstate these teachings for the benefit of mankind.

From his own mind Manjushri projected a giant golden tortoise, causing it to arise from the depths of the primal ocean. From his bow he unleashed a golden arrow which pierced the side of the tortoise, impaling it and causing it to roll over onto its back. On its undershell Manjushri inscribed the astrological diagram, revealing to mankind the astrological teachings and prognostications of the myriad destinies that were to come to pass throughout all future times.

Plate 64

The central motif of the divinatory diagram of the great gold tortoise Rubal is believed to have been the original tortoise diagram which the Chinese princess W'en cheng introduced into Tibet around AD 642.

At the centre of the drawing is the astrological diagram which Manjushri inscribed on the undershell of the tortoise. In the inner central circle are the Tibetan numerals one to nine arranged into a 'magic square' known as the 'nine *mewas*' (Tib. *sme ba*), with the number five at the centre and the other eight numbers arranged around it so that their digits add up to fifteen – horizontally, vertically, and diagonally. In the second circle are eight lotus petals, each containing one of the eight possible combinations of trigrams formed from the *yin* (broken) and *yang* (firm or continuous) lines which create the eight trigrams (Tib. *spar kha*) used in Chinese divination. These eight trigrams follow the 'King Wen' system or sequence as used in the Chinese divinatory *I Ching* (Book of Changes), with south at the top, west on the right, north at the bottom, and east on the left. Rotating from the top (south) clockwise these eight trigrams are: south – fire (*li*); south-west – earth (*k'un*); west – lake (*tui*); north-west – heaven (*ch'ien*); north – water (*k'an*); north-east – mountain (*ken*); east – thunder (*chen*); and south-east – wind or wood (*sun*). This sequence gives the Chinese names and elements of the 'King Wen' arrangement.

The third outer circle of the tortoise shell is divided into twelve lotus-petal segments, each containing one of the twelve animals of the 'twelve-year cycle' – derived originally from the Chinese system of the 'twelve terrestrial branches'. The twelve branches are employed chronologically in horary calculations to denote the particular qualities or influences arising in the hours, days, months, and years. The Chinese twelve-year cycle commences with the rat (or mouse) in the north (bottom) and moves clockwise through each of the following eleven years. The Tibetan twelve-year cycle commences with the hare in the east (left). This is because the Tibetans began their cycle in AD 1027, with the establishment of the Kalachakra cycle; this was already three years into the continuing Chinese cycle – which recommenced its sixty-year cycle in the year 1024. Moreover, whilst the Chinese favoured a north–south axial alignment, the Tibetans followed the traditional Indian model with an east–west axis of orientation. The Tibetan cycle of twelve animals is as follows (where it

differs, the Chinese animal equivalent is given in brackets): mouse (rat); ox (cow); tiger; hare; dragon; snake; horse; sheep (goat); monkey; bird (cock); dog; and pig (boar).

The orientation of these twelve animals places two animals in each of the cardinal directions, with the remaining four animals occupying the intercardinal directions. Thus the tiger is in the first eastern section, the hare in the second eastern section, the dragon in the north-east (intercardinal), the snake in the first northern section, and the horse in the second northern section, etc.

The twelve cyclic animals are believed to be of Central Asian or Turkic origin, which later combined with the original four directional animals of ancient China – the tiger, dragon, bird, and tortoise or 'black warrior'. According to a Buddhist legend these twelve animals were believed to have come to pay their last respects to Shakyamuni Buddha before he passed into *paranirvana* at Kushinagara.

Outside of the animal–lotus circle the thin rippled edge of the tortoise's shell can be seen within a circle of flames that envelops his body. These flames symbolise a protective circle which immolates any evil influences. His head, tail, and four limbs emerge from the shell. His ferocious head is crowned with three half-*vajras*, and another half-*vajra* seals his tail. The central half-*vajras* at the top of his head and tail symbolise the central channel ascending through his body on the '*brahma*-line', which forms the central axis of all symmetrical deity thangkas and mandalas. The two half-*vajras* to the left and right on his head symbolise the lunar and solar channels; the two snakes coiled around them and facing inwards represent the merging of these two channels with the central channel. His four limbs, pointing towards the intercardinal directions, take the form of human hands. In each hand is a wooden stake on which a frog is impaled, representing the 'four quarters' of the earth element. These four 'golden frogs with turquoise spots' are the 'soil spirits' (Tib. *gnyan*) of the earth. The small outlined squares in each of the four intercardinal directions also represent the square bases of the element earth (Tib. *sa*). Above the head of the tortoise emerges a flame, representing the element fire (Tib. *me*) in the south. Below his tail is a small triangular lake representing the element water (Tib. *chu*) in the north. To the left and right of his lower hands are drawn a tree and a flaming iron sword. The tree represents the element of wood (Tib. *shing*) in the east, and the sword the element of metal (Tib. *lcags*) in the west.

The five elements of wood, fire, earth, metal, and water, which occupy the five directions of east, south, centre, west, and north, are assigned the five colours of green, red, yellow, white, and blue-black. Each of the elements are accorded characteristics which interrelate with the eight trigrams, seven planets, five seasons, and times of the day, and the five qualities, activities and vital organs of the body. The five elements combine with the cycle of twelve animals to create the sixty-year cycle known as the 'cycle of Jupiter' or the 'cycle of Cathay'. In addition each of the five elements is accorded a male and female polarity for alternating years, derived from the Chinese *yang* (masculine) and *yin* (feminine) principles. Even-number years are male, and odd-number years are

Plate 64: The Tibetan astrological diagram

female. Thus for example the year 2000 is the male iron-dragon year; 2001 the female iron-snake year; 2002 the male water-horse year; 2003 the female water-sheep year; 2004 the male wood-monkey year, etc. The Tibetans 'jumped in' to the Chinese calendar cycle in AD 1027, and both systems remain identical in their polarity, element and animal cycles.

The complex interrelationship between the five elements with their polarity pairings, the twelve cyclic animals, the eight trigrams (Tib. *spar kha*), and the nine numbers and colours of the nine *mewas* creates an astronomical number of possible permutations. When these are combined with the seven great planets, the two nodes of the moon (the 'invisible' eclipse planets Rahu and Ketu), and the twenty-seven or twenty-eight lunar mansions of the Tibetan and Chinese systems, the possible number of astrological progressions and aspects becomes infinite.

The symbols of the seven great planets and Rahu are represented in a vertical column below the lake at the tortoise's tail. From the top downwards they are: the red disc of the Sun; the white crescent of the Moon; the red eye of Mars; the turquoise hand of Mercury; the green dagger of Jupiter; the white arrowhead of Venus; the yellow fibre-bundle of Saturn; and the blue-black raven's head of the eclipse planet Rahu.

At the top of the diagram are the three great bodhisattvas – Manjushri (centre), Vajrapani (left), and Avalokiteshvara (right). As Lords of the Three Families they represent the trinity of Buddha's divine qualities of wisdom, energy, and compassion. Since Manjushri emanated the tortoise diagram from his wisdom-mind he is placed at the centre and slightly above the other two bodhisattvas. The auspicious conjunction of the crescent moon and sun are placed to their left and right.

In the upper left corner is the monogram of the ten stacked syllables of the Kalachakra mantra. As the seal of Kalachakra it embodies the entire protective symbolism of the 'great wheel of time'. The ten syllables also represent the ten powers of a bodhisattva, especially Manjushri in this diagram. In the upper right corner the nine *mewas* are arranged in the same magic square sequence of numbers and colours as appears in the centre of the tortoise diagram. Short prayers are inscribed on each of the nine squares to protect against the possible occurrence of negative aspects of the *mewas*. This magic square is said to have been devised by Padmasambhava, and is here exalted to the status of a deity by its placement on a lotus throne with a surrounding aura, in counterbalance with the Kalachakra monogram in the opposite corner.

At the bottom left and right are the two protection wheels (Tib. *ngan pa kun thup*) of elemental astrology (Tib. *'byung rtsis*), devised by an early Nyingma scholar named Khyung Nag Shakdar. The left protection wheel is inscribed on the underside of a small tortoise that holds the four jewels of the earth element in its hands. The outer circle is inscribed with the fifty Sanskrit vowels and consonants written in Tibetan script. There then follows a long prayer which continues around the outer circle and then fills the inner circle. This prayer makes offerings and seeks protection from the goddess Kali and the Tathagata (Shakyamuni Buddha).

It continues, "As Buddha has explained the cause and cessation of all things, protect us from the hostility of the planets, stars, earth spirits, *nagas*, etc." The third circle contains the eight trigrams, arranged again in the Chinese 'King Wen' sequence. At the centre are *bijas* or seed-syllables, which protect against the malevolent influences of the nine *mewas*.

The circle at the lower right is known as the 'charm of *mewa*'. Its outer rim consists of a protective prayer beseeching refuge for all beings in the three worlds. The Tibetan script on each of the inner eight petals and central hub consists of prayers to each number and colour of the nine *mewas*, seeking protection from evil. The four eight-faceted jewels across the bottom of the drawing decoratively represent the four intercardinal directions of the earth element.

On either side of the main tortoise diagram are two vertical stacks of protective talismans, depicting symbols of the *nagas*, earth spirits, mountain spirits, gods and goddesses who influence all divisions of time. These are composed of protective seals and tetragrams formed by the addition of one horizontal line to each of the eight trigrams of the King Wen system. These create pictographs of each of the eight trigrams depicting the eight 'elementals' of fire, earth, lake, heaven, water, mountain, thunder, and wood.

On the upper left side beneath a jewelled parasol is the protective seal for the twelve-year cycle, with a triangular metal dagger (Tib. *phur bu*) vase, and treasure vase at its base – symbolising stability and good fortune. Beneath this and below another parasol is the protective seal for the retinue of gods and goddesses of the 'serpent-belly lords of the soil' (Tib. *sa bdag*). Very much like the *nagas* in appearance, these are earth spirits which control the positive and negative geomantic influences of any location.

In the upper right column, again under a parasol, is the protective seal against malevolent influences caused by the three classes of spirits: the spirits of the underworld, spirits of the soil or earth, and the spirits that inhabit all places on or above the earth (Tib. *klu; sa bdag; gnyan*). Beneath this are three jewel-topped talismans, which represent protection for the whole field of astrology itself.

The Tibetan astrological tortoise diagram is not actually used for divinatory purposes. Although it contains the main components used for astrological calculations, a large number of other diagrams, charts, and complex calculators fashioned from rotating dials, fulfil these purposes. The main function of the tortoise diagram is to act as a very powerful amulet for protection against all astrological and spirit afflictions. It is frequently hung on doorways to protect a building or homestead from evil spirits. To create auspicious circumstances it is prominently displayed at major events or transitions, such as birth, marriage, moving or building a house, illness and death. Many thangkas contain errors in the sequence of the trigrams, which should follow either the Tibetan or the Chinese 'King Wen' arrangements.

Tibetan astrologers practise several different systems of calculation and interpretation. The 'white astrology' (Tib. *dkar rtsis*) derived from Indian sources employs mathematical calculations, and in this respect is similar to the Western astrological tradition. The 'black astrology' (Tib. *nag rtsis*)

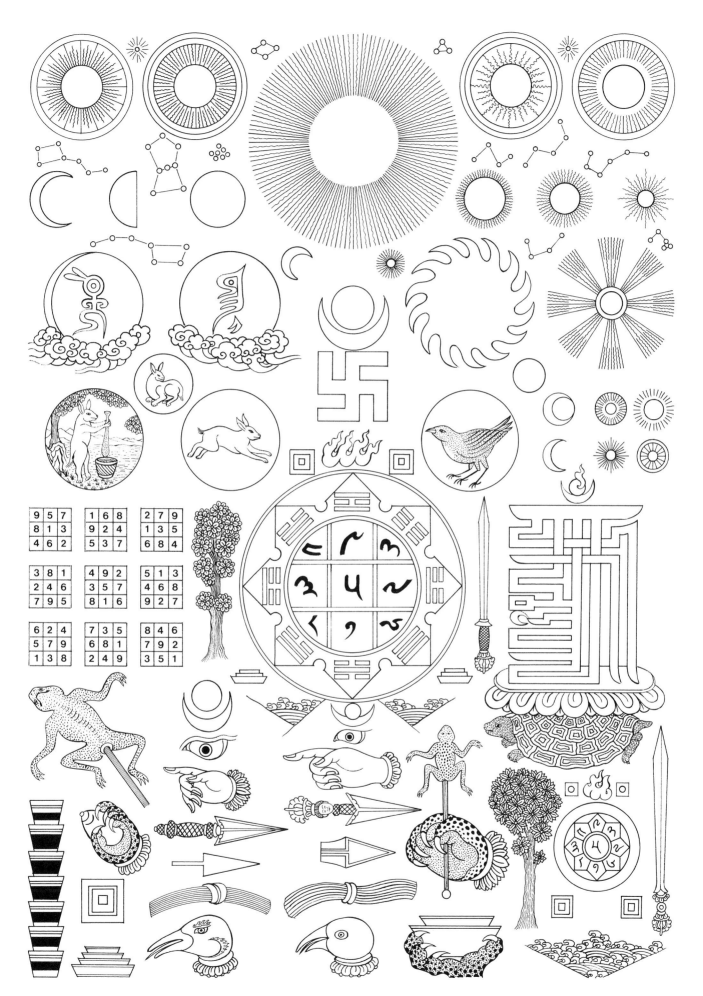

Plate 65: Astrological symbols

derived from Chinese sources employs minimal calculations and is more psychologically interpretive. The system 'arising from the vowels' (Tib. *dbyangs 'char*), is also akin to Western astrology in its use of calculations; it recognises nine planets (including Rahu and Ketu), and employs numerology in its calculations. The Kalachakra system (Tib. *dus 'khor*), derived purely from the *Kalachakra Tantra*, omits the planet Ketu (the descending or southern node of the moon) and employs only eight planets in its calculations. Elemental astrology (Tib. *'byung rtsis*), based on the precise time of birth, is most commonly used to forecast a horoscope.

Tibetan astrology is an extremely profound metaphysical science, and to assume that one can derive much insight from simply knowing the qualities of the twelve animal signs is akin to reading the horoscope columns in popular newspapers. It requires many years of study to become an accomplished master of astrology. In learning the science of Tibetan medicine all students must undergo a thorough basic training in the principles of Tibetan astrology.

Plate 65

This drawing depicts various astrological symbols. At the top centre is a large thousand-rayed sun; its radiating lines are drawn alternately as straight and waving lines. To the left and right of this central sun appear drawings of the moon and sun. The two full moons on the left are painted as pure white (or silver) discs with white, silver or gold radiating lines. The two suns to the right are painted as gold discs with gold radiating rays and halo; the gold of the disc and halo is outlined in vermilion. In the second row left, the three lunar phases of a crescent, half and full moon illustrate the first, eighth, and fifteenth day of the lunar month. Both the Indian and Tibetan calendars are based on the lunar month, with the fifteenth day being a full moon and the thirtieth day the new moon. This produces a year of 360 days. Between these upper moons and suns are drawn auspicious star groupings and constellations. The early Buddhist *Manjushrimula Tantra* states that there are 1,624 constellations. Shown here are the bright star groups of the plough (Ursa Major), Orion, and the Pleiades on the left, and Cassiopeia, Ursa Major and Ursa Minor on the right. Although of course these constellations are not identified by their Greek names and mythology, they naturally form conspicuous stellar groupings due to their magnitude of brightness and spatial proximity. In Tibet the pole star (Polaris) is known as the 'fixed star of the north', and in India the seven bright stars of the plough are known as 'the seven great *rishis* or sages'. On the right of the third row a clockwise rotating solar disc appears like a circular saw blade, whilst to its right a smaller sun emanates rays to the eight directions like a windmill. The moiré pattern effect caused by squinting the eyes, or when the sun is seen between near physical objects, such as trees or foliage, creates a clearly visible network of fine shimmering light rays. Although modern science would describe this as an optical effect produced by the eye, to the ancients it was clear evidence of the sun's physical rays.

In the third row from the top on the left, two orbs borne upon clouds contain the Chinese pictograph for the 'hare of the moon' and the 'red three-legged bird of the sun'. These pictographs are cleverly designed from the Chinese characters for moon and sun. In the fourth row left are three representations of the hare in the moon. In Western folklore the shapes formed at or near full moon by the dark lunar patches or 'mares' (once believed to be oceans), resemble the proverbial shape of 'the man in the moon'. The Chinese and Tibetan astronomers saw this shape as a hare, due perhaps to the moon's lower angle of declination in more southerly latitudes. In the first illustration the hare is shown pounding the nectar of immortality beneath a cassia tree. This image derives from a Chinese legend, where the lunar goddess Heng-O consumes the nectar produced by the hare and becomes an immortal toad. The inner symbolism of the hare pounding *amrita* refers to the Taoist sexual or alchemical practice of raising the white seminal fluid (*bodhichitta*) to the 'moon' within the crown centre.

In Indian Buddhism a *Jataka* legend relates how Buddha was born as a hare in one of his previous lives, and in order to test his endurance Indra drew an outline of this hare on the moon, where it has since remained. Two other hares are illustrated in the smaller and larger moon discs. On the right is depicted the Chinese three-legged red bird or crow of the sun, his three legs representing the number three accorded to the *yang* or masculine principle of the sun. The red three-legged bird is very rarely represented in Tibetan art; I have only seen it depicted in three thangkas of Sino-Tibetan origin. But the outline drawing of the hare in the moon, usually seated as in the smaller drawing, is quite frequently portrayed in Tibetan art. The patches visible in the full moon are also compared to the skin markings of a deer in both the Tibetan and Chinese traditions. In Hinduism the white-rumped antelope is one of the vehicles of the moon god, Chandra or Soma.

To the right of the three-legged bird is a group of three small moons and four suns. Contrary to the natural laws of light the crescent moon is usually painted facing away from the sun (as illustrated), with the two horns or cusps of the moon's crescent pointing towards the sun's disc. This motif is considered to be an 'auspicious conjunction' in the Tibetan tradition. A group of three or four stars, known as the 'lucky constellation', is also commonly painted near the moon. Below the large central sun at the top is an auspicious emblem, formed by a clockwise or right-turning swastika surmounted by a crescent moon and sun. This protective design is commonly painted on doors or above doorways to bring good luck to the household and avert evil influences. The swastika is a symbol of stability, and a swastika design or print is invariably laid in the foundations of a new building. As a Buddhist symbol its four limbs and eight hands turning to the right symbolise the turning of the wheel of dharma, revealing the Four Noble Truths and the Noble Eightfold Path of the Buddha. The sun and moon symbolise the union of wisdom and compassion. The inner symbolism of this motif refers to the union of the solar and lunar winds dissolving into the central channel, or the union of the female egg (sun) and male sperm (moon) creating new life (swastika).

In the alchemical tradition of ancient Chaldea and Egypt, the conjunction of the sun above the crescent moon formed the apex of the 'philosopher's stone', which is believed to have been inscribed on a small emerald stone. Here the moon and sun represent the transmutation of mercury into gold.

At the centre is the circular hub of the astrological tortoise diagram, enclosing an eight-pointed *chakra* sealed with the eight trigrams (Tib. *spar kha*), and with an inner circle containing the Tibetan numbers from one to nine arranged in a sequence to create the 'magic square of fifteen'. The arrangement of the eight trigrams in this drawing is based on a thangka housed in the Potala Palace in Lhasa, and follows the Tibetan astrological system with south at the top, west to the right, north at the bottom, and east on the left. Rotating clockwise from the top (south), the eight trigrams are: south – fire (Tib. *me*); south-west – earth (Tib. *sa*); west – metal (Tib. *lcags*); north-west – sky (Tib. *gnam*); north – water (Tib. *chu*); north-east – mountain (Tib. *ri*); east – wood (Tib. *shing*); south-east – wind (Tib. *rlung*). Outside of this *chakra* circle the flame at the top represents the heating activity of the element fire (south); the iron sword on the right represents the cutting activity of the element metal (west); the two triangles of water at the bottom indicate the liquidity of the element water (north); and the tree on the left represents the movement of the element wood (east). The two triple-squares on either side of the southern flame, and the two three-tiered mandala bases placed above the lower triangles of water, represent the solidity of the element earth which is assigned to the four intercardinal directions. The four intercardinal trigrams related to these four earth symbols are: earth in the south-west, sky in the north-west, mountain in the north-east, and wind in the south-east. Each of the eight trigrams also represents a spirit or deity, derived from the eight classes of spirits. The trigrams rotate around the centre from year to year creating an eight-year natal or birth-year cycle similar to the twelve-year cycle, and the family relationships of the trigrams follows a pattern similar to the *I Ching*, with a father; mother; first, second, and third son; and first, second, and third daughter.

As already explained the '*mewa* square of fifteen' consists of the numbers one to nine arranged in a specific sequence which add up to fifteen horizontally, vertically, and diagonally. The numerical equivalent of the Tibetan numbers in the central hub can be seen at the centre of the group of nine magic squares to the left, with the number five occupying the central position. The term *mewa* (Tib. *sme ba*) refers to a 'blotch' or skin blemish, mole or birthmark. This probably derives from the ancient Indian system of divination or omen interpretation based upon where moles or birthmarks occur on a person's body. The Chinese almost certainly had a similar system of birthmark divination. Each *mewa* is accorded a colour, an element, and a direction: one is white (metal) in the north; two is black (water) in the south-west; three is blue (water) in the east; four is green (wood) in the south-east; five is yellow (earth) in the centre; six is white (metal) in the north-west; seven is red (fire) in the

west; eight is white (metal) in the north-east; and nine is red (fire) in the south. The nine *mewas* arise as the nine 'influencing deities' derived from the cyclic influences of the nine great 'owners of the earth' (Tib. *sa bdag*).

The magic square of fifteen was also known to the Hebrew, Arabic, and Western magical traditions, where it forms the mystical insignia of the 'great seal of Saturn' when a pathway of lines are drawn through the numbers one to nine. In the Chinese tradition this pathway sequence is known as the 'nine paces of Emperor Yu', the legendary emperor who is said to have received the tortoise shell bearing the nine-*mewa* sequence, and to have travelled through the nine provinces of China following this sequential pathway. Numerologically a perfect symmetry is derived from this magic square of fifteen: the base of three muliplied by the central five totals fifteen; the central five is midway between one and nine; the numbers on either side of the central five are balanced (plus or minus) in their relationship to five; and the central five multiplied by nine produces forty-five, which is the total sum of the digits of this magic square. Nine as the square of three occurs as a unique perfect number in numerology: any number multiplied by nine produces a number the sum of whose digits is also multiple of nine.

4	9	2
3	5	7
8	1	6

A. The magic square of fifteen

B. The path sequence of the nine *mewas* from one to nine as 'the nine paces of Emperor Yu'

C. The symbol of the great seal of Saturn

Each of the eight *mewas* placed around the central five has a relationship with the trigram placed in the same direction, and each year the numerical sequence of the nine *mewas* changes by rotation, with the central number moving from one through to nine in a nine-year cycle. Throughout life the *mewa* for one's year of birth (Tib. *skyes sme ba*) remains constant, and prognostications for a particular year of one's life may be determined by comparison with one's birth *mewa* and the particular year in question. Harmonics of the *mewa* rotation cycle are also assigned to each month and day, with comparative calculations arising as permutations of the natal *mewa*, year, month, and day *mewa* in question. The nine *mewas* combine with the twelve cyclic animals in a ruling ratio of three *mewas* to four animal signs. Natal *mewas* also arise as the 'four categories of life', with the actual natal-year *mewa* representing the vitality or life energy (Tib. *srog*) of the body, a second *mewa* predetermining the individual's health (Tib. *lus*), a third the financial disposition (Tib. *dbang thang*), and a fourth revealing the individual's luck or success as the 'windhorse' (Tib. *rlung rta*). A fifth category is sometimes added representing the individual's intelligence or 'soul'. A complete cycle of the interrelationships between the nine *mewas*, the five elements, and the twelve cyclic animals occurs over a period of 180 years, equivalent to three sixty-year 'Jupiter' or 'Cathay' cycles.

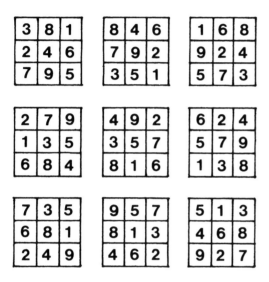

The Chinese *lo shu*, or 'master square of eighty-one'

To the left of the central hub with its eastern tree is the Tibetan arrangement of the nine magic squares of each of the central *mewa* numbers from one to nine, placed in their specific positions with north at the bottom centre. These nine magic squares, with a total of eighty-one individual digit squares, represent the group of eighty-one 'lords or owners of the earth' (Tib. *sa bdag*), who manifest in nine groups of nine, with a specific colour arrangement in each of their nine centres, cardinal and intercardinal directions. This system of a 'master square of eighty-one' is derived from the migrating series of magic squares (*lo shu*) of Chinese astrology. In the Chinese system of *lo shu*, illustrated in the diagram above, the eight numbers surrounding the five in the central square migrate to form the central number of the eight magic squares placed in each of the cardinal, and intercardinal directions. For example, the four positioned in the south-east corner of the central magic square becomes the central four in the outer magic square assigned to the southeast. A divinatory dial-plate is designed from either the Tibetan or Chinese arrangements, with the central magic square at its hub and eight radiating spokes of the eight outer surrounding numbers of the eight magic squares placed in each of the directions. The eight numbers of the surrounding central hub provide the missing central numbers in the radiating arms of the dial. A dial-plate designed in the Chinese arrangement is shown below.

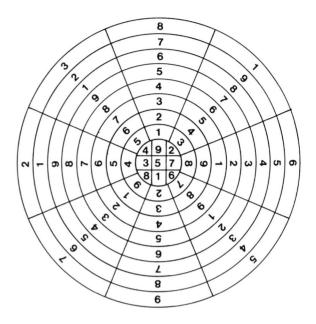

In the Tibetan system illustrated on Plate 65, the central numbers one to nine occur in numerical sequence from the top left (south-east) to the bottom right (north-west), following a linear pattern from left to right and top to bottom across the three rows. The same sequence is followed on each of the eight digital directional squares of all nine magic squares. Mathematical analysis of these two systems, based on the Chinese and Tibetan models, reveals their magical complexity. For example, the magic square of twelve placed in the eastern direction (centre left) of the Tibetan system on Plate 65, adds up to twelve in its horizontal, vertical, and diagonal directions when the number nine at its lower centre is omitted.

To the right of the central hub is the 'three-legged' mystical monogram of the ten stacked syllables of the Kalachakra mantra, which is placed upon a lotus throne resting on the back of a tortoise. In Chinese cosmology the tortoise represents the universe, its lower shell symbolising the expanse of earth, and its upper shell the firmament of the starry heavens. Below the tortoise is another representation of the nine *mewas* arranged in a circular *chakra* formation with the number five at its centre. Surrounding this circular hub are the five elements: water in the north (below), wood as a tree in the east (left), fire in the south (top), iron as a sword in the west (right), and earth as a square placed in the four intercardinal directions.

To the left of the tree at the bottom are two details of the cosmic tortoise's hands holding symbols of the element earth. In the upper drawing a spotted frog is impaled on a wooden stick, which pierces the frog's anus and penetrates along its central channel. This frog represents the specific spirit of the earth (Tib. *gnyan*), which is described as a golden frog with turquoise spots. Like most vividly-coloured natural animal markings its golden body and turquoise spots indicate its poisonous or malevolent nature. Its impalement on a stick symbolises the nailing or pinning into stability of the earth spirit of the element earth. In the hand of the lower tortoise is a square two-tiered base of the element earth. Four further examples of the earth element are drawn in the second column from the lower left corner and below the group of nine magic squares. At the top is another drawing of the impaled golden frog with turquoise spots. Below this is a tortoise's hand holding a golden jewel obtained from the earth. Below again are the inscribed golden square of earth, and a four-tiered square stack representing the base of Mt Meru. In the bottom left corner is a stack of seven black tiers (Tib. *thur ma*). It consists of seven separate segments or 'knuckles', and is used as a time measuring device to determine the astrological ascendant sign of a child born in the hours of daylight. Since watches and clocks were virtually non-existent in rural Tibet, the seven knuckles of the *thurma* served as a sundial, indicating from its base and six ascending knuckles the six two-hour shadow periods of each of the six ascending zodiac signs during the twelve hours of daylight.

Below and to the left of the central hub are illustrated two stacked columns representing the seven great planets as the days of the week, with the raven's head of the eclipse planet Rahu at the bottom. In depictions of the astrological tortoise diagram these pictographs of the planets are always placed at the bottom centre. At the top of each of these two columns are the round red discs of the Sun representing Sunday (Tib. *gza' nyi ma*). The Sun has the nature of the fire element, and in Sanskrit is known as Aditya or Surya. Next is the white or pale yellow crescent of the Moon representing Monday (Tib. *gza' zla ba*). The Moon has the nature of the water element, and in Sanskrit is known as Chandra. Next is the baleful red eye of the planet Mars representing Tuesday (Tib. *gza' mig dmar*). Mars has the nature of the fire element, and in Sanskrit is known as Mangala. Next is the turquoise blue hand, with a pointing index finger making the threatening *tarjani* gesture, of the planet Mercury representing Wednesday (Tib. *gza' lhag pa*). Mercury has the nature of the water element, and is known as Budha in Sanskrit. Next is the golden or green ritual dagger (Tib. *phur bu*) of the planet Jupiter representing Thursday (Tib. *gza' phur bu*). Jupiter has the nature of the wind element, and is known as Brhaspati in Sanskrit. Next is the golden, white, or multicoloured arrowhead of the planet Venus representing Friday (Tib. *gza' pa sangs*). Venus has the nature of the earth element, and is known as Shukra in Sanskrit. Next is the golden-yellow or black-red bundle of fibre of the planet Saturn representing Saturday (Tib. *gza' spen pa*). Saturn has the nature of the earth element, and is known as Sani in Sanskrit. At the bottom is the blue-black raven head of the invisible eclipse planet Rahu (Tib. *sgra gcan*), the 'wild god of the sky'. Rahu's decapitated raven head is sealed with an open lotus neck-choker, his beak is made of tempered meteorite iron, his tongue is a blazing sword, his teeth are knives, and a poisonous mist of illnesses issues from his mouth. His head is extremely poisonous, and his eclipse shadow causes epileptic fits on whomever it falls. As mentioned already, Rahu chases and swallows the sun during a solar eclipse, but since his head has been severed from his body the sun again reappears from the open orifice of his

neck. Rahu's headless body forms the secondary eclipse planet Ketu (Tib. *mjug rings*), which devours the moon during a lunar eclipse. Rahu and Ketu correspond to the northern and southern nodes of the moon in Western astrology, where they are known as the 'dragon's head' and 'dragon's tail' respectively. Ketu means 'brightness' in Sanskrit, and 'long-tailed' (Tib. *mjug rings*) in Tibetan, and Ketu as the 'ninth planet' is also identified with a great comet – possibly Halley's comet, which throughout recorded history has often made a spectacular return on its seventy-six-year elliptical orbit around the sun. The later Kalachakra astrological system recognised that eclipses of the sun and moon actually occur by the shadows of the moon and earth passing over their respective discs. As symbols Rahu and Ketu appear as the sky-blue head and tail of a dragon in the Kalachakra system. Since their sky-blue colour renders them invisible, it is only when the sun and moon enter the mouth or tail of the dragon and turn dark red in colour that their precise astronomical position can be seen.

The nine planets are classified into peaceful and wrathful forms. The Moon, Mercury, Venus, and Jupiter are the peaceful, 'white', compassionate planets. The Sun, Mars, Saturn, Rahu, and Ketu are the wrathful, 'red', dynamic planets. The Chinese related the five elements to the 'wandering' planets: Mercury, being the fastest moving planet, is the water planet; Venus, being the brightest, is metal; Mars, being the red planet, is fire; Jupiter, being the planet of growth, is wood; and Saturn, being the slowest-moving planet, is earth. In ancient Indian astrology these nine planets (*navagraha*) have been worshipped, propitiated, and appeased since time immemorial. As pure abstract symbols they are accorded a geometric shape, colour, and direction. As deities they are represented in two-armed form with specific colours, vehicles, and attributes.

A final group of astrological symbols, which occur on astrological diagrams but are not illustrated here, are the four auspicious and inauspicious signs. The four auspicious signs are a swastika, jewel, *vajra*, and endless knot. The four inauspicious signs are a human limb, a ritual dagger (Tib. *phur bu*), a triangular wedge, and the 'five demons' or black spots of a dice.

THE 'ALL-POWERFUL TEN' INTERLOCKING SYLLABLES
(Tib. *spungs yig rnam bcu dbang ldan*)

Plates 66 and 67 illustrate four examples of the ten interlocking or stacked syllables of the Kalachakra mantra (*Om Ham Ksha Ma La Va Ra Ya Sva Ha*), commonly known as the 'all-powerful ten'. The interlocking body of this mystical monogram is composed of the seven syllables *Ham Ksha Ma La Va Ra Ya* written in Lantsa characters. Lantsa is an Indian Buddhist script – probably of late Pala origin although certain scholars date it as late as the seventeenth century – which is specifically used for mantra syllables and the titles of sacred texts. This stylised and beautifully ornate script was devised from the Sanskrit alphabet and used extensively in Nepali Buddhism. Above the broad horizontal bar which crowns these seven interlocking consonant syllables is a crescent moon, a sun disc or dot, and a dissolving flame-tip – which completes the ten stacked syllables. An eleventh symbol, the vowel syllable *A* – representing the element of space – is not depicted, but it merges with all of the consonant sounds as the musical drone of the tonic note gives life to the melodic structure of a musical composition. In Vajrayana or Mantrayana (more precisely *mantranaya*) Buddhism an elaborate and complex symbolism and theory are applied to the vowel and consonants sounds, known as '*ali*' and '*kali*'.

The seven consonant syllables, *Ham Ksha Ma La Va Ra Ya* are always written in a vertical column, even in conventional Tibetan script. These syllables are composed of vertical 'legs' (Tib. *rkang pa*), and horizontal 'arms' (Tib. *lag pa*), which interweave like basketwork. Plate 66 and the left-hand drawing on Plate 67 illustrate the full form of the all-powerful ten syllables with seven vertical legs and seven horizontal arms. Two condensed versions of this monogram are at the centre and right of Plate 67, depicting a simpler variation with three legs and three arms.

The entire symbolism of these stacked syllables is extremely complex, encapsulating meanings which relate to all three aspects of the *Kalachakra Tantra* – the external, internal, and alternative. The external aspect deals with cosmology, astronomy, and astrology; the internal aspect deals with the subtle energy systems of the individual's mind and body interrelationships; and the alternative aspect deals with the actual deity practice of Kalachakra. However the main symbolism of the 'all-powerful ten' relates to the cosmology of Mt Meru and its surrounding universe according to the *Kalachakra*, and to the complex geometrical mandala palace of the deity Kalachakra and his retinue of 722 deities.

At the base on the left is the *Ya* syllable, symbolising the disc of wind or air on which the mandala rests. This *Ya* syllable is black and composed of the first vertical leg which rests on the lotus throne, and another black inner vertical line which runs parallel to the first leg from its double-line, plough-shaped, consonant form. The second leg represents the red disc of fire, formed by the single pointed red syllable *Ra.* The third leg is white and represents the white disc of water formed by the U-shaped white consonant *Va.* The fourth leg is yellow representing the disc of earth, and forming the lance and crescent shape of the yellow syllable *La.* The fifth leg is red and terminates in the oval shape of the syllable *Ma.* This oval, divided into four quadrants, represents Mt Meru and the mandala palace itself; the four sides of the oval are coloured red on the right, yellow at the bottom, white on the left, and black at the top – which correspond to the four directions of south (red), west (yellow), north (white), and east (black) of Mt Meru according to the Kalachakra system of cosmology. The sixth leg of the syllable *Ksha* is green and represents the green or multicoloured eight-petalled lotus placed above Mt Meru, the gods of the desire and form realms above Mt Meru, and the deities of the mandalas of enlightened body, speech, and mind. The seventh leg of the syllable *Ham* is dark blue and geometrically forms both the sixth horizontal arm and

'head' (Tib. *mgo bo*) of these seven stacked consonants. This broad dark blue head is shaped like the cross-section of a lotus blossom and symbolises the four formless god realms above Mt Meru, and the deities of the mandala of enlightened wisdom.

The crescent moon, solar dot, and triple curving flame-tip above the head of the seven stacked syllables symbolise the three psychic channels, and the deities of the mandala of great bliss, which crowns the centre of the Kalachakra mandala. These three symbols commonly occur above many *bijas* or seed-syllables and are known as the *visarga, anusvara,* and *tilaka* (dot) or *nada* (disappearing flame) respectively. The *visarga* is the aspirated first consonant sound of a seed-syllable, the *anusvara* is the last nasal consonant sound, and the *tilaka* is the central vowel sound. The crescent moon, which may be coloured white or red, is the *visarga* of the first consonant '*h*' sound of the syllable *Ham,* and represents the left lunar energy channel. The solar dot – which may be coloured red, yellow, or white – is the *anusvara* of the last '*m*' sound of the syllable *Ham,* and represents the right solar energy channel. The flame-tip – which is dark blue, green, or black in colour – is known as the *tilaka* (or *nada*) or vowel sound, and represents the central channel as the eclipse planet Rahu.

In the external Kalachakra system the ten syllables represent the four disc elements of air, fire, water, and earth; Mt Meru; the eight-petalled lotus; the form and formless god realms; and the sun and moon of the outer cosmos. In the internal Kalachakra system the ten syllables represent the four internal elements; the spinal column; the sexual centre; the three psychic channels, and the arising of bliss. In the alternative Kalachakra system the ten syllables, including the underlaying *A* vowel sound of the disc of emptiness or space, combine with the *tilaka* flame-tip to represent the eleven stages of initiation performed in the Kalachakra initiation. The first seven of these are the 'childhood initiations' of: water, crown, silk ribbon, *vajra* and bell, conduct, name. and permission. The last four are the higher initiations of: vase initiation, secret initiation, knowledge-wisdom initiation, and provisional word initiation.

In relation to the geometric symbolism of the painted or coloured sand mandala of Kalachakra the multicoloured outer flame-circle is the disc of wisdom; the inner black *vajra*-circle is the disc of space; the green outer section of the mantra and wheel-circle is the disc of wind, and its red inner section the disc of fire; the white wave-design circle is the disc of water; and the inner yellow swastika-circle is the disc of earth. In the central palace of the mandala, resting on the four-coloured base of Mt Meru, are the triple mandalas of enlightened body, speech, and mind, the mandala of enlightened wisdom, and the innermost mandala of enlightened great bliss. At the very centre of the great bliss mandala are a stack of five identical discs bearing on their uppermost surface a blue *vajra* symbolising the deity Kalachakra, and a small yellow-orange disc placed to the right of the *vajra* symbolising his consort Vishvamata. These five coloured discs symbolise the lotus base crowned by the four planetary discs of a white moon, red sun, blue-black Rahu, and orange or golden Kalagni. The white moon

Plate 66: The all-powerful ten syllables of the Kalachakra mantra

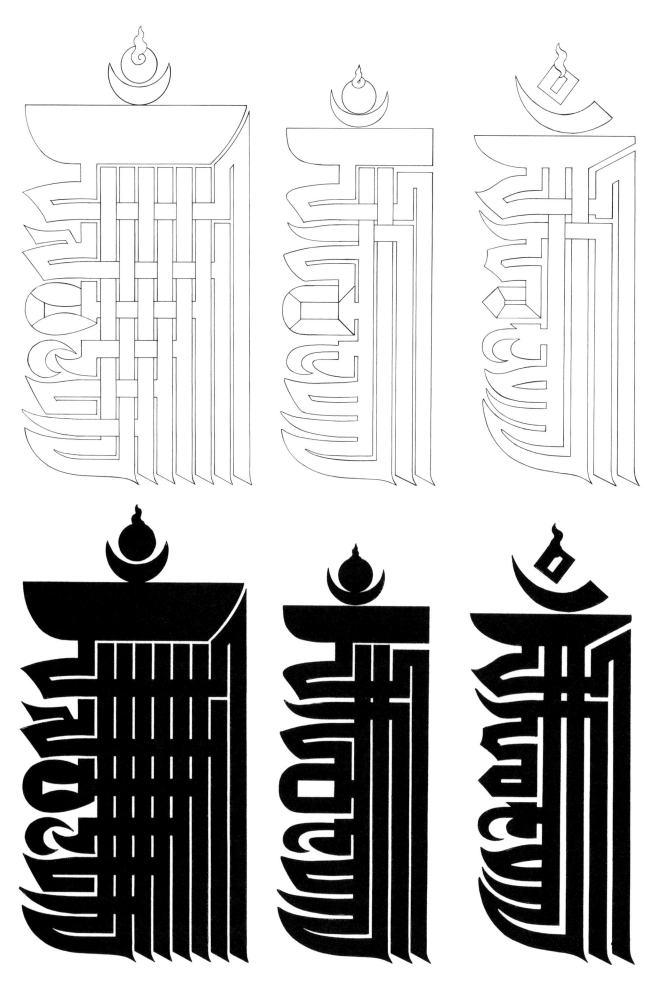

Plate 67: Variations of Kalachakra's all-powerful ten syllables

and the red sun correspond to the left lunar white channel (Tib. *rkyang ma*) and the right solar red channel (Tib. *ro ma*), which in the Kalachakra system cross and knot around the central channel at the navel centre. The central channel (Tib. *dbu ma*) corresponds to Kalagni below the knot at the navel centre, and Rahu above the navel centre. These five discs are represented below the ten stacked syllables by the lotus throne base – whose eight petals represent the heart *chakra* – above which are stacked the four planetary discs of a white moon, red sun, blue-black Rahu, and orange or golden Kalagni. On either side of the ten stacked syllables in Plate 66 are the Lantsa syllables '*e*' on the left and '*vam*' on the right, which combine to produce the *bija* or seed-syllable *Evam*. The '*e*' syllable on the left is coloured blue representing the *vajra* of Kalachakra, and the '*vam*' syllable is coloured orange to represent the lotus (*padma*) of Vishvamata. Surrounding the monogram of the ten stacked syllables is a golden deity aura composed of scrolling jewels.

The ten syllables also represent the ten aspects, aims and powers of Kalachakra, along with the ten psychic winds, the ten 'doors' or apertures where psychic winds may enter the central channel, and the movements of the ten planets within Kalachakra's cosmological system.

Within the subtle consciousness of the '*vajra* body' (see page 142) the four discs of wind, fire, water, and earth are positioned above the sexual *chakra* of the preservation of bliss; the *Ma* syllable represents the spine; the *Ksha* syllable represents the throat to the *ushnisha*; and the syllable *Ha*, crescent moon and *bindu* drop are the three main psychic channels or *nadis*. Within the 'body of experiential joy' – where the four descending and ascending joys are experienced as increasing levels of great bliss (see page 331) – the four discs of wind (*Ya*), fire (*Ra*), water (*Va*), and earth (*La*) correspond respectively to the forehead, throat, heart, and navel centres; the *Ma* syllable is located at the 'secret place' four finger-widths below the navel; *Ksha* is the secret lotus of the sexual centre; and the syllable *Ha*, crescent moon, and *bindu* drop are again the three main psychic channels.

Although any mantra of a major Buddhist deity may similarly be compounded into an interweaving vertical monogram of Lantsa letters, the stacked syllables of Kalachakra's all-powerful ten are the only form commonly represented, and are by far the most symbolically complex and profound.

THE STUPA (Tib. *mchod rten*)

Three 'receptacles' represent the body, speech, and mind of the Buddha: a painted image or statue of an enlightened Buddha, or deity, forms the receptacle of body; a religious text forms the receptacle of enlightened speech; and a stupa forms the receptacle of Buddha's enlightened mind.

The stupa is essentially the earliest form of the Buddha image, built to commemorate the major events in his life and to mark the sacred places where these events occurred, and to house his relics as well as those of his spiritually advanced disciples.

Burial mounds are common to most neolithic, bronze and iron age cultures, and Vedic India was no exception to this almost universal practice. Domed tombs or *samadhis* erected over the buried bodies of Indian saints or kings function as free-standing sacred sites which the devotees can circumambulate, absorbing the blessings or *darshan* of the great spiritual 'presence' entombed within. Great Indian saints are traditionally buried – cremation is not deemed necessary as they have already passed through the fire of spiritual purification.

Early Indian Buddhism, with its immediate reliance on the doctrines of the Buddha, developed the stupa form at its inception, giving rise to a popular cult of relics and pilgrimage centres with circumambulatory sites. Two sets of eight great stupas were built shortly after Shakyamuni Buddha's *parinirvana*. One set is known as the 'Tathagata stupas of the eight sacred places': these stupas commemorate the eight major events of his life. The second set is known as the 'eight great relic stupas of the cities': these contained the eightfold division of Buddha's physical relics – his cremated mortal remains. The Buddhist emperor Ashoka (third century BC) restored and rebuilt many of these great stupas. He is said to have constructed 84,000 other stupas from their original relics within his lifetime.

These great early Indian stupas were of a large monumental design forming a vast dome known as an *anda* or egg. This dome was raised above a round circumambulatory base, frequently balustraded with four gates and steps leading up to a higher circular terrace. The dome of the stupa was crowned by a square structure known as a *harmika*, in which the relics were enshrined. Above the *harmika* a wooden axle-pole known as a *yasti*, supported a series of diminishing circular wheels or umbrellas known as a *chattravali*. The Indian prototype of the vast domed stupa – consisting of a base, dome, *harmika*, axle-pole, and umbrella-wheels – underwent a varied metamorphosis in its aniconic shape in all of the lands to which Buddhism spread. It appeared in the forms of the Chinese and Japanese pagoda, the Sri Lankan dagoba, the Indian stupa or chaitya, and the Tibetan chörten (Tib. *mchod rten*). Circumambulation of Buddhist stupas and shrines always revolves in a clockwise direction; adherents of the Tibetan Bon tradition always circle in an anticlockwise motion.

Shakyamuni Buddha is believed to have given the basic design for the stupa within his own lifetime. A *sutra* story relates that the relics of Shariputra, one of Shakyamuni's closest disciples, were enshrined in a lay disciple's house for veneration. One day the layman went away locking his door, and the devotees were disappointed not to be able to worship the relics. When it was brought to the attention of Shakyamuni, he decreed that an external reliquary should be constructed housing Shariputra's relics, to which all people could have continuous free access. He described its construction as having four gradually ascending steps, a circular vase base, a vase dome, a square *harmika*, an axle-pole, a rain cover, and from one to thirteen stacked umbrella-wheels. In ancient India thirteen umbrellas or parasols was the highest emblem of royalty, an honour accorded only to the *chakravartin* or 'universal monarch'. This number may have symbolised the earth as a central point with the twelve surrounding solar houses of the year, or the overcoming of the three primary poisons at the central hub of the didactic 'wheel of life' surrounded by the twelve links in the circular chain of dependent origination.

Shakyamuni was later questioned about stupa designs for other disciples and for his own eventual reliquary stupa. He instructed that the Tathagata's stupa should be of full design, having at least thirteen umbrella-wheels. For the reliquary stupas of *pratyekabuddhas* five umbrellas were assigned, for an *arhat*'s stupa four umbrellas, for a non-returner (*anagamin*) three umbrellas, for a once-returner (*sakrdagamin*) two umbrellas, for the stream-enterer (*shrotapanna*) one umbrella, and for the unordained lay practitioner no umbrellas were prescribed. Early *sutras* of Buddha's spoken words also record the evolution and development of the stupa's basic form. A walled enclosure with four directional *torana* gateways both sanctified the enclosed stupa grounds and kept animals at bay. The spire, upper parasol, and rain cover were also adapted to prevent water damage, staining, and bird excrement. The finest surviving examples of the enormous early Indian stupas are to be found at Sanchi and Sarnath.

Throughout the centuries stupa designs continued to evolve. In Burma, Thailand and South East Asia the stupa designs became delicate and slender, with a long bell-shaped central vase or dome. In China the stupa evolved into the pagoda, whilst in Nepal the great stupas of Bodhnath and Swayambhu retained the hemispherical breast-like shape of their Indian prototype, particularly that of the Sanchi stupa. Later Nepali stupas inherited the ornate decorative elegance of the twelfth-century Pala style from Eastern India, incorporating the images of the Five Buddha Families. The Tibetan variant (Tib. *mchod rten*) also assumed various stylistic designs, but from the Kadampa tradition there evolved the common inclusion of the Buddha's enlightenment throne base, which provided a strong element of uniformity to the various classes of stupa. Early Kadampa designs of small moulded clay images stamped from a metal mould (Tib. *tsha tsha*) depict votive stupas mainly in a bell-shaped design with a square *harmika* above, and often the eight great stupas positioned in relief around the central dome. But these images were subject to the limits of clay impression moulding, which technically precluded the casting of recesses or tapering spires. These impressed images of stupas or of tutelary and longevity deities are commonly fashioned from clay mixed with auspicious substances and usually three grains of barley, which symbolise the Three Jewels of Buddha, dharma, and sangha. Reliquary *tsha tsha* often contain the cremation ashes of a lama or respected lay practitioner.

The rituals involved in constructing a stupa are extremely elaborate. The site has to be carefully chosen and permission from the 'serpent-tailed earth spirit' established. Weapons and coins are frequently buried under its base, whilst thousands of rolled mantras and moulded clay images (Tib. *tsha tsha*) are placed in the dome along with an enormous array of offerings. In the *harmika* are placed the relics of great lamas or teachers, together with a specific mandala for the stupa's design. This mandala is usually engraved into a slab of stone or slate, according to instructions given in two texts known as the *Rashmivimala* and *Vimaloshnisha*. The wooden axle-pole is fashioned from a specific tree trunk, and placed in the same directional orientation as when the tree grew in the wild. This follows an old oriental tradition of timber construction, whereby wood that grew on the north, south, east, or west slopes of a hill would be incorporated into a wooden building in the same directions on each of its four sides, as the wood had naturally weathered and seasoned in that direction. A small stupa is carved at the top of the axle-pole and a half-*vajra* at its base, which rests above the centre of the *harmika*'s engraved mandala of stone or slate. Many mantras are carved or bound along the length of the axle-pole. The siting, pegging of the ground, elimination of negativities, construction by prescribed stages, and final consecration of the stupa follow an extremely elaborate ritual procedure.

Although the original purpose of the stupa was to enshrine relics of great spiritual teachers, they are also constructed for many other auspicious reasons. At sacred sites they commemorate major events; at crossroads, mountain passes and on pilgrimage routes they provide a focus for religious devotion. As stabilisers, removers of hindrances, illnesses and epidemics, they bring peace to strife-torn lands, longevity to the local inhabitants, and a sense of harmony to the whole environment.

The mummified bodies of highly realised masters, such as the previous Dalai Lamas, are sometimes enshrined in lavishly gilded and jewelled stupas. The large reliquary stupa of the great Fifth Dalai Lama inside the Potala Palace is gilded with over three-and-a-half tons of gold leaf and embellished with thousands of large precious stones and pearls. The equally precious reliquary stupa of Lama Tsongkhapa (1357–1419), at Ganden monastery near Lhasa, was plundered during the Cultural Revolution by Chinese Red Guards who reduced the whole monastic city of Ganden to rubble. According to various witnesses the perfectly preserved body of Tsongkhapa caused great consternation amongst the Chinese cadres. They threw the body into a river, but apparently it remained floating on the surface. Tsongkhapa's body was eventually burned with kerosene, and amongst his ashes only a single tooth survived. Stamped clay impressions of this tooth were produced by the thousand and secretly distributed to those of the Buddhist faith. To kill a living faith is not an easy thing, as the Chinese are still discovering, and to try to do so is proverbially a crime before which even murder pales.

The Symbolism of the Stupa

As the receptacle of Buddha's enlightened mind the stupa encapsulates a multitude of symbolic meanings that reveal his enlightened qualities. Firstly, although it is not actually described in any Tibetan text on stupa symbolism, the stupa has 'assumed' the representation of the five purified elements. The square base or lion throne represents the four cardinal sides and four intercardinal corners of the element earth. The hemispherical dome or vase (Tib. *bum pa*) represents the circle or drop of the element water. The conical spire of thirteen umbrellas represents the element of fire. The upper lotus parasol and crescent moon represent the element of air; and the sun and dissolving point, the element of space.

As a representation of the Buddha's body, the square base of the stupa – composed of a plinth, three steps, main facade, cornice, edge, and cap – is measured to the same iconographic proportions as the Buddha's lion throne. Thus the square base is the throne on which Buddha sits. The four square steps rising above the throne's cap represent the Buddha's legs locked into *vajrasana* or 'reversed' full-lotus posture. The four sides of this square section evoke the solidity and stability of earth. Two sides represent Buddha's thighs, one his back, and the fourth his forelegs and feet folded into *vajrasana* posture. The vase or dome symbolises the torso of the Buddha; the arched niche or window in which an image of a deity is placed at the dome's centre is situated in the exact position of Buddha's heart. The *harmika* above the dome represents the Buddha's face and eyes – which gaze out over the four directions; frequently on Nepali stupas a pair of Buddha eyes are painted onto each side of the square *harmika*. The conical spire of thirteen wheels represents the Buddha's *ushnisha* or head protuberance and his crown. The upper parasol is an emblem of royalty floating above his head, with the pinnacle of moon, sun, and flame symbolising his enlightenment. The wooden axle-pole represents Buddha's spinal column or central channel.

The three parts of the stupa – throne base, dome, and *harmika*-spire – also symbolise the body, speech, and mind of the Buddha. Taken as a single unit the stupa itself represents the *dharmakaya* as the ultimate nature of the fully enlightened mind.

The architecture of the stupa is divided into three classes corresponding to the three early Buddhist paths of Shravaka, Pratyekabuddha, and Mahayana. The Shravaka stupa is described as resembling the possessions of a Buddhist monk or *shravaka*. The four steps above the throne base represent his robes neatly creased into a fourfold pile, the dome represents his upturned alms bowl, and the *harmika*, spire, and pinnacle represent the form of his *khakkhara* (Tib. *'khar gsil*) or the iron staff of a Buddhist mendicant (see Plate 105). The Pratyekabuddha stupa has a square throne base, a square dome, and twelve circular umbrella-wheels crowned by an eight-spoked *dharmachakra*. The dome of the Mahayana stupa is shaped either like an inverted alms bowl, vase, or bell. Included in the Mahayana category are the eight great stupa designs, the square-based temple or gateway stupa, and the mandala-palace stupa – the finest surviving Tibetan example of which is the magnificent Gyantse Kumbum stupa.

The typical form of the Tibetan stupa (Tib. *mchod rten*) is illustrated in the enlightenment stupa at the top centre of Plate 68, and in the outline of the stupa's proportions on Plate 69. The lion-throne base of the Buddha that forms the lower support of the stupa is common to most Tibetan stupa designs, and its symbolism is not included in the description of the stupa that follows. On Plate 69 the lion throne forms the first sixteen units of the stupa's height.

Above the lion-throne base the lower part of the typical Tibetan stupa consists of four ascending steps, the vase base, vase dome, and the square *harmika*. This lower structure is known as the 'causal stupa' (Tib. *rgyu'i mchod rten*). The upper part of the stupa – consisting of the lotus umbrella support, the axle-pole, the thirteen umbrella-wheels, the upper umbrella, rain cover, and pinnacle of sun, moon, and flame – is known as the 'resultant stupa' (Tib. *'bras bu'i mchod rten*).

The first of the lower four steps symbolises in its four sides the 'four close contemplations' of body, feeling, mind, and dharma. The second step symbolises the 'four perfect abandonments' of non-virtuous actions. The third step symbolises the 'four legs of miraculous power' attained through the renunciation of contemplative aspirations of desire, mind, effort, and analysis. The fourth step symbolises in its four sides and top the 'five moral faculties' of faith, perseverance, mindfulness, concentration, and wisdom. The narrow circular dome base above these steps symbolises the power of these five moral faculties. The dome or vase (Tib. *bum pa*) represents the seven conditions of enlightenment: perfect mindfulness, wisdom, joy, effort, suppleness, concentration, and equanimity. The square *harmika* above with its eight corners symbolises the Noble Eightfold Path of right view, right intentions, right speech, right conduct, right livelihood, right effort, right mindfulness, and right concentration. The axle-pole symbolises the 'ten knowledges': of phenomena, others' thoughts, dharma, karma, suffering, cessation, origination, paths, exhaustion, and non-action or creation. Around the axle-pole are the thirteen wheels, the first ten of which symbolise the 'ten powers' of the Buddha: clear thought, full karmic responsibility, meditative knowledge, perception of others' faculties, perception of others' mental inclinations, knowledge of others' mental faculties, knowledge of all paths, knowledge of all previous lives, knowledge of all deaths and rebirths, and knowledge of karmic cessation. The three top wheels symbolise the 'three close contemplations': that the Buddha does not experience pleasure when all his disciples listen with respect, that he does not experience anger when none of his disciples listen with respect, and that he experiences neither pleasure nor anger when some disciples listen with respect and others do not. The umbrella above these wheels symbolises Buddha's great compassion and his modes of teaching for disciples of narrow, medium, and great scope. The rain cover symbolises the four formless realms. When a *makara* or crocodile-headed banner (*makaradhvaja*) is placed above the umbrella it symbolises victory over the four Maras: emotional defilements (*skandhamara:* Brahma); passion (*kleshamara:* Yaksha); death (*mrityumara:* Yama); divine pride and lust (*devaputramara:* Indra).

The waxing crescent moon symbolises the aspiration to enlightenment and increase of *bodhichitta*. The sun disc symbolises wisdom and emptiness. The union of moon and sun represents the co-emergence of method and wisdom, or relative and absolute *bodhichitta*. The ethereal jewel-flame of enlightenment at the pinnacle symbolises on an inner level the lunar and solar channel winds igniting the goddess Chandali, and her ascent through the central channel.

A specific stupa with seven steps and seventeen umbrella-wheels alludes to the cosmology of Mt Meru. The twelve corners of the three throne base steps are the four main continents and eight subcontinents surrounding Mt Meru. The seven upper steps are the seven rings of mountains which encircle Mt Meru. The thin bangle-like decorative vase base represents the *naga* king, Vasuki, who encircled Mt Mandara in the churning of the ocean legend. The stupa vase represents Mt Meru itself. The axle-pole is the wish-fulfilling tree. The six stages of the *harmika* are the six form realms of desire (*kamaloka*). The seventeen wheels are the seventeen levels of form realms without desire (*rupaloka*), and the upper umbrella symbolises the highest four formless realms (*arupaloka*).

The Proportions of the Stupa

Many great Tibetan masters produced texts on stupa construction, the most famous probably being Butön Rinpoche (1290–1364), Desi Sangye Gyatso (1653–1705), and Mipham Rinpoche (1846–1912).

Desi Sangye Gyatso was for twenty-six years the regent to the great Fifth Dalai Lama and one of the most outstanding scholars in the history of Tibet, equivalent perhaps to Leonardo da Vinci in his visionary versatility. Under his supervision the Potala Palace was rebuilt to its present size, he founded Chakpori Medical College on the Iron Hill adjacent to the Potala, he kept the death of the Fifth Dalai Lama secret for many years, and built the priceless reliquary stupa which eventually entombed his mummified body. Besides being a monk, a diplomat and polititian, Desi Sangye Gyatso also compiled two comprehensive illustrated treatises on Tibetan medicine and astrology, known as the *Vaidurya Ngonpo* (Blue Beryl), and the *Vaidurya Karpo* (White Beryl). The seventy-seven beautifully illustrated medical thangkas of the 'Blue Beryl', together with Desi's codified editing of the *Gyuzhi* (Four Medical Tantras), reveal the genius of this great scholar's profound vision.

Plate 69 is based on the theoretical proportions of the stupa of enlightenment as explained by the recent Tibetan polymath, Mipham Rinpoche.

Plate 68

This drawing depicts the construction grid for the sixty-four-unit measure of the stupa of enlightenment.

The majority of Tibetan traditions base their proportion on the sixty-four-unit stupa. A squared grid is drawn of sixteen large units in height and ten large units in width. Each of these large units is then divided into four small units, to give a grid of sixty-four units in height and forty units in width. In Mipham's plan the plinth or base of the stupa is forty-two units in width and three units in height. Above this are the three tiered stairs, of one unit each, which support the

main facade, which is six units in height. Surmounting this are the facade cornice in two steps, of one unit each, and the base's cap measuring thirty-two units in width and two in height.

This lower section of the stupa measures sixteen units in height and forms the lion-throne base on which the seated iconic image of the Buddha is depicted, or above which his aniconic form as the stupa arises. As the painted *asana* or throne of the Buddha, the lion throne is richly decorated (see Plate 56), with golden, jewel-encrusted, spiralling roundel patterns or lotus border designs on its steps and cap. In depictions of Shakyamuni, two lions enclosed by *vajra*-pillars are painted on each side of the main facade. When one of the Five Buddhas is individually represented on such a throne, his particular animal mount is painted here. In the case of the whitewashed stupa the steps are usually undecorated, but the main facade may bear auspicious symbols such as the *dharmachakra*, *vajra*, or lions.

Above the cap is the one-unit-high step of 'ten virtues', and above this again the four two-unit steps. Above this is the one-unit-high circular vase base from which the dome or vase (Tib. *bum pa*) arises. At the centre of the vase is a niche or window which contains the image of the Buddha or a deity. The long-life goddess Ushnishavijaya is frequently placed within this alcove, denoting longevity in this or a future life. The exact centre of the stupa falls in the heart of this enshrined deity. The trefoiled aura which surrounds this window is commonly decorated in entwined gold patterns which enclose five coloured jewels representing the Five Enlightened Buddhas. In Mipham's design the vase is twelve units in height, corresponding to the major divisional unit of the Buddha's iconographical form, where twelve units or finger-widths are equal to the measure of his face and hands.

Above the vase is the narrow *harmika* base, the square *harmika*, and the lotus umbrella base which support the thirteen tapering wheels above. Together these measure four units. The umbrella-wheels, usually fashioned of gilded metal, measure seventeen units in height and are divided into wide 'male' wheels with narrower 'female' wheels in between. Above the wheels are the protective umbrella and rain cover, each measuring one unit in height. Both the umbrella and rain cover are usually decorated with lotus-petal designs. The pinnacle of crescent moon, sun, and flame, crown the top of the stupa and measure three units in height. Small sharp iron spikes are usually welded into the pinnacle components to prevent birds alighting on the stupa.

The lower part of the stupa from the lion-throne cap to the *harmika* measures twenty-five units in height and is known as the 'causal stupa' (Tib. *rgyu'i mchod rten*). The upper part of the stupa from the lotus umbrella support to the tip of the pinnacle is known as the 'resultant stupa' (Tib. *'bras bu'i mchod rten*).

Plate 69

This illustration depicts the theoretical relationship between the iconographical grid (Tib. *thig tshad*) of the seated Buddha

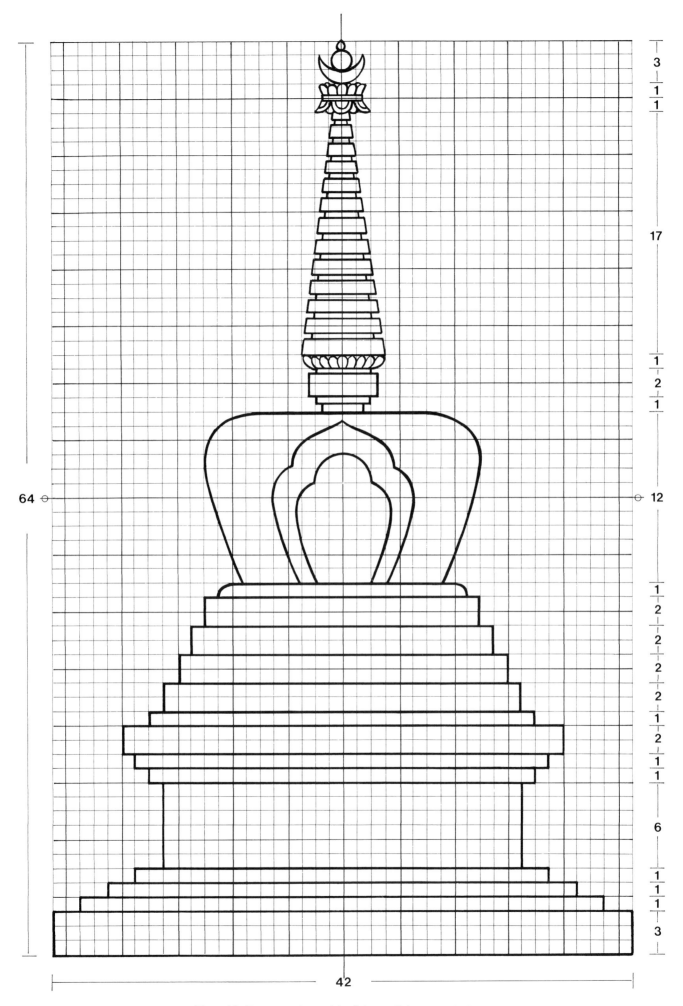

Plate 68: Construction grid of the enlightenment stupa

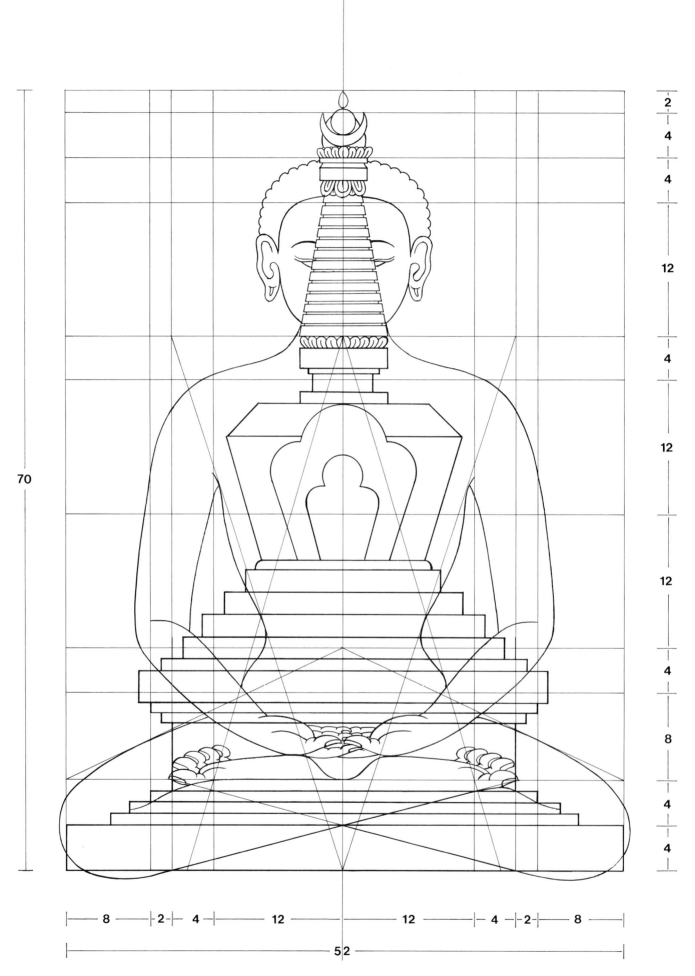

Plate 69: The theoretical relationship between the Buddha image and the stupa

and the stupa of enlightenment. It must be emphasised that this drawing has been improvised and does not originate from any Tibetan textual sources. This theoretical grid is based upon the seated Buddha's height of seventy units, and width of fifty-two units.

The lower lion throne of the Buddha corresponds at its plinth base to the fifty-two units' width of Buddha's crossed legs; its central facade corresponds to the thirty-two units' width of Buddha's crossed feet; and its upper cap corresponds to the thirty-eight units' which define the width of Buddha's arms.

Above the lion-throne pedestal the one-unit step of 'ten virtues', the four main two-unit steps, and the one-unit circular vase base, ascend towards the centre of Buddha's torso. Above these rises the vase of the stupa, with its central window or niche precisely centred at Buddha's heartline. Above the vase is the *harmika* base, the square *harmika*, and the lotus-umbrella base – which collectively ascend into the throat of the Buddha.

The thirteen umbrella-wheels occupy the thirteen facial units of the Buddha from his chin to hairline. Although Buddha's face is specified as measuring twelve units, an extra half unit is traditionally extended for both his chin and hairline. The upper lotus-wheel and rain cover occupy the four-unit thickness of Buddha's hair, and the rain cover's upper lotus, crescent moon, sun disc and dissolving flame correspond to the top six units of Buddha's head protruberance (*ushnisha*) and golden flame crest.

The distance between the top of the *ushnisha* and the point between the eyebrows (*urna*), the throatline, the heartline, the navel line and the secret place line, all measure twelve units, and correspond to the placements of the crown, forehead, throat, heart, navel and sexual centres.

The Eight Great Stupas

Plate 70

Illustrated in this drawing are the eight great stupas which commemorate the major events of Shakyamuni Buddha's life. At the centre is a fully-ornamented enlightenment stupa with *vajras* on the plinth, *dharmachakras* on the main facade, and the syllable *Hum* in the vase window. Two long silk pendants hang from the upper parasol. Traditionally flower garlands were hung from hooks or pegs in the parasol, but as these flowers quickly wilted they were replaced by jewel and silk tassles. Prayer flags are now traditionally strung from pegs placed under the upper parasol of large stupas, such as at Bodhnath stupa in Kathmandu. Surrounding this central stupa are the eight great stupas. I have based the textual dates and eight simplified events in the life of Shakyamuni on the group of eight stupas consecrated by Dilgo Khentse Rinpoche at Sechen Gompa in Boudha, Kathmandu. Variously similar listings are given in all of the many pan-Asian Buddhist traditions.

At the top left hand corner is the 'stupa of heaped lotuses' (Tib. *pad spungs mchod rten*), commemorating the Buddha's birth in the royal Lumbini gardens on the seventh day of the fourth lunar month in the year 563 BC. His father, Shuddhodana, is said to have erected a stupa in this design to commemorate this event. At birth Buddha took seven steps in each of the four directions from which lotuses sprang, symbolising his immediate resolve to embark on the path of the four 'immeasurables'. The four steps of this stupa are circular and decorated with lotus-petal designs. A tradition also exists of constructing seven heaped lotus steps to represent Buddha's first action. This stupa is also known as the 'lotus blossom stupa' or the 'birth of the Sugata stupa'.

In the top centre is the 'stupa of the conquest of Mara' (Tib. *bdud 'dul mchod rten*), or 'enlightenment stupa' (Tib. *byang chub mchod rten*), commemorating Shakyamuni's defeat of the temptation and attack of the hosts of Mara under the bodhi tree at Bodh Gaya, when he was thirty-five years old. King Bimbisara is said to have erected a stupa of this design. This stupa has the traditional unadorned four square steps, often with a slight overhang along the top of each step.

In the top right corner is the 'stupa of many doors or gates' (Tib. *sgo mang mchod rten*), commemorating the Buddha's first turning of the wheel of dharma at the Deer Park in Sarnath near Varanasi, when he was thirty-five years old. His first five mendicant disciples are said to have built a stupa of this design. Each of the four square steps are decorated with many small door frames which express the many avenues or methods of Buddha's teachings. A series of four, six, eight, or twelve doors on each side of the steps symbolises respectively the Four Noble Truths, the six perfections, the Noble Eightfold Path, and the twelve links in the chain of dependent origination.

At the middle left is the 'stupa of great miracles' (Tib. *cho 'phrul mchod rten*), commemorating the Buddha's display of inconceivable miracles in the first half of a lunar month at Shravasti, when he was fifty years old. Here he overpowered the *maras* and heretics (*tirthika*) at the Jetavana Grove. The stupa of miracles or 'conquest of the *tirthikas*' was built by the Lichavi tribe to commemorate this event. The stupa of miracles has projecting central sections on each of its four steps and sides, which also project slightly by one third of their height.

At the middle right is the 'stupa of descent from the god realm' (Tib. *lha babs mchod rten*), commemorating Buddha's descent from the heaven of the thirty-three gods (Trayastrimsa), when he was forty-two years old. Here he spent the summer retreat in Tushita heaven teaching the dharma to the reincarnation of his mother, in order to repay her kindness in having borne him just before she died. He descended at the city of Sankasya, and the local inhabitants built a stupa in this design to commemorate the event. The descent from the god realm stupa is characterised by a central projection in each of its four sides containing a triple ladder or 'projected steps'. The central projections follow the plan of the miracle stupa with middle buttresses which project by one third of their height. The 'projected steps' which form a triple receding ladder were said to have been constructed for the Buddha by the celestial architect Vishvakarman. They often have three rows of thirty-three steps symbolising the

Plate 70: The eight great stupas

god realms. Laddered stairways in this design are frequently built at temple entrances; the central stairway is reserved exclusively for distinguished or incarnate lamas, the right stairway is for the ordained sangha, and the left stairway for lay practitioners. Triple flights of wooden stairs at the Potala Palace are very worn down on their right and left sides, but completely unworn in their central section – as this stairway was only used by the Dalai Lamas.

At the bottom left is 'the stupa of reconciliation' (Tib. *dbyen mchod rten*), commemorating Buddha's reconciliation of the disputing factions within the sangha which had been divided by the enmity of his cousin Devadatta. Buddha reunited the sangha at the Veluvana bamboo grove at Rajagriha (Rajghir), and the local inhabitants of the kingdom of Magadha constructed a stupa in this design. The reconciliation stupa is characterised by its four octagonal steps with equal sides. Various symbolic meanings are given for the four levels of eight-sided steps, which total thirty-two in number.

At the bottom centre is 'the stupa of complete victory' (Tib. *rnam rgyal mchod rten*), commemorating Buddha's prolongation of his lifetime by three months. This event occurred at the city of Vaisali when Buddha was eighty years of age by the supplication of the lay devotee Tsundra. The celestial beings are said to have erected a stupa of this design. The complete victory stupa is characterised by having only three steps, which are circular and unadorned.

At the bottom right is 'the stupa of nirvana' (Tib. *myang 'das mchod rten*), commemorating Buddha's passing away 'beyond sorrow' into his final *parinirvana* at Kushinagara between two *sal* trees when he was eighty years old. The Malla tribe of Kushinagara erected a stupa in this design. The nirvana stupa is characterised by its circular bell-shaped dome which rests directly on the circular base of the ten virtues with no ascending steps. Usually this bell-shaped dome is not ornamented, except occasionally when the base or mouth of the dome is decorated with an ornate ring of inscribed circles. Its simplicity and the absence of steps symbolises the Buddha's complete absorption into *parinirvana*, where all conceptual qualities merge into the unqualified state of pure emptiness as the *dharmakaya*. There is a touching poignancy in the shape of the dome as an unstruck bell, a silent reliquary vase, or an upturned alms bowl, which represents by its inversion the physical death of an enlightened renunciate and his having transcended the need for sustenance.

None of the original eight great commemorative stupas of the Tathagata have survived intact to the present day, although the five sites at Kushinagara, Sanchi, Sarnath, Bodh Gaya and Lumbini are well known. Over the course of the centuries the stupas began to crumble into disrepair, and restorations were accomplished by building larger stupas over the previous remains. Encased within the large stupa at Sarnath may be several generations of earlier stupas, hidden away like hollow wooden babushka dolls in the largest and final version. Nor are all the Indian, Tibetan, and Chinese Buddhist listings of these stupas, their locations and builders in full agreement, although their geographical locations are in close enough accord.

After Shakyamuni Buddha's *parinirvana* and cremation a dispute arose amongst the various Indian tribes over possession of his ashes as relics. This dispute is said to have been amicably settled by a Brahmin named Drona who mediated that the relics be divided into eight portions for each of the eight claimant tribes. Thus eight reliquary stupas were subsequently erected in the capitals of these tribal kingdoms, where they became known as 'the eight relic stupas of the eight cities'. Their locations also vary according to different listings and the changing of names of these early Indian cities, but most likely they were located at Kushinagara, Rajagriha, Kapilavastu, Vaisali, Allakappa, Pava, Vishnudvipa, and Ramagama.

Eight great white stupas are also directionally placed in the eight great cemeteries of the mandala (one in each), where they are positioned on the summits of eight specific mountains. Here the mountains symbolise the immovability of meditative stability placed single-pointedly on the union of great bliss and emptiness. The stupas on their summits symbolise the unity of the three *kayas* or three bodies of the Buddha, with the stupas' throne bases representing the *nirmanakaya* or 'form body'; the causal stupa of the dome and *harmika* representing the *sambhogakaya* or 'enjoyment body'; and the resultant stupa of the umbrella-wheels and pinnacle representing the *dharmakaya* or 'body of absolute truth'.

The placement seqence of the stupas of the eight great cemeteries is as follows: the *vajra*-stupa on multicoloured Mt Lhunpo in the east; the created *vajra*-stupa on yellow Mt Malaya in the south; the established *vajra*-stupa on white Mt Kailash in the west; the black *vajra*-stupa on green Mt Mandara in the north; the mind *vajra*-stupa on black Mt Ishvara in the north-east; the body *vajra*-stupa on the yellow incense mountain in the south-east; the jewel *vajra*-stupa on the white snow mountain of Kongchen in the south-west; and the dharma *vajra*-stupa of blue Mt Paljiri in the north-west.

THE CHANNEL-WHEEL SYSTEMS
(Skt. *chakra*; Tib. *rtsa 'khor*)

The complex subjects of the Hindu Kundalini Yoga *chakra* system and the Buddhist channel-wheel systems are extremely profound, and can only be briefly and inadequately explained here. The symbolism of the Buddhist channel-wheel system is, however, of great importance for a deeper understanding of Vajrayana ritual and deity symbolism, since on a conceptual and numerological level they arise as the inner essence of the 'body mandalas' of all deities.

Although the complexities of the *chakras*, *nadis*, winds, and drops are conceptually described here, and may be interpreted within the confines of an individual's imagination and intelligence, their ultimate nature is purely experiential and may only be realised within the visualisation practices of the 'completion stage' of Highest Yoga Tantra (*anuttarayoga tantra*), or at the time of death. Like sugar to one who knows not of sweetness, the truth lies in the tasting and not in any verbal description. The menu and the meal are two different things; the one whets the appetite by making you think, the other takes the hunger away.

The Sanskrit term *nadi* (Tib. *rtsa*) means channel or psychic nerve, and is in certain respects similar to the median channels or meridians which occur in acupuncture. The 'subtle' or *vajra* body, as the vital 'life energy' of consciousness within the physical body, is believed to be permeated with an elaborate network of these psychic channels, which form an etheric counterpart to the physical arteries, veins, and nerves. The energies which move through these channels are referred to as 'winds' (Skt. *prana*; Tib. *rlung*), and the subtle essences of consciousness carried through the channels on these winds are referred to as 'drops' (Skt. *bindu*; Tib. *thig le*). The terms 'chakra', 'channel-wheel', and 'centre' used throughout this text are synonymous. In the Hindu tantric traditions the term *chakra*, meaning 'wheel', is most commonly used, although in many texts the Sanskrit term *nadi-chakra*, meaning 'channel-wheel', is given. The *chakras* are more commonly referred to as channel-wheels (Tib. *rtsa 'khor*) in the Buddhist tantras. The *chakras* or channel-wheels are plexuses where the main channels or *nadis* emanate from constrictive points along the subtle body's median nerve or central channel. In the West, the theory of the *chakra* systems has been widely misunderstood and diluted, and the *chakras* tend to be 'factually' viewed as a concrete bodily reality, and perhaps naively envisioned as irridescent lotuses spinning around a central pole – in the manner of a neon carousel within the astral realms of the body's inner amusement park.

The conceptual ideology of the *chakra* system was first brought to the attention of the Western World by the 'universal brotherhood' of the Theosophical movement, under the inspiration of Madame Blavatsky (1831–91) and Colonel Olcott (1832–1906). With his translation of *The Serpent Power* in 1918, Arthur Avalon (Sir John Woodroffe) made a valuable contribution to an understanding of the esoteric complexities of the Kundalini Yoga doctrine, and put in perspective the earlier simplistic monograph on the *chakras* by the theosophist Rev. C.W. Leadbeater (1910). In a seminar on Kundalini Yoga Dr Carl Gustav Jung (1875–1961) observed, "These symbols have a terribly clinging tendency. They catch the unconscious somehow and cling to us. But they are a foreign body in our system. I have seen too often how dangerous their influence may be." Jung actually derived his psychological concepts of the anima and animus from the polarity symbols of Kundalini and Shiva; none the less he viewed Kundalini Yoga merely as an alien import into Western psychology. Yet Jung was correct in perceiving that these symbols have a way of clinging, and clung they have since the early years of the Theosophical movement, permeating Western New Age culture with a plethora of therapeutical practices and concepts.

The Hindu Kundalini Yoga Chakra System

Kundalini Shakti, who is personified as a goddess coiled and sleeping in the form of a snake, represents the ego or individual self (*ahamkara*). As long as Kundalini sleeps, karma activates the outer reality of being in the world.

Throughout conscious life Kundalini's head closes the door of the central channel, and the unactivated *chakras* remain dormant, closed, and downward-facing.

When Kundalini awakens and begins to turn inwards, the dissolution of the notion of an individual self begins to occur, reaching its ultimate cessation in Kundalini's final merging with her consort Shiva in the thousand-petalled lotus (*sahasrara*) of the crown *chakra* at the top of the head. Her power is such that when the temporary bliss of sexual orgasm is experienced it is described as only one hundredth of the bliss which arises when Kundalini enters and ascends the central channel, as the psychic nerves (*nadi*) which carry the winds (*prana*) of sexual orgasm either cross over the mouth of the central channel or momentarily enter it. In this context the actual ascent of Kundalini and the opening of the *chakras* is simply indescribable.

When the great Hindu sage Shri Ramakrishna (1836–86) would experience the arising of Kundalini, his voice would cease when she reached the throat *chakra*. As she ascended to the forehead or *ajna chakra* he would pass into the stillness of formless absorption (*nirvikalpa samadhi*). It was obvious to Ramakrishna's assembled devotees that they were in the presence of Bliss incarnate, though some modern sceptics have tried to equate Ramakrishna's *samadhi* with epilepsy.

Shrichakra or Shriyantra

Jung cannot be blamed for recoiling from and rejecting these tantric concepts. To unleash such an infinity of visionary experiences as Kundalini's light illuminates – a veritable Pandora's box of the personal subconscious and the collective unconscious – was more than the rational human mind could bear.

The practice of Kundalini Yoga in its true Indian setting has to be accomplished under the meticulous guidance of a competent guru who has himself raised Kundalini to the *sahasrara*, and such masters are extremely rare. However,

Plate 71: The Hindu Kundalini Yoga chakra system

Kundalini can also be 'stirred' or awakened spontaneously by factors beyond the control of the individual. Metanoia, or the 'turning about of the mind in the seat of consciousness', can often result in a 'kundalini crisis'. Such an experience can be triggered by a variety of causes, such as severe trauma or bereavement, an emotional or mental breakdown, psychosis and paranoia, chemical imbalance or psychedelic drugs. Here objective and subjective realities, or waking and symbolic realities, compete with one another for attention. Personality disintegration, reintegration, and redisintegration can occur with such rapid oscillations and profound changes that an individual may be metaphorically cast adrift in a leaky conceptual boat on an endless ocean of possibilities. Once awakened, the genie cannot be put back in the bottle, and there is no return to consensus reality. There is no going back; one must succumb to the process or learn to live with it. Suppression by drugs, or direct self-inquiry into the nature of mind are perhaps the only remedies, but few have the strength of mind to follow the latter. Since each person's ego or sense of individuality are different, then their experience of ego or personality disintegration is likewise unique. Although proverbially one cannot discover new continents until one has the courage to lose sight of the familiar shore, the voyage through a 'kundalini crisis' is rarely one of calm sailing, even if you have a competent guru to protect you. Or, as Dr Ramamurti Mishra observed, one may end up in the situation where, "Neurotics build castles in the air, psychotics live in them, and psychiatrists call by to collect the rent".

Plate 71

In this drawing of the Hindu *chakra* and *nadi* system a yogin is depicted, seated in *vajrasana* with his hands behind his thighs and long matted hair or *jata*. Ascending through the axial centre of his body, and corresponding to the spinal column as Mt Meru, is the central channel or median psychic nerve, known as *sushumna-nadi*. The name *sushumna* means 'most refined'. The term *nadi* – meaning vein or channel – is derived from the Sanskrit root *nad* – meaning 'movement', indicating the movement of the vital winds or *prana* through the channels of the subtle body. *Sushumna* is usually described as being red in colour, of the nature of fire, and a thousand times as fine as a human hair. It extends from the base of the spine, in the region of the sacral plexus near the second vertebra, to the cranial fissure or 'aperture of Brahma' (*brahmarandhra*), at the crown of the skull. Certain traditions maintain that the *sushumna-nadi* itself is composed of sheaths, with three further internally enclosed *nadis* known as *vajra-nadi*, *chitrini-nadi*, and *brahma-nadi*, the last being the actual channel through which *kundalini* ascends. The root of *sushumna* is usually described as arising in the *muladhara chakra* at the base of the spine, but in the drawing the central channel of *sushumna* extends to the tip of the yogin's penis.

On either side of the central channel ascend the two main subsidiary psychic channels which carry the subtle (*sukshma*) polarised psychic currents or energies of the subtle body. To the left of the central channel is the *ida-nadi* or 'channel of comfort', which carries the white cooling energies of the moon (*chandra*). To the right of the central channel is the *pingala-nadi* or 'reddish-brown channel', which carries the red heating energies of the sun (*surya*). These two channels arise in the left and right testicles of a man, and the left and right Fallopian tubes or ovaries of a woman. In the drawing the symbols of a crescent moon and sun disc are depicted in the yogin's testicles.

The importance of these polarity energies in both the female and male reproductive systems emerges in Buddhist tantric theories of conception, described below. In the Bengali tantric tradition the mother's menstrual cycle is symbolised by the three-and-a-half coils of the goddess Kundalini, which represents the three-and-a-half days of the menstrual cycle as the 'coils' or apparent rotations of the moon around the earth during this period.

From the sexual organs these two subsidiary channels ascend alongside the central channel until they curve below the crown of the head and then descend to the left and right nostrils. At various points along their ascent they cross over the central channel of *sushumna*, creating knots or junctions. In the drawing these knots occur at each of the six ascending *chakras* along the central channel, but the most important knots are said to occur in the sacral base or *muladhara chakra*, the heart or *anahata chakra*, and the forehead or *ajna chakra*. These knots are likened to the meeting place of the three sacred Indian rivers, known as *triveni*, where the River Ganges (*pingala-nadi*) and the River Yamuna (*ida-nadi*) meet with the hidden underground River Sarasvati (*sushumna-nadi*).

At different times of the day and night one of the two nostrils predominates in breath inhalation and exhalation. When the left or lunar nostril predominates, the body relaxes and cools, and one is more receptive and submissive. When the right or solar nostril predominates, the body energises and heats, and one is more creative and sensual. The yogic practice of breath control or *pranayama*, meaning 'breath extension', utilises techniques of inhalation, retention, and exhalation to control the psycho-physical organism by regulating the winds on which 'mind' travels as *prana*. When the psychic winds from the lunar and solar channels are forced into the central channel at their junction in the base or *muladhara chakra*, the goddess Kundalini is awakened and begins her ascent through the central channel. As Kundalini pierces each of the ascending *chakras* she releases the knots which constrict the central channel, causing the closed and downward-facing 'lotuses' of each *chakra* to open upwards as she ascends. With the blossoming of each ascending lotus, progressively deepening levels of bliss (*anada*), meditative absorption (*samadhi*), and psychic powers (*siddhi*) arise. Supreme bliss arises when Kundalini Shakti unites with her lord Shiva in the *sahasrara padma* or thousand-petalled lotus at the crown of the head; here the sense of individuation – personified by Kundalini Shakti – merges into the absolute as Shiva and Shakti unite.

The subtle body is described as being permeated with 72,000 *nadis*, although differing numbers of both *nadis* and *chakras* are affirmed in various tantric traditions. Most of these *nadis* arise or terminate at the sensory doors of the eyes, ears, mouth, nostrils, genitals, and anus; although most yogic traditions assert that all of the major *nadis* arise in the egg-shaped bulb or *kanda*, which is located in the perineum between the anus and urethra. Other traditions place the *kanda* or bulb in the *anahata chakra* at the heart. Purification of these 72,000 *nadis* is attained through the yogic practices of *pranayama* and Hatha Yoga. The term Hatha Yoga, meaning 'forceful or violent union', is composed of the two *bija* syllables *Ha* and *Tha* of the sun and moon, symbolising the red solar energy of the *pingala-nadi* and the white lunar energy of the *ida-nadi,* being forced into union (*yoga*) in the *sushumna-nadi* or central channel. When these united psychic winds enter with full potency into the central channel, the dualism of the individual and absolute as polarity symbols begins to dissolve. With the cessation of individuation the karmic cycles of birth and death as concepts of time dissolve also, as time – symbolised by the cyclic nature of the lunar and solar channels – is consumed in the fire of the central channel as *kalagni*, the 'fire of time'.

The six ascending *chakras* are strung along the *sushumna-nadi* like pearls. They are assigned a varying number of petals, each of which are sealed with a syllable of the Sanskrit alphabet. In total there are fifty *chakra* petals, which correspond to the fifty Sanskrit letters. Each syllable is a mantra of Kundalini, and collectively they encompass the totality of speech or sound. Symbolically the lotus petals represent plexuses of converging *nadis,* and their syllables, the vital energies which emanate from these focal points. The pericarp or centre of each lotus also bears the symbols of a presiding deity, a goddess, an animal, and an element shape, colour and seed-syllable or *bija*.

The six ascending *chakras* also represent the six *lokas* or realms of existence, and the first five *chakras* the five great elements.

At the base of the central *sushumna-nadi* in the perineum is the *muladhara chakra*, in which the goddess Kundalini lies coiled and sleeping. She is symbolised as a female serpent, as bright as a million suns, and coiled around the *kanda* or bulb with her head closing the entrance to the central channel. Usually three-and-a-half, five, or eight coils are described. When she is awakened her head enters the central channel and ascends like a thread passing through a hollow reed. The *muladhara chakra* has four petals and bears the yellow square of the earth element on its pericarp. Within this square are the symbols of a downward-pointing radiant triangle enclosing the syllable *Lam* of the earth element, and a golden Shiva *lingam* around which Kundalini is coiled. The *muladhara*'s presiding deity is Ganesha, its goddess Dakini Shakti, and its animal an elephant.

Above this, and located in the pubic region, is the *svadhisthana chakra* with six red petals. On its red pericarp is a white lunar crescent and the syllable *Vam* of the water element. Its presiding deity is Brahma, its goddess Rakini, and its animal a *makara*.

Above this, at the navel centre, is the *manipura chakra* with ten petals coloured like blue-grey storm clouds. Its pericarp is sealed with a red triangle and the syllable *Ram*

of the fire element. The *manipura*'s presiding deity is Vishnu, its goddess Lakshmi, and its animal a ram.

Above this, at the heart centre, is the *anahata chakra* with twelve red petals. On its pericarp is a blue-black, six-pointed star, which is sealed with the syllable *Yam* of the air or wind element. Its presiding deity is Rudra, its goddess Kakini, and its animal a deer.

Above this, at the throat centre, is the *vishuddha chakra* with sixteen purple petals. On its pericarp is a white circle which resembles the full moon, enclosing the syllable *Ham* of the space element within a downward-pointing triangle. Its presiding deity is Sadashiva, its goddess Shakini, and its animal an elephant or swan.

At the forehead centre between the eyebrows, at the point commonly known as the 'third eye', is the *ajna chakra* with two grey or white petals. The *ajna chakra* is sealed with none of the five great elements but with the subtle essence of consciousness, for it is here that the lunar and solar channels meet and descend towards the nostrils. The *ajna chakra*'s two petals symbolise these two channels. Its pericarp is a pure white circle with the syllable *Om* enclosed in a downward-pointing triangle. The presiding deity is the supreme form of Shiva known as Paramashiva, its goddess Hakini, and its animal a swan.

The seventh *chakra* of *sahasrara padma*, or the thousand-petalled lotus, is located at the crown of the head above the six lower *chakras*. It arises at the terminal point of the *sushumna-nadi* in the 'pure realm' (*sattvaloka*), where Shiva and Kundalini Shakti unite. Its thousand pink or white petals are *yoga-nadis*, which symbolically bear the fifty Sanskrit syllables in twenty radiating circles of lotus petals.

The three 'secret *chakras*' of *golata, lalata*, and *lalana* – located respectively on the uvula at the back of the throat, above the *ajna chakra*, and within the soft upper palate – are also illustrated in the drawing. In alchemical yogic traditions a *lingam* of solidified mercury is often placed within the cavity formed in the soft upper palate. Its purpose is to 'irradiate' the nectar in the brain. These three *chakras* and their highly esoteric yogic practices are employed in the 'inner coitus' yogas of *khechari mudra*.

The yogin's eyes glance upwards and inwards towards the *ajna chakra*, in the concentrative gaze known as *bhrumadya drishti*. From his nostrils extend 'pathways' of breath or *prana*, which reach to a distance of twelve finger-widths from the nostrils. The *prana* of the lunar channel on his left is white, and terminates on the insignia of a crescent moon on his left earring. The *prana* of the red solar channel on his right is patterned in the drawing, and terminates in the disc of the sun on his right earring. The Sanskrit term for earring is *kundala*, which has the same root as *kundalini*, meaning coiled or circling. Mahasiddhas are often described as wearing the sun and moon as ear ornaments.

The Buddhist Channel-Wheel System

Sexuality, Conception, and Birth

According to the Tibetan medical tantras the onset of puberty occurs around the age of twelve for a girl, and around sixteen for a boy. Symbolically these ages represent the solar aspect of wisdom for a girl, with the sun's twelve months and zodiac houses; and the lunar aspect of compassion for a boy, with the moon's sixteen 'digits' or phases between new and full moon. For this reason tantric deities in sexual union are described as being like sixteen-year-old virgins in the full flush of their first sexual embrace, symbolising the bliss that arises in their face-to-face union as consummate father and mother (Tib. *yab yum*). The swelling with blood of the glans of the penis represents expansion into great bliss, and its *vajra*-shaft, form; the open 'lotus' of the vagina represents wisdom, and its enclosing nature, emptiness. The three petals of this lotus, formed from the clitoris and the two labia folds enclosing the vulva, symbolise the three lower openings of the three main channels. The 'giving' of the mother to the father, as bride to groom, symbolises the marriage of formlessness and form, the union of wisdom and compassion, and the consummation of emptiness and great bliss.

With the arising of the female menstrual cycle with its monthly release of stored ova, and the continuous generation of semen in the male, the first two primary conditions for conception arise. When these two primary causes are in optimum fertility, the close proximity of the consciousness of a being seeking rebirth – which is the third primary cause for conception – may enter into their union. The secondary causes for conception are the balance of the five elements, without which physical development of an embryo would be impossible. The karmically driven and 'disembodied' consciousness of a being seeking rebirth enters on the breath of the father by way of the mouth during copulation, and exits through the penis and into the mother's womb during ejaculation. Two other 'doors' of conception are by way of the crown of the father's head, and directly into the mother's womb.

From the intermediate state of seeking rebirth, the incoming consciousness perceives only the dream-like vision of its future parents' sexual organs, which causes attraction and aversion to arise. If a boy is karmically destined to be born, the consciousness is attracted to the mother and experiences aversion towards the father, causing it to self-identify with the 'white drop' of the father. The consciousness of a karmically predestined girl will experience the reversal of these emotional states, and self-identify with the fertile 'red drop' of the mother.

As it transmigrates through the three intermediate states (Tib. *bar do*) between death and rebirth, the consciousness of a being seeking rebirth can self-identify with any form throughout the six realms of existence, according to its karmic propensity. Human beings tend to speculate only on human rebirths, but the accounts of Shakyamuni Buddha's previous lives in the voluminous *Jataka* tales testify to the importance placed on non-human rebirths in early Buddhist beliefs. In certain Buddhist doctrines a human rebirth is said to be as rare as the chances of a turtle surfacing directly into the centre of a cork ring floating somewhere on the surface of the great ocean. Rebirth in one of the six realms is karmically determined by the seeds of extreme pride,

jealousy, desire, ignorance, craving or miserliness, anger and hatred, coming to fruition within the god, *asura,* human, animal, *preta*, and hell realms respectively. These realms are also 'visited' in the *bardo* of dreaming by the movement of the psychic winds within the body during the dream state (see page 34). On a psychological level they may also be viewed as metaphors for the states of consciousness which beings experience in the *bardo* of waking life, but this is a simplistic understatement of the actual process involved.

The union of the three primary causes of conception – a flawlessly fertile sperm and ovum uniting with the consciousness of a being seeking rebirth – sets the chain of embryonic life in motion by forming the 'indestructible drop'. This 'indestructible drop' is believed to remain in the heart centre of the body throughout conscious life, until it 'departs' at the time of death. Here the life force of the 'subtle consciousness', impelled by its karmic propensities or 'causal body', interacts with the indestructible drop to create a 'blueprint' of the embryo's future development as the 'subtle body' of the incarnating consciousness. The white drop of the father's semen is described as giving rise to the creation of the solid white bone tissue, marrow, the brain, and spinal cord, whilst the red drop of the mother's 'uterine blood' is described as generating the soft red matter of blood, muscle tissue, and the solid and hollow organs or viscera. The consciousness of the being seeking rebirth gives rise to the development and consciousnesses of the sense organs – the 'doors' by which, ultimately, the mind will experience and interact with the external world.

The five subtle elements of earth, water, fire, air, and space, originate the pattern of cell division into muscle and bone tissue (solidity); blood and humidity (liquidity); warmth and complexion (vital heat); breath (respiration); and the orifices of the body (space). Soon after conception the central channel, with its two subsidiary channels, arises at the heart; and the umbilical cord, with its right and left channels, connects with the uterus to facilitate the development of the embryo. In the first four weeks after conception the embryo passes through the stages of 'mingling, clotting, solidifying, and rounding'. In the fifth week the umbilical cord and placenta are formed. In the sixth week the channel of life arises just behind the central channel itself, and parallels in its ascent the less subtle physiological energy winds of its ethereal and extremely subtle precursor. The 'essences' of the merged white and red drops in the indestructible drop begin to migrate from the 'heart centre' at the mid-point of the central channel. The upper white essence moves up to establish the brain or crown centre at the top of the head, and the lower red essence moves downwards to the navel centre. The indestructible drop, as the seat of consciousness, remains at the heart centre; even though we intellectually conceive of the brain as being the nucleus of the mind and its thoughts, it is actually only the receiver. Primal thought as 'mind' arises from the heart centre and becomes conceptual in the brain. Our involuntary indication in pointing to ourself or 'I' is to touch the centre of the breast, and not the forehead. Some modern Tibetan philosophers believe that if brain transplants were possible, the personality of the recipient would still dominate, reinstating its original mind into the confines of a new brain.

Within the conceptual framework of the Tibetan medical tradition the human embryo continues its development, passing through the stages of 'fish, turtle, and pig', or the periods described respectively as 'limbless, limbs and head, and consuming impure food'. The male foetus is believed to be positioned on the right side of the mother's womb, a female foetus on the left, and a hermaphrodite in the middle. Twins occupy both sides of the womb, and like triplets are conceived by a karmically driven 'psychic wind', which divides the original 'indestructible drop'. Just before birth certain psychic winds, which have remained static in the heart centre of the central channel, begin to dissolve into the two subsidiary channels via the navel centre, and pass out through the nostrils. At the moment of birth and the taking of the first breath, *prana* – which is the vital energy of the breath – vitalises the winds within the subtle body, causing the mind to identify with the sensory consciousness of 'being in the world'. *Prana,* which carries the essence of 'mind', is said to occur in five primary and secondary forms as 'winds', which ride on the delicate network of psychic channels or *nadis*, and give rise to an infinite array of manifestations of physical, emotional, mental, psychological, philosophical, and spiritual consciousnesses.

Throughout life the indestructible drop remains contained within the 'knot' at the heart centre. It is described as being about the size of a mustard seed, white on its upper half and red on its lower half, and enclosing the 'very subtle mind and wind' of the life force or consciousness within it. The migration of part of the 'essence' of the white and red drops to the crown and navel centres continues as the child grows. At puberty these white and red drops reach full maturity, with the onset of the female menstrual cycle around the age of twelve, and the male generation of semen around the age of sixteen. These refined essences of semen and menstrual blood are known as the white *bodhichitta* and red *bodhichitta*, and from their respective centres at the crown and navel they spread throughout the body's network of *nadis*.

The Death Process

At the time of a natural death the five inner elements of earth, water, fire, air, and space gradually begin to dissolve into one another. As earth dissolves into water the body becomes weaker, and a vision like a shimmering mirage arises. As water dissolves into fire the bodily fluids are experienced as dehydrating, and an internal vision like smoke arises. As fire dissolves into air the heat from the body's extremities withdraws into the heart, and an internal vision like sparks or fireflies arises. As air dissolves into space the breathing ceases, and a vision like a dying butter lamp or candle arises. Then space itself dissolves into wisdom, as the gross conceptual mind along with its pervasive winds becomes extremely refined and withdraws into the heart centre on the 'life-holding' wind.

The knots in the central channel – which throughout conscious life have restricted the entry of winds into the central channel – now unravel, allowing the white *bodhichitta*

at the crown to descend within the central channel. As this white *bindu* or *bodhichitta*-drop slowly descends towards the indestructible drop at the heart centre, a 'white appearance' like the vision of moonlight on a clear autumn evening arises. When the 'white appearance' dissolves, there next arises the 'red increase' as the red *bodhichitta* drop at the navel slowly ascends towards the indestructible drop, producing a vision like a clear autumn sky illuminated by the red glow of sunlight. As the white and red drops approach and completely enclose the indestructible drop the stage of 'black near-attainment' arises, which is experienced as the vision of complete darkness, like a black and empty sky.

Finally the indestructible drop at the heart centre opens, revealing the extremely subtle consciousness and its wind as the 'clear light of death', which arises as an exceedingly clear and bright vision, similar to the sky at dawn. After the breaking open of the indestructible drop the consciousness of the deceased, riding on the very subtle wind which serves as its vehicle, departs through one of the nine apertures of the body into its karmically predestined next realm of rebirth. If the consciousness escapes through the anus it signifies rebirth in the hell realm; through the sexual organ, the animal realm; through the mouth, the hungry ghost realm; through the nose, the human or spirit realm; through the ears, the *asura* realm; through the navel, the desire god realm; through the eyes, the form god realm; through the top of the head, the formless god realm; and through 'the aperture of Brahma' at the crown of the head, directly into the paradise realm of Amitabha Buddha known as Dewachen.

Deprived of its sustaining life force or consciousness, the white and red *bodhichitta* at the heart centre now separate, with the white *bodhichitta* usually descending and leaving the body through the sexual organ, and the red *bodhichitta* ascending and leaving through the nostrils. Clinical death has now reached its conclusion.

There are said to be six different 'intermediary states' (Tib. *bar do*), three of which are experienced in life, and three which are experienced in death. The first is that of waking life (Tib. *skyes gnas bar do*); the second is that of the dream state (Tib. *rmi lam bar do*); the third is that of meditative experience (Tib. *bsam gtan bar do*); the fourth is that of the death process as described above (Tib. *'chi kha bar do*; the eight visionary appearances described above mark its eight stages); the fifth is that of the after-death intermediary state (Tib. *chos nyid bar do*); and the sixth is that of seeking rebirth (Tib. *srid pa bar do*). The last three of these *bardo* states, experienced between death and rebirth, are graphically and symbolically described in the *Bardo Thodol* (Tibetan Book of the Dead, more accurately translated as, The Great Liberation by Hearing in the Intermediate State).

The Generation and Completion Stages of Highest Yoga Tantra

The eight visionary appearances of the death process are also said to arise daily on transition from the waking state into the state of deep sleep, although they are not recognised by most human beings due to their lack of awareness of the more subtle levels of consciousness. Since this process occurs every day and is not recognised, it follows that during the actual death process the consciousness of the deceased will have little or no control over the death process, intermediary visionary state, and future rebirth.

A specific aspect of Tibetan Vajrayana Buddhism which is not found in other forms of Buddhism is that of reincarnate lamas (Tib. *sprul sku*) who can consciously control the death experience in order to take human rebirth in the most beneficial and continuing conditions. This implies complete control over the three *bardos* of the death process, intermediary state, and future rebirth, within the context of a bodhisattva's altruistic aspiration to attain the highest enlightenment for the compassionate benefit of all beings.

Vajrayana meditation techniques are essentially composed of 'formless' practices which are utilised to develop the awareness of emptiness or *shunyata*, or as the 'visualised form' branches of Deity Yoga. Deity Yoga employs highly refined techniques of creative imagination, visualisation, and photism in order to self-identify with the divine form and qualities of a particular deity as the union of method or skilful means and wisdom. As His Holiness the Dalai Lama says, "In brief, the body of a Buddha is attained through meditating on it".

In the practices of Highest Yoga Tantra (*anuttarayoga tantra*) two stages of meditational practice are employed in order for the practitioner to attain supreme enlightenment by the process of actual transformation into the form of the deity. The first stage is known as the 'generation stage' (Tib. *bskyed rim*) or 'creation stage', which is perfected by dissolving one's mind into emptiness and generating the vivid form of the particular meditational deity (Tib. *yi dam*), with the visualised 'clear appearance' of the deity and the quality of the 'divine pride' of actually being the deity.

The second stage is known as the 'completion stage' (Tib. *rdzogs rim*), which is perfected by causing the psychic winds to enter, abide, and dissolve into the central channel of the subtle or *vajra* body, and release the indestructible drop at the heart centre. With the opening of the indestructible drop and the dawning of the 'clear light', emptiness is consciously realised as the 'blissful mind of clear light'. This gives rise to the 'illusory body' which manifests in the form of the deity. The union of 'clear light' and 'illusory body' – as the pure empty form of the deity meditating on emptiness – rapidly results in the accumulation of wisdom and method which leads directly to the full enlightenment of Buddhahood. The sign which indicates the transition from the generation stage to the completion stage is the practitioner's ability to draw the winds into the central channel. Highest Yoga Tantras are divided into 'mother tantras' (*yoganiruttara tantras*) and 'father tantras' (*yogottara tantras*), which emphasise respectively the development of 'clear light' (wisdom) and 'illusory body' (method), yet each of these tantric systems lead to the same goal of full enlightenment. The Six Yogas of Naropa – consisting of the yoga of vital heat (Tib. *gtum mo*); illusory body yoga; dream yoga; clear light yoga; transference of consciousness (Tib. *'pho ba*); and yoga of the intermediate state (Tib. *bar do*) – also employ techniques for controlling the winds and drops within the *vajra* body.

In the advanced practices of Highest Yoga Tantra the three *bardos* or stages of the death experience – the *bardo* of the death process with its eight visionary appearances, the *bardo* of the intermediate state, and the *bardo* of seeking rebirth – are 'brought into the path' by consciously simulating the death experience and transforming it into the three *kayas* or bodies of the Buddha. The eight visionary appearances of the generation stage culminate in the dissolution of the winds into the indestructible drop at the completion stage. The resultant body attained at this stage of 'clear light' is the *dharmakaya* or formless 'truth body' of the Buddha. Arising from emptiness in the symbolic form of a seed-syllable in the generation stage culminates in the attainment of the illusory body in the completion stage, and the resultant body attained is the *sambhogakaya* or visionary 'enjoyment body' of the Buddha. Arising as the deity in the generation stage culminates in the attainment of 'taking the old body' as the *nirmanakaya* or 'emanation body' of the Buddha in the completion stage. The *nirmanakaya* or 'form body' is known as *tulku* (Tib. *sprul sku*) in Tibetan, a term which is also applied to reincarnate lamas who have consciously taken rebirth as the physical 'form body' of the Buddha.

The three *bardo* states of the death process, intermediate state, and rebirth, are thus transformed into the three divine bodies of the Buddha as the *dharmakaya*, *sambhogakaya*, and *nirmanakaya*. The three *kayas* also correspond to the three states of deep sleep, dreaming, and awakeness throughout conscious life. With the attainment of the three *kayas*, death itself is transformed into the state of full enlightenment.

Plate 72

Illustrated in this drawing is a Buddha form seated in *vajrasana* posture, with his hands in the *dhyana mudra* of meditative equipoise. Within his body are drawn the three main *nadis* and channel-wheels according to the *Guhyasamaja Tantra* system. Most of the completion stage practices of Highest Yoga Tantra (*anuttarayoga tantra*), such as those of the of *Chakrasamvara*, *Vajrayogini*, *Vajrabhairava* and *Hevajra Tantras*, follow the pattern of the early *Guhyasamaja* system; although there are variations in the emphasis placed on certain channel-wheel centres in specific practices, and in the knots, drops, and winds which arise from the three main channels. The *Kalachakra Tantra* describes an alternative system of channel-wheels, *nadis*, winds, and drops, an account of which is given below.

In the *Guhyasamaja* system the central channel, known in Sanskrit as the *avadhuti* or *sushumna nadi* (Tib. *rtsa dbu ma*), ascends like a vertical pole from the tip of the sexual organs to the crown of the head. From the crown it arches over the skull and forehead to its point of origination between the two eyebrows. Its vertical location within the body is described as being slightly in front of the thicker 'channel of life', which ascends in front of the spinal column. The central channel is very straight, subtle, clear, transparent, and delicate, and is often described as being blue or white

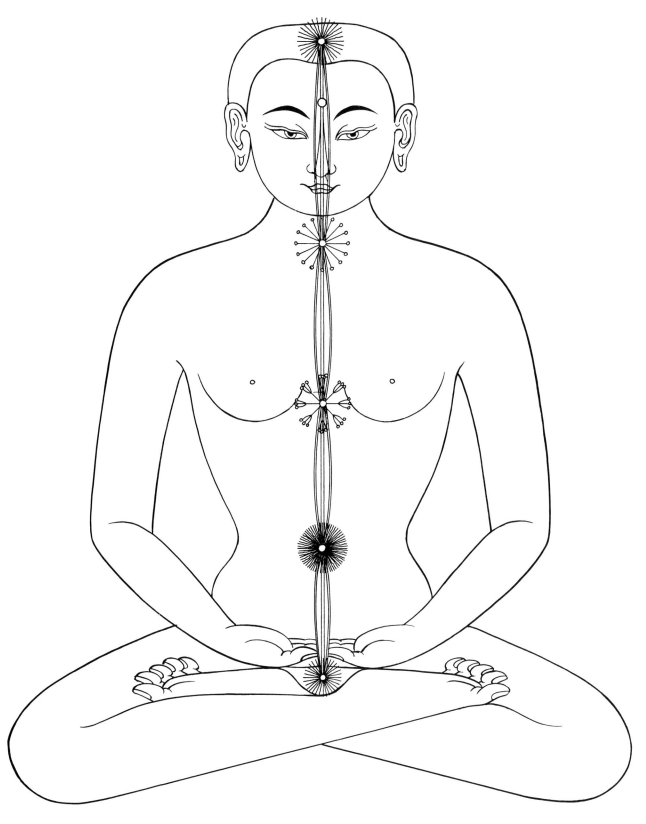

Plate 72: The Buddhist channel-wheel system

on the outside and blood-red in its interior. In many practices the central channel is visualised as extending only from the crown of the head to a point which is located four finger-widths below the navel centre.

Running parallel and in contact with the central channel in its vertical ascent, are the right and left channels of the sun and moon. Both of these channels arise at the two nostrils, arch over the crown of the head, and descend adjacent to the central channel until the navel centre. From here the right solar channel curves slightly away from the central channel and terminates at the anus, where its function is to control defecation. The left lunar channel curves away slightly to the right and terminates at the tip of the sexual organ, where its function is to control urine, semen, and menstrual blood. The white left lunar channel corresponds to the *ida nadi* in the Kundalini Yoga system, and in Buddhist Sanskrit is known as *lalana* or 'caressing woman' (Tib. *rtsa rkyang ma*). The red right solar channel corresponds to the *pingala nadi*, or *rasana* meaning 'tongue' (Tib. *rtsa ro ma*). These three main channels – left, right, and centre – are also known as the channels of body, speech, and mind.

In the 'rosary' of Sanskrit seed-syllables (*bija*) the white vowel sounds (*ali*) arise in the white drops of the lunar channel, the red consonants (*kali*) in the red drops of the solar channel, and the non-dual union of the crescent moon dot (*aksara*), placed above the seed-syllables, arises in the fire of the central channel. The rosaries of the sixteen white vowels and forty red consonants of the Sanskrit alphabet are commonly visualised circling in both clockwise and anticlockwise motions; their doubling symbolises the thirty-two major and eighty minor marks of an enlightened Buddha or bodhisattva. The white lunar channel is male – representing the *vajra*, method (*upaya*), and semen (*sukra*). The red solar channel is female – representing the lotus, wisdom (*prajna*), and blood (*rakta*). The central channel, which is empty and of the nature of fire, unifies the polarities of male and female, *vajra* and lotus, method and wisdom, semen and blood, as the enlightened consciousness of the deity in the indestructible drop within the heart centre.

At various points along the central channel the white lunar and red solar channels cross and coil around the central channel, forming constricting knots (Tib. *rtsa mdud*). These 'knots' occur at the five main channel-wheel centres, with a single knot formed from the double coiling of the left and right channels at the secret place, navel, throat, and crown centres, and a triple knot at the heart centre. The six overlapping coils of the triple knot of the heart centre enclose the 'indestructible drop' in a constricting cage. The dawning of the 'clear light' at the last stage of death when the indestructible drop opens, releases the most subtle consciousness from this 'cage' into its future rebirth. In the *Guhyasamaja* system the two openings of the central channel at the forehead and tip of the sexual organ are also closed by constricting knots which effectively seal the central channel.

The channel-wheels are the five main plexuses of constriction along the central channel, where the knots arise and where various *nadis* emanate like petals or the spokes of a wheel. They are visualised like the spokes of an umbrella, which alternately arch towards each other along the central channel. The four upper channel-wheels of crown, throat, heart, and navel are the ones most commonly visualised in meditation practices. At the crown is the 'wheel of great bliss'; it arches downwards with thirty-two white spokes. At the throat is the 'wheel of enjoyment', which arches upwards with sixteen red spokes. At the heart is the 'wheel of phenomena', with its eight white spokes arching downwards in the eight directions. At its centre is a circle of space enclosing the indestructible drop within the six coils of its triple knot. At the navel is the 'wheel of emanation'; it arches upwards with sixty-four red spokes and a triangular centre. The 'secret place' channel-wheel, which is located in the sexual area, is known as the 'wheel of the preservation of bliss', and has thirty-two red spokes which arch downwards.

These five channel-wheels at the crown, throat, heart, navel, and secret place are sealed by the syllables *Om A Hum Sva Ha*, and represent the body, speech, mind, qualities, and activities of an enlightened being. The first three syllables *Om A Hum*, are always painted on the back surface of a thangka at the forehead, throat, and heart centres of the main deities – representing the body, speech, and mind of the deity.

There are many variations in different Vajrayana practices, which makes it impossible to present a definitive system of the three main *nadis*, channel-wheels, and knots. The four main channel-wheels of crown, throat, heart, and navel are only employed in specific practices; whereas up to seven – including the forehead, secret place, and sexual tip or 'jewel centre' – are visualised in others. Many traditions assert that the solar and lunar channels should be reversed for male and female practitioners, with the lunar channel being on the right 'method' side for men, and on the left 'wisdom' side for women. In the *Vajrabhairava Tantra* system a double knot is formed at the navel centre, and here all three channels are white in their interiors. In the practice of 'inner heat' (Tib. *gtum mo*) the central channel is often visualised with the thickness of an arrow shaft, and the right and left channels, with the thickness of wheat stalks running parallel to it, but with a separation of around half an inch on either side. The crown centre may also be located at the upper-back of the head, as the aperture at the top of the head is held to be the doorway into the formless god realm.

Common to most Buddhist traditions, however, is the belief that the subtle body is permeated with 72,000 *nadis*, as in the Hindu Kundalini Yoga system. These 72,000 *nadis* are derived from the eight *nadi* petals or spokes of the heart channel-wheel. Each of these eight main *nadis* have a name, a function, and a supporting wind. From the end of each arise three branching *nadis* coloured white, red, and blue – representing body, speech, and mind – and which carry the white *bodhichitta* drops, the red *bodhichitta* drops, and the supporting winds. These twenty-four *nadis* travel to different parts of the body, and outwardly form the twenty-four sacred places of the 'Heruka body mandala' wherein reside the twenty-four 'heroes' (*viras*) and 'heroines' (*yoginis*). The twenty-four sacred pilgrimage sites (*pithastana*) of the *Chakrasamvara Tantra* are derived from the sad legend of Shiva's first wife, Sati, whose dismembered body was divided into twenty-four parts by

Vishnu, and scattered across India. Each of these twenty-four *nadis* again divide into three, making a total of seventy-two channels, which likewise carry white drops, red drops, and winds. These seventy-two channels then divide into a thousand branches, giving a final total of 72,000 *nadis*. These *nadis* carry the impure winds of the conceptual mind which dissolve into the central channel at the time of death, and which are brought under control during the 'generation stage' (Tib. *bskyed rim*) of meditational practice. During the 'completion stage' (Tib. *rdzogs rim*) of Highest Yoga Tantra, their refined energy winds enter the central channel and release the constricting knots.

There are five primary winds (Skt. *prana*; Tib. *rlung*) and five secondary winds which flow through the channels. The five primary winds are: the 'life-supporting wind', which maintains life; the 'downward-voiding wind', which releases faeces, urine, semen, and menstrual blood; the 'upward-moving wind', which controls breath, swallowing, and speech; the 'equally-abiding wind', which controls heat and digestion; and the 'pervading wind', which controls the physical activity of the body. Each of these winds is assigned a colour, direction, element, location, and function, which accord with the Five Buddha Families of Akshobhya, Ratnasambhava, Amitabha, Amoghasiddhi, and Vairochana respectively.

The five secondary winds arise from the life-supporting wind at the heart centre and govern the sensory consciousnesses. These secondary winds are also assigned the colours of the Five Buddhas, with the sequence of blue – sound; yellow – smell; red – sight; green – touch; and white – taste. These winds arise on three levels as gross, subtle, and very subtle. The gross and subtle winds carry the coarse and refined emotional and mental consciousnesses, and the very subtle wind carries the very subtle mind which transmigrates from life to life. The life-supporting wind is the essential wind of the heart centre which supports life itself, and is the most important in the inner yoga practices.

The drops or *bindu* (Tib. *thig le*) are spread throughout the channels in their gross form, and within the indestructible drop in their subtle form. The white *bodhichitta* drop at the crown is the source of white seminal fluid, and the red *bodhichitta* drop at the navel is the source of all fecund blood. The equally-abiding wind, which has its seat in the navel centre, creates the vital heat of the body which is responsible for warmth and digestion. In the yogic practice of 'inner heat', a breath-retention technique known as 'vase breathing' is employed to compress the air at the navel centre, distending the abdomen into the shape of a vase or pot. This fans the inner fire at the navel centre, causing it to ignite and blaze upwards through the central channel like a twisting needle of fire and to melt the white *bodhichitta* at the crown, causing great bliss to arise in the blazing and melting. *Chandali* in Sanskrit means the 'fierce one' or 'female outcaste', and a physical by-product of its accomplishment is the yogin's ability to withstand the bitter cold, to melt snow, or dry wet blankets on his naked body. The melting of the gross drops and their movement through the channels creates the experience of ordinary bliss. Sexual intercourse agitates the motion of the downward-voiding wind,

creating the experience of sexual pleasure. This agitation ignites the 'ordinary fire' and causes the gross drops in the lower body to melt, descend, and flow through the sexual organ during orgasm. The temporary bliss of orgasm does not, however, arise in the central channel; yet it forms a sexual metaphor for the enduring great bliss created by the actual melting of the *bodhichitta* in the practice of 'inner heat', or other *anuttarayoga tantra* practices. The visualised ascent of the white *bodhichitta* drop, which enters and ascends the central channel from the tip of the sexual organ, produces the sublime experience of the 'four joys' as it moves through the navel, heart, throat and crown centres.

The Kalachakra Channel-Wheel System

The *Kalachakra Tantra* channel-wheel system presents an alternative inner cosmology of the three main channels, winds, drops, and channel-wheels to the *Guhyasamaja*, *Hevajra*, and *Chakrasamvara* model described above.

In the *Kalachakra* system the central channel arises between the eyebrows, arches to the crown, and then descends vertically to the tip of the penis or clitoris. The left, white lunar channel and the right, red solar channel arise at the two nostrils, and following the path of the central channel terminate one finger-width below the central channel in the sexual bulb or *kanda*. From here the left channel controls the release of urine and sexual fluids, and the right channel the function of excreting. At each of the six channel-wheel centres of crown, forehead, throat, heart, navel, and sexual *chakra*, constricting knots are formed by the coiling of the lunar and solar channels. At the navel centre the single knotted loops of the two side-channels creates a specific plexus which corresponds to the sixfold scheme of Kalachakra's six elements . Here the central channel above the navel *chakra* is identified with the energy of the eclipse planet Rahu, and below the navel *chakra* with the energy of Kalagni, the 'fire of time'. Rahu represents the green element of space, and carries wind in the central channel above the navel. Kalagni represents the sixth blue element of wisdom, and carries semen below the navel centre. The lower extent of the left lunar channel below the navel represents the black eastern element of air, and carries urine; above the navel it represents the white northern element of water, and carries semen. The right solar channel below the navel represents the yellow western element of earth, and carries excrement; above the navel it represents the red southern element of fire, and carries blood. This sixfold scheme creates a mandala of Kalachakra's six elements of earth, water, fire, air, space, and wisdom. Kalachakra's left and right legs are coloured white and red to represent the lunar and solar channels. His three necks are coloured white, black, and red to symbolise the lunar, central and solar channels; and his four faces are coloured; black at the front (Rahu), yellow at the back (Kalagni), white on the left (Moon), and red on the right (Sun). These four planets also arise as the four stacked discs of Moon, Sun, Rahu, and Kalagni, on which Kalachakra stands.

The constricting knots along the central channel allow a minimal movement of energy winds to pass within the central channel, unlike the *Guhyasamaja*-related systems where the central channel is normally empty. Like the *Guhyasamaja* model the eight spokes of the heart channel-wheel branch into twenty-four, seventy-two, and finally 72,000 *nadis*.

The five principal and five secondary winds in the *Kalachakra* system follow a similar scheme to the *Guhyasamaja*'s ten winds. The five principal winds are: life-sustaining; downward-voiding; fire-accompanying; upward-moving; and pervasive. The five secondary winds relate to the five senses and elements, and are known as: the 'moving wind' of the yellow earth element and sight; the 'fully-moving wind' of the white water element and sound; the 'perfectly-moving wind' of the red fire element and smell; the 'extremely-moving wind' of the black wind element and taste; and the 'certainly-moving wind' of the green space element and touch. Each of these ten winds arise consecutively during the ten months of the foetus's gestation within the womb.

Unlike the *Guhyasamaja* system, with its two drops of white and red *bodhichitta*, the *Kalachakra Tantra* describes four kinds of drops. These arise in the crown, throat, heart, and navel centres, and correspond to the 'four states of existence'. The 'body drop' is located in the crown centre and gives rise to the waking state; the 'dream or speech drop' arises in the throat centre and gives rise to the dream state; the 'deep sleep drop' is located in the heart centre and gives rise to the state of deep sleep; and the 'deep awareness drop' arises in the navel centre and gives rise to the state of sexual ecstacy.

The six channel-wheel centres of the *Kalachakra* system similarly arch towards each other in pairs, like the upward and inverted curving spokes of an umbrella. At the crown centre is the 'wheel of great bliss' with four spokes; at the forehead is the 'wheel of wind' with sixteen spokes; at the throat is the 'wheel of enjoyment' with thirty-two spokes; at the heart is the 'wheel of phenomena' with eight spokes; at the navel is the 'wheel of emanation' with sixty-four spokes; and at the 'secret place' or sexual centre is the 'wheel of preservation of bliss' with thirty-two spokes.

The Numerical Symbolism of the Channels and Channel-Wheels
The esoteric symbolism of the two wind energies of the lunar and solar channels entering, abiding, and dissolving into the central channel, forms a potent polarity symbol in Vajrayana Buddhism. The dualities of male and female, sperm and egg, *vajra* and lotus, moon and sun, method and wisdom, great bliss and emptiness, all merge into the non-dual union which is the pristine 'unborn' state of enlightenment.

In Tibetan thangka painting the central axis or 'brahma-line', which is centred precisely at the crown centre of the main deity, divides the thangka into two vertical halves, with the male method side placed to the right side of the deity under a full moon, and the female wisdom side to the left of the deity under a sun. For a viewer, the left side of a thangka is the method side, and the right the wisdom side. In certain practices, especially those which emphasise the 'mother tantra' aspect of the development of wisdom, these polarity symbols may be reversed. The moon represents 'relative *bodhichitta*', which is the spontaneous aspiration towards enlightenment; and the sun represents 'ultimate *bodhichitta*',

or the ripening effect of discriminating awareness (*prajna*) which directly realises emptiness (*shunyata*). In the completion stage of Highest Yoga Tantra, the moon represents the attainment of the 'illusory body', and the sun the realisation of 'clear light'. As colours the white and red *bodhichitta* drops of moon and sun arise as the silver and gold metal ornaments, and the pearl and coral mineral ornaments, which adorn the forms of peaceful deities.

The goddess Palden Lhamo is depicted with a blazing sun at her navel, and the moon at her crown. Shaivite-related deities, such as Chakrasamvara, have a one-day-old crescent moon at their crown, symbolising the increase of white *bodhichitta*. The goddess Troma Nagmo is described as having a red sun disc as her right eye, a white moon disc as her left eye, and as her third or 'wisdom eye' the reddish-white union of sun and moon. The familiar tantric symbol of a white skull-cup filled with blood represents the union of great bliss and emptiness as the father and mother's *bodhichitta* drops creating the bone and blood at the crown and navel *chakras*. In the ancient Indian alchemical tradition the white *bodhichitta* symbolises the semen of Shiva as mercury, and the red *bodhichitta* the menstrual blood of Parvati as cinnabar or sulphur. The crucible is the navel *chakra*, the distillation flask the central channel, the fire Chandali, and the bellows the vase-breathing exercises.

As a trinity the lunar, solar, and central channels – coloured white, red, and blue – represent the body, speech and mind of the deity, and correspond to the three syllables *Om A Hum*, which arise in the crown, throat, and heart centres as the three *kayas* or 'bodies' of the Buddha. In the symbolism of the *khatvanga* or 'tantric staff', which represents the form of the deity or Heruka himself, the three impaled heads – coloured white as a dry skull, red as a freshly severed head, and blue as a decaying head – symbolise the three channels, three syllables, and the three main *chakras* as the body, speech, and mind of the deity. The three prongs of the trident, and the three visible prongs of the *vajra*, also represent these three channels. The meeting place (*triveni*) of the three sacred Indian rivers, the Ganges and Yamuna merging with the invisible subterranean river Sarasvati (symbolising the central channel), reveals the ancient origin of this tantric concept.

The visualisation of deities which arise at the heart centre is generated from a *bija* or seed-syllable, which arises from a moon and sun disc placed above an eight-petalled lotus. Here the eight-petalled lotus is the heart channel-wheel of phenomena, the moon and sun discs are the two halves of the indestructible drop, and the *bija* syllable which transforms into the deity is the pure consciousness which resides in the indestructible drop. In peaceful deity visualisations the predominant colour scheme is of a white male deity in sexual embrace with his red female consort. This represents the union of the fertile white semen and red uterine blood creating new life as pure consciousness. In wrathful forms the predominant colours are of a blue-black male embracing a red consort, this represents the blue-black poison and red sacrificial blood of ego-death, selflessness and the 'death' or cessation of conceptualisation.

The *Hevajra Tantra* states, "Then there are *ali, kali*, sun and moon, the sixteen phases, the sixty-four periods, the thirty-two hours and the four watches. So everything goes in fours." Numerically the *nadis* of the channel-wheels are derived from the doubling of the base number four, which produces the eight, sixteen, thirty-two, and sixty-four spokes of the various *chakras*. In the geometric mandala layout, which forms a common design in most deity practices, this numerical sequence is expressed in the placement of deities in the body, speech, mind, great bliss, and emanation wheels which occur in the lotus circles and protection wheels of the mandala. The eight-petalled lotus, which is usually placed at the mandala's centre, represents the eight spokes of the heart *chakra* as the 'mind wheel' of *dharmakaya*. The sixteen petals of the surrounding lotus circle – which may embody eight directional deities with their consorts, the sixteen offering goddesses or the sixteen arhats – represent the throat *chakra* as the 'speech wheel' of *sambhogakaya*. The sixty-four variegated lotus petals on the innermost of the outer protective circles, represents the sixty-four spokes of the navel *chakra* as the 'emanation wheel' of *rupakaya*. The thirty-two golden *vajras* which encircle the next protective circle of the black '*vajra*-tent', symbolise the thirty-two major marks of an enlightened being. The thirty-two variegated coloured flame-banks of the 'fire mountain' (Tib. *me ri*) in the outermost protective circle, symbolise the thirty-two spokes of the crown *chakra* as the 'body wheel of great bliss' of the *nirmanakaya*.

The 'eight great charnel grounds', which frequently form a fourth protective circle of the mandala, encapsulate the complex symbolism of both the sutra and tantra paths. The symbolism of the eight great charnel grounds and the twenty-four sacred places is described and explained on page 251.

The main channel-wheels are also numerically illustrated in the six bone ornaments worn by wrathful forms and semi-wrathful deities. At the crown is a netted bone chain with thirty-two loops which encircle the top hair-knot. At the throat is a bone necklace with sixteen hanging net loops. At the heart is an eight-spoked bone wheel, with four double strands of two hundred bone beads which form a cross around the upper body, symbolising the 72,000 *nadis* which emanate from the eight spokes of the heart channel-wheel. Around the waist is a bone belt with sixty-four net loops, representing the sixty-four spokes of the navel channel-wheel. Bone bracelets, armlets, and anklets form the fifth bone ornament; and a pair of bone earrings, representing the lunar and solar channels, forms the sixth. These six bone ornaments are shaped to correspond with Vajrasattva and the Five Buddhas: with jewel-shaped pendants on the upper torso, lotus-shaped bones at the heart, a *vajra*-shaped bone at the centre of the back, crossed *vajras* at the navel, noose-shaped loops at the waist, and wheel-shaped bones on the bracelets, armlets and anklets. Wrathful deities also display a mandala of cemetery unguents on their faces, with cremation ash applied to the forehead, blood smeared on the 'three bulges' of the nose and cheeks, and human fat applied to the chin or throat.

The following passage is a footnote from David Snellgrove's translation of the *Hevajra Tantra*. Although this was written at a very early date in the field of modern tantric studies, this footnote expresses an important point as to how the subject of visualisation practices as a whole, and the inner channel-wheel cosmology in particular, should be approached in order to gain a clearer perspective of their subject matter and actual practice:

Of the actual method of controlling the physical functions the text tells nothing directly. They are, however, clearly implied in the more general statements. The Taoists treating of similar practices, are certainly more explicit …The various processes are here described explicitly, whereas in the Indian texts one is presented primarily with schemes and patterns. Nor is any distinction made between an imagined and an actual physical process, because no such distinction is recognised. One surmises that the real process was elaborated to conform with a theoretical scheme, just as the master's responsibility towards his pupil is elaborated into the theory of the five families. This has the effect of concealing what is actually involved, and I doubt whether this particular problem is soluble. To ask what may appear to us an all-important question: "Are the chakras within the body conceived of as real psychic centres, or are they an imagined device like the external mandala?" is to bring contradiction into the whole basic theory from the standpoint of the texts. For them the whole process, internal and external, is bhavana (mental production), and the mandala, although imagined (bhavita) exists on a higher plane of reality than the phenomenal world it represents. Likewise the idealised representation of the body, consisting of the nadis and chakras, exists on a higher plane than the normal physical structure of the body. Then, finally, these higher stages themselves are dissolved. The same applies to the divine forms. They are not pure symbol as we might interpret them. We regard them as unreal in the beginning. The Buddhists, however regard them as real in the beginning, more real than flesh and blood. Hence arises the need of insisting that the divine form too consists of just something that comes into existence. In fact the very power of these gods as means of purification (vishuddhi) resides in the initial belief that they instilled. They are the essence of samsara, and one must learn to conceive of them in terms of their non-existence. To call such use symbolic is not adequate, for as pure symbol they would be powerless. Nor is any real distinction to be made between an esoteric and exoteric interpretation, between the few who know all these things are symbols, and the many who place faithful trust in them. They all, siddhas and prithagjanas alike, believe in these gods. The siddhas have, however, trained themselves to regard them as though they were non-existent. It clearly only becomes possible to understand these texts thoroughly by accepting their Weltanschauung complete, and this is probably an impossibility for a modern European. To think one has done so is not sufficient. One is then placed in the predicament of explaining away much that is unaccept-

able, and one manner of doing this is an appeal to symbolism and esoteric interpretation; but these are notions that have no meaning in a genuine tradition. A distinction is made, it is true between an inner (adhyatmika) and outer (bahya) interpretation with regard to the actual rites, but they remain rites none the less, and the distinction arises from no embarrassment with regard to them, or desire to explain them away. On the contrary the outer sense is usually commended as necessary to lead men to the inner, which is precisely their use. The position is completely reversed by certain European and modern Indian exponents of these doctrines, who commend them to us for their esoteric significance, as though one could dispense with all else. Such an interpretation is historically inaccurate. Those Buddhists believed, and it was necessary for their whole scheme of 'release' that they should believe, in those gods and magical practices for their own sakes, before they began to use them as means. There was no short-cutting of this way, or the means would have been completely ineffective; nor indeed were they inclined to believe otherwise. The task now of trying to understand becomes very much more difficult, and can only be attempted when one has amassed sufficient knowledge of the historical and religious setting of the times to permit one to see certain practices in sufficient context. Such a view can scarcely be perfect, but it is the only possible approximation…

(Snellgrove 1959, Vol. 1: 33–4)

Chapter Six
Mudras

The Sanskrit term *mudra* (Tib. *phyag rgya*) has a variety of meanings. Its primary meaning as 'seal' implies stamping, impressing, marking, or printing, as in the stamping of coins or currency, the impressing of a signet ring, the marking or engraving of a sign, and the printing of an image or text.

In yogic practices, especially those of Hatha Yoga, *mudra* implies specific yoga postures, breathing practices, concentrations, and looks or gazes. The large conch or ivory earrings worn by the Hindu Kanphata or 'split-ear' sect of Hatha yogins are also known as *mudras*.

In the highly symbolic 'left-hand' tantric ritual of *panchamakara* (the 'five M-letters'), which is of great significance in Hindu tantras, *mudra* refers to parched grain as one of the five M-letters. The five ingredients of this left-hand ritual are: wine (*madya*), meat (*mamsa*), fish (*matsya*), parched grain (*mudra*), and sexual intercourse (*maithuna*). On an outer level the consumption of the first four ingredients generates the sexual energy which is expended in the fifth as sexual union (*maithuna*). On an inner level wine symbolises the divine intoxication of love; meat, the body; fish, the retention of breath; parched grain, the retention of sexual fluids; and sexual intercourse, the full arousal of the goddess Kundalini. In the practice of *khechari mudra* meat symbolises the tongue, parched grain the soft upper palate, fish the retention of the breath, sexual union the churning of the tongue into the 'tenth door' or cavity formed within the upper palate, and wine the descent of *bodhichitta* or nectar from Shiva located in the brain centre – which floods the yogin's body with divine bliss. Several small New Age American pharmaceutical companies have endeavoured to reproduce this inner nectar as a by-product of Serotonin. But true spiritual experience cannot be synthesised in a laboratory; its substance is not physical and its experience is not mechanistical.

The Buddhist term Mahamudra, meaning 'great seal', refers to the perfection of realisation attained through the synthesis of the Mahayana and Vajrayana paths.

In Vajrayana sexual yoga practices *mudra* refers to the female consort taken for the generation of spontaneous bliss and emptiness. Here the *mudra* as female consort arises on an outer, inner, and secret level: as the outer consort she manifests as the physical form of the goddess or *dakini*; as the inner consort she manifests as Chandali, the goddess of inner heat located below the navel *chakra*; and as the secret consort she arises as the consummate union of the white and red *bodhichitta* drops (*bindu*), as the ultimate merging of coincidental bliss and emptiness.

Mudra as hand gesture has its origin as the spontaneous natural sentiment or expression of innate pristine awareness, where the subtle hand movements 'just come into existence' as a manifestation of the state of realisation. Body language is now a familiar concept in modern psychology, where awareness of a person's mental state is communicated unconsciously and without recourse to verbal analysis. Shakyamuni Buddha's right hand just reached down and touched the ground when he called the earth goddess, Sthavara, as witness to his enlightenment. Buddha's *mudra* happened spontaneously and was not a contrived act. When my eldest daughter, Carrina, was born in 1982, she was graced with exquisite artistic hands, which bore an uncanny resemblance to the sculptural hands of Buddha and bodhisattva images. For the first few months of her life her waking hours were characterised by an endless display of the most sublime hand movements, which revealed the whole spectrum of iconographic and dance *mudras*. Intuitively I learned far more from the mesmerism of these spontaneous hand and finger gestures than from any number of artistic manuals on the canons of proportion. I have witnessed the same phenomena in the hands of Indian and Sufi saints who are in a state of divine rapture or ecstatic union. Herman Hesse once wrote, "Children live on one side of despair, the enlightened on the other". There is a ring of truth in these words.

Hand gestures, as conveyors of the language of implied meaning, have appeared throughout the historical ascendencies of world cultures, especially where oral traditions have been maintained. They appear in Egyptian hieroglyphs, in early Christian art, in Native American traditions, and in the various symbolic hand clasps of secret societies, such as the Freemasons. The familiar V for Victory sign, which becomes an obscene gesture when the palm is reversed, has its origin in the amputation of the first two fingers of captured medieval European archers, where the victors would display their intact first two fingers as a gesture of triumph.

An early *Jataka* legend of one of the Buddha's previous lives describes how he enquired of the marital status of a woman by displaying a closed fist; in reply she showed him her empty hand. However it was not until the advent of Indian sculpture, around the third century BC, that the *mudra* became an expression in classical Indian art. The first Buddhist images were sculpted in Mathura and Gandhara around the second century AD, and it was only during this period that the *mudra*, or indeed any physical representation of the Buddha image, came to prominence. The Mahayana period of Buddhist art, exemplified in the early cave temples of Ajanta and Ellora, display a great simplicity in the depictions of Buddhist hand *mudras*. Here the main *mudras* which appear on sculptural forms are the five basic hand gestures of the Buddha, which later became the defining *mudras* of the Five Buddha Families.

Early tantric literature, such as the *Guhyasamaja Tantra* (*circa* sixth or seventh century AD), reveals a tradition of secret signs, phrases and glances of initiates within a particular tantric lineage. Most of the main Buddhist tantras were revealed during the eighth and ninth centuries, and during this period the various systems of *mudras* evolved as ritual expressions of different lineages.

In later Vajrayana Buddhism, with its all encompassing symbolism, the *mudra* variations proliferated to accomodate an increasing number of ritual symbols and metaphysical meanings. Several hundred *mudras* are probably defined within the Vajrayana pantheon, although only a small number are prominent in iconographical forms. Lists of twenty-four or thirty-six different *mudras* are common in Hindu, Buddhist, and Jain tantric traditions.

In classical Indian dance and the martial art traditions of India and the Far East, the various *mudras* also evolved into highly sophisticated gestural languages. The Newari Vajracharya dance tradition of the Kathmandu valley, now nearing the brink of extinction, exemplifies the ritual use of *mudra, asana,* and dance movement to the accompaniment of ritual song and melodic structure (*raga*) in its invocation of the Newari Buddhist deities. The eight great *mudras* (*ashta mahamudra*) listed by the Newari tradition are the *mudras* of Vajradhatu, Vajrasattva, Amitabha, Vairochana, Vajradhara, Dharmachakra, Abhaya, and the *vajra*

mudra. The Japanese Buddhist tradition also commonly lists eight principal *mudras*.

Certain hand gestures are known as *hasta* (Tib. *phyag*), meaning 'hand', and are not included in the lists as Buddhist *mudras*. Both Hindu and Buddhist traditions describe the twenty digits of the hands and feet as the four thumbs and sixteen fingers. Various symbolic meanings are applied to these, such as the four immeasurables (compassion, love, sympathetic joy, and equanimity), the sixteen emptinesses (*shunyata*), and the sixteen digits or days of the moon between new moon and full moon. Taken as a group of ten fingers, the hands represent the Five Buddhas (right) and their consorts (left), the ten symbolic prongs of the *vajra*, the ten stages and powers of a bodhisattva, the ten perfections, and the ten virtues.

In Buddhist tantra, the right hand symbolises the male aspect of compassion or skilful means, and the left hand represents the female aspect of wisdom or emptiness. Ritual hand-held attributes, such as the *vajra* and bell, *vajra* and lotus, *damaru* and bell, *damaru* and *khatvanga*, arrow and bow, curved knife and skull-cup, sword and shield, hook and rope snare, etc., placed in the right and left hands respectively, symbolise the union of the active male aspect of skilful means with the contemplative female aspect of wisdom.

In Hindu tantra a similar distinction is made between the 'male' right hand and the 'female' left hand, where the tantras of the god Ishvara (Shiva) are known as the 'right-hand path' (*dakshina marg*), and those of the goddess Devi (Shakti), as the 'left-hand path' (*vama marg*). The clockwise right-hand path is considered auspicious, and in Indian society men and their male attributes are always positioned on the right. The anticlockwise female left-hand path is considered inauspicious, and is taken to its extreme in the left-hand rituals of Shakti worship, as rituals for the dead, black magic, and the necromantic rites performed in cremation grounds on the dark nights of the moon. In both Hinduism and Buddhism the goddess is always placed on the left side of the male deity, where she 'sits on his left thigh, while her lord places his left arm over her left shoulder and dallies with her left breast'. The widespread taboo and deprecation accorded to the left hand as dark, female, inferior, and 'not right', makes a fascinating study. In Latin the right hand is known as 'dexter', suggesting dexterity, skill, adroitness and ability. The left hand is known as 'sinistral', meaning sinister, malignant, or of evil omen. In Vajrayana Buddhism the right-hand path represents the 'father tantra' aspect emphasising skilful means, and the left-hand path represents the 'mother tantra' aspect emphasising wisdom. In representations of the Buddha image, the right hand often makes an active *mudra* of skilful means – the earth-touching, protection, fearlessness, wish-granting or teaching *mudra*; whilst the left hand often remains in the passive *mudra* of meditative equipoise, resting in the lap and symbolising meditation on emptiness or wisdom.

In Vajrayana Buddhism each of the five fingers on each hand represents one of the Five Buddhas, with their corresponding colours, directions, elements, syllables, attributes, and qualities. The thumb is identified with the syllable *Om*

Plate 73: *Mudras* made by combining both hands

representing Vairochana; the first or forefinger has the seed-syllable *Hum* of Akshobhya; the second or middle finger has the syllable *Tram* of Ratnasambhava; the third or ring finger has the syllable *Hri* of Amitabha; and the fourth or little finger has the syllable *A* of Amoghasiddhi. When the tips of the four fingers are closed or grouped around the top of the thumb and viewed from above, they form a natural mandala with the central thumb tip representing Vairochana, and each of the four fingertips representing Akshobhya, Ratnasambhava, Amitabha, and Amoghasiddhi in their respective mandala positions. Similarly each of the five fingers represents a psychic nerve (*nadi*), which connects with a channel-wheel and carries the energies of the five winds, elements, aggregates, senses, delusions and wisdoms.

The hands of the deity Kalachakra have a highly symbolic meaning. The fifteen individual finger and thumb joints of each of Kalachakra's twenty-four hands give rise to a total of 360 phalanxes or finger joints. This symbolises the 360 days of the year as a twelve-month lunar cycle, and the 360 divisions of the day – each divided into sixty breaths, making a total of 21,600 breaths in a twenty-four-hour day. Half of this number during a twelve-hour period – 10,800 – gives rise to the sacred number of 108. Each of Kalachakra's fingers is coloured black, red, and white on the underside of their phalanxes from the palms outwards, symbolising the mind (black), speech (red), and body (white) of the deity. The back of Kalachakra's fingers are coloured to represent the five elements and their attributes. The thumb is yellow representing the earth element, the first finger is the white of the water element, the middle finger is the red of the fire element, the ring finger is the black of the air element, and the little finger is the green of the space element. The *Kalachakra Tantra* differs from most other tantric systems in its placement and colours of the five elements, Five Buddhas, and their attributes and qualities.

The *nirmanakaya* and *sambhogakaya* forms of Buddhas and bodhisattvas are endowed with the thirty-two major signs or marks of enlightened beings, several of which refer to the hands and feet. The soles of the feet are level indicating equanimity, and marked with a thousand-spoked wheel representing the thousand *dharmas* or methods of the Buddha's teachings. The palms and soles are rounded and soft, indicating great compassion and freedom from prejudice. The arms and hands of a Buddha reach to below his knees, symbolising his boundless generosity. The hands and feet are pliant, indicating service to others, and healing abilities. The fingers are long and slender, indicating virtue. And the fingers and toes have a fine skin webbing at their bases, the eight webs between the fingers symbolising the Noble Eightfold Path which leads to the attainment of Buddhahood.

On painted images the palms of the hand are rarely marked with any of the major lines of the human hand, although occasionally the heart, head, and life lines may be depicted on sculpted images. Most commonly a curved 'X-shape' is outlined in the centre of the palm, indicating the union of the mound of Venus – defined by the crease of the lifeline around the base of the thumb – with the Lunar mound on the outer edge of the palm. A diamond shape may also be outlined in the palm, formed from the union of the two lower mounds of Venus and the Moon with two upper mounds formed from the union of the Jupiter and Saturn mounds under the first and second finger, and the Sun and Mercury mounds under the third and fourth fingers. This symmetrical diamond indicates the four major hand lines of life, fate, head, and heart. The auspicious insignia of an eight or thousand-spoked wheel is often painted within this diamond, or at the centre of the open palms and soles of divinely marked Buddha forms. The slender and subtle shape of the palm, fingers and fingernails, represents the refined qualities of the artistic, psychic or spiritual hand. The palms and soles of deities are often painted in a complementary and lighter tone than the general skin colour of the deity. This is probably derived from the paler skin pigmentation found on the hands and feet of dark-skinned Indian peoples, and also from the female practice of staining the palms with henna dye. On dark wrathful forms this colour contrast may be sharply delineated.

Plates 73 and 74 illustrate the principal *mudras* and hand gestures (*hasta*) depicted in iconographical images of the deities. The extensive and continuous gestures and movements of the hands employed during liturgical rituals have a highly symbolic fluidity of meanings. There are gestures to represent *bija*-syllables, such as *Om A Hum* symbolising body, speech, and mind, or *Dza Hum Bam Ho* symbolising the evoking, absorbing, stabilising, and dissolving of the meditational deity. And there are *mudras* to represent such listings as the Lords of the Three Families, the Five Buddhas, the principal offerings of the mandala, and the eight or sixteen offering goddesses.

Plate 73

Illustrated on this page are examples of the major *mudras* formed by combining both hands. Across the top row are four examples of the *mudra* of 'turning the wheel of dharma' or *dharmachakra mudra* (Tib. *chos kyi 'khor lo'i phyag rgya*). This teaching *mudra* derives from Shakyamuni Buddha's first sermon on the Four Noble Truths at the Deer Park in Sarnath. The thumb and index finger of both hands touch at their tips to form a circle, representing the wheel formed from the union of wisdom and method or skilful means. The three extended fingers of the right hand – the middle, ring, and little fingers – symbolise the three *yanas* or vehicles of the Buddha's teachings: that of the *shravaka* or 'hearers', of the *pratyekabuddhas* or 'solitary realisers', and of the *mahayana* or 'great vehicle'. The three extended fingers of the left hand symbolise the three scopes or capacities – small, medium, and large – of beings following these three *yanas*. The three fingers of both hands also symbolise the Three Jewels of Buddha, dharma, and sangha. The hands are held in front of the heart with the right palm facing outwards, representing the 'method' aspect of the transmission of the teachings to others, and the left palm facing inwards indicating the 'wisdom' aspect gained through realisation of the teachings within oneself. On early Buddha images the left hand often holds a corner of Buddha's monastic robe, symbolising the inner teaching of renunciation. In Sarnath museum near Benares the guides explain, with the aid of a loosely knotted handkerchief, how the 'knot of appearances' may be untied by the rotation of the hands in *dharmachakra mudra*, whilst holding each end of the handkerchief between both fingers and thumbs. The *dharmachakra mudra* is the principal teaching *mudra* of the Buddha, reflecting his teachings from the heart. Many Buddha forms, such as Vairochana, Shakyamuni, Dipankara, and Maitreya, display this *mudra*, along with many Indian and Tibetan masters, such as Atisha, Asanga, Tsongkhapa, and Sakya Pandita. The drawing in the upper right corner shows the hands reversed in *dharmachakra mudra* and holding the stems of two lotus blossoms, which may bear the particular emblems of the lama or teacher depicted. This reversal emphasises the simultaneous teachings of wisdom and compassion. The first three drawings in the second row illustrate variations of the *dharmachakra mudra,* indicating the gestures of explanation and argumentation.

The drawing on the far right of the second row and in the third row below it show two examples of the enlightenment *mudra* of Vairochana Buddha, known as *bodhyangi mudra* (Tib. *byang chub mchog gi phyag rgya*), or *vajra mudra* (Tib. *rdo rje phyag rgya*). Here the index or 'vajra' finger of the left hand, representing the *vajra* nature of Akshobhya, is held within the 'lotus' of the right fist in a gesture of sexual union. This symbolises the perfection of wisdom – as the *vajra* finger of the left hand – in union with the five perfections of skilful means, which is represented by the enclosing fingers of the right hand. A variation of this *mudra* has the thumb enclosed within the centre of the closed fist, symbolising Vairochana at the centre of the mandala surrounded by the Buddhas of the four directions. When Vairochana appears as one of the Five Buddhas in mandala he is represented in *dharmachakra mudra*, but when he appears as the primordial or Adi Buddha in the Yoga Tantra mandalas he displays the *bodhyangi mudra* as Lord of all Five Buddha Families. This *mudra* is also known as *jnana mudra* (Tib. *ye shes phyag rgya*), as the five fingers symbolise the knowledges or wisdoms of all Five Buddhas. The somewhat general term 'vajra mudra' takes a variety of forms. In Newari Buddhism the *vajra mudra* is formed by joining the tips of the first and fourth fingers in the meditative gesture of *dhyana mudra*, whilst holding down the second and third finger of each hand with the thumbs.

The four drawings on the centre left of rows three and four illustrate examples of the *vajrahumkara mudra,* formed by the crossing of the right wrist over the left wrist with the palms facing inwards. The name *vajrahumkara* (Tib. *rdo rje hum mdzad*) denotes the wrathful form of Samvara or Shiva, who is also known as Humkara or Trailokyavijaya. Humkara means sounding the syllable *Hum,* and *kara* also refers to a wrist bracelet. The prefix *vajra* means, belonging to the Vajra Buddha Family, of which Akshobhya is the lord. Many of the semi-wrathful *yidam* deities that emanate from Akshobhya, such as Chakrasamvara, Vajrahumkara, Hevajra, Kalachakra, and Guhyasamaja display the *vajrahumkara mudra,* usually

with their main arms locked around their consorts in divine embrace – whilst holding the polarity symbols of *vajra* and bell as the union of method and wisdom. Vajradhara, the *dharmakaya* form of the Adi Buddha who reveals the tantric transmissions, also displays this *mudra* whilst holding the *vajra* and bell. The posture adopted in *vajrahumkara mudra* is one of power, as in the stance of a warrior sounding the syllable *Hum* of Akshobhya – the lord of *vajra*-wrath, energy, and transmuted anger. As the *mudra* of the great embrace or 'seal' of the consort, the 'male' right hand crossing over the 'female' left hand at the wrist symbolises the union of compassion or skilful means with wisdom, the union of great bliss and emptiness, and the attainment of 'clear light' (Tib. *'od gsal*) and the 'illusory body' (Tib. *sgyu lus*) in the completion stage of Highest Yoga Tantra. In the upper two drawings on the left of the third row the hands are drawn in the *vajrahumkara mudra* without the attributes of the *vajra* and bell. The first drawing shows unadorned hands, with the middle finger and thumb touching in the gesture of 'snapping the fingers', or sounding the syllable *Hum.* The second drawing shows empty, braceleted hands, with the index finger and thumb nearly touching, making the symbolic gesture of holding the *vajra* and bell. The crossing of the right arm over the left reflects the interlocking leg posture of *vajrasana*, or 'reversed full lotus' posture. In the fourth row below are illustrated two drawings of hands holding the *vajra* and bell in *vajrahumkara mudra*. The dominance of the right '*vajra*' hand over the left 'bell' hand represents the outward manifestation of method, compassion, or skilful means, over the inner left hand of wisdom or meditation on emptiness. When the palms of the hand face outwards the *mudra* is known as *trailokyavijaya mudra* (Tib. *'jig rten gsum las rnam par rgyal ba'i phyag rgya*), or *mudra* of 'victory over the three worlds'.

Second from the right in the third row and on the far right of the fourth row are two variations of *trailokyavijaya mudra*, known either as *bhutadamara mudra* (Tib. *'byung po 'dul byed phyag rgya*), or *humkara mudra* (Tib. *hum mdzad kyi phyag rgya*). Bhutadamara, meaning 'spirit subduer', is a four-armed form of Vajrapani, who makes this *mudra* with his two principal arms. *Humkara,* as in the previous example, means sounding the syllable *Hum.* In this *mudra,* illustrated, the palms of the hand are held outwards, with the little fingers linked to form the shape of a chain. The two hands resemble Garuda's wings, with the index fingers of Akshobhya's syllable *Hum* pointing outwards in a threatening gesture. The upper drawing in the third row shows the right wrist forward, whilst the lower drawing in the fourth row shows the left wrist forward in the *mudra* of Bhutadamara Vajrapani, the subduer of spirits.

Between the fourth and fifth rows are drawn three single hands. On the left is drawn the *varada mudra* (Tib. *mchog sbyin phyag rgya*), or 'boon-granting' *mudra* of supreme generosity and accomplishment. This *mudra* is formed by the right hand being held palm open with the fingers extended; it usually rests upon the right knee of seated deities. It is the *mudra* of Ratnasambhava, the yellow Buddha of the south, and of deities that hold wish-granting objects – such as the citron fruit of Jambhala, the stem of myrobalan of the Medicine Buddha, or the auspicious jewels and substances held by a host of other deities. Both Green and White Tara make this boon-granting gesture with their right hands, which symbolises the bestowal of the realisation of the 'two truths' – relative or conventional truth (Tib. *tha snyad bden pa*), and ultimate truth (Tib. *don dam bden pa*). The hand in the centre, with the first three fingers extended and the thumb and little finger joined, is a variation of the *tripitaka mudra* (Tib. *sde snod gsum phyag rgya*) or *triratna mudra* (Tib. *dkon mchog gsum phyag rgya*). *Tripitaka* means the 'three baskets', or the collections of Buddhist teachings on ethics (*Vinaya Pitaka*), meditation (*Sutra Pitaka*), and wisdom (*Abhidharma Pitaka*). *Triratna* refers to the Three Jewels of Buddha, dharma and sangha. The third drawing on the right shows a right hand with the thumb and second finger touching. This hand gesture (*hasta*), is commonly depicted on deities holding ritual implements – a bow, an arrow, a rope snare, or the shaft of a weapon such as a trident, spear, axe, or hammer.

In the fifth row are drawn four examples of hands held with the palms facing together. The first drawing on the left shows the palms pressed together in the gesture of salutation, adoration, or prayer. This *mudra*, commonly known as the *namaskara mudra*, is probably the earliest of all Indian *mudras*. As a gesture of respectful greeting or *namaskar* in Indian society, this gesture parallels the Western handshake in its common usage. The palms folded together at the heart is a symbol of friendship, supplication, respect, devotion, and non-violence. In Buddhism it forms the *anjali mudra* (Tib. *thal mo sbyar ba phyag rgya*), or *samputanjali mudra* of prayer or adoration, which is most specifically represented in the iconography of the four, eight, and one-thousand armed bodhisattva of compassion, Avalokiteshvara. The second, third, and fourth drawings from the left of the fifth row illustrate three variations of Avalokiteshvara's hands holding the wish-fulfilling jewel to his heart.

The first drawing on the left of the bottom row shows the 'treasure box' *mudra* (Tib. *sgrom bu phyag rgya*), or the 'space treasury' gesture of *akashanidhana mudra* (Tib. *nam mkha' mdzod phyag rgya*), symbolising the *dharmadhatu* or 'sphere of the dharma' within Buddha's heart. The second drawing from the left again shows Avalokiteshvara's hands in *anjali mudra* holding the precious jewel. Third from the left are two drawings illustrating interlocking *mudras*. The upper drawing illustrates a raised form of the *dhyana mudra* (Tib. *mnyam bzhag phyag rgya*) of meditative contemplation, created by forming the circle of method and wisdom with the index fingers and thumbs whilst interlocking the remaining three fingers. The lower drawing depicts the *mandala mudra* (Tib. *dkyil 'khor phyag rgya*), symbolising Mt Meru and its four continents. The second and little fingers are held down by the index fingers and thumbs respectively – representing the four continents; whilst the two ring fingers are placed upwards back-to-back, symbolising Mt Meru at the centre. The last drawing in the bottom right corner illustrates the *jalandhara mudra*, which is a specific Hatha Yoga posture adopted by the Buddhist and Hindu mahasiddha, Jalandhara.

Plate 74

Illustrated in this drawing are examples of mainly single hand *mudras*. In the top row are drawings of the 'earth-pressing' *mudra* (bhumisparsha), or 'earth-touching' *mudra* of *bhumi-akramana mudra* (Tib. *sa gnon phyag rgya*), more commonly known as the 'earth witness' *mudra*. This *mudra*, formed with all five fingers extended to touch the ground, symbolises the Buddha's enlightenment under the bodhi tree, when he summoned the earth goddess, Sthavara, to bear witness to his attainment of enlightenment. The right hand, placed upon the right knee in earth-pressing *mudra*, and complemented by the left hand – which is held flat in the lap in the *dhyana mudra* of meditation – symbolises the union of method and wisdom, samsara and nirvana, and the realisations of the conventional and ultimate truths. In this posture Shakyamuni overcame the obstructions of Mara whilst meditating on emptiness. *Bhumisparsha mudra* is characteristic of many Buddha, deity, and human forms, particularly those of Shakyamuni and Akshobhya Buddha. The first four drawings in the top row show examples of the *bhumisparsha mudra* with fingers extended. The second four drawings to the right show the thumb and first finger touching, with both right and left hands holding the stems of lotus blossoms.

The second row shows four examples of the left hand which is placed in the lap in the *dhyana mudra* (Tib. *mnyam bzhag phyag rgya*), or *samahita mudra* of meditation, symbolising the female left-hand principle of wisdom or meditation on emptiness. Ritual objects, such as a text or *vajra*, may be placed upon the open palm, or more commonly an alms bowl in the case of Buddha forms, symbolising renunciation. The third and fourth rows show seven variations of both hands held in the posture of *dhyana mudra*. The left hand is placed below the right in all seven drawings, symbolising that the accomplishment of method or skilful means has to arise from a direct understanding of wisdom or emptiness. In several of these drawings the tips of the thumbs are placed together; this represents the union of the 'mind of enlightenment' as the two psychic channels of white and red *bodhichitta* which terminate in the thumbs.

The first two drawings on the left of the fifth row depict examples of the *nidrata hasta* gesture of 'royal ease', where the inclined body of a seated deity is supported by a hand placed flat on the ground. The third drawing shows the threatening forefinger of *tarjani* gesture (Tib. *sdigs mdzub*), with the raised index finger of Akshobhya's syllable *Hum* pointing in a threatening manner. On certain wrathful forms, such as Vajrakilaya, a tongue of flames twists around the raised index finger in *tarjani* gesture, symbolising the ability to destroy the five obscuring emotions. The fourth drawing shows the second, third, and fourth fingers curled inwards with the index finger making the shape of a hook. This gesture is known as *ankusha hasta* (Tib. *lcags kyu*) or 'iron hook', symbolising the goad used by the mahout or elephant driver to control an elephant. The fifth drawing shows the *vyala hasta*, of pointing towards an object or indicating a principle. The

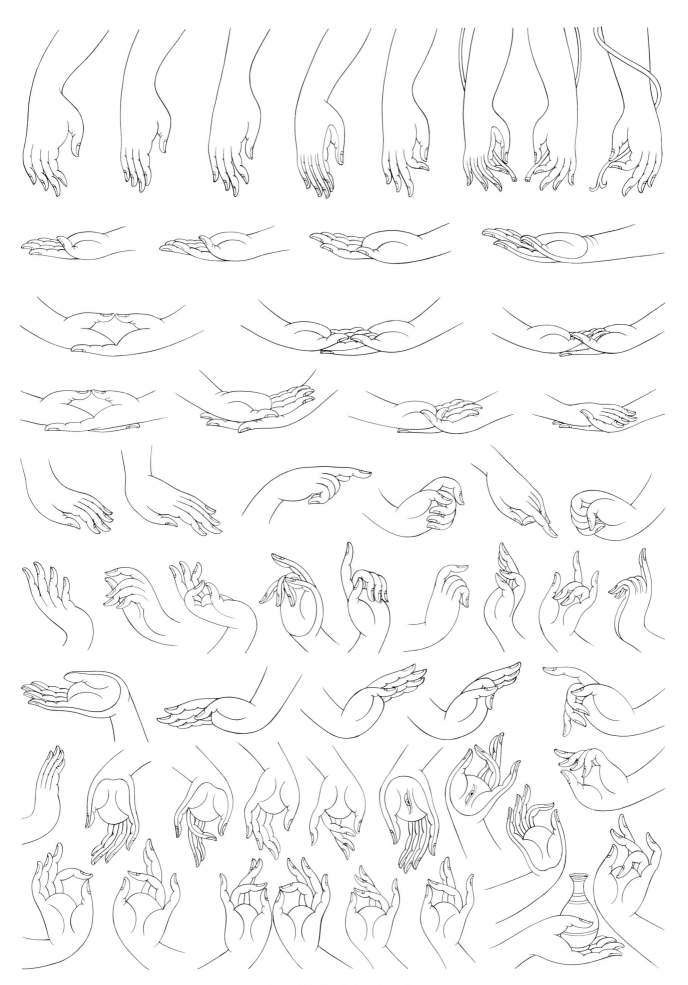

Plate 74: Single hand *mudras*

last drawing on the right of the fifth row depicts the closed fist of the 'stopping or repelling' *mudra*.

The sixth row illustrates nine drawings of the hands of deities in various non-specified iconographical postures. At the centre are two examples of hands making the threatening pointed index finger of *tarjani* gesture. The *tarjani* (Tib. *sdigs mdzub*) or 'threatening pointer' is not actually classified as a *mudra*, and is referred to here as a 'gesture'.

The first drawing on the left of the seventh row shows an open-palmed hand facing upwards in the *abhaya mudra* (Tib. *mi 'jigs pa'i phyag rgya*) of protection, fearlessness, or giving refuge. The second and third drawings show the *varada mudra* (Tib. *mchog sbyin gyi phyag rgya*) of generosity or boon-granting, with the palm facing downwards and the fingers extended. Divine beings, such as the goddess Mahalakshmi, may be depicted circling the hand in this *mudra* and producing a rain of jewels or nectar from the palm. The fourth drawing shows a variation of the *abhaya mudra* of giving refuge, with the thumb and forefinger uniting in the circle of method and wisdom, and the three extended fingers representing the Three Jewels. The last drawing on the right shows another example of the threatening *tarjani* gesture.

In the eighth row, or second row from the bottom, the first drawing on the left shows a right hand held at the heart in *ardha-anjali mudra*, or the gesture of bestowing blessings or half (*ardha*) salutations. The second and fourth drawings depict a right and left open hand in the *varada mudra* of generosity. The third and fifth drawings show two left hands in the *abhaya mudra* of giving refuge. The sixth drawing depicts an open-palmed hand in the *varada mudra* of generosity or boon granting, with an eye in the centre of the palm. Such eye-endowed hands are specific to the deities White Tara and Thousand-Armed Avalokiteshvara. The five extended fingers symbolise the five perfections (*paramita*) of method or skilful means: generosity, morality, patience, effort, and meditative concentration. The eye in the palm symbolises the sixth perfection of wisdom or insight, and its placement in the palm represents how the five perfections of method depend upon, or originate from, the sixth perfection of wisdom. The seventh drawing depicts the left hand of White Tara, with an eye in the palm forming the *abhaya mudra* of protection or giving refuge. Again, the thumb and ring finger touching represents the coincidence of method and wisdom, and the three extended fingers symbolise taking refuge in the Three Jewels of Buddha, dharma, and sangha. The eighth drawing, placed slightly below, shows a right hand with the index finger and thumb forming the teaching gesture of *dharmachakra mudra*. The last drawing on the right depicts a hand in the typical pose of holding a ritual implement.

On the left of the bottom row two pairs of hands are illustrated in the *virtaka mudra* of reasoning, argumentation, or explanation of the teachings. The *virtaka mudra* is formed in the same manner as the *dharmachakra mudra* with the index finger and thumb touching; or in the manner of the *varada mudra* with the third finger and thumb touching. The next two drawings show two left hands in *virtaka* or *varada*

mudra, with the third finger and thumb touching. The last drawing in the bottom right corner illustrates a right hand holding a crystal vase of nectar, whilst the left hand makes the gesture of snapping the fingers.

Plate 75

Illustrated in this drawing are examples of hands holding ritual implements. Across the top row are six variations of hands holding a five-pronged *vajra*, which symbolises the ultimate realisation of all Five Buddha wisdoms. The first drawing on the left shows the *vajra* held vertically at the level of the heart. The second drawing shows the *vajra* extended outwards. The third drawing shows the *vajra* held downwards at the level of the knee. The fourth drawing illustrates the right hand of a wrathful deity performing the activity of circling the *vajra* in the ten directions. The long curved nails of this wrathful hand come to a sharp point, like tiger's claws. The fifth drawing shows the hand in *vajra mudra*, with the index and little finger pointing upwards. The sixth drawing in the upper right corner illustrates Vajrasattva's *mudra* of holding the five-pronged *vajra* upright at the level of the heart.

The first drawing in the second row depicts Vajrasattva's gesture of holding the inverted bell or *ghanta* (Tib. *dril bu*) at the level of his hips or navel *chakra*. To the right of this are two further drawings of the bell held outwards and horizontally. In the centre and below the horizontally-held bell is the braceleted hand of a semi-wrathful deity holding a rope noose or *pasha* (Tib. *zhags pa*). Invariably the raised index finger of a hand holding a noose makes the threatening *tarjani* gesture. Rings are worn on the thumb and third finger of this depicted hand. Certain deity descriptions may mention rings being worn on two, three, or all five fingers, which correspond to the colours of the elements or planets. In the Indian tradition rings made of copper are worn to placate the Sun and Mars, brass for Mercury, silver for Venus, gold for Jupiter, bronze or conch for the Moon, lead for Rahu and Ketu, and a hammered iron nail from a horseshoe for Saturn. Above and to the right is a hand displaying and holding a *vajra* at its base. To the right of this is the hand position of Manjushri, holding the hilt of his flaming sword of wisdom. Below this is a left hand in *dhyana mudra* holding a conch shell, symbolising the proclamation of the dharma. Two other hands holding the shafts of ritual implements are drawn to the right and left of the centre in the upper area of this drawing.

Across the upper middle row are four drawings of hands holding ritual daggers, and a skull-cup with curved knife. The first drawing on the left shows the two principal hands of the deity Vajrakilaya holding a three-bladed dagger or *kila* (Tib. *phur bu*), which Vajrakilaya rolls between his palms, its rotating point destroying all malevolent forces, hostile enemies, and obstructions. This dagger is described as being as vast as Mt Meru, representing the pinning down or nailing of the phenomenal universe as Buddha's activity. Around Vajrakilaya's wrists are two bracelets entwined with

Plate 75: Hands holding ritual implements

great *naga* kings or *nagarajas.* The second and third drawings show alternative positions for the single hand-held dagger; in both drawings the threatening *tarjani* gesture is shown. The fourth drawing on the right depicts Mahakala's hands, holding the blood-filled skull-cup in the left hand and the curved flaying knife or *kartri* (Tib. *gri gug*) in the right. The right hand holding the *vajra*-topped *kartri* is in *vajra mudra,* whilst the left hand holding the skull-cup displays the *tarjani* gesture.

Across the lower middle row are examples of hands holding the *damaru* and skull-cup. On the left the right hand of the goddess Vishvamata holds the brocade handle of a *damaru* whilst making the *tarjani* gesture. In the second drawing the *damaru* is held at its centre. To the right are a group of hands holding blood-filled skull-cups. The tilting of the skull-cup in order to drink the blood reflects the Indian custom of pouring liquid from a container directly into one's mouth to avoid contamination or defilment. Below on the right are three drawings: of a hand holding the shaft of a ritual implement, a hand holding a paintbrush, and a left hand in *dhyana mudra* holding the base of a bowl or vase. In the lower right corner are examples of hands holding Tibetan religious texts. The two drawings in the right corner show two left hands in *dhyana mudra* holding folios of Tibetan texts.

In the bottom left and centre are a group of hands playing musical instruments. At the left of the second row from the bottom, are the hands of the mahasiddha Lilapa playing the Indian *shenai* or its Tibetan equivalent (Tib. *rgya gling*). This oboe-like instrument is played with the fingers of the left hand stopping the higher notes, in reverse fashion to the Western oboe or flageolet. To the right of this are the hands of the mahasiddha Naropa playing a short horn (Tib. *rkang gling*), fashioned from an antelope horn. Below this are the hands of one of the offering goddesses of music fingering a transverse bamboo flute. To the right are two drawings of hands fingering the necks of two four-string Central Asian lutes. In the lower left corner is a drawing of the singing posture of the Tibetan yogin Milarepa, or his disciple Rechungpa. A modern theory asserts that Milarepa is pressing with his thumb on a certain nerve behind the right ear, but this practice of pressing the ears forward is a well-established tradition in Indian folk and classical music, and in the ancient Bengali *doha* tradition of singing spontaneous songs of realisation.

Plate 76

Illustrated here are examples of foot postures. In the upper left corner are the feet of the Buddha bearing auspicious marks. The drawing on the left shows the mark of the *dharmachakra* wheel on the sole. The detailed drawing on the right shows swastikas on each of the toes, a thousand-spoked wheel on the upper sole, a jewel-tipped trident on the mid-sole, and an eight-petalled lotus design on the heel. The trident symbolises the Buddhas of the three times – past, present, and future, and the Three Jewels of Buddha, dharma, and sangha. Other designs, such as the eight auspicious symbols or the seven royal jewels, may be depicted on Buddha's footprints – which are frequently carved on stone. The *Vinaya Sutra* relates that these precious marks were formed from the tears of Buddha's repentant female devotee, Amrapati, who wept at his feet.

In the upper right corner are the outlines of the hands and feet of a highly venerated lama, which are occasionally painted on the back surface of an important thangka as part of a consecration ritual (Tib. *rab gnas*). A stupa design inscribed with prayers is more commonly found on the back surface of a consecrated thangka. The hand and foot outlines of a great lama, such as the Dalai Lama or Panchen Lama, may also be painted as an actual thangka. Here the hands and feet are painted in gold, and usually surround the central image of the figure or deity portrayed. The left hand and foot in the drawing are marked with the eight-spoked *dharmachakra.* In the mid-centre is a small drawing of the sole of a foot with splayed toes. The toes of the unshod Indian foot, which have not been constrained by the lifelong habit of wearing constricting shoes, are naturally splayed.

Across the upper mid-centre are two drawings of feet locked in the 'adamantine posture' of *vajrasana* or *vajra-paryanka* (Tib. *rdo rje skyil krung*), with the right foot forward over the left thigh. In the Hindu Hatha Yoga tradition this posture is reversed, with the left foot forward over the right thigh in *padmasana* or 'full lotus' posture. The drawing on the right depicts the outline of the soles and undertoes, which are painted in a paler colour tone than the general body colour.

In the lower half of this page are illustrations of feet in a variety of postures and stances.

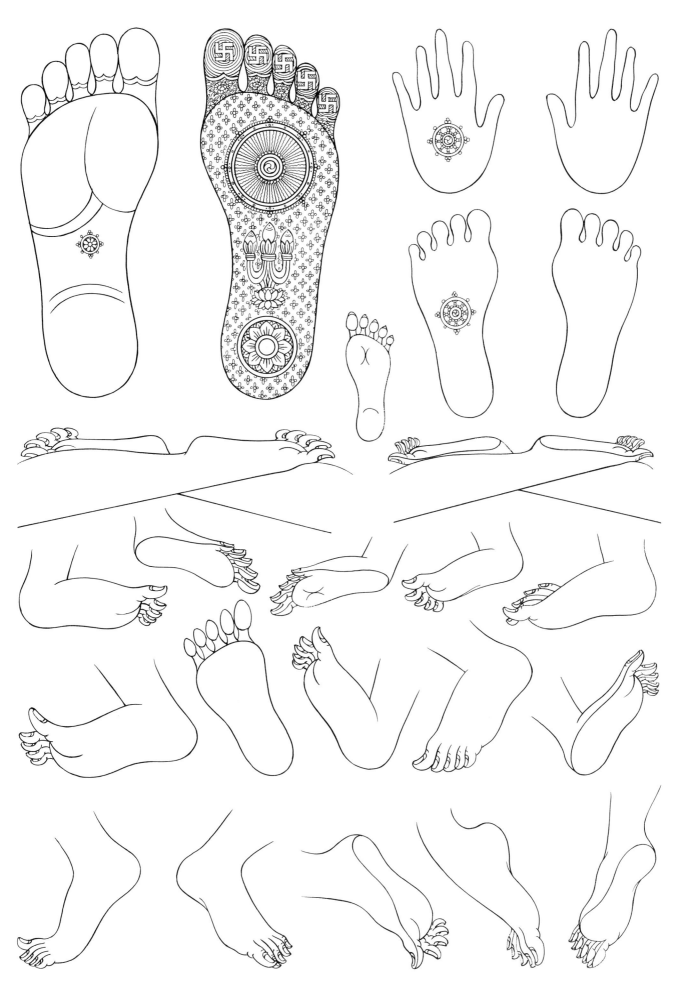

Plate 76: Footprints, handprints and foot postures

Chapter Seven
The Chakravartin and his Seven Precious Possessions

The term *chakravartin*, usually translated as 'universal monarch or emperor', literally means 'wheel-turner' or 'a wheel that travels everywhere without obstruction'. The prefix '*chakra*' or wheel, has various interpretations. It can refer to the fiery wheel of the sun, or the sun god's chariot of two wheels (heaven and earth), which rides through the sky drawn by seven horses, representing the seven days of the week. As an emblem of Vishnu it is the discus, which appears as an auspicious sign on the palms and soles of divine beings. As a unit of land measure the *chakra* refers to the whole of a land's surface area, from coast to coast. This is implied in descriptions of the *chakra* touching the rim of the horizon, or the encircling perimeter of land seen as a disc from a central vantage point. The turning of the wheel symbolises both secular and religious authority; it denotes change, movement, extension, conquest, and the formation of a new ethical and moral order. The deliverance and transmission of the Buddhist teachings are known as 'turning the wheel of dharma'.

When Shakyamuni Buddha was born the great seer Asita interpreted the miraculous events and auspicious marks on the baby's body as divine indications that the child was destined to become either a *chakravartin* or an enlightened Buddha; temporal or spiritual sovereignty lay in the child's destiny. There was a choice, the pendulum could swing either way. It was for this reason that Shakyamuni's father, King Shuddhodana, endeavoured to keep his son away from the harsh realities of life, cocooning him in the opulence of sensual gratification and the illusion that youth, vitality, and beauty are eternal delights. Curiosity beckoned the young prince to venture beyond his golden cage, where he witnessed the god-sent apparitions of old age, disease, and death. The realisation that suffering was man's lot tore asunder the illusory veil of eternalism. What could it profit a man to gain the whole world if in the end one's soul was

lost to old age, disease, and death? In the face of such blatant impermanence there was no longer any choice for the young prince. World domination was the ultimate illusion; only self-enquiry into the root cause of suffering and the nature of the mind – the eternal quest – could lead to the ultimate understanding of reality.

The concept of the *chakravartin* probably arose from the Vaishnavite ideal of the *mahapurusha* or 'great man', which in turn had its origins in the Vedic and Puranic epics of ancient India. Such a being is destined to become a world leader and, like the Buddha, there can only be one *chakravartin* in the world at any one time. Auspicious events and astrological configurations precede the birth of a *chakravartin*, reminding one of the journey of the three Magi to Jesus's birthplace seeking the one 'who would be born king of the Jews'. The role of the Messiah in ancient Judaism also referred to both a temporal and spiritual sovereignty.

Thirty-two major marks and eighty minor marks appear on the body of a *chakravartin*. These include: slightly webbed fingers and toes; retracted sexual organs; a fleshy protuberance (*ushnisha*) on the head; lion-like chest, thighs, and jaws; soft smooth skin; pliant hands and feet; and a thousand-spoked wheel mark on the soles of the feet. The mother of a *chakravartin* usually dies shortly after his birth, as was the case with Queen Maya, Shakyamuni's mother. A total eclipse of the sun is believed to coincide with the death of the *chakravartin* as the sun itself is represented as the personification of the *chakravartin*. The Asiatic concept of the 'solar death' of the *chakravartin* finds a parallel in the midday darkness at Jesus's crucifixion, which is believed to have been caused by a total eclipse of the sun.

The birth of a *chakravartin* heralds the onset of seven wealths or abundances which arise in the realm: a wealth of faith, morality, honesty, modesty, learning, renunciation, and wisdom. At the time of his birth his seven precious jewels or possessions also appear simultaneously: the precious wheel, jewel, queen, minister, elephant, horse, and general. These seven possessions (described in detail below) are the 'property' of the *chakravartin*, and karmically come into existence as his 'mandala'. The wheel and jewel are both symbols of his temporal and spiritual majesty, and the miraculous means of its accomplishment. The horse and elephant, as symbols of inexhaustible speed and strength, are his vehicles. The queen, minister and general are his trinity of love, wisdom, and power; their fidelity, his blessing.

An auxiliary or lesser group of seven royal jewels also accompanies the rule of the *chakravartin*. These are the sword, the *naga* skin, the throne, the robes, the boots, the royal house or palace, and the palace gardens. These seven secondary jewels represent the material inheritance or attributes of the *chakravartin*.

A third group of seven auspicious royal jewels also occur as insignia or emblems of the *chakravartin*'s possessions. These comprise the rhinoceros horn, the square earrings of the minister, a branch of precious coral, the round earrings of the queen, the insignia of the general, a pair of elephants tusks, and a triple-eyed gem enclosed in a trefoil gold mount. These seven symbols represent the precious horse, minister, wheel, queen, general, elephant, and jewel respectively. As a single or composite group these seven insignia are very commonly placed as offerings before deities, usually appearing amongst piles or lines of coloured, oval-shaped jewels.

The investiture of the *chakravartin* as ruler was ceremoniously conferred by anointing him with water drawn from the four directional oceans or lakes surrounding his realm. Similarly tantric initiation into a mandala requires the disciple to be sprinkled with water from five vases placed at the mandala's centre and four cardinal directions. The mandala palace itself is modelled on the divine four-gated palace of the *chakravartin*. The Dravidian temples of southern India, the Mesopotamian ziggurat, the Chinese imperial palace of the forbidden city, and the royal Persian palace, all comprise architectural ideals comparable to the divine abode of the *chakravartin* or universal monarch.

Alexander the Great, whose thirteen-year conquest extended his empire westward from Greece and Egypt to the Indus river, may have been seen as a secular *chakravartin*. Yet his untimely death from fever in 323 BC, at the age of thirty-three, put an end to his potential divinity. The Indian Buddhist emperor Ashoka, who ruled over two thirds of India between 273 and 232 BC, was a far more worthy candidate. A bloodthirsty military campaign sickened the victorious Ashoka. Renouncing violence he adopted Buddhism, and from his capital city of Pataliputra (near modern day Patna in Bihar state) he sent out Buddhist monks to proclaim the dharma in all directions. Historically, after Shakyamuni himself, the emperor Ashoka was the most important figure in the propagation of Buddhism. Around the beginning of the second century AD, Kanishka, the emperor of the Kushana dynasty, advanced Ashoka's example. From his capital city of Purushupura (now Peshawar), Kanishka introduced Buddhism into Afghanistan and the Swat,

Gandhara, and Kashmir areas of northwest India (now Pakistan). From Gandhara some of the earliest Buddha images evolved, interestingly sculpted in the Greek style by the descendants of Alexander the Great.

The *chakravartin* is, first and foremost, a righteous universal monarch who rules purely through compassion and wisdom. The divine human form realises its perfection in the non-dual identification of the *chakravartin* and bodhisattva ideals.

Just as the *sambhogakaya* forms of bodhisattvas and goddesses are endowed with the thirty-two major and eighty minor marks of a divine being or *chakravartin*, so are they likewise attired in the silk robes and ornamental gold jewellery of the ancient Indian kings, princes or princesses. Bodhisattvas are the 'spiritual sons' or princes of the Five Buddhas, they are crowned by them, and as symbols of their investiture bear the image or syllable of their parent Buddha on the crown of their heads. Their golden thrones are modelled on the square-based pedestal thrones of ancient Indian kings, and frequently placed before their thrones are the seven insignia of the *chakravartin*. Bodhisattvas and goddesses are apparelled in the thirteen *sambhogakaya* ornaments of a *chakravartin*, five of which are fashioned of coloured silk, and eight of which are wrought of precious stones and metals. The five silk attires consist of a white upper bodice with gold-embroidered patterns made from Benares silk or muslin (*kashikamsuka*); a 'rainbow' or multicoloured skirt or dhoti (*panchalika*); a yellow silk scarf worn as a sash over one shoulder; a variegated ribbon binding the crown or tiara; and a long blue scarf draped over the shoulders.

The eight precious jewellery ornaments consist of a five-jewelled tiara made of natural and divine jewels; golden earrings; a short necklace around the neck; a medium necklace reaching to the level of the heart; a long necklace reaching below the navel; bracelets and armlets; anklets; and a jewelled belt with little silver bells. On peaceful bodhisattvas and goddesses these eight jewelled ornaments are usually condensed into a group of six, representing the six perfections or *paramitas* of patience (earrings), generosity (necklaces), discipline (bracelets, armlets, and anklets), effort (belt), meditation (jewelled tiara), and wisdom (a divine or flaming jewel above the hair-knots). Semi-wrathful male deities wear the equivalent earrings, necklaces, bracelets, armlets, and anklets, and belt, as bone ornaments, with a bone wheel at the crown of the head symbolising meditation, and cemetery ash applied to the forehead symbolising wisdom. Semi-wrathful female goddesses wear only the five bone ornaments; they are not adorned with cemetery ash as their form itself symbolises the perfection of wisdom.

The attributes of the *chakravartin* are very ancient symbols, dating back to before the time of Shakyamuni – more than two and a half thousand years ago. Other auspicious groups, such as the eight auspicious symbols and the eight symbols of good fortune, originated at a similar point in time. Their meaning and relevance have inevitably become diluted over the course of more than twenty-five centuries; the concept of monarchy itself has virtually collapsed over the last few decades. Yet the transposition of these symbols has remained intact, even though their original utilitarian purposes may now seem extremely redundant.

When Buddhism entered Tibet from India its entire symbolic content entered simultaneously. The depiction of Indian Buddhist deities dressed in the flimsy silks of Indian royalty was a foreign import into Tibet. The same is true of its vast array of jewelled ornaments, offerings, symbols, and motifs. They became indigenous by the philosophical values placed upon them as 'pure symbols', self-existent in their own right as visual encapsulations of the Buddhist teachings. Some fashions change, other traditions endure; hopefully the Buddhas will never be depicted in denim and trainers. The wheel moves on, yet it is always circular and cannot exist without its hub, spokes, and rim.

THE SEVEN POSSESSIONS OF THE CHAKRAVARTIN

The Precious Wheel
(Skt. *chakraratna*; Tib. *'khor lo rin po che*)

The precious thousand-spoked wheel or *chakra* is the first and greatest possession of the *chakravartin*. It is extremely bright and made of the gold found in the Jambud river of our world continent, Jambudvipa. Its thousand spokes symbolise the thousand dharmas of the Buddhas, and the thousand Buddhas of our present era (*bhadrakalpa*). Yet pictorially the wheel is usually depicted as an eight-spoked wheel, representing the eight directions and the Noble Eightfold Path which the Buddha set in motion.

The wheel is described as being vast, five hundred leagues (*yojanas*) in diameter, and with a radiance like the sun. It is actually the vehicle or chariot of the *chakravartin*, its magnificence overwhelms everything which comes within its path. On its hub the four divisions of the *chakravartin*'s army – infantry, cavalry, elephants, and chariots – may traverse vast distances across the heavens, travelling a hundred thousand leagues in one day. It is also capable of inter-dimensional travel. With its aid the *chakravartin* is able to journey to all of the continents surrounding Mt Meru. Like our present day flying saucers, 'a modern myth of discs seen in the sky', the precious wheel seems capable of making a 'quantum leap' into other parallel universes – co-existent, yet invisible.

The *Kalachakra Tantra* describes one such 'parallel universe' – the kingdom of Shambhala. Theoretically calculated to be located in Baghdad, Central Asia, Russia, Mongolia, or Tibet, the kingdom of Shambhala preserves the pristine lineage of the *Kalachakra* teachings which Shakyamuni revealed to Suchandra (or Chandrabhadra), the first king of Shambhala. The Shambhala lineage passes through seven great religious kings, and twenty-five Kulika kings, or enlightened universal monarchs (*chakravartins*). Each of these rulers has a lifespan of one hundred years. Our present time coincides with the reign of the twenty-first Kulika king. It is predicted that a great battle will take place during the reign of the last of the twenty-five kings, around the year AD 2327,

when the 'believers' (Buddhists) will triumph over the 'barbarians' or 'non-believers' (Moslems).

The golden wheel is a symbol of both temporal and spiritual sovereignty. The creator god, Brahma, presented Shakyamuni with a thousand-spoked wheel immediately after he attained enlightenment. It is an emblem of Tibet's great religious kings, and an attribute of many of the previous Dalai Lama incarnations.

The Precious Jewel (Skt. *maniratna*; Tib. *nor bu rin po che*)

The eight-faceted precious jewel or wish-granting gem fulfils all of the desires of the *chakravartin* and those who come within its sphere of radiance. Like the red Kaustubha gem, which surfaced during the churning of the ocean, and which Vishnu and later Krishna wore as a breast ornament, the precious jewel possesses eight magical qualities: its radiance illuminates the darkness of night; it cools when the days are hot, and warms when the days are cold; it causes rain to fall or a spring to appear when one is thirsty; it brings to fruition everything that its holder desires; it controls the *nagas*, preventing floods, hailstorms, and torrential rain; it emits various coloured lights which heal emotional afflictions; its radiance cures all of the diseases of those who are in its range of healing light; it prevents untimely death, ensuring that death by natural causes occurs in the auspicious sequence of grandfather, father, and finally son.

The jewel is described as being smooth, eight-faceted, as radiant as the sun, and fashioned of lapis lazuli like the *vaidurya* jewel. It is often borne on the back of the precious horse, or held in the right hand of the precious minister.

The Precious Queen
(Skt. *raniratna*; Tib. *btsun mo rin po che*)

The precious queen is the most beautiful of women. Her body has the natural scent of camphor, and her breath has the fragrance of the *utpala* lotus exuding its sweetness at night. She possesses the thirty-two marks of a divine woman, which include long and gentle fingers; a straight body; clear bright eyes; eyelashes like the 'finest of cows'; dark curving eyebrows; pure red lips; forty neatly arranged teeth; a slim soft tongue; beautiful black hair; three creases on her neck; and long ear lobes. She has firm round breasts, soft protruding red nipples, a lotus-shaped navel, and a pubic mound like the back of a tortoise. She is youthful and lusty, like a sixteen-year-old virgin.

Luckily she also possesses the eight perfect qualities of a lady. She is faithfully devoted to her lord, the *chakravartin*, and thinks of no other man. She is not jealous if the *chakravartin* displays amorous favour towards other women. Her womb will bear many healthy sons. She works for the welfare of all in her lord's kingdom. She has an innate feminine wisdom, and always supports her lord's plans. She always speaks the truth and uses no frivolous words. She is not attracted to sensual objects or stimuli, and she holds no false views.

The precious queen is adored by her subjects, and she in turn worships and respects her husband, the *chakravartin*.

Together they bring peace, prosperity, and happiness, establishing stability and harmony in the kingdom, their unity and a lineage of male offspring providing hope for the future.

The Precious Minister
(Skt. *parinayakaratna*; Tib. *blon po rin po che*)

The precious minister is endowed with the eye of the gods, which can see beyond a thousand leagues. His intelligence is as sharp as a razor, with a great patience and listening ability which assure perfect counsel to the *chakravartin*. The minister desires to do only good works to promote the dharma, protecting and benefitting all beings. In the service of his lord he is able to locate buried treasure to swell the royal coffers. In this capacity he is also known as the 'minister for home economics'. A cultured diplomat, he excels at political economy, affairs of state, social welfare, religious duties, and ethics, clearly understanding the wishes of the *chakravartin*. The precious minister often bears a wish-granting gem or treasury box in his right hand.

The Precious Elephant
(Skt. *hastiratna*; Tib. *glang po rin po che*)

The precious elephant has the strength of a thousand ordinary elephants. He is the lord of all bull elephants, as large as a mountain; his skin as white as snow. The fragrance which exudes from his forehead glands entices all other elephants towards him. He possesses seven limbs – four legs, a trunk, and two powerful tusks. His trunk, tail and scrotum reach to the ground – which is a curious description as an elephant's genitals are naturally retracted. One of the thirty-two major signs of a Buddha's body is that his sexual organs are 'retracted like an elephant's'. Sometimes the precious elephant is also described as having six tusks like Airavata, Indra's elephant, which arose at the churning of the ocean.

In battle the precious elephant is inexhaustible, fearless, and unassailable, with an endurance and gait that make him capable of circumambulating the continent of Jambudvipa thrice in a single day.

In peacetime he is wise and dignified, his step serene and gentle, possessing great majesty and beauty. As a ceremonial mount of the *chakravartin*, he is perfectly obedient to his master, following his mental directions with perfect telepathic accord. He wears a golden jewelled necklace around his neck and can be led by the thinnest of cords. Often he is depicted carrying the precious wheel or the cloth-covered alms bowl of Shakyamuni Buddha on his back.

The Precious Horse
(Skt. *ashvaratna*; Tib. *rta mchog rin po che*)

The precious horse bears the thirty-two marks of a divine steed. Like the windhorse he travels fast and tirelessly, and is capable of encircling the continent of Jambudvipa three times in a single day. His body is white like a swan, and adorned with the golden jewelled trappings of the gods. In some traditions he is described as being the blue-black colour of a peacock's neck, with the ability to traverse all of the four continents in an instant.

His form is perfect, endowed with a soft mane of ten thousand hairs, and a long flowing tail like a comet. He speedily bears the *chakravartin* with royal ease; his tireless hooves are silent, light, and unfaltering. The precious horse often bears the precious jewel on his saddle, representing the spreading of auspicious blessings throughout the *chakravartin*'s realm, for wherever the jewel travels it brings all of its divine qualities in its wake.

The Precious General
(Skt. *senapatiratna*; Tib. *dmag dpon rin po che*)

The precious general wears the armour and helmet of an ancient warrior, forged of metal plates bound together with leather thongs. In his right hand he holds an upraised sword and in his left a shield, symbolising his readiness both to wage war and defend the kingdom. His military prowess ensures that he is never defeated in battle, having attained mastery of the sixty-four strategic arts of war. His will is attuned to that of the *chakravartin*, knowing the exact wishes of his ruler. He fights for truth and justice; having abandoned unvirtuous acts he causes no harm to other beings. When the righteouness of dharma has been established throughout the realm, and the peace of wisdom and compassion prevails, the general removes his armour and appears as the 'precious householder'.

THE SEVEN SECONDARY POSSESSIONS OF THE CHAKRAVARTIN

The seven secondary possessions of the *chakravartin* comprise a sword, *naga* skin, palace, robes, gardens, throne, and boots. These seven Buddhist symbols of royalty were adopted from the ancient Indian concept of the seven emblems of royalty, known as the *rajakakuda*. These seven original Indian emblems were a sword, a white umbrella, a crown, boots, a fly whisk, a sceptre, and a throne.

Although these objects may seem commonplace in the affluence of the modern world, their importance to an ancient Indian king should not be underestimated. European fairytales, folklore, and the romantic and chivalrous legends of the dark and middle ages are replete with tales of wondrous swords, talismans, clothes, shoes, thrones, palaces, and gardens.

The Sword (Skt. *khadga*; Tib. *ral gri*)

The precious sword of the *chakravartin* is usually depicted upright, its blade coloured in the dark blue of tempered iron or occasionally in burnished gold. Its embellished golden handle, graphically detailed in a knot or double lotus-petal design, is surmounted by a five-pronged *vajra* or jewel. Like Manjushri's flaming sword of wisdom, a slender tongue of flame usually entwines the double-edged blade forming a crest of flames at the tip. The flame symbolises the *vajra* nature of the sword: it is unbreakable, adamantine, invincible. Like King Arthur's sword Excalibur it possesses magical qualities and can only be held by its rightful owner. Its flame illuminates the darkness, both physically and spiritually, and terrifies the hosts of *maras* and demons.

In the Western tradition, investiture of a sovereign is ritually conferred by the touch, blessing, and presentation of a sword. It is the main material emblem of a monarch symbolising not only sovereignty, power, and authority, but also justice, mercy, discriminating wisdom, and insight.

The *chakravartin*'s sword is a weapon of enormous power. Without spilling blood it vanquishes all foes, penetrating deep into the heart of ignorance – just the sight of the sword causes enemies to surrender.

The *Naga* Skin (Skt. *nagacharman*; Tib. *klu pags pa*)

The precious *naga* skin is likewise a miraculous talisman with magical powers. It is the skin of a great *naga* king obtained from the ocean depths, having the appearance of a large lustrous snakeskin. By its power the *chakravartin* can subdue all manner of *naga* spirits, causing them to bend before his will. Through control of the *nagas* the *chakravartin* gains control of the weather also. He is able to conjure forth rain in times of drought, halt torrential downpours, and usher in warm breezes on cold days or cool the heat of a blazing summer. Afflictions such as dropsy, leprosy, skin diseases, and mental or psychic disturbances, caused by the demonic possession of *naga* spirits, are banished from the realm.

Pearl, conch, and coral – the *naga* treasures of the ocean – are yielded to the *chakravartin* in times of financial need. The *naga* skin has power over the terrestrial *nagas* also, who likewise submit their mineral wealth to the *chakravartin*. The *naga* skin is an object of great power and, like the alchemical salamander, is impervious to the destructive activity of wind, fire, and water.

The Royal House (Skt. *harmya*; Tib. *khang bzang*)

The precious house or palace of the *chakravartin* possesses all of the divine qualities attributed to an ancient Indian royal palace. Naturally it is fashioned of the finest woods, precious metals, and gemstones. It is spacious, harmonious, divinely proportioned, with doorways and windows which face in the four cardinal and four intercardinal directions, panoramically overlooking the *chakravartin*'s realm. Supernaturally it is impregnated with divinity, radiant with the joys and pleasures of the god realms. Divine music, perfumes, visions, caresses, and tastes manifest within its walls. It is invigorating, restful, embracingly gentle as a mother's love. Its peaceful chambers know not of death or illness; sleep comes both sweetly and easily with beautiful dreams of the highest of the god realms.

The Robes (Skt. *chivara*; Tib. *gos*)

The various robes of the *chakravartin* are usually illustrated by the outer ceremonial robe of a lama or imperial dignitary.

The robes of the *chakravartin* are woven from the finest silks and cotton muslin. Traditionally these are likely to have been Indian silks woven in Benares (Kashi), which as a pilgrimage city has from time immemorial been an important centre for the weaving of rich silk brocades, fine silk scarfs, embroidered shawls, and homespun cotton and muslin. The great fifteenth-century poet-saint, Kabir, came from a background of weaving castes in Benares, already a famous and ancient sacred city at the time of Shakyamuni. Chinese brocade would have provided another source of reference for artists in Tibet. Many of the gold brocade designs employed in Tibetan art are based on traditional Indian patterns, such as floral roundels or regular gold dot patterns.

The *chakravartin*'s robes possess the magical qualities of endurance, lightness, climate and temperature regulation, and are also a panacea for physical and mental weaknesses. They are always clean, soft, fragrant, and impervious to the attack of weapons, fire, water, insects, and the corruptions of dust or curses.

The Royal Gardens (Skt. *vana*; Tib. *tshal*)

The precious gardens are an appropriate adjunct to the royal house. All varieties of fragrant trees, fruit trees, flowers and lotuses blossom perennially in the gardens. Streams of cool clear water weave amongst the ornamental banks, filling pools whose surface is covered with lotus blossoms, and ponds where exotic fish and water birds dwell. The trees are alive with colourful birds, butterflies, and bees gathering nectar. The divine music of the gods is heard and perfumes waft on the soothing breezes. Just like the heavenly desire realms of the gods, all is beautiful and vibrant with form and colour. A road of golden sand leads to the palace steps.

Here the *chakravartin* dwells in blissful meditative absorption, with beautiful maidens to delight his eyes, the nectar of fruits always in season, the fragrance of a thousand blossoms, and the gently inspiring music of divine musicians and tender birdsong to fulfil his sensual desires.

The Throne (Skt. *sayana*; Tib. *mal cha*)

The precious throne or couch is an object of exquisite craftsmanship and majesty. It is accomodating, spacious and comfortable, its presence creating a sacred atmosphere within the throne room. In spite of its grandeur it is light and portable, capable of being moved to any area of the *chakravartin*'s realm. Like the sacred seat (*sthan*) of a realised being, it produces a state of meditative absorption in the sitter. The three root poisons of ignorance, desire and aversion are banished in its presence. On its sumptuous cushions the *chakravartin* is able to remain absorbed in a state of royal ease and one-pointedness of mind, with an impeccable mental clarity and discernment. Like one's favourite armchair or shamanistic 'power spot', it is positioned exactly at the positive energy centre of the *chakravartin*'s universe. It relaxes, refreshes, and eliminates all fatigue and malaise.

The Boots (Skt. *pula*; Tib. *lham*)

The precious boots are proverbially comfortable, soft, light, strong, enduring, and again thermostatically beneficial. They cause no fatigue; with their aid the *chakravartin* is able to travel vast distances at great speed over land or water. Their soles were probably fashioned of rhinoceros hide, a very durable leather used on shields, which also bears the magically virile and defensive properties of the rhinoceros.

Plate 77

This drawing is based on a detail from a very fine, early twentieth-century thangka of a Gelugpa Assembly Tree.

In a grove of jewel-hung, wish-fulfilling trees is the royal palace with a solitary jewel-tree growing in front of it. The precious minister kneels at the left, with a turbaned head and brocade robes. In his left hand he holds the eight-faceted precious jewel, with his right hand in the *abhaya mudra* of protection and benevolence. The queen kneels on a lower throne, her hands joined in the *anjali mudra* of veneration and prayer. Behind her and within the curtained pavilion is the precious golden wheel with eight spokes. The horse and elephant are to the right of the queen. The horse is saddled and frisky; the elephant carries on his back a flaming jewel on a lotus. Behind is the precious general, dressed in armour with his sword upraised.

To the right of the general and just outside the pavilion are the seven secondary jewels. The throne, robes, boots, and sword are grouped together. The *naga* skin hangs over a balustrade in the lower right. Placed in the foreground are groups of jewels and a flat bowl containing medicinal pills. In the background, steps lead up to an enclosed lotus pool with a gabled gate and open doors. A pavement surrounds the lotus pool and a walkway or pergola surrounds the raised walls. A thicket of varied fragrant fruit and flower trees defines the extended royal gardens. The sun is directly above the solitary wish-granting tree, which symbolises the presence of the *chakravartin*.

Plate 78

This drawing of an assembly of the *chakravartin*'s possessions is based on a detail of an extremely beautiful nineteenth-century offering thangka to Palden Lhamo, now in the Rijksmuseum, Leiden.

The precious queen, minister, general, horse, and elephant all face towards the unrepresented majesty of the *chakravartin*. The queen holds the precious wheel in a silken cloth, respectfully acknowledging its unblemished purity. She wears silk robes and an entwined floral tiara. The turbaned minister folds his palms together in the *anjali mudra* of prayer and supplication. The precious general, in his ornate armour, helmet, and boots, holds the upraised sword in his right hand and the circular shield in his left. The precious horse is shown in all his finery, with bridle and bit, a

pennant-edged saddle blanket, silk pennants, jewelled straps, yaktail choker, and a long knotted tail showing his alertness. He bears the flame-enhaloed precious jewel upon his saddle. The submissive elephant wears a silk brocade back-cover, a single jewel crown, and a neck rope with a spherical golden bell hanging from it.

The secondary possessions of sword, *naga* skin and boots are in the left foreground; the throne, robes, royal pavilion, and gardens are in the background. The flaming sword stands upright and rises from a lotus, symbolising both its magical qualities and purity. At the bottom right are a row of eight circular jewels with the seven insignia of the *chakravartin* placed behind them. From left to right they are: elephant's tusks; jewel insignia; rhinoceros horn (horse); queen's round earrings; coral (wheel); general's insignia; and minister's square earrings.

Plate 79

Illustrated in this drawing are the seven secondary possessions and the seven gems or insignia of the *chakravartin*. Across the top row are the *chakravartin*'s seven secondary possessions of sword, *naga* skin, throne, palace, and royal gardens at the centre; and the robes and boots to the right.

In the second row are the seven gems (Skt. *saptaratna*; Tib. *nor bu cha bdun*) or insignia of the *chakravartin*. From left to right these are: the unicorn or rhinoceros horn (Tib. *bse ru*), symbolising the precious horse; the tusks of the precious elephant (Tib. *glang chen mche ba*); the round golden earrings of the precious queen (Tib. *btsun mo rna cha*); the square golden earrings of the precious minister (Tib. *blon po rna cha*); the crossed gems (Tib. *nor bu bskor cha*), crossed swords, or military insignia of the precious general; the triple-eyed gem (Tib. *nor bu mig gsum pa*) symbolising the precious jewel; and a branch of coral (Tib. *byu ru*) symbolising the precious wheel.

Although originating in Buddhist India, this group of seven insignia has been absorbed into Tibetan Buddhist iconography from Chinese art. There appears to be no original Tibetan source material that describes or defines these symbols, and as a result different traditions identify these seven gems with varying correlates amongst the seven precious possessions of the *chakravartin*. The rhinoceros horn and elephant's tusks are always specifically identified with the precious horse and elephant. But the round earrings are often identified with the king's earrings or the wish-granting gem. The square earrings may be assigned to the minister or queen. The crossed swords or jewels are invariably assigned as the insignia of the general. The triple-eyed gem may be identified with the precious wheel, and the coral branch as the queen or precious gem.

In the third row an alternative arrangement of the seven gem insignia is drawn, with an eight-spoked wheel as the *chakra*; a three-faceted gem as the jewel; the round earrings of the king or *chakravartin*; the square earrings of the minister; the crossed tusks of the elephant; the rhinoceros horn of the horse; the crossed swords or Chinese emblem of the general; and the coral branch of the precious queen.

Plate 77: The seven precious possessions of the *chakravartin*

Plate 78: The seven precious possessions of the *chakravartin*

Plate 79: The seven secondary possessions and the seven insignia of the Chakravartin

Plate 80: Jewel heaps and the seven insignia of the Chakravartin

The fourth row from left to right shows six examples of the various styles in which the triple-eyed gem is drawn. In Chinese art the triple-eyed gem is identified with *jui'i* as the Chinese sceptre or *vajra* (see Plate 160). The first two of these drawings show the three points or heads of this gem. The second two drawings depict the triple-eyed gem as a 'wheel of joy or pleasure' (Tib. *dga' 'khyil*), with three swirling faces. The last two drawings show a triform gold frame enclosing the three-eyed gem. To the right are examples of the rhinoceros horn, elephant's tusks and coral branches, with flat golden pedestals or three-legged Chinese stands at their bases. The centre of the fifth row illustrates five examples of the Chinese military insignia of the precious general, appearing in abstract forms as crossed swords, crossed jade bars, or crossed measuring rulers.

In the lower half of the illustration are four rows of multicoloured jewels supporting the seven royal gems or insignia. These jewel-heaps are commonly depicted on deity thangkas, where they are placed as offerings before the deities as attributes of their identification with the *chakravartin*. The elephant tusks are usually placed in pairs at either end of the jewel row, and no specific sequence is followed in the placement of the other six insignia within the jewel-heaps. Other ritual offerings, such as a conch, flaming jewel, *dharmachakra*, or vase, are also commonly included at the summits of the jewel-heap pyramids.

In Tibetan the unicorn and rhinoceros are known by the same term (Tib. *bse ru*). In the Chinese tradition the unicorn is known as the *chi-lin* or dragon horse, which is identified with the windhorse (Tib. *rlung rta*) of the Tibetan tradition. In Chinese medicine the rhinoceros horn is known as 'dragon's tooth', and again equated with the unicorn or *chi-lin* as the only animal with a single defensive central horn. In Oriental medicine rhinoceros horn, as a phallic symbol of erect virility, is highly esteemed as an aphrodisiac or male tonic. The simulacra of a human form within the cross-section of a rhinoceros horn is believed to vastly increase its medicinal potency. Whole horns were often carved into drinking vessels in ancient China, as the liquid was believed to absorb the medicinal essence of the horn. Such drinking vessels were also credited with the peculiarity of sweating in the presence of poison.

Plate 80

Illustrated in this drawing are further compositions of jewel-heaps containing the seven royal insignia, along with various other assorted symbols. In the centre of the top row is a jewel-heap with the seven royal gems and a *dharmachakra* at the centre. On either side of this in the left and right corners are the ends of stacked Tibetan texts with silk covers. Below the top centre is a small jewel-heap with a large *dharmachakra* at its centre and elephant tusks paired at either end. To the left and below are an eight-faceted flaming jewel, and a small jewel-heap enclosing a vase of immortality between paired elephant tusks. In the lower mid-centre is a flaming eight-faceted jewel, with a group of six jewels to its lower right. Above this are a double pyramid heap of seven jewels with paired elephant tusks at either end, and behind a wish-granting jewel on a stand, a conch shell, and a cluster of many-branched coral. Surrounding this whole central area are the two halves of an entwined-jewel aura of a peaceful deity. The intricate scrolling design of this aura is difficult to draw, and is usually accomplished with a repeated back-tracing technique. The jewels within the golden entwined scrolls are painted in the colours of the Five Buddhas.

In the lower half of the drawing are four rows of jewel-heaps. On the left side of the upper row a treasure casket, coral branch, flaming jewel, conch shell, and skull-cup are positioned around two pyramids of three jewels. On the right hand side the seven royal gems are placed behind a jewel row with the addition of a wish-granting gem and conch shell. In the second row a central eight-faceted jewel divides two jewel-heaps containing the seven royal gems, with the addition of flaming jewels, conch shell, wish-granting gem, treasure vase, and a perfume-laden conch shell. In the third row the seven royal gems are distributed on the left and right in jewel-heaps. Across the bottom row six pyramids of flame-topped jewels are surmounted by a central flaming eight-faceted jewel.

Chapter Eight

Auspicious Symbols

The drawings on Plates 81 to 95 illustrate the three main groups of auspicious symbols and offerings that appear in Tibetan Buddhist art. These are the eight auspicious symbols, the eight auspicious substances, and the offerings of the five sensual enjoyments. The eight auspicious symbols form the most well-known group of Buddhist emblems, and their origin can be traced back to the advent of Buddhism in India. The eight auspicious substances date back to the same period, although they are less well known as an auspicious group. The offerings of the five senses were probably incorporated into Buddhist imagery at a later date; they are first referred to as a symbolic group in the *Guhyasamaja Tantra*, which was revealed between the sixth and eighth centuries AD. As ritual symbols of the five sensory enjoyments, however, they probably occurred in different representational forms from the early Vedic period.

THE EIGHT AUSPICIOUS SYMBOLS
(Skt. *ashtamangala*; Tib. *bkra shis rtags brgyad*)

The eight auspicious Buddhist symbols (Tib. *bkra shis rtags brgyad*) consist of: a parasol, a pair of golden fishes, a treasure vase, a lotus, a white right-spiralling conch shell, an endless knot, a banner of victory, and a golden wheel. Originally these formed a grouping of early Indian symbols of royalty which were presented at such ceremonies as the investiture or coronation of a king. The earliest Indian grouping of these eight precious objects probably comprised: a throne, a swastika, a handprint, a hooked knot or hair-curl, a vase of jewels, a water libation flask, a pair of fishes, and a lidded bowl. A south Indian listing includes: a fly whisk, a pair of fishes, an elephant goad, a mirror, a

drum, a banner, a water vase, and a lamp. The Jains also adopted a list of eight auspicious symbols, which included a treasure vase, a water flask, two golden fishes, a swastika, an endless knot, a hair-curl, a mirror, and a throne. In Nepal the Newar Buddhist form of the *ashtamangala* replaces the golden wheel with a pair of fly whisks (Skt. *chamara*), and most commonly the eight symbols form a composite vase-shaped arrangement.

In Buddhism these eight symbols of good fortune represent the offerings made by the gods to Shakyamuni Buddha immediately after he attained enlightenment. Brahma, the great god of the form realm, was the first to appear with an offering of a thousand-spoked golden wheel, requesting Shakyamuni to turn the teaching wheel of the dharma. The great sky god Indra appeared next, presenting a white, right-spiralling conch shell as a symbol of the proclamation of the dharma. The earth goddess Sthavara (Tib. Sayi Lhamo), who had borne witness to the Buddha's enlightenment, presented Shakyamuni with a golden vase full of the nectar of immortality. Iconographically Brahma and Indra are frequently represented to the left and right of Buddha's enlightenment throne, offering the golden wheel and the white conch shell.

Early Buddhist aniconic representations of Buddha's footprints invariably depicted auspicious symbols as divine marks on the soles of his feet. These included the lion throne, victory banner, *vajra*, water flask, elephant goad, hair-curl, eternal knot, swastika and conch shell; but the most common of these marks were the lotus and wheel. As an insignia of the *chakravartin* an eight- or thousand-spoked wheel adorns the palms and soles of Buddha images or bodhisattvas. One of the meanings of the word *deva* is 'auspiciously drawn', referring to the body markings on the palms, soles, breast or

Plate 81: The eight auspicious symbols

throat of divine beings or gods. Indra, for example, bears the insignia of the *shrivatsa* or eternal knot on his breast.

In early Indian Vajrayana Buddhism the eight auspicious symbols were deified into eight goddesses, known as the Ashtamangala Devi, who each carry one of the auspicious symbols as their attribute.

In his book *The Buddhist Tantras* Alex Wayman quotes the commentary of the Indian master Buddhaguhya on the eight auspicious symbols, "Yoga displays itself as the eight emblems on the true nature of body. The eight emblems of good luck are: the endless knot (*shrivatsa*) which is lotus-like; the wheel (*chakra*) which is frightening; the banner (*dhvaja*) which is victorious; the umbrella (*chattra*) which is dignified; the lotus (*padma*) which is luminous; the flask (*kalasha*) of acute mind; the conch (*shankha*) of purity; the golden fishes (*matsya*) of auspicious mind."

In Chinese Buddhism these eight symbols also represent the eight precious vital organs of the Buddha's body: the parasol indicates the spleen, the two golden fishes are the kidneys, the treasure vase is the stomach, the lotus indicates the liver, the conch is the gall bladder, the endless knot forms the intestines, the victory banner represents the lungs, and the wheel arises as the heart. An eight-spoked wheel – fashioned from bone or gold – adorns the breast of many Buddhist deities and symbolises the eight spokes or lotus petals of the heart *chakra*.

A Tibetan tradition identifies the eight auspicious symbols as forming the body of the Buddha, with the parasol representing his head, the golden fishes his eyes, the lotus his tongue, the treasure vase his neck, the wheel his feet, the victory banner his body, the conch his speech, and the endless knot his mind.

Artistically the eight auspicious symbols may be depicted individually, in pairs, in fours, or as a composite group of eight. When illustrated as a collective group they often assume the simulacra form of a vase-shape, in which case the treasure vase may be omitted as the other seven symbols form the outline of the vase. Designs of these eight symbols adorn all manner of sacred and secular Buddhist objects, such as carved wooden furniture, embellished metalwork, wall panels, carpets and silk brocades. A beautiful Chinese brocade design depicts a pair of dragons holding the eight symbols in their claws. The eight auspicious symbols are frequently drawn on the ground in sprinkled flour or coloured powders to welcome visiting religious dignitaries to monastic establishments.

Plate 81

Here the eight auspicious symbols are illustrated in two columns. From the top of the left column are: the parasol (Skt. *chattra*; Tib. *gdugs*); the golden fishes (Skt. *suvarnamatsya*; Tib. *gser nya*); the vase (Skt. *kalasha*; Tib. *bum pa*); the lotus (Skt. *padma*; Tib. *pad ma*). From the top of the right column are; the right-spiralling conch shell (Skt. *dakshinavartashankha*; Tib. *dung g.yas 'khyil*); the endless knot (Skt. *shrivatsa*; Tib. *dpal be'u*); the banner of victory (Skt. *dhvaja*; Tib. *rgyal mtshan*); and the wheel (Skt. *chakra*; Tib. *'khor lo*).

Plate 82

In the upper half of the illustration are the eight auspicious symbols enclosed in circular motifs. The parasol, pair of fishes, treasure vase, and eight-petalled lotus design are drawn from left to right across the top row; and the conch shell, endless knot, banner of victory, and eight-spoked wheel are drawn across the second row. The lower half of the drawing depicts a detailed set of the eight auspicious symbols arranged in the same order as above.

Plate 83

Illustrated in this composition are some stylised variations of several of the auspicious symbols. In the upper mid-centre is a graceful and elaborate banner of victory. On its pinnacle is a flaming eight-faceted jewel. The small white canopy below the jewel is supported by a golden crest-bar, over which a white silk scarf (Tib. *kha btags*) is knotted and looped. Below the crest-bar hangs a double row of coloured pendants, and below this again are two billowing banner-drapes of creased silk. A lotus-mounted pole, hanging golden chains, and the swirling ends of the white scarf complete the victory banner's form. In the upper right corner are four examples of white conch shells, three of which are decorated with knotted silk scarfs. Further examples of the conch shell are illustrated and described on Plate 87. To the left of and below the victory banner are two lotus flowers. As an auspicious symbol the lotus is usually painted white with pink shading towards its centre. The knot of eternity or endless knot (Skt. *shrivatsa*), is drawn in two forms at the upper left corner and centre-left. The upper drawing shows the knot in its most conventional form, whilst the lower drawing depicts an unusual and intricate form. Both knots are entwined with silk cloth. Further examples of endless knot designs are illustrated on Plate 158. In the lower half of the illustration are eight drawings of the two golden fishes.

The Lotus (Skt. *padma*; Tib. *pad ma*)

The lotus, which blossoms unstained from the watery mire, is a symbol of purity, renunciation, and divinity. The symbolism of the lotus is described in Chapter Two and illustrated in Plates 26–28.

The Endless Knot (Skt. *shrivatsa*; Tib. *dpal be'u*)

The term *shrivatsa* means 'beloved of the goddess Shri'. Here Shri refers to Lakshmi, the consort of Vishnu, and the *shrivatsa* is an auspicious triangular mark or curl of hair which adorns the breast of Vishnu – originally as an eight-looped knot. Krishna, as the eighth incarnation or *avatara* of Vishnu, also bears the *shrivatsa* at the centre of his chest. Lakshmi's insignia on Vishnu's breast represents the devotion in his heart, and as Lakshmi is the goddess of wealth and good fortune the *shrivatsa* forms a natural auspicious

Plate 82: The eight auspicious symbols

Plate 83: Variations of some of the eight auspicious symbols

symbol. Another name for this hair-curl is *nandyavarta*, which means 'curl of happiness'. It is shaped like a Greek hooked cross or swastika. Another early Indian form of the endless knot appears as a *naga* symbol, where two or more entwining snakes form the familiar knot design. The eternal knot overlaps without a beginning or an end, symbolising the Buddha's endless wisdom and compassion. As a secular symbol it denotes continuity or dependent origination as the underlying reality of existence.

The Golden Fishes (Skt. *suvarnamatsya*; Tib. *gser nya*)

The Sanskrit term *matsyayugma* means 'a pair of fishes'. They originated as an ancient pre-Buddhist symbol of the two main sacred rivers of India, the Ganges (Ganga) and Yamuna. Symbolically these two rivers represent the lunar and solar channels, which originate in the nostrils and carry the alternating rhythms of breath or *prana*. In Buddhism the golden fishes symbolise happiness, as they have complete freedom in the water. They represent fertility and abundance as they multiply very rapidly. Fish often swim in pairs, and in China they represented conjugal unity and fidelity, where a brace or pair of fishes would often be given as a wedding present. As fish were so plentiful in China and formed an important part of the staple diet, the Chinese word *yu* – meaning both 'fish' and 'great wealth' – became synonymous with material prosperity.

The two golden fishes are often drawn in the form of carp, which are commonly regarded as sacred in the Orient on account of their elegant beauty, size and lifespan. At sacred lakes, such as Tsho Pema in northwest India which is believed to be the birthplace of Padmasambhava, the giant golden carp eagerly accept food from the hands of pilgrims.

The pair of fishes form a common auspicious symbol in the Hindu, Jain and Buddhist traditions. In ancient Egypt a pair of fishes symbolised the River Nile. Early Christianity adopted the paired fishes as an emblem of Christ, the 'fisher of men'. The symbolism of Christ's feeding of the five thousand with five loaves of bread and two fish, is sometimes viewed in esoteric astrology as the conjunction of five major planets in the sign of Pisces. In Christian art the fish, along with wine and unleavened bread, represent the eucharist and the last supper. (These three ingredients, along with meat and sexual intercourse, form the 'eucharist' of the tantric *panchamakara* ritual.) In the Latin Church, fish is traditionally eaten on a Friday; this has its origin in the early goddess cults of Isis, Venus, and Ishtar or Astarte. Fish was consumed on their sacred day of Friday in honour of their fecundity. In Buddhist art the two golden fish are often depicted touching nose-to-nose; in Hinduism this symbolises the female sexual organ or *yoni*.

The Parasol (Skt. *chattra*; Tib. *gdugs*)

The parasol or umbrella is a traditional Indian symbol of both protection and royalty. Its shadow protects from the blazing heat of the sun, and the coolness of its shade symbolises protection from the heat of suffering, desire, obstacles, illnesses and harmful forces. In ancient warfare the royal parasol (*chattra*), large parasol (*atapatra*), and victory banner (*dhvaja*), were borne on battle chariots. In its early form the umbrella was made from silk cloth stretched over a fixed frame with spokes; the familiar folding umbrella or parasol with bamboo spokes and an oiled paper canopy, was developed in China around the fourth century AD.

Originally the parasol was a symbol of secular wealth or royalty, as the greater the number of parasols carried by bearers in the entourage of an affluent dignitary, the higher his social rank would appear. Traditionally thirteen umbrellas appear to have defined the status of a king, possibly representing the central sun and its twelve zodiac houses. Early Indian Buddhism adopted the emblem of thirteen royal umbrellas as a symbol of the sovereignty of the Buddha as *chakravartin* or universal monarch. Thirteen stacked umbrellas form the conical spire of the Buddha or Tathagata stupa (see page 128). The *Vinaya Pitaka* (collective 'basket', *pitaka*, of Buddha's monastic discipline, *vinaya*), states that the Buddha's stupa has thirteen umbrella-wheels, the stupa of the *shravaka* has a number equal to his attainment, and that of the *pratyekabuddha* has seven umbrellas. The great Indian Buddhist master Dipankara Atisha, who revived Buddhism in Tibet during the eleventh century following its persecution by the Bonpo king, Langdarma, was reputed to have qualified for a retinue of thirteen umbrellas. The Indian mahasiddha, Kanhapa, was miraculously accompanied by seven umbrellas and hand drums (*damaru*), which would float in the air above him.

In ancient India umbrellas were often stacked one above another on a single pole as a symbol of royalty, and it is probable that the tapering conical design of the stupa's axle-pole and umbrella-wheels were derived from this emblem. The later definitive design of the Tibetan stupa developed the early Indian rain-cover – originally placed above the umbrella-wheels to provide protection – into the elaborate form of the lotus umbrella with its finial of moon, sun and flame. Early non-figurative representations of the Buddha often depict his footprints, throne, parasol and bodhi tree. As the umbrella is held above the head it naturally symbolises honour and respect. A jewelled umbrella is said to have been offered to the Buddha by the king of the *nagas*; it was fashioned of gold with *amrita*-emitting jewels around its edges, was hung with sweetly tinkling bells, and had a handle made of sapphire. Depictions of the Buddha often display an elaborate and large umbrella above his head, and in Vajrayana Buddhism this large umbrella (*atapatra*) was later deified into the thousand-armed, -headed and -footed goddess Sitatapatra (Tib. gDugs dkar), whose name literally means 'the white umbrella'. Above Sitatapatra's thousand heads are seven stacked umbrellas and a crown of seven million Buddhas. Her main left hand holds the shaft of a large white umbrella at the level of her heart; its function is to protect all beings from all fears. The two-armed form of this goddess bearing a white umbrella is often depicted above painted images of the Buddha.

Buddhist descriptions of a thousand-spoked umbrella have a symbolic affinity to the Hindu thousand-petalled

Plate 84: The parasol or umbrella

lotus (*sahasrara padma*) at the crown *chakra*, with its axle-pole representing the central channel.

The Tibetan version of the parasol was adopted from its royal Indian and Chinese prototypes, and fashioned from a wooden, spoked frame with a domed silk cover and hanging silk pendants or valances. Its function is to protect from the sun's heat rather than the rain – as the words 'parasol', meaning 'to hold off the sun', and 'umbrella', meaning 'little shade', similarly imply. The Sanskrit term *chattra* also means 'mushroom', in reference to the parasol's capped mushroom and stem shape.

The structure of a typical Tibetan parasol consists of a thin round wooden frame with eight, sixteen or thirty-two thin arched wooden spokes. Through its centre passes a long wooden axle-pole embellished at its top with a metal lotus, vase and jewel finial. Over the domed frame is stretched white, yellow or multicoloured silk, and from the circular rim of the frame hangs a folded or pleated silk skirt with eight or sixteen hanging silk pendants attached. The pendants are usually fashioned from folded silk brocade strips, stitched together in a single, double or triple valance design, and they hang to the same level as the pleated skirting. Their purpose is both decorative and to stabilise the hanging silk skirt in the wind. The parasol dome symbolises wisdom, and the hanging skirt, compassion. A ceremonial silk umbrella is usually over four feet in diameter, with a long axle-pole which enables it to be held at least three feet above the head. Octagonal and square parasols are also common, symbolically representing the Noble Eightfold Path and the four directional quarters. A square parasol invariably crowns the sedan chair in which dignitaries and important lamas are carried in procession. A square or circular yellow or red silk parasol may be suspended over the central sculpted or bronze image of a Buddha or bodhisattva on monastic shrines. A round yellow parasol is usually suspended from the centre of the ceiling in monastic assembly halls, with another parasol often suspended over the throne of the monastery's presiding lama. The white or yellow silk parasol, as described above, forms the ecclesiastical or monastic symbol of religious sovereignty. Secular sovereignty is more commonly represented in the peacock-feather parasol. As both spiritual and secular leaders, the Dalai Lama and the Panchen Lama frequently display both the silk parasol and peacock-feather parasol in their ceremonial processions.

Plate 84

Illustrated in this drawing are eight forms of the parasol or *chattra* (Tib. *gdugs*) such as are commonly depicted in thangka painting. Auspicious symbols, such as the parasol, victory banner, conch, wheel, mirror and vase are often held by the cloud-borne gods of the form realms in the upper heaven of a thangka, or by a group of gods that stand behind a central Buddha image. When the parasol is painted above the head of a Buddha or deity, it is usually depicted without an axle-pole, floating miraculously in the sky.

The drawing in the upper left corner shows a typically ornate Tibetan-style parasol. A gold-encased jewel crowns the top of the white silk canopy, which is embellished on its perimeter with a gold crest-bar, ornamented at either end with *makara*-tail scrolls. From the crest-bar hang a circle of silk pendants or valances with triangular ends tipped with pearls, jewels, or round gold or silver bells. These embroidered brocade pendants are usually coloured yellow and red alternately, symbolising the Hinayana and Mahayana paths. If a double row of pendants is depicted the colours are usually blue and green on the upper row, and yellow and red on the lower row, representing the colours of the four directions, or the Five Buddhas when the central white of the canopy is included. Below the pendants is a red or orange silk skirt, which billows outwards as if lifted on a breeze. Underneath the skirt is a long hanging silk scarf, which gracefully loops at its centre and twists upwards at its extremities. A garland of jewels hangs behind the central loop of the scarf. The long axle-pole is usually painted in the red of fragrant sandalwood, or may be specifically described as being fashioned from a precious mineral, such as red coral or lapis lazuli.

In the upper right corner is a similar white-canopied parasol, with a circle of radiating peacock feathers below the row of silk pendants. Such a white parasol is usually held above the head of the Buddha by a beautiful god or goddess; the white canopy symbolises his spiritual sovereignty, and the peacock feathers his secular power as *chakravartin*.

In the centre of the second row is a smaller drawing of a parasol with a tigerskin spread over its white silk canopy. This parasol has a semi-wrathful appearance, as it combines the qualities of the spiritual parasol with the warlike tiger skin of the victory banner.

In the central row are two further examples of parasol designs. The white canopy on the left drawing is convoluted, indicating a four-sided or square parasol. A flaming three-faceted jewel forms the pinnacle, with an ornate flowing apron below. The drawing on the right illustrates the very elaborate parasol of the Buddha, with peacock feather and brocade valances, hanging four-colour brocade pendants, double scarfs entwined in the four directions, hanging jewel garlands, and a pair of jewel chains with white yaktail fly whisks at their ends.

In the centre of the fourth row is the peacock-feather parasol which floats above the head of the goddess Palden Lhamo. The secular nature of the peacock feathers illustrate her power over all realms of existence, transmuting the three poisons of ignorance, desire and hatred into the feathers' beautiful golden and blue-black eyes. The eyes symbolise wisdom, and the many golden strands, method. Together they represent Palden Lhamo's ability to perform countless activities for the benefit of all beings. Sometimes, on traditional white parasols, the finial is decorated with an auspicious bundle of peacock feathers.

In the bottom left corner is a circular parasol with sixteen spokes and a radiating spoked support wheel on its axle-pole. Two hanging silk pendants are looped onto the golden, *makara*-tail crest-bar, and an eight-faceted flaming jewel forms the finial. In the bottom right corner is a narrow

Plate 85: The victory banner

parasol which is shaped like a banner of victory with a Chinese-style radiating spoked support on its axle-pole. Iconographically the parasol and victory banner may occasionally appear to have a similar representational form, as both are invariably depicted with white canopies.

The Victory Banner (Skt. *dhvaja*; Tib. *rgyal mtshan*)

In Sanskrit the banner or sign of victory is known as the *dhvaja*, meaning banner, standard, flag or ensign. Originally the victory banner was a military standard carried in ancient Indian warfare; it often adorned the back of a great warrior's chariot. The Indian chariot also bore the large umbrella (*atapatra*) as protection from the sun, or in the case of the chariot of a prince or king, the royal umbrella (*chattra*). The victory banner bore the specific ensign of its champion: Krishna's chariot was adorned with a garuda-topped banner; Arjuna's bore the device of a monkey; whilst Bhishma's bore the emblem of a palm tree. The *dhvaja* is also specifically identified as the banner of Shiva, whose emblem is the *lingam* or 'sign' of his erect phallus as the 'giver of seed'. The word *dhvaja* also refers to the erect male penis. An ancient Indian rite known as *dhvajaropana* or 'banner planting', in which a springtime tree was decorated with flower garlands, leaves and flags, bears a distinct resemblance to the Western fertility ritual of the maypole. The *dhvaja* was also the name given to the skull-topped staff carried by Shaivite Kapalika or 'skull-bearing' ascetics, which is more commonly known as the *khatvanga*.

As the battle-standard of military supremacy the victory banner was adopted by early Buddhism as an emblem of the Buddha's victorious enlightenment and his vanquishing of the armies of Mara, whose demonic warriors bore the *dhvaja* as an emblem. The hosts of Mara personify hindrances and defilements, and in Tibetan Buddhism the victory banner is said to symbolise eleven methods for overcoming these defilements: the development of knowledge, wisdom, compassion, meditation and ethical vows; taking refuge in the Buddha; abandoning false views; generating spiritual aspiration, skilful means and selflessness; and the unity of the three *samadhis* of emptiness, formlessness and desirelessness. Within the Tibetan Buddhist tradition a list of eleven specific forms of the victory banner are given for overcoming the powers of evil.

In ancient Indian warfare the *dhvaja* took on many forms as a military standard or banner, many of which were designed to instil terror in the enemy. The impaled head and flayed hanging skin of a human victim formed one such horrific emblem. The heads and skins of ferocious animals, particularly of the tiger, crocodile, wolf and bull, were also commonly employed as battle-standards. The crocodile, wolf and bull-headed banner are illustrated in Plate 133. In his book *Oracles and Demons of Tibet*, Nebesky-Wojkowitz lists eleven animal heads which stylistically crown the various victory banners: the *makara* or crocodile, tiger, wolf, otter, goose, cat, peacock, frog, snake, scorpion and tortoise. The *makaradhvaja,* or crocodile-headed banner, appears as an early Buddhist emblem in the ornamentation of the stupa,

where four *makaradhvajas* are placed in the four directions symbolising Buddha's victory over the four Maras. The four Maras (Skt. *chaturmara*; Tib. *bdud bzhi*) are: the Mara of emotional defilements (Skt. *skandhamara*; Tib. *phung po' i bdud*); the Mara of passion (Skt. *kleshamara*; Tib. *nyong mongs pa'i bdud*); the Mara of death (Skt. *mirtyumara*; Tib. *chi bdag gi bdud*); and the Mara of divine pride and lust (Skt. *devaputramara*; Tib. *lha'i bu' i bdud*).

The victory banner is said to have been placed on the summit of Mt Meru, symbolising the Buddha's victory over the entire universe. In the mandala offering the parasol and victory banner are the two auspicious symbols which are placed to the south and north of Mt Meru respectively, and paired with sun and moon in the north-east and south-west. An early form of the Mt Meru 'victory banner of the ten directions' is described in the form of a triple pennant (see Plate 85). The handle of this victory banner is fashioned of jewels and crowned at its pinnacle with a crescent moon and sun. The triple pennant hangs below the jewelled support of the crescent moon, and is fashioned from coloured silk which bears the emblems of the 'three victorious creatures of harmony' depicted in Plate 48.

In Vajrayana Buddhism the *dhvaja* became an attribute of many deities, particularly Vaishravana (Tib. *rNam thos sras*), the great guardian king of the north. Vaishravana is identified with Kubera, the king of the *yaksha* spirits, as a wealth deity whose warlike form holds the victory banner and a jewel-spitting mongoose, symbolising the possession of wealth through victory. The 'secret' form of Vaishravana holds a victory banner made from the head and skin of a tiger. A tigerskin apron is frequently incorporated into the victory banner as a symbol of triumph over anger and aggression.

The Tibetan Buddhist form of the victory banner is usually constructed on a cylindrical wooden frame, which is capped with a small jewel-tipped parasol and vertically draped with layers of silk valances, hanging aprons, jewel nets and silk scarfs. Cylindrical victory banners made of beaten copper are traditionally placed at the four corners of monastery and temple roofs, symbolising the Buddha's victorious dharma radiating to the four directions and his triumph over the four Maras. These roof ornaments usually take the form of a small circular parasol surmounted by the wish-fulfilling gem, with four or eight *makara* heads at the parasol's edge supporting little silver bells. From the parasol descend a series of hanging fronds or aprons of beaten metal, which are encircled with repoussé nets of hanging jewels. A smaller victory banner fashioned on a beaten copper frame, hung with black silk, and surmounted by a flaming trident is also commonly displayed on the roofs of protector chapels or small temples, particularly those of the Nyingma or Bon traditions.

Plate 85

Six designs of the victory banner are depicted in this drawing. The banner in the upper left corner is crowned by a wish-fulfilling gem, which emanates from a small canopy fashioned of either white silk or gilded bronze. Around the edge of this canopy are three decorative rings painted in gold and red, with a lower black ring embossed with golden circles. Below this are two hanging silk aprons which may be painted in yellow, red, green, blue or black, according to the quality or definition of the banner. From the upper apron hang little strings of golden jewels or pearls. The lower skirt, which flares outwards, is usually depicted in red with a light green or yellow underside. Hanging below this skirt is a white or yellow silk scarf, with a red flagstaff tipped with a jewel at its base.

The drawing in the upper centre depicts a jewel-topped victory banner with seven hanging layers of five-colour silk valances. The top of the canopy may be coloured white or gold, with a gold and red decorative edging from which descend small nets of golden jewels or pearls. The valances are usually coloured in an alternating sequence of yellow, red, green, white and blue, representing the Five Buddha wisdoms; or a two-colour sequence of yellow and red; a three-colour sequence of yellow, red and blue; or a four-colour sequence of yellow, red, blue and green. This form of banner probably originates from the Indian royal ensign of stacked umbrellas, where usually an odd number of levels are represented, such as three, five, seven, nine or thirteen. This form of silk-strip banner (Tib. *ba dan*) occurs as a common decoration in monastic assembly halls as a freely suspended ceiling-banner. The multitude of silk valances symbolise the countless activities of the Buddhas.

In the upper right corner is a jewel-topped victory banner with a single row of silk valances and a white silk scarf bound around its centre. Below the scarf hangs a strip of tiger skin and two silk aprons. The colour scheme usually follows a red and blue, or orange and green sequence for the silk valances. The two hanging aprons are usually coloured in red with yellow interior folds.

An elegant five-coloured silk victory banner is drawn in the lower left corner, with an eight-faceted flaming jewel at the centre of its white canopy, *makara*-tail scrolling on its crest-bar, and a white silk scarf looped from its extremities. A double row of silk valances coloured in sequences of red and blue, and orange and green, hang below the crest-bar. Three yellow, blue and red aprons hung with jewels, and a twisting white scarf descend below.

The victory banner at the bottom centre has a white canopy with a central flaming jewel at its apex, and with four directional gems placed around the canopy's circumference. A tigerskin frieze and a gilded bronze band, embellished with a diamond-shaped repoussé design, form the upper cylinder of the banner. A double row of multicoloured silk valances, two red aprons hung with jewels, and a twisting white or yellow silk scarf descend below. The flagstaff is tipped with a five-pointed *vajra* at its base.

In the bottom right corner is a short victory banner, tipped with a flaming eight-faceted jewel placed above a white silk canopy with a *makara*-tail crest-bar. A tigerskin frieze, a single row of silk valances, and two billowing aprons descend below.

The wish-fulfilling jewel crowns each of the six victory banners illustrated, symbolising the complete victory of the Buddha's enlightenment, and corresponding to the crowning jewel on the heads of deities or the golden flame which emerges from the Buddha's head protuberance or *ushnisha* (Tib. *gtsug tor*).

The Treasure Vase
(Skt. *nidhana kumbha*; Tib. *gter gyi bum pa*)

The golden treasure vase or 'vase of inexhaustible treasures' is modelled on the traditional Indian clay water pot or *kumbha* with a flat base, round body, narrow neck and fluted upper rim. The typical Tibetan treasure vase is usually represented as a highly ornate golden vase with lotus-petal motifs radiating around its various sections, and a single flaming jewel or group of jewels protruding from its upper opening. The great treasure vase (Tib. *gter chen po'i bum pa*) as described in the mandala offering is fashioned of gold and decorated with a multitude of gems. Around the neck is tied a silk cloth from the god realm and its upper opening is sealed with a wish-granting tree, the roots of which retain the water of longevity and create all manner of treasures. As the divine vase of inexhaustible treasures it possesses the quality of spontaneous manifestation: however much is removed from it the vase remains perpetually full. Wealth vases, sealed with precious and sacred substances, are commonly placed upon altars and on mountain passes, or buried at water springs, where their presence attracts wealth and brings harmony to the environment.

Plate 86

This illustration depicts various examples of the treasure vase, triple pennants, hanging tassles, banners and flags. In the upper half of the drawing are three golden treasure vases supporting flagstaffs, which are crowned with jewels and hanging silk valances. As an auspicious symbol the emblem of a triple pennant (Tib. *phan rtse*), mounted above a treasure vase, is commonly placed above the outer wall in the geometric mandala layout, along with the victory banner and parasol. The triple pennant represents the trinities of the three jewels; the three *yanas*; the three aspects of body, speech and mind; and victory over the three realms. Triple pennants are commonly represented on ritual implements such as the *damaru, khatvanga,* trident and triple banderole. When nine pennants are depicted they may represent the nine *yanas*. These comprise the three 'common' *yanas* of the *shravaka, pratyekabuddha,* and *bodhisattva* (or Mahayana); the three 'outer' *yanas* of *kriya, charya* and *yoga tantra*; and the three 'inner' *yanas* of *anuttarayoga, mahayoga* and *atiyoga*.

In the first vase on the left a jewelled pole is hung with two triple pennants, which are divided into nine coloured sections. The second central drawing of a double-handled treasure vase displays an ornate circular hanging banner of silk valances (Skt. *pataka*; Tib. *ba dan*). The pinnacle of this banner is crowned with the dissolving point, sun and moon

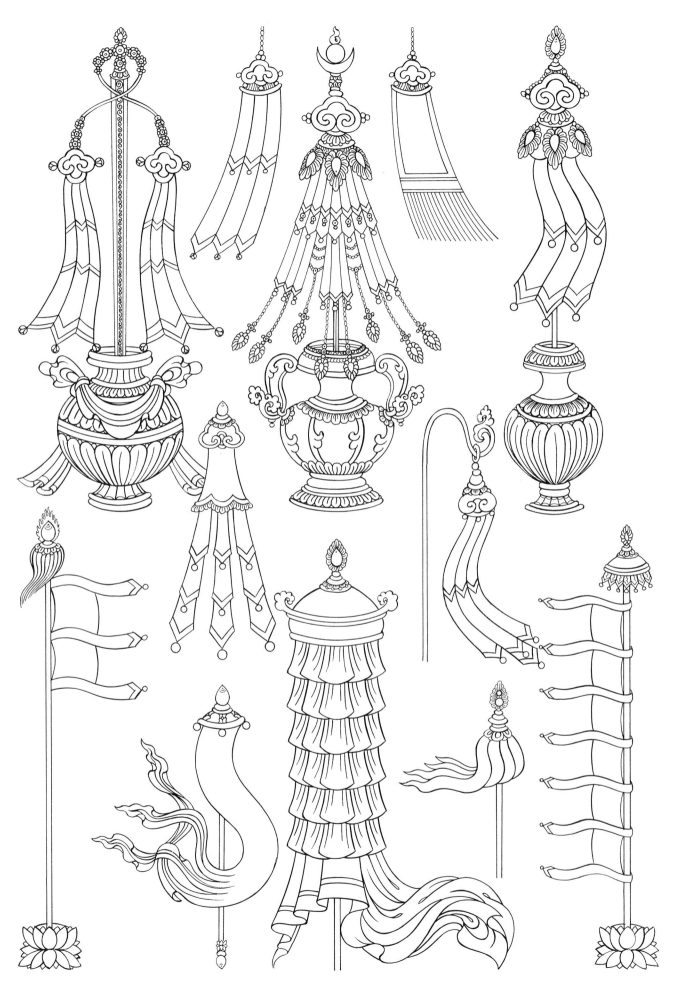

Plate 86: Treasure vases, pennants, banners and flags

emblem, below which is the insignia of the triple-eyed gem, with four gold-mounted jewels radiating below. From this jewelled finial hang a circular frieze of silk valances, which extend into four groups of triple pennants radiating into the four directions. Extending below the valances are hanging jewels suspended on golden chains. The treasure vase in the third drawing on the right supports a triple banderole which is crowned with a jewel-topped finial similar to the preceding drawing.

The trefoil form of the triple-eyed gem occurs on many of the tassles and valances illustrated in this drawing, and its depiction as one of the seven secondary gems or insignia of the *chakravartin* is illustrated in Plate 79 (see also Plate 158). As a symbol of the Three Jewels of Buddha, dharma and sangha, its trefoil form is similar to the cloud scroll or classical *jui'i* design of Chinese art, which is probably derived from the Taoist trinity or the head of the *vajra* (*jui'i*) of Manjushri. The Hindu trinity of Brahma, Vishnu and Shiva, and the Buddhist trinity of Manjushri, Avalokiteshvara and Vajrapani as the Lords of the Three Families occur as parallels to the Taoist trinity of the gods of the three heavens (Yu huang, Tao chun and Lao tzu). The crowning insignia of the triple-eyed gem, or a trefoil cloud motif enclosing a single gem, occur on many hanging silk banners adorning monastic assembly halls. An alternative form arises in the *kirtimukha* face, whose flattened head and two hands form the shape of a triple-arched cloud motif.

To the upper left and right of the central vase are a triple valance banderole (Tib. *phan rtse*), and a flat silk banner with a multicoloured fringe (Tib. *phan*). To the lower left and right of the central vase are a jewel-topped triple valance, and a triple valance banderole mounted on a curved, crook-like, metal handle. The triple valance in this form, decorated with the images of the 'three victorious creatures of harmony' (see Plate 48), may appear as a victory banner.

At the bottom centre is a cylindrical form of the victory banner, consisting of a jewel-topped canopy with a *makara*-tail rim, and six aprons of folded multicoloured silk. At the base of the banner is a flowing red silk apron, which is usually coloured yellow on its underside. This is similar to the valance banner depicted at the top centre of Plate 85.

To the lower left of the central banner is a circular banner crowned by a wish-fulfilling gem placed above a six-spoked golden or bone wheel. A tubular apron or hose of silk hangs below the wheel, which divides into three separate streamers at its end. To the lower right of the central banner is a jewel-tipped circular banner which bears four coloured silk streamers. These two forms of banner are most commonly represented in Bon iconography, where many forms of banners and flags are carried by protective deities. The three colours of the pendants are often red, white, and green or blue, corresponding to the elements of fire, water, air or space.

In the bottom left and right corners are two long flags (Tib. *phan*), consisting of squares of cotton or silk interwoven with longer valances or streamers. This form of flag may have originated in Central Asia or Mongolia, where it served as a standard for Mongol warlords such as Genghis Khan,

Gushri Khan and Kublai Khan. Or, it may have been of Indian Buddhist origin, since similar standards appear to have travelled with the spread of Buddhism into Burma and Cambodia. In Tibet such tall flagstaffs are commonly positioned at sacred sites near temples, monasteries, stupas, mountain passes and other auspicious geomantic locations. Printed prayer flags are sewn within the square sections, although often a long single strip of white cotton printed with prayers extends along the length of the flagstaff. The poles are usually capped with a small circular dias and a flaming sword, symbolising penetrative wisdom as Manjushri's emblem. Alternatively a small parasol or victory banner, a jewel, trident, yaktail or wool tuft, may also serve as a finial. The sword, spearhead or trident emblem originate from the spear-flag (Tib. *mdun dar*) or trident-flag (Tib. *ru mtshon rtse gsum*), which are illustrated on Plates 125 and 126. The Tibetan national flag usually bears a small victory banner as the crowning emblem on its flagstaff. Certain banners and flags have a specific association with various protective deities, and are venerated as religious treasures in the temples which enshrine them.

The three-valance flag on the left is crowned with a jewel and yaktail, whilst the seven-valance flag on the right is crowned with a small parasol.

Hanging banners occur in many different forms within the Tibetan tradition, and their many variations are extensively used to decorate walls, pillars, and beams, and as ceiling hangings in temples or monastic assembly halls. They are often named after their predominant colour, with a five-colour sequence of yellow, red, green, white and blue representing the Five Buddha wisdoms. One such continuous frieze is composed of numerous layers of alternating five-colour silk valances, arranged in sequence to create a zigzag pattern (Tib. *bkra shis bkras ring*).

The White Conch Shell (Skt. *shankha*; Tib. *dung dkar*)

The precious white conch shell of India has survived as the original horn trumpet since time immemorial. Ancient Indian epics describe how each hero of mythical warfare carried a mighty white conch shell, which often bore a personal name. The conch is one of the main emblems of Vishnu, and Vishnu's conch bore the name of Panchajanya, meaning 'having control over the five classes of beings'. Arjuna's mighty conch was known as Devadatta, whose triumphant blast brought terror to the enemy. As a proclaiming battle horn the conch is akin to the bugle. It is an emblem of power, authority and sovereignty, whose blast is believed to banish evil spirits, avert natural disasters, and scare away poisonous creatures.

Early Hinduism classified the conch into male and female varieties, with the thicker-shelled bulbous conch occurring as the male or *purusha,* and the thin-shelled slender conch as the female or *shankhini*. The fourfold caste division was also applied, with the smooth white conch representing the *brahmin* caste, the red conch the *kshatriya* or warrior caste, the yellow conch the *vaishya* or merchant caste, and the dull grey conch the *shudra* or labourer caste.

Plate 87: The conch shell

Vedic Brahmanism and later Buddhism adopted the conch as a symbol of religious sovereignty and an emblem which fearlessly proclaimed the truth of the dharma. One of the thirty-two major signs of a Buddha's body is his deep and resonant voice, which is artistically symbolised in images of the Buddha by three conch-like curving lines on his throat. The conch also appears as an auspicious mark on the soles, palms, limbs, breast or forehead of a divinely endowed being.

The natural white conch shell is obtained from the Indian Ocean and Arabian Sea. Ancient conch shells are also unearthed in the Himalayan region and on the Tibetan plateau, as this high altitude region was once an ocean floor. The marine conch belongs to the *Strombidea* family of gastropod molluscs, occurring as a spiralling white shell with thick walls and usually a wide frontal opening. Shells which spiral to the right in a clockwise direction are considered especially sacred, although they are a rarity in nature. The right-spiralling conch is known as a *dakshinamukha,* with the lower opening positioned to the right of the spiral tip. The left-spiralling conch, with an opening to the left, is known as a *vamavarta.* Auspicious blowing-horns are fashioned from the right-spiralling white conch (Tib. *dung dkar g.yas 'khyil*), by cutting off the tip of the shell. The right-hand spiralling wind passage thus created acoustically symbolises the true or 'right-hand' proclamation of the *buddhadharma.* As a Tibetan ritual musical instrument the conch is ornamented with a metal mouthpiece, and an ornamental metal casing extending from the shell's mouth. This copper, bronze, silver or gold casing is embellished with auspicious symbols and designs.

The right-spiralling movement of the conch is echoed in the celestial motion of the sun, moon, planets and stars across the heavens. The hair whorls on Buddha's head spiral to the right, as do his fine bodily hairs, the long white curl between his eyebrows (*urna*), and the conch-like swirl of his navel.

Conch-shell earrings and finger rings are worn by certain siddhas or yogins, as astrologically conch shells have an affinity with the moon's planetary influence. The ears of elephants were frequently adorned with whole hanging conch-shell earrings, which were known as *shankhakila,* or 'conch spikes'. The Sanskrit word *kundala* means both 'earring' and 'spiral coil', and is derived from the same root as 'Kundalini', the coiled serpent goddess.

Plate 87

Illustrated in this drawing are thirty-two examples of conch shells. On the far left of the upper row are two precious right-spiralling conch shells, with their lower mouths opening to the right of their spiral tips. Next, to the right, are three common left-spiralling conch shells, with their mouth openings to the left of their spiral tips. The last drawing on the far right of the top row shows a right-spiralling conch with a lotus-petal design beneath the lower edge of its coiling tip. The spiral tip of the conch shell commonly spirals in a

right-hand or clockwise motion as it widens, yet in artistic representation the very tip may emphasise a right- or left-hand spiralled centre. The second row depicts three right-spiralling conch shells with silk scarfs threaded through their split ends, and two small right and left-spiralling conch shells placed on either side of the centre. The third row depicts conch shells with elongated projecting tips; these graceful shells are usually classified as the slender feminine *shankhini* variety. The two drawings on the left of the fourth row show two examples of a right and left-spiralling conch with an uneven corrugated surface. Next to this is a precious red conch shell with speckles on its surface; two further examples of the speckled red conch are drawn lower on the page. Across the bottom row and in the lower right section are horizontal conch shells containing aromatic liquids or perfumes. Saffron, musk, sandalwood, camphor and nutmeg are the five common liquid perfumes employed in Tibetan conch-shell offerings. The essences (*attars*) of flowers or woods, such as rose, jasmine, magnolia, *champaka*, sandalwood, and sacred lotus, were more common as Indian Buddhist offerings. Further examples of the perfumed conch shell are illustrated on Plate 95.

The Wheel (Skt. *chakra*; Tib. *'khor lo*)

The wheel is an ancient Indian symbol of creation, sovereignty, protection, and the sun. As a solar symbol it first appears on clay seals unearthed at archaeological sites of the early Indus Valley or Harappan civilisation. In Vedic Hinduism the six-spoked wheel became the main attribute of Vishnu, and was known as the Sudarshana Chakra. It identified Vishnu with the sun as the central hub around which the wheel of creation and preservation arises as the phenomenal universe. The wheel represents motion, continuity and change, forever moving onwards like the circular wheel of the heavens. As an ancient Indian weapon a wheel of sharp blades was rolled into the ranks of the enemy, swung on a rope as a vicious rotating weapon, or hurled as a discus. Six, eight, or twelve spokes formed the radiating poles of a cart or chariot wheel, and also the number of blades of the wheel as a weapon.

Buddhism adopted the wheel as a symbol of the Buddha's teachings and as an emblem of the *chakravartin* or 'wheel turner', identifying the wheel as the *dharmachakra* or 'wheel of the law'. The Tibetan term for *dharmachakra* (Tib. *chos kyi 'khor lo*) literally means 'the wheel of transformation' or spiritual change. The wheel's swift motion symbolises the rapid spiritual transformation revealed in the Buddha's teachings, and as a weapon of change it represents the overcoming of all obstacles and illusions. Buddha's first discourse at the Deer Park in Sarnath is known as 'the first turning of the wheel of dharma'; here he revealed the truth (dharma) of the Four Noble Truths – the truth of suffering, its origin, its cessation, and the truth of the Noble Eightfold Path, which leads to the cessation of suffering. His subsequent discourses at Rajghir and Shravasti are known as the 'second and third turnings of the wheel of dharma'.

The hub of the wheel symbolises moral discipline, the eight spokes symbolise analytical insight, and the rim, meditative concentration. The eight spokes point to the eight directions and symbolise the Buddha's Noble Eightfold Path of the Aryas or righteous beings, which comprises right understanding, thought, speech, action, livelihood, effort, mindfulness and concentration.

Plate 88

Six drawings of the golden wheel or *dharmachakra* are represented in this illustration. At the top centre is an eight-spoked golden wheel supported on a lotus base, and encircled with a pear-shaped ornamental surround fashioned into a golden scroll design. At its centre is a rotating hub (Tib. *dga' 'khyil*) of four *yin yang* shaped sections, which are usually coloured to match the four directions, and which symbolise Buddha's Four Noble Truths and the four elements. The eight directional spokes which emanate from the hub represent the Noble Eightfold Path, and their depiction as *vajra*-spokes

indicates their indestructible nature in cutting through all obstacles on the path to the cessation of suffering. The background quadrants behind the eight spokes are often painted in the traditional mandala colours of the four directions and elements, with white or blue in the bottom quadrant, yellow to the left, red at the top, and green to the right. Alternatively the whole circular background may be painted white like the surface of a mirror. The top centre drawing of the *dharmachakra* with a pear-shaped, golden surround is the most commonly represented form of the wheel as depicted in Tibetan art.

To the left and right of this central wheel are two *dharmachakras* ornamented with white silk scarfs. Each have eight spokes which terminate in golden balls or jewels beyond their rims. At the centre of each is a triple *yin yang* design known as a 'wheel of enjoyment' (Tib. *dga' 'khyil*), symbolising the trinity of Buddha, dharma and sangha, and the overcoming of the three poisons of ignorance, desire and aversion.

At the bottom left is a representation of the thousand-spoked golden solar wheel of the *chakravartin*, fashioned

Plate 88: The golden wheel

Plate 89: The wheel and deer emblem

from gold found in the Jambud River of our world continent, Jambudvipa. Its thousand spokes, like the shining rays of the sun, represent the thousand Buddhas of this cosmic cycle or *kalpa*, and the thousand *dharmas* or teaching methods revealed by Shakyamuni Buddha.

The small wheel at the bottom centre is made of white pearls or bone, and is worn as a breast ornament by many deities, symbolising the eight spokes of the heart centre. In the lower right corner is a double sixteen-spoked wheel which may represent the sixteen emptinesses or *shunyata*, or the thirty-two major marks of an enlightened being.

Plate 89

This drawing shows two examples of the wheel and deer design, which is derived from the Buddha's first turning of the wheel of dharma in the Deer Park at Sarnath, and which occurs as one of the main emblems of the Buddhist teachings. Gilded three-dimensional representations of this motif are commonly placed at the centre of monastery and temple roofs as a crowning gold emblem of the *buddhadharma*. On the geometric mandala design the wheel and deer emblem is placed over the mandala's four gateways.

The origin of this early emblem possibly predates Buddhism, as both the insignia of the wheel and the motif of two deer flanking the deity Shiva Pashupati are found on clay seals unearthed at Mohenjo-Daro in the Indus Valley. Shiva as Pashupatinath or 'Lord of the Animals', possibly alludes to a connection between early Shaivism and the first disciples of the Buddha. The Deer Park at Sarnath, to which Shakyamuni returned after his enlightenment at Bodh Gaya, and where he delivered his first discourse to his five ascetic companions, was probably a sacred grove dedicated to Shiva Pashupati where Shaivite yogins lived and practised. Sarnath is very close to the ancient city of Kashi, the 'city of light' considered sacred to Shiva, and known later as Varanasi or Benares. It is possible that with the establishment of the great stupa and monastery at Sarnath the emblem of Pashupati flanked by two deer was replaced by the wheel, as an emblem of the supremacy of the Buddha's teachings over its early Shaivite predecessor. The monastic

academy at Kushinagara, where the Buddha was cremated, is believed to have borne the insignia of a funeral pyre between two *sal* trees, and it may be that each of the sacred sites connected with the major events in the life of Buddha displayed specific emblems to commemorate these events. However the wheel and deer design eventually became the standard emblem of an establishment where the Buddha's teachings are transmitted, and where the enduring wheel of the dharma continues to turn.

The two deer, which peacefully rest in attentive obeisance on either side of the *dharmachakra*, are depicted as a male on the right side and a female on the left in the traditional Indian system of polarity placement. On Tibetan bronze castings the genitals of both deer are invariably depicted. In the drawing on the right the male deer has the single horn of the mythical unicorn. The gentleness and grace of the deer represent the qualities of the true renunciate, as does its lifestyle as a homeless wanderer never resting in the same place on two consecutive nights.

THE EIGHT AUSPICIOUS SUBSTANCES
(Skt. *ashtamangaladravya*;
Tib. *bkra shis rdzas brgyad*)

The eight auspicious substances, lucky articles, or bringers of good fortune, which form the second group of early Buddhist symbols, consist of a mirror, precious medicine, yoghurt or curds, *durva* grass, the *bilva* fruit, a white conch, cinnabar or vermilion powder, and white mustard seeds.

Like the eight auspicious symbols, these eight objects are probably also of pre-Buddhist origin and were adopted into early Buddhist symbolism during the period of its initial inception. They are believed to represent events in the Buddha's life, and like the eight auspicious symbols were later deified in Vajrayana Buddhism to form a group of eight offering deities.

The mirror represents the offering goddess of light, Prabhavati or 'cicle of light', who presented Shakyamuni with a stainless mirror, symbolising the clear karmic vision of all his previous lives. The medicine (*gorochana*), derived from the brain glands of an elephant and personified as a precious white elephant holding a jewel-tray, symbolises the offerings made by the elephant guardian of the land at Bodh Gaya. The curds represent the offering of milk rice made by the virtuous lady Sujata to Shakyamuni before he sat under the bodhi tree. Sujata had previously received the boon of a son from the spirit inhabiting the bodhi tree. The *durva* grass represents the eight handfuls of grass presented to Shakyamuni as a meditation mat by the grass-cutter Sotthiya or Mangala. The *bilva* fruit was presented to Shakyamuni by Brahma, and the white right-spiralling conch, by Indra (Shatakratu). The cinnabar powder was presented to the Buddha by a brahmin king, and the mustard seed, by the powerful bodhisattva, Vajrapani.

The eight auspicious substances listed above essentially represent the four *karmas* or activities of an enlightened being. The mirror, medicine and yoghurt represent peaceful activities; the *durva* grass, *bilva* fruit and conch represent activities of increase; the vermilion powder represents the activity of magnetising or empowering; and the mustard seed represents destructive activity.

Like the eight auspicious symbols these eight precious objects may be represented individually – often with each object appearing in a separate bowl – or they may be collectively grouped behind jewels, in the branches of a small tree, or in a tray or shallow bowl. Plates 90 and 91 illustrate various examples of the eight auspicious substances.

The Mirror (Skt. *darpana, adarsha*; Tib. *me long*)

The mirror's function is to enable one to see oneself clearly, and as a cosmetic accessory or household object its auspicious importance is obvious. In Buddhism the mirror is the perfect symbol of emptiness or pure consciousness – it is clear, bright and shining, it reflects all objects impartially, and yet remains completely unaffected by the images which arise in it. It reveals all phenomena to be void in essence; like a passing show it reflects all objects of the phenomenal world but reveals them to be without substance.

In ancient Indian rituals of cleansing or bathing a sacred image, the reflection of the sacred image in a mirror would often be washed by pouring water over the mirror. This rite is known as *pratibimba*, which literally means 'reflected'. In Tibet this ritual is known as the 'bathing ceremony of the deity' (Tib. *khrus gsol*), where water is sprinkled over the reflected image of a statue or thangka. The water, having bathed the form of the deity, is thus considered consecrated water. The mirror is also used in divination rituals (see Plate 121), and in many shamanic rituals of healing and exorcism. Further examples of the mirror are depicted on Plate 93.

The Medicine (Skt. *gorochana*; Tib. *gi wang*)

The precious medicine is derived from the liver, intestinal or gallstones found in certain animals, particularly elephants, bears and cattle. The name *gorochana* (Tib. *gi wang*) refers specifically to the stones or bezoars found in cattle (Skt. *go*) – the bull, cow, ox and yak. The presence of bezoars is believed to be indicated by the noises the animal makes in its sleep.

A Vedic legend relates how the god Indra cast the five precious gemstones – gold, silver, coral, turquoise and pearls – into the ocean. These precious substances were consumed by elephants, bears, snakes, frogs, peacocks, vultures, geese and pigeons, and formed bezoars within their bodies. The intestinal stones obtained from these creatures consequently have different colours and medicinal potencies. The medicinal properties of these bezoars are reputed to counteract poisoning, promote clear thoughts, and to alleviate fevers and contagious diseases. The superior, mediocre and inferior forms of these stones are reputed to cure seven, five or three patients who have been poisoned.

The word 'bezoar' is derived from the Persian *pad-zhar*, meaning 'protecting against poisoning', and its general meaning is 'antidote'. In early Western medicine animal bezoars were highly esteemed as an antidote against poisoning. Particularly valued were the 'Oriental bezoars' obtained from the East, which consisted of organic resin layers formed around a hard foreign body. The common Indian antelope is known as the bezoar antelope, and the wild Persian goat as the bezoar goat. In Turkestan bezoars are also ritually employed to bring rain. In Tibet small mineral stones, of a white or orange colour, are found near hot springs as calcium and sulphur accretions, and are believed to possess similar medicinal qualities as the animal bezoar.

The finest quality of *gorochana* is said to be obtained from the brain or forehead of an elephant, and the second best quality is obtained from the cow. In size and appearance *gorochana* is said to resemble the yellow yoke of a boiled egg, and the yellow pigment obtained from it is used as a tonic and sedative, and is applied as a sacred mark (*tilaka*) to the forehead. When mixed with honey and applied to the eyes, *gorochana* is believed to bestow clear vision, enabling one to see all the treasures of the world. The grey or white stone obtained from the crown of a king cobra's head is believed to enable a snake-charmer to control all lesser serpents, and bestows immunity to their venom. The occidental 'toadstone', obtained from the skull of a toad, was similarly credited with the antidotal qualities of serum.

In Tibetan art this precious medicine is represented in many ways: it appears in the form of pills, or in the shape of an egg, bean, spiral, fruit, gland or fungus. It is usually coloured white or yellow, and is often illustrated as a solid oval shape suspended in a viscous white liquid.

Curds or Yoghurt (Skt. *dadhi*; Tib. *zho*)

Curds have always been regarded as a nourishing food in India, and in ancient times was probably one of the most important elements of the diet. In Ayurvedic medicine it is highly esteemed as a digestive stimulant, and prescribed as a remedy for diarrhoea and emaciation. Curds made from colostrum – the first milk that a cow gives after delivering a calf – are considered especially regenerative. Its pure white nature symbolises spiritual nourishment and the abandonment of all negative actions.

The 'three white substances' derived from the sacred cow – milk, yoghurt and ghee – are viewed as the concentrated essence of plants. Curds, as one of the eight auspicious substances, recalls the forty-nine-mouthful meal of milk-rice which the fasting Buddha received from the cowherd girl, Nandabala or Sujata, which gave him the strength to attain enlightenment under the bodhi tree and to recognise with clarity the truth of the 'middle way'. For this reason white curds are usually represented in the iron begging bowl of the Buddha. The Indian monsoon or rainy season, which occurs in the months of July and August, was traditionally a period in which the Buddhist sangha would undergo a seasonal meditation retreat. Curds were ritually consumed as the first celebratory meal after this rainy season retreat. In Tibet this practice found continuity in the 'curd festival' or Shoton, held at great monasteries such as Sera and Drepung, in which the monks would enjoy curds at the end of their hundred-day summer retreat.

Milk, curds and ghee, as the 'three whites' derived from the cow, form three of the five 'nectars' of the cow, the other two being urine and dung. The cow's urine and dung are collected in vessels before they touch the ground, and are then mixed with the three white substances in a bronze vessel. This mixture is then boiled, and when cool the upper scum and lower sediment of the viscous liquid are discarded, leaving only the middle section, which is then spread and dried in the sun. The dried powder is then blended with saffron and made into pills (Tib. *ba byung lnga'i ril bu*). These pills are employed in ritual practices along with consecrated medicinal pills (Tib. *bdud rtsi ril bu*). The cow should be pregnant, of a golden or orange colour, and endowed with intestinal stones or bezoars, from which the precious medicine *gorochana* is obtained.

Durva Grass (Skt. *durva*; Tib. *rtsva dur ba*)

Durva, durba or *darbha* grass is a common grass with many common names. In the Western World it is known as Bermuda grass (*Capriola dactylon*), Bahama grass, scutch grass or devil grass, and commonly grown as pasturage. In the East it is known as 'panic grass' (*Panicum dactylon*) or 'bent grass'. It also grows as a white species of grass, known as *chanda*. *Durva* grass is very hardy, growing as a trailing grass with a knotty stalk culminating in leafy heads. Its natural habitat is marsh or wetlands, but such is its durability that even when dry it will put out new shoots on contact with water.

Durva grass was a prerequisite ingredient in the Vedic sacrifice or *yagna*, the Vedic altar itself being constructed of cow dung bricks bound together with knots of *durva* grass. In rites of propitiation of the gods the Vedic priest wore a finger ring woven from *durva* grass, which was believed to have been formed from the hair of Vishnu.

The sacredness of *durva* grass is believed to have originated with the accidental spilling of *amrita* at the legendary churning of the cosmic ocean, when a few drops fell onto *durva* grass. A similar legend concerns the sacredness of *kusha* grass (*Poa cynosoroides*), where Garuda carries *amrita* to the *nagas* as a ransom payment for the release of his mother. Indra removed the vessel of *amrita* from where it rested in a grove of *kusha* grass, and the *naga* serpents, believing the *amrita* to

be on the *kusha* grass, licked the sharp edges of the grass; their tongues split into the forked tongues of serpents.

Durva and *kusha* grass became synonomous in their sacredness; both are commonly known as *darbha* grass. *Kusha* grass is a long brush-like grass which grows to around two feet in height. In India a bundle of *kusha* stalks are bound together with a coiled rope handle to produce the common household broom. Traditionally *kusha* grass was used to purify defilements, and brahmins would sleep in a grove of *kusha* grass when ritual purification was required. The sharp points of a stalk of *kusha* grass proverbially symbolise a keen intellect or intelligence. In Buddhism *kusha* grass is believed to enhance the clarity of visualisation and meditation. In many tantric initiations, such as the Kalachakra, two stems of *kusha* grass are used to reveal clear dreams on the night prior to the initiation, with a long stem being placed lengthwise under the mattress and a shorter stem being laid horizontally under the pillow. Water soaked in *kusha* grass often provides the sacred water for oblations, and the sacrificial fire is built over a bundle of dried *kusha* grass.

Shakyamuni Buddha probably sat on a mat of *kusha* grass when he attained enlightenment under the bodhi tree. From Vedic times a mat of woven *kusha* grass (*kushasana*) served as a sacred mat in religious ceremonies, and Shakyamuni was following an age old tradition in the use of *kusha* grass as his seat or *asana*. Iconographically many Buddhist ascetics, yogins and siddhas are depicted on such a woven *kusha* grass mat. The name of Kushinagara, the ancient capital of the Malla kingdom where Shakyamuni was finally cremated, derives from the 'city of *kusha* grass'.

Both *durva* and *kusha* grass are represented with many stylistic variations in Tibetan art.

The Bilva Fruit (Skt. *bilva*; Tib. *bil ba*)

The *bilva* fruit (*Aegle marmelos*) is also known as the *bel* or *bael* fruit, and as the Bengal quince. It is a large round fruit about the size of an orange, with a hard skin and a dappled reddish-brown colour. When, in the early nineteenth century, British botanists were confronted by a bewildering array of exotic Indian fruits and plants with unpronounceable Indian names, they chose to name many of these fruits after the English apple, creating such names as the pineapple, custard apple, rose-apple, and thorn apple. The *bilva* fruit, with its tough, wood-like, skin, was appropriately named the 'wood-apple'. Medicinally it is a potent astringent, and highly regarded for its purifying qualities in traditional Indian folk medicine. The unripe interior of the fruit, especially when made into a jam, was the best known cure for diarrhoea and dysentry.

In ancient India the *bilva* was regarded as the most sacred of all fruits, and served as the main offering to temple deities. Only in comparatively recent times has the coconut superseded the *bilva* fruit in its role as the principal fruit of religious offering or as a symbol of self surrender. The *bilva* tree is considered sacred to many Hindu deities, particularly Shiva, Parvati, Lakshmi, Durga and Surya. In one

Hindu legend the *bilva* tree is said to have originated from drops of sweat from the forehead of the goddess Parvati which fell onto Mt Mandara, the sacred hill used as a churn in the Vedic creation legend. Its trifoliate leaves symbolise both the trinity of Brahma, Vishnu and Shiva (creator, preserver and destroyer), and the trident of Shiva. The tree is especially sacred to Shiva, who is often represented with a trifoliate *bilva* leaf crowning his matted hair. Wet *bilva* leaves are often placed upon a Shiva lingam as a cooling offering during the heat of an Indian summer. The tree is also the abode of the various *shaktis* or emanations of the goddess Parvati, and the breast-like *bilva* fruit is believed to contain the milk of the mother goddesses (*matrikas*). The *bilva* fruit is also known as Shriphala, 'the fruit of the goddess Shri', symbolising her breast milk (see Plate 131).

Much of the Shiva and Shakti symbolism applied to the *bilva* fruit and tree arose during the Hindu tantric period, and at a far later date than the time of Shakyamuni Buddha. Whatever its pre-Buddhist symbolism may have been, the *bilva* fruit has been enduringly regarded as the most sacred of all fruits. Brahma is said to have presented Shakyamuni with the *bilva* fruit, and in this gesture of veneration and supplication he humbles himself before a wisdom and enlightenment greater than his own. Iconographically Brahma is usually represented offering the golden wheel to Shakyamuni, but occasionally the wheel may be replaced by a tray containing *bilva* fruit. In Tibetan art the *bilva* fruit is usually depicted like a pomegranate with a rounded nipple-like tip; the trifoliate leaves of the *bilva* may be depicted in a variety of stylised forms.

The Right-Spiralling Conch
(Skt. *dakshinavartashankha*; Tib. *dung g.yas 'khyil*)

The conch appears in the group of eight auspicious symbols, in the group of the eight auspicious substances, and as a vessel containing perfume in the five sensory offerings. The white conch shell is illustrated and described on Plate 87.

The white right-spiralling conch symbolises the Buddha's mighty proclamation of the dharma, and its presentation by Indra, the supremacy of Buddha's doctrine. The white conch shell is said to have been presented to Shakyamuni by the great sky god Indra. In Vajrayana Buddhism Indra was deified as a god offering a conch shell to the Buddha, and coupled with Brahma who offers the golden wheel. Indra in this form is known as Shakra, the 'king of the gods' or Shatakratu, an epithet of Indra which means 'mighty' or 'one who has performed the sacrifice a hundred times'.

The Vermilion Powder (Skt. *sindura*; Tib. *li khri*)

Vermilion powder is said to have been presented to the Buddha by the brahmin king or merchant, Kargyal. This orange or red powder is sometimes identified as cinnabar (Tib. *cog la ma*) or natural vermilion (Tib. *mtshal*), which are forms of mercuric sulphide derived from naturally-occurring mineral deposits. Mercury is extracted from cinnabar by a heating process which separates it from its sulphur content, and

this process can be carefully reversed by recombining sulphur and mercury to produce crystalline cinnabar. The transmutation of cinnabar into mercury and back to cinnabar again revealed the mutability of the elements, and gave rise to the Indian and Chinese traditions of alchemy.

In Sanskrit, vermilion powder is known as *sindura* (Tib. *li khri*), and is identified as the mineral minium or 'red lead', the red oxide of lead which is used as a pigment. The Tibetan materia medica defines three forms of minium – coarse minium from stones, soft minium from earth, and minium extracted from wood. A more general interpretation of the word *sindura* defines it as red lead, cinnabar, vermilion, or sacred ash.

Both cinnabar and minium have been used as vermilion, red or orange pigments since ancient times. In India, *sindura* is the red powder pigment that is used to adorn sacred images, and for a variety of religious purposes and rituals. Along with yellow saffron (*kumkum*), red sandalwood (*chandan*), and white ash (*vibhuti*) made from burnt cow dung, *sindura* is used to apply the sacred marks or *tilaka* to the foreheads of devout Hindus. Traditionally a circular red *tilaka* of *sindura* on the forehead of a woman indicates that her husband is still alive and that she is not a widow. Such a mark provides an important visual statement in the social order of orthodox Hindu society. The marking of the forehead or other parts of the body dates back to Vedic times, and elaborate systems of caste and sect marks have developed over the course of time. The marking or 'sealing' with a *tilaka* is another meaning of the word *mudra*.

Vermilion powder was certainly of great ritual significance during the time of Shakyamuni Buddha. Its red colour symbolises power, especially the magnetising power of love and desire, which later arose in the form of Vajrayana goddesses such as Vajrayogini and Kurukulla. Vermilion powder is used in the creation of sand mandalas, and as a paint in the decoration of monasteries, temples, shrines and furniture.

Mustard Seed (Skt. *sarshapa*; Tib. *yungs 'bru*)

White mustard seed was offered to Shakyamuni Buddha by the wrathful form of the bodhisattva Vajrapani. It was a common household commodity at the time of the Buddha, as his parable of asking a distressed widow to obtain mustard seed from a house in which no one has died reveals. Every householder possessed mustard seed, but none had been spared the grief of bereavement. As she listened to their harrowing stories the widow's own distress came to be alleviated.

Mustard seed was cultivated to produce oil for cooking and for fuelling oil lamps. It occurs in two varieties – white mustard (Tib. *yungs dkar*), and black mustard (Tib. *yungs nag*). In Buddhism mustard seed is a wrathful substance used in destructive rites against negativities and hindrances, which arise as obstructive demons. Mustard seed may be empowered with mantras of exorcism and burned or cast away to eliminate ghosts or malignant spirits. A certain form of spirit which possesses young children is known as a *sarshaparuna*,

Plate 90: The eight auspicious substances

or 'red mustard spirit', referring perhaps to leprosy. In Vajrayana rituals of destructive activity mustard seed is one of the main 'magical ingredients' (Tib. *thun*) used in ritual weapons against harmful spirits. These weapons may take the form of a ritual cake offering (Tib. g*tor ma*), a skull-cup, or an animal horn engraved with the images of poisonous creatures, such as the snake, scorpion and frog (see Plate 134). Mustard seed is also employed as a burnt offering in the 'fire *puja*' or *homa* ceremony (Tib. *sbyin sreg*) for destructive activity, and in rituals of weather control, where hailstorms are often conjured forth or prevented. The mustard seed offered to the Buddha by Vajrapani symbolises the Vajra Buddha Family, whose quality of activity is to destroy all harmful influences.

In *Oracles and Demons of Tibet*, Nebesky-Wojkowitz describes a Tibetan magical instrument known as the 'mill of the Shinje', located at Khardo Gompa near Lhasa. This weapon consists of a double millstone with powerful mantras chiselled on its upper surface, whose function was to kill the leaders of a hostile party. The presiding lama appointed for this task would first catch the 'life essence' (Tib. *srog snying*) of the enemy, and bind it into a few grains of white mustard seed, which would then be ground under the millstone with specific mantras. This process was evidently extremely dangerous, as people who handled the mill often had the habit of dying soon afterwards.

Plate 90

Across the top two rows of this drawing the eight auspicious substances are individually depicted in offering bowls with a lotus petal design. The silver mirror is in the upper left corner, embellished with a circular golden frame and a silk cloth. Next are three egg-shaped spirals of the precious medicine obtained from the forehead of an elephant. In the third drawing is a curd-filled wooden vessel with metal edges and handles. In the upper right corner are crossed stalks of *durva* grass, which are stylistically represented in the form of *kusha* grass stalks. In Tibetan art *durva* grass is often depicted as long *kusha* grass stems, since the two grasses are often confused or identified as *darbha* grass. Three large *bilva* fruit with hook-shaped navels and serrated leaves are illustrated on the left of the second row. Next are the white conch shell, the vermilion powder, and the bowl of mustard seed.

On either side of the third row are two larger bowls which each contain four of the eight auspicious substances. The bowl on the left contains the mirror, the *bilva* fruit, tied stalks of *durva* grass, and an alms bowl filled with yoghurt. The bowl on the right contains the white conch, the vermilion powder to the left, the mustard seed to the right, and the medicine in an avocado-like form at the front.

The drawing across the middle of the page depicts a row of multicoloured jewels forming a pyramid at the centre and crowned with a flaming gem. At either end are a pair of elephant's tusks. The large vase on the left contains pills made from the precious medicine, and the bowl to the right of it contains heaps of vermilion powder. Behind is the *bilva*

fruit, and above the fruit is the silver mirror. On the right hand side of the flaming jewel are the white conch, the bundle of *durva* grass, a cloth-covered alms bowl containing yoghurt, and a bowl full of mustard seed.

In the lower section of the drawing are two lotus-supported bowls containing the five sensory offerings on the left, and the eight auspicious substances on the right. The five sensory offerings appear as a mirror for sight, cymbals for sound, a perfumed conch for smell, fruit for taste, and a silk cloth for touch. At the centre of the bowl containing the eight substances on the right is a mirror, with a wooden vessel containing yoghurt positioned behind it. In front of the mirror are mustard seeds arranged in rows so that they appear like strands of rope fibre. On the left are fruit-like bezoars of the precious medicine, with vermilion powder heaped behind and a conch shell rising above. On the right are the *bilva* fruit and another heap of vermilion powder. Arranged behind the vermilion powder on either side are stalks of *durva* grass.

At the bottom of the page is a wide tray draped with silk cloth and containing the eight auspicious substances. At its apex is the conch shell, which rests above a bowl of yoghurt placed above the mirror. On the left end of the tray are three heaps of mustard seeds, and on the right three heaps of vermilion powder. Between these two are a mound of medicinal pills, with crossed stalks of *durva* grass behind, and *bilva* fruit in the background.

Plate 91

Illustrated in this drawing are five different examples of each of the eight auspicious substances. The top row depicts five common forms of the mirror. The second row illustrates five forms of the medicine as bezoars. The medicine, said to be derived from the forehead or brain of an elephant, is commonly depicted as white, and possibly alludes to the glands that produce rutting-musk secretions from an elephant's forehead, located in the elephant's temples. The bezoars derived from cows and geese are yellow and oval shaped. The first bowl depicts medicine which looks like fungus, the second bowl contains avocado-shaped bezoars in a lymphatic juice, the third bowl depicts kidney-bean shaped bezoars, the fourth bowl spiral bezoars, and the fifth bowl contains small round bezoars or medicinal pills. The third row depicts the yoghurt, with the familiar cloth-covered alms bowl at the centre. The fourth row depicts stylised variations of the *durva* grass; the closest example to the actual appearance of *durva* or Bermuda grass is represented in the fourth bowl. The other bowls show examples which are closer to *kusha* grass. The fifth row illustrates variations of the *bilva* fruit, several of which depict its trifoliate leaves. The *bilva* is not an indigenous Tibetan tree, and stylistically it received much artistic license at the hands of Tibetan artists. The sixth row illustrates further examples of the conch shell, the seventh row, of vermilion powder, and the eighth row, of mustard seed.

Plate 91: Offering bowls containing the eight auspicious substances

THE FIVE OFFERINGS OF SENSORY ENJOYMENT
(Skt. *panchakamaguna*; Tib. *'dod yon sna lnga*)

The five offerings of sensory enjoyment represent the most beautiful objects which attract the five senses: sight or form (Skt. *rupa*; Tib. *gzugs*); sound (Skt. *shabda*; Tib. *sgra*); smell (Skt. *gandha*; Tib. *dri*); taste (Skt. *rasa*; Tib. *ro*); and touch (Skt. *sparsha*; Tib. *reg bya*). These offerings invariably take the form of: a mirror for sight; cymbals, gongs or a lute for sound; an incense-laden conch shell for smell; fruit for taste; and a silk cloth for touch.

As objects of the most delightful sensory pleasures they are presented as offerings to the deities or gurus, symbolising both the desire to please the enlightened beings and as a gesture of sensual renunciation on the part of the donor. In thangka painting they are usually depicted as offerings to the peaceful deities, and placed before them either as separate symbols or as a composite group of five objects within an offering bowl. In rituals of request they are often momentarily presented and touched by the presiding lama, and usually take the form of a mirror or wheel, a pair of cymbals, incense or a conch shell, fruit, and a silk cloth. Small painted images of the sense offerings, or of any of the other important groups of offerings, may be represented as rectangular miniature paintings (Tib. *tsak li*). Butter sculptures, modelled in the most exquisite detail and colours, are also made of the various offering groups for specific rituals or festivals. The most impressive ceremony of butter sculpture images was held in Lhasa on the full moon of the first month during the Great Prayer Festival or 'Monlam Chenmo', when the various monasteries would compete to create the finest butter sculpture. These butter sculptures, shaped like ritual cake offerings (Tib. *gtor ma*), were usually around ten feet in height and the product of many weeks of intensive work. The competition was held at night outside Lhasa's Jokhang temple, and the winning image was judged by the Dalai Lama.

The five sensory offerings are related to the Five Buddhas as the faculties of the five senses. Vairochana represents form as the faculty of sight, symbolised by the mirror. Ratnasambhava represents feeling as the faculty of sound, symbolised by the lute or cymbals. Amitabha represents perception as the faculty of smell, symbolised by incense or a perfumed conch. Amoghasiddhi represents motivation or will as the faculty of taste, symbolised by fruit. Akshobhya represents consciousness as the faculty of touch, symbolised by the silk cloth.

In Vajrayana Buddhism these five sensual offerings are deified into a group of five offering goddesses who bear the five objects of the senses as attributes.

Plate 92

Illustrated in this drawing are examples of the five sensory offerings appearing mainly in groups. At the top centre is a graceful composition of the mirror, lute, perfumed conch shell, fruit and silk cloth, contained within a double lotus which rests upon a lotus leaf. The lute is fretted with movable bronze frets which are bound around the neck of the instrument with silk thread. Its upper peg-box is crowned with a carved *makara* head, and a three-coloured silk valance hangs from the top of the fingerboard.

In the upper left and right corners are two rows of five jewels with the seven insignia of the *chakravartin* divided between them. Behind the jewels in the drawing on the left are the mirror, the lute, and the silk cloth, which is tied around the neck of the lute. In the upper right drawing the conch shell full of perfume and three *bilva* fruit are depicted behind the jewels.

Below the drawing in the upper left corner is a bronze bowl containing the mirror, fruit, perfumed conch, and a pair of brass cymbals joined together with a silk cloth. A second silk cloth is draped over the front of the bowl. Below this composition is a perfume-filled conch in a bowl, and to the right of this are the blossoms and leaves of fragrant flowers in a basin. To the right of this is another composition of the five sensual objects grouped in a metal tray. The four-stringed lute has a silk cloth tied on its upper neck, and behind are the mirror, conch and fruit. Above the neck of the lute is a round mirror in a bowl. On the face of this mirror are small embossed circles; the five circles at the centre are arranged in the form of a cross to represent the centre and the four directions. Below the head of the lute is another small mirror, and below the lute's sound box is a bowed ribbon of silk cloth.

The lower half of the drawing is dominated by five assemblies of the sense offerings, four of which have the eight-spoked golden wheel at their centres, representing form as the object of sight. The composition at the middle left depicts a large lotus leaf on which are placed the golden wheel, a pair of cymbals joined by silk cloth, a perfumed conch, and a group of three fruits. The compact composition on the centre right has an ornate golden wheel, conch, fruit, and silk cloth. To the right of the fruit is a small Chinese gong (*lo*), with a wooden striking stick. Below the large lotus leaf on the left is a group of four Chinese gongs or Mongolian gongs (*dudaram*), which are now more commonly known as 'Tibetan singing bowls'. To the right of the gongs is a bowl of peaches.

The lotus pedestal in the lower left corner bears the five sensory offerings on its upper moon disc. In the bottom left corner is a pair of small finger-cymbals (Tib. *ting shag*), which are made from bronze bell-metal and resonate with an enduring high pitched tone. In the lower right corner are another group of the five sense offerings in a metal bowl. Above are a group arranged on an altar with an eight-spoked golden wheel at the centre.

The wrathful form of the offering of the five senses is illustrated on Plate 140.

The Mirror (Skt. *adarsha, darpana*; Tib. *me long*)

The mirror represents consciousness and the element of space. It is clear, pure and bright, and reflects all phenomena with impartiality. Whatever appearances arise as

Plate 92: The peaceful offering of the five senses

reflections, be they beautiful or ugly, inherently good or evil, the mirror passes no judgement on them. It remains completely unaffected, untarnished and unchanged. Similarly pure consciousness is unaffected by the beautiful or ugly, good, neutral or evil nature of the thoughts which arise and pass. Like reflections in a mirror their essence is void, without substance, and yet they continue to manifest on the 'screen' of consciousness or within the emptiness of the mirror. Like a wild animal that sees and attacks an apparent rival in its own reflection in a still pool or mirror, the mind self-identifies with its own projected imagery.

Clouds come and go across the sky, but the nature of the sky remains unchanged; it is clear, void, without substance. Images come and go within the surface of a mirror, but the mirror remains unchanged. As a Zen patriach once observed, "The wild geese do not mean to cast their reflection. The water does not intend to reflect the wild geese".

Plate 93

This drawing illustrates various examples of the mirror as depicted in Tibetan art. Traditionally oriental mirrors were fashioned from polished metal, usually silver, bronze or bell-metal. The finest mirrors were made of pure silver, or from an alloy of silver and tin. Silver naturally tarnishes, but a silver mirror could be returned to a high reflectivity by polishing with rouge, which served as a common cosmetic in Tibet. The bronze mirror evolved in ancient China and was cast in 'speculum metal', consisting of one part tin to two parts copper, with the possible addition of a little arsenic, antimony or zinc to increase the mirror's whiteness. Bell-metal is cast by varying the proportions of copper and tin, producing a predominantly gold or silver-coloured alloy. An alloy known as *panchaloha*, consisting of five metals – copper, tin, iron, zinc and silver – was traditionally used in ancient India.

The four mirrors in the top row of the drawing are decorated with an aureole of peacock feathers and a knotted silk scarf. Such mirrors are commonly held by the attendant gods as a form offering to the Buddhas or bodhisattvas, and are borne aloft on long shafts. The peacock feathers and the silk scarf enhance the beauty of the appearances which arise in the mirror. The half-moon shaped mirror on the right may also function as a fan. Within the mirror is sometimes painted the reflection of a divine landscape of clouds, lakes and mountains, or the form of a Buddha or bodhisattva. The image of Tara or Avalokiteshvara is often painted in the mirror held above Buddha's mother in the 'birth of the Buddha' composition. In very fine thangkas the whole composition of the painting may be depicted as a miniature reflection in the mirror. More commonly the mirror is white, symbolising the reflection of all phenomena as emptiness.

The two small mirrors on the left of the second row are divination mirrors, which are utilised to obtain prophetic visions through the oracular intervention of certain deities. The silk cloth attached to the mirror is coloured white, yellow or red, and five small embossed circles are arranged in the form of a cross on the mirror's surface. Divination arrows and mirrors are described in Plate 121.

Below the second mirror is a bowl with a dark interior filled with water, whose reflective surface functions as a mirror. In the water's surface are reflected the moon, the stars and the sun, believed to empower the water with healing astrological essences. Mercury may also be used as a reflective liquid, and in the Indian alchemical tradition the tinctures or 'oils' of various metals may be 'clarified' by exposing them to the nocturnal light of the 'mirror' of the full moon.

The large mirror at the centre of the second row is embossed with five small circles, which symbolises the wisdoms of the Five Buddhas and their directions. To the right of this are two oval mirrors, the first of which rests upon a stand, whilst the second has a handle.

The bottom row illustrates four circular mirrors with ornate golden frames and stands. The two mirrors on the left have silk scarfs and are embossed with small circles on their surfaces. The second mirror has a central embossed circle and four groups of three circles positioned in the cardinal directions. These twelve circles may represent the continents and subcontinents of Mt Meru, the twelve animals of the Chinese zodiac, or the Buddhas of the four directions along with their bodhisattvas and consorts. Ancient Chinese bronze mirrors were commonly embossed with astrological designs on their back surface, depicting the four supernatural creatures, the eight trigrams, the twelve cyclic animals or zodiac signs known as the 'terrestrial branches', and the twenty-eight lunar mansions or constellations. A circular Chinese mirror represents the heavens, and a square mirror the earth. In *feng shui* a mirrored plaque, with a *yin yang* design at its centre and the eight trigrams encircling its perimeter, is used to deflect negative or evil influences. Mirrors are also placed above doorways to repel evil spirits, the belief being that when an intruding spirit sees its own reflection it will take flight in terror. Ancient Chinese bronze mirrors were believed to possess magical qualities on account of the wisdom they had absorbed.

During the symbolic 'judgement of the dead', described in the *Bardo Thodol* (Tibetan Book of the Dead), Yama, the Lord of Death, holds up the mirror of karma in which all one's deeds are reflected. Here Yama's mirror of karma represents the clarity of seeing all of one's actions in the nakedness of pure humility, where the self-cherishing attitude which originates in primordial ignorance is revealed in all its inescapable and consequential realities. Here self deceit and lying are of no avail; one's own karmic reflections determine the destiny of the future rebirth. By contrast, the mirror as depicted in Tibetan art reflects the empty clarity of Buddha nature: as one of the prime symbols of Dzogchen it reflects the state of pure awareness; as a symbol of Mahamudra it reflects the 'great seal'. By whatever name it is known the white mirror is empty of appearances, pure and bright, and eternally umblemished.

Plate 93: Offering of sight – the mirror

Musical Instruments (Stringed Instruments, Flutes, Cymbals, and Tibetan Singing Bowls)

Plate 94

Illustrated in this drawing are examples of stringed instruments, hand drums, cymbals and flutes which may be depicted as the musical offerings of sound. Then follows a discussion of the evolution of the various Asiatic stringed instruments that are generally classified as 'the lute' in Tibetan art. Next follows a section on the melodic scales of the Indian ragas and their importance in the song and dance traditions of early Vajrayana Buddhism. Flutes and cymbals are described next, and the section concludes with a discussion of 'Tibetan singing bowls'.

In the upper left corner of Plate 94 is a four-stringed Central Asian lute with its peg-box ornamented with a carved head of a garuda. Its four strings are made of wound silk and usually tuned in fifths and an upper fourth (C.G.G.F.) from the bass string upwards. Its body is carved from a single piece of hardwood, with a hollow sound box covered with a tight and percussive white goatskin. Its fingerboard, fitted over a hollowed neck, is made of a very hard wood such as ebony or rosewood. In this form the Central Asian lute became the prototype for the Afghan and Indian *rabab*, which later developed into the north Indian *sarod* with metal strings and a polished metal fingerboard.

In Tibetan the lute is known as the *pi wang*, in Chinese, as the *ch'in*, and in Sanskrit, as the *vina*. The three large lutes illustrated across the top row are the usual form in which this instrument is represented in Tibetan art, where it is held by deities such as Sarasvati, the goddess of knowledge and wisdom, Shabdavajra, the offering goddess of sound, Vinadhara, the offering goddess of music, Dhritarashtra, the white guardian king of the east, and the *gandharvas* or celestial musicians.

The second drawing to the right shows a smaller lute with a round sound box and *makara*-tail scrolling carved at the top of the peg-box. A long silk scarf is tied around the middle of the lute's fingerboard. Below this small lute are four examples of picks or plectrums made from wood, coconut-shell, tortoiseshell or horn. To the upper right of this lute is a small *damaru* or hand drum (see Plate 117).

The third lute illustrated has four silk strings and a *makara*-tail and leaf design peg-box. The fourth drawing of a small pear-shaped lute with a silk cloth tied around its fingerboard is the prototype of the Chinese lute known as the *p'ip'a* or 'balloon guitar'. Below this instrument is a small hourglass-shaped Indian hand drum, known as a 'monkey drum' or *dugdugi*. This double-headed drum has skins which are strung together with thin rope, such that the pitch of the drum may be raised by squeezing the ropes at their centre. This drum is 'rattled' like the *damaru* by twisting the hand back and fore rapidly, which causes the two knotted thongs of rope to alternately strike the two skins. To the right of this drum is another example of a later version of the Central Asian lute with five strings instead of four.

The last drawing on the far right is modelled on an unusual nineteenth-century Tibetan lute or guitar (Tib. *dram snyan*). This instrument is unusual in having two skin-covered sound boxes, the lower of which is an innovative addition to the standard form of Tibetan guitar. Like the European guitar it has six equally-spaced silk strings, five of which originate in the *makara*-headed peg-box, whilst the sixth originates from the first octave position on the fingerboard. This reveals an influence from Indian stringed instruments such as the *vina, sitar, surbahar* or *sarod,* which have one or two short strings – known as *chikari* strings – tuned a single or double octave higher than the tonic note of the instrument. The traditional Tibetan folk guitar has a single sound box and six silk-wound strings, which are paired into three main playing strings running in double courses. These identically pitched double strings are tuned at intervals of a third to C.E and G from the bass string upwards.

The transmission and evolution of stringed instruments throughout the Eastern, Islamic and Western Worlds makes a fascinating comparative study. The Chinese classified their musical instuments into eight categories comprising wood, bamboo, clay, metal, stone, skin, silk and gourd. Stringed instruments formed the 'silk' category. The strings of Asian lutes were traditionally made of wound silk thread, and in the case of certain bowed instruments, of twisted, stretched and dried goat intestines. Metal strings of drawn brass, bronze, phosphor-bronze and steel are a comparatively recent Western invention. Indian instruments are often named after the number of strings they possess, from the simple one-stringed *ektara* with its coconut-shell and split-bamboo neck, to the more sophisticated double-stringed lute or *dotara,* the intricate seven-stringed *sitar,* and the extremely intricate *sarangi* – meaning 'a hundred (tonal) colours'.

Drawn horizontally across the upper centre of the page is the divinely jewelled lute of the celestial musicians of the gods – the *gandharvas, apsaras* and *kinnaras.* This divine instrument is fashioned of the five precious substances of gold, silver, lapis lazuli, coral and pearl. Its oval, skin-covered sound box has a black edge in the drawing, representing the dark blue colour of lapis lazuli. It has an open fingerboard, with four tuning pegs and four silk strings. The neck is fashioned of gold and silver studded with pearls, coral and other gems, and its head is crowned with a lotus-mounted, eight-faceted, flaming jewel.

Beneath the divine lute is a four-stringed Tibetan horse-head fiddle (Tib. *go phong*), modelled after the two-stringed Mongolian horse-head fiddle known in Mongolian as the *morin khur* or *khil khur.* The Mongolian horse-head fiddle usually has a trapezoid-shaped sound box, a thin square wooden neck crowned by a carved horse's head, and its two bowed strings are tuned a fifth apart to C and G. The Tibetan horse-head fiddle, as illustrated, has a round sound box, a lute-like neck, and is also crowned with a carved horse's head. Its four strings are made from goat-gut or wound horsehair, and tuned at intervals of either fourths or fifths. The wooden bow is tensioned with many strands of horsehair, which are rubbed with resin to create the resistance needed to resonate the strings. The strings are stopped with

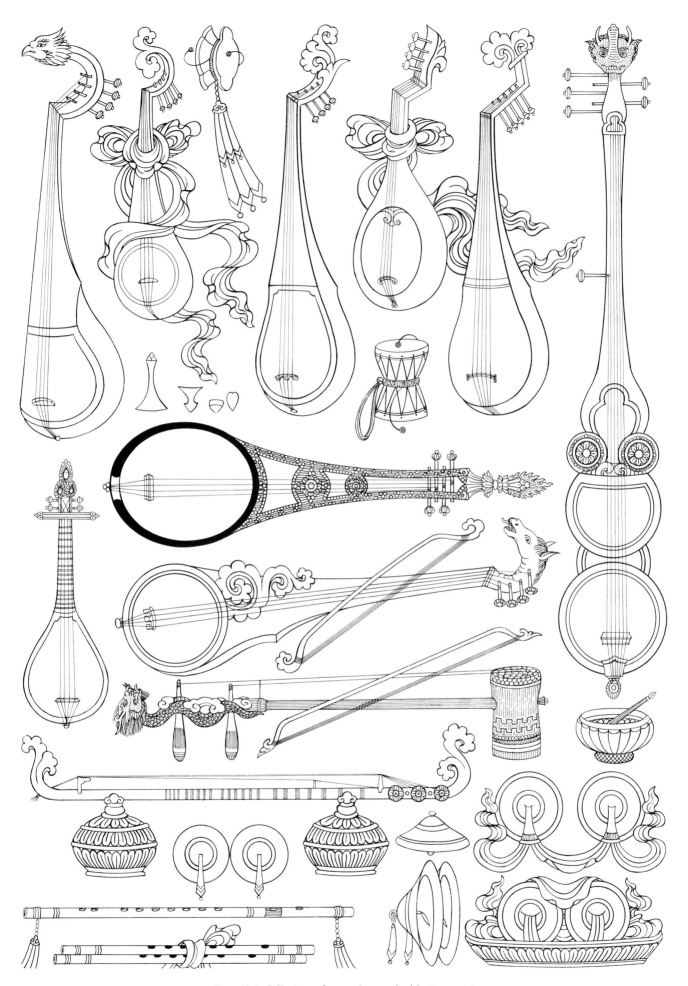

Plate 94: Offering of sound - musical instruments

the fingertips, and the neck of both the Tibetan and Mongolian horse-head fiddle is often bridged with a capo made from a thin strip of movable gut which allows the pitch to be raised when required.

Below the horse-head fiddle is the two-stringed Chinese fiddle, known as the *erh hu* or *hu ch'in*. This instrument has a hexagonal, octagonal or cylindrical wooden sound box, through the middle of which runs a round wooden or bamboo pole, which is usually decorated at its end with an intricately carved wooden dragon. The sound box is usually covered with snakeskin, and it has a small bone bridge. The horsehair bow passes between the two strings, which are sounded simultaneously and tuned a fifth apart to D and A. The strings are stopped with the fingertips, and an adjustable metal loop or S-shaped holder forms the upper bridge. The *erh hu* is very popular with Tibetan folk musicians, and is known in Tibetan as a *ye*.

Illustrated vertically on the left is a small fretted lute which later possibly evolved into the Chinese 'moon guitar' or *yueh ch'in*. This plucked instrument has a small pear-shaped body made from redwood with a spruce soundboard. Its raised frets are fashioned from hardwood, ivory or bone, and its four strings were probably tuned as the *p'ip'a* or 'ballon guitar' as A.D.E and A.

Below the Chinese fiddle is a horizontal drawing of the north Indian *vina* or *bin*. This instrument is fashioned from a tube or tubular section of bamboo with two large calabash resonating gourds. A Hindu legend relates that the *vina* was originally fashioned by Shiva, who modelled its design on the sleeping form of his consort, Parvati. The long bamboo neck resembles Parvati's slender body, the two gourds her breasts, the metal frets her bangles, and its sound her rhythmic breathing. The north Indian *vina* or *Sarasvati vina* is the instrument of the goddess of wisdom, Sarasvati, and often bears the image of her swan vehicle on its peg-box, or may incorporate the body and head of a swan as a small sound box with a swan's tail forming the embellishment on the peg-box. The *vina* depicted in the drawing, however, has the familiar Tibetan *makara*-tail scrolling as its terminal decorations, and is a fretless instrument with bound silk threads marking the notational positions on the instrument's neck. In this form the instrument depicted closely resembles the north Indian *vichitra vina*, which is played by sliding an egg-shaped glass ball along the playing strings in the manner of a Hawaiian or slide guitar, whilst plucking the strings with wire plectrums (*mizrab*) placed over the fingertips of the right hand. The four main playing strings of the *vina* are tuned upwards as C.G.C.F. with an upper octave *chikari* string tuned to high C. This *chikari* string is depicted passing over a small ivory peg to the left of the *vina*'s upper bridge and tuning pegs. The lower ivory bridge has a slightly convex extension which produces the reverbating twang or *jawari* effect which is so characteristic of Indian stringed instruments such as the *sitar*, *tamboura* and *surbahar*.

The Indian scale has seven major notes forming the sequence *Sa, Re, Ga, Ma, Pa, Dha, Ni*, corresponding to C.D.E.F.G.A.B. in Western notation, with *Sa* as the tonic and *Pa* as the fifth. The second (*Re*), third (*Ga*), sixth (*Dha*), and

seventh (*Ni*) also occur as flattened or *komal* notes, whilst the fourth (*Ma*) also arises as a sharp or *tivra* note. This produces a chromatic series of twelve tones which are likened to the cries of various animals and birds. The melodic structure of Indian classical music or raga is realised with variations of ascending and descending notes, defined phrases and characteristic modes, and performed at specific times of the day. Although the musical genius of the Moghul influence evolved into what is now recognised as classical Indian music, its pre-Mughal form as *dhrupad* music consisted more purely of aesthetic and philosophical invocations to the Hindu deities.

Early Indian Vajrayana Buddhism incorporated the melodic structures of the Indian ragas into the *charyagiti* tradition of mystical songs of spontaneous realisation or *dohas*. Most of these are attributed to the lineages of the eighty-four Mahasiddhas, and are composed in an allegorical and vernacular 'twilight language' (*sandhabhasha*) which concealed various levels of inner meaning. Vajrayana Buddhism flourished under the patronage of the Eastern Indian Buddhist Pala kings (eighth–twelfth centuries AD); its final flowering culminated just prior to the iconoclastic Muslim invasion which swept into Eastern India at the end of the twelfth century. The Mahasiddhas, who flaunted their miraculous powers (*siddhi*) with impeccable precision and improvised *doha* songs with spontaneous insight, were the original instigators of the Vajrayana traditions which revealed the Buddhist tantras. With the rapid demise of the Vajrayana under the converting onslaught of the monotheistic Muslim sword, the legacy of the *charyagiti doha* tradition was absorbed into the later Muslim Sufi and Hindu Bhakti traditions, and still survives within the Baul lineages of itinerant poets, singers and musicians of Bengal. In Tibet the evolution of the *charyagiti doha* poetic form perhaps found its most famous expression in the *Hundred Thousand Songs of Milarepa*.

The importance placed upon dance and song in tantric rituals is revealed in such texts as the *Hevajra Tantra*, and in the dance postures assumed by many of the dynamic Vajrayana gods and goddesses. The only surviving Buddhist ritual tradition of musical invocation based on the Indian ragas is to be found in the *charyanritya* dance rituals of the Newari Buddhist *vajracharyas* of the Kathmandu valley. In the *charyanritya sadhanas* descriptive prayers of the deities are sung in specific ragas and rhythmic cycles (*tala*) to accompany a dance which evokes the qualities of the deity through *mudra*, dance movements, costumes and masks. The Newari *charyanritya* tradition may date back as far as the eighth century, in direct transmission from its Indian Pala origins. Sadly this ancient tradition is rapidly disappearing amidst the commercialisation of modern Kathmandu, and the greatest living master of the *charyanritya* lineage, Ratnakaji Vajracharya, receives little recognition for the wealth of knowledge that he alone carries.

In the lower left corner are two examples of Chinese and Indian bamboo flutes. The upper drawing depicts a long transverse Chinese flute known as a *ti*, which originated in Central Asia and is believed to have been introduced into

China during the Western Han dynasty (206 BC–AD 9). The *ti* has six or seven fingerholes, with two separate auxiliary end holes, which were originally threaded with a silk tassle that served as a carrying handle. At the right end of the flute are two mouth holes, the lower of which is covered by a thin bamboo membrane that resonates with the passage of the breath, producing the characteristic kazoo-like nasal tone of the Chinese flute. Below the *ti* are two six-holed Indian bamboo flutes bound together with a silk cloth. The simple transverse bamboo flute, plugged with resin or wax at the mouthpiece end and with six fingerholes produced by burning with a red-hot iron poker, has endured as a common Asian folk instrument since time immemorial.

In Tibetan art the Central Asian lute, the long Chinese membrane flute (*li*), the two-string Chinese fiddle (*erh hu*), the hand cymbals (Tib. *ting shag*) the kettledrum or *mirdangam* (Tib. *lda man*), and the double-ended *madal* drum are frequently depicted in the celestial orchestra of the offering goddesses of music, song and dance.

Below the *vina* are a pair of small bronze hand cymbals (Tib. *ting shag*), which measure about three inches in diameter and are usually joined by a leather thong which connects their centres. These are similar to the traditional Indian hand cymbals or *talam* used by devotional singers. Below the head of the *vina* is a single hand cymbal, viewed from the side, showing its bell-shape. Below this, is a pair of bell-shaped Chinese cymbals or *hsing erh*. To the right are depicted two pairs of Tibetan cymbals which are joined by silk cloths, the lower pair appearing in a shallow bowl. As a sense offering to peaceful deities the cymbals appear as the flat cymbals (Tib. *zil snyan*) used in peaceful rites, rather than the domed cymbals (Tib. *rol mo*) used in wrathful rites. Cymbals and other instruments used in Tibetan monastic music are described in Plate 106.

Above the upper pair of Tibetan cymbals on the lower right of Plate 94 is a Chinese gong (*lo*) or Mongolian gong (*dudaram*) fashioned from sonorous bronze or bell metal, with its wooden striking stick placed in its interior, and a cloth ring underneath, to sustain its resonance when struck. Several other examples of these gongs are depicted on Plate 92 as part of the assembly of the five sensory offerings. Monastic gongs are used in virtually all Buddhist traditions and countries, and their presence in Tibetan art shows that Tibet also incorporated them into its religious traditions.

In recent years the musical technique of playing 'Tibetan singing bowls' has become both a fashionable and pseudo-mystical form of entertainment; this modern mythology – grafted onto Tibetan tradition like so many other New Age phenomena – needs some clarification. The colourful bazaars of modern India and Nepal are wonderful places to wander, browse or bargain. Everything is on view and up for sale – everything from crude brass copulating couples to enormous crystal, gold and silver *phurbas*, embellished with a mass of Buddhist symbols but no collective meaning. Visually stunning mandala paintings lavishly burnished with gold and silver details are compositionally devoid of any iconographical significance. When you need to sell something no one speaks English; when you want to buy,

everyone does. The tourist areas of Delhi or Kathmandu are now stacked with locally manufactured Buddhist ritual objects. This includes thousands of 'Tibetan singing bowls', even though in the early 1970s, when genuine Tibetan artifacts were quite abundant, there was not a single Tibetan singing bowl in any of these places; although bell-metal gongs of Chinese or Mongolian origin would very rarely appear on Tibetan refugee stalls. Demand created the commodity, and their true place of origin was in the Western imagination. As highly stacked as these stalls of Tibetan singing bowls may be, taller still are the bizarre bazaar tales told by the merchants of the origin of these items. Like a conjuring trick their real appeal is that they are very easy to play, and when they reverbate harmonically within the human voice-box they sound extremely impressive. Traditionally they would be struck as a monastic or lay gong not rubbed around the edges with a wooden striker to create a 'singing' overtone. The same effect can be produced with crystal wineglasses, though no one can reasonably claim that wineglasses are manufactured to create meditational music.

Perfume and Incense Offerings

In India a conch shell mounted on a small tripod serves as the water oblation vessel in *pujas* or rituals, and is known as a *shankhapatra*. As a Buddhist oblation or offering vessel the conch is usually filled with saffron-scented water, or water perfumed with the five fragrant substances of saffron, sandalwood, musk, camphor and nutmeg. Rosewater, aloe or *champaka* flowers (*nagi*) are also used in India as liquids for 'conch perfume' (*shankhanakha*). As with many natural substances or herbs used in Vajrayana rituals the water should be collected from a waterfall by a pre-adolescent child. Iconographically the perfumed water is represented as a 'swirling offering', and depicted as pale blue with white waves which form crests, symbolising the fragrance of the liquid.

The basic ingredient of Tibetan incense (Tib. *bsang*) is powdered juniper leaves, which is commonly burned in charcoal-fired braziers or incense burners. Traditional Tibetan stick incense (Tib. *spos*) is hand-rolled from a paste of juniper powder mixed to various formulas with medicinal herbs, saffron, sandalwood, aloes. musk and other fragrant substances. Traditional Indian incense is known as *dhup*, and is mixed as a waxy paste from flower and wood essences.

Fruit and Food Offerings

Offerings of food may consist of offerings of fruit or ritual cakes (Tib. *gtor ma*). The Tibetan ritual cake offering is derived from the sacrificial offering (Skt. *bali*) of ancient India, which consisted of various food offerings presented to the deities. In early Buddhist Tibet the Indian tradition of *bali* amalgamated with the Bon tradition of offering sacrificial cakes made of butter and barley flour. In Vajrayana Buddhism the varieties of sacrificial cakes developed into an elaborate ritual pantheon, with specific shapes, colours and designs for different deities and the various classes of spirits (see Plate 139).

Silk Cloth

Silk fabrics are invariably depicted in flowing graceful movements, as if the cloth or scarf is floating on a divine breeze. Indian silk merchants often demonstrate the fineness of their silk by passing the width of a bolt of silk, or a sari, through a finger ring. The gossamer thread of divine silk is described as being so fine that a square which could cover Mt Meru can be drawn beneath a fingernail. Traditionally a white silk scarf is presented as an auspicious offering to a lama or teacher, symbolising the offering of a pure mind, heart and motivation.

Artistically there are no specific rules for the depiction of silk offerings, although they are usually painted in white, yellow or red as heavenly silk ribbons. White, yellow and red cloth symbolise the three activities or *karmas* of pacifying, enriching and magnetising. Black, as the fourth *karma* of destructive activity, is never represented as a cloth offering to peaceful deities, as it symbolises and draws malignant spirits or energies. In the wrathful offering of the five senses (see Plate 140), a small black silk banner is fastened to an arrow which pierces a human heart, representing touch. Rainbow-coloured silk of white, yellow, red, green and blue represents the Five Buddhas, and a specifically coloured silk ribbon may be depicted as an offering to an emanation of one of the Five Buddha Families. In certain traditions silk garments coloured white, blue and red represent the Vajrayana, Mahayana and Hinayana paths. The three-coloured silk brocade frame of thangkas – forming a rainbow-like surround of red, yellow and blue – also represents the Hinayana, Mahayana and Vajrayana traditions.

Plate 95

This composition depicts images of the three sensory offerings of touch, taste and smell. In the top area of the drawing are scarfs, ribbons, and bolts of silk, representing the faculty of touch. The reef-knot illustrated in the silk ribbon or belt in the second drawing on the left of the top row is particularly associated with the bodhisattva Avalokiteshvara. The peacock feather and small feather on the left are occasionally depicted as representations of touch. In the upper right corner are two drawings of cylindrical bolts of rolled silk, which are often illustrated in narrative thangkas as ceremonial offerings.

In the central section are offerings of fruit and ritual cakes (Tib. *gtor ma*) as representations of taste. At the centre is a bowl of mangoes, and to its right three fruits rest upon a leaf plate. To the lower left of the central bowl is a small tray with a pyramid stack of balls made of roasted barley flour (Tib. *tsam pa*) and butter. As a specific offering or attribute of the elephant-headed deity Ganapati, these balls take the form of a sweetmeat known as *laddu* or *ladduka*, consisting of fried gram flour mixed with ghee, sugar and spices. Below the central tray are coconuts (Tib. *be ta*), and to the right a pineapple.

Above the leaf plate at the left are six stylised examples of fruits – a lemon, mango, persimmon, peach, guava and wild strawberry. To the right is a bundle of sugar cane tied with a silk cloth. The hollow tubers of sugar cane, along with the plantain or banana plant are symbols of Mahamudra, as they have no solid centre. For this reason plantain leaves and stems are often depicted surrounding the great Mahamudra teacher and translator, Marpa. To the right of the sugar cane is a large spotted red mango, with cherries above and to its right, and a group of three berries below. To the right above the mango is an apricot within a cluster of eight leaves, then a bunch of grapes with three bananas, and a persimmon below. To the right again are two bowls containing peaches above, and *bilva* fruit below. A few other stylised and spotted fruits are depicted around these bowls.

On the right are three trays containing examples of ritual cake offerings (Tib. *gtor ma*), which are commonly depicted as offerings to wrathful or semi-wrathful deities. The three examples illustrated in the drawing are hand moulded from butter and barley flour coloured with dyes. Their conical or heart-shaped forms are decorated with discs of the sun and moon, four-petalled flowers, a lotus base, and dissolving-point finials known as *nada*. Various ingredients may be incorporated, such as medicinal substances (Tib. *bdud rtsi*); the 'three whites' of milk, curd and butter; the 'three sweets' of sugar, molasses and honey; or the twenty-five precious ingredients known as the 'five times five' (see vase description on Plate 103).

In the lower third of the page are drawings of conch shells containing perfumed water, and incense as offerings representing fragrance as the sense of smell. Across the page are drawn four white conch shells supported on metal bases or cloth rings, with three right-spiralling conch shells on the left, and a left-spiralling conch on the far right.

Below the conch shells are various forms of incense burners (Tib. *spos phor*). In the bottom row on the left are three typical bronze incense burners mounted on small tripods, and with the curling smoke of the incense wafting above. To the right of these is a wooden incense burner, shaped as a decoratively carved oblong box or casket. Stick incense is burned on a bed of ashes or grain placed upon a metal tray within the box, and the incense smoke rises from carved perforations in the lid of the box. In the bottom right corner is a large stupa-shaped incense burner (Tib. *bsang khung*) in which juniper leaves and branches are burned. Such incense burners are constructed of whitewashed clay and built upon rooftops as household shrines or near the entrances of temples and monasteries.

In between the bottom row and the conch shells are small drawings of incense burning vessels. On the left is a small bronze incense vessel mounted on a tripod. To the right is a wrathful triangular iron box containing burning human flesh as an incense offering to wrathful deities. Next are three incense sticks in a rice or barley-filled bowl. Next are a bundle of incense sticks bound with thread, which are commonly carried as a fragrance offering in processions. The last drawing shows a hanging incense burner which is swung in a monastic procession, and is very similar in design to the frankincense burner used in the Christian Church.

Plate 95: Offerings of touch, taste and smell – cloth, fruit, perfume and incense

Plate 96: The seven offering bowls

Chapter Nine
Various Peaceful Offerings, Jewels and Ritual Implements

This chapter illustrates and describes various forms of offerings and ritual implements, many of which are not included amongst the groups of auspicious symbols described in Chapter 8. The subjects covered in this chapter include: the Three Jewels, the seven offering bowls, alms bowl and vase offerings; jewels, *gzi* stones, rosaries, *rudraksha* beads, and plant attributes; ritual vases; hand-held insignia; assorted objects and offerings; the possessions of a monk and ritual musical instruments. Plates 103, 104 and 107 are drawn as collages of ritual implements and offerings to include many miscellaneous objects.

THE THREE JEWELS
(Skt. *triratna*; Tib. *dkon mchog gsum*)

The central offering on a Buddhist altar are the Three Precious Jewels of Buddha, dharma and sangha, which represent the body, speech and mind of all the Buddhas. They form the three aspects or 'receptacles' of 'taking refuge' in the Buddhist teachings. Conceptually the Buddhist trinity of body, speech and mind refer to the purified conduct, speech and thought of enlightened beings.

An image or statue of the Buddha is placed at the centre of the altar, representing the enlightened body of the Buddha or fully realised teacher. A scriptural text is placed to the left of the Buddha image, representing the Buddhist teachings of enlightened speech or dharma. A stupa is placed to the right of the Buddha image, representing enlightened mind as the sangha or spiritual community. Traditionally scriptural texts, being the spoken words and teachings of the Buddha, are placed on the highest level of the altar. The Buddha image, being the manifest representation of the Buddha's form, is placed at the central point. The stupa,

representing the spiritual community or sangha, is placed beneath the Buddha image. During the refuge taking ceremony, where one formally becomes a Buddhist, the Buddha image, text and stupa are placed, momentarily, in sequence upon the disciple's head. In the preliminary tantric initiations, refuge is also taken in the 'three roots' (Tib. *rtsa ba gsum*) of the guru, *yidam* deity, and *dakini*.

THE SEVEN WATER BOWL OFFERINGS
(Tib. *ting phor*)

The seven water bowl offerings are traditionally made on a Buddhist altar each day, and placed in front of and a little below the representations of the Three Jewels. The bowls are normally made of brass, bronze or silver, about three or four inches in diameter, and are often ornamented with auspicious designs in repoussé gold or silver inlay. The seven bowls represent the 'seven limbed practice' (Skt. *saptanga*; Tib. *yan lag bdun pa*) for purifying negative tendencies and accumulating merit, which consists of prostrations; making offerings; confession of non-virtuous actions; rejoicing in the positive actions of oneself and others; requesting the Buddhas to teach; requesting the Buddhas to remain in this world; and the dedication of merit.

Before they are placed on the altar, a little water is poured into each of the cleansed bowls: as a preliminary offering this ensures that the bowls are not presented empty. The clean stacked bowls are held in the left hand before placement, consecrated by reciting the three syllables *Om A Hum*, and the top bowl is partially filled with water. Then most of the water from the top bowl is poured into the second bowl before it is placed on the altar. This process is repeated until all seven bowls form a straight line from left to right. The distance between each bowl should be approximately equal to the thickness of one barley grain. If they touch each other it augurs that one may become mentally dull; if they are placed too far apart it augurs that one may become separated from one's guru.

The pure, clean water used to fill the bowls is said to be poured 'like a barley grain' from the water vessel's spout. This indicates that the stream of water is thin or slow at the beginning, thick or faster in the middle, and tapering off to a narrow stream at the end. The bowls are filled to within a barley grain's thickness of the top of each rim. Overflowing the rim's top is believed to result in ethical detriment, and too low a level of water augurs a decline in prosperity. One should not breathe on the water bowl offerings, as this creates defilement.

The seven bowls can also be arranged to form the 'seven offerings'. The seven offerings are presented to the deities in the manner in which an honoured guest would have been welcomed to one's house in ancient India. The first bowl contains pure water for drinking and rinsing the mouth. The second bowl contains water for washing the feet, as in the traditional Indian custom of entering the threshold of a house barefooted. The third bowl contains fresh flowers, representing the custom of presenting a male guest with a flower garland, and a female guest with flowers for her hair adornment. The fourth bowl holds incense to please the sense of smell. The fifth bowl holds an oil or butter lamp to represent the illumination of wisdom. The sixth bowl contains rosewater or perfumed water for refreshing the face and breast; and the seventh bowl contains delicious food for the honoured guests. The Tibetan food offering usually consists of a red or white conical sacrificial cake (Tib. *gtor ma*), made from roasted barley flour (Tib. *tsam pa*), dyes and butter. An eighth offering of music is included in the list, represented by a lute, flute, cymbals, a conch or a *damaru*, but the music offering is more commonly visualised and not actually represented with the seven offering bowls. In certain tantric practices or *sadhanas* the first two water bowls may be combined into one bowl, and a *damaru* or small conch placed in the seventh bowl to represent the offering of music. When all eight bowls are prescribed they may form a correspondence with the eight offering goddesses (see Plate 113) – the four intercardinal goddesses of flowers, incense, light and perfume (the third to sixth bowls), and the four cardinal goddesses of beauty, garlands, song and dance (the pairs of bowls at each end).

When the offerings have been arranged they are consecrated by dipping a stem of *kusha* grass into the water vessel and sprinkling the offerings, whilst reciting the syllables *Om A Hum*, three or seven times. At the end of the day the offerings are removed. The water from the bowls is gathered, and the flowers and food offerings dispersed into the natural environment for the benefit of passing animals or hungry spirits. The seven bowls are wiped clean and stacked upside down ready for the next day.

Another practice of water offering is performed in the water-*puja* ritual, where a water offering set (Tib. *gtor chas*) is used to propitiate the *nagas* and certain wealth deities.

This set consists of four metal implements: a small shallow pouring vessel with a spout, a wide containing bowl, a small tripod which rests within the containing bowl, and a smaller flat bowl which rests on the tripod. Ritual water is repeatedly poured into the small bowl above the tripod and then emptied into the lower containing bowl.

Plate 96

Illustrated here are three drawings showing the arrangement for the seven offering bowls. If only water is used in the seven bowls, then a lighted butter lamp is usually placed in front of the middle bowl.

Plate 97

Examples of various alms bowls, offering bowls and vases, containing fruit, flowers and jewels are represented in this drawing. Such offerings are commonly illustrated in thangkas, particularly those depicting Buddhas, arhats, Indian masters, or Tibetan lineage holders, lamas and gurus.

The two top rows depict twelve variations of the traditional Indian Buddhist alms bowl or *patra* (Tib. *lhung bzed*). The *patra* is made from cast iron and depicted in the deep blue colour of this metal. Its interior is usually white – indicating milk or yoghurt as the milk-rice food offering which Shakyamuni Buddha consumed prior to his enlightenment. In certain deity descriptions the *patra* is described as being fashioned of a precious blue mineral, such as turquoise for Amitabha, and lapis lazuli or blue beryl for the Medicine Buddha. The alms bowls depicted here are mounted on gilded bronze or gold stands embellished with lotus-petal designs. At the left of the top row is an alms bowl with the earth base and four tiers of Mt Meru placed above. The second alms bowl contains yoghurt, and the third alms bowl holds three myrobalan fruits. Myrobalan is the attribute of the Medicine Buddha, who holds an alms bowl containing myrobalan in his left hand, and a triple stem of the fruit in his right hand (see Plate 102). Below the bowl are peaches and artemisia leaves, symbolising longevity and health. The next three bowls to the right contain the triple fruit and leaves of the wild strawberry, *bilva* fruit, and peach respectively.

On the left of the second row is an alms bowl full of setting curds, with a white silk cloth draped over its aperture as a protection against insects and dust. The second alms bowl to the right contains wild mushrooms and edible green leaves. The third bowl contains peaches and berries. The fourth bowl holds three peaches, with a second offering bowl containing jewels and cinnabar to its left. The fifth bowl contains curds with a white cloth cover, and the sixth bowl contains *bilva* fruit.

On the left of the third row is a golden bowl resting on a large round lotus leaf, and containing an arrangement of fruit, leaves, and budding flowers. At the centre is a lotus pedestal with a moon and sun disc above it, and a golden

Plate 97: Alms bowls, offering bowls and vases

tripod base below. On the moon disc are: a bowl of fruit, a jewel, and a water flask, with three fruits and a skull cup containing medicinal pills placed behind. The next drawing on the right shows a flower vase containing a lotus flower. To the right of this is a golden treasure vase with a lotus-petal design and a white silk scarf draped around its neck.

Below the centre on the far left are two drawings of jewel trays or basins (Tib. *gzhong pa rin po che*). The upper tray is made of gilded bronze and embellished with the imperial Chinese wave and rock design. It contains three pyramidal stacks of multicoloured jewels with a flaming jewel at the centre, elephant's tusks, fruit, and a perfumed conch shell on the left, and a sacrificial cake (Tib. *gtor ma*) surrounded by medicinal pills on the right. The lower tray displays the wave and rock design, and rests upon a double lotus base of sixty-four petals. It contains a pyramid of jewels, elephant's tusks, flowers, leaves and fruit.

To the right of the trays are a pair of flower vases containing peonies. Next is a larger vase, draped with a silk scarf and containing two fully-blossoming peonies. On the right is a shallow basin which also contains three peonies. Below is another small basin full of fruit and berries. In the bottom right corner is a basin of fruit, leaves and flowers, which rests upon a large convoluted lotus leaf.

In the bottom left corner is a low wooden altar with the seven offering bowls placed in sequence from left to right. At the centre above the altar is a bronze tray containing fruit, jewels, flowers, leaves, coral, elephants' tusks, and a sacrificial cake; a long silk scarf swirls upwards on either side of the tray. To the right of the tray is a basin of conch-shaped jewels and leaves.

Depictions of ceramic basins, bowls, cups and vases in Tibetan art often reveal a great attention to detail in their accuracy of design and motif illustration. The models on which these designs are based were copied from Chinese ceramic imports of the Yuan, Ming and Qing dynasties, as the Tibetans relied upon China for their trade supply of porcelain chinaware. Extremely rare Ming porcelain designs may be illustrated on fine Tibetan thangkas. This incorporation of faithfully reproduced ceramic designs reveals that there were strong elements of 'still life' composition within Tibetan art.

JEWELS
(Skt. *ratna*, *mani*;
Tib. *rin po che*, *rin chen*, *nor bu*)

Tibetan art abounds with depictions of precious jewels, which occur as the offerings and adornments of deities, and as decorative embellishments on thrones, buildings and architectural structures. Jewels appear to permeate the whole visionary landscape with their celestial light and spectral radiance. The mineral pigments employed in Tibetan art, the fauvist purity of their vivid primary colour combinations, and the minimal use of sombre colour tones or chiaroscuro effects, all enhance the other worldly jewel-like quality embodied in the essence of Tibetan art. The pure primary colour powders used in the creation of sand mandalas are compared to, or composed of, precious gems, semi-precious minerals, or their synthetic colour equivalents.

The Tibetan word *rinpoche*, meaning 'jewel' or 'precious one', is also the term or title used for incarnate lamas as the embodiment of the precious jewel of the *buddhadharma*. The terms *rinchen* and *norbu*, meaning 'of great value' and 'jewel' respectively, are also commonly used as names amongst both the Tibetan laity and sangha. The comparison of the precious rarity of the 'wish-fulfilling gem', which fulfils all desires, to the enlightened nature of highly realised teachers attains its full expression in the Three Jewels of Buddha, dharma and sangha.

In the Tibetan Buddhist tradition five or seven precious substances are listed – gold, silver, coral and pearl form the first four; and lapis lazuli, turquoise or 'gemstones' the fifth. Crystal sometimes replaces silver in certain listings, and emerald may arise in the place of gemstones. When a list of seven precious substances is given they usually follow the sequence: gold, silver, coral, pearl, lapis lazuli, diamonds and gemstones. The wish-fulfilling tree, for example, is described as being composed of the seven precious substances, with gold roots, a silver trunk, lapis lazuli branches, coral leaves, pearl flowers, gemstone buds, and diamond fruit. The wish-fulfilling cow is described as having a gemstone body, horns of diamond, hooves of sapphire, and a tail resembling a wish-fulfilling tree.

The precious metals of gold and silver are commonly found as natural deposits in Tibet, and surface-mined or river-panned gold were to be found in abundant supply. The Roman historian 'Pliny the Younger' (*circa* AD 62–113), and the legendary Venetian explorer Marco Polo (1254–1324), both relate the legend of how giant ants mined for gold in the frozen wastelands of the Tibetan Changtang highlands. A gold nugget, the size and shape of a dog, is reputed to have been unearthed in a goldfield close to Lake Manasarovar in Western Tibet. The then ruling Dalai Lama is said to have decreed that this large nugget should be returned to its original site and marked with a stupa named Khyiro Serpo or 'golden dog's body' (Tib. *khyi ro gser po*). Gold dust, often in substantial quantities, was frequently presented as an offering for religious teachings or an initiation.

Indigenous gold was mainly obtained from the goldfields in the Kailash-Manasarovar area of Western Tibet, known as the kingdom of Guge. The Tibetan materia medica lists various qualities, colours and sources of gold, such as white and light-yellow gold from India, yellow gold from Western and Central Tibet, red-yellow gold from the province of Kham, red gold from China, and green gold from Mongolia. But the finest quality of gold was believed to be from Sri Lanka. Gold and silver are weighed in *tola*, and the gold pigment used in Tibetan painting is bought and sold in *anna* and *tola* quantities. One *tola* equals approximately twelve grams or 180 Troy grains, and is equivalent to the weight of an Indian silver rupee coin; a sixteenth part of a *tola* is known as an *anna*, as monetarily sixteen *anna* coins equalled a rupee in value. An estimation of the gold needed for a particular thangka was often an important consideration in the commissioning of a painting.

Pure gold is such a malleable metal that it can be beaten into almost translucent sheets of gold leaf, which are virtually weightless, highly static, and only a few microns thick. The malleability of gold makes it extremely difficult to grind into a fine powder, as its particles tend to adhere together like wax. The Newars of Kathmandu have for centuries possessed secret techniques of grinding gold pigment from its twenty-four carat absolute. Newar 'drop gold' pigment is used in Tibetan thangka painting. It is produced by grinding beaten gold leaf to an extremely fine grade in a mortar and pestle with the addition of a soluble mineral grinding agent. At the end of each day's grinding the mortar is filled with water and stirred, quickly poured off into another container, and the fine suspended gold particles allowed to settle overnight. When all of the gold has been finely ground it is mixed with a plant-derived liquid binder or glue, and dropped and dried as small hemispherical pellets. In comparison to Newari 'drop gold' the finest quality of powder-gold pigment obtainable in the west, known as 'shell gold', is extremely coarse. In medieval Western art a fine gold powder was produced from evaporating a gold leaf and mercury amalgam, but this technique was lost over the course of time. Gold leaf was also ground with salt or honey to produce the fine powder pigment used in illuminated manuscript painting. Synthetic gold substitutes, such as copper or bronze powder, are poor imitations for real gold pigment. Unlike these metals, gold is inert and does not oxidise or tarnish, and its matt surface may be intricately burnished to a luminous and permanent lustre.

Gold, as the first of the five precious substances, is symbolic of the Buddha's radiant enlightenment, and any deity form or image may be painted or gilded in a pure gold skin colour.

As gold is the 'hot' metal of the sun, silver is the 'cool' nocturnal metal of the moon, which is metaphorically derived from solidified moonbeams. In Chinese art the crescent moon and the milky way are known as the 'silver sickle' and 'silver stream'. Tibetan silver was most easily obtainable from India in the form of Indian silver rupee coins. The Tibetan materia medica lists silver obtained from Indian, Nepali, Russian and Bhutanese coins, Chinese ingots shaped like crescents, Mongolian ingots shaped like walnuts, and native Tibetan ingots shaped like horse or sheep hoofs. White, red, or green silver alloys may be produced by adding tin, copper or lead respectively. Silver is widely used in the casting and gilding of statues, ritual objects, jewellery and household utensils.

Silver pellets of ground silver pigment are also produced by Newari goldsmiths, but it is rarely used in thangka painting as silver tarnishes by oxidising, and is considered an inferior colour to gold. The tourist market of Kathmandu now displays many glittering and cheap imitations of black thangkas (Tib. *nag thang*), painted in burnished gold and silver line on a black background, but since these compositions are invariably iconographically inaccurate they serve only as decorative ornaments.

Silver is used in the same gilding processes as gold, with a silver leaf and mercury amalgam being used for 'hot gilding', where the heated mercury evaporates at a lower temperature leaving a fine matt gold or silver deposit. Like gold, silver can be burnished to a high reflectivity, or beaten into sheets of thin silver leaf between stacked 'sandwiches' of paper. Oriental gold and silver leaf tend to have a richer lustre than their European equivalents, which tend to be more reflective and less matt.

Red coral (Tib. *byu ru*) and white pearl (Tib. *mu tig*) are the two main organic substances which are classified as jewel ornaments and worn by many deities. As the aquatic correlates of gold and silver, coral and pearl similarly symbolise the sun and moon, the solar and lunar channels, and the red female and white male *bodhichitta* or 'seminal drops' (Skt. *bindu*; Tib. *thig le*). The esoteric symbolism of the *bodhichitta* drops is revealed in very specific deity descriptions where the jewel ornaments are described as being of merged or 'fused' coral and pearl, referring to the 'indestructible drop' at the heart centre (see Plate 72).

Coral is naturally formed in a variety of hues and shapes such as red, white, or black branch coral, blue coral, brain coral, and organ-pipe coral. Red branch coral (*Corallium rubrum*), which often takes the form of a cylindrical branched tree, is considered the most sacred and precious by Tibetans, and is widely fashioned into beads and jewel ornaments. Coral was imported into Tibet from India, China, Russia and Japan, and even from as far afield as the Italian Adriatic Sea, which provides a rich harvest of precious red coral. White, red and white, and black branched coral stems are also valued as religious offerings, and are used for medicinal purposes – particularly in the treatment of blood, liver, and poison-induced fevers.

White seed pearls (Tib. *mu tig dkar po*), strung in rows or clusters, form one of the most common ornaments in both secular jewellery and deity descriptions. Ocean pearls, derived from the pearl-oyster (*Pinctada*) or pearl-mussel (*Margaritifera*), were imported into Tibet from India and China. Cultivated river pearls from the freshwater mussel were harvested in China, and as an innovation a miniature clay image of the Buddha could be introduced into the mussel as the irritant foreign-body around which a layer of pearl would grow. The Chinese believed that pearls embodied the *yin* essence of the moon, and like the Indians believed that pearls protected against fire as the *yang* essence of the sun. The Chinese symbol of the 'dragon pearl' is described in Plate 43.

The Tibetan materia medica lists a variety of unusual organic pearls: green pearls derived from rainwater accumulations on the leaves of East Indian plantain trees; blue pearls from the leaves of a certain South Indian tree; sacred red pearls derived from legendary creatures; red and grey pearls from the heads of snakes; white elephant pearls or bezoars; freshwater pearls from Amdo province and China; and blister pearls obtained from mother-of-pearl or oyster shells. Tibetan pearls are also classified into smooth-surfaced 'male' pearls, and 'female' pearls with protruding 'eyelets' that resemble breasts.

The enduring suffering experienced by the oyster in its pearl cultivation has universally identified the pearl as a symbol of sorrow and purity. In the Christian tradition the pearl (Margarita) represents the body of Christ, and mother-of-pearl the Virgin Mary. In the celebration of the Christian Mass both the chalice and the particle of bread or 'Host' – which is dropped into the consecrated wine – are known as the Margarita or 'pearl', and symbolise the union of the body of Christ with his sacred blood.

Turquoise (Tib. *g.yu*), as the fifth alternative precious substance, is probably the most common stone worn as a jewel ornament amongst the Tibetans. Native turquoise is found in all of the regions of Tibet, although it was also imported from Persia, Afghanistan and China. The most superior quality of turquoise occurs in a deep blue colour, and in forms tinted with red or white. Turquoise stones with many black striations or a pale green colour are considered to be of inferior quality. Medicinally turquoise is believed to purify the blood and absorb the toxins which accumulate in the liver. Turquoise is also believed to change its colour according to the health of its wearer, becoming duller or paler as the owner's health deteriorates.

Gemstones, as the fifth inclusive group of precious substances, includes diamond, sapphire, lapis lazuli, tournaline, beryl, topaz, ruby, emerald, jade, amber, crystal, and chalcedony or agate as *gzi* stones (see Plate 99).

The diamond, although rarely found in Tibet, was synonymous in Indian Buddhism with the adamantine *vajra* as 'the lord of stones' (Tib. *rdo rje*). As the hardest, clearest and most brilliant of precious stones the diamond symbolises the indestructible, indivisible, infallible, incorruptible and unchangeable nature of the enlightened mind, and became synonymous with the Vajrayana as the tantric path of the 'indestructible vehicle'.

The most famous of Indian diamonds, the Koh-i-noor or 'mountain of light', was first mentioned in the epic legends of the *Mahabharata* (*circa* 2000 BC). This legendary stone passed through the hands of many great Indian, Persian and Mughal emperors, culminating in Ranjit Singh (1780–1839), the Punjabi founder of the Sikh kingdom. With the annexation of the Indian Punjab in 1849, the Koh-i-noor was presented to Queen Victoria and passed into British hands.

Sapphire, emerald and ruby were mainly mined in Burma, Sri Lanka and India; topaz and beryl in Russia; jade and amber in Central Asia and China; and lapis lazuli in Persia and Afghanistan. Lapis lazuli (Tib. *mu men*) is frequently referred to in iconographical descriptions or gem-like comparisons as the fifth alternative precious substance. The pure azure blue of this mineral equates it with sapphire as the bluest of stones. The mineral pigment (lazurite) obtained from ground lapis lazuli is commonly believed to have been used extensively in both oriental and occidental medieval art, but since lazurite becomes extremely pale when finely ground its actual use was limited by the coarseness of its particle size and the expense involved in obtaining deep blue lapis from Persia. The mineral azurite was much more commonly used to create the deep blues found in medieval painting. In Western art azurite was later superseded by the development of synthetic ultramarine, so named because Asiatic lapis lazuli was brought to Europe from 'beyond the sea' (ultra-marine).

Amber was obtained from Yunnan province in China, and its Chinese name, *hu p'o*, meaning 'tiger's spirit', is derived from the belief that the spirit of a dead tiger enters the ground and transforms itself into amber. Opaque yellow or orange amber is commonly worn as a bead or jewel ornament by the Tibetan laity and, along with *gzi*, turquoise, red coral and white pearls, forms one of the five most popular Tibetan costume jewels. The opaque orange amber favoured by Tibetans is considered to be of a superior quality and age (approximately twenty million years) to the translucent amber found in the Baltic area of Eastern Europe. Amber is formed from the fossilised resin of coniferous trees, and possesses electrostatic properties when rubbed. Powdered amber is used medicinally and as an incense.

Gemstones are commonly believed to have medicinal and protective qualities, and are assigned astrologically to planetary and zodiacal influences. Powdered gemstones form an important ingredient in the composition of many Tibetan medicines, particularly 'precious pills', such as 'the precious wish-fulfilling jewel' (Tib. *rin chen ratna bsam 'phel*).

Plate 98

Illustrated in this drawing are examples of various jewels and compound gemstones. Across the top area of the drawing are hanging loops of pearls and jewels. The two inner rows consist of gold ornaments on chains, or strings of small jewels or seed pearls. The next three rows show pearls of a uniform size, alternating large and small pearls, and a string of graded pearls which increase in size towards their centre. At the upper centre and corners are leaf-ornamented gold roundels, from which hang jewelled pendants and two loops of graduating pearl or amber ovals. At the centre of the left loop is a seven-eyed *gzi* stone, and at the centre of the right loop are three jewels encased in golden lotus-petal mounts. The pendants hanging from the central roundel are embellished with little silver bells, sun and moon symbols, and terminate in jewelled tips. Two white yaktail tassles hang to either side of the central pendant.

Below the central roundel is a pyramid stack of multi-coloured jewels in a golden tray. Pyramid jewel stacks, which resemble the triangular formation of pool or billiard balls, are stacked in a decreasing square sequence to form the four faces of Mt Meru as a pyramid formation. To the left of this is an eight-faceted flaming jewel mounted on a jewel-tipped handle, which is held as a hand emblem by certain deities – particularly those associated with wealth. To the upper left of this gem is a lotus-mounted crystal that radiates rays of light. Two other drawings of rock crystals are depicted on the left edge of the drawing.

In the transmission of the Dzogchen or Great Perfection teachings, rock crystal (Tib. *man shel*) is symbolically revealed during initiation to introduce the disciple to the perfect clarity of his own mind. The clear transparency of rock crystal,

Plate 98: Jewels and gemstones

which both reflects and refracts the prismatic spectrum of sunlight into brilliant rainbow-coloured rays, symbolises the Great Perfection as the natural state of the unconditioned mind. Namkhai Norbu Rinpoche, in his book *The Crystal and the Way of Light*, describes how a mirror, a crystal, and a crystal ball are used in Dzogchen to illustrate the 'three conditions' of essence, nature and energy – where the mirror reflects unconditionally, the crystal refracts light's essence unconditionally, and the crystal ball appears to hold the image within itself.

Small reliquary stupas, statues and ritual implements, such as the *vajra* or *phurba,* are traditionally carved from clear rock crystal as a symbol of their 'diamond' or *vajra* nature. The Hindu *Yogini Tantra* states that the deity may be worshipped as an image, a mandala, or a *yantra.* In the Hindu tantric tradition three-dimensional *yantras* are commonly carved from rock crystal and worshipped as a manifestation of a specific god or goddess. The *yantra,* which means 'instrument' or 'device', is usually carved as a stepped base symbolising Mt Sumeru, with a square 'earth city' (Skt. *bhupura*) of four flat mandala gateways on its summit – which encloses concentric lotus-circles containing an inscribed inner geometric design of interlocking triangles and/or squares. For peaceful rites *yantras* of rock crystal or inscribed birch bark are used; for enriching rites *yantras* of gold, silver or copper plate are used; for magnetising or empowering rites red sandalwood or smeared saffron paste are employed; and for destructive rituals *yantras* constructed of iron, lead, bone or skin are used. The stylus used for *yantra* inscription may be specified as a gold, silver or iron needle; a bone splinter; or an acacia, datura, or 'poison-wood' thorn.

The occult properties of rock crystal are well established in the occidental magic traditions, where crystal balls are used for fortune telling in crystal-gazing or scrying. The contemporary interest in crystal healing, and the modern use of quartz crystal in the 'magic' of microchip technology attests to its enduring fascination. In many cultures rock crystal is believed to be a form of petrified ice, and the aboriginals of Australia and New Guinea utilised rock crystal in rain-making rituals.

To the upper right of the jewel tray in the upper centre are two jewel-topped treasure vases, and to the right of these are five drawings of jewel-spitting mongooses. The mongoose (Skt. *nakula*; Tib. *ne'u le*) is a common attribute of wealth deities such as Vaishravana, Jambhala and Kubera. The symbol of a jewel-raining, -spitting, or -vomiting mongoose, which produces treasures when squeezed, has its origin in the Central Asian custom of using a mongoose skin as a jewel container or money-purse, where coins, precious stones or cowrie-shells could be squeezed upwards through the empty skin and ejected from the mongoose's mouth. The mongoose is also the traditional enemy of snakes, which as *nagas* are the guardians of treasures and wealth. The Indian or Central Asian mongoose is often incorrectly identified as an 'ichneumon' (*Herpestes ichneumon*), which is the native mongoose species of North Africa.

In the area below and to the left of the jewel tray are drawn various examples of single flaming jewels; the triple-eyed gem; the Three Jewels of Buddha, dharma and sangha; and the flaming eight-faceted gem. Below the tray are five examples of the single jewel, supported mainly on lotus bases. The large single flaming jewel at the lower centre has a spiral curl of flame at its base and rests upon a lotus stand. As the precious wish-fulfilling gem (Skt. *chintamani*; Tib. *yid bzhin nor bu*), the flames represent the radiance of its adamantine *vajra* nature, which shines forth in five rays of coloured light as the Five Buddha wisdoms. Precious gems are usually represented in a pear-shaped form with small spiralling flame-points at their tips and three or more concentric arcs outlined below, which echoes the spiral of the conch shell or the three curved crease lines on the throats of enlightened beings. Occasionally precious gems are depicted with a fountain of rainbow light emanating from their tips or, in the case of water-borne or *naga*-jewels, with a fountain of water. Jewels are shaded from a light tone at their tips to a dark colour tone at their bases, and are usually painted in the four colours of blue, red, green, and orange. When rows of pyramid-stacked jewels are represented, such as are depicted at the bottom of the drawing, the alternating colour sequence of each row is usually blue and red, with a green and orange sequence occurring across the next row. This colour scheme follows the model of the multicoloured lotus.

Twelve examples of the flaming eight-faceted jewel are depicted in this drawing. The eight-faceted jewel is usually composed of a pyramid formation of six visible and elongated jewels which taper towards their cylindrical bases or a lower-middle waistline. This waist may be encircled by a golden band or coloured silk scarf which appears to bind the individual tapering facets together. The jewel is often supported on a moon, sun, and lotus base. The eight facets are theoretically arranged in a square group of four at the base, with a triangular group of three above and inside, and a single central jewel crowning the tip. Artistically they are depicted as a lower row of three tapering cylindrical jewels, with two jewels in the middle row and a single jewel at the top – such that only six of the eight facets are visible. The colour sequence is usually red, blue, red across the bottom row, green and orange across the middle row, and red or blue at the top. The eight facets of this jewel – which is usually identified as lapis lazuli – symbolise the eight *nadis* of the heart *chakra,* the eight directions, and the Noble Eightfold Path.

Above the stacked jewels at the bottom of the drawing are several spiralling circular motifs of the conch-shell tip, which occurred as a common decorative jewel motif in early Tibetan art and symbolised the jewel-like quality embodied in heavenly landscape elements, such as flowers and leaves. On either side of the central jewel pyramid are the triple-jewel spirals of the 'wheel of joy' (Tib. *dga' 'khyil*).

GZI STONES OR BEADS

The banded or etched agate, known in Tibetan as a *gzi* stone, is worn as a protective amulet against afflictions of disease, strokes, misfortune, spirit possession and malignant planetary influences. *Gzi* stones are commonly worn as ornaments around the neck, and often sawn in half lengthwise to embellish the crowns of sacred images, such as the Jowo Rinpoche statue in Lhasa. They are generally classified into two forms: the cylindrical brown (or black) and white banded agate with circular eyes (Tib. *mig*), and the rounded chalcedony or cornelian variety with a spiralling red ochre, white or gold band. *Gzi* are also classified by shape into female *gzi* – which are slender and tapering, and male *gzi* – which are thicker or barrel-shaped. In Sanskrit the *gzi* is known as *mechaka*, a precious blue-black stone which is said to resemble the eye of a peacock.

The cylindrical brown (or black) and white variety are usually marked with white 'eyes' or rings, which form a symmetrical angular pattern with their bands. The circular eyes can number more than twelve, but those with nine eyes are considered the most precious as a protective talisman against demonic possession. Nine-eyed stones are extremely rare and expensive, their trade value in Tibet being equivalent to a modest farmhouse or several pounds weight of silver ingots.

The origin of these stones is shrouded in mystery. Similar forms of etched agate are found in the Himalayan region and across the plain areas of India, Pakistan, Afghanistan and Iran. Techniques of etching agate stones are believed to have been known across the wide area of land between the Indus valley and the Tigris River delta since the third millenium BC. Yet Tibetan *gzi* dealers maintain that Tibetan *gzi* are of a much harder stone and exhibit different qualities from their Central Asian equivalents. Since they are often found near ancient grave sites or in ploughed fields, they are believed to be of prehistoric origin.

Tibetan sources ascribe several origins for the *gzi* stone. One belief is that they are living creatures or worms, which petrify into stone when they are first seen or touched. Since they are nearly always imperfect, it is also believed that the sky gods discard and drop them to earth when they become worn, damaged and chipped, or that they are the fallen fruits of the celestial wish-fulfilling tree. Another belief is that they are the scattered treasure trove of the legendary hero Gesar of Ling, who plundered them from the treasury of the king of Tajik (Persia). A lesser known belief is that they are the droppings of the fabulous bird Garuda, which fall to earth as he flies across the skies.

In the Indus valley area the following technique was used for etching patterns into cornelian, chalcedony, and opaque agate or quartz. The design would first be applied using a thick solution of sodium carbonate (washing soda) painted on with a reed pen or brush. When dry, the stone was buried in hot embers and baked for a short time. When cool and cleaned this would leave a white design glazed or fused into the darker stone.

A reverse design process could be accomplished by coating the whole stone in sodium carbonate solution, firing it until it was bleached, then etching it with a copper nitrate solution to produce a black on white pattern. The earliest *gzi* patterns were probably of a banded or pentagonal design. The best stones are unchipped, opaque, with the pattern embedded deep within the stone, and with a smooth lustrous patina.

The Tibetan word *gzi* actually means 'brightly burnished' or 'etched'. Tibetan artists use a polished and pointed fragment of *gzi* stone, mounted like a brush with a silver ferrule and wooden handle, to burnish the gold applied in thangka painting. The use of *gzi* as an auspicious agate burnishing tool is believed to lend a luminous and sacred quality to the painted gold work on thangkas and statues.

Powdered *gzi* stone is mixed with ground gold, silver and pearl to produce medicinal pills (Tib. *ril bu*), with potent healing properties.

Gzi stones have been prolifically imitated in the last century. Copies are now made out of porcelain, plastic, resin, yak horn, and glass, and produced in India, China, Nepal and Tibet. Extremely fine copies are now being made in Taiwan, using the original fire-etching process. These beautiful Taiwanese copies are very costly, but genuine Tibetan *gzi*, particularly those with nine eyes or rare designs, sell for very high prices. In the modern oriental marketplace these prices have now become astronomical, with absurd fables grafted onto the origin or uniqueness of these stones – such as being one of the keys to the treasure chest of Gesar of Ling. It is commonly understood amongst Tibetans that the 'pedigree' of a *gzi* should be scrupulously investigated; some *gzi* may become more of a curse and less of a blessing. In recent years several murders are said to have occurred during the theft of these stones. Like the ill-omened gemstones of the Western tradition, which reputedly bring a legacy of misfortune to their new owners, karmically blemished *gzi* can attract all of the negative influences they are supposed to repel. In J.R.Tolkein's *Lord of the Rings*, the great ring of Sauron was a thing of enchanting beauty, but it could very easily become too precious!

Plate 99

This illustration depicts 55 different varieties of *gzi* stone patterns or designs:

1–5. Illustrates five variations of nine-eyed *gzi* stones.
6. Shows a rounded *gzi* with a double lotus and lotus-heart motif.
7. *Gzi* with a double-ringed single eye.
8. Four-eyed *gzi* with central lotus or wave pattern.
9. Six-eyed banded *gzi* with symmetrical pattern.
10. Six-eyed *gzi* with aligned triple-eye design.
11. Rectangular 'earth door' design with double-eye.
12. 'Male' five-eyed *gzi* with swastika arm pattern.
13. 'Female' five-eyed *gzi*.
14. Symmetrical *gzi* with double sun and moon motif.
15. Wide barrel *gzi* with early domed pentagonal design.
16. Rare '*vajra*-hook' in lotus petal design.
17. '*Damaru*' or hand drum design
18. Two-eyed *gzi* with double ring.
19. Transverse 'arrowhead' design.

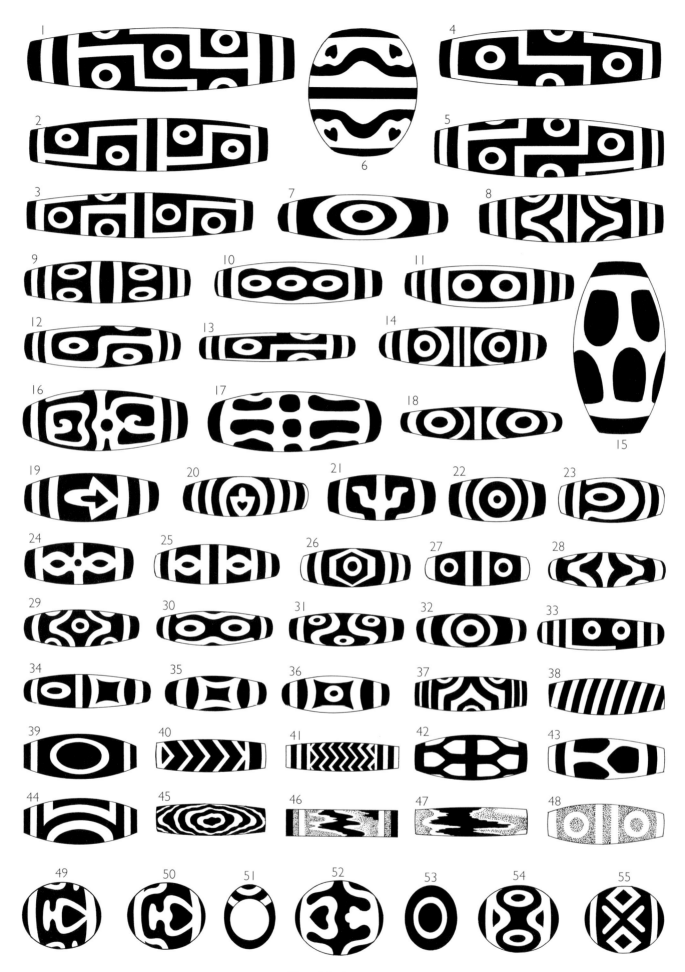

Plate 99: *Gzi* stones

20. 'Arrowhead' design within a circular motif.
21. Rare 'trident' design.
22. Single-eyed *gzi* with radiating circles.
23. Sun and moon, designed as a lotus-petal band.
24, 25. '*Vajra*' designs.
26. Hexagonal 'mouth' enclosing central eye.
27. Small four-eyed symmetrical *gzi*.
28. Four-eyed *gzi* with central spear or arrowhead axis.
29. '*Makara*-mouth' design.
30–33. Variations of eye patterns.
34. 'Heaven door and earth door', based on the Chinese symbols of a circle for heaven, and a square for earth.
35. 'Earth door' design.
36. 'Heaven door' within 'earth door' design.
37. '*Makara*-mouth' design.
38. *Gzi* with a banded spiral pattern.
39. Single-eyed *gzi*.
40, 41. Two examples with etched wave or zig zag pattern.
42, 43. Two examples of pentagonal design made by positive and negative etching.
44. Barrel-shaped 'heaven and earth door'.
45. Naturally occurring agate stone with eye formation.
46. '*Chung gzi*', meaning 'opaque *gzi* stone'. A naturally-occurring banded agate with annealed end sections.
47. A typical '*chung gzi*' with natural striations of white quartz within an ochre, brown, and black agate amalgamation.
48. Translucent *gzi* with light ochre pattern embedded in the stone.
49. Round '*bumpa*' or vase design.
50. '*Bumpa*' with lotus-petal design.
51. Finger ring carved from a *gzi* stone.
52. Rounded lotus and lotus-leaf design.
53. Single-eye *gzi* worn as a stone on a finger ring.
54. Rounded eye and lotus wave motif.
55. Diamond and arrow tip design.

THE ROSARY (Skt. *mala*; Tib. '*phreng ba*)

Traditionally a Buddhist rosary or *mala* of 108 even-sized beads is used for mantra recitation. The sacred number of 108 predates Buddhism, being the classical number of the Hindu names assigned to a deity or god. As a multiple of twelve and nine it represents the nine planets in the twelve zodiac houses. As a multiple of twenty-seven and four it also represents the four quarters of the moon in each of the twenty-seven lunar mansions or constellations. Nine is also a 'magic' number. A number multiplied by nine results in a number the sum of whose digits is also a multiple of nine. In Pranayana Yoga it is calculated that a human being takes 21,600 breaths in a twenty-four-hour cycle consisting of sixty periods of 360 breaths; a twelve-hour 'day' cycle therefore equals 10,800 breaths. The 108 beads also ensure that at least a hundred mantra recitations have been completed in a full rosary turning.

Mantras are recited to accomplish the four *karmas* or enlightened activities of pacifying, enriching, magnetising, and destroying. Although various numbers of beads are specified below, a *mala* of 108 beads is invariably used by most practising Buddhists.

In the peaceful rites of appeasing, the beads should be made of crystal, pearl, mother of pearl, white lotus seed, moonstone, conch shell, or ivory. The beads should be clear or white, numbering one hundred or 108. In the enriching rites of increase, the beads should be of bodhi seed, lotus seed, gold, silver, bronze or copper, and should number 108. In the magnetising rites of attracting or drawing power into one's sphere of personal influence, the beads should be made of red coral, carnelian, red sandalwood or saffron-scented redwood, and should number twenty-five. In the wrathful rites of destructive or forceful activity, the beads are made from *rudraksha* seeds, human or animal bone, iron, or lead, and should number sixty. Alternative numbers of beads for various practices are given as: 1,008, 108, one hundred, sixty, fifty-four, forty-two, twenty-seven, twenty-five, and twenty-one. For the practice of Vajrayogini, beads made from red coral and carnelian are especially prized. For the Medicine Buddha practice, beads made from lapis lazuli are auspicious.

Fashionable beads made from amber, ruby, turquoise, amethyst, beryl, tiger's eye, onyx, rose quartz, and rock crystal are now commercially popular, but traditionally bodhi seed and red sandalwood are considered to be universally auspicious for all practices. Human and animal-bone *malas* should only be used by accomplished yogins, as karmic influences are believed to be inherent in ritual objects made of bone.

An early Buddhist text known as the *Susiddhi Tantra*, which is based on the early Vajrayana concept of only Three Buddha Families (see page 92), states that for increase rites of the Lotus Family lineage, lotus-seed beads should be used (see below). For wrathful rites of the Vajra Family lineage, *rudraksha* seeds should be used. For pacifying rites of the Buddha Family lineage, seeds of a wild plant named Putranjiva (*Putranjiva roxburghii*) should be used; these small seeds are worn as necklaces by children in India to protect their life force and health. Traditionally *mala* seeds were consecrated or purified by cleansing in a mixture of the five products derived from an orange-coloured cow – milk, butter, yoghurt, urine and dung.

The threads which are strung through a *mala* represent the continuity of the *buddhadharma* piercing the 108 worldly passions. Traditionally the thread is wound from three or nine individual strands, which should be spun by a young virgin girl belonging to the tantric lineage of the specific Buddha Family. Three strands represent the Three Jewels of Buddha, dharma and sangha; nine strands symbolise Vajradhara and the eight bodhisattvas. A single strand should not be used, in case of sudden breakage.

A typical Tibetan *mala* will consist of 108 beads on a triple-strand thread, with different colour beads at the twenty-seven, fifty-four, and eighty-one bead points, dividing the mala into four equal sections. Coloured beads may also be placed at the ten and twenty-one points for mantra counting.

Plate 100: The Buddhist rosary

Attached to the mala are two tassled counter strings, each threaded with ten small ring beads made of metal – usually silver, gold or bronze – and sealed at their separate ends with a small metal *vajra* and bell. These small counters, strung on a double plaited cord, are used for counting the tens and hundreds of complete rosary recitation cycles. A third counter for the thousands may also be used; this is commonly sealed with the symbol of a wheel or jewel. Its thread loop may be moved from bead to bead along the *mala* to count the tens of thousands of mantra recitations performed. On completion of a full cycle of 108 mantra recitations, the mala is turned around and the next mantra cycle is counted in reversed order along the beads.

The 'guru' beads at the end of a rosary – one round and the other cylindrical – symbolise the wisdom which cognizes emptiness and emptiness itself. The shape of the two beads also symbolises the enlightenment stupa of the Buddha.

Plate 100

Illustrated across the top row of this drawing are, from left to right: threaded crystal beads, which are employed in pacifying rites; lotus or bodhi seeds, employed in rites of increase; red sandalwood beads, employed in magnetising rites; and *rudraksha* beads and bone disc beads, used for rites of forceful activity.

Underneath these are illustrated from left to right: a wrist *mala* of twenty-seven beads; a *mala* of 108 beads with *vajra* and bell counters, and guru bead; and a *mala* of dried human skulls, as held by the protective deity, Mahakala.

Below these are drawn a simple unadorned bead *mala*, and a detail of a guru bead.

Rudraksha Beads

The dried berry of the *rudraksha* tree (*Elaeocarpus ganitus*) is named after the wrathful god Rudra, an early Vedic manifestation of Shiva. *Rudraksha* beads are especially sacred to Shiva, and are worn by Shaivite sadhus or holy men as rosaries, hair bands, bracelets or as singly strung amulets. In Buddhism they are employed in the mantra recitations of wrathful deity practices.

Rudraksha means the 'eye' (*akshu*) of Rudra, symbolising the third eye in his forehead. The name Rudra is derived from the Sanskrit root *rud* meaning 'to cry tears', and is based on a legend of how Rudra cried because he had been given no name when he was created from the wrath of Brahma. Tears also refer to Shiva, who cried at his own destructive activity.

Rudraksha seeds are formed in a hard woody shell, which when broken open reveals a round pitted seed with granular protuberances. The seeds are naturally divided by radial grooves into a number of segments known as *mukha* or 'faces'. The most common number of faces is invariably five. Very rarely they are found with a varying number of faces, from one to upwards of twenty-one. The rarest beads are the twenty-one-faced, and the one-faced *rudraksha*, which is known as *ekamukha* – 'single-faced'; such beads are extremely sacred and very costly. It is believed that after an *Elaeocarpus* tree produces a one-faced *rudraksha* its vitality is exhausted, and the tree remains barren and fruitless for several years.

Rudraksha seeds are found in three colour varieties – red, white and black – which are said to be produced from the solar eye, the lunar eye, and the third or 'fire eye' of Shiva. Again these colours symbolise the solar, lunar, and central (or fire) channels of the subtle body. The yellow *rudraksha* is added as a fourth variety, and a correspondence is made between the four Hindu castes and these four colours: white beads should be worn by the priestly *brahmins*; red beads by the *kshatriya* or warrior caste; yellow beads by the *vaishya* or merchant caste; and black beads by the low caste *shudras*. Specific mantras are employed for the numerical faces of a *rudraksha*, and various Shaivite traditions prescribe specific numbers to be worn on different parts of the body: a *rudraksha mala* of 108 beads is worn around the neck, and a twenty-one-bead *mala*, known as an *Indramala,* is used for *japa* or mantra recitation.

Rudraksha beads vary from a quarter to more than an inch in diameter, and in the present day are grown in Indonesia, Nepal and India. Many imitation rare *rudrakshas* are carved

Plate 101: *Rudrakasha* beads

from larger beads or from a similar species of Elaeocarpus known as the *bhadraksha* or 'auspicious-eyed' tree.

Plate 101

The two rows of this drawing illustrate some of the auspicious marks or simulacra found on *rudraksha* beads, and their numerical faces or *mukha* numbering from one to fourteen. The first three seeds on the left of the top row illustrate the auspicious symbols of the Hindu syllable *Om*, the Shiva lingam, and the trident, which along with the snake are believed to be miraculously self-manifested on rare one-faced *rudraksha* seeds. Kali Baba, a contemporary saint from South India believed to be over a hundred years old, is said to wear a *rudraksha mala* which has spontaneously manifested 108 different deity forms on its beads. Underneath these in the second row are illustrated a binary or double *rudraksha* with single faces, and a double bead with multiple faces. These very rare double beads symbolise the union of Shiva and his consort Parvati (Umadevi). The extremely rare triple-joined bead symbolises Shiva, Parvati, and their son, Ganesha.

Illustrated in the two rows of seven beads on the right are beads with between one and fourteen faces. Their symbolism is as follows:

1. One face: represents Shiva. Possession of such a bead confers great fortune.
2. Two faces: Shiva and Parvati united into one body as Ardhanarishvara – the 'god who is half man'.
3. Three faces: the trinity of Brahma, Vishnu and Shiva; the fire god Agni; the goddess Sarasvati; the merging of the three sacred rivers (*triveni*) – the Ganges, Yamuna and Sarasvati.
4. Four faces: the four heads of Brahma.
5. Five faces: the five faces of Shiva as Pashupatinath, or 'Lord of the Animals'.
6. Six faces: Kumara or Kartikeya, the second son of Shiva, who was born with six faces.
7. Seven faces: the seven Great Rishis.
8. Eight faces: Ganesha; the eight directional guardians.
9. Nine faces: the nine planets.
10. Ten faces: the ten incarnations (*avataras*) of Vishnu.
11. Eleven faces: Ekadasa Rudra – the eleven faces of Shiva as Lokeshvara, 'The Lord of the Realms' – which Buddhism developed as eleven-faced Avalokiteshvara.
12. Twelve faces: Aditya or Surya, the sun god, with his twelve zodiac houses.
13. Thirteen faces: Kamadeva, the god of love; Indra the sky god.
14. Fourteen faces: Hanuman; Paramshiva.

Rudraksha faces numbering fifteen to twenty represent various other gods. The twenty-one-faced seed represents the wealth god Kubera, and is said to bestow great material riches on its owner.

HAND-HELD PLANT ATTRIBUTES

Illustrated in Plate 102 are ten varieties of plants with specific ritual or symbolic significance, or which occur as the hand-held attributes of certain deities. The main botanical hand emblem of most Vajrayana deities is of course the red, white, or blue lotus, but the hand-held lotus is not illustrated here as it is described in Chapter 2.

Within the complex esoteric and alchemical symbolism of Hindu tantra, virtually all plant species have a ritual significance since they are all manifestations of the 'divine'. Alchemically the 'three realms' of mineral, vegetable and animal existence correspond to the three qualities (*gunas*) of inertia (*tamas*), activity (*rajas*), and purity (*sattva*), as the attributes of body, soul and spirit. The 'soul' of plants is alchemically released through the extraction of plant essences or essential oils. The Indian, Tibetan, and Chinese medical traditions have studied the qualities of all plant-derived medicines in great detail. Within the tantric traditions the interrelationship between the mineral, vegetable, and animal realms was developed into a highly esoteric science, where the 'souls' of plants could be 'liberated' at specific astrological times and geomantic places in order to focus their spiritual qualities for specific tantric rituals. The Vedic ritual of the sacred *soma* sacrifice (see page 335) was an important precursor to this body of tantric knowledge.

Plate 102

The top row of this drawing illustrates ten varieties of plants that have specific ritual or symbolic significance, or that occur as the hand-held attributes of certain deities.

The first drawing on the left depicts the red-flowering *ashoka* tree (*Saraca indica*; Tib. *mya ngan med pa'i shing*) under

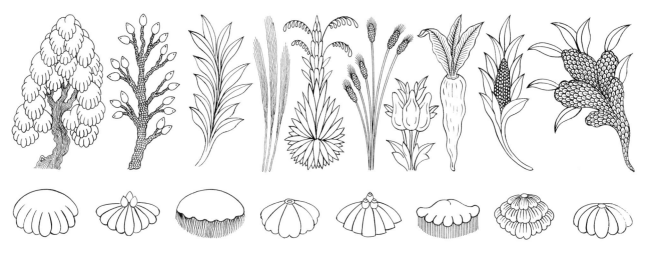

Plate 102: Plant and grain attributes

which Vipashyin (Tib. rNam gzigs), the first of the Six Universal Buddhas of the previous epochs, attained enlightenment. A flowering branch of the *ashoka* tree is also a hand emblem of the goddess Marichi (Tib. 'Od zer can ma), who along with Ekajata forms one of the two attendants of Khadiravani Tara. Three of the twenty-one forms of Tara – *siddhi*-bestowing Tara, boon-granting Tara, and sorrow-dispelling Tara – also hold a flowering branch of the *ashoka* tree as a hand attribute.

The second drawing depicts a 'jewel-twig' or a branch of the 'heavenly tree'. The jewel-twig (Tib. *rin po che'i lcug phran gyi*) is held by the bodhisattva Manidharin, who accompanies the four-armed form of Six-Syllable Avalokiteshvara. The heavenly tree is a healing attribute of the goddess Blue Parnashabari.

The third drawing depicts a bunch of fresh leaves (Tib. *shing lo gsar pa'i sbrang yab*) which is held by the goddesses Yellow Parnashabari and Black Parnashabari. A bundle of fresh leaves is also used as a fly whisk (see Plate 103).

The fourth drawing shows three stems of *kusha* grass, the symbolism of which is described in Chapter 8 (see page 189).

The fifth and central drawing depicts a rice plant (Tib. *'bras*). An ear of rice (Tib. *'bras kyi sne ma*) is an attribute of several forms of the wealth goddess Vasudhara (Tib. Nor rgyun ma).

The sixth drawing depicts ears of corn (Tib. *'bru'i sne ma*), which are an attribute of the main form of Vasudhara as a wealth goddess.

The seventh drawing depicts three fruits of the sacred medicinal tree myrobalan (*Terminalia chebula*; Skt. *haritaki*; Tib. *a ru ra*), which is the main attribute of the Medicine Buddha (Skt. Bhaishajyaguru; Tib. Sangs rgyas sman bla). The myrobalan fruit or 'cherry-plum' is an astringent fruit that resembles a prune when dried, and which is used as a yellow dye and for tanning leather. In both the Indian Ayurvedic and Tibetan medical systems myrobalan is highly esteemed as a preventative and curative panacea for all diseases. In Tibetan it is known as the 'king of all medicines' (Tib. *sman mchog rgyal po*), and various parts of the tree – its roots, stem, branches, bark, leaves, and fruit – are used to cure diseases of

the bone, muscle, blood vessels, skin, viscera, vital organs, and heart respectively. Various legends relate the mythological origins of myrobalan, including several based on the spilling of the drops of *amrita* in the 'churning of the ocean' legend (see page 109). The Tibetan materia medica lists eight varieties of *arura*, and the Indian Ayurvedic system lists eleven varieties of *haritaki*. Each of these varieties have differing properties, tastes, qualities, colours, shapes and ridges, and the fruit may be stylistically depicted in a variety of forms.

The eighth drawing depicts a white radish (*Raphanus sativus*; Skt. *mulaka*; Tib. *la phug*), which is the favoured vegetable of the elephant-headed god, Ganapati (Tib. Tshogs rje), and a triple-leafed white radish is held in his right hand as an emblem. The radish symbolises the essence of the element earth, and along with meat, garlic and onions forms one of the *tamasic* or 'black foods' which are forbidden in pure or *sattvic* ritual practices of the 'right-hand path' (*dakshinamarg*). Ganapati's other favourite food, the sweet *ladduka* (Tib. *la du*) – deep fried balls mixed from gram flour, milk, sugar and spices – is sometimes depicted in Ganapati's trunk or left hand. In early Vajrayana Buddhism Ganapati, the Hindu 'remover of obstacles', was identified as the 'Lord of the *ganas*' or 'hindering demons', and is commonly depicted being trampled underfoot by Mahakala.

The ninth drawing depicts an ear of barley (Tib. *nas*) which forms the main crop of Tibetan agriculture, and which as roasted barley flour (Tib. *tsam pa*) is a staple food of the national diet. The thickness of a barley grain (Tib. *nas*) is used as a unit of measure in Tibetan iconography, where eight barley grains are equal to a finger-width (Tib. *sor*) or 'small measure' (Tib. *cha chung*), and twelve *sor* or finger-widths are equal to a 'face' (Tib. *gdong*) or 'large measure' (Tib. *cha chen*).

The tenth and last drawing on the right depicts the huskless crop of cereals or grains that grow as the 'abundant harvest' on Mt Meru's northern continent of Uttarakuru. The uncultivated harvest of this fertile land is said to spontaneously regenerate within the very day that it is reaped. The huskless 'fruit' of this crop is described as being clean, perfect, beautiful, tasty, satisfying, and easy to pick.

218

In the bottom row of the drawing are eight examples of multifoliate leaf formations which are commonly depicted on stylised trees or as rock mosses and lichen. Several of these leaf clusters resemble the early-spring leaf formation of the horse chestnut tree. These leaf drawings are not related to the hand attributes listed above.

ASSORTED RITUAL IMPLEMENTS

The illustrations on Plates 103, 104 and 107 were drawn as collages of miscellaneous ritual implements and offerings, and the subjects they include do not correspond to any recognized groupings of Buddhist symbols. Plate 103 begins with a lengthy discussion of the ritual vases used during ritual practices, initiations, and ceremonies.

Plate 103

On the left half of the top row are three drawings of the sacred water vases or flasks (Skt. *kalasha*; Tib. *bum pa*) used during ritual practices and initiations. The first drawing on the left shows a side view of an unadorned water vase with a slender pouring spout. In ritual practices two kinds of water vases are used which have an identical appearance but are often differentiated by a circular lotus-band of Sanskrit syllables or the symbols of the Five Buddhas (*dharmachakra*, *vajra*, jewel, lotus, *vishvavajra* or sword), which are inscribed around the top of the vase or around the detachable peacock-feather sprinkler which fits within the vase's top. These two vases or flasks are known as the 'chief or main vase' (Tib. *gtso bum*), and the 'action or working vase' (Skt. *karma kalasha*; Tib. *las kyi bum pa*). The chief vase embodies or contains the visualised mandala of deities within its consecrated water; the action vase – which is placed facing the practitioner on the altar, along with specified ritual objects such as the inner offering (see Plate 141), *damaru*, *vajra* and bell – is used as the actual pouring or 'working' vase for water purification during the stages of the ritual. The chief vase is empowered by removing the peacock-feather sprinkler and replacing it with a *vajra* bound around its centre with a five-coloured variegated thread. The end of this thread is then held at the heart of the practitioner and the 'action mantra' recited 108 times whilst visualising the entry of the deities into the vase water by way of the heart, thread and *vajra*. The five-coloured thread (Tib. *gzungs thag*) represents the light-ray blessings which emanate from the hearts of the Buddhas and bodhisattvas to form a mantra-rosary within the vase.

In ritual use the vase is held at the neck between the thumb and middle fingers, and the water is poured in a tapering stream 'like a barley grain'. A white, blue, yellow, red, or green silk ribbon (Tib. *bum dar*) is tied around the neck of the vase to accord with the particular Buddha Family lineage to which the meditational deity is assigned. During the stages of tantric empowerment (Skt. *abhisheka*; Tib. *dbang bskur*) – such as the water, crown, *vajra* and bell

initiations – a coloured silk ribbon of the same particular Buddha Family adorns each of the ritual objects.

The second drawing shows the 'all-victorious vase' (Skt. *vijaya kalasha*; Tib. *rnam rgyal bum pa*), which is used during empowerments as the central deity vase of the mandala. It is again coupled with the action or working vase which is used to sprinkle the mandala and consecrate the offerings and disciples during the empowerment ritual. The victorious vase depicted in the drawing has no pouring spout as it functions as the 'chief vase' (Tib. *gtso bum*), whose consecrated water is mixed with, and poured from, the spouted action vase (Tib. *las bum*) during ritual use. The bulbous body of this 'deity vase' is adorned, like a deity, with a multicoloured silk brocade apron (Tib. *bum khebs*), symbolising the all-purpose spectrum of activities of the Five Buddhas. Victorious vases are also employed in the consecration of sand mandala bases or during the foundation-laying ceremonies of monastic buildings, where five or ten vases containing water from the centre and four directions are empowered by a five-coloured thread which the ritual master touches to his heart. The central mandala vase is crowned with a conch shell containing water from all of the surrounding vases, which symbolises the essence of all of the mandala's deities. This ritual of consecration has its origins in the investiture or 'water-sprinkling' (Skt. *abhisheka*) of an ancient Indian king.

The third drawing depicts a *bumpa* with its water spout facing towards the practitioner in an easterly direction, and adorned with the multicoloured silk apron (Tib. *bum khebs*) and the neck-tied silk ribbon (Tib. *bum dar*) of the specific Buddha Family colour.

The fourth drawing shows the detachable metal sprinkler (Tib. *kha rgyam*) which is used to sprinkle or flick water during consecration or empowerment rituals. The hollow conical tube of the sprinkler (Tib. *kha*) is filled with a bunch of peacock feathers, whose 'eyes' symbolise the wisdoms of the Five Buddhas. The sprinkler may also contain stems of *kusha* grass (see Plate 90) which is known as a 'life-increasing substance' (Tib. *tshe 'phel rdzas*) symbolising longevity; alternatively twigs and leaves of fruit trees, like the mango, may be placed in the open neck of the vase, symbolising abundance or fruition.

In ritual practice the interior of the empty vase is first purified with incense smoke, and its exterior washed with saffron water mixed with various ingredients – such as milk, curd and ghee (the 'three whites'); sugar, molasses and honey (the 'three sweets'); or sesame or mustard seed – depending on which of the four 'activities' (Skt. *karma*; Tib. *las kyi*) is being emphasised during the ritual. The vase is then filled two-thirds full with pure water coloured with saffron (Tib. *gur gum*). The two-thirds measure of water symbolises the combination of the *nirmanakaya* as the 'form or emanation body' with the pure visionary appearance of the *sambhogakaya* or 'enjoyment body', and the one-third of empty space above symbolises the formlessness of the *dharmakaya* or 'truth body'.

The saffron water is mixed with or contains the twenty-five 'vase substances' (Tib. *bum rdzas*) or the 'five times five'

Plate 103: Ritual vases and assorted ritual implements

ingredients, which symbolise the body, speech, mind, activities, and qualities of the Five Buddhas as the embodied mandala of deities. There are said to be two types of vase substances – those used in the practice of *kriyatantra* (Tib. *bya ba'i rgyud*) or Action Tantra, and those used in *anuttara-yoga tantra* (Tib. *rnal 'byor bla na med pa'i rgyud*) or Highest Yoga Tantra – but various listings of the twenty-five substances are occasionally given in different ritual practices and traditions. These substances may be obtained in the form of pills (Tib. *ril bu*) mixed with *tsampa,* which are available from Tibetan medical institutions or tantric colleges, and are crushed before mixing with the saffron water.

The aspect of body is represented by five varieties of medicinal herbs; speech is represented by the five fragrant incenses of sandalwood, aloewood, pine resin (amber) or juniper, camphor, and *ushira* root (*Andropogon muricatus*); and the mind is represented by the five essences of sesame, salt, ghee, molasses, and honey. Here sesame represents the essence of earth, salt the essence of water, ghee the essence of cattle, molasses the essence of plants, and honey the essence of flowers. The activities are represented by the five grains of mustard seed, rice, pulses, barley, and sesame seed. These correspond to the four activities of pacifying, enriching, magnetising or subjugating, and destroying, which along with spontaneous activity create a fivefold scheme. Here mustard seed pacifies hindrances, rice brings increase, pulses empower, barley gives strength, and sesame seed destroys evil activities. The qualities are represented by the five precious substances of gold, pearls, crystal, coral, and lapis lazuli, which correspond to the wisdom qualities of the Five Buddhas.

The vase is traditionally fashioned of beaten bronze or silver, and embellished with floral motifs, auspicious symbols, encircling lotus petals, and a *makara*-head at the base of its spout. In deity descriptions, where the vase forms a hand-held attribute, it may be described as fashioned of crystal, gold, ruby, lapis lazuli, or other gemstones. According to one list of activities the vase is described as being fashioned of crystal for pacifying rites, silver for enriching rites, copper for magnetising rites, gold for wealth-attracting rites, iron for causing enmity, human bone for slaying, clay for petrifying, and wood for concealing or veiling with illusions.

On the right of the top row are three drawings of the 'long-life vase' (Tib. *tshe bum*) filled with the 'nectar (Skt. *amrita*; Tib. *bdud rtsi*) of immortality'. This vase is the attribute of the longevity deity Amitayus (Tib. Tshe dpag med) whose name means 'infinite life'. Amitayus is an emanation of the red Buddha of the western direction, Amitabha (Tib. 'Od dpag med), the lord of the Lotus Buddha Family – whose name means 'infinite light'. Amitayus, along with White Tara and the goddess Ushnishavijaya, form a trinity of long-life deities. The long-life vase is employed in longevity rituals, often to increase the lifespan of revered lamas or teachers. The golden vase is filled to its top with saffron water containing the twenty-five substances as described above, and is richly adorned with jewel ornaments and covered with a red half-moon – symbolising fullness (water) and increase (half-moon). In certain long-life

empowerments (Tib. *tshe dbang*) the descriptive vase is filled with barley or rice beer (Tib. *chang*) instead of water, and sealed with a 'long-life teat' bound with a five-coloured thread and four *Hri* syllables around its top.

The top of the long-life vase is adorned with four cascading leaf-shaped pendants embellished with jewels and symbolising the overflowing of the nectar of immortality, the four directional seals of Amitabha's seed-syllable *Hri,* and the Buddhas of the four directions with Amitabha at their centre. The first drawing has an oval aura or *torana* (*prabhatorana*) at its top, which would contain an image of Amitabha or Amitayus as the presiding long-life deity. The second drawing has a wish-fulfilling tree at its top, which embodies the essence of Amitabha or his syllable *Hri*; according to one legend the wish-fulfilling tree – always in leaf, flower and fruit – belongs to Amitabha. The third drawing in the upper right corner has the leaf cluster of a mango tree with three mango fruits at its centre. Fresh fruit leaves and twigs often adorn the long-life vase as symbols of abundance and longevity. A bowl of consecrated long-life pills (Tib. *tshe ril*) made from medicinal herbs mixed with *tsampa,* the 'three whites' (milk, curd and ghee), and the 'three sweets' (sugar, molasses and honey), are also offered and distributed in long-life ceremonies.

The first two drawings on the left of the second row depict two further examples of the long-life vase. The first is crowned by a red jewel or ruby representing Amitabha, and the second is sealed with Amitabha's syllable *Hri*. The third drawing shows a long-life vase overflowing with fresh fruit leaves in the form of an 'all-victorious vase' with a multi-coloured brocade apron. The next three drawings to the left depict examples of the golden 'treasure vase' (Skt. *nidhana kumbha*; Tib. *gter gyi bum pa*) which is described in Plate 86. The third treasure vase is adorned with a silk ribbon (Tib. *bum dar*) around its neck, coloured to correspond to one of the Five Buddha Families. The last drawing on the right shows a small image of red Amitabha Buddha seated on a lotus and holding his turquoise alms bowl; this image of Amitabha is held as an attribute in the second right hand of the longevity goddess Ushnishavijaya (Tib. gTsug tor rnam par rgyal ma).

On the left of the third row are five drawings of the treasure casket (Skt. *nidhana petaka*; Tib. *gter sgrom*), illustrated as three small round caskets and two rectangular boxes. Such treasure caskets are depicted in the hands of 'treasure finders' (Tib. *gter ston*) as receptacles of hidden treasure (Tib. *gter ma*). These *termas* or '*dharma*' treasures' consist of relics, ritual objects and texts which were originally concealed by Padmasambhava and his consort Yeshe Tshogyel and were later miraculously discovered by great Nyingma masters such as Terdak Lingpa, Guru Chowang, Nyima Özer, Pema Lingpa, Thangthong Gyalpo, Jigme Lingpa, or Longchenpa. The various 'concealed treasure traditions' list several hundred treasure finders who lived between the eleventh century and the present day. The *terma* tradition has its origin in Indian Buddhism, as in the case of the *Prajnaparamita Sutra* – which was entrusted by Shakyamuni Buddha to the *nagas* and 'revealed' many centuries later by Nagarjuna – the great first or second-century Indian Buddhist master and founder of the Madhyamaka or 'middle way' philosophical school. *Termas* may be revealed in material form as sacred images, as ritual objects (often made of meteorite iron), or as texts written in archaic or sacred cryptographic scripts. These mysterious treasures are found buried in the earth, within sealed rock cavities, on mountains and in lakes, by highly realised and designated *tertons.* In visionary form they are revealed as texts which arise in the sky or, through transmission, directly into the mind of the *terton*. The most well known *terma* is probably the *Bardo Thodol* (Tibetan Book of the Dead), which was discovered as a *terma* text hidden within a hill by the great fourteenth-century 'Northern treasure finder' Rigdzin Karma Lingpa.

On the far right of the third row are two skull-cups containing the long-life vase (Tib. *tshe bum*) full of the nectar of immortality. The first vase is surrounded by four coloured jewels, which, along with the red jewel of Amitabha surmounting the vase, forms a mandala of the Five Buddhas. The second skull-cup contains an ocean of *amrita* in which a long-life vase arises like Mt Meru; this attribute is held in the left hand of Padmasambhava as an emblem of the unborn and undying 'lotus-born guru' who bestows the immortal nectar of the *buddhadharma.*

On the left of the fourth row is a small jewel-topped treasure vase. To the right of this is a Chinese porcelain cup standing on a repoussé silver base, and containing a heap of saffron-coloured rice which is sprinkled or cast during empowerments as a consecrated blessing substance. The third drawing depicts a bowl full of multicoloured jewels (Tib. *nor gzhong*). The fourth drawing shows a tray of consecrated *tsampa* balls mixed with the 'three whites' and the 'three sweets', which are offered and distributed during a tantric 'feast offering' (Skt. *ganachakrapuja*; Tib. *tshogs kyi 'khor lo*). The next two drawings depict the lapis lazuli alms bowl containing three myrobalan fruits, and the stem of three myrobalan fruits, which are held in the left and right hands of the Medicine Buddha and are described in Plate 102. The next drawing depicts the hand-held Tibetan prayer wheel (Tib. *ma ni lag 'khor*), which is inscribed around its circumference with the Tibetan or Lantsa syllables of the famous mantra of Avalokiteshvara, *Om Mani Padme Hum,* and contains within its interior thousands of mantras printed on rolled paper. Its tip bears the emblem of a 'jewel in a lotus' (Tib. *ma ni pad me*), and a small jewel-lotus weight on a chain enables the prayer wheel to be rotated clockwise by the pious Tibetan laity, who incessantly intone this mantra. Large cylindrical prayer wheels – which strike a bell on each clockwise rotation – are commonly found on either side of the entrances to temples or monasteries. Circumambulatory rows of hundreds of wall-mounted prayer wheels often surround monastic compounds and stupas, such as the great *stupas* of Bodhnath and Swayambhu in Kathmandu, which during the early mornings and evenings are thronged with a colourful array of Buddhist pilgrims. Sturdy water-driven prayer wheels are also erected over streams, and more fragile wind-driven prayer wheels bestow their silent mantras onto the prevailing wind. Delicate household paper prayer wheels, mounted as drums on a central metal needle, are fan-driven by the rising convection of a butter lamp or candle placed underneath.

The last drawing on the far right of the fourth row depicts a hanging jewel ornament, consisting of gold-encased jewels suspended on chains or loops of pearls with three pendants ornamented with bells, sun and moon union, and jewelled tips. Several other jewel pendants are drawn in the lower right corner of the illustration.

On the left of the fifth row is a golden finial which crowns the roofs of temples, and incorporates the symbols of the bell-shaped Kadampa or nirvana stupa, the lotus, and the vase or *bumpa* crowned by a wish-fulfilling jewel. To the right of this is a rectangular wooden writing board (Tib. *sam ta*), and next to this a bamboo pen and a paintbrush with a small rectangular block of Chinese ink (Tib. *snag tsha*) below. Beneath the paintbrush is a small recessed wooden ink-pad with a felt top, which is used for stamping seals. To the right of this ink-pad and beyond the *stupa* spire is a small cylindrical Tibetan metal seal stamp. The seal (Tib. *the'u tse*), which is usually between three and four finger-widths in height, is commonly made of gilt bronze or silver and is intricately decorated with entwined floral motifs, lotus bands, and auspicious symbols. A thin ribbon is often tied around the recessed waist above its barrel, which is crowned with a jewel or triple-gem decorative top. Seals either have a square or round cross-section and their base is etched with a central 'seal script' insignia surrounded either by a square block or a circular design of cloud or lotus-petal motifs. Seal script is written as a rectilinear stylisation of the Tibetan alphabet, where the characters are inscribed in a continuous 'ladder' of wide horizontal and narrow vertical lines, creating a unique calligraphic system. The Mongolians developed a similar rectilinear script, and Tibetan seal imprints bear a strong resemblance to the vermilion or black seal 'signatures' found on Chinese scroll paintings or Japanese woodblock prints. Official seals were often impressed in sealing wax (Tib. *la cha*) on locks or sealed documents, and ink-stamped paper seals were impressed with carbon-black or vermilion powder mixed as an ink with glue or oil.

To the right of the paintbrush is the hand-held emblem of an eight-spoked wheel mounted on a handle. To the right of this is a Bon emblem of a swastika, which in the Bonpo tradition corresponds to the Buddhist *vajra*.

To the right of the swastika emblem is a white yaktail fly whisk or 'chowry' (Skt. *chamara*; Tib. *rnga yab*). The chowry is one of India's ancient symbols of royalty, and was waved as a fan by the attendants of a regal personage to drive away mosquitoes and other flying insects, which in the Indian climate are particularly abundant. Early Buddhism adopted the symbol of the fly whisk as an emblem of sovereignty and compassionate activity, as by its use insects are not harmed. The Jain religion, with its emphasis on the principle of non-harming (Skt. *ahimsa*), prescribed the *chamara* as a requisite attribute for its ascetics, who would sweep insects from their path and even wore gauze face-masks to avoid the inhalation of minute insects. Likewise Shakyamuni Buddha decreed that every ordained monk should carry a fly whisk. In early Buddhism, however, the *chamara* was primarily a symbol of religious authority and protection, and along with the parasol formed two of the main protective attributes held by attendants of the Buddha. Three of the Sixteen Arhats (Angaja, Vanavasin and Vajriputra), and one of their two attendants (Upasaka Dharmatala), carry the fly whisk in their right hands as an attribute of spiritual power, protection, and the bestowing of blessings. In Taoism and Chinese Buddhism the *chamara* is ceremoniously held by the presiding master during religious discourses or debates. In Newari Buddhism a pair of fly whisks replaces the *dharmachakra* as the emblem of the Buddha's sovereignty in representations of the eight auspicious symbols. In early Tibetan art the motif of a pair of fly whisks with a throne-base and text, form a symbolic representation of the Indian Buddhist master Atisha (see below).

The Tibetan name for the yaktail, chowry, means 'father of tails' (Tib. *rnga yab*), and bleached yaktails were one of the main Tibetan exports to India from the earliest of times. In ancient India the white tail of a deer was also used as a chowry, and in Central Asia horsetails, sheeps' wool and foxtails were also employed. The Mongolian warlords took as an emblem the military standard of nine yaktails. The incorporation of the yaktail into Central Asian weapons such as the spear and trident is illustrated in Plates 124, 125 and 126.

Three further examples of the *chamara* are drawn to the right of the first vertical fly whisk, which is mounted on a wooden pole and crowned with a jewel. Three yaktails are suspended from the *chamara* in the second drawing, which is embellished with a *vajra* and a *makara*-head on its handle. The third *chamara* below has a flexible jewel-embellished handle, and the fourth drawing to its upper right depicts a yaktail suspended by a ring from a short handle. To the right of the first *chamara* is a bundle of fresh leaves which is utilised as a fly whisk. One tree which featured prominently in early Indian Buddhist sculpture (apart from the bodhi tree), was the variegated Bauhinia (*Bauhinia variegata*), which is known as the *champavidala* or *chamarika,* meaning 'chowry-tree'. The heart-shaped leaves of the *chamarika,* which grow in clusters and resemble the shape of a yaktail, may have originally served as a convenient fan or fly whisk. In modern India, Bauhinia leaves are used as the dried 'paper' covers for hand-rolled cigarettes or beedies.

To the right of the leaf bundle are three drawings of the Tibetan amulet-box (Tib. *ga'u*), and two further drawings of the *ga'u* are depicted on either side of the yaktail handle at the bottom centre. The *ga'u* is usually fashioned as a small round, square or *torana*-shaped metal amulet-box with a detachable back, and made of beaten bronze or silver. Its front is highly decorated with an intricate repoussé design of auspicious symbols and entwining jewel, flower, cloud, or lotus motifs – which may be gilded in gold or silver and inlaid with small turquoise, coral, amber or pearl jewels. The front centre of the *ga'u* usually has a *prabhatorana* or aura-shaped opening or window in which a small clay or metal image of a deity may be displayed; behind this its interior is packed with small sacred objects, such as relics,

precious stones, protective or astrological charms, and folded paper sheets of printed mantras. The *ga'u,* as a protective amulet, was traditionally worn concealed within the clothing, usually above the heart, and as an object of personal protective power and therefore prone to influences was not to be handled by another person – particularly someone of the opposite sex. In recent times the *ga'u* has increasingly become a visible article of jewellery and is nowadays commonly worn around around the neck on a ribbon, chain, or necklace attached to the small handles at its sides.

To the right of the three upper *ga'u* is a cylindrical leather, bamboo, or wooden container full of divination sticks. This form of stick divination is derived from the Chinese yarrow-stalk method, where a sealed tube of inscribed yarrow stalks is shaken until one falls out of a small hole in its lid, and its meaning is then deciphered from an accompanying divination text. A similar form of 'golden urn' (Tib. *ben ba*) and ivory-stick divination was recently employed by the Chinese authorities during their controversial selection procedure to determine the candidate for the Tibetan reincarnation of the Panchen Lama. To the right of the divination container is a small curved flint or striking-iron (Tib. *me cha*), the spark of which is used to kindle a fire. The flint is usually worn suspended from the belt, and is an indispensable possession for the nomadic traveller or pilgrim.

In the lower right corner are three examples of the triple pennant, as described in Plate 86. As a hand-held attribute of the wrathful deity Yamantaka (Skt. Vajrabhairava; Tib. rDo rje 'jigs byed), the triple pennant (Tib. *ba dan rtse gsum pa*) symbolises the illusory nature of all phenomena, as like a flag its form continually changes with the wind. Each of the triple-pennants depicted are fastened to a handle, which is sealed with a *vajra* or jewel at its base and with *makara*-tail scrolling at its top. One of the pennants is crowned with a jewel-topped vase of *amrita,* and another with a half-*vajra* above a conjunct sun and moon. Like the *chamara* the triple-pennant may be used to bestow blessings during empowerment ceremonies by the touching of its silk valances to the disciples' heads.

At the bottom centre, below the three upper *ga'u,* and near the right corner are several drawings of Tibetan religious texts (Skt. *pustaka;* Tib. *glegs bam*). Tibetan texts are woodblock-printed onto individual sheets of long rectangular wood-pulp paper, which are modelled on the early Indian tradition of inscribed palm-leaf manuscripts. The text of each individual woodblock is carved in reverse, then the blocks are inked with a carbon-black ink roller; next a paper sheet is carefully laid on the block and pressed with a clean roller and the printed page gently lifted off. The pages of text are invariably enclosed within a narrow rectangular printed border which defines the edge of the woodblock, as is illustrated in the drawing below the three upper *ga'u.* The title page is often printed in vermilion in both Lantsa and Tibetan script, and the edges of each folio may be vermilion dyed. Precious texts or original biographies may also be handwritten in gold pigment on indigo, black, or vermilion dyed paper. Ornately carved wooden book covers (Skt. *pustakakashtha;* Tib. *glegs shing*) are used to protect and enhance the preciousness of such sacred texts; more commonly a block-printed text is wrapped into a large square of red or yellow cloth, with a smaller square corner decoration of contrasting yellow or red cloth, and a binding ribbon at its final folding corner. The drawing at the bottom centre shows a cloth-wrapped text enclosed within a wooden cover; the small rectangle on its left edge displays the book's title.

During the fourteenth century the great Tibetan scholar and encyclopaedist, Butön Rinpoche (1290–1364), compiled the two great collections of translated texts known as the *Kangyur* (Tib. bKa' 'gyur) and *Tengyur* (Tib. bsTan 'gyur). The *Kangyur* comprises of 108 volumes on *vinaya, sutra* and *tantra*, which form the transmitted precepts of Shakyamuni Buddha; the Tengyur comprises of 225 volumes on the philosophical works and commentaries of Indian Buddhist scholars. As the definitive collection of the spoken words of the Buddha (*Kangyur*) and the commentaries (*Tengyur*), the entire collection forms the traditional monastic library and is commonly housed in specially constructed shelves around the main altar.

In the bottom left corner are two drawings of a basket containing texts and a stupa, which are the attributes of the great Indian scholar Atisha (982–1054), and are represented at the left and right sides of his lotus seat. Dipankara Atisha (Tib. Mar me mdzad, or Jo bo rje – meaning 'noble lord') was a leading scholar from Vikramashila monastic university in Bengal who was invited into Western Tibet by King Yeshe Ö in 1040. Under Atisha's guidance Buddhism was revived in Tibet following its persecution by the ninth-century Bonpo king, Langdarma. Atisha and his main disciple, Dromtonpa (1005–64), established the Kadam (Tib. bKa' gdams) or 're-formed school' of Tibetan Buddhism, which later developed into the New Kadam or Gelug (Tib. dGe lugs) – the 'virtuous school' – founded by Tsongkhapa (1357–1419).

Atisha and his two attributes, a basket of texts and a stupa represent, the 'three receptacles' of the body, speech, and mind of the Buddha respectively. The specific form of Atisha's stupa is known as the Kadampa stupa, which has a bell-shaped base supporting a lotus-based nirvana stupa with thirteen umbrella-wheels. Atisha was said to be entitled to a retinue of thirteen umbrellas, which honorifically elevated his spiritual status to that of a Buddha in the eyes of the reformed school of Tibetan Buddhism.

The basket (Skt. *pitaka*; Tib. *za ma tog* or *sde snod*) of texts – which is frequently depicted to the right or left of early Indian Buddhist masters – represents 'spiritual nourishment' as the 'three baskets' (Skt. *tripitaka*; Tib. *sde snod gsum*). The 'three baskets' are the threefold division of Shakyamuni Buddha's teachings into the *Vinaya Pitaka* or 'basket of discipline', which is concerned with the ethical code and vows of the ordained sangha; the *Sutra Pitaka* or 'basket of discourses', containing the verbal teachings of the Buddha concerned with meditation; and the *Abhidharma Pitaka* or 'basket of realised knowledge', concerned primarily with the development of wisdom. Iconographically the scholar's basket is represented as an ornate, round or egg-shaped container, with decorative

bands and designs around its circumference. Its top is commonly crowned with a lotus-mounted jewel, and its upper dome may be festooned with a silk scarf. Three small baskets are sometimes drawn to represent the *Tripitaka*, but more commonly a single basket is depicted on one side of an Indian or Tibetan scholar, and a stack of texts on the other side. Several drawings of stacked texts are illustrated in the upper corners of Plate 80.

Plate 104

Depicted in this composition are small reliquary stupas, assorted ritual objects, vessels, receptacles, butter lamps and offerings. In the upper left corner are six hand-held stupas or *chaityas*. The first, a Kadampa or nirvana stupa, appears on a white lotus base. The second and third stupas are drawn in the styles of the Mt Meru stupa (see page 130), and the enlightenment stupa respectively. On the left of the second row is a depiction of Mt Meru in the form of a throne-based stupa. To the right are two further examples of a bell-shaped *vijaya* or victory stupa and a nirvana stupa.

In the upper right hand corner are the three ritual implements of a skull-cup full of blood, a curved flaying knife, and a hand drum or *damaru*. These three implements are described in Plates 119, 118 and 117 respectively. Below the central stupa is a wooden *tsampa* bowl (Tib. *tsam phor*), with a detachable lid that serves as a teacup, and a lotus-decorated lower *tsampa* bowl. To the upper right of the *tsampa* bowl is a silver-lidded Chinese porcelain teacup (Tib. *shal dkar*) on a silver stand; another ornately decorated teacup set is depicted below the *damaru*'s pennant. To the left of the pennant is a large silver grain container or vase (Tib. *'brus phor*), in which consecrated rice or grains are kept for ritual use or mandala offerings. To the left of this is a shallow silver bowl on a tripod, which is used for holding a 'sacrificial cake' (Tib. g*tor ma*). To the left of this is another small wooden *tsampa* bowl with a jewel-topped lid. On the far left is a decorated silver sheath containing the eating utensils of chopsticks and a sharp knife.

On the left of the middle row is a butter lamp ornamented with five dry skulls. Large wrathful butter lamps, decorated with a full array of weapons and wrathful offerings, are sometimes used to illuminate the gloomy interiors of protector chapels. The lamps offered to protective deities are described as having a wick made from twisted corpse's hair, and are fuelled by human fat (see Plate 138). In place of the long-life vase, which is normally found on ornate butter lamps, the wrathful lamp displays a 'death vase' fashioned of skeletons and flayed human skins, with four hanging skeletons replacing the pendant leaves that usually descend from its top.

To the right of the lamp is a silver or bronze teapot (Tib. *gsol tib*) with a hinged lid; such a vessel may also be used for rice or barley wine (Tib. *chang*). To the right of this is another teapot with a *makara*-headed spout. On the far right is a ceremonial jewelled spoon for sacred liquid oblations.

Plate 104: Assorted ritual implements

In the second row from the bottom are seven examples of butter lamps (Tib. *mar me*). These are usually made of bronze or repoussé silver, and decorated with auspicious symbols, a lotus-petalled base, and a central waist shaped like a long-life vase. The chalice form of the butter lamp possibly derives from the communion chalice of the Nestorian Christians, who took refuge in Central Asia during the fifth century. Nestorius was branded a heretic, and exiled to the Egyptian desert in AD 435. The Nestorian 'heresy' was the direct transmission of the original Nazarene Judaic-Christian tradition, based on the lineage founded by Jesus the 'Nazarene'. Nestorian Christianity evolved into the Egyptian Coptic Church, and the Persian Church of the East. Its 'trade route' was the ancient Silk Road, which began in China and ended in Alexandria. Many ritual aspects of Nestorian Christianity have a strong parallel with the Tibetan Buddhist tradition. These include the sacrament, iconic image of blessing, brocade robes and hats, insignia of religious status, the hanging incense burner, and the arrangement and consecration of the altar.

The wick of a butter lamp consists of cotton wound around a tapered wooden stick. Butter lamps, symbolising the light of wisdom, are essential offerings on a Buddhist altar. For specific ceremonies a hundred, a thousand, or a hundred thousand butter lamps are offered. The lamp is extinguished by ladling melted butter over the wick; the spoon above is also used for this purpose.

On the left of the bottom row are four drawings of precious coral offerings. Coral occurs in four forms: precious red coral, red coral with white roots, white coral, and black coral. Three, five, seven, eight, or nine-branched coral stems are considered most auspicious.

In the bottom right corner are three examples of ritual metal water pots or flasks (Skt. *kalasha* or *kundika*; Tib. *spyi blugs*) used for liquid oblations. The drinking water flask (Tib. *phud tib*) in the right corner is derived from the Persian water flask. The two other conical topped flasks to the left also show a Persian or Mughal influence, and are used for ritual cleansing. Two further water flasks are depicted in Plate 105.

THE POSSESSIONS OF AN ORDAINED MONK

In ancient Buddhist India those who originally took the vows of monastic ordination were compelled to live the life of a true renunciate, having very few material possessions. The earliest list of a monk's possessions numbered only eight, but later this list was extended to thirteen items to accomodate the climatic conditions in the colder mountainous areas of India. These original eight items comprised the three robes of a monk, a begging bowl, a mendicant's staff, a water sieve, a water pot, and a blanket or towel.

The three robes of a fully ordained monk consisted of a yellow or red ceremonial outer robe made from many sewn patches and known in Sanskrit as a *sanghati* (Tib. *nam sbyar*), a yellow upper garment known as an *uttarasangha* (Tib. *bla sos*), and a lower robe known as an *antaravasaka* (Tib.

mthan gos). These three robes symbolise the attainments of discipline, meditation and wisdom. There were very specific measurements for the size of these garments, and for their number of folds or pleats.

Later additions to the list of garments included two under-robes, a daytime shawl (Tib. *zen*), a nightime blanket, a small face towel, a larger towel for the shaving of the head, and a sitting mat (Tib. *gding ba*) for meditation. Monks were also permitted to carry a belt, a needle and thread, and a razor for shaving the face and head.

Plate 105

Illustrated in this drawing are some of the thirteen possessions of an ordained monk or *bhikshu*. These images are drawn from a diagram that frequently appears as a fresco on monastery walls depicting a monk's possessions as prescribed by the monastic discipline (*vinaya*) established by Shakyamuni Buddha.

On the left are three variations of the Buddhist mendicant's staff, known as a *khakkhara* (Tib. *'khar gsil*) or *hikkala*. This staff had a threefold function: it served as a walking stick; its metallic noise frightened away snakes and small creatures in the mendicant's path; and its shaking announced the presence of a begging Buddhist mendicant. Since the monk or *bhikshu* was frequently under a vow of silence, and was forbidden by the *vinaya* rules to either address or raise his eyes to a woman, the rattling of the *khakkhara* would announce to a householder the presence of a Buddhist *bhikshu* seeking alms. A monk would rattle his *khakkhara* three times before a householder's threshold; if this produced no result then five and seven rattles would follow. If this also produced no response then the mendicant would walk silently on. The *khakkhara* has its parallels amongst the Vaishnavite and Shaivite ascetic mendicants or sannyasins of Hindu India, who likewise carry symbolic staffs of their lineages. Western scholars have sometimes identified the *khakkhara* with the ancient Egyptian 'sistrum', which was a metal ringed staff shaken by priests in the worship of the goddess Isis.

The *khakkhara* possesses a complex symbolism which embodies the thirty-seven aspects of the path to enlightenment (*bodhipakshadharma*) which are listed on pages 240, 242. The upper part of the *khakkhara* is made of iron, fashioned into a curved oval frame. Within and above the oval frame are two stupas, possibly representing the enlightenment stupa and the stupa of reconciliation amongst the sangha. Attached to the bottom of the oval frame are the metal rings which produce the rattling sound. As symbols of renunciation the rings probably derive from the earrings, bracelets, and anklets which Shakyamuni discarded when he renounced his worldly bonds. Bracelets are still placed on Shaivite tridents at Hindu shrines as symbols of renunciation and betrothal to Shiva. The number of iron rings on a Buddhist *khakkhara* is usually six, but four, eight and twelve are also represented. Four rings symbolise the Four Noble Tuths of a *bhikshu*. Six rings represent the 'six perfections'

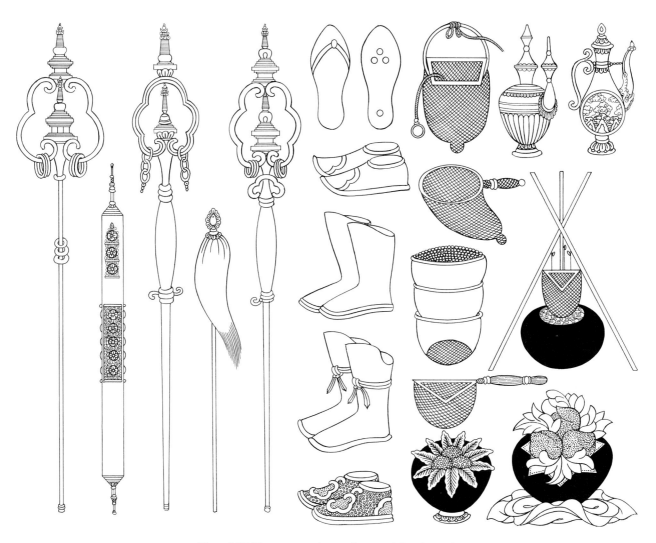

Plate 105: The possessions of an ordained monk

(*paramitas*) of a bodhisattva. Eight rings represent the Noble Eightfold Path followed by an arhat. Twelve rings represent the 'twelve links' in the chain of dependent origination (see page 240), and the twelve deeds of a fully enlightened Buddha. The staff of the *khakkhara* is usually fashioned of wood with a leather-bound handle and metal tip.

In between the first and second *khakkhara* is illustrated the heavy wooden staff-of-office of the proctors of Drepung monastery in Lhasa. Between the second and third *khakkhara* is a yaktail fly whisk or *chamara* (see Plate 103), which the Buddha decreed should be carried by *bhikshus* to harmlessly brush away mosquitoes, flies and other insects.

The next row on the right shows the permissible items of footwear. Traditionally a *bhikshu* wandered barefoot, yet certain footwear was allowed for specific conditions. At the top are shown the upper and under-soles of wooden or leather sandals to protect the feet on rough ground. The thick wooden peg or leather thong, which holds the sandal in place between the first and second toes, is believed to press on certain nerves which control sexual desire. Certain celibate Hindu ascetics (*brahmacharya*) can still be seen wearing such heavy wooden sandals in present-day India. The traditional Indian sandals, with leather rings for the big toe

and over-straps for the upper arch of the foot, are commonly represented in Tibetan thangkas depicting Indian Buddhist monks.

The second footwear drawing illustrates simple leather or cloth shoes, which protect the wearer from snake and insect bites, or when walking on rough ground. The third drawing shows unadorned calf-length boots, used when walking through long grass and again to protect from snake and insect bites. The fourth drawing shows calf-length boots with an upper lace-tie to protect the feet in cold weather, or against leeches in the rainy season. The fifth drawing shows fashionably ornamented boots, which should not be worn by ascetic Buddhist monks.

The next row to the right illustrates examples of sieves. These were used in ancient India to strain water, milk or fruit-juice, and in the cooking of grains. An early *vinaya* rule also decreed that a *bhikshu* should only consume foodstuffs that would pass through a sieve. The sieve was made of a finely woven gauze or cheesecloth, often with a small 'teat' or filter bulb on the bottom. As a water filter the sieve removed foreign particles from water and especially saved the lives of small drowning insects. As a strainer the sieve could also be used for boiling rice or other grains.

At the top of the last row are illustrated two water vessels (*kundika*). The first vessel, with capped lids to protect from dirt or insects, is used for washing the mouth and hands. This form of water flask (Tib. *spyi blug*) is an attribute of the bodhisattva Maitreya. The second ornate vessel (Tib. *phud tib*) is used as a vessel for drinking water. In ancient India the Buddhist monk would have more commonly used a brass water pot (*lota*) for washing and toilet hygiene, and a skin water bottle or gourd for carrying drinking water.

Below these is drawn a wooden or metal tripod supporting a sieve over an iron alms bowl, illustrating the common technique for straining water. At the bottom are two alms bowls, containing the auspicious offering of the 'three fruits'. After his enlightenment Shakyamuni Buddha was offered four beautiful alms bowls by the great guardian kings of the four directions. Shakyamuni rejected these as being too ostentatious for a renunciate, and fashioned his own alms bowl from the most inferior of these four bowls. Traditionally a *bhikshu*'s alms bowl is shaped like the inverted head protuberance of a Buddha, and there are three separate ways of representing it in Tibetan art. The alms bowl is traditionally made of iron for durability and for cooking over an open fire. Clay bowls or coconut shells are also used as alms bowls. In the case of a tantric yogin a human skull-cup is more common. In thangkas, alms bowls are painted in the deep blue colour of iron, often with spiralling white yoghurt, water, rice, fruit or myrobalan inside. There is a certain irony in the fact that traditional Buddhist alms bowls now sell for high prices at oriental auction houses.

MONASTIC AND CEREMONIAL MUSICAL INSTRUMENTS

Plate 106 depicts the musical instruments used in monastic rituals and ceremonies. The unique vocal chanting and ritual music of Tibet is believed to have originally been transmitted by the *dakinis* (Tib. *mkha' 'gro ma*), the realised female yoginis of the pure realms. Its strange rhythm structures and atonal melodies are extremely complex, requiring years of training to perfect. Each monastery has its own specific ritual repertoire, with different modes of musical expression for liturgical ceremonies, and for the rites of peaceful deities, lamas, *yidams*, *dakinis* and wrathful protective deities.

The musical modes are also classified to correspond to the four activities of pacifying, enriching, magnetising and destroying. The four activities find expression within the spectrum of the 'nine sentiments' or *rasa* (Tib. *nyams dgu*) of classical Indian music, drama, and dance. These nine sentiments are grouped into three groups of three representing the body, speech, and mind. These are: strong, heroic, and severe (body); wrathful, energetic, and awe-inspiring (speech); and compassionate, dignified, and serene (mind). The notation for each individual instrument is handwritten

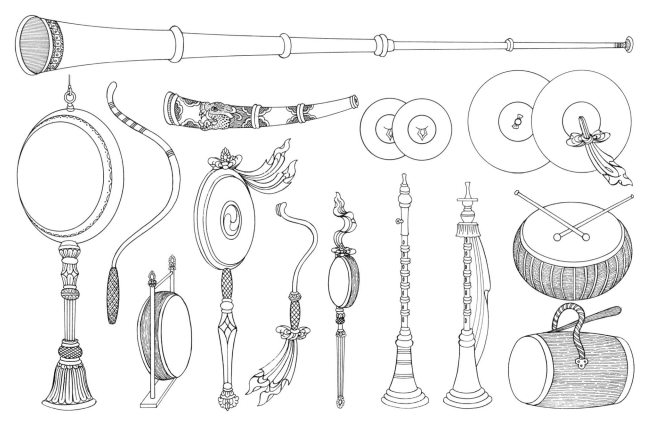

Plate 106: Monastic and ceremonial musical instruments

with graceful calligraphy, which is visually suggestive of the curving wave-motion of the music.

Plate 106

Across the top of this drawing is the long brass trumpet known as a 'long horn' (Tib. *rag dung* or *dung chen*). The *dung chen* are always played in pairs, and usually measure around ten to twelve feet in length. For portability they are fashioned of five or six separate sections which telescope into each other. When they are played in a stationary position a vertical wooden frame supports their trumpet ends. When they are played in procession, their ends are usually physically supported by the shoulders of a pair of monks who walk in front of the musicians.

On the lower right is the hanging drum known simply as the 'drum' (Tib. *rnga*) or 'hand drum' (Tib. *lag rnga*). Its wooden pedestal base supports it from below, whilst a metal ring tied to an overhead roofbeam supports its top. It is beaten with a wooden sickle-shaped striker or drumstick, which is illustrated to the right of the drum. The sickle-shaped drumstick has a padded skin tip and handle.

Next, to the lower right, is the suspended 'big drum' (Tib. *rnga chen*). This double-sided drum is often more than three feet in diameter and hangs within a wooden frame. It is played with a similar sickle-shaped drumstick.

Next to this is the ceremonial drum (Tib. *rnga yak*) or hand drum (Tib. *lag rnga*) which is used in processions. This is a smaller portable version of the hanging drum depicted on the left. It has a long decorated wooden handle tipped with a *vajra*, a silk scarf often hangs from its top, and it is ornamented with a triple-coloured 'wheel of joy' (Tib. *dga' 'khyil*) which represents Mt Meru. Its sickle-shaped wooden striker is also shown with a silk scarf decoration.

Next to the right is a smaller hand drum (Tib. *lag rnga*), derived from the divinational or 'magical' drum of the Bonpo shamans. Such a drum is depicted in the hands of Bonpo siddhas, and divine beings such as *devas*, *dakinis*, *gandharas* and *kinnaras* – the celestial singers and musicians.

In the lower right corner are two other drums used in ritual processions. The upper kettledrum is known as a *mirdangam* or *tudum* (Tib. *lda man*). The transverse lower drum is known as a *dhola*, *madal* or *mirdanga*. These two drum forms are common throughout Asia, although in India the transverse drum is also known as a *mirdangam*. These drums are also played by two of the sixteen offering goddesses – Lasya, goddess of dance, and Gita, of song.

To the left of these two drums are two upright drawings of the Tibetan reed shawm or oboe (Tib. *rgya gling*). This shawm is made from a hardwood bore, such as teak or black rosewood. It is highly decorated with an elaborate, gilded copper, bell-shaped trumpet end, and a reed mouthpiece with a small resonator made of beaten metal. Its wooden bore has six or seven holes with an upper back-hole for the thumb, similar to the Western recorder. However, unlike the Western recorder or oboe, it is played with the hands reversed, the left hand fingering the lower notes and the right

hand the upper. The wooden bore is decorated with copper wire, coiled between each of the holes, and the holes are actually stopped with the middle pad of each finger, rather than the finger tips. The Tibetan *rgya gling* derives from the north Indian *shenai*, which in turn is of Arabic origin. The *rgya gling* has a variable pitched tuning, and is a very difficult instrument to master. Like the long horns (Tib. *dung chen*) and the short horns (Tib. *rkang gling*), the *rgya gling* are always played in pairs.

The short Tibetan horn (Tib. *rkang gling*) is illustrated below the middle of the long horn. The *rkang gling* bears the same name as the human thighbone trumpet, yet as a monastic instrument it is usually fashioned from beaten brass. It is highly decorated, often with a *makara* head near the horn end. Its mouthpiece is either rounded like the thighbone trumpet (as illustrated), or has a circular lipped mouthpiece.

To the right of the *rkang gling* are the two main sets of monastic cymbals used in peaceful and wrathful rituals. The smaller pair of cymbals are the flat cymbals (Tib. *sil snyan*) with a low central boss, which are held vertically and used in the rites of peaceful deities. The larger high-domed cymbals to the right (Tib. *rol mo* or *sbug cal*), are held horizontally and used in the rites of wrathful deities. The domed *rol mo* look rather like a hat when viewed from the side. Both pairs of cymbals have cloth handles issuing from their centres, and are played with clashing, rolling, rotating and muting techniques. Cymbals and drums are played together to accompany vocal chanting.

Tibetan instrumental music is divided into four orchestral sections: percussive (drums), ringing (hand bells and cymbals), wind (horns and conches), and plucked (stringed instruments). String instruments are not actually employed in ritual music, but their harmonic presence is acoustically imagined.

The ensemble of a ritual monastic orchestra consists of up to thirteen different instruments. The hand bell (Skt. *ghanta*; Tib. *dril bu*), the double-sided hand drum (Tib. *damaru* or *da chung*), and the pair of conch-shell horns (Skt. *shankha*; Tib. *dung dkar*) are added to the above instruments to create the full monastic ensemble. The flat cymbals (Tib. *sil snyan*), the shawm (Tib. *rgya gling*), and the conch horn (Tib. *dung dkar*) are played together in the rites of peaceful deities.

Musical instruments are also described on Plate 94. The *damaru* and thighbone trumpet are described on Plate 117, and the conch is described on Plate 87.

Plate 107

Illustrated in this drawing are an assembly of ritual objects and peaceful offerings. Dominating the upper and lower centre are two drawings of the offerings of the five senses, which are described in Plate 92.

In the upper left corner are small jewel chains, beneath which are positioned a parasol and a victory banner. Below the parasol is a wooden temple-gong and a pair of small cymbals. Below again are a five-pointed *vajra*, an open nine-pronged *vajra*, a *ghanta* or bell, and a *mala* or rosary.

Plate 107: Peaceful offerings and ritual objects

The representations of the five sense objects are depicted in the mirrors (sight) on the left of the page, a lute and cymbals (sound) in the upper right corner; and two perfumed conch shells (smell), a silk cloth (touch), and fruit (taste) arranged across the top of the page.

To the right of the small mirror in the fourth row are the seven offering bowls, which are described in Plate 96. Between the middle bowls and under the bowls on either side are three drawings of Tibetan texts or scriptures. Above the bowls on the right is a large rounded orange conch shell, known as a Ganesha shankha. This form of conch shell is sacred to the elephant-headed god Ganesha, on account of its elephant-like shell, vermilion colour, and short tail. On the far right of the line of offering bowls is a white yaktail fly whisk, with an embellished golden handle and chain.

Below the seven offering bowls are the eight auspicious substances or objects: the mirror, the precious medicine, yoghurt in an iron alms bowl, two bundles of *durva* grass, a bowl of *bilva* fruit, a white conch, cinnabar powder, and mustard seed (see Plates 90 and 91). To the left and below the mirror and precious medicine are: a tray of *bilva* fruit, a round metal hand-mirror, a twelve-spoked wheel in a square golden frame, a jewel-topped treasure vase, and a Tibetan text. Small drawings of jewels, a jewel tray, mirror, wheel, flower, water flask, and yaktail are placed above the lower sense offerings and around the sword and book motif, which is known as the 'emblem of the three bodhisattvas'.

Below the five sense offerings are the seven gems or insignia of the *chakravartin*. From left to right they are: the unicorn or rhinoceros horn, the interlinked square earrings, the eight-branched coral, the queen's round earrings, the crossed gem insignia of the general, the elephant's tusks, and the three-eyed gem. These seven gems are described on Plate 79. Below are five small groups of coloured jewels. In the centre of the bottom row are a line of jewels forming a central pyramid, with the seven gems or insignia of the *chakravartin* arranged behind. In the bottom left corner are the Three Jewels or *triratna*. In the bottom right corner is an eight-faceted flaming jewel on a lotus base, an arrow, and a divination or long-life arrow with silk ribbons and a small mirror.

To the right of the five sense offerings is the 'emblem of the three bodhisattvas'. This design – of a lotus, book and sword, flanked by two double-headed birds – is both an insignia of the three great bodhisattvas, and of the early transmission of the Buddhist teachings into Tibet.

As the emblem of the three great bodhisattvas, Manjushri is represented by the lotus-borne book of wisdom, and his flaming sword which cuts through the darkness of ignorance. The bodhisattvas Vajrapani and Avalokiteshvara are represented respectively by the two-headed green parrot to the right, and the two-headed orange duck to the left. As a trinity they symbolise the wisdom, power and compassion aspects, or the body, speech and mind of an enlightened being.

As an emblem of the early (Nyingma) Buddhist transmission into Tibet, five important masters of the time are represented in the design. The lake at the bottom from which the lotus rises symbolises Shantarakshita, whose name means 'lake of serenity'. The lotus itself symbolises Padmasambhava, meaning 'the lotus born'. The book and flaming sword of wisdom symbolise the first great Buddhist king of Tibet, Trisong Detsen (Tib. Khri srong lde btsan), who was considered to be an emanation of Manjushri. The two-headed orange duck symbolises the Indian master Vimalamitra, and the two-headed green parrot the Tibetan master Vairochana. The two eyes and beaks of each bird, facing in opposite directions, symbolises both the transmission of the teachings from India into Tibet, and their translation from Sanskrit into Tibetan.

Plate 108: The nine-pronged *vajra*

Chapter Ten
The Wheel of Sharp Weapons

This chapter illustrates and describes the array of ritual implements and weapons that occur as hand-held attributes of the deities. Many of these weapons and implements have their origins in the wrathful arena of the battlefield and the funereal realm of the charnel grounds. As primal images of destruction, slaughter, sacrifice, and necromancy these weapons were wrested from the hands of the evil and turned – as symbols – against the ultimate root of evil, the self-cherishing conceptual identity that gives rise to the five poisons of ignorance, desire, hatred, pride, and jealousy. In the hands of siddhas, *dakinis*, wrathful and semi-wrathful *yidam* deities, protective deities or *dharmapalas* these implements became pure symbols, weapons of transformation, and an expression of the deities' wrathful compassion which mercilessly destroys the manifold illusions of the inflated human ego.

This long chapter is divided into three main sections. The first part explains the symbolism of the *vajra*, the *vishvavajra*, the ritual bell, and the dagger – illustrated in Plates 108–114. The second section explores the origin and symbolism of the tantric staff or *khatvanga*, the drum, the thighbone trumpet, the curved knife, and the skull-cup – illustrated on Plates 115–119. The third section deals with the vast array of hand-held weapons, beginning with the bow and arrow, and ending with the specific or unique attributes of particular deities.

The symbolism accorded to many of these weapons in Vajrayana Buddhism often displays a certain uniformity. I have therefore chosen to explore their historical origins in the context of Hindu mythology and ancient Indian warfare. This may at first glance appear to be an approach that is in apparent contradiction to the tenets of Buddhism which advocates the principles of absolute non-violence, yet the main symbolic context of the wrathful deities arises from the art of war. Their 'wrath' is explicitly the wrath of war;

the 'enemy' are the personified armies of *maras* and *rudras* who create the notion of the individual self, and veil the citadel of innate Buddha nature behind the clamour and smokescreen of illusion.

A wrathful deity such as Yamantaka tramples upon the lords of these illusions with his sixteen feet, crushing their apparent reality into the sixteen *shunyatas* or emptinesses; his nine heads glare and snarl in all directions, bellowing in the triumph of the nine Buddhist *yanas*; his thirty-four arms circle as an impenetrable wheel of sharp weapons, and combine with his body, speech, and mind as the compassionately wrathful thirty-seven practices of a bodhisattva. All of these weapons are of Indian origin, and any symbolic meaning grafted upon them does nothing to blunt their sharp edges.

THE VAJRA (Tib. *rdo rje*)

The *vajra* or *dorje* is the quintessential symbol of the 'diamond vehicle' or Vajrayana Buddhist path, becoming both its namesake and the appellation or prefix of a host of *vajra*-named divinities, attributes, and qualities. The Sanskrit term *vajra* means 'the hard or mighty one', and its Tibetan equivalent *dorje* (Tib. *rdo rje*) means 'the lord of stones', implying an indestructible hardness and brilliance like the diamond (Tib. *pha lam*), the adamantine stone which cannot be cut or broken. The *vajra* essentially symbolises the impenetrable, immovable, immutable, indivisible, and indestructible state of enlightenment or Buddhahood as *vajra* mind.

As the adamantine sceptre of peaceful divinities and the indestructible weapon of wrathful deities, the *vajra* symbolises the male principle of method or skilful means. It is held in the right or male hand. When coupled with the *ghanta* or bell – which symbolises wisdom and is held in the left or female hand – their pairing represents the perfect union of method and wisdom, or skilful means and discriminating awareness. As a sexual symbol the *vajra* is coupled with the lotus as a metaphor for the penis and vagina.

The primordial or Adi Buddha, Vajradhara ('the bearer of the *vajra*'), is regarded as the supreme *dharmakaya* manifestation of Shakyamuni Buddha. Vajradhara is the primordial source from which the Five Buddha Families and all of their fivefold qualities emanate. Vajrasattva ('*vajra*-being' or hero) and Vajrapani ('*vajra*-in-hand'), are two other tantric deities that assumed pre-eminence in the early tantric transmissions.

The form of the *vajra* as a sceptre or a weapon appears to have its origins in the single or double trident, which arose as a symbol of the thunderbolt or lightning in many ancient civilisations of the Near and Middle East. Occidental parallels are postulated between the meteoric hammer of the Teutonic sky-god Thor, the thunderbolt and sceptre of the Greek sky-god Zeus, and the three thunderbolts of the Roman god Jupiter. As a hurled weapon the indestructible thunderbolt blazed like a meteoric fireball across the heavens, in a maelstrom of thunder, fire and lightning.

The historical *vajra* was probably both a weapon and a sceptre. As a weapon it could be flung or hurled, or, as interpreted by martial-arts enthusiasts, it could be used in the closed fist as a 'tantric knuckle-duster'. As a sceptre or symbol of royalty, its arched cluster of four prongs converging on a central axis parallels the prototype for the coronation crowns of European kings, and many other royal insignia, becoming the 'crowning glory' on heraldic standards, emblems and devices.

In ancient India the *vajra,* as a thunderbolt, became the chief weapon of the Vedic sky-god Indra whose *vajra* controlled the forces of thunder and lightning, breaking the monsoon storm clouds that bring the welcome rains to the parched plains of an Indian summer. According to legend Indra's thunderbolt was fashioned from the bones of the great Rishi, Dadhichi, who temporarily assumed the head of a horse before he was decapitated by Indra. The sacrifice of Dadhichi's 'indestructible' skull-bones gave Indra the most powerful of adamantine weapons, for by their energy Indra slew 'nine times ninety' *vritras* or dragons. In mythological descriptions Indra's thunderbolt or *vajra* is shaped either like a circular discus with a hole at its centre, or in the form of a cross with transverse bladed bars. The *Rigveda*, the earliest of the four Hindu *Vedas* composed around 1500 BC, identifies the *vajra* as a notched metal club with a hundred or a thousand spikes, which was fashioned for Indra by the divine craftsman, Tvashriti. According to a Buddhist legend Shakyamuni took the *vajra* weapon from Indra and forced its wrathful open prongs together to form a peaceful Buddhist sceptre. As the prime symbol of *shunyata* or emptiness, the Buddhist *vajra* absorbed the unbreakable qualities of the diamond, the indestructible power of the thunderbolt, and the indivisible transparent clarity of empty space.

Meteoric iron or 'sky-iron' (Tib. *gnam lcags*) is the supreme substance for forging the physical representation of the *vajra* or other iron weapons, since it has already been tempered by the celestial gods in its passage across the heavens. The indivisibility of form and emptiness is a perfect metaphor for the image of a meteorite or 'stone fallen from the sky', manifesting out of the voidness of space as a shooting star or fireball, and depositing a chunk of fused 'sky-iron' on the earth below. Many of the *vajras* held by deities as weapons are described as being forged from meteorite iron, and Tibet, with its high altitude, thin atmosphere and desolate landscape, received an abundance of meteorite fragments. Tibetan *vajras* were often cast from meteorite iron, and as an act of sympathetic magic a piece of the meteoric iron was often returned to its original site. A similar tradition occurs with the famous Balinese '*kris*' knives, which are also forged from meteorite iron and are each protected by an ethereal captive spirit. In South East Asia triangular iron points or blades are believed to be found impaled within trees after a severe lightning storm; these are thought to be meteorites produced by fork-lightning. In Tibetan iconography the meteorite is represented by a triangular iron *phurbu* blade. Meteorites are often depicted amidst a fall of hailstones, descending like darts from the electrical storms produced by dragons. Since the spark of a lightning flash can produce temperatures six times hotter than the surface of the sun, and since the return stroke of lightning can travel at speeds approaching half the speed of light, then perhaps anything is possible within this realm of extremities.

In early Indian and Central Asian art the *vajra* is often depicted in the form of a bar or club, with a cluster of three or five prongs at either end. The standard form of the Tibetan *vajra* is believed to have been modelled on a large golden *vajra* installed at Sera Monastery near Lhasa, which was formerly carried in an annual procession through the streets of Lhasa and was believed to have miraculously flown over the Himalayas from India. This legend reveals the Indian origin of the ornately stylised Tibetan *vajra.*

The Tibetan words for diamond (Tib. *pha lam*) and sky-iron (Tib. *gnam lcags*) or thunderbolt, are distinct from the term *dorje,* meaning 'lord of stones'. Although diamond, adamantine and thunderbolt are three terms synonomous with the *vajra,* its metaphysical substance exists more in the realm of alchemical transformation than in any material or chemical creation. The *vajra,* as 'lord of stones', may in this respect be viewed as the alchemical 'philosopher's stone' .

The *vajra* may be represented with one, two, three, four, five, six, or nine prongs at either end, five and nine-pointed *vajras* being the most common in the Indo-Tibetan Vajrayana tradition.

A single-pointed *vajra* represents both the central channel as Mt Meru's central axis, and the union of all duality symbols conceived of as non-dual. These include wisdom and compassion, emptiness and bliss, absolute and relative truths.

A three-pointed *vajra* symbolises the trinities of the three times (past, present and future); the three main psychic channels or *nadi*; the three realms; destruction of the three root delusions (ignorance, desire, and aversion); the three *kayas* or 'bodies' of the Buddha; the 'three gates' of body, speech and mind.

The five-pointed *vajra* arises as the crowning symbol on many ritual implements and weapons. As the prime symbol of enlightenment it represents the indistinguishable perfection of the Five Buddha wisdoms, and the attainment of the five *kayas* of the *anuttarayoga tantras*, as the *vajra* body of spontaneous great bliss.

The nine-pointed *vajra* mainly symbolises the Five Buddhas of the five directions (Vairochana – east or centre; Akshobhya – centre or east; Ratnasambhava – south; Amitabha – west; and Amoghasiddhi – north), with the four intercardinal prongs symbolising the 'four mothers' or consorts of the four directional Buddhas (with Lochana in the south-east; Mamaki in the south-west; Pandara in the north-west; and Tara in the north-east). The nine-pointed *vajra* also symbolises the nine 'vehicles' or *yanas* (see page 236); the centre and eight directions; and all other groups of eight surrounding a central principle; such as the eight great charnel grounds, or the Buddha and his Noble Eightfold Path.

Painted representations of both the five and nine-pointed *vajras* have only three prongs depicted at each end. A visual distinction is made between the five-pointed *vajra* – which has closed or uniting prongs, and the nine-pointed *vajra* – which has open prongs that form the shape of a trident and do not unite with the central prong. Gold is the most common colour for depicting both five and nine-pointed *vajras*. Alternatively the dark-blue colour of iron is used, where iron or meteoric iron is specified for many wrathful forms symbolising the *vajra*-wrath that cuts through conventional anger. Extremely wrathful deities may sometimes be depicted with lightning bolts or flames emanating from the tip of their *vajra*, symbolising its indestructible power. Other colours, such as the white of rock crystal, may also be specified for certain individual deities. In visualisation practices where the form of the deity is 'generated' from a seed-syllable (*bija*) which transforms into a lotus, sun and moon disc, and *vajra* – the *vajra* is often specifically coloured to accord with the form of the deity.

The Iconography and Symbolism of the Five-Pointed Vajra

The five-pointed *vajra* is said to measure twelve units in length, subdivided into three sections of four units. The central section consists of a central four-unit hub with a lotus and moon disc on either side, and is sealed at both ends with a crown of five extending prongs, each measuring four units in length. The standard unit of measure is known as an *angula* or 'finger-width' (Tib. *sor*). This is the distance across the middle finger below the second knuckle. Twelve *angulas* are equal to one 'face' or large measure – the distance in finger-widths from the chin to the hair line. The *vajra* is said to measure twelve units as it annihilates the twelve links in the chain of causation, or the twelve links of dependent origination (see page 240).

At the centre of the *vajra* is a rounded hub or flattened sphere representing the *dharmata* (Tib. *chos nyid*), as the 'expanse or sphere of actual reality'. This sphere or *bija* is sealed within by the syllable *Hum*, whose three component sounds represent freedom from causation or karma (*Hetu*), freedom

from conceptual thought or reasoning (*Uha*), and the groundlessness of all *dharmas* (*M*).

On either side of the central hub are three rings which encircle the lotus bases like bracelets of pearls. These three rings symbolise the spontaneous bliss of Buddha nature as emptiness, signlessness, and effortlessness. Emerging from the three rings on either side are two eight-petalled lotuses. The sixteen petals of the lotuses represent the sixteen modes of emptiness (*shunyata*). The eight upper lotus petals also represent the eight bodhisattvas, and the eight lower petals, their eight female consorts. Above the lotus bases are another series of three pearl-like rings, which collectively represent the six perfections (*paramitas*) of patience, generosity, discipline, effort, meditation, and wisdom. A full-moon disc crowns each of the lotuses, symbolising the full realisation of absolute and relative *bodhichitta*.

Emerging from the moon discs are five tapering prongs forming a spherical cluster or cross. These consist of an axial square central prong and four inward-curving prongs which unite with the central prong near its tip. The four curved prongs, positioned in the cardinal directions, face inwards towards the central prong, symbolising that the four aggregates of form, feeling, perception, and motivation, depend upon the fifth aggregate of consciousness. The five upper prongs of the *vajra* represent the Five Buddhas (Akshobhya, Vairochana, Ratnasambhava, Amitabha and Amoghasiddhi), and the unity of their omniscient wisdoms, attributes and qualities. The five lower prongs represent the female consorts of the Five Buddhas (Mamaki, Lochana, Vajradhatvishvari, Pandara, and Tara), and the unity of their qualities and attributes. The Five Buddhas and their consorts symbolise the elimination of the five aggregates of personality. The ten prongs together symbolise the ten perfections (the six *paramitas*, plus the perfections of skilful means, aspiration, inner strength, and pure awareness); the ten 'grounds' (Skt. *bhumi*; Tib. *sa*) or progressive levels of realisation of a bodhisattva; and the ten directions (four cardinal, four intercardinal, zenith, and nadir).

Each of the four outer prongs arise from the heads of *makaras*, which face outwards. The mouths of the *makaras* are wide open, and the curved arcs of the upper part of the prongs emanate like *vajra*-tongues from their mouths. The four *makaras* symbolise the four 'boundless states' or 'immeasureables' (compassion, love, sympathetic joy, and equanimity); the four doors of liberation (emptiness, signlessness, wishlessness, and lack of composition); the conquest of the four Maras (emotional defilements, passion, death, divine pride and lust); the four activities or *karmas*; the four purified elements; and the four joys (joy, supreme joy, the joy of cessation, and innate joy).

The tips at either end of the central prong may be shaped like a tapering pyramid or four-faceted jewel, which represents Mt Meru as the axial centre of both the outer macrocosm and inner microcosm. The twin faces of the symmetrical *vajra* represent the unity of relative and absolute truth.

The above iconographic description reveals the symbolic meanings attributed to the *vajra*. There follows a description of the *vajra* as an insignia or seal that marks the crown of wrathful deities, and a description of the stages of the visualised generation of certain deities where its inner symbolism is revealed.

The vast number of Vajrayana deities that emanate from the mandala principle of the Five Buddha Families are each described as being crowned with the 'seal' (*mudra*) or insignia of their particular Buddha Family, which is worn as an image or syllable at the crown of their heads. This derives from the *ushnisha* (Tib. *gtsug tor*) or wisdom protruberance on the crown of the Buddha's head. Peaceful deities and bodhisattvas usually bear a small image of their Buddha lord, or a small *torana*-shaped aureole inscribed with their lord's seed-syllable. Amitayus, for example, is crowned with a small image of Amitabha Buddha or Amitabha's seed-syllable, *Hrih*. Wrathful forms may likewise be described as bearing the seal or mark of their particular Buddha lord on their crowns, but usually this takes the form of a half-*vajra* insignia, the hub of which contains the seed-syllable or image of their parent Buddha. In the case of the wrathful blue-black deities, which mainly emanate from Akshobhya Buddha, the central hub of the half-*vajra* is sealed with Akshobhya's wrathful syllable, *Hum*.

In the visualisation practice of deity generation, a seed-syllable is usually described as arising out of emptiness at the heart. This seed-syllable may then transform into a lotus, upon which arises a moon or sun disc. Above this disc arises another syllable which transforms into a *vajra* – with another seed-syllable at its centre – which then finally transforms into the form of the deity. These three syllables are known as the three '*vajra* stages': the first is the arising of the seed-syllable from emptiness, the second is the arising of the wisdom mind (*vajra*), and the third stage is the transformation of the *vajra* into the form of the deity. The lotus, which is often described as eight-petalled, represents the heart *chakra*. The moon and sun discs, as method and wisdom, represent the white and red drops as the union of relative and absolute *bodhichitta*. Both ends of the *vajra*'s central prong represent the central channel, and their eight surrounding prongs, the eight *nadis* which emanate from the heart *chakra*. The three rings on either side of the central hub represent the three knots which constrict the central channel at the heart *chakra*. The central hub of the *vajra*, which embodies the ultimate seed-syllable from which the deity arises, represents the 'indestructible drop' at the heart centre, from which the most subtle consciousness of the practitioner arises as the 'clear appearance' of the visualised deity.

Plate 108

The central motif of this composition, depicting an 'open' nine-pronged *vajra* enhaloed in flames and resting upon a moon disc and lotus base, was originally drawn as a logo for Shambhala Publications.

In the four corners are four five-pronged 'closed' *vajras*, bound with silk cloths that are coloured to represent the Buddhas of the four cardinal directions.

The flames and open prongs of the central *vajra* depict its wrathful quality of destroying anger, which may identify it with the dark-blue Buddha Akshobhya (Tib. Mi bskyod pa) at the centre of the mandala. Akshobhya, whose name means the 'immutable one', is the Lord of the Vajra Family, representing the transmutation of anger into spacious or mirror-like wisdom.

The nine-prongs of the open *vajra* here represent the centre and eight directions as the nine Buddhist *yanas* or 'vehicles' of the path to enlightenment, based on the Nyingma or 'ancient school' of Tibetan Buddhism. The nine *yanas* are divided into three groups of three: the three 'causal' *yanas* derived from the sutra vehicles – shravaka, pratyekabuddha and *bodhisattva-yanas*; the three 'outer tantra' vehicles – *kriya tantra*, *charya tantra* and *yoga tantra*; and the three 'inner tantra' vehicles – *mahayoga*, *anuyoga*, and *atiyoga* or *dzogchen* (Tib. *rdzogs chen*).

Plate 109

Iconographically the Tibetan *vajra* is invariably represented in a stylised and simplified artistic form, largely due to the fact that as a hand-held or crowning emblem it is usually depicted as a small-scale object. The central hub is commonly drawn as a circle; the three rings on either side of the lotus pedestals are drawn as single solid segments; the eight lotus petals themselves appear as bands of three or five petals; the *makara*-heads are stylised to a curved leaf-shaped motif; and the prongs are drawn in a flat two-dimensional form – with the central prongs arising like double-edged swords, with diamond-shaped motifs at their centres and tips – and two embellished side prongs arching inwards to meet below the central tips.

Across the top row of this illustration are four drawings of the *vajra*. The two drawings on the left depict the five-pronged *vajra*, with two closed outer prongs meeting below the tip of the central prong. The two drawings on the right depict the nine-pronged or 'wrathful' *vajra*, with open prongs that form the shape of a trident.

On the left and right sides of the centre row are two drawings of the single-pointed *vajra*. Their four-faced central prongs are shaped like squared sword blades with sharp four-faceted tips. The lethal nature of its double-ended spike, which protrudes from a clenched fist is obvious. The spokes of the *dharmachakra* as a pacified 'wheel of sharp weapons' are also depicted in the form of *vajra*-spikes (see Plates 88 and 131).

Inwards, on either side of the single-pronged *vajras*, are two drawings of the nine-pronged *vajra* depicted in three-dimensional form. The drawing on the left shows the three encircling bands below and above the eight-petalled lotus pedestals that emanate from the central hub. The eight upper and lower arching prongs are depicted in a front-elevation of five prongs which emanate from lotus-petal bases; these represent the eight bodhisattvas above and their eight female consorts below (see Plate 113). The nine-pronged *vajra* on the right again depicts the two sets of three concentric

Plate 109: The various forms of the *vajra*

Plate 110: *Vajras*, crossed-*vajras* and *vajra*-chains

rings above the lotus pedestal and flattened central hub. Here the rings appear as continuous bands of pearls. When cast in bronze these three rings are commonly depicted as impressed circles of pearls or small lotus petals. Frequently only the central ring may be impressed, with the upper and lower rings unadorned. The *makara*-heads are depicted rising above the flat moon-disc which crowns the lotus pedestal; these heads should always face outwards from the central axis and moon-disc, as they 'emanate' the four or eight qualities that they represent.

At the centre is a five-pronged *vajra* draped and bound with a coloured silk scarf, representing one of the Five Buddha wisdoms or activities. Below this is a horizontal drawing of a wrathful open-pronged *vajra*, with sharp points in the form of a trident.

Across the bottom row are five drawings of the closed five-pronged *vajra,* showing several stylistic variations of its inward curving prongs. Three of these drawings show *makara*-head motifs at the bases of their prongs. The *makara*-mouths, from which the prongs emanate like tongues, symbolise indestructible strength and tenacity. The drawing at the centre of this row has an interior leaf-shaped design on the inner curves of its prongs.

Plate 110

This drawing illustrates a variety of stylised *vajras,* as may be depicted in Tibetan painting. Across the top row, and bounded by two single-pronged *vajras* at either end, are six five-pronged *vajras* and one open-pronged *vajra*.

Across the second intermediate row are drawn, from left to right: a crossed-jewel insignia (Skt. *vishvaratna*; Tib. *nor bu rgya gram*); two half-*vajras* mounted above crescent moons; and a crossed *vajra* or *vishvavajra*. The crossed jewels, derived from the earth and coloured to represent the four mandala directions, symbolise stability and the activities of enrichment. The half-*vajra* above the crescent moon symbolises the union of absolute *bodhichitta* (half-*vajra*) and relative *bodhichitta* (as the waxing or 'increase' of a one-day-old crescent moon). This insignia is commonly depicted on two-dimensional mandala designs on the inner edges of the 'offering goddess platform', which is placed outside of the five-coloured walls that encompass the inner square and four gateways of the mandala palace. It is also depicted in the four corners of the geometrical designs for the ritual fire-hearth of the *homa* offering, illustrated in Plates 143–45. The half-*vajra* is often painted in gold or red, and the moon in white, symbolising the union of absolute and relative *bodhichitta* as the union of the red and white drops or *bindu*.

The third row illustrates five further examples of the *vajra*, with a crossed-jewel motif on the left edge and a crossed *vajra* on the right. The fourth row depicts five small examples of the crossed *vajra* (the crossed *vajras* depicted here and on the following two plates are usually represented with their axes of orientation in the cardinal directions, rather than in their diagonal or intercardinal form as shown here;

I have drawn them diagonally so as to incorporate them in the page design).

The bottom half of the drawing shows six *vajra*-chains (Skt. *vajrashrinkhala*; Tib. *rdo rje lcags sgrog*) or *vajra*-rosaries (Skt. *vajramala*; Tib. *rdo rje 'phreng ba*). A lattice of *vajra*-chains is visualised as forming a protective '*vajra*-tent', which encloses the whole structure of a mandala palace like a great hemispherical dome over the mandala's sky. This *vajra*-tent is represented by the protective *vajra*-fence circle (Skt. *vajraprakara*; Tib. *rdo rje ra ba*) inside the five-coloured flame ring or 'rosary of light' (Skt. *prabhasamala*; Tib. *'od 'phreng*), which encircles the mandala's perimeter. In mandala visualisation practices a triple protective hemisphere – composed of a dome of five-coloured flames, a *vajra*-tent, and a 'womb' of pure lotuses – encompasses the mandala palace. These three hemispheres are represented by the flame, *vajra*, and lotus circles on the mandala's outer perimeter, which prevent negative influences, vow breakers, and those with impure *karma* from entering the sanctity of the mandala's pure realm.

Small chains of five-pronged *vajras* connect the five jewels or five skulls which adorn the tiara-crowns of many deities. These *vajra*-chains are often represented by a *vajra* design along the golden tiara-base that encloses the deity's hairline. Certain deities also wear a long rosary of fifty or fifty-one *vajras* around their necks, symbolising the purification of speech as the fifty Sanskrit vowels and consonants, and the purification of mind as the elimination of the fifty-one thought processes (see Plate 137). The bottom row of the drawing depicts a chain of single-pointed *vajras*. The deity Kalachakra is described as wearing a long rosary of single-pointed *vajras*, although iconographically Kalachakra's rosary is more often depicted as a long chain of five-pronged *vajras* with a crossed *vajra* at its lower centre.

THE CROSSED VAJRA
(Skt. *vishvavajra*; Tib. *rdo rje rgya gram, sna tshogs rdo rje*)

The *vishvavajra*, as the crossed or 'universal' *vajra*, which underlays the foundation of Mt Meru's universe, represents the principle of absolute stability, characterised by the solidity of the element earth. Bodh Gaya, where Shakyamuni Buddha attained the realisation of enlightened '*vajra* mind' (Tib. *thugs rdo rje*), is also known as Vajrasana (Tib. *rDo rje gdan*) or '*vajra*-seat'. The posture in which he sat, and in which the vast majority of seated deities are also depicted, is known as '*vajra*-posture' (Skt. *vajraparyarika*; Tib. *rdo rje skyil krung*) with the legs crossed in the opposite manner to the Hindu 'full-lotus' posture of *padmasana*. The raised wooden throne on which sit high lamas, such as the Dalai Lama, is usually decorated on its front with a hanging silk brocade square which displays the image of the *vishvavajra* at its centre, often with four swastikas in its corners. This emblem represents the indestructible reality of Buddha's *vajra* mind as the unshakeable throne or ground of enlightenment. In the Bonpo iconographical tradition an anticlockwise swastika (Tib. *g.yung drung*) replaces the Buddhist *vajra* as a symbol of the eternal adamantine reality. The relationship between the crossed *vajra* and the swastika, as stability symbols of the element earth, also finds expression in the visualisation or drawing of a *vishvavajra* or swastika under a practitioner's meditation seat during retreat. Similarly the emblem of a crossed *vajra* is inscribed upon the metal base that is used to seal deity statues after they have been consecrated. If the vertical *vajra* represents the visualised generation of the deity, the horizontal *vishvavajra* represents the visualised generation of the deity's mandala palace, symbolising the stability of the *vajra*-earth upon which it rests.

The *vishvavajra* is usually depicted in the five-colour scheme of the Five Buddha mandala with blue at its central hub, white in the east, yellow in the south, red in the west, and green in the north. The five directional colours symbolise the elements and qualities expressed in the symbolism of the Five Buddhas. The four sets of prongs of the *vishvavajra* symbolise the four activities or *karmas* of pacifying, enriching, magnetising, and destroying, representing the Buddha's activities in the four directions. The *vishvavajra*, or the sword, is the attribute of the green Buddha of the north, Amoghasiddhi, and represents his all-accomplishing wisdom as Lord of the Karma Family of activity.

A mandala palace rests upon a huge *vishvavajra*, which in turn stands upon the disc of earth as the unshakeable foundation of the deity's palace. The *makara*-heads and prongs of this *vishvavajra* extend beyond the outer wall of the palace in the four directions, and are coloured correspondingly. The four central prongs of this *vishvavajra* just touch the base of the outer lotus circle, symbolising the union of great bliss or method (*vishvavajra*) and emptiness or wisdom (lotus circle), as a sexual metaphor for the 'jewel (*vajra*-tip) in the lotus'. According to different mandala descriptions this *vishvavajra* may be represented as a three-dimensional five-pronged *vajra*, symbolising the Five Buddha wisdoms in each direction; or it may be represented as a flat two-dimensional three-pronged *vajra*. The twenty spokes of the five-pronged *vishvavajra* symbolise the purification of the 'twenty deluded views' of the five aggregates, conceived as a group of four self-misconceptions.

The twelve spokes of the three-pronged *vishvavajra* symbolise the purification of the 'twelve links of dependent origination' (Skt. *pratityasamutpada*; Tib. *rten 'brel yan lag bcu gnyis*). These 'twelve links' are graphically depicted in the outer circle of the 'wheel of life' painting. Rotating clockwise from the top the illustrations symbolise:

1. Primordial ignorance (*avidya*), represented as a blind man.
2. Conditioned activity (*samskara*), as a potter making pots.
3. Consciousness (*vijnana*), as a playful monkey attracted by objects.
4. Name and form (*namarupa*), as two men in boat.
5. The five senses and the mind (*ayatana*), as a house with five windows and a door.
6. Contact and its desire for an object (*sparsha*), as a couple kissing or making love.
7. Sensation (*vedana*) or desire giving rise to feelings of pleasure and pain, as a man blinded by an arrow in one eye.
8. Thirst or attachment to desire (*trishna*), as a man drinking alcohol.
9. Grasping (*adana*), as a monkey plucking fruit.
10. Becoming (*bhava*) or maturing towards rebirth, as a pregnant woman or a hen roosting on eggs.
11. Birth (*jati*) leading to endless rebirth, as a woman giving birth.
12. Ageing and death (*jaramarana*) leading to endless cycles of life and death, as an old man with a stick, and a corpse being carried to a cemetery.

The conceptual framework of the twelve links of dependent origination is one of the most important philosophical doctrines on the Buddhist view of causation and interdependence. Its deep metaphysical meanings according to the different Buddhist philosophical schools are of the most profound and subtle nature, and this subject can only be briefly alluded to here in relation to the symbolic interpretation placed upon the number twelve or to groups of twelve attributes. When Shakyamuni Buddha first taught the doctrines of dependent origination and the twelve links, one of his most advanced disciples believed he had fully understood it. The Buddha mildly chastised this disciple, saying that if a person fully understood this wonderful doctrine, then that person would have attained nirvana and be completely free of the endless cycle of existence portrayed in the 'wheel of life'.

Another symbolic listing of the number twelve refers to the twelve deeds of the Buddha, which are:

1. His descent from the Tushita heaven.
2. His entry into his mother's womb.
3. His birth.
4. His mastery of arts and skills.
5. His marriage and fathering of a child.
6. His renunciation.
7. His practising of austerities.
8. His resolve to meditate under the bodhi tree.
9. His conquest of Mara.
10. His enlightenment.
11. His turning of the wheel of dharma.
12. His death and *parinirvana*.

The nine-pronged *vishvavajra* has a total of thirty-six prongs, which along with the central hub symbolise the 'thirty-seven aspects of the path to enlightenment'. These aspects are grouped into seven categories:

1. The four mindfulnesses of body, feelings, mind, and phenomena.
2. The four complete abandonments of negative thoughts and actions, and their transformation.
3. The four 'legs of miraculous power' (aspiration, effort, intention, and analysis).
4. The five faculties of confidence, effort, mindfulness, one-pointedness and intelligence.

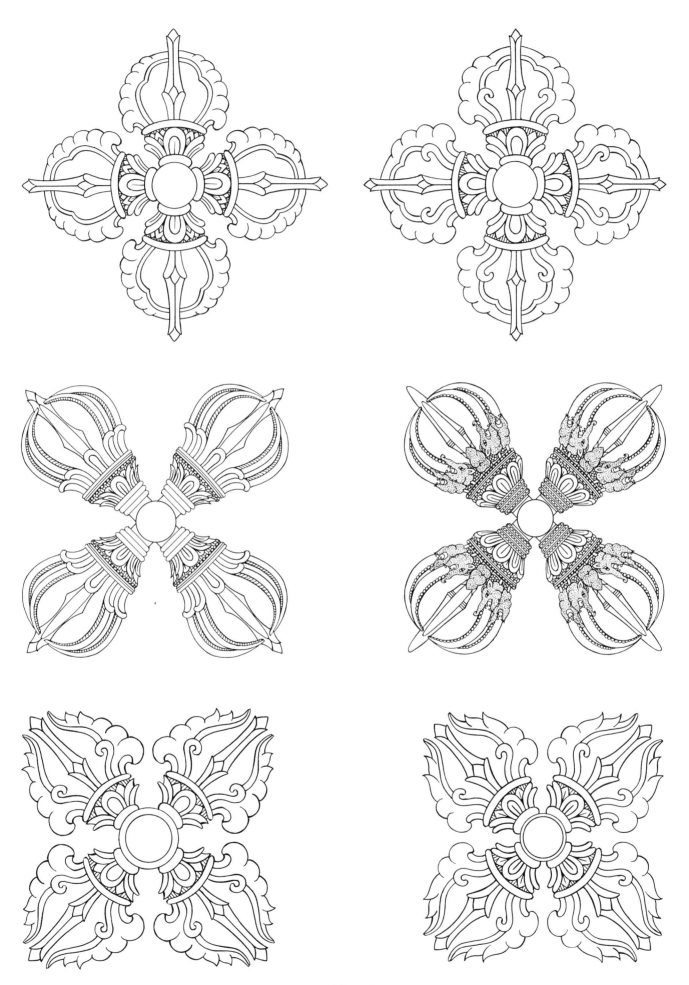

Plate 111: The *vishvavajra*

Plate 112: The *vishvavajra*

5. The five powers, which are the expression of the previous five qualities.

6. The seven branches of enlightenment (perfect mindfulness, analysis, effort, joy, adaptability, meditation, and equanimity).

7. The Noble Eightfold Path of right view, intention, speech, action, livelihood, effort, mindfulness, and meditation.

Plate 111

Depicted in this illustration are six examples of the *vishvavajra* (the lower four drawings are again drawn on a diagonal axis in order to accomodate them onto the page).

The top row shows two closed five-pronged *vishvavajras*, with a total of twenty prongs. On the central row are two nine-pronged *vishvavajras*, with a total of thirty-six prongs. On the bottom row are two open three or five-pronged *vishvavajras*, with a total of twelve or twenty prongs.

Plate 112

Depicted in this drawing are seventeen variations of the *vishvavajra*, mainly in its closed five-pronged form. The two drawings across the top show the *vishvavajra* in a half-section, as depicted on the tantric staff or *khatvanga* (see Plates 115 and 116).

The Bell (Skt. *ghanta*; Tib. *dril bu*)

The ritual hand-bell or *vajra ghanta* (Tib. *rdo rje dril bu*) represents the feminine principle as the 'perfection of wisdom' (Skt. *prajnaparamita*) which directly realises emptiness (*shunyata*). The *vajra* and bell are the two main ritual implements that symbolise the perfections of method or skilful means (*vajra*), and wisdom or emptiness (*ghanta*). When paired, the *vajra* is held in the right hand, and the bell in the left, representing the inseparable union of method and wisdom. Plates 73 and 75 show the principal hand gestures or *mudra* in which the *vajra* and bell are held.

The bell is described as 'proclaiming the sound of emptiness', which arises from the voidness of its form, radiates in all directions, and dissolves back into silence or emptiness. Its hollow or 'mouth' is emptiness; its clapper or 'tongue' is form. As a sexual symbol the hollow 'lotus' of the bell represents emptiness as the vagina, and the prongs of the *vajra* – symbolising the four *nadi* which emanate from the 'jewel-wheel *chakra*' at the tip of the male sexual organ – represent form or appearance. Their union is the coincidence of great bliss and compassion as pure emptiness and form.

Tibetan bells are traditionally individually cast from bronze bell-metal by a skilful technique of sand-casting. An inner and outer mould are made for the bell casing, made of fine compacted sand which is bound with radish juice or raw brown sugar as a cohesive. A plain 'blank' bell is used to model the moulds, and the embellished external designs of the bell are carefully impressed into the outer sand mould before casting. This is accomplished with a series of metal embossing stamps, imprinted with the various motifs that decorate the bell. The upper design of the lotus circle and syllables are engraved onto the upper shoulder of the blank, as they will not damage the outer mould when the blank is removed. The upper bronze handle of the bell is cast separately by the lost wax method of bronze casting, and the two parts of the bell are joined together with pitch-resin.

The Iconography and Symbolism of the Bell

The ritual set of a *vajra* and *ghanta* essentially symbolise the practitioner's personal tutelary or *yidam* deity and the deity's mandala. The bell, as the deity's mandala, is proportioned with equal measures in its upper handle, lower casing, and the width across its mouth or bottom rim. The pitch of a bell rises as its surface area decreases, and the thickness of its walls increase.

At the base of the bell is the inward-tapering rim, from which the 'sound of emptiness' arises as vibration. This rim represents the disc of space. Above the rim are an embossed ring of upright *vajras* enclosed between two rows of pearls or 'conch-rosaries' (Tib. *dung 'phreng*). The lower rosary of pearls symbolises the outer protective wheel of five-coloured flames or 'rosary of light' which surrounds the mandala. The ring of *vajras* – which may number twelve, sixteen, twenty-four, or thirty-two, and occasionally depicts a single *vishvavajra* at its front – symbolises the *vajra*-fence protection wheel. The upper rosary of pearls symbolises the thirty-two or sixty-four petals of the 'lotus-womb' protection circle. Above these lower motifs is an open unadorned area, which symbolises the earth-disc of the mandala. Above this open area is a frieze of eight 'monster-heads' or *kirtimukhas* (Tib. *'go pa thra*), which symbolise the eight *makara*-heads of the *vishvavajra* on which the mandala palace rests. An alternative symbolism for the eight *kirtimukhas* is given as the mandala's eight great charnel grounds or cemeteries. From the mouths of the *kirtimukhas* hang a connecting frieze of jewel-loops and jewel-pendants (Tib. *dra ba dra phyed*), which symbolise the decorations on the outer wall of the mandala. Above the upper arcs of the jewel-loops, and positioned between the *kirtimukha* faces, are the eight symbols of the eight bodhisattvas, which are also represented by the eight lotus petals placed above the shoulder at the top of the bell's casing. These eight symbols may take the form of *vajras*, wheels, or lotus flowers, and are described in one standard sequence below. Above the *kirtimukha* frieze is another double row of pearls, enclosing either eight or sixteen horizontal *vajras*. These represent the inner walls and inner protection circle of the mandala, and symbolise the eight or sixteen emptinesses (*shunyata*).

On the top shoulder of the bell casing, and inside the upper rosary of pearls, is the eight-petalled lotus-dias of the eight bodhisattvas and their female consorts as the eight offering goddesses. The eight petals, which symbolise the bodhisattvas, and the eight syllables, which symbolise the eight offering goddesses, are illustrated in the lower right of Plate 113. Their sequence, beginning with the eastern petal at the bottom and rotating clockwise is as follows:

East – the bodhisattva Kshitigarbha (Tib. Sa yi snying po) and his consort Lasya (Tib. sGeg pa ma), the goddess offering beauty, represented by the syllable *Tam.*

South-east – the bodhisattva Maitreya (Tib. Byams pa) and his consort Pushpa (Tib. Me tog ma), the goddess offering flowers, represented by the syllable *Mam.*

South – the bodhisattva Akashagarbha (Tib. Nam mkha'i snying po) and his consort Mala (Tib. 'Phreng ba ma), the goddess offering garlands, represented by the syllable *Lam.*

South-west – the bodhisattva Samantabhadra (Tib. Kun tu bzang po) and his consort Dhupa (Tib. bDug spos ma), the goddess offering incense, represented by the syllable *Pam.*

West – the bodhisattva Avalokiteshvara (Tib. sPyan ras gzigs) and his consort Gita (Tib. Glu ma), the goddess offering song, represented by the syllable *Mam.*

North-west – the bodhisattva Manjughosha (Tib. 'Jam dpal dbyangs) and his consort Aloka (Tib. Mar me ma), the goddess offering light, represented by the syllable *Tsum.*

North – the bodhisattva Vajrapani (Tib. Phyag na rdo rje) and his consort Nritya (Tib. Gar ma), the goddess offering dance, represented by the syllable *Pam.*

North-east – the bodhisattva Sarva-nivarana-vishkambhim (Tib. sGrib pa rnam sel) and his consort Gandha (Tib. Dri chab ma), the goddess offering perfume, represented by the syllable *Bhrum.*

The arrangement of the eight offering goddesses, placed within the eight directional lotus petals, follows the same sequence as in the mandala offering (see Plate 62 and 63). The *Bardo Thodol* lists the eight offering goddesses in a similar sequence, but transposes Gandha to the north and substitutes Nritya with Narti, as the goddess offering food in the north-east.

An alternative arrangement of the syllables places the four 'mothers' (Skt. *matrika*; Tib. *yum*), or consorts of the four directional Buddhas, in the four cardinal directions, and four of the offering goddesses in the intercardinal directions. Mamaki (*Mam*), the consort of Akshobhya is in the west; Lochana (*Lam*), the consort of Vairochana is in the south; Pandara (*Pam*), the consort of Amitabha is in the north; and Tara (*Tam*), the consort of Amoghasiddhi is in the east. The intercardinal directions are occupied by the goddess Pushpa (*Mam*) offering flowers in the south-east; Dhupa (*Pam*) offering incense in the south-west; Dipa or Aloka (*Tsum*) offering light in the north-west; and Gandha (*Bhrum*) offering perfume in the north-east.

Another sequence places the eight female bodhisattvas on the lotus petals, with the goddess Prajnaparamita (Tib. Sher phyin ma) – meaning 'Perfection of Wisdom' – at the centre. The most common list of the eight female bodhisattvas is: Sarasvati, Chunda, White Tara, Khadiravani Tara, Sitatapatra, Marichi, Ushnishavijaya and Parnashabari. The syllable sequence may vary, according to the tradition or

ritual specifications for which the bell was cast, but the sequence illustrated on Plate 113 is found on most bells.

The most common sequence of bodhisattva symbols that occur between the *kirtimukha* faces, and correspond to the eight syllables is as follows: front or east (*Tam*), a wheel; south-east (*Mam*), an *utpala* flower; south (*Lam*), a jewel; south-west (*Pam*), a wheel; west (*Mam*), a lotus; north-west (*Tsum*), a *vajra*; north (*Pam*), a sword; north-east (*Bhrum*), a lotus.

Within the eight-petalled lotus circle is a central dias of sixteen, twenty-four, thirty-two, or forty lotus-petals or spokes, from which the stem of the bell rises. These occur in groups of two, three, four, or five, within each of the eight outer lotus-petals. Above the stem is the upper handle of the bell, which is bronze-cast separately from the base of the bell, and sealed with resin into the cavity of the stem.

At the base of the upper handle are usually a series of three pearl rings, which combine with the upper three rings – above the lotus pedestal of the *vajra* at the bell's top – to symbolise the six perfections. Above these three lower rings is either the square (representing an earth base) or the round base of a nectar-vase or a long-life vase (Tib. *tshe bum*) with four leaf-shaped pendants. This vase symbolises the 'nectar of accomplishment', and represents the nectar-filled body of the goddess Prajnaparamita above. On certain bells the vase may be replaced by an open ring through which the middle or ring finger is inserted; this represents the wisdom of Prajnaparamita's body as emptiness. The single face of the goddess Prajnaparamita (Tib. Shes rab kyi phar phyin) represents the perfection (*paramita*) of the absolute non-duality of all the Buddhas' wisdoms or discriminating awarenesses (*prajna*). Her hair is tightly bound in a bun at the back, representing the binding of all views into non-dual reality. The five wisdom-jewels of her crown overlap onto the five frontal petals of the upper *vajra*'s eight-petalled lotus pedestal. The symbolism of the half-*vajra* at the top is the same as for the five or nine-pointed *vajra*, described in the preceding section.

Plate 113

On the left and centre of this illustration are two frontal view drawings of the ritual bell or *ghanta*. The bell on the left has a lower '*vajra*-fence' circle of thirty-two vertical *vajras* between the two 'pearl-rosaries' at its base, and an upper circle of sixteen horizontal *vajras* below the bell-casing's shoulder. *Vajra* emblems are also depicted between the ring of eight *kirtimukha* faces on the bell's casing. The circle of eight lotus petals and their contained syllables are depicted in perspective above the shoulder of the bell. Above the cylindrical stem is a long-life vase (Tib. *tshe bum*) with its four hanging leaf-shaped pendants, and the face of the goddess Prajnaparamita.

The central bell drawing has a lower circle of sixteen *vajras* – with a central *vishvavajra* at its front, positioned on the axial line of Prajnaparamita's face – and an upper circle of eight *vajras*. The emblems of a jewel and a wheel are drawn between the *kirtimukha* faces, following the sequence of

Plate 113: The ritual bell

bodhisattva emblems as described above. Above the stem is a plain golden nectar-vase and the face of Prajnaparamita.

The upper drawing on the right shows a cross-section of the bell's casing, with the clapper suspended from a cast half-ring within the inner roof of the bell. The circular drawing below depicts the top view of the bell-casing, with an inner dias of sixteen lotus-spokes surrounding the bell's stem, then the eight-petalled lotus with its eight syllables, and finally the upper protection ring of sixteen *vajras* at its perimeter. From the bottom (east) rotating clockwise the inscribed syllables follow the sequence: *Tam Mam Lam Pam Mam Tsum Pam Bhrum.*

THE RITUAL DAGGER
(Skt. *kila*; Tib. *phur bu*; *phur pa*)

The triple-bladed dagger, nail or spike – known as a *kila* in Sanskrit and a *phurba* in Tibetan – has its origins in Vedic India as the stake or post to which domestic animals, or those intended for ritual sacrifice, were tethered. The position of the Vedic altar was determined by repeatedly throwing the peg (Skt. *shamya*) of an oxen's yoke towards the east, until it remained upright in the ground. The purpose of this ritual was to divine the stable point of the earth, whereby the head of the invisible 'earth-serpent' below the ground is transfixed or pinned down to create stability. The movement of the earth-serpent progresses by one degree a day in a geomantic compass-circle, in accord with the 360 days of the lunar year. This divinatory ritual is still performed in India, where the Vedic astrologer determines the precise point where the earth-serpent's head is located before a building can be constructed, and hammers a small peg of acacia wood into the ground at this point using a coconut as a mallet.

An almost identical ritual procedure is performed in the foundation rites of a Tibetan Buddhist monastery, temple or stupa, whereby a chart of the 'serpent-tailed earth deity' (Tib. *sa bdag*) is constructed on a grid of ninety square sections in each of the four seasonal directions, totalling the 360 days of the lunar year. The auspicious 'rectangle' of the earth deity's body is determined from the chart and excavated for geomantic signs. Treasures are then buried in this hole, and the land is purified through '*phurba* rituals' of staking the ground to create stability and protection as 'hallowed ground'. The marking out of sacred ground with wooden stakes and thread, endowed the stakes with the magical qualities of establishing protective boundaries that repelled all negative influences and evil spirits. In many tantric rituals a protective circle is created around the practitioner by the 'nailing' (Skt. *kilana*) of wooden pegs into the ground, and binding their perimeter with mantras and thread of a certain colour.

A comparable practice of establishing magic circles and pentagrams was also well known in the Western occult tradition.

In Vedic mythology the *kila*, as 'Indrakila', is specifically identified with the central *kila* or spike of Indra's *vajra*. In an early variation of the Hindu creation myth, Indra hurls his *vajra* at the great dragon-serpent Vritra, who encircles the floating rock island of Mt Mandara and sleeps with his head pressed over the pool containing the water of life. The central prong of Indra's *vajra* transfixes the head of Vritra, cleaving the rock of Mandara and allowing the waters of creation to flow, whilst simultaneously acting as a *kila* to nail Mt Mandara to the ocean floor and create stability on the earth. Mt Mandara, which was used as the churning pole in the 'churning of the ocean' legend, is also known as Indrakila or 'Indra's spike'. In this legend the symbolic allusions to the awakening of Kundalini Shakti in the *muladhara* or earth-*chakra* are quite obvious.

Indrakila is also the name given to the wooden axle-pole that runs through the centre of a Buddhist stupa, and the axis which ascends through the centre of a Buddha or deity statue, symbolising the central channel. Tibetan tent pegs (Tib. *phur 'gyur*) act as *phurbas* in the erection of a tent, and the Tibetan yogin, when erecting a retreat tent, visualises all hindering demons as being pinned by the pegs in a spread-eagled posture under the earth. One form of the protective deity Mahakala is known as Panjaranatha or 'Lord of the Tent'. This form of Mahakala has garuda wings, and his feet take the form of sharp *phurbas* which pierce the heart of an enemy. An early form of Mahakala with *phurba* legs was propitiated in Khotan, and the earliest forms of wooden *phurbas*, carved in the forms of deities, have been unearthed in the Khotan region of Central Asia. The earliest written text of a *phurba* ritual was recently discovered in an ancient Buddhist stupa at Gilgit, in the Indus valley of northern Pakistan. This palm-leaf manuscript dates back to the fifth century AD.

In the historical annals of early Buddhist Tibet the princess Wen cheng Kongjo, the Chinese wife of King Songtsen Gampo, is credited with determining through *feng-shui* how to pin down the 'supine demoness' of Tibet, in order to subdue her obstructive nature and facilitate the expansion of Buddhism into Tibet. Thirteen stupas and shrines were erected to pin down the invisible demoness's wrists and ankles, elbows and knees, shoulders and hips, with a central shrine to pin down her heart. It is written that, "The pillars of the heart (sited at the sacred Jokhang temple in Lhasa) were fashioned in the form of *phurbas*, and the tantrics rejoiced."

In the biography of Padmasambhava it is recorded that he travelled to the northern land of Kashakamala, where the cult of the *phurba* or magical dagger prevailed. Later, whilst meditating on the deity Yangdak Heruka (Skt. Vishuddha Heruka) in the 'Asura Cave' at Parping in the Kathmandu valley, he experienced many obstructions from the *maras*, and in order to subjugate them he requested the *Phurba Vitotama Tantras* to be brought from India. Having established the first Tibetan monastery at Samye, the first transmission that Padmasambhava gave to his twenty-five 'heart disciples', in order to eliminate the hindrances to the propagation of the *buddhadharma* in Tibet, were the teachings of the *Vajrakilaya Tantra*. From its early Nyingma origins the practice of Vajrakilaya as a *yidam* deity with the power to cut through any obstructions was absorbed into all schools of Tibetan Buddhism.

The evolution of the wrathful *yidam* deity Vajrakilaya (Tib. rDo rje phur pa), or Vajrakumara, into its definitive form as a three-headed, six-armed deity with *vajra*-wings, who rolls the 'Mt Meru *phurba*' between the palms of his hands, or whose lower body assumes the form of a *phurba*, reveals a complex mythological derivation from the legends of the subjugation or taming of the wrathful hindering demon, Rudra. In order to subdue Rudra, the Buddhas of the three times manifested countless wrathful deities such as Yamantaka, Hayagriva, Yangdak Heruka, Amrita Kundalin, and Vajrakilaya, which respectively represent the compassionately-wrathful aspects of the body, speech, mind, qualities, and activities of all the Buddhas. As the emanation of enlightened activity, Vajrakilaya embodies the supremely wrathful Buddha activity of destroying the hatred, hindrances, and negativities projected by the personified demons as *maras* and *rudras*. This wrath is emphasised in Vajrakilaya's *sadhana*, which describes how his skin is armoured with an impenetrable network of *vishvavajras* representing his perfect Buddha activites, with each of his body hairs crowned by a minute half-*vajra*, and from every pore of his skin emanate a stream of tiny incandescent *kilas* which spark throughout space like meteorites. The form of Vajrakilaya, with three faces and six arms – symbolising the vanquishing of the three root poisons of ignorance, desire and hatred, and the accomplishment of the six perfections – manifests the essence of all the wrathful Heruka deities with three faces and six arms. The term 'Heruka' means: emptiness (*he*), great compassion (*ru*), and their indivisibility (*ka*).

As the ultimate weapon which cuts through hatred and stabs demonic obstructions, the *phurba* realises its most symbolic form as the representation of Vajrakilaya, with three heads, six arms, and his lower body forming the blazing triple-sided blade of a pointed dagger. As a hand-held weapon the *phurba* more commonly takes the form of an eight-sided shaft surmounted by a knot and three wrathful deity faces, with a lower knot, *makara*-head, *naga*-tails, and a triple-sided blade forming the lower extremity. The *phurba* may be fashioned in many variant forms and constructed of many materials, including mined or meteorite iron, acacia wood, black rosewood, red or white sandalwood, thorn wood, monkey or human bone. The following materials are prescribed for the four activities (*karmas*) or rituals of tantra: soft or sappy white woods are specified for pacifying rituals, *sirisa* wood for rituals of enrichment, acacia or *khadira* (*Acacia catechu*) wood for rituals of subjugation, and iron for destructive or wrathful activities. Many *phurbas* – particularly those found as *termas* or hidden treasures – are fashioned of meteorite iron (for a discussion of the Tibetan depiction of the meteorite as a triangular iron blade see page 234).

The *phurba* is frequently held in a pointing or stabbing gesture in the right hands of Nyingma gurus and *tertons*, or may also be tucked into their belts. When the *phurba* is coupled with the *vajra* or *vajra*-hammer as hand-held implements, it is always held in the left hand. The symbolic placement of an upright *phurba* into a triangular wooden or iron receptacle (Tib. *'brub khung*), represents the pinning or 'grinding to dust' of obstructing demons in a triangular iron prison. In rituals of extremely wrathful activity the effigy of an enemy or hindering spirit may be placed within the iron receptacle, pinned down with four small *phurbas* at the shoulders and knees, and with a large central *phurba* piercing the heart. Here the four small *phurbas* represent the 'four immeasurables' of compassion, love, sympathetic joy, and equanimity, with the central *phurba* representing pure *bodhichitta*, as the altruistic aspiration to attain enlightenment for the benefit of all sentient beings.

The Iconography and Symbolism of the Phurba

The wrathful *phurba* is depicted in the dark-blue colour of iron, symbolising its unchangeable and indestructible *vajra* nature. *Vajra*-flames often emanate along the edges of its blades, as the *phurba* is described as blazing with fire when it is stabbed in the ten directions. The lower half of the dagger represents method or skilful means, and its upper shaft symbolises wisdom. The point of its blade metaphorically presses on the hell realms beneath the earth, and its upper shaft ascends through the god realms. The 'Mt Meru *phurba*', held by Vajrakilaya and rolled between his palms, represents both the 'grinding to dust of enemies' and the pinning-down or stabilising of Mt Meru – as the full manifestation of the Buddhas' activities throughout the phenomenal universe.

The triple blade of the *phurba,* which is described as 'a ferocious striker issuing from the jaws of a *makara*', symbolises the overcoming or cutting through of the three root poisons of ignorance, desire, and hatred. The properties of its triangular shape, representing the element fire, symbolise wrathful activity. The tenacious grip of the *makara*-head at the top of the blade represents its ferocious activity, and the inseparable union of method and wisdom as the fearlessness and certainty of its accomplishment. The six entwined *naga*-tails – three pairs of which emanate from the *makara*'s mouth and coil down the blades – symbolise the six perfections of the *phurba,* as the six-armed deity Vajrakilaya. As the *phurba* is mainly used in earth-subjugating rituals, *nagas* – which cause afflictions such as leprosy and water-related illnesses – are one of the main targets of the *phurba*'s wrathful activities. The garuda wings and *naga*-ornaments, embodied in the *phurba* as Vajrakilaya, also represent his hostility towards the *nagas*. The three blades also represent control over the three times of past, present and future, and control over the three realms – above, on, and below the earth's surface.

The two knots on either end of the eight-faceted shaft probably derive from the tethering rope used to tie animals to a fixed pillar or stake, or from its use in *kilana* rituals, as the tying or sealing of a sacred area. Several symbolic interpretations are applied to these knots and the shaft. The 'Northern treasure tradition' (Tib. Byang gter) states that, "Samsara and nirvana are enclosed within the vast knots (Skt. *mahakanda*) at either end of the handle. The eight sides of the handle radiate with the splendour of all creation." Another interpretation places the heavens of the desire gods

(*kamadhatu*) in the lower knot, those of the form-gods (*rupadhatu*) in the lower half of the eight-sided shaft, the formless gods (*arupadhatu*) in the shaft's upper half, and the realm of the Buddhas in the knot above. The eight-sided shaft also symbolises the *chakras* and *nadis* of the *vajra* body, or more specifically the eight *nadis* of the heart *chakra* enclosed by its constricting knots. Like the *khatvanga* (see Plates 115 and 116), the eight facets of the shaft radiating to the eight directions may symbolise the Noble Eightfold Path and the circle of the eight great cemeteries. As a mandala of Vajrakilaya the eight facets also symbolise the 'deities of the eight transmissions' which surround Vajrakilaya.

The three wrathful faces above the upper knot embody such three-faced *yidam* deities as Vairochana, Amrita Kundalin, Hayagriva, Yamantaka, and Vajrakumara, who are invoked to dwell within the *phurba*. These three faces destroy the afflictions of ignorance (Skt. *moha*), desire (*raga*), and hatred (*dvesha*). They may be identified with Yamantaka (body), as the white right face which destroys anger; Hayagriva (speech), as the left red face which destroys desire; and Amrita Kundalin (mind), as the central blue face which destroys ignorance. These three faces also symbolise the three *kayas,* and the binding of their hair into a single topknot symbolises the binding of all extremes and contentions into the single nature of reality, and the binding of their commitments or pledges (Skt. *samaya*; Tib. *dam tshig*). Their nine eyes symbolise the nine wisdoms of the *dharmata* or ultimate truth, as the unified wisdoms of the Five Buddhas and the Four Mothers. They also symbolise the nine vehicles (*yanas*) of the Buddha's teachings. The twelve projecting skulls, which encircle their combined crown, represent freedom from the twelve links of dependent origination (see page 240). The half-*vajra* which surmounts the topknot represents the Five Buddha wisdoms, and encloses the image or seed-syllable of the presiding Buddha, which for the majority of *phurba* deities is Akshobhya or his bodhisattva, Vajrapani.

The artistic representation of the *phurba* in thangka painting invariably follows the form described above, and depicted in Plate 114, although its three-dimensional sculptural form is often subject to a variety of iconographical representations. The upper torso of the central *phurba* deity may be depicted with two hands rolling a small *phurba* at his heart, or often with another four outer hands which also hold small *phurbas*. Alternatively each of the three *phurba* deities which reside in the *phurba* may be represented with six-arms, in the posture of Vajrakilaya, and with *phurbas* in each of their hands. The form of garuda may also be incorporated into the *phurba* below the upper torsos of the three *phurba* deities, or the head of a garuda may replace the *makara*-head at the top of the triangular blade. A central five-pronged *vajra* between the two knots may replace the eight-sided shaft; or the knots – which may include a third central knot, joined by two interspaced eight-sided shafts – may be sculpted in regular octahedral forms as cubes, with their corners cut away. In this form the knots may be depicted in an interlocking basket-weave design; alternatively the knots may be hollow in their interior.

Plate 114: The ritual dagger

Plate 114

This illustration depicts five examples of the *phurba*. The first drawing on the left depicts the most common representation of the triangular-bladed *phurba*. Its central blade points to the front and is crowned by the *makara*-head disgorging entwined serpents' tails, which descend along the inner surface of its blades. The two woven knots above are separated by the eight-faceted shaft, and crowned at the top by the three faces of the *phurba* deities, with a half-*vajra* above their central topknot.

The second drawing depicts a similar design of *phurba*, but with a five-pronged *vajra* replacing the central eight-sided shaft.

The third drawing depicts a *phurba* with a large *makara*-head and small *vajra*-flames emanating from the edges of its blades. The top of this *phurba* is surmounted by a flattened topknot, which serves as the 'nail head' of the *phurba*

as a '*vajra*-spike', when it is symbolically hammered into the effigy of an enemy, or ritually hammered into the ground as part of a sacred protective boundary.

The fourth drawing depicts a simplified artistic representation of the *phurba* consisting of a three-sided blade, two ellipsoid knots, an eight-sided shaft, and a surmounting half-*vajra* at the top. *Phurbas* in this form are commonly drawn as the small hand-held implements of deities, siddhas, gurus and teachers.

The fifth drawing depicts the side-view of a *phurba* crowned by the horse-head of the wrathful *yidam* deity, Hayagriva (Tib. rTa mgrin). As one of the main *phurba* deities, Hayagriva (whose name means the 'horse-necked') is represented with either a single or triple horse-head crowning his three faces above his topknot. The top of the horse's head on this drawing is crowned by the half-*vajra* containing the syllable of the patron Buddha, which in Hayagriva's case is usually Amitabha or Amoghasiddhi. The side-view of the *makara*'s head above the blade illustrates how the serpents' tails entwine on each of its three faces. The stand or receptacle into which the *phurba* point penetrates holds the implement in an upright position. Triangular wooden receptacles – which are often decorated in a wrathful form as a black triangular 'iron prison', with red flames and an array of wrathful weapons encompassing the bound effigy of

On painted wooden *phurbas* 'totem animals' and weapons – garudas, tigers, lions, *vajras* and *chakras*, or fortress doorways containing armies (see Plates 127 and 128) – may be depicted on the diamond-shaped faces of the knots and on the octagonal faces of the shaft.

248

an enemy (see Plate 133) – commonly serve as ceremonial or ritual stands for *phurbas*.

Often a group of ten *phurbas* – positioned in the ten directions and representing the ten wrathful wisdom deities (Tib. *ye shes khro bo*) of the Vajrakilaya mandala – form a protective circle or sphere in the ritual activities of 'staking out' (Skt. *kilana*) a sacred building or mandala. The ten wrathful wisdom deities of Vajrakilaya's mandala are: Krodhavijaya (east); Niladanda (south-east); Yamantaka (south); Achala (south-west); Hayagriva (west); Aparajita (north-west); Amrita Kundalin (north); Trailokavijaya (north-east); Krodhahumkara (zenith); and Mahabala (nadir).

THE HINDU KAPALIKAS, PADMASAMBHAVA, AND THE BUDDHIST MAHASIDDHAS

The social rigidity of the ancient Hindu caste system dictated that one's status in life was predetermined by one's birth. A seemingly inflexible doctrine of spiritual evolution – based upon karma and transmigration and coupled with an unquestioning devotion to a fixed religious belief system – maintained both social and religious law. Yet, as Buddhism was to prove by its major impact on the Brahminical hierarchy, in any fixed system based upon and bound by destiny there is always an escape clause based upon free will.

For the crime of inadvertently killing a brahmin the penalty was social ostracism. The penitent was prescribed to dwell in a forest hut, at a desolate crossroads, in a charnel ground, or under a tree; to obtain their food by begging; to practise austerities; to wear a loincloth of hemp, dog or ass-skin; to sleep upon a bed of grass; and to carry the emblems of a human skull as an alms bowl, and the skull of the brahmin they had slain mounted upon a wooden staff as a banner. The miscreant's sentence of social exile was imposed for a period of twelve years. The Sanskrit name given to these ascetics, who soon evolved into a sect of yogins, was Kapalika or 'skull-bearers'.

Dwelling as an outcaste in the charnel grounds, consuming the food offerings presented to the dead and wearing their shrouds as clothing, the penitent was projected into an imaginal reality which blurred the distinction between the world of men and the realm of ethereal beings. Besmeared with human ashes, wearing bone ornaments, intoxicated with divine madness, *bhang* (marijuana paste), or alcohol, eating from a human skull-cup, brandishing a skull-topped club (*khatvanga*), and warning away human beings with the rattle of his double-skull drum (*damaru*), the outcaste automatically assumed the traditional guise of the yogin. With only the company of *chandalis* (disposers of corpses), jackals, cemetery dogs, vultures and carrion crows, the yogin entered the twilight world of the dead, and crossing over the borderlands inhabited by disembodied spirits and ghosts, he gained the allegiance of the great spiritual denizens of the charnel grounds, the wrathful *dakas* and

dakinis. From the *sambhogakaya* level of this transcendental reality, the yogin received through direct mind transmission the revelations or instructions enabling him to penetrate into the very heart of darkness – to go beyond the conceptual cage of self-identification where human beings are imprisoned by their limitations, inhibitions and fears – and to emerge into the dazzling light of great immaculate nakedness, beyond hope, beyond fear, beyond conceptualisation, beyond doubt and certainty.

Some of the practices that were performed in the charnel grounds penetrate deeply into the 'black arts' of necromancy. Many necromantic archetypes which surge as the most potent fears of the collective unconscious – ghouls, vampires, spirits of the undead, zombies, succubi and incubi, changelings and werewolves – originated in the most extreme recesses of the 'left-hand path' of ancient Indian witchcraft.

The 'corpse-ritual' (Skt. *shavasadhana*), for example, was employed to invoke a powerful spirit into a human corpse in order to gain the *siddhi* or psychic power of that spirit. The corpse chosen for a specific *shavasadhana* ritual had to be of a certain kind, such as a 'twice-born brahmin', a virgin teenager, or a pregnant woman. On a dark night of the moon the practitioner prepared the corpse in a prescribed way and turned its tongue backwards into the throat (see *khechari mudra*, page 110). He then filled its opened mouth with specific ingredients, such as iron and copper filings, oil and a wick, or a piece of camphor. Sitting on the chest of the corpse he would light the wick or camphor in the corpse's mouth and commence his ritual with invocations, *mudras*, and mantras. When the spirit took possession of the cadaver or 'corpse-seat', the corpse would reanimate with a ferocious power. It was the yogin's task to physically subdue the zombie (Skt. *vetala*; Tib. *ro langs*) and capture its 'life essence' by biting off its protruding tongue with his own teeth, thereby gaining the *siddhi* of that spirit.

The construction of the great Indian Buddhist monastery of Odantapuri in ancient Magadha (modern Bihar) was believed to have been funded by a *shavasadhana* ritual. When the Buddhist *bhikshu* who had been coerced into performing this ritual by a tantric yogin named Narada succeeded in biting off the tongue of the zombie, the tongue transformed into a magical sword, whilst the corpse itself became solid gold. Using the magical '*siddhi* of the sword' to fly through the heavens, the *bhikshu* flew over Mt Meru and observed its formation. Upon this vision he based his design of Odantapuri monastery, whilst using the self-replenishing supply of gold from the corpse to fund its construction. The name Odantapuri means 'the city that is flown over'.

Although spirit-subduing rituals, such as *shavasadhana*, *vetala siddhi*, *munda siddhi* and *pishacha siddhi*, are believed to have died out with the decline of the tantric era in India, secret lineages of transmission still continue to the present day. But such topics should not be discussed here; it is enough that they are alluded to in passing, as they concern the aquisition of mundane or worldly *siddhis*, which pale to insignificance in the light of Mahamudra *siddhi* or the Buddha's enlightenment. These topics are extremely esoteric, and open to the most deviating of misinterpretations when taken out of their cultural context.

The charnel grounds (Skt. *smashana*) have always been a traditional site for the most potent development of renunciation, where the vivid realities of impermanence, suffering, grieving, disease, death, decay, and emptiness confront the mendicant in a blatant and ceaseless cycle. At Manikarnika burning ghat in Benares, the perpetual flame used to light the funeral pyres dates back to the founding of the city. Manikarnika is the site of the longest-burning flame in mankind's history. Manikarnika – meaning 'jewel earrings' – is according to legend one of the twenty-four sacred sites where the dismembered body parts of Sati, the first wife of Shiva, were scattered across India by Vishnu.

Even in the time of Buddha the practice of frequenting cemeteries was one of the 'twelve observances' of a *bhikshu*. Yet an early Buddhist text, the *Lalitavistara* (*circa* second century AD), reveals the enormous spiritual schism between the orthodox 'right-hand' Buddhist sangha, and the unorthodox 'left-hand' tantrics of the charnel grounds. It describes the Kapalikas as, "… fools who seek purification by smearing their bodies with ashes, wearing red garments, shaving their heads, and carrying a trident staff, a pot, a skull, and a *khatvanga*".

Yet it is from this grass-root level of Indian culture, and the Kapalika traditions in particular, that the Hindu, Jain, and Buddhist tantras simultaneously emerged. The instigators of the tantras were the mahasiddhas of India, many of whom practised their *sadhanas* for twelve symbolic years in the 'eight great charnel grounds', where they often received transmissions directly from the *dakinis*. Iconographically they are often represented with the Kapalika adornments of an animal skin, matted hair, and bone ornaments; they are smeared with ashes, and bear the two main Kapalika attributes of a skull-cup and *khatvanga*.

In the hagiographies of the early Buddhist mahasiddhas and their numerous lineages of transmission, the importance of the eight great charnel grounds as places of spiritual attainment is explicitly revealed. The legends of many of these charismatic siddhas portray them as divine madmen or powerful sorcerers who recklessly displayed their psychic powers. Yet paradoxically their written works often reveal the most subtle nuances of spiritual understanding and philosophical thought.

Padmasambhava was the most famous of these Buddhist mahasiddhas, and almost single-handedly is credited not only with establishing Buddhism in Tibet, but with displaying countless miraculous activities, such as concealing thousands of 'hidden treasure teachings' (Tib. g*ter ma*) which continue to be revealed into the present day. Yet his early activity in India clearly links him to the Kapalika tradition. His iconographic attributes of a trident-topped *khatvanga*, and a skull-cup containing a vase, clearly refer to the trident, *khatvanga,* skull-cup, and pot carried by the Kapalikas. The only attribute borne by Padmasambhava which distinguishes him from a Kapalika is his *vajra*, which symbolically identifies him as a practitioner of Vajrayana Buddhism. Many of the Buddhist siddhas and *dakinis* carry the Kapalika attributes of the trident-topped *khatvanga*, skull-cup (*kapala*), and *damaru*.

Episodes in the life of Padmasambhava bear a striking similarity to many of the legends of the eighty-four Buddhist mahasiddhas. In his biography Padmasambhava karmically causes the death of a minister's wife and two infants and is sent into exile, where he takes up residence in the 'Cool Sandalwood Grove' charnel ground near Bodh Gaya. For five years he lives the life of a Kapalika, using corpses for his meditation seat, consuming human flesh, giving and receiving teachings from the *dakinis,* and subduing countless ethereal beings. From the Cool Sandalwood Grove, Padmasambhava then practises in each of the other seven great charnel grounds. These events are explicitly described in his biography, and along with his other accomplishments of a more wordly nature reveal the spiritual practices from which his legendary powers arose.

THE EIGHT GREAT CHARNEL GROUNDS
(Skt. *ashtamahashmashana*; Tib. *dur khrod chen po brgyad*)

The Indian tradition of the eight great charnel grounds dates back to the schematic placement of eight cemeteries around a great city, in order to accomodate the various funeral rites of the different castes of Hindu society. Under the rigid caste laws, even in death all were not equal. The sanctity of a brahminical cremation site, for example, could not be polluted by the 'unclean' disposal of a *shudra* or outcaste corpse.

Mythologically the origin of the eight great cemeteries derives from a legend which relates how the demon Rudra was slain and his dismembered body cast down from Mt Malaya. The four vital parts of Rudra's body – the 'energy centres' of his head, heart, guts, and genitals – fell in the four cardinal directions, and his severed arms and legs fell in the four intercardinal directions. Eight kinds of great trees then grew from Rudra's dismembered body parts (see page 50), and around these trees evolved the 'other worldly' sanctuaries of the eight great charnel grounds. These eight trees – which symbolise the subtle body's central channel – are iconographically depicted in each of the eight great cemeteries, which form part of the protection wheel in most *anuttarayoga tantra* deity mandalas. Eight 'field' or realm protectors appear above their branches, and eight directional protectors beneath them. Eight specific mahasiddhas, stupas, *nagas*, jewels, fires, clouds, mountains, and lakes are also directionally assigned to each of the charnel grounds. Vultures, crows, owls, jackals, wolves, dogs, tigers and snakes roam within these cemeteries devouring corpses, whilst yogins and yoginis, human and divine 'knowledge holders' (Skt. *vidyadhara*) practise amidst *yakshas*, spirits, zombies, hungry ghosts, ogres, cannibals and ethereal beings. The great cemetery is said to be 'perfect' if it contains the four kinds of corpses. These are fresh corpses; mutilated, hanging or decaying corpses; skeletons; and 'mindless corpses' or zombies. The symbolism of these elements, as explained in the *Vajrabhairava* or *Yamantaka Tantra*, is as follows:

Cemeteries: the complete paths of the *sutra* and *tantra* vehicles.

Fresh corpses: cyclic existence; the impermanence and sufferings of birth, sickness, old age and death.

Impaled, hanging, dismembered and decaying corpses: ego annihilation. The revolting imagery which is an antidote to attachment.

Skeletons: emptiness.

Zombies or mindless corpses: selflessness.

Devouring animals: realisation of the 'generation stage' (Tib. *bskyed rim*), as the animals devour the 'corpses' of ordinary appearances and conceptions.

Nagas: cultivation of the six or ten perfections.

Gems held by nagas: the four ways of gathering disciples.

Trees: the central channel.

Lakes: conventional *bodhichitta*.

Clouds: the white *bodhichitta*-drops at the crown of the head.

Fires: the 'inner heat' (Tib. *gtum mo*).

Directional protectors: the 'downward-voiding wind', located just below the navel.

Realm protectors: the 'life-supporting wind', located at the heart.

Mountains: the immovability of medative equipoise placed single-pointedly on the union of great bliss and emptiness.

Stupas: the attainment of the three *kayas* or bodies of the Buddha.

Yogins and yoginis: those who uphold the tantric commitments.

Human and divine knowledge holders: those who have attained the realisation of the 'generation stage' (Tib. *bskyed rim*).

Mahasiddhas: the tantric practitioners who have attained the realisation of the 'completion stage' (Tib. *rdzogs rim*); the attainment of the eight great *siddhis*.

The protection wheel of the eight cemeteries: the experiencing of the sixteen joys; the eight joys generated by the descent and ascent of the white *bodhichitta* drop as it enters each of the four main *chakras*, and the eight joys generated by the ascent and descent of the red drop.

The eight cemeteries are divided into the four cardinal 'cemeteries' (Skt. *shmashana*) and the four intercardinal 'nearby cemeteries' (Skt. *upashmashana*). Collectively they form the 'body mandala of Chakrasamvara' – who is also commonly known as Heruka – which is situated beneath the earth. Heruka's 'speech mandala', which is located on the earth, is geographically conceived as the eight great 'fields', which are again divided into the four 'fields' (Skt. *kshetra*) and 'nearby fields' (*upakshetra*). Heruka's 'mind mandala', which occupies the heavens, is formed from the eight great 'seats' or sacred sites, divided into the four 'seats' (Skt. *pitha*) and four 'nearby seats' (Skt. *upapitha*). Further subdivisions of these sacred sites occur as: the 'meeting places' (Skt. *melapaka* and *upamelapaka*) where tantric 'festivals' (Skt. *mela*) are held (e.g. the four sacred sites of the Hindu Kumbha Mela); the 'unobstructed places' (Skt. *pilava* and *upapilava*); and the 'desirable places' (Skt. *chandoha* and *upachandoha*). Geographically these twenty-four sacred pilgrimage places are located across the Indian subcontinent with outlying sites in the Himalayas,

Nepal, and Tibet, and correspond to various parts of the human body, and the places where deities reside. The 'twenty-four *viras*' (heroes) and 'twenty-four yoginis' dwell at these sacred sites (Skt. *pithasthana*), which are simultaneously located within the yogin's subtle body. Chakrasamvara's full mandala consists of sixty-two deities, which are all named and located at these twenty-four sacred places (see pages 254–255).

These twenty-four *pithasthanas* of the *Chakrasamvara Tantra* are identically listed in one of the 'parallel passages' found in the early Shaivite tantras. However, a single mistake in the transposition of a sacred site with its corresponding body part in the *Chakrasamvara Tantra*, reveals that it was in fact derived from an earlier Shaivite tantra. The implications of this simple but 'irrefutable proof' are enormous, since it turns inside-out the conventional belief amongst Buddhists that the Hindu tantric systems were inferior plagiarisms from earlier Buddhist sources. Future scholarly research will undoubtedly draw these seemingly disparate traditions into a closer and more mutually dependent relationship.

Many of the Buddhist mahasiddhas who 'revealed' the tantras are also renowned within the Hindu siddha lineages, especially that of the nine Nath Siddhas. Some are described, even in Buddhist sources, as being 'Hindu by day, and Buddhist by night'. In certain surviving Indian siddha and alchemical lineages a belief is maintained that, with foresight, the early Indian siddhas deliberately hid many of their esoteric teachings in Tibet prior to the Islamic invasion, so that they would be preserved.

Within the various Hindu tantras the number of *pithasthanas* varies between four and 110, although the Shaivite and Shakti tantras commonly list twenty-four, which are based upon the legend of Sati's dismemberment (see page 145). The Buddhist *Hevajra Tantra* lists thirty-two, which correspond to the thirty-two main psychic channels (*nadi*) of Hevajra's subtle body system.

However many these *pithasthanas* numbered, their importance within all of the Highest Yoga Tantras was enormous. On an external level of symbology they were 'power places' where tantrics and yogins gathered, where secret signs, glances and *mudras* were exchanged within particular lineages of transmission, where highly esoteric initiations and rituals were performed in *ganachakras*, or group assemblies as 'circles of offerings'. On an internal level they were the abodes of the various classes of spirits, the power places of the *dakinis* and goddesses, and the mandala palaces of the deities – many of whom were said to have originated, resided, or been 'brought' from these places. On a secret level they are all of these things within the yogin's own transformed body; the divine inner cosmology wherein all deities and mandalas reside within the blissful emptiness of the siddha's enlightened mind. Herein lies one of the greatest and most sublime of mysteries revealed in the allegorical 'twilight language' (Skt. *sandhyabhasha*) of the tantras. As the great Mahasiddha Saraha sang, "I have visited in my wanderings *kshetra*, *pitha* and *upapitha*, yet I have not found another place of pilgrimage as blissful as my own body."

THE HINDU RITE OF CREMATION

In the traditional Hindu cremation ritual the presiding priest carries a bell in his left hand and a *damaru* in his right. The corpse is wrapped in a shroud, laid on a bamboo bier, and bound with ropes to pegs on the bier. A white silk drape is laid over the bier and garlanded with flowers in the shape of a cross (see Plate 141). The bier is then devoutly circumambulated seven times, the mourners bow respectfully to the corpse's head, and the body is carried feet first towards the cremation grounds. Here the bier is ritually cleansed with river water, or most auspiciously immersed in the most sacred of all Indian rivers, the Ganges.

The bier is then laid upon the cremation pyre, the eyes and forehead are anointed with ghee, and the astrological chart of the deceased (prepared at his birth), is wrapped around the corpse's forehead. A piece of camphor is then placed into the open mouth of the corpse. The sacred flame is carried in a sheath of burning *kusha* grass, and ritually ignites the 'purifying hearth' of the camphor in the corpse's mouth before the wood of the funeral pyre is ignited.

During the cremation an important ritual is traditionally performed by the eldest son, who uses a stick or bamboo pole to crack open the burning skull of his parent, releasing the spirit of the deceased into a higher rebirth. Having performed this last rite of passage, the son turns his back to the funeral pyre and walks away without looking back. To witness this ritual often reveals the meaning of the word 'dignity'.

The spiritual symbolism enshrined within these funeral rites is extremely profound, but is perhaps too tangential to explain here. However, one important symbol relates to the cremation pole which is used in the Advaita Vedanta tradition as a spiritual metaphor to illustrate the practice of self-enquiry. This pole, which cracks open the corpse's skull, is then used by the cremation ground attendants to stir the funeral pyre until the body is burned to ashes. The stick itself is then finally thrown into the fire and becomes one with the ashes. Metaphorically this represents Advaita's method of self-enquiry, which consumes the 'corpse' of an individual's self-identity until only the 'pole', as the question, "who am I?" remains. This ultimate question is then consumed in the absolute realisation of the Self.

THE TANTRIC STAFF
(Skt. *khatvanga*; Tib. *kha tvam ga*)

Etymologically the root of the Sanskrit term *khatvanga*, meaning a tantric staff or club, derives from the term *khatva* (or *charpai*) meaning an Indian cot-bed and *anga* meaning the leg. The *charpai*, fashioned as a woven rope bedstead within a rectangular wooden frame and supported by four sturdy wooden legs, has since time immemorial served as the standard Indian bed. *Charpais* and bamboo or wooden funeral biers were a common feature of important charnel grounds, as the *charpai* was itself often used as a bier. It is easy to imagine tantrics who dwelled within these fearful charnel grounds – the Kapalikas, Aghoris, Kalamukhas,

Nagas and Kanphats – using a heavy wooden *charpai* leg as a club or mallet to break bones, coconuts, and *bel* fruit, or as a ritual tool or weapon. The very shape of the lathe-turned cot-leg, which consists of a tapering wooden leg capped by one or more decorative bulbs, a thick cubic section into which the corners of the bed frame join, and a large surmounting circular wooden knob, is extremely suggestive of the *khatvanga*'s form. When the brahmin-victim's skull is united through the skull's 'aperture of Brahma to the wooden knob of the cot-leg by the thin iron shaft of the Kapalika's trident, the theoretical form of the *khatvanga* is clearly revealed. It consists of a trident, skull, vase (round knob), *vishvavajra* (square section), upper shaft (bulbs), and lower shaft (tapering leg). Early artistic depictions of the Buddhist *khatvanga* portray it as a sturdy skull-topped club with a short tapering shaft or leg, rather than the long, thin and delicate ritual implement portrayed in later Buddhist art. In the hands of Tibetan artists the vast majority of Indian weapons took on a much more refined and aesthetic quality, and these weapons then became ritual objects depicted in the hands of deities. The forms of the skull-topped trident illustrated on Plate 126, and the skull-topped clubs illustrated on Plate 127, are all derived from the composite form of the *khatvanga*.

In Shaivism the *khatvanga* is an emblem or weapon of Shiva, and is variously described as a skull-topped club, a skull-mounted trident, or a trident-staff on which three skulls are impaled. Iconographically, Shiva's trident – with or without a mounted skull – invariably shows his double-sided *damaru*, which hangs by a cloth strip of red or white cemetery-shroud from the prongs of his trident.

In Vajrayana Buddhism the *khatvanga* essentially represents the union of Heruka Chakrasamvara with his consort Vajravarahi, or the inseparable union of great bliss and emptiness, as 'ultimate *bodhichitta*'. The iconographic parallels between Chakrasamvara and Shiva – who is also known by the names Samvara, Sambara or Shambu – reveal their mutual interdependence and common origin. Chakrasamvara himself 'arises' from the prostrate forms of Shiva as Bhairava (Tib. 'Jigs byed), and Parvati (Uma) as Kalarati (Tib. Du than ma). For the practitioner of Chakrasamvara, any site dedicated to Shiva or Shakti is a sacred site, as the feet of his *yidam* deity also rest and arise from there. The hand-held emblems of the *khatvanga*, skull-cup, *damaru*, trident, and four-faced head of Brahma are common to both deities, as are their body emblems of a crescent moon, cemetery adornments, bone ornaments, skull-crown, skull and head garlands, blue skin, matted and coiled hair, their 'nine modes of expression' (see page 228), and their adornments of flayed elephant, tiger, and human skin. Other *anuttarayoga tantra* deities also bear the attributes of the wrathful form of Shiva. One such deity is Yamantaka as Vajrabhairava (Tib. rDo rje 'jigs byed) who even bears the name of the wrathful form of Shiva (Bhairava).

The Shaivite Kapalika emblem of the *khatvanga* was first introduced into Tibet by Padmasambhava, the great tantric master of the charnel grounds, whose 'hidden elephant' retreat cave below Nyenri Gompa in the western valley of Mt Kailash looks straight onto the snow-capped dome of the heavenly abode of both Shiva and Chakrasamvara. Mt Kailash is the supreme abode of Shiva for Hindus, and of Chakrasamvara for Buddhists. Both share the same twenty-four sacred sites: the Hindu *shaktipithasthanas* of Shiva's dismembered consort, Sati, and the Buddhist body, speech and mind mandalas of Chakrasamvara.

The Iconography of the Khatvanga

The khatvanga is the divine body; prajna is the sound of
    the damaru.
The lord who holds the vajra is day; the yogini is night.
          Charya song of the Mahasiddha Luipa

Firmly holding the central channel as the khatvanga; the
    unstruck sound of the damaru resounds with the
    ultimate sound of emptiness.
Having adopted the conduct of a Kapalika-yogin,
    Kanhapa roams about in the city of the body, being
    of one disposition towards all beings.
          Charya song of the Mahasiddha Kanhapa

The *khatvanga* symbolises ultimate *bodhichitta* as the union of great bliss and emptiness. It is iconographically described as having an equal length to the god or goddess who holds it. For standing male *yidam* deities, such as Chakrasamvara, its full length is equal to his height of 120 finger-widths or *angulas* (Tib. *sor*). For standing goddesses, such as Vajravarahi, its length is equal to her height of 108 *angulas*. For seated deities, such as siddhas or yogins, its length is shortened for aesthetic reasons to either seventy-two or eighty-four *angulas*. As a hand-held implement in the hand of a many-armed *yidam* deity, its length is usually forty-eight or thirty-six *angulas*.

The goddess Vajrayogini, in her form as 'Naropa's Dakini' (Skt; Nada khechari; Tib. Na ro mkha' spyod ma), carries the *khatvanga* balanced across her left shoulder, held at an inclined horizontal plane by the crook of her left arm. Due to her leaning stance and inclined head, her total height is iconographically reduced from 108 to ninety-six *angulas* or units, and her *khatvanga* is correspondingly shortened to ninety-six units. On her specific iconographical grid (Tib. *thig tshad*) the *khatvanga* is precisely divided into half (forty-eight units) by the vertical axis or '*brahma*-line' that runs through the centre of her body. This symbolises the equilibrium or unity of method and wisdom. The forty-eight-unit division of the *khatvanga*'s lower staff is again precisely divided into half (twenty-four units) by the outer grid line that traverses precisely through the crook of her left arm. This point symbolises the perfection of her wisdom, as the *khatvanga* (Heruka) is held in an inseparable embrace in the crook of her left arm. Although this iconographical description may be difficult to comprehend without an accompanying illustration, it does reveal a little of the complexity of the precise measurements used to create the 'divine proportions' of individual deities.

As a symbol of the consort, the *khatvanga* is always held in the crook of the left arm. When it is held by male deities it

symbolises the female consort as wisdom; when held by female deities it represents the male consort as method. Seated gurus, lineage masters, siddhas, *dakinis*, yogins, and yoginis always hold the *khatvanga* in the crook of the left arm. However, as a hand-held attribute of multiple-armed *yidam* deities, it may appear either in the left or right hands. It is held in the left hand by deities such as Chakrasamvara, Kalachakra, and Buddhapalita, and in the right hand by deities such as Vajrabhairava and Nilambara.

The shaft of the *khatvanga* is often described as being fashioned of white sandalwood, or occasionally 'white sandalwood tinged with red' – symbolising the white and red merging of the *bodhichitta* drops. The shaft is shaped in an octagonal section with eight faces. At its base is either a five-pronged half-*vajra*, or a single-pronged half-*vajra*, coloured either in gold or blue, depending upon the deity's description. An ornamental handle, fashioned like the shaft of a *phurba* with two enclosing knots or lotus-bulbs, may sometimes be positioned near the top of the long shaft; often the shaft is unadorned or terminates in a single lotus-bulb. A lotus-handle or bulb is commonly fashioned on sculptural forms of the *khatvanga*, but on painted representations the thin white shaft either ascends behind the lower prongs of its crowning *vishvavajra*, or is covered by the folds of the hanging white silk ribbon which descends from above.

The top of the long lower shaft is crowned by a golden five-pronged *vishvavajra*, which may be painted in the four directional colours of the mandala. On sculptural forms the *vishvavajra* is fully modelled in the round, but on painted forms it is usually depicted in a half-section, with a full five-pronged *vajra* pointing downwards to the front and the cross-sections of half-*vajras* on either side (see Plates 115 and 116 for the variations in the *khatvanga*'s form).

Above the *vishvavajra* is a small golden vase or flask containing *amrita*. On painted images this usually appears as a simple golden vase with lotus-petal designs, but on sculptural forms or meticulously painted thangkas it often appears as a long-life vase with four descending leaf-shaped pendants.

Above the vase are two impaled heads and a skull. The lower head is a freshly severed head, the second head is a decaying head, and the skull above is dry and white. Two colour sequences for the two heads are given in different deity descriptions. The freshly severed head may be red, with a green or blue decaying head above; or the freshly severed head may be green, blue or black, and the decaying head above red. The reasons given for these variations is firstly that a freshly severed head is full of red blood when cut, and then turns green or blue-black when the blood coagulates, and secondly that a freshly cut head is green or blue-black from the trauma of decapitation, and then turns red on decaying. The symbolism of these colour schemes is explained below.

These three qualities (fresh, decaying, and dry) and their colours (red, green, and white) also occur in the three 'cemetery unguents' of fresh blood, human fat, and human ashes, which adorn the cheeks and nose (red blood), chin and neck (green fat), and the forehead (white ash), of wrathful deities.

Certain deities also hold a *khatvanga* fashioned from human bone, all the components of which are painted white. This form of *khatvanga* has three impaled skulls, which are described as: 'dripping', indicating that the skull has been freshly skinned; 'wet', indicating that the skull-bone is soft and still drying; and 'dry', meaning that the skull is hard and old. The white bone *khatvanga* represents the full descent of the white *bodhichitta* drops, which flood the yogin's body with great bliss; the same symbolism applies to the yogic practice of smearing the whole body with human ashes, which is also believed to be an antidote to the arising of sexual passion.

The khatvanga: Outer Symbolism

As a representation of the physical universe the *vishvavajra* of the *khatvanga* symbolises the earth base of the Mt Meru mandala. Its twelve visible prongs represent the four main continents and eight subcontinents surrounding Mt Meru. The eight-sided shaft with its top (zenith) and bottom (nadir) represents Mt Meru's central axis and the ten directions. The vase represents Mt Meru, and its four leaf-shaped pendants, the four faces of Mt Meru. The vase's top represents Indra's palace above Mt Meru, with the visualised wish-fulfilling tree at its centre. The fresh red head above the vase represents the six heavens of the desire-god realms (*kamaloka*), as red is the colour of desire. Blue or green symbolises the decay or death of desire, and the decaying green or blue head represents the eighteen heavens of the pure form realms (*rupaloka*) of the desireless gods. The fleshless dry white skull represents the four highest formless realms (*arupaloka*). The crowning *vajra* at the top symbolises the paradise realms of the Buddhas. If a trident crowns the *khatvanga*'s top it represents the Three Jewels, and the Buddhas of the three times – past, present and future. The hanging *damaru* and bell symbolise the union of method and wisdom. The hanging pendants of sun and moon represent these planets circling Mt Meru. The triple-valance pendant represents the victory banner placed at Mt Meru's summit; and the hanging white scarf which is tied around the vase symbolises Mt Meru's encircling mountains and the great salt ocean.

The Khatvanga: Inner Symbolism

As the *khatvanga* symbolises the unchangeable essence of Heruka, and is described as being 'continually held', it represents the inseparable embrace of the consort as the coincidence of method and wisdom, or great bliss and emptiness. The white eight-sided shaft symbolises the purity of the Buddha's Noble Eightfold Path. The *vishvavajra* represents the four purified elements of earth, water, fire, and air; the four activities or *karmas*; and the 'four doors of liberation' (emptiness, signlessness, wishlessness, and lack of composition). The small golden vase of *amrita* symbolises the nonconceptual awareness that mind is identified with the perfection of wisdom as the 'nectar of attainment'. The white silk ribbon that billows in the wind represents the various teachings of the different Buddhist vehicles or *yanas*, which

may be received according to the capacities of different practitioners. The hanging three-coloured silk valance represents the union of the Hinayana (yellow), the Mahayana (red), and the Vajrayana (blue). The hanging *damaru* and bell represent the teachings of method and wisdom; and the union of sun and moon signifies the realisation of method and wisdom.

The three impaled heads represent the three *kayas*. The *nirmanakaya* is respresented by the freshly severed head, the *sambhogakaya* by the decaying head, and the *dharmakaya* by the dry white skull. They also symbolise the three doors of liberation: emptiness of cause (red head), effect (green head), and phenomena (white skull). In reverse order they symbolise the three doors of body, speech and mind, with the dry skull as the white syllable *Om* at the crown (body); the decaying head as the red *A* at the throat (speech); and the fresh head as the blue *Hum* at the heart (mind).

The half-*vajras* at the top and bottom of the *khatvanga* symbolise the indistinguishable perfection of the Five Buddha wisdoms, and the five *kayas* of the *anuttarayoga tantras* (*dharmakaya, sambhogakaya, nirmanakaya, abhisambodhikaya, vajrakaya*). If a full golden *vajra* is depicted at the top, it symbolises all of the enlightened qualities of the *vajra*. If a flaming blue iron trident is placed there, it symbolises the Three Jewels, three Buddhas, three times, and victory over the three realms (heavens, earth, and underworld).

On a more esoteric level the trident symbolises the union of the three main channels or *nadi,* with the flames around the central prong symbolising the ascent of the inner fire (Tib. *gtum mo*) through the central channel. The white eight-sided shaft symbolises the central channel flooded with white *bodhichitta* from the melting of the drops at the crown (white skull), and the shaft's eight sides are the eight *nadi* emanating from the heart *chakra*. The five ascending elements are represented by the golden *vishvavajra* (earth); the flask of *amrita* (water); the red head (fire); the green head (air); and the white skull (space). The half-*vajra* above the skull represents wisdom as the sixth element. The pairing of sun and moon as a hanging pendant symbolises the united energies of the solar and lunar channels entering the central channel by way of its entwined thread. The pairing of the bell and *damaru* similarly symbolises the union of wisdom and method. The white silk cloth represents the melting and descent of the white *bodhichitta* drop, flooding the yogin's body with the experience of simultaneously born bliss.

The Khatvanga: Secret Symbolism

In the 'completion stage' yoga of Chakrasamvara, the visualised form of the deity, which arises as the clear appearance in the 'generation stage', transforms into the 'body mandala' of Chakrasamvara, and his *khatvanga* transforms into the sixty-two deities which reside in the Chakrasamvara mandala.

From his two legs spread in the shape of a bow arises the bow-shaped wind mandala. The triangular form of his erect penis and two testicles next arise as the triangular fire mandala. The circular shape of his stomach next arises as

Plate 115: The *khatvanga* or tantric staff

the circular water mandala. The square shape of his chest next arises as the square earth mandala, and his spine arises as Mt Meru. The thirty-two petals of his crown *chakra* arise as the mandala's lotus circle. The equal span of his outspread arms and body arise as the four walls of the mandala palace. His limbs arise as the eight pillars of the palace (the eight bones of his two legs and arms), and his thirty-two major and eighty minor marks arise as the embellishments of the mandala palace.

The *khatvanga*, as the essence of Chakrasamvara, symbolises his sixty-two deity mandala. The golden vase at the *khatvanga*'s 'heart' symbolises Chakrasamvara's mandala palace. The *amrita* contained in the vase represents Chakrasamvara himself as the 'essence of great bliss' (Skt. *mahasukha*). The *vishvavajra* represents the eight deities of the 'commitment wheel', which arise as the channels of tongue, navel, sex tip, anus, brow, ears, eyes and nostrils. The lower blue head represents the sixteen blue deities of the 'mind wheel'. The middle red head represents the sixteen red deities of the 'speech wheel'. The white skull above represents the sixteen white deities of the 'body wheel'. The five-pointed *vajra* represents the four directional deities of the 'great bliss wheel', which surround the union of Chakrasamvara and Vajravarahi. Collectively the deities of these five wheels comprise the sixty-two deities of Chakrasamvara's mandala. The eight-sided white sandalwood shaft symbolises the eight great charnel grounds, and the half-*vajra* at its base symbolises the *vajra*-tent protection wheel which encircles the charnel grounds.

Plate 115

This illustration depicts the upper sections of three *khatvangas*. The first *khatvanga* on the left depicts the golden *vishvavajra* in its stylised half-section, with the golden vase arising from the semi-circular hub of the *vishvavajra*. The white silk ribbon is tied around the neck of the golden vase and loops in front of the lower shaft, with its two ends descending from behind the vase and flowing towards the right. The truncated lower section of the eight-sided shaft is capped by a wider bevelled extension, which is visible behind the lower prongs of the *vishvavajra*. The bell with the sun and crescent moon conjunction, and a snakeskin-covered *damaru*, hang upon two separate silk threads to the left, whilst a pair of small yaktail pendants hang to the right. Above the top of the vase are the two impaled heads, which may be coloured red and blue-green depending upon the sequence in which the fresh and decaying heads are arranged, and above is the dry white skull, crowned by a full five-pronged golden *vajra*.

The second and central drawing shows the *khatvanga* crowned by a flaming blue-iron trident, bearing two rings. The sequence of the skull, decaying head, fresh head, golden vase, and half-sectioned *vishvavajra* are arranged below. An eight-sided *vajra*-prong arises from the circular hub-knot at the top of the eight-sided shaft. This *khatvanga* is not adorned with a white silk ribbon, and the emblems of the *damaru*,

bell, and sun-moon conjunction descend to the right on a single jewelled-thread.

The third drawing on the right shows another trident-crowned *khatvanga*, with its long white silk ribbon looping and billowing below. The *damaru*, bell, moon-sun conjunction and jewel pendant hang to the right from a single thread.

Plate 116

This illustration shows six variations of the *khatvanga*. The first drawing on the left depicts a full-length *khatvanga* with a jewel at its lower end. The eight-sided shaft has an upper handle ornamented with two golden knots and a knurled upper shaft. The knotted, looped and billowing white ribbon is tied to the upper shaft, and the *damaru*, bell, and sun-moon emblems extend on a single thread to the right. The two heads and the skull face towards the three directions of centre, right, and left, and are crowned by an ornate flaming iron trident with two hanging yaktail pendants.

The second drawing to the lower right depicts the upper section of a trident-topped *khatvanga* with no silk ribbon. The *damaru*, sun-moon conjunction, and triple-valance hang upon one thread, whilst the bell and yaktail pendant hang upon another.

The third drawing to the upper right shows the upper section of a *khatvanga* crowned by a golden half-*vajra*. In this drawing the *vishvavajra* is positioned above the golden vase, and is depicted as a full-*vajra* forming a cross with the vase top and lower head. The white silk ribbon is knotted below the vase, and the pendants of the *damaru*, bell and sun-moon hang towards the left, whilst a pair of yaktail pendants hang towards the right. The upper part of the eight-sided shaft is decorated with a knurled cap enclosed by golden rings.

The fourth drawing at the centre shows a full-length *khatvanga*, which is sealed with a half-*vajra* at its lower tip and a knurled handle on its upper shaft. The looped and flowing white silk ribbon is tied below the vase which crowns the top of the shaft, and the emblems of the *damaru*, bell, and moon-sun conjunction are suspended upon a single hanging thread. The *vishvavajra* is again positioned above the vase, and appears in three-quarter form as a fully crossed five-pronged *vajra*. The two heads and dry skull are crowned by a full five-pronged golden *vajra*.

The fifth drawing to the lower right depicts the upper section of a flaming trident-crowned *khatvanga*, with a long knotted white silk ribbon tied beneath the *vishvavajra* and billowing towards the right. The *damaru*, bell, and yaktail pendant are suspended upon a single thread, with the symbol of the sun-moon conjunction not depicted.

The sixth drawing on the far right illustrates a trident-topped *khatvanga*, with the components of the skull, two heads, golden vase, *vishvavajra*, white ribbon, eight-sided shaft, and lower half-*vajra* seal in their conventional positions. Two threads descend towards the right, the upper of which carries a triple-valance, and the lower the emblems of the *damaru*, bell, and moon-sun conjunction.

Plate 116: The *khatvanga* or tantric staff

Not illustrated in these two plates of drawings is the pure white bone *khatvanga* with three impaled skulls, described as dry, soft, and dripping.

THE HAND DRUM
(Skr. damaru; Tib. *da ma ru, rnga chung*)

The double-sided hand drum or *damaru* is first recorded amongst the artifacts and clay seals unearthed from the ancient Harrapan civilisation of the Indus valley, where it first appears as an early Shaivite emblem. Shiva is invariably depicted with his *damaru*, which usually hangs silently from his trident – revealing the passive nature of the Hindu male principle – in contrast to the dynamic female energy of his Shakti or consort. In his form as Nataraja, or 'King of the Dance', Shiva vibrantly sounds his *damaru* in one of his right hands, creating the male rhythm (Skt. *tala*), which underlies the female melody (Skt. *raga*) as the fabric of the universe. The hourglass shape of Shiva's *damaru* represents Shiva and Shakti in union, as the interpenetration of the male (*lingam*) and female (*yoni*) genital or polarity triangles.

The Indian *damaru* or 'monkey drum' is commonly used by itinerant traders and street performers to announce their presence or 'drum up' an audience. The term 'monkey drum' derives both from the dance that a captive and tamed monkey performs to its rhythm, and from its resemblance to, and occasional construction from, a pair of joined monkey skulls. The hourglass-shaped, wooden Indian *damaru* or *dugdugi* is described in Plate 94. Its two small goatskin drumheads are tensioned with a threaded length of string, such that its pitch may be raised by squeezing the bunched strings at the *damaru*'s waist.

The Buddhist *damaru* or 'little drum' (Tib. *rnga chung*) has a similar form to its early Shaivite prototype, but it is more compressed in shape, and its double skins are glued to the drumheads rather than being tied with a latticed tension-string. Its double-hemispherical body is commonly turned from wood into a perfectly round section, or hand-carved into a slightly oval or trapezoid shape. This shape is modelled on the oval form of the Kapalika *damaru*, which was fashioned from the sawn-off cranial sections of two human skulls. The Kapalika or 'tantric *damaru*', as held by wrathful and semi-wrathful Buddhist deities, is described as being fashioned from the joined skulls of a fifteen or sixteen-year-old boy and girl, or a sixteen-year-old boy and a twelve-year-old girl. On deity depictions the left side of the double-skull *damaru* is often drawn smaller to represent the pubescent girl's skull. The magical qualities possessed by these skulls symbolises the virginal ripening to fullness of the male and female *bodhichitta* essences. In tantric rituals the properties of human bone and other substances are often explicitly prescribed, to endow the ritual implement or 'power object' with the peaceful or wrathful affinities of the deities being propitiated (see also thighbone trumpet below; skull-cups on Plate 119; and skulls on Plate 138).

Tibetan *damarus* fashioned from human skulls obtained from the charnel grounds or 'sky-burial' sites were once relatively abundant, but now such ritual objects are rare and command high prices in the oriental art market. Modern 'forgeries' are now more readily available in the form of *damarus* made from skulls salvaged from unclaimed Indian accident victims, cremation ground debris, or 'water-burials' washed ashore on the mouth of the River Ganges. But according to tantric specifications these skulls are virtually powerless for the rituals they are intended to serve. Small *damarus*, fashioned from monkey skulls, are also obtainable.

The size of a *damaru* varies from about four inches in diameter to the large wooden drum (Tib. *gcod rnga*), which may measure up to twelve inches. The typical *damaru* made of two human skulls measures approximately six inches in diameter. The interior surfaces of a *damaru* are often inscribed with mantras before the skins are stretched and glued, and its exterior may be laquered, wood-stained, or decoratively painted with symbols. The small trapezoid wooden *damaru* may be painted in the four directional colours on its exterior. The two glued goatskins are commonly painted green; on small *damarus* they may be of snakeskin or even fishskin. Both skins are cut from the same piece of vellum, then water-soaked before glueing, so that the same pitch is attained on both skins when dried. The central waist of the *damaru* is encircled with a decorative brocade, leather, or metal band, from which its cloth or jewelled handle hangs. On either side of this central band hang the two oval silk-embroidered or crocheted beaters, which are usually attached by two twisted red or black silk threads, occasionally knotted at their central points. From the *damaru*'s padded-cloth or jewelled handle hangs the silk valance 'tail', which commonly consists of a padded-cloth top shaped into a trefoil 'cloud scroll' or *jui'i* design, from which descends a five-colour silk valance. Attached to the alternating tips of the valances, and to its upper and lower edges, are silk-thread tassles, usually with a five-colour tassle sequence descending from the lowest silk valance. On painted representations of the *damarus* held by deities, the handle usually consists of a jewel-chain, terminating in a 'cloud scroll' pendant with a triple-valance tail. When not in use, the long tassled tail is coiled around the waist and the *damaru* is stored in a drum-shaped padded-cloth bag, which is cross and rib-stitched into a geometric or lotus design and decorated at its circular centres with three-coloured 'wheels of joy' (Tib. *dga' 'khyil*).

The *damaru* is held and played in the 'male' right, or 'method', hand by yogins and yoginis, siddhas and deities, and its function is to summon or invoke all of the Buddhas, inspiring them with supreme joy. Just as the (female) bell – held in the left or 'wisdom' hand – proclaims the 'sound of emptiness', the male *damaru* proclaims the 'sound of great bliss'. As internal or 'unstruck sounds' (Skt. *anahata nada*), these correspond to the 'ringing' of the nervous system and the 'drumming' of the blood circulation, which are heard when the yogin sits in complete silence. When the *damaru* and bell are paired, they symbolise the union of method and wisdom as the simultaneous sound of great bliss and emptiness. The two faces of the *damaru*, as adolescent male and female skulls 'sounding together' in sexual union symbolises the union of relative and absolute *bodhichitta*.

The large *damaru* used in the Tibetan 'cutting practice' or *chöd* (Tib. *gcod*) proclaims the 'sound of impermanence', and summons all of the *dakas* and *dakinis* to the 'dance' of ego-annihilation, and all spirits and ethereal beings to the 'great feast' of the practitioner's own body. The *chöd* rite – introduced from India by the siddha Padampa Sangye and transmitted through his famous female Tibetan disciple Machig Labdrön (1055–1152) – seeks to cut through the attachments of dualistic egotism and self-cherishing by means of the technique of visualising one's own dismembered body being offered to the spirits and hungry ghosts in order to fulfil one's karmic debts. This potent practice for severing attachment is traditionally performed at night in a desolate or haunted place, such as a charnel ground.

This Tibetan rite has its parallel in the extremely powerful Indian tantric practice of *kanda yoga*, where the limbs and head are visibly seen to be temporarily severed from the 'bulb' (*kanda*) of the torso. Shirdi Sai Baba and the legendary Telang Swami of Benares (who is recorded to have lived to the ripe old age of 370 years!), are two of India's most famous modern siddhas who secretly practised the full 'five-limbed' severance (Skt. *panchanga*) of *kanda yoga*. The legend of the Hindu and Buddhist Nath siddha, Chaurangipa (meaning the 'four-limbed') contains a veiled account of the transformation or 'illusory body' *siddhi* of *kanda yoga*. This extremely esoteric yogic practice bears no relation to the hypnotically-induced or spirit-assisted 'miracles' of the Indian magicians or fakirs, who publicly perform acts such as the 'Indian rope trick' or the horrific and bloody 'apparent' mutilation of a child assistant.

The Tibetan yogini Machig Labdrön is depicted in naked dance posture sounding a large *chöd damaru* (Tib. *gcod rnga*) in her right hand, and ringing a bell with her left. Her guru, Padampa Sangye, carries the attributes of a *damaru* and thighbone trumpet in his right and left hands.

THE THIGHBONE TRUMPET
(Tib. *rkang gling, rkang dung*)

The white thighbone trumpet is mainly an attribute of the practitioners of the *chöd* lineages, and siddhas, yogins, and yoginis associated with the great charnel grounds. As a hand-held ritual object it is only carried by a small number of protective deities, such as 'Red Mahakala with the thighbone trumpet' (Tib. *mGon dmar rkang gling can*), and the wrathful Tibetan goddess Troma Nagmo, in her *chöd* aspect as the 'protectoress of the charnel grounds'. However, in the assembly of ritual offerings presented to wrathful deities, and in their ritual music invocations, the thighbone trumpet assumes a prominent role as its sound is said to be pleasing to the wrathful deities, but terrifying to evil spirits. Tibetan shamans (Tib. *sngags pa*) – either of the Buddhist or Bon traditions, or of both – employ the thighbone trumpet in many rituals of exorcism and weather control. Here the instrument's threatening drone is said to unhinge the powers of the malignant spirits who possess a human's personality, or of the *nagas* and local weather gods who

vengefully withhold or unleash the elemental powers of thunder, wind, hail, and rain. The deity's possession of a thighbone trumpet symbolises victory over the three realms.

The Tibetan thighbone trumpet is usually held in the left or 'wisdom' hand, and is often paired with the *damaru* held in the right or 'method' hand. In the tantric tradition the left femur of a sixteen-year-old brahmin girl was considered to be the most effective in controlling spirits and elementals. The femur of a 'twice-born' brahmin was the next best kind of bone, followed by the thighbone of a murder victim, then a person who died from a sudden accidental death, then one who died from a virulent or contagious disease. The bones of a person who died from old age or 'natural causes' was considered virtually powerless in its efficacy against the powers of evil spirits. The femur of a tiger (Tib. *stag gling*) was believed to embody the powerful qualities of this animal, and was also used as a thighbone trumpet.

The ball-joint end of the femur was partially sawn-off to create the wide single or double mouth of the thighbone trumpet. The mouthpiece is often bound with wire or encased in a metal ferrule, and the trumpet's mouth may also be adorned with a metal casing. The marrow-canal of the thighbone serves as a natural hollow bore for the instrument. As a musical instrument used in monastic ceremonies, it may also be fashioned from bronze in the form of a human thighbone (see example on Plate 106).

Plate 117

This drawing illustrates examples of the *damaru* in the upper area, and examples of the thighbone trumpet below.

The first drawing in the upper left corner shows an end-view of a wooden *damaru*, revealing its *vajra*-decorated central waist-band, connecting cloth and jewel handle, and its intricate valance and jewel-chain tail. The two crocheted and padded beaters swing from the threads emerging from the centres of the *vajras* depicted on the mid-points of the waist-band.

The second and third drawings on the right show two examples of the double-skull *damaru*, with the cranial fissure lines stained with vermilion dye. The first *damaru* has its beaters in motion, whilst they hang pendant in the second drawing. The drawing in the top right corner depicts a double-skull *damaru*, with the smaller female cranium to the left. Below the first drawing of the *damaru* in the upper left corner is a double-skull *damaru* with double beaters striking each face. Each of these five *damarus* in the upper area has the 'cloud scroll' or *jui'i* trefoil design at the end of their jewel handles. The variations of handles and triple-valance tails depicted in these drawings are commonly found on painted representations of the *damaru*. Above and below the tail of the *damaru* in the upper right corner, are two examples of the small *damaru* that is suspended from the upper shaft of the *khatvanga*. The lower of these drawings shows the four-faced form of the trapezoid-shaped skull *damaru*.

Across the central area of the illustration are four further examples of the *damaru*. The large round *damaru* on the

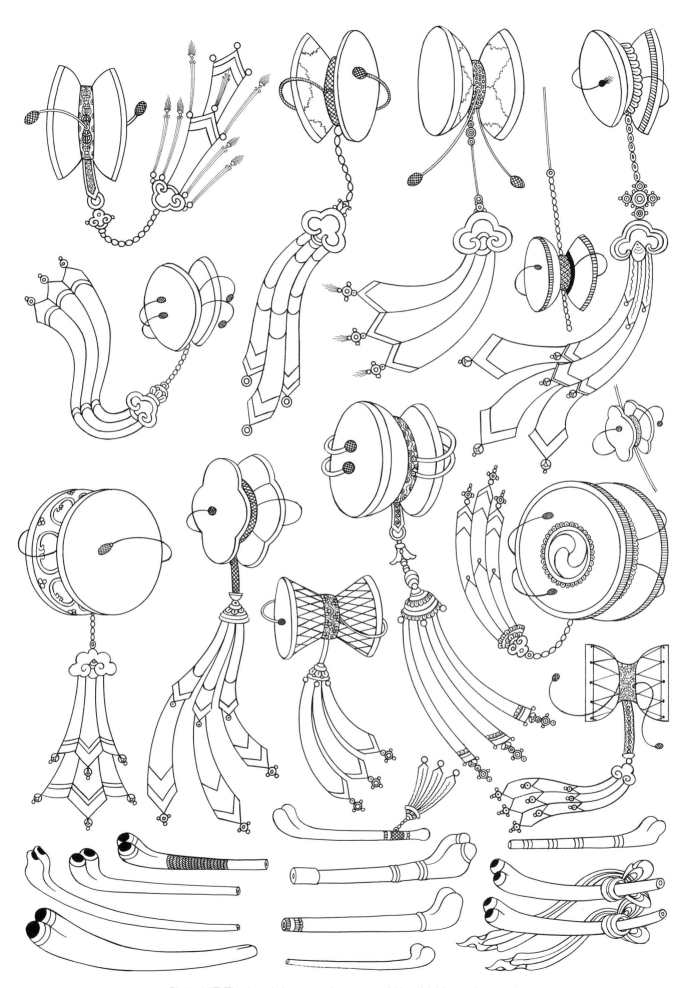

Plate 117: The hand drum or *damaru* and the thighbone trumpet

left is the *chöd* drum (Tib. *gcod rnga*) used in the *chöd* rite. Its round wooden body is decorated with lotus-petal motifs, which would either depict in painted miniatures the iconography of the eight great charnel grounds or the eight forms of Padmasambhava, or both of these subjects combined. Mantras of the *chöd* practice would be inscribed upon the inner body of the drum. The drawing on the opposite right of the page shows another form of this drum, with double beaters and a three-coloured 'wheel of joy', here symbolising Mt Meru, at its centre. The two beaters are shown striking in their correct positions on the 'great salt ocean' (the outer area of the drum skin) which surrounds Mt Meru.

Between these two *chöd* drums are two regular *damarus*. The one on the left is shaped as a quatrefoil with four curved edges. The one on the right has a thick wooden body and double-beaters. The jewel handles and tails of these *damarus* show the variations in its iconographical form. Below the two central *damarus* and the *chöd* drum on the right are two examples of the Shaivite 'monkey drum', showing its hour-glass shape and string-tensioned drumskins. The strings are threaded through holes around the edges of the drumskins, and should more correctly appear as straight connecting threads, which are bound together with the long end of the string at the drum's waist. But the two representations shown here are commonly depicted in painted stylisations of the Shaivite *damaru*.

At the bottom of the page are eleven examples of the thighbone trumpet. The group of four on the left are all illustrated with twin black holes on the femur's ball-joint or mouth, and with tapering bores and unadorned mouthpieces. The top trumpet has a coiled silk thread around its central section as a handle, and the third drawing below depicts a long and graceful stylisation of the instrument. The four thighbone trumpets in the central row are depicted without black holes on their ball-joints. The top drawing is decorated with a triple valance, and the second and third drawings both depict metal mouthpieces and upper bronze rings. The three drawings on the bottom right show a femur decorated with four metal rings at the top, and a pair of cloth-bound thighbone trumpets fashioned from the left femur of a sixteen-year-old brahmin girl, and the right femur of a sixteen-year-old brahmin boy.

THE CURVED KNIFE OR CHOPPER
(Skt. *kartri*; Tib. *gri gug*)

The *vajra*-topped curved knife or flaying knife is also known as the 'knife of the *dakinis*'. The *dakinis* (Tib. *mkha' 'gro ma*), whose name means 'sky-goers' or 'space-travellers', are the enlightened yoginis, or female counterparts to the male Heruka deities (Skt. *daka*). The metaphorical term 'space-traveller', means one who is immersed (a traveller) in the realisation of emptiness (space). The modern translation of *dakinis* as 'sky-dancers', suggests one who delights (dances) in the experience of emptiness (sky). The three main hand-held attributes of the *dakinis* in general are the skull-cup, the curved knife or the *damaru*, and the *khatvanga*. The skull-

cup of blood which is held in the left hand of important *dakinis*, such as Vajrayogini, Vajravarahi, and Nairatma, symbolises 'method' as the cultivation of great bliss; the curved knife held in the right hand symbolises 'wisdom' as the severing of all conceptualisations; and the *khatvanga* symbolises the inseparable union of bliss and emptiness, as the consort (method) held in the *dakini*'s (wisdom) perpetual embrace (union), by the crook of her left arm.

The curved flaying-knife of the *dakini* – which is either held aloft or extended in her right hand, or held above the skull at the level of her heart – is modelled on the Indian flaying-knife or 'the knife of the butchers', used for skinning animal hides. The scythe-shaped blade is made from iron honed to a sharp edge, and the gibbous crescent of its blade – which terminates in a sharp point or curved hook – combines the flaying implements of a cutting-knife and scraping blade, and the piercing activity of a dagger or pulling-hook. The blade's crescent is used for cutting through flesh and scraping it clean, separating the outer and inner as 'appearance and emptiness'. The sharp hook or point of the blade is used for the more delicate acts of flaying: the initial incising of the carcass, the pulling out of veins and tendons, and cutting around the orifices of the skin. Iconographically the sharp blade is depicted in the dark-blue colour of iron; its upper edges are embellished with a thin leaf-shaped golden mount that emanates from the wide-open mouth of a golden *makara*. A central hub or shafted-handle rises above the *makara*'s head, which is crowned by a golden half-*vajra*.

The *dakinis* perform the activity of circling the curved knife towards the ten directions, which symbolises their destruction of all negative forces, as the wisdom consciousness that terrifies all *maras* or emotional defilements and severs all conceptualisations. The blade's sharp edge, which divides into two everything it cuts, symbolises the cutting through of the two 'veils' or obscurations (Skt. *avarana*; Tib. *sgrib ba*): the veil of emotional defilements (Skt. *kleshavarana*; Tib. *ngon mongs sgrib pa*), which arises as the obscuration to liberation; and the veil of ignorance or conventional knowledge (Skt. *jneyavarana*; Tib. *shes bya'i sgrib pa*) which arises as the obscuration to the knowledge of emptiness. The veil of emotivity arises both as the gross delusions of the five poisons of ignorance, desire, hatred, pride, and jealousy, and as the more subtle psychological delusions which form karmic seeds for their future continuity. The veil of ignorance arises as the dualistic appearance of 'self and other', as the individual's inner consciousness (self) and the outer phenomenal world (other). As the knife's blade severs all tangible and abstract conceptualisations, it also cuts through the six hindrances to meditative contemplation: pride, lack of belief, lack of devotion, distraction, inattention and boredom.

The 'female' pairing of the skull-cup and curved knife – as polarity symbols of the yogini or *dakini*'s method (skull-cup) and wisdom (curved knife), held in her right and left hands respectively – is reversed in the case of male deities, such as Herukas and protective deities, where the skull-cup symbolises wisdom and the curved knife symbolises

Plate 118: The curved knife and chopper

method. Yamantaka, and many of the seventy-five forms of Mahakala, for example, hold the curved knife in their right hand above the skull-cup in their left hand, with both hands held at the level of their hearts. Here the curved knife symbolises method, as the severing of all conceptions; and the skull-cup symbolises wisdom, as the consumption of the 'blood and guts' of conceptualisation. The placement of the 'method knife' above the 'wisdom skull-cup' symbolises that method arises from, and is permeated with, wisdom. In Yamantaka's symbolism their placement or union at his heart means that he demands a heartfelt commitment to his *samaya* or tantric vows (Tib. *dam tshig*) and 'revives' those who have broken their vows by metaphorically consuming their blood. In Mahakala's symbolism the curved knife cuts through the life veins (Tib. *srog rtsa*) of enemies such as the *maras,* oath-breakers, and other hindering spirits; and his skull-cup is filled with the heart-blood of these enemies and *maras*.

The curved knife held by Mahakala is usually described as a 'chopper' rather than a flaying knife. This chopper has two distinct forms: one is the conventional form of the *dakini's* hooked knife, and the other is that of a flaming crescent-shaped or semi-circular chopper. The latter is held by the dwarf form of 'Black-Cloaked Vajra Mahakala' (Tib. rDo rje ber nag chen), who is the main protector for the Karma Kagyu tradition. In his *Principles of Tibetan Art* Gega Lama states that there are two schools of thought on the representation of the hooked knife and crescent chopper. One view holds that the hooked knife is the attribute of female deities, and the crescent chopper the attribute of wrathful male deities. The other view holds that the hooked knife is held by deities of the 'mother tantras', which emphasise the cultivation of wisdom, and the crescent chopper is held by deities of the 'father tantras', which emphasise the development of method.

The crescent-shaped chopper, held by deities such as Mahakala, corresponds in shape to the cavity of the skull-cup and functions to make 'mincemeat' of the hearts, intestines, lungs, and life-veins of enemies hostile to the dharma. A similar crescent-shaped hand cleaver is used in oriental cuisine to chop meat and dice vegetables. Certain forms of Mahakala wield a cleaver of copper, depicted with a golden blade in its painted form. The flaming chopper has a thin row of flames that lick around the edge of its sharp blade and emanate into the ten directions, revealing its *vajra* or indestructible nature.

An interesting but somewhat disturbing legend is related about the Mahakala 'protector chapel' (Tib. *mgon khang*) at Samye monastery in Central Tibet. Traditionally, this forbidding chapel was kept locked for most of the year and entry into its precinct was rarely permitted. The attendant monk who supervised the chapel would each year ceremoniously replace an iron chopper and wooden chopping-board which had become blunt and worn down by its nocturnal activity. Even though the chapel was locked and empty, at night the screams of the ethereal miscreants hacked under Mahakala's chopper could be clearly heard from outside the chapel.

Plate 118

This illustration shows seventeen examples of the curved knife. At the top centre is the flaming crescent-shaped chopper held by the protective deity Dorje Bernagchen. Its semi-circular iron blade is capped by a golden central hub and half-*vajra*. To the right and left of this are two examples of the curved knife of the *dakinis*.

At the upper and lower centre of the page are two drawings of a curved knife with a *makara*-head mount and faceted handle. The upper drawing displays a subtle curve on its hooked blade, and depicts how the golden leaf-shaped blade-mount extends from the *makara's* snout and jaw. The lower drawing depicts a curved knife held above a blood-filled skull-cup. The *makara*-head mount on this blade is especially expressive, and is crowned by a knot, knurled handle, and *vajra*.

To the upper right of the paired knife and skull-cup are two curved knives with eight-faceted handles and enclosing knots similar to those on a *phurba*. Above these are two examples of knives crowned by open-pronged or wrathful *vajras*. The upper drawing depicts another *makara*-head mount.

The rest of the illustration depicts further examples of the curved knife, showing especially the variations in its blade shape and golden blade-mount. The chopper in the bottom left corner has a semi-circular blade shaped like an axe-head or half moon.

THE SKULL OR SKULL-CUP
(Skt. *kapala*; Tib. *thod pa, ban dha*)

The skull-cup (Skt. *kapala*; Tib. *thod phur*) – fashioned from the oval upper section of a human cranium – serves as a libation vessel for a vast number of Vajrayana deities, particularly wrathful and protective deities, *yidam, dakinis,* siddhas and tantric lineage holders. In the hands of these deities and human emanations the symbolic meanings placed upon the skull-cup are both complex and multifaceted.

The Kapalika attributes of the *khatvanga, damaru,* and *kapala* or skull-cup, have already been referred to. Just as the qualities inherent in certain kinds of bone of the thigh-bone trumpet are said to vary, so too do the qualities of skulls. The skull of a murder or execution victim is believed to possess the greatest tantric or spirit power; the skull of one who has died from a violent or accidental death, or from a virulent illness, possesses a medium magical power; the skull of a person who died peacefully in old age has virtually no occult power. The skull of a child who died during the onset of puberty also has great potency, as do the skulls of a miscegenated or misbegotten child of unknown paternity, born from the forbidden union of castes, out of wedlock, from sexual misdemeanour, or particularly from incest. The 'misbegotten skull' (Tib. *nal thod*) of a seven or eight-year-old child born from an incestuous union is considered to possess the greatest power in certain tantric rituals. Here the vital force or potential of the skull's 'previous owner' is embodied within the bone as a spirit, rendering it as an effective power-object for the performance of left-hand tantric rituals.

As the libation vessel of the Vajrayana practitioner the *kapala* essentially parallels the clay pot (Skt. *kumbha*) of the Vedic sacrifice, the alms bowl (Skt. *patra*) of the Buddhas, and the sacred water vase (Skt. *kalasha*) of the bodhisattvas. As a receptacle for sacrificial offerings, such as the 'sacrificial cakes' (Tib. *gtor ma*) presented to wrathful deities, the *kapala* parallels the precious tray or bowl containing auspicious substances – the jewels, flowers, or fruit presented to peaceful deities. In its most benign symbolism, as the begging bowl or food vessel of an ascetic, the *kapala* serves as a constant reminder of death and impermanence, the ephemeral transitoriness of life that engenders renunciation.

The three Kapalika attributes of the *khatvanga, damaru,* and *kapala* are commonly held by both male siddhas and yogins, and female *dakinis* and yoginis. These three attributes represent the body, speech and mind of the deity, although alternative identifications are placed upon these implements in relation to their body, speech and mind aspects in different tantric traditions. Certain traditions also maintain that the *kapala* held by male deities is an old or 'dry' skull, whilst the *kapala* held by goddesses is a fresh or 'wet' skull. These qualities may also be accorded to an *anuttarayoga tantra* deity as belonging either to the 'father tantras' – which emphasise the cultivation of method and the realisation of the 'illusory body', or to the 'mother tantras' – which emphasise the development of wisdom and the realisation of the 'clear light'. However, in deity descriptions or *sadhanas*, the distinction between a male and female skull, or a dry or wet skull, are not usually applied to the *kapala*. Here the skull-cup is simply referred to as a skull-cup, and the only distinction between dry and wet skulls occasionally occurs within the symbolism of the rosary of fifty or fifty-one skulls worn by both male and female deities (see page 317). The five-skull crowns (Tib. *cod pan*), worn by both male and female wrathful deities, are commonly described as being fashioned of dry skulls – which on an exoteric level symbolise the 'drying up' of the five aggregates and poisons and their transmutation into the five wisdom-awarenesses, and on an esoteric level, the arising of the illusory body from the state of clear light.

The white skull-cup full of red blood is almost invariably held in the left hands of both male and female deities, often at the level of the deity's heart, symbolising the importance placed upon the left-handed performance of activities in the mother tantras. In the tantric view of conception, the father's semen creates the solid white organs of bone, brain, marrow, and spinal cord; the fertile blood of the mother gives rise to the soft red organs of viscera, muscle tissue, and blood. The skull or 'crown' is the seat of the white male *bodhichitta*, symbolised by the moon, and created by the semen of the father. The navel is the seat of the red female *bodhichitta*, symbolised by the sun as the vital heat, and created by the fecund uterine-blood of the mother. Their placement at the level of the heart represents

the union of the white and red *bodhichitta* as the mind of the deity, or as the indestructible drop at the heart centre.

As polarity symbols the white and red *bodhichitta* drops are commonly depicted in two separate skull-cups, placed as offerings in front and to the left and right of a *yidam* or protective deity. In the case of a deity of the father tantra class, a skull-cup of white or pale-blue *amrita* – representing method as white *bodhichitta*, or the 'nectar-medicine' (Tib. *bdud rtsi sman*) of male semen (Skt. *kunda*) – may be depicted on the lower left side of the thangka; and a skull-cup full of red blood (Skt. *rakta*) – representing wisdom as red *bodhichitta*, or fertile uterine blood – may be depicted on the lower right side of the thangka. In the case of a mother tantra deity, these polarity symbols may be reversed, as may the positions of the moon and sun at the top of the thangka. At the lower centre of the thangka and between these two skull-cups, is also commonly depicted a third skull-cup containing the wrathful offering of the five senses. Collectively these three skull-cups symbolise the three primary causes for conception and the formation of the indestructible drop, with the white and red 'nectars' representing the fertile semen and uterine blood of the parents, and the five sense organs representing the consciousness of the being seeking rebirth. As a procreative image this symbolises the arising of the enlightened mind from the sexual union of the deities in *yab yum*. An example of this symbol is illustrated at the bottom left corner of Plate 140.

In the case of wrathful protective deities, the male skull-cup may be full of blue-black poison, and the female skull-cup full of sacrificial or heart-blood. Here the image symbolises annihilation rather than procreation, as the death of the ego and the transmutation of the five poisons into nectar.

One of the main *anuttarayoga* mother tantras is that of Chakrasamvara and his consort Vajravarahi. In this tantra the symbolism placed upon the blood-filled skulls held by both deities is of great significance. Chakrasamvara represents appearance and method as great compassion, and Vajravarahi represents emptiness and wisdom as great bliss. The skull-cup of blood, held in one of Chakrasamvara's left hands, symbolises the mental continuum or the mind of the deity (white skull) being filled with great bliss (red blood). The skull-cup of blood, which Vajravarahi offers to the mouth of Chakrasamvara's rear face, symbolises the fusion into 'one-taste' (Skt. *ekarasa*) of the illusory body (white skull) and the clear light (red blood). This symbolism is further emphasised by the *kapala* of Vajravarahi being full of both red blood (clear light) and intestines (illusory body), representing the union of absolute and relative truth as the 'cultivation of great bliss'. The symbolism of intestines, representing the illusory nature of phenomena; blood, representing desire; and skull-cup, representing hatred; also signify the overcoming or consumption of the three primary poisons of ignorance, desire, and aversion.

In her form as Naro Khajoma, Vajrayogini is depicted pouring blood from an upraised skull-cup into her own mouth, whilst blood also trickles from her mouth and vagina, symbolising that she consumes, and is consumed with,

Plate 119: The skull-cup

great bliss. In the secret *sadhana* of this goddess the blood is described as the 'fecund drops of the mother', meaning her own menstrual blood which blazes and drips through her central channel as 'inner heat'.

The skull-cup of blood (Skt. *rakta purna*; Tib. *thod khrag*) is usually depicted as a 'swirling-offering', with the blood forming waves and crests like turbulent water or boiling liquid. This symbolises the 'blazing and dripping' of the red *bodhichitta* as 'inner heat', since a liquid offering of blood or nectar is said to boil in the presence of a wrathful deity, *yidam* or goddess. The blood or *amrita* of a swirling offering spirals in an anticlockwise motion in mother tantra practices, and in a clockwise direction in the father tantras.

In the iconography of wrathful protective deities the skull-cup, held at the level of the heart, may also be paired with the curved knife or chopper which may be held above the *kapala*. Here the chopper is the weapon that severs the life veins and vital organs of demonic enemies, and the *kapala* is the oblation vessel in which the blood and organs are collected as the deity's sustenance. Descriptions of the contents of a wrathful deity's *kapala* include warm human blood, blood and brains, blood and intestines, human flesh and fat, the heart or the heart and lungs of an enemy, the heart of Mara, the blood of the four Maras, the blood of Rudra, or magical 'charm blood' (Tib. *thun khrag*).

Certain other deities may hold other attributes within their skull-cups – a *torma*, a *vajra*, or jewels. Padmasambhava, for example, holds a skull-cup described as an ocean of nectar, in which floats a longevity vase. Hevajra holds sixteen skull-cups containing animals and gods, which collectively symbolise the sixteen emptinesses or *shunyata*. Other examples of skulls and skull-cups are illustrated on Plates 135, 138, 140.

Plate 119

This page shows various drawings of the skull-cup. In the upper left corner is a drawing of Mahakala's curved knife held above a skull-cup containing the warm blood and heart of an enemy. At the upper centre of the page is a similar drawing showing the curved knife of a *dakini* held above a blood-filled skull-cup. In the hands of a male deity, such as Mahakala, the curved knife held in the right hand is an attribute of method, and the skull-cup in the left hand, an attribute of wisdom. In the hands of female goddesses this polarity symbolism is reversed, with the curved knife representing the wisdom that cuts through conceptualisations, and the skull-cup representing method as the 'preservation of bliss' (white *bodhichitta*).

To the right of the *dakini*'s skull-cup is that of Padmasambhava, with a long-life vase at its centre which overflows to create an ocean of blue nectar. Below and to the right is a skull-cup full of *amrita* with a *vajra* at its centre. The attribute of a *vajra*-marked skull is linked to several *anuttarayoga tantra* deities that belong to the Vajra Family lineage of Akshobhya Buddha, such as Buddhakapala, Samvara, Mahamaya and Yogambara.

The cranial fissures depicted on skull-cups usually form the pattern of a Y-shaped crack at the centre and two semicircular cracks on the skull's sides. These fissures – which are depicted in angular red zigzag lines – divide the *kapala* into five sections, representing the Five Buddha wisdoms, or the five goddesses. On the 'inner offering' skull-cup (illustrated on Plate 141), only a single vertical fissure is depicted, symbolising the indivisibility of great bliss and emptiness.

In the upper right corner is a blood-filled skull-cup with no cranial fissures, and with its hot blood appearing as wave crests. The top of this skull-cup – like the majority of the drawings on this page – is ornamented with a leaf-shaped golden edging. This decorative edge is the overlap of a sheet of beaten gold or copper that lines the interior of the skull-cup, and often has an inscribed *vajra* on its inner base. Here the white bone of the skull represents method, the gold lining represents wisdom, and the *vajra* their indestuctibility and indivisibility. Across to the upper left of the page is a similar *kapala*, and below this a small drawing of three flame-tipped conical *tormas* in a skull-cup.

At the upper centre, and below the *dakini*'s skull-cup and curved knife, is a skull-cup with a stream of turbulent blood pouring out towards the left. This drawing represents Vajrayogini's upraised *kapala*, from which she consumes fresh blood. To the right of this is a smaller *kapala* mounted upon a triangular stand of three skulls, with its content of blood rising like a fountain. In a row across the upper centre of the page are four *kapala* drawings. The first on the left is mounted upon a similar stand of three skulls, with its content of blood swirling upwards. The second drawing shows a large *kapala* with five cranial fissures. The third drawing shows a plain white *kapala* with no fissures, and its blood or nectar offering depicted as spiralling swirls. The skull-cup is sometimes metaphorically described as a 'conch ocean' (Skt. *shankha samudra*). Its contents represent an 'ocean of blood' on an outer level; the 'truth of no-birth' on an inner level; and the 'fertile drops of the mother' on a secret level. The fourth drawing shows a large skull-cup full of blood mounted upon a stand of three skulls, with another variation of this drawing depicted below. The three skulls and their triangular metal stand serve as a tripod to hold the *kapala* upright, with the triangular stand representing the wrathful element of fire as a blazing fire mandala, and the three skulls forming the cornerstones of its hearth. The three skulls represent annihilation of the three poisons, victory over the three realms and times, and the unity of the three *kayas* as the purified body, speech, and mind of the deity.

Below and to the left are two drawings of skull-cups mounted upon triangular vessels with three severed-head cornerstones. The *kapala* on the left contains a flaming triangular *torma*, and has two tongues of flame emanating from its sides. The lower *kapala* has a single fissure arising from its base, and contains the substances of the 'inner offering' (see pages 327–333). In the bottom right corner is an ornate form of the ritual vessel which holds the 'inner offering', such as may be depicted upon the offering table or altar of a tantric practitioner. The intricate base of this vessel represents the wind and fire mandalas which melt the inner offering. The *kapala* placed above this base is a natural skull, and therefore depicted without the single fissure of its visualised form. The *kapala* is covered with a golden lid, decorated with the emblems of a two-dimensional *vishvavajra* with a central *vajra* arising as its crowning seal.

To the left of the inner offering is a skull-cup full of nectar, which rests upon a golden vase supported by a lotus. This form of vase is commonly used in the empowerment rituals of wrathful or semi-wrathful deities, where the *kapala* replaces the conch shell as the oblation vessel (see Plate 103). The *kapala* and vase are first purified with the smoke of black frankincense (Skt. *guggula*; Tib. *gu gul*), which is said to pacify and please the wrathful deities. The twenty-five substances are mixed with the consecrated water in the vase and *kapala* to produce *amrita*. The deities of the mandala are invoked and represented by grains of white mustard seed that are placed in the *kapala*, transmuting the vessels into the mandala palace and retinue of the deity.

To the left of the vase is a wrathful offering of light, fashioned as a skull-cup full of human fat with a wick made from the twisted hair of a corpse. Above this is a *kapala* containing the heart and blood of Mara. To the left and above the drawing of the two monkeys are: a blood-filled *kapala* on the left; a *kapala* mounted upon three skulls and containing three triangular *tormas*; and a *kapala* containing three flame-tipped *tormas* to the right.

The drawing of two monkeys standing on their hands in the lower left corner, shows the two *pishacha* spirit attendants of the wrathful deity, Kshetrapala (Tib. Zhing skyong), the 'Protector of the Fields'. Kshetrapala is a dark-blue *yaksha* emanation of Mahakala, who has the face of a lion and rides upon a horse, wielding a skull-cup and spear-flag in his left and right hands. His two monkey attendants are known as Dudtri, meaning 'messenger', and Putri, meaning 'daughter'. These two messenger spirits stand upon their hands, each holding a *kapala* containing three triangular red *tormas* in their 'crow-like' feet. These red *tormas* are employed to subjugate the 'nine-headed Chinese demon', who periodically threatened and invaded Tibet in the form of the Chinese militia. Dudtri and Putri perform handstands with their tails entwined, and wear human skins around their waists.

An interesting parallel to their iconographical representation was related to me by a Bengali Baul friend. The Bauls are itinerent poets and musicians who travel around the villages of Bengal, composing and singing *dohas*, or songs of spiritual realisation. On a dark night of the moon this friend was returning with some other Bauls to their village home in West Bengal, when, attracted by a strange glow in a remote wooded copse, they decided to investigate. In a clearing within the wood they came upon a naked Bengali woman, who having kindled a charcoal fire was performing a left-handed tantric ritual. Standing upon her hands, this woman was holding an iron pan of burning charcoal in her feet, and from her behaviour she appeared to be possessed by the spirit of a monkey. One of the Bauls realised that she was performing a *pishacha sadhana* to invoke a spirit. Having grown up in a culture saturated with spirit tales and superstition, the Bauls took fright and retraced their

steps as quickly as possible. *Pishacha sadhana* is usually performed to gain the *siddhi* of prophecy or clairvoyance. The allegiance of an ethereal spirit is gained by the practitioner or *sadhaka*, who reveals the past events and future destiny of any questioner who seeks consultation. The most prominent *pishacha sadhana* is that of *Karna pishachini* – 'she who whispers in the ear' – and an extremely explicit account of one form of this *sadhana* is given in Sudhir Kakar's *Shamans, Mystics and Doctors*.

Although there may well be no connection between this story and the iconography of Kshetrapala's monkey messengers, it is perhaps interesting to note that one of Kshetrapala's titles is 'Lord of the Pishachas', and he is described as being accompanied by a retinue of ten-million *pishacha* spirits.

HAND-HELD WEAPONS AND THE RITUAL IMPLEMENTS OF SPECIFIC DEITIES

This section illustrates and describes the various weapons of conventional warfare, along with the magical weapons and ritual implements held by particular deities. It begins with the bow and arrow as symbols of the union of wisdom and method, and then progresses through the spectrum of right-hand 'method weapons', and left-hand 'wisdom weapons' – illustrated on Plates 120–132. Plates 133 and 134 depict miscellaneous weapons and implements.

ARCHERY

When an archer is shooting for nothing, he has all his
  skill.
If he shoots for a brass buckle, he is already nervous.
If he shoots for a prize of gold, he goes blind or sees two
  targets.
He is out of his mind!
His skill has not changed, but the prize divides him.
He cares. He thinks more of winning than of shooting.
And the need to win drains him of power.
    From the poem 'Need to win' by Chuang Tzu

From the most primitive of rainforest, desert, prairie or snow-bound tribes to the most sophisticated of military empires, the humble bow and arrow have always been regarded as the supreme of mankind's early weapons. Prehistoric cave paintings and stone carvings from ancient Egypt, Assyria, Babylonia, Phoenicia, Minoa, and Greece, reveal the importance placed on the bow and arrow in their depiction of hunting and warfare scenes. The short composite or 'union bow' – made from two separate and laterally joined materials, usually wood and horn – is depicted in Egyptian stone carvings dating back to the time of Akhenaten (*circa* 1378 BC). The earliest known example of the composite bow dates back to neolithic age fragments found in Denmark.

In ancient Indian warfare both the 'self bow' or long-bow (made from a single piece of wood), and the shorter 'union' or composite bow (made from joined wood and horn), were employed. The longbow, which fired cane arrows of five hand-spans in length (approximately three feet), was probably used by infantry archers. The composite bow, which fired shorter arrows, was used by charioteers and cavalry archers. In the Indian system the length of a 'bow' was a unit of measure equal to a 'fathom' or the height of a man, which was equivalent to ninety-six finger-widths (Skt. *angula*; Tib. *sor*) or four cubits (a cubit, the distance from the elbow to the middle-finger, measured twenty-four *angulas*).

The epic heroes of Indian mythology all bore mighty bows and arrows, which were inscribed with the names of their master along their shafts. Vishnu, Krishna, and Rama's bow was known as Sarnga; Shiva's bow as Ajagava; Indra's bow as Vijaya; Arjuna's bow as Gandhiva; Brahma's bow as Parivita; and Kama's bow as Pushpadhanvan (see Plate 122). The bows of these epic heroes were kept unstrung, and such was their legendary might that they could not be strung by mere mortals.

This symbolic motif, which appears in the Greek legend of Odysseus, also occurs in the early life of the Buddha as Prince Siddhartha. In an archery contest for the hand of Princess Yashodhara, the young Prince Siddhartha triumphs over his cousin and rival, Devadatta, by unleashing a single arrow which speeds right through the bull's eye of the distant target and continues unimpeded, flying beyond the range of sight. This single arrow was fired from the ancient bow of a legendary hero, which no one else had been strong enough to string, let alone shoot. As Buddha is considered the ninth of Vishnu's ten incarnations in the Hindu tradition, it is possible that this bow was Sarnga – the bow of Vishnu – and also that of Rama and Krishna as the seventh and eighth of Vishnu's incarnations.

In Bhutan archery has been the national sport for centuries, the bamboo longbows and the steel-tipped arrows of the male archers should reputedly not be touched by a woman, for fear of bringing bad luck in a contest. Similarly archery featured as a national sport in Tibet, where skilled archers would notch and shoot arrows at a target whilst galloping at full speed on a horse. These skills descended onto the Himalayan plateaus from the legendary legacy of the Mongol overlords, who were masters not only of horsemanship and archery, but in their powerful combination as mobile warfare.

THE BOW (Skt. *dhanus, chapa*; Tib. *gshu*)

The Indian bow (made of wood or bamboo, or as a composite bow of wood and horn) is known by a variety of Sanskrit names (*dhanus, chapa, sarasana, kodanda, karmuka, sarnga*). The term *karmuka* refers to a particular kind of wood obtained from the *krimuka* tree, and the term *sarnga* – also the name of Vishnu's bow – refers to a bow made of horn.

The conventional Tibetan bow (Tib. *gshu*) was made from a shaped flat section of thick bamboo. The compound bow was made from sections of yakhorn glued between joints of bamboo. Its shape was that of the typical hunting bow, found throughout most of the world's indigenous cultures. The bow as represented in Tibetan art, however, is most commonly depicted in the form of the 'classical bow' from ancient Greece – as held by Cupid – with an inward curve at its centre.

The bow and arrow are attributes of many Vajrayana deities, where they are most commonly paired as separate 'left' and 'right' hand-held implements. The bow is naturally held in the left wisdom hand, and the arrow in the right method hand. As symbols of wisdom and method or compassion, their pairing symbolises that wisdom 'projects' skilful means, or that the perfection of wisdom 'launches' the other five perfections (*paramita*) of method – generosity, discipline, patience, effort, and concentration. When the bow and arrow are held together in the left hand, vertically and undrawn – as in the forms of the eight-armed or thousand-armed Avalokiteshvara – they symbolise the coincidence of wisdom and method, or the union of wisdom and concentration. Similarly when they are strung and drawn together for shooting, with the bowstring pulled outwards by the right hand, they symbolise the concentrated and spontaneous activity of wisdom and method aimed precisely at the heart (symbolising the *dharmakaya*) of an enemy. Here the bow symbolises triumph over the three realms, and the arrow the transfixing of false views, such as superstition and conceptual thought.

Plate 120
On the left of the top row are four drawings of the bow as depicted in Tibetan art, in the style of the 'classical bow' with an inward-facing curve at the centre. The first drawing shows a wood or bamboo bow with a central leather handle, and its bowstring (Tib. *gshu rgyud*) tightly strung and bound. The second drawing shows a plain wood or bamboo bow with leaf-shaped bow ends (Tib. *gshu mchog*). The third drawing shows a more ornate wooden bow, with a central handle and bound silk threads positioned at intervals along its length. The ends of this bow have gracefully curving leaf-shaped designs over which the bowstring is strung. The fourth drawing shows a composite or union bow, made from bamboo on its underside or 'belly' and yakhorn on its outside or 'back'. The fifth drawing to the right depicts a wood or bamboo longbow, drawn and notched with an arrow.

On the left of the second row is a leopardskin quiver containing five arrows. Five arrows are often depicted in a quiver, where they symbolise the transfixing of the five passions (see page 276). The quiver (Skt. *ishudhi*; Tib. *mda' shubs*) is often depicted as being made of leopardskin, and frequently paired with a bow-case made of tigerskin. The 'female' leopardskin symbolises wisdom as a 'sheath' for the 'male' method arrows (see leopard and tigerskin symbolism on page 316). To the right of the quiver is a long composite hunter's bow, with the upper and lower halves of a

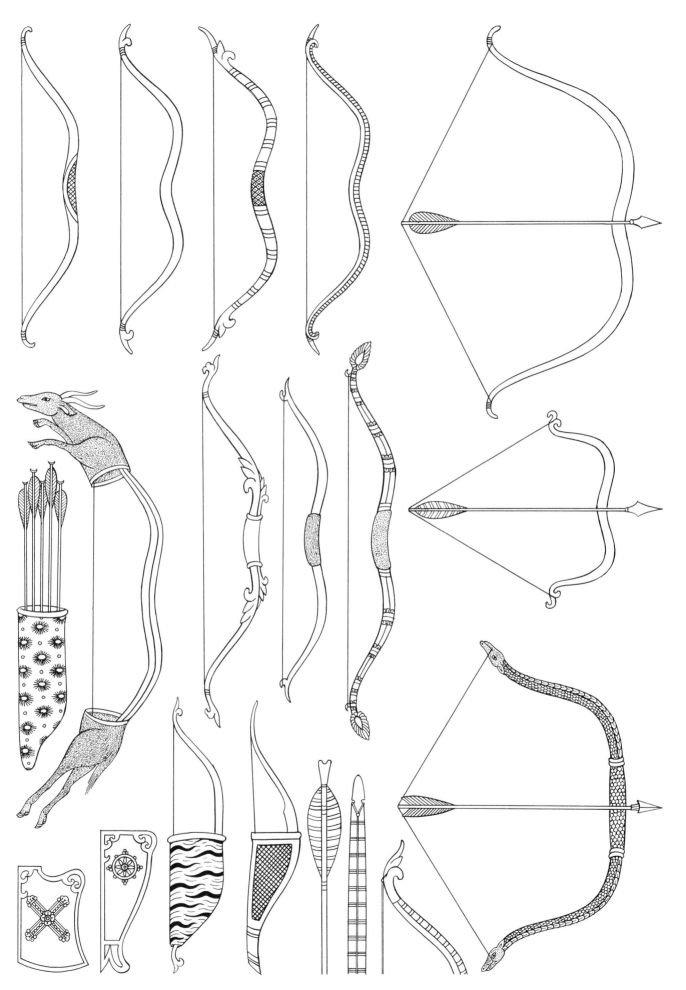

Plate 120: The bow

deerskin at its top and bottom ends. This form of bow is sometimes depicted in the hands of the mahasiddha hunter, Shavaripa; or it may be depicted in narrative thangkas of Milarepa, where a deer, a hunter, and his dog take refuge and receive teachings from Milarepa in his cave.

To the right of this hunting bow are three more drawings of strung bows. The first depicts an ornately carved bow, with leaf-shaped decorations and a composite section of yakhorn at its handled centre. The second drawing depicts an iron bow (Tib. *lcags gshu*), with a padded leather and felt handle. The third drawing shows a composite jewelled bow, fashioned from gold and silver with jewel ornaments at its ends. Both the iron and jewel bows have small hooks on their tips for attaching the bowstring. Across to the far right is a short bow that is drawn back to its full extent and notched with an arrow. Rahula is often depicted with such a bow, aiming an arrow at the heart of an enemy. This symbolises the coincidence of wisdom and method which perceives the phenomenal world as the empty manifestation of the *dharmakaya* – represented by the enemy's heart as the 'centre' of mind.

On the left of the bottom row are two bow-cases made of leather with metal edging. The first is ornamented with the cross insignia of a Chinese military commander, and the second shows a fitted bow-case ornamented with a *dharmachakra* of precious metal. The next drawing to the right shows a bow in a tigerskin bow-case, symbolising the union of wisdom and skilful means. The fourth drawing shows a bow sheathed within a leather and metal bow-case. To the right of this is a detail of an arrow-flight, with the steering-feathers crowned by a notched and tapering end. Tibetan arrows are often depicted with a widening, notched end, which protects the arrow from splitting from the tension of the bowstring. Alternatively the arrow's notched end may be bound with glued coloured silk thread.

In archery there are three main methods of arrow-release. Primary-release is performed by holding the bowstring with the ball of the thumb and the second joint of the forefinger; Mediterranean or Greek release is performed by pulling the bowstring back with the upper joints of the first three fingers; and Mongolian-release is performed by drawing the bowstring with the second joint of the thumb held over the hooked forefinger, with the arrow's end resting in the hollow of the thumb. In Mongolian archery a leather thumb protector is commonly worn. The next drawing shows the typical method of stringing a longbow, with the looped ends of the bowstring held by by two notched grooves in the bow's ends. To the lower right of this is a detail of a looped bowstring held in place by the leaf-shaped ornaments on a Tibetan bow. The last drawing on the right shows a black-serpent bow (Tib. *sbrul gshu nag po*) as may be drawn by Rahula. The bowstring is held in the mouths of the two serpents at either end, and the central handle is fashioned of snakeskin.

THE ARROW (Skt. *sara, ish, bana*; Tib. *mda'*)

The arrow of Indian warfare was known by many different Sanskrit names (*sara, ishu, bana, bhalla, naracha, nalika, vipattha,*

and *vaitastika*). The first four names refer to 'reed-arrows' made of cane or bamboo, with iron or bone tips, and steering-feathers made from vulture wings bound with sinew or thread. The terms *naracha* and *nalika* refer to arrows made of iron, which because of their weight had only a short shaft and range. Short iron arrows, smeared with grease, were probably used in warfare to kill elephants at close range. Greased arrows appear to have been commonly used in Indian warfare, the grease acting as a lubricant to enable the arrow to pierce deeper into the flesh. The *vipattha* appears to have been a long arrow made of wood, which measured five hand-spans in length. The *vaitastika* was a very short wooden arrow, dart, or bolt, measuring only one span, which was fired from a small composite bow or crossbow. Incendiary or fire-arrows (Skt. *agnibana*; Tib. *me'i mda'*), covered in burning oil or resin, were also used in Indian warfare, and are described in the Vedas as *agneya* or 'fire-weapons'. Poison-tipped arrows were known as *alakta, digdha* and *lipta*.

Indian wooden arrow-shafts were probably fashioned of a variety of woods, such as were obtained from the ironwood, axle-wood and *jujuba* trees. Cane or bamboo was, however, the traditional wood for Indian, Chinese, Mongolian and Tibetan arrows. American Indian arrows were made from the sourwood and viburnum trees, and European arrows from the alder buckthorn and other species of birch. The shaft of a long bamboo arrow consisted of three bamboo joints or sections, which were sanded smooth to ensure eveness and straightness.

The Tibetan arrow also had a variety of names and forms, such as the cane or bamboo arrow (*myug mda'*); the iron arrow (*lcags mda'*); the poison-tipped arrow (*dug mda'*); the long arrow (*mda' chen*); the magical arrow (*thun mda'*); the fire-arrow (*me'i mda'*); the flower arrow (*me tog mda'*); and the powerful arrow (*mda' po che*).

The design of the Tibetan arrowtip (*mda' rtse*) or arrowhead (*mda' mde'u*) is not specified, other than being sharply-pointed, and may take the form of a triangular blade, a curved spear-like tip, or a barbed point. The steering-feathers (*mda' sgro*) are most commonly made from the long wing-feathers of a vulture – particularly the soaring Himalayan bearded vulture or lammergeir – which are cut lengthwise and either glued into grooves on the arrow's shaft, or glued and bound with silk thread. Three steering-feathers are used on the arrow's flight, providing stability and accuracy for the true flight of the arrow. The flight end is scored with a deep notch (*mda' stong*) into which the bowstring (*mda' rgyud*) is fitted. Auspicious five-coloured silk threads are often glued and bound to the end of the arrow.

Besides their use as weapons, arrows are widely used in ritual. Tibetan ritual arrows are fashioned in many forms, with different coloured shafts, hanging silk ribbons, adornments and steering-feathers. Divination arrows (*mo mda'*), and silk-arrows (*mda' dar*), are illustrated and described on Plate 121.

The symbolism of the arrow is revealed in such legends as that of the mahasiddha Saraha and his *dakini* consort, who was a master arrowsmith. Saraha is usually depicted as sighting along an arrow's shaft to determine its smoothness and straightness. Here the arrow-shaft represents the central channel, and the smoothness of the three bamboo joints symbolises the untying of the psychic knots that constrict the flow of wind into the central channel. The three sections of the bamboo shaft and the three steering-feathers represent the trinities of body, speech, and mind; the three *kayas*; the three times, realms, and poisons. The four splits made in the bamboo shaft for the arrowhead symbolise the four concentrations; mindfulnesses; immeasurables or boundless states; activities or *karmas*; and the four joys, four moments, and four levels of tantra. The sharp *vajra*-point of the arrowhead symbolises the concentration of wisdom as penetrating awareness or single-pointedness of mind. The sinews or threads represent the binding of tantric commitments. The five-coloured threads, which are bound and glued at the flight-end of the shaft, represent the binding of the Five Buddha wisdoms, and the five perfections of method (generosity, discipline, patience, effort, and concentration) with the bow representing the sixth perfection (wisdom). The two sides of the arrow's releasing-notch represent the union of relative and absolute truth, and the union of conventional and ultimate *bodhichitta*.

As a male symbol of method, compassion, or skilful means, the arrow is commonly held in the right or 'method' hands of deities, and frequently coupled with the bow which is held in the female left or 'wisdom' hand. Multiple-armed deities, such as Yamantaka and Kalachakra, usually display the male penetrative weapons (e.g. sword, trident, hammer, mallet, or pestle, axe, iron hook, spear, club, and arrow) as right hand or method implements. As weapons, these implements are naturally held in the right or 'dextrous' hands.

As a male symbol the Tibetan arrow is paired with the female spindle in ritual magic, especially in rites of 'ransoming' (Tib. *glud tshab*) the health, life, property, or vital forces of a man or woman, by means of an effigy or painted substitute.

Plate 121

Illustrated in this drawing are examples of the divination mirror, divination arrow, and various forms of arrows.

In the top left and right corners are three examples of the divination mirror (Tib. *mo me long*) or 'magical mirror' (Tib. *'phrul gyi me long*). The circular divination mirror is made of silver or polished bell-metal, and marked with five small inscribed circles in the centre and cardinal directions, forming the shape of a cross and symbolising the Five Buddha wisdoms. In divination rituals – such as are performed to the goddess Dorje Yudonma (Tib. *rDo rje g.yu sgron ma*) – the mirror is placed upright in a container of barley or grain, and covered with five coloured silk cloths representing the Five Buddhas. A young virgin boy or girl acts as the medium of divination, seeing images or syllables which may arise on the mirror's uncovered surface, and which are then interpreted by the ritual master. As a hand-held attribute the magical-mirror is held in the left hand of Palden Lhamo, in her four-armed form as the 'Self-arisen Queen' (Tib. Rang

byung rgyal mo), symbolising her ability to clearly perceive the activities or *karmas* of the three realms.

A circular silver, bronze, or gold divination mirror also adorns the breast and costume of oracular deities and certain protectors, such as the Nechung and Gadong oracles, and the *dharmapalas* Begtse, Dorje Dragden, and Tsiu Marpo. Placed above the heart of the oracle or *dharmapala*, this mirror is known as the 'mirror of mind' (Tib. *thugs kyi me long*), which represents the mind of the deity and is often sealed with the deity's inscribed seed-syllable.

The drawing in the upper left corner shows a small divination mirror in a gold surround, with four inscribed circles on its surface and a silk ribbon tied onto its base. When a single ribbon adorns a mirror it is commonly coloured to accord with the deity being propitiated. White, yellow, and red silks correspond respectively to rituals of pacification, enrichment, and empowerment or subjugation. A black silk ribbon is never employed, as this would 'cloud' the mirror with the influences of malignant spirits, such as the *maras* (Tib. *bdud*) and disease-causing spirits (Tib. *ma mo*). The second drawing to the right of this shows a *vajra*-handled mirror, with five inscribed circles on its surface and a group of five silk ribbons hanging from its base, coloured in the Five Buddha sequence of white, yellow, red, green, and blue. The third drawing in the upper right corner depicts a similar mirror, with a single white or yellow silk ribbon tied onto the small handle on its base. Below and to the left is a fourth divination mirror, with five dots inscribed on its surface, and five coloured silk ribbons tied behind.

The divination arrow (Tib. *mda' mo*) or 'silk-arrow' (Tib. *mda' dar*) are employed in the divination or longevity rituals of deities such as Gesar, Dorje Yudonma, Tseringma, Amitayus, and Padmasambhava. As a hand-held implement the divination arrow is carried by many indigenous Tibetan deities of non-Buddhist origin, many of whom are said to have been subjugated by Padmasambhava.

One method of arrow-divination involves the shaking of a tubular container full of numbered arrows. When an arrow falls out of the container its number is looked up in a divination manual, which should accord a direct or metaphorical answer to the question posed. This form of divination is derived from a Chinese system employing yarrow-stalks.

Tibetan divination arrows take several forms. The following list draws from the account of divination arrows given by Nebesky-Wojkowitz.

The 'long-life silk arrow' (Tib. *tshe sgrub mda' dar*) has an iron arrowhead and red shaft which terminates in a five-pronged flight. Each prong is adorned with three steering-feathers from the wings of a vulture. The shaft-ends of the flights are painted in the five-colour mandala sequence, with corresponding silk ribbons attached to their ends. A small silver divination mirror is tied to the shaft below the flights, and the arrowhead is positioned vertically within a container of grain. The long-life arrow (Tib. *tshe mda'*) is employed in rituals of propitiation to Amitayus, Tseringma, and Padmasambhava. Iconographically the long-life arrow is held in the right hands of deities such as Amitayus and Mandarava, where it is rotated in all directions and paired with the long-life vase (Tib. *tshe bum*) held in the left hand.

The 'auspicious silk arrow' (Tib. *g.yang sgrub mda' dar*) is fashioned with an iron arrowhead and a single-ended shaft adorned with three steering-feathers. The shaft may be coloured to correspond to the deity being propitiated, with three or five coloured silk ribbons, and placed point-downwards into a wooden 'granary' (Tib. *'bru mdsod*) containing an abundance of grain and precious substances. For auspicious rituals of pacification the shaft and ribbons are coloured white, and for increase rituals of prosperity they are coloured yellow. Five-coloured silk ribbons are employed for all-purpose activities. A small mirror and a white conch-shell are hung from the upper shaft. The shaft symbolises the deity's body, the conch symbolises the deity's speech, and the mirror symbolises the deity's mind. The seed-syllable of the deity invoked may be inscribed in coloured powder upon the mirror, or for all-purpose activity the syllable *Om* may be inscribed. The auspicious-arrow or 'arrow of good luck' (Tib. *g.yang mda'*) is used in the Tibetan marriage ceremony to hook the collar of the bride and pull her away from her female companions. Here the arrow, as a male symbol, represents the groom's capturing of the bride. An arrow, wrapped in a white silk scarf, is also touched to the bride's forehead during the marriage ceremony.

The 'wealth-attracting silk arrow' (Tib. *nor sgrub mda' dar*), is fashioned with a copper arrowhead, red painted shaft, three steering-feathers, and five silk ribbons coloured white, yellow, red, green and blue. This form of divination arrow is employed in rituals propitiating the magnetising, or attracting goddesses, Vasudhara and Kurukulla. For specific rituals the arrow's shaft may bear the attributes of a mirror, conch shell and three divination dice.

The 'silk arrow of the fire god' (Tib. *me lha 'bod pa'i mda' dar*) is fashioned with an iron arrowhead, a red shaft, three steering-feathers, a single red silk ribbon, and a small square red pennon bearing the syllable *Ram* of the fire god. This arrow is placed upright into the earth in a south-easterly direction from where a ritual ceremony is being performed, in order to propitiate the fire god, Agni (Tib. *me lha*), who resides in the south-east.

The 'silk arrow of the wind god' (Tib. *rlung lha'i mda' dar*), is fashioned in a similar manner to the arrow of the fire god described above, but with a green shaft and green pennon bearing the syllable *Yam* of the wind god. This arrow is placed into the earth in a north-westerly direction to propitiate the wind god, Vayu (Tib. *rlung lha*).

Specific silk arrows (*mda' dar*) are also accorded to the eight classes of spirits, with specifically coloured shafts and silk ribbons, and their steering-feathers obtained from birds which bear a relationship with these spirits, such as the raven, vulture, hawk and owl. These 'spirit-arrows' are often positioned upright in the construction of the complex thread-crosses (Tib. *mdos*) employed in rituals of spirit subjugation.

The divination mirror and arrow are also used in a form of 'psychic surgery' by Tibetan shamans to cure illnesses or rabies. The mirror is firstly passed over the patient's body

to determine the precise 'seat' of the illness. The shaman then places the tip of the arrow on the body point located, and begins to suck on the end of the arrow's shaft. Often a large quantity of blood, puss, and diseased body tissue will be sucked out by the shaman, who then spits this foul matter into a bowl. In the case of rabies, a piece of flesh in the shape of a dog will also be sucked out of the patient's body by the shaman. A female shaman who becomes possessed by the spirit of a dog-headed deity in the retinue of Chakrasamvara – now performs this technique of psychic surgery at Bodhnath in Kathmandu. Many years ago a friend's young child was bitten by a rabid dog and cured of rabies by this method. Several years later the child was again bitten and again contracted rabies; the shaman's technique proved ineffective the second time, and the child died.

In the upper area of the drawing are seven examples of the divination arrow (Tib. *mda' mo*) or 'silk-arrow' (Tib. *mda' dar*). At the top centre of the page are three drawings of divination arrows, adorned with silver mirrors and silk ribbons. The first drawing on the left shows the five-coloured silk ribbons fastened behind the mirror, with their upper ends falling as a short apron below the mirror, their mid-points knotted and folded above the mirror, and their tapering lower ends flowing outwards towards the left. The second drawing shows a similarly festooned silk arrow, with the five-coloured silk ribbons hanging symmetrically below. The third drawing shows an arrow with three silk ribbons and three separate vulture feathers at the top. An arrow in this form is commonly held in the right hand of Mandarava, the Indian princess who along with Yeshe Tsogyal was one of the consorts of Padmasambhava. Three splayed vulture feathers also adorn the crest of Padmasambhava's hat, symbolising his mastery over the three *yanas*, the three times, the three realms, and the union of the three psychic channels.

To the right of these three divination arrows is a detail of an arrow flight with its steering-feathers made from the 'wisdom eyes' of the peacock or painted with the eyes of an owl. The owl is a 'messenger bird' of the flesh-eating *rakshasa* spirits (Tib. *srin po*), and an arrow of this kind may be used in thread-cross rituals or depicted in images of the wrathful assembly of offerings (Tib. *rgyan tshogs*). As a stealthy bird of prey, nature has endowed the soft and delicate wing-feathers of the owl with the quality of noiseless flight (see also Plate 134). Another arrow, with the painted eyes of an owl and a single silk ribbon, is depicted on the left centre of the page. Above and to the left of this arrow is another divination arrow with a mirror and five silk ribbons. Across to the right of the owl-eyed arrow is a divination arrow with four silk ribbons tied behind its mirror. Their tapering ends emanate or 'rotate' towards the four directions. Across to the right of the page is the last of the seven illustrated divination arrows, with a single silk ribbon twisting below its mirror. The black silk arrow is also depicted in the 'wrathful offerings of the five senses', illustrated on Plate 140.

At the centre of the page are two drawings of fire-arrows (Skt. *agnibana*; Tib. *me'i mda'*) with flames emanating from their sharp tips, and across to the right are a group of three

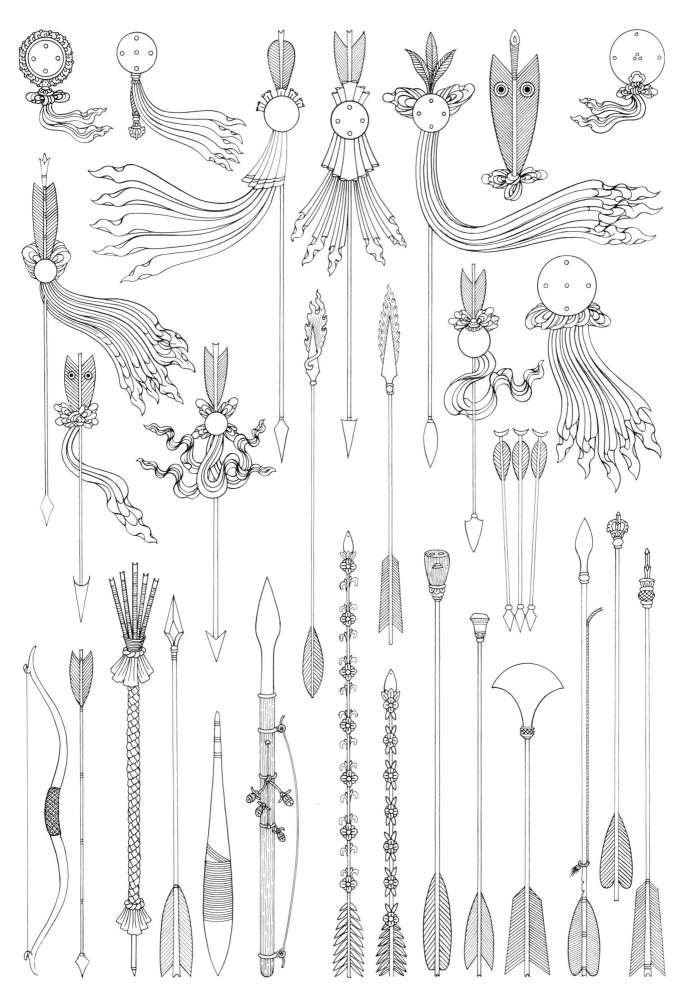

Plate 121: Arrows, divination arrows and mirrors

short arrows (Tib. *gsum mda'*) with crescent-moon caps above their steering-feathers. These implements are depicted as alternative attributes, held in the fifth right hand of Kalachakra, and paired with the bow held in his corresponding left hand. A difference of iconographic opinion exists as to which of these two attributes Kalachakra holds. Some say that it is a fire-arrow propelled by gunpowder, or that it is an arrow made of fire, or that it is red like fire with a sharp fire-like tip. Others say that it is a group of three arrows, with which Kalachakra transfixes and slays the three poisons of the three realms. In Tibetan the fire-arrow (Tib. *me'i mda'*) is also a term used to describe the cannon or firearm. Since the application of gunpowder as an explosive was already known at the time of the introduction of the *Kalachakra Tantra* (AD 1024), it is possible that the fire-arrow refers to either a bamboo rocket, or an arrow – possibly of iron – that was propelled by gunpowder. The Swedish explorer Sven Hedin mentions his discovery of fire-bearing Chinese arrows at a second-century Buddhist site in Central Asia.

On the left of the bottom row are a bow and arrow, as paired symbols of wisdom and compassion. The next drawing depicts the auspicious 'good luck arrow' (Tib. *g.yang mda' dar*) with a five-pronged flight. The five prongs are arranged in the mandala sequence of a central prong and four directional prongs, each of which is painted in the colours of the Five Buddhas and bound with silk threads in the same colours. Below the flight is a small five-coloured apron, and its bamboo shaft is plaited with long silk ribbons of the five colours with a second apron near its tip. This arrow, which symbolises the blessings of the Five Buddhas, is presented at the Tibetan New Year (Tib. *lo gsar*) ceremony as an auspicious offering of good fortune for the coming year.

To the right of this silk arrow are the paired attributes of an arrow and a wooden spindle (Tib. *'phang shing*). The pointed arrow represents the male principle as the emblem of a man as a hunter; the spindle used by Tibetan women for spinning woollen yarn represents the female principle. As a sacrificial object, portrayed in the assembly of wrathful offerings (Tib. *rgyan tshogs*), the 'female' spindle (Tib. *'phang bkra*) is wound with variegated colour thread. These two emblems are depicted upon the wooden tablets (Tib. *rgyang bu*) or ransom effigies (Tib. *glud tshab*), which are used in shamanic rituals as 'substitutes' to avert the influences of malignant spirits (these wooden tablets are illustrated on Plate 139).

To the right of the spindle is a 'postal-arrow' or 'letter-arrow' (Tib. *mda' yig*), used by Tibetan couriers to convey important letters, documents, or governmental edicts. The sealed document, in the form of a scroll, is contained within the hollow tube of the postal-arrow and tied with officially stamped seals that are impressed upon sealing wax (Tib. *la cha*). The leather strap of the postal-arrow enables the courier to carry it over his shoulder whilst riding on horseback. It symbolises speed of delivery. Documents conveyed by a relay of archers as fired arrows were also known as letter-arrows.

To the right of the postal-arrow are two drawings of the red *utpala*-flower arrow of the goddess Kurukulla (also

illustrated and described in Plate 122). The next drawing to the right shows a 'whistling-arrow' with a small clay ocarina as its arrowhead. The velocity of the wind forced through the apertures of this flute-like whistle produces a high-pitched single or double-tone note. This arrow was of Chinese origin and adopted by the Mongols as a weapon. When fired over the heads of the enemy and their battle animals, the screeching of the arrow instilled fear and panic. The next drawing shows a 'stunning-arrow' with a flat hammer-like metal head, which was used for rendering an opponent or animal unconscious. The next drawing shows a 'cutting-arrow' (Tib. *mda' phyed byas pa*), with a sharp axe-like, semi-circular blade that was used for severing ropes or limbs. In Indian warfare this weapon was known as a 'half-moon' (Skt. *ardhachandra*) arrow, and said to be capable of severing a head from a body. The next drawing depicts a 'notched arrow' (Tib. *mda' nag khram*) or hurled javelin (Tib. *be mdung*), which is propelled by a knotted string. The knot at the end of the string is placed in a notch in the base of the arrow's shaft and looped once around the shaft to secure it. The string is then pulled taut along the length of the shaft and thrown in the manner of a javelin, the string acting as a sling to propel the arrow a great distance. The notched arrow was probably used as a method of improvised weaponry when an archer's bow was broken in battle, where the bowstring could be adapted as a catapult. The last two drawings in the lower right corner depict two *vajra*-tipped arrows; the first with a five-pronged *vajra*, and the second with a single-pronged *vajra*.

The Flower Attributes of the Bow and Arrow, Hook and Noose

The attributes of a bow and arrow made of flowers derives from a legend of Kamadeva – the Vedic god of love – who like Eros and Cupid unleashes the arrow of love from his bow. According to this legend, Kamadeva fired five arrows at the austere and meditative form of Shiva, in order to arouse passion within his heart for the goddess Umadevi (Parvati). The first of Kamadeva's two arrows missed their target and failed to arouse thoughts of desire in Shiva's mind; the second two arrows entered Shiva's mind and caused his meditation to waver; whilst the fifth arrow pierced Shiva's heart and unleashed the full force of the ascetic lord's desire. In great wrath Shiva emanated a blaze of wisdom-fire from his third eye, immolating the physical form of Kamadeva and rendering him eternally bodiless, as the invisible 'power of love'.

Kamadeva is known by a variety of epithets including Maya (the destroyer), Ananga (the bodiless), Makaradhvaja (the *makara*-banner), Pushpadhanus (bow of flowers), and Pushpasara (arrow of flowers). Kamadeva's bow is either described as a bow of flowers or as a bow made of sugar cane (Skt. *ikshukodanda*), with a honey-soaked bowstring (Skt. *madhukara*) covered in bees. Kamadeva's five arrows are described as being fashioned from five different flowers – the white lotus, the *ashoka* flower, the mango flower, jasmine, and the blue lotus. Kamadeva's five arrows (Skt. *panchasara*) are

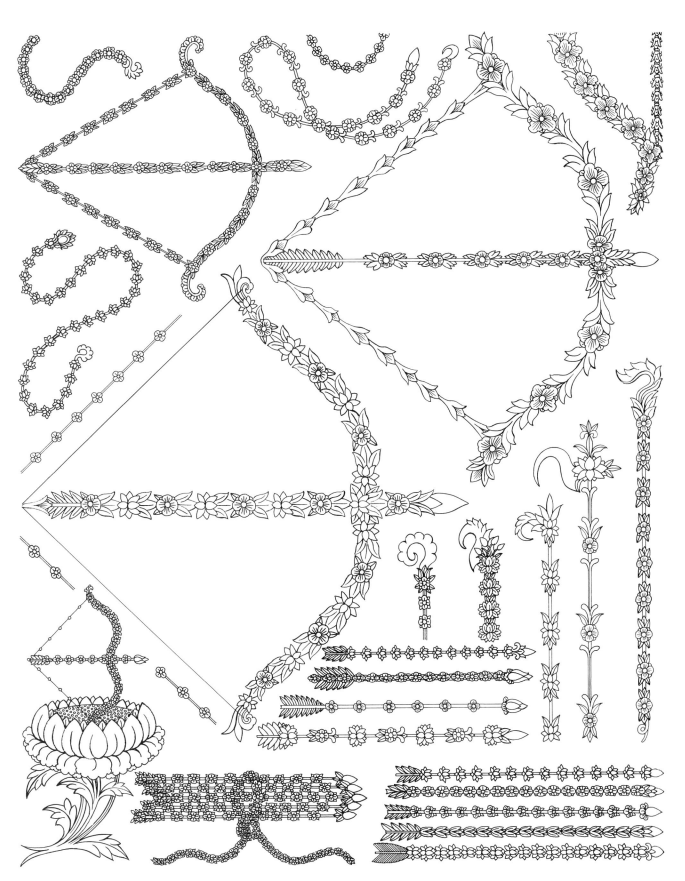

Plate 122: Flower bows and arrows

identified with the 'five passions' (Skt. *pancharaga*). These are sexual ecstasy (*unmadana*), burning (*tapana*), unconsciousness (*sammohana*), bewitching (*soshana*), and paralysing (*stambhana*). Within their multiple levels of meaning in the Hindu tantras, these five passions find one level of poetic expression as the stages of romantic or erotic love – gazing into each other's eyes, holding hands, embracing, kissing, and sexual union.

In early Vajrayana Buddhism the 'five passions' were also used as sexual metaphors for the 'five classes of tantra' (*kriya, charya, yoga, yogattara, anuyogattara*), although traditionally, and in later Vajrayana Buddhism, only 'four classes of tantra' are listed. Smiling or holding hands represents *kriya tantra*; gazing into each other's eyes, *charya tantra*; embracing and kissing, *yoga tantra*; and sexual consummation, *anuttarayoga tantra*. The five passions also correspond to the five poisons of ignorance, desire, aversion, pride, and jealousy; the five senses and their objects of sight, sound, smell, taste, and touch; and the five aggregates of form, feeling, perception, motivational factors, and consciousness.

The five arrows are also associated with Manjushri, representing – like the five protuberances on his head – the Five Buddha wisdoms. Manjushri's five arrows – like the five prongs of the *vajra* – transfix the five passions in their psychic centres. Ignorance is transmuted at the crown; desire, at the throat; anger, at the heart; pride, at the navel; and jealousy, at the secret place.

In Vajrayana iconography Kamadeva, as the 'god of desire' (Tib. 'Dod pa'i lha), is depicted being trampled upon by the deities Kalachakra and Kurukulla. In the iconography of Kalachakra, Kamadeva is personified as the red demon (Tib. *bdud*) of desire, whose four arms hold the subjugating attributes of a bow, five flower-arrows, a noose, and a hook. Kamadeva lies prone upon his back under the right foot of Kalachakra, whilst his consort tries to lift Kalachakra's foot from the chest of Kamadeva. This symbolises Kalachakra's triumph over, and his exhaustion of, the hosts of Mara.

The goddess Kurukulla is an aspect of Red Tara, who is invoked for the controlling activities of subjugating, magnetising, and attracting. She is extremely seductive: her red colour and subjugating flower-attributes emphasise her more mundane activity of enchanting men and women, ministers and kings, through the bewitching power of sexual desire and love (Skt. *vashikarana*). The eroticism of her symbolism is further enhanced through the imagery described in her *sadhana*. For attracting or subjugating a man, the flower-hook and red *utpala* arrow are visualised as piercing his heart; and for attracting a woman these attributes are visualised as penetrating her vagina. From a red eight-petalled lotus at the practitioner's heart arise eight red bees, which are visualised as flying out from his nostril and entering the nostril of the person to be subjugated. Here they suck the vowel syllables from that person's heart with their 'pollen-gathering sucking-tubes', then return with their 'nectar' to their 'hive' in the practitioner's heart. The symbolism of red bees intoxicated with honey, of red *utpala* flowers laden with fragrant nectar, and of the snaring, hooking, and

piercing activities of Kurukulla's flower-attributes, reveal the sexual magnetism of this seductive goddess.

In her red four-armed form, Kurukulla holds the attributes of a flower-bow (Skt. *pushpadhanus*; Tib. *me tog gshu*); a flower-arrow (Skt. *pushpasara*; Tib. *me tog mda'*) with a red *utpala* flower arrowhead; a flower-hook (Skt. *pushpankusha*; Tib. *me tog lcags kyu*); and a flower-noose (Skt. *pushpapasha*; Tib. *me tog zhags*). These four attributes are described as being fashioned from flowers, or more specifically from the flowers of the red *utpala* lotus or water-lily (Tib. *ut pa la dmar po*).

The two-armed form of the goddess Red Tara, holds the stem of a red *utpala* blossom in her left hand at the level of her heart. The root of this stem forms a noose, and the flower blossoms at the level of her left ear and bears the attributes of a drawn flower bow and arrow.

Plate 122
This illustration depicts the flower-attributes held by the goddesses Kurukulla and Red Tara, and by the Vedic god of love, Kamadeva.

Dominating the illustration are three drawings of Kamadeva's flower bow and arrow, which are held by the goddess Kurukulla. Each of the three arrows loaded and drawn in these bows are tipped by an arrowhead of a red *utpala* flower, with a shaft made of flowers and a flight made of leaves. The two upper bows are depicted with bowstrings made of flowers and leaves, whilst the lower bow has a rope bowstring.

Within the upper left area are three drawings of Kurukulla's flower-noose, which terminates in a hook and ring made from leaves or red *utpala* buds. In the upper right corner is a detail of Kamadeva's bow, with a bowstring fashioned from pollen-gathering bees. To the right of the lower bow and arrow are four horizontal drawings of different forms of flower-arrows, and five vertical drawings of Kurukulla's flower-hook.

At the bottom centre and right are two drawings of the five arrows of Kamadeva. The drawing on the left shows a group of five identical flower-arrows bound together in a cluster. The drawing on the bottom right depicts these five arrows as fashioned from the flowers of the white lotus, the *ashoka* flower, the mango flower, the jasmine flower, and the blue lotus. The drawing in the bottom left corner depicts the small red flower bow and arrow held by Red Tara. These attributes are held within a red *utpala* lotus, which arises from a noose formed from its lotus-root in Tara's left hand, and which blossoms at the level of her left ear.

THE SWORD (Skt. *khadga, asi*; Tib. *ral gri*)

In the Western chivalric tradition the sword, as the weapon of heroes, gods, and demi-gods, represents justice, might and authority, and is a symbol of the king's sovereign investiture. As a 'sword of destiny', King Arthur's Excalibur possessed the discriminating awareness to release itself only into the hand of the rightful king. The magical powers inherent in a legendary or heroic sword often endowed its owner with the ability to detect treason, betrayal, and enemies, as the blade would glow or heat in warning. This medieval motif of the 'divine sword' was revitalised by J.R.Tolkein in *The Lord of the Rings*. In *Genesis* the flaming swords of Eden guarded the gates of Paradise against mankind's defilement, whilst in *The Book of Revelations* the 'Son of Man' proclaims the Last Judgement with a sharp two-edged sword emerging from his mouth.

In ancient Indian warfare the sword was second in importance only to the bow and arrow. As a weapon of close combat its swiftness and versatility could easily undermine the lethal weight of the club, mace, and battleaxe. In Vedic mythology the unvanquishable sword of Vishnu was named Nandaka, and Indra's sword was named Paranjaya. In Sanskrit the sword is known as *khadga, asi, karavala* or *karavali*. Besides the shorter hand-sword (*khadga*), there was the long sword (*mahakhadga*), which measured at least thirty *angulas* or finger-widths (approximately twenty-four inches) along its blade. The term *khadga* also means rhinoceros, and this mighty animal with its penetrating single horn and almost impregnable hide was both a symbol of masculine virility and military invulnerability. The thick hide plates of the rhinoceros were employed in defensive warfare as shields, spear-guards and body armour. Early Buddhism identified the rhinoceros with the *pratyekabuddha* or 'solitary realiser', who according to an early sutra 'fared as lonely as the rhinoceros'.

As a protective symbol of the Buddhist doctrine the sword represents the victory of enlightenment over the attack of the hosts of Mara, as the hindering forces of ignorance. The *Bodhicharyavatara* states, "As the blade of the sword does not cut itself, neither does the mind know itself". As a symbol of wisdom the sword cuts through the veils of ignorance, severing the knots of illusion that bind beings to delusion and obscure the absolute truth.

Manjushri, the bodhisattva of wisdom, holds aloft in his right hand the flaming sky-blue sword of awareness that 'cuts through the net of misunderstanding'. He is said to abide at the Chinese five-peaked mountain of Wu Tai Shan, which geomantically symbolises the Five Buddha wisdom protuberances (*ushnisha*) on Manjushri's head. In Nepal, Manjushri is credited with having created the Kathmandu valley, by cutting through the surrounding mountains at Chobar Gorge with his sword, thereby draining the lake which filled the valley. According to legend the 'self-created' hill of Swayambhu, which emerged as the waters receded, is the site from where Nagarjuna received the *Prajnaparamita Sutra* from the guardianship of the *nagas*.

The flaming sword of Manjushri is sealed with a *vajra*-handle and Manjushri's syllable, *Dhih*, and represents the discriminating wisdom that realises emptiness. Its sharp double edge represents the indivisibility of relative and absolute truth; its fine point, the perfection of wisdom; and its fiery *vajra*-flames which emanate to the ten directions, the blazing of the wisdom-awareness fire of full enlightenment. In his left hand Manjushri holds the stem of a blue *utpala*

flower at the level of his heart, which blossoms near his ear and bears the text of the *Prajnaparamita Sutra* (Perfection of Wisdom) in 100,000 stanzas. The emblem of Majushri – either an upright sword resting upon this text, or the sword and book resting upon two *utpala* flowers held in his right and left hand – is borne as an insignia by many human emanations of Manjushri, such as Trisong Detsen, Sakya Pandita, Tsongkhapa, and Longchenpa. As an emblem of the Karma Buddha Family, the sword or *vishvavajra* is an attribute of Amoghasiddhi, the green Buddha of the north.

A vast number of semi-wrathful and wrathful deities hold the sword as a weapon, almost exclusively in their right or 'dextrous sword-hands'. These swords may be depicted with or without flames, with curved single-edged or straight double-edged blades, and with varying styles of hilt decorations. The sword blade is depicted mainly in the dark-blue colour of iron, but descriptions of crystal, copper, gold or lapis lazuli are sometimes given, particularly in the case of a warrior-deity surrounded by a retinue of four directional manifestations. Extremely wrathful activity is sometimes expressed in the form of a scorpion-hilted sword, a sword fashioned from a the tongue of a resuscitated corpse (Skt. *vetala*; Tib. *ro lang*), or the blazing sword of fire of a demonic *rakshasa* (Tib. *srin po*). However wrathful the sword is depicted, its main symbolism is the destruction of ignorance and enemies, personified in the form of evil spirits and demons who create obstacles to the development of wisdom.

In the right hands of *anuttarayoga tantra* deities, such as Yamantaka, a sword also symbolises the granting of the the eight *siddhis* (Skt. *ashtasiddhi*; Tib. *grub chen brgyad*) or powers of psychic attainment. The 'sword-*siddhi*' (Skt. *khadga siddhi*) is the first of these: it bestows the power to vanquish enemies with the sword of discriminating awareness. The second, *anjana siddhi*, bestows clairvoyant vision through the 'eye salve' of omniscience. The third, *padalepa siddhi*, bestows fleetness of foot as the 'foot ointment' of speed-walking. The fourth, *antaradhana siddhi*, bestows invisibility and the miraculous ability to disappear. The fifth, *rasayana siddhi*, is the alchemical power of transmutation which bestows immortality and the ability to transform matter. The sixth, *khechara siddhi*, enables one to fly through the sky. The seventh, *bhuchara siddhi*, bestows the power of translocation and multiple manifestation. The eighth, *patala siddhi*, enables the siddha to traverse all realms of existence. The eight great *siddhis* are variously listed in different tantric traditions, but the list given above is the most common.

The Scorpion and the Scorpion-Hilted Sword

The Indian scorpion (Skt. *vrishchika*; Tib. *sdig pa*) – armoured in glossy black skin segments with two pincers and a poisonous sting in its tail – presents a formidable image of aggression and malice. The mating scorpion's 'dance of death', wherein it stings itself to death within a ring of fire or becomes imprisoned within an invisibly inscribed 'magic circle', have rendered it a favoured 'familiar' of Indian fakirs who have gained the minor *siddhi* of controlling poisonous snakes and scorpions. Three species of scorpion are believed to be indigenous to Tibet.

The sting of the scorpion's whip-like tail transfixes and poisons its prey, and in this respect it is identified with the wrathful activity of the ritual dagger or *phurba*. Padmasambhava's biography relates how he received the *siddhi* of the *phurba* transmission at the great charnel ground of Rajgriha from a gigantic scorpion with nine heads, eighteen pincers and twenty-seven eyes. This scorpion reveals the *phurba* texts from a triangular stone box hidden beneath a rock in the cemetery. As Padmasambhava reads this *terma* text spontaneous understanding arises, and the heads, pincers, and eyes of the scorpion are 'revealed' as different vehicles or *yanas* of spiritual attainment. Here, at Rajgriha, Padmasambhava is given the title of 'the scorpion guru', and in one of his eight forms, as Guru Dragpo or Pema Dragpo ('wrathful lotus'), he is depicted with a scorpion in his left hand. As an emblem of the wrathful *phurba* transmission the image of the scorpion took on a strong symbolic meaning in the early development of the Nyingma or 'ancient school' of Tibetan Buddhism.

Milarepa's biography describes how in his early life he reaps vengeance on his spiteful relatives by resorting to the black arts. In the midst of a wedding feast attended by thirty-five of his relations a swarm of poisonous reptiles and insects suddenly manifests, and a giant scorpion 'as big as a yak' pulls down the central pillar of the house, killing them all. Simultaneously at his retreat cave Milarepa is presented with the bleeding heads and hearts of these thirty-five relatives by the wrathful deities he had invoked.

The image of the wrathful scorpion also arises in the iconography of certain protective deities, and many of the multitudinous forms of the eight classes of spirits who appear in their retinues. Certain spirits may have the head and pincers of the scorpion, and wear its black skin as armour; or they may hold a scorpion as an attribute, or wield a scorpion-hilted sword. In protective or sympathetic magic the painted or drawn image of the scorpion is also employed for spirit subjugation. The image of a scorpion devouring a 'spirit king' (Tib. *rgyal po*), for example, is created to protect against the harm inflicted by such spirits. The manacled effigies of other classes of spirits (Tib. *btsan, mdud, dam sri*, for example), are depicted being devoured by scorpions in drawn protective diagrams (Tib. *ling ga*), which are used as charms against their malevolence.

The *dam sri* spirits appear as dwarfs who inflict plagues and cattle diseases. Amongst the spirits and demonic forms that inflict plagues (Tib. *gnyan*), many are represented in the form of scorpions. In certain necromantic rituals the bone of a plague victim may be carved into a *phurba* to cause the death of an enemy. The wrathful female deity Palden Lhamo or 'Remati', in her form as the 'goddess of plagues' (Tib. dPal ldan lha mo gnyan gyi re ma ti), holds a human corpse and a scorpion-hilted sword in her two right hands. One form of the wrathful goddess Ekajati also wields the scorpion-hilted sword. Both of these goddesses emanate a poisonous mist from their mouths, nostrils, and lower orifices. The wrathful warrior-protector, Begtse, also wields the scorpion-hilted sword, representing his destructive activities of spreading disease and pestilence upon the battlefield.

Plate 123

This illustration depicts drawings of the scorpion-hilted sword, the scorpion, and various examples of both magical and wisdom swords. Across the left of the top row are five examples of the flaming scorpion-hilted sword, held by deities such as Begtse. The blade of the sword emerges from the mouth of the scorpion like a sharp double-edged iron tongue, whilst its pincers may grip the base of the blade forming the cross-guard of the hilt. In the first two drawings on the left the six or eight legs of the scorpion are not depicted on the sword's grip or handle. The fourth drawing shows an eight-legged scorpion with eyes all over its body. The *vajra*-flames which envelop these swords entwine, like serpents, around their blades.

In the upper right hand corner are three drawings of scorpions. The image on the left shows the two halfs of a scorpion's body forming the *vajra*-hook and ring of a noose (Skt. *pasha*; Tib. *zhags pa*) or snare (see also Plate 130). The scorpion in the upper right corner is depicted in its 'natural' stylised Tibetan form with eight legs. The large scorpion below this has nine heads and eighteen pincers, and devours a naked male and female figure in his nine mouths. This image represents the destructive activity of the nine ritual *phurbas*, which are nailed into the centre and eight directions in *kilana* rites of spirit subjugation.

Below this large scorpion are four illustrations of swords. The first drawing on the left shows an example of a flame-scroll coiling around the tip of a sword blade. The second drawing depicts a short *vajra*-hilted sword with a mass of wisdom fire blazing around its tip. The third drawing shows a long flat sword with a straight blade and *vajra*-tipped grip. The last drawing on the right shows a long double-edged sword with a tapering blade.

The first drawing on the left of the bottom row depicts a sword fashioned from threaded and tied Chinese coins. Such 'spirit swords' were used in China to protect newborn children from the spirits of deceased barren women, who were believed to be abductors of small children. This sword is often hung above babies' cots, and may also be found in Tibetan protector chapels. The blade, cross-guard, and pommel of the sword are constructed from the overlapping of flat coins bound tightly together through their central holes, whilst the handle is made from stacked and strung coins. In *feng shui* these swords are used to deflect evil spirits away from a building.

The second drawing depicts an iron sword which has been bent into a loop by an oracle. The psychic technique of 'metal-bending' was often demonstrated during the trances of Tibetan oracles, who would often tie a knot in a thick iron sword blade, or rapidly twist the blade into the shape of a Tibetan syllable. Twisted or knotted swords are commonly found in protector chapels, and are hung above doorways or entrances to repel evil spirits.

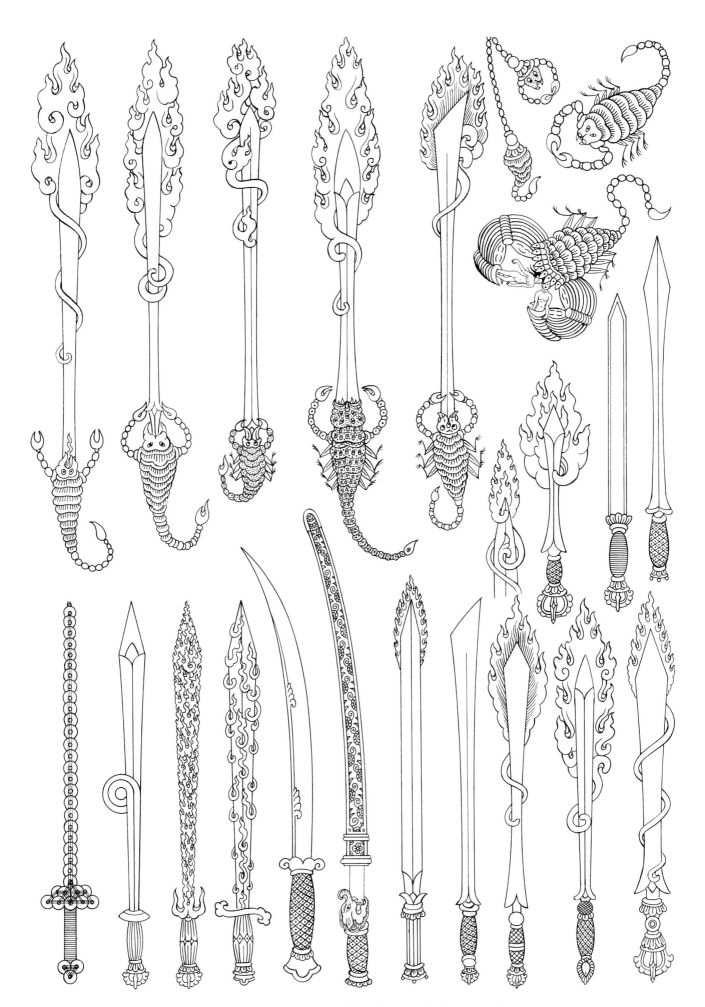

Plate 123: Scorpion-hilted, flaming and wisdom swords

The third and fourth drawings show two examples of the flaming *rakshasa* sword wielded by male and female demons (Skt. *rakshasa / rakshasi*; Tib. *srin po / srin mo*) or malevolent spirits who often take the form of goblins. The first sword has a blade made of fire, a flaming trident cross-guard, and an eight-faceted handle sealed with a half-*vajra*. The second is depicted with small tongues of flame licking around its blade.

The fifth drawing depicts a sabre (Tib. *shang lang*), with a curved single-edged blade and sharp tip. The sixth drawing depicts a curved *makara*-handled sword being drawn from its sheath or scabbard. Virudhaka, the great blue guardian-king of the south, is often depicted unsheathing such a sword with both hands. The seventh drawing depicts a flaming sword of wisdom with a parallel-sided blade and eight-sided handle. The eighth drawing shows a cutlass with an acutely angled tip.

The last three drawings on the right show three variations of the flaming wisdom sword with *vajra*, jewel, and *vajra* handles, respectively. The flames commonly coil around the blade, enveloping it in a blaze of wisdom fire. Ten tongues of fire are often painted in the upper flame mass to represent the sword's wisdom radiating to the ten directions. Amongst artists it is believed that the sharper the point of the wisdom-sword is painted, then the greater will be the wisdom achieved by the artist.

THE TRIDENT-PIKE, CADUCEUS, DART, AND OTHER BLADED WEAPONS

Plate 124

Illustrated in this composition are examples of the trident-pike, the trident-caduceus, darts, fish or water-knives, sword blades, daggers, scissors, and scythes.

On the left side of the page are a group of four tridents or pikes. The first and fourth drawings from the left depict two trident-pikes with impaled human heads and flowing flags. These wrathful tridents are held by protective deities, such as Trakshad Mahakala and the blue 'Soul Releasing' Four-Faced Mahakala. The trident-shaped head of this weapon incorporates the three blades of an axe, a spear, and a curved knife or iron hook; it performs the functions of cleaving, lancing, cutting, and hooking. The spear tips on both of these weapons emanate *vajra*-flames, and the upper shafts of the pikes impale the decapitated head of an enemy through the mouth. The first drawing shows the flayed skin of the enemy coiled below its head and trailing in the wind as a flag. The fourth drawing clearly shows the combined forms of the axe, spear, and hooked blade emanating from a flame-enveloped skull. The tongue of the enemy's severed head protrudes in this drawing, indicating that the enemy is a resurrected corpse (Skt. *vetala*; Tib. *ro lang*). A long battle-flag streams from below its head. The shaft-ends of these two pikes are sealed with half-*vajras*.

The second drawing from the left shows a double-bladed trident (Skt. *trishula*; Tib. *rtse gsum*), the outer blades of which are sharpened in the form of a double axe. Below the trident's iron top is a central skull-hub with a small red blood-stained yaktail hanging below. To the right of this trident is a smaller pike (Skt. *shula*; Tib. *rtse*) with twisting prongs at its left and centre, and an axe-head as its right prong. A bloodstained yaktail and black pennants hang below. The fifth drawing from the left shows a small double battleaxe or 'axe-lance' (Tib. *dgra sta mdung*), with its three blades emanating from a rectangular iron hub. This hand-held weapon functions primarily as a battleaxe, which may also be used for lancing.

At the top centre of the page is an entwined serpent-trident (Tib. *sbrul rtse gsum*) or caduceus. The trident in this form is an emblem of Shiva as Lokeshvara, the 'Lord of the Realms'. It was adopted into early Mahayana Buddhism as an emblem of the bodhisattva Avalokiteshvara in his form as Simhanada or 'Lion's Roar'. Simhanada's trident – which rises behind the right side of his body – has a green shaft, with a white snake coiled around it that drips red blood from its mouth. Shiva's serpent-trident is also green or blue in colour and has two symmetrically entwined serpents coiled around it. These two serpents are red and white, symbolising the solar and lunar channels coiling (Skt. *kundala*) around the green or blue central channel. The red yaktail pennant and white skull at the top of the shaft symbolise the ascent of the red serpent-goddess Kundalini, rising to unite with her white lord, Shiva, in the crown centre of the skull. Emerging from the skull's crown centre is a flaming trident, which symbolises the solar and lunar channels dissolving into the fire of the central channel.

The caduceus, as an emblem of the alchemical god Mercury or Hermes, first originated within the ancient Assyrian, Hittite, and Phoenician cultures as a sun-moon symbol, consisting of a central rod crowned by a sun disc with two lunar horns on either side. As the Greek staff of Hermes, the 'messenger of the gods', it aquired the entwined serpent and wing-topped motif now familiar as a healing symbol. Through its magical power Hermes was able to resuscitate the victims of Hades. Medicinally the two serpents symbolise poison and its antidote, or venom and serum as the homeopathic principle of 'like cures like'. Alchemically the two serpents symbolise cinnabar and mercury, or menstrual blood and semen, which through their transmutation create the 'elixir of immortality'. The Greek caduceus is described as being fashioned from green olive-wood and adorned with gold ornaments of sun, moon, wings, and serpents.

Across the top right half of the page are four drawings of the peacock-feathered dart or *shakti*-dagger, held by deities such as Yamantaka and the goddess Palden Lhamo, in her form as Somo Remati (Tib. *gTso mo re ma ti*). Yamantaka's dart (Skt. *bhindipala*; Tib. *bhi dhi pa la*), consists of a three-sided iron *phurba* blade with a flight of three peacock feathers. The three-sided blade symbolises the pinning down of the three poisons of ignorance, desire, and hatred, and the three peacock feathers represent Yamantaka's triumph over the three realms. The triangular blade and its feathered flight also symbolise the purification of both objective and subjective conceptualisation. Palden Lhamo's dart is

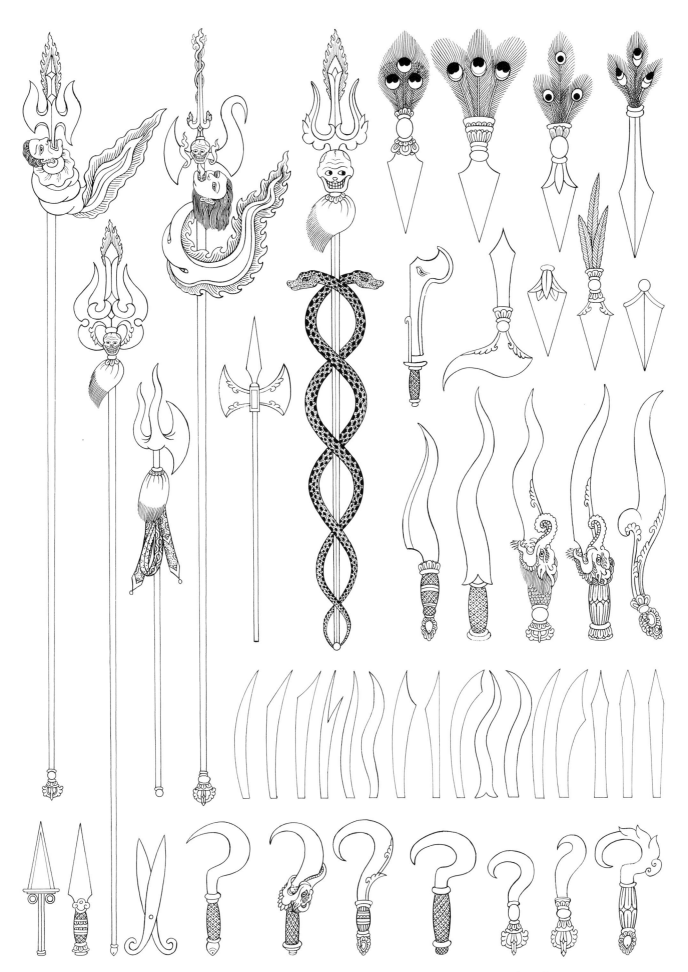

Plate 124: The trident pike, caduceus, dart, water-knife, sword blades and scythes

identified as a *shakti*-dagger (Tib. *shag ti*), and likewise symbolises her victory over the three poisons (triple-sided blade) of the three realms (three peacock eyes). The term *shakti* refers to a spear (described in Plate 125); and the *shakti*-dagger was probably fashioned from a conventional spearhead sealed with a peacock-feather handle or flight, which could be used both for stabbing and throwing.

The Sanskrit term *bhindipala* refers to a short javelin or arrow, thrown either by hand or from a tube (see also Plates 121 and 125). This suggests that the dart could be launched from a thick bamboo throwing-tube, to give it greater velocity and distance, though probably less accuracy. In ancient Indian warfare the 'iron dart' (Skt. *ayashula*; Tib. *lcags gsum*), could be hurled at an opponent with great precision, or cast skywards to fall into the massed ranks of the enemy. The peacock-feathered dart or *bhindipala* is often mis-identified with the *phurba*, as both these weapons are held by different forms of the goddess Palden Lhamo. In Yamantaka's iconography the *bhindipala* is sometimes identified as the conical peacock-feather sprinkler (Tib. *kha*) which crowns the ritual vase or *bumpa* (see Plate 103).

The four upper drawings of the *bhindipala* illustrate its various forms, with the last drawing on the right depicting the dart as a sword blade. Below these and to the right are three drawings of the iron dart's head, with the central image having a flight of three long eagle or vulture-wing feathers. To the left of these three drawings is a 'sword-knife' (Skt. *khadgakartrika*; Tib. *ral gri gug*), a weapon combining the thrusting and slashing powers of the sword and razor. To the left of this is the Indian sacrificial cleaver known as a *kartrika*; a weapon wielded by the wrathful Hindu Mahavidya goddesses, Kali and Tara. The *kartrika* is used in ritual sacrifices to the Hindu mother goddesses (Skt. *matrikas*), on festival days such as Durga Puja, when male goats, buffaloes, oxen, and chickens are sacrificially beheaded. The single eye on the blade of the *kartrika* symbolises the wrathful wisdom aspect of the goddess.

Below these weapons and across the central right area of the illustration are five examples of the razor known as a 'fish knife' or 'water knife' (Skt. *churika*; Tib. *chu gri*). The *churi* or *churika* is still used in India for gutting, heading, tailing, and scaling fish. Around the coastal fishing villages of the subcontinent, regional variations of the *churika* as a curved or wave-shaped knife are commonly found. These knives are often mounted upon a wooden base which can be held between the feet, leaving both hands free to manipulate the slippery fishes. In Tibetan art this knife appears as a long wave-shaped razor, which emerges from the crocodile grip of a *makara*'s mouth, with a short embellished handle often terminating in a *vajra* or jewel insignia. The blade is depicted in the dark-blue colour of iron, and its decorative *makara* handle is made of gold. The Tibetan form bears a strong resemblance to the meteorite-iron Balinese 'kris' or 'spirit-knife', which must draw blood when it is unsheathed.

The water knife is held by deities such as Yamantaka, and many of the attendant spirits that form the retinues of wrathful and protective deities. As a razor it symbolises the 'shaving away' of evil karmas and defilements. As a water or fish knife it symbolises the cutting away of 'cyclic existence' (Skt. *samsara*; Tib. *'khor ba*). The Sanskrit term *samsara* literally means 'to flow or pass through', and implies the endless cycles of births and rebirths as the metempsychosis of suffering. Fishes are symbols of samsara, representing the abundance of beings flowing aimlessly in the ocean of cyclic existence (see Plate 83). The symbolism of the fish knife, which cuts away the guts (the emptiness of inherent existence), scales (phenomenal appearances), heads (the cycle of births and rebirths), and tails (karmic propensities) of sentient beings, represents the severing of the repetitive cycle of existential suffering which imprisons beings within samsara.

Below the caduceus and water-knives is a row of sixteen different sword-blades, such as are held by the vast retinues of spirit-warriors of the various classes of spirits (see page 284), who accompany warrior deities such as Gesar, Begtse, Tsiu Marpo, Tsangpa, and Pehar. The first, fifth and twelfth of these blades are shaped like a sabre (Tib. *shang lang*). The second, third, and eighth blades from the left have a shape akin to the Western scimitar or cutlass. The bifurcated fourth blade is used for blocking and breaking an opponent's sword. The sixth, tenth and eleventh blades are shaped like the water knife. The seventh, ninth, and thirteenth blades are shaped like the 'butcher's knife' or cleaver (Tib. *gshan gri*). The last three blades on the right are shaped like the double-edged sword (Skt. *khadga*; Tib. *ral gri*).

On the left of the bottom row are two daggers. The first depicts the Indian and Islamic dagger known as a *katari*, which either has a handle with two finger-rings (as illustrated), or a small ladder-like hand grip with two cross-rungs. The second drawing shows a 'gutting-dagger' (Tib. *rgyu gri*) used for disembowelling. Next to this is a pair of Indian scissors, which are held by the Hindu Mahavidya goddesses, Kali and Tara. To the right of the scissors are seven examples of the curved sickle (Tib. *dgra zor*), which is used as a weapon to sever limbs and decapitate opponents. The sickle symbolises the cutting away of all evil karmas, 'overturning the world above the ground' in the process of reaping, in contrast to the ploughshare which 'overturns the world below the ground' in the process of sowing. The sickle has a sharp blue-iron blade and is mounted in a golden handle, often with *makara* and *vajra* embellishments.

THE SPEAR, LANCE, JAVELIN, HARPOON, AND PIKE

The hand-held or hurled spear or lance was one of the most important weapons of ancient Indian warfare. It appears to have had many specific forms, judging by the many Sanskrit names given to it (*shakti, rathashakti, tomara, kunta, shanku, bhindipala, kanapa, kampana, shula, pattisha*). These weapons are no longer identifiable though, and one can only speculate about how they differed. *Shakti* (Tib. *shag ti*) was the most common name given to the long hand-held lance or spear. The *rathashakti* means 'chariot-spear', and appears to have been a long thrusting-lance, possibly bearing a small pennon or triangular flag. The *tomara* and *kunta* are simply

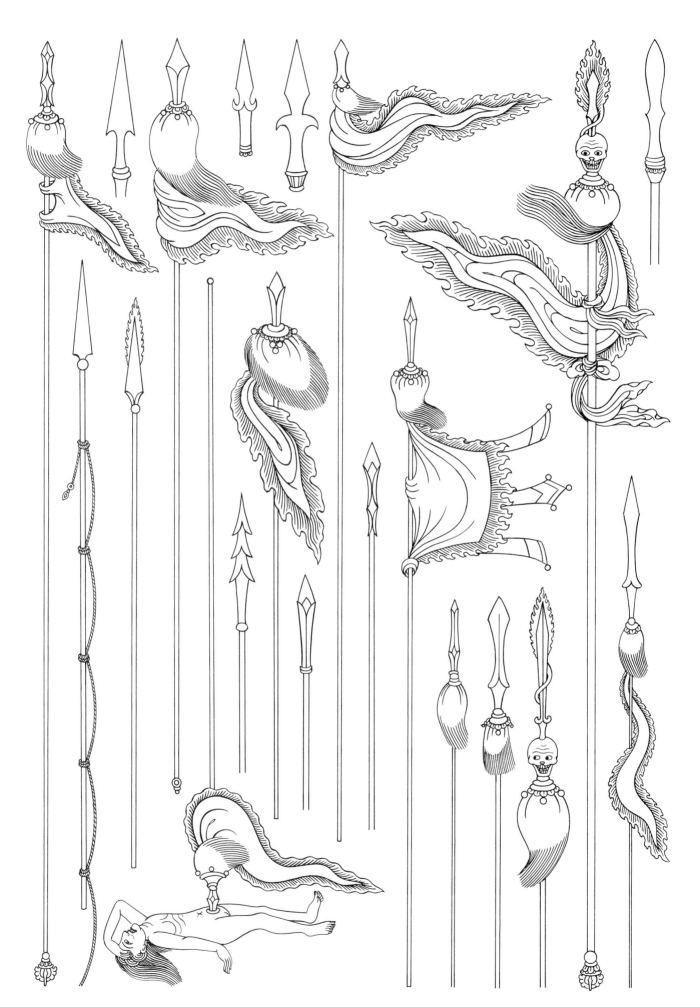

Plate 125: The spear or lance

defined as lances, clubs, or spears. The *shanku, kanapa,* and *bhindipala* appear to have been short javelins or throwing darts. The *kampana,* meaning 'shaking' or 'trembling', appears to have been a bamboo-shafted javelin, which trembled like an arrow when it struck its target. The *pattisha* may have been a trident-topped spear, and the *shula* or 'blade' was a single-pointed lance.

Tibetan uses two terms (Tib. *mdung, shag ti*) for the spear, lance, javelin, or pike. Artistically the spear is usually depicted with a sharp blue-iron tip, shaped either like a pointed sword, a *vajra*-spike, or an arrowhead. The spearhead is commonly mounted in a decorative golden hub, from which hangs a small yaktail that is usually stained red with blood and billows to one side. Hanging from the shaft below may be a long triangular flag, made from coloured silk with serrated cloth, skin or leather edges. This triangular flag – whose shape symbolises the destructive or wrathful activity (Skt. *krodhakarma*) of war – is known as a 'military insignia' (Tib. *ru dar*), a 'divisional standard' (Tib. *ru mtshon*), or a 'spear-flag' (Tib. *mdung dar*).

The triangular spear-flag is the common military standard of the Tibetan army, and forms the battle-ensign for mounted warrior-deities such as Gesar, Vaishravana, and Karmaraja. The colour or material of the flag is not usually specified, although Ganapati Mahakala is described as brandishing a trident-topped spear-flag which is 'poppy coloured'. Yamantaka likewise holds a spear with a red cloth-flag, and Vaishravana holds a red-jewelled spear. The *dharmapala,* 'Treasure Club Mahakala' (Tib. mGon po beng gter ma), is described as holding a long spear made from the thighbone of a *rakshasi* (Tib. *srin mo*) – tall ogressses or cannibal demonesses, and one of the Tibetan 'eight classes of spirits' (the original inhabitants of Tibet are said to have descended from a monkey emanation of Avalokiteshvara who mated with a *rakshasi* dwelling in a mountain cave).

The hand-held spears or lances carried by multiple-armed *yidam* deities are usually depicted with a sharp blue-iron point, a small golden hub, a red yaktail and flag pennon, and a long red sandalwood shaft tipped by a *vajra* or jewel. The battle-spear is usually equal in height to the warrior who bears it, and in Kalachakra's description his spear is described as equalling the height of two or three men.

The specific lances of protective deities may be fashioned of precious substances, such as gold, silver, copper, lapis lazuli, crystal, or coral.

The lances held by other spirits of the 'eight classes' are variously described, such as: the 'red lance of the red *btsan* demons', which has bloodstained pennants; the 'white lance of the *dbal* demons'; and the jewel-fashioned lances of the *rgyal po,* or treasure-guarding 'spirit-kings'. The iconographic forms of the various listings of the eight or nine classes of spirits creates the most complex pantheon of ethereal beings, and cannot be included within the scope of this book; Nebesky-Wojkowitz's monumental work provides a very good introduction to the complexities of this subject. The eight classes of spirits most commonly listed are: *lha, btsan, bdud, gza, dmu, srin po, rgyal po, ma mo*. The Bon tradition lists nine classes of demons, only four of which appear

in the list above. Essentially these eight or nine classes embody the pantheons of major spirits, but the categories of minor spirits are said to number up to 84,000 – corresponding to the 84,000 *dharmas* of the Buddhas.

The sharp point of the spear symbolises the piercing or impaling of all false notions and distorted views.

Plate 125

Illustrated in this drawing are various examples of the spear or lance and its iron spearhead. The first drawing on the left depicts a long lance with an iron *vajra*-spike, a decorative gold hub above a flowing yaktail, a triangular spear-flag (Tib. *mdung dar*) of war, and a long shaft tipped by a golden half-*vajra*.

The second drawing to the right and below depicts a harpoon (Tib. *ka na ya*), or 'fishing spear', with a long rope line attached to its shaft. The harpoon is held in one of the right or 'method' hands of Yamantaka, and symbolises the piercing of ignorance with discriminating awareness or wisdom, which overcomes the faults of body, speech, and mind. The *I Ching* describes pigs and fishes as being the most difficult creatures to influence, and the fish – with its short-term memory and tendency to be easily caught – was possibly an early symbol of ignorance. Coincidentally the main prey of the Western hunting-spear was the wild boar. The sharp point of Yamantaka's harpoon – which is described as a single-pointed *vajra* – symbolises penetrative insight, and the rope represents the power of mindfulness or recollection.

The next drawing on the right depicts a light spear or javelin (Skt. *shanku* or *kanapa*) with a *vajra*-flame tip. The javelin, as the Olympic Games reveal, is a weapon that can be cast far into the ranks of the enemy. As a simple and disposable weapon it probably consisted only of an iron spearhead and a short wooden or bamboo shaft. The notched javelin, launched with a knotted string (see Plate 121), had a much greater trajectory than the hand-thrown javelin.

The fourth drawing depicts another spear with a short sword-like spearhead. To the upper left and right of its tip are three examples of spearheads with different forms of barbs. The fifth vertical drawing depicts a *vajra*-tipped spear-flag piercing the abdomen of a demoness. Across to the right of this are a barbed triple-pointed spearhead; another spear-flag with a short head and large yaktail; a long spear-flag with a small *vajra*-pointed spearhead; and the top of a spear with a sword-bladed head.

To the right again is a sword-pointed spear with a rectangular flag adorned with three silk valances. Below and to the right are three further examples of spearheads, the first with a *vajra*-point; the second with a sword-point; and the third with a flaming sword arising from the crown of a skull. To the right again is a long spear-flag with a *vajra*-flame spearhead; an impaled skull; a golden mount and bloodstained yaktail; a triangular flag, secured with silk ribbons; and a long shaft, tipped with a half-*vajra*. On the far right are two further examples of a spear and a spearhead.

THE TRIDENT (Skt. *trishula*; Tib. *rtse gsum*)

In Western mythology the trident was the attribute of the Greek god Poseidon, the aquatic god of the seas, storms and earthquakes, who later became the Roman maritime god, Neptune. The watery planet Neptune is represented astrologically by the trident, which as a fish-spear formed the most versatile implement for spearing fish. In early Christian art the trident formed a symbol for the trinity of Father, Son, and Holy Ghost, but later the trident was identified with Satan or Lucifer, and his trident became the pitchfork of the denizens of hell.

The symbol of the trident – meaning 'three teeth' – first appeared on Mesopotamian clay seals, and on early Shaivite seals unearthed from the ancient Harappan civilisation of the Indus valley. In Vedic mythology the three points of the *trishula* – meaning 'three iron spikes or stakes' – are identified with the three prongs of Indra's *vajra* or 'thunderbolt', and early representations of Indra's *vajra* often depict it as a double-ended trident. The three points symbolise the Hindu trinity of Brahma, Vishnu and Shiva, and the three vibrational sounds – *A U M* – of the sacred syllable *Om*. As the main emblem of Shiva, the *trishula*'s three points represent his transcendence over the three *gunas* or qualities of nature: *rajas* – the dynamic or passionate quality of Brahma as creator; *sattva* – the wisdom or pure quality of Vishnu as preserver; and *tamas* – the inert or dark quality of Shiva as destroyer. Shiva's trident also symbolises his control over the three realms of heaven, earth, and underworld; his triumph over the three times of past, present, and future; and his form as the 'Lord of the Three Rivers' or 'triple braid' (Skt. *triveni*). *Triveni* refers to the sacred site of Prayaga (modern Allahabad), where the two rivers of the Ganges and Yamuna unite with the hidden underground river of Sarasvati. Esoterically this symbolises the 'third eye' point between the eyebrows, where the lunar and solar channels unite with the central channel. The shaft of the *trishula* represents the central channel of *sushumna*, by which the goddess Kundalini ascends to unite with her lord, Shiva, in the 'thousand-petalled lotus' (*sahasrara chakra padma*). As the median nerve, or as the axis of Mt Meru, which rises from the earth into the heavens, the shaft serves as a conduit between the devotees of Shiva and their lord. The iron *trishula* is found in every Shaivite shrine scattered throughout India, and is often adorned with the bangles of female devotees as a supplication for fertility, the birth of a son, or as a symbol of betrothal to Lord Shiva. The evolution of the Shaivite *khatvanga* and *trishula* into the Vajrayana *khatvanga* is decribed in Plates 115 and 116.

In early Indian Buddhism the trident formed one of the first aniconic representations of the Buddha image, occurring as the emblem of the 'crown of Brahma' on Buddha's footprints, and as a finial surmounting the crowning *dharmachakra* on the gateways of the great stupa of Sanchi. Here the symbolism essentially represents the Three Jewels (*triratna*) of Buddha, dharma, and sangha; or the 'three baskets' (*tripitaka*) containing the Buddha's collective discourses on ethics, meditation, and wisdom.

In Vajrayana Buddhism the Shaivite and Kapalika trident was adopted as a weapon, particularly in the hands of semi-wrathful *yidam* deities and wrathful protective deities with an affinity to Shiva. Such deities include Chakrasamvara, Vajrabhairava, and Mahakala. The dry skull of the *khatvanga*, and the yaktail pendant and flag of the spear, are both commonly incorporated into the form of the Buddhist trident to identify it as a *khatvanga*-trident, trident-spear, or trident-staff.

As a weapon the trident symbolises the destruction of the three poisons of ignorance, desire and aggression within the three realms; omniscience over the three realms and the three times; the union of the three 'divine bodies' (*kayas*), and the unified emptiness of body, speech, and mind; the teachings of the Buddhas of the three times; and the Three Jewels of Buddha, dharma, and sangha. The Tibetan term for the trident means 'three points' (Tib. *rtse gsum*), and is linked to the term meaning 'three roots or veins' (Tib. *rtsa gsum*). Here the three roots refers to the Mahayana trinity of Buddha, dharma, and sangha, and to the Vajrayana trinity of *guru*, *yidam*, and *dakini*. Esoterically the shaft represents the central channel; the flaming central prong represents enlightenment as the unified energies of the two subsidiary channels dissolving into the fire of the central channel; the dry white skull represents the full increase of the white *bodhichitta*; the red yaktail pendant the ascent of the red *bodhichitta*; and the flowing silk ribbon the union of relative and absolute *bodhichitta*. The *vajra*-flame crowning the central prong symbolises the wisdom-fire which completely immolates ignorance as the primordial poison. The hanging links which may descend from the two side prongs of the trident symbolise the breaking of the twelve links of dependent origination or karmic causation. The two side prongs uniting in the flaming central prong also symbolise the unity of method and wisdom; the abandonment of the two extremes of samsara and nirvana; and the ultimate union of absolute and relative truth.

Plate 126

This illustration depicts nineteen examples of the trident, showing its stylistic variations. The first drawing on the left shows a full-length trident, with a half-*vajra* at its base, an upper dry white skull, golden lotus pedestal, red yaktail pennant, and a flowing silk ribbon at the shaft's top. Its flaming blue-iron head is adorned with two small jewel pendants. Across to the right of this drawing are two simple trident heads, the first with a flaming central prong and the second with two leaf-shaped side prongs.

Across to the lower right of the first drawing is a trident-flag (Tib. *ru mtshan rtse gsum*), with an angular iron head surmounting a red yaktail pennant, and a long triangular pennon or ensign coiling below. The trident-flag is held by many protective deities, and the flag is usually coloured red with a green edging, and mounted upon a red sandalwood staff. One form of Trakshad Mahakala is described as holding a trident with a black flag and a hanging human head; this form of trident is illustrated on the left of Plate 124.

Plate 126: The trident

To the lower right of this trident-flag is a trident-banner (Tib. *rgyal mtshan rtse gsum*), which may adorn the roofs of protector temples (Tib. *mgon khang*). The cylindrical form of this banner is commonly fashioned of a bronze frame draped with black silk, and with a green, red, or black hanging silk ribbon or apron. Across to the right of this is an iron trident with a short tubular base, mounted upon a skull and yaktail. Above and to the left is a large skull-topped trident, with a flaming sword-shaped central prong and its two side prongs ascending like horns from within the crown of the skull.

The second full-length trident to the right of these drawings has a flaming wisdom sword as its central prong, from which emerge two stylised side prongs with leaf-shaped decorations. Three green and blue silk valances hang from a small golden lotus pedestal beneath the trident's head, and a tied green silk ribbon flows below. To the lower right and at the centre of the page is an ornate skull and yaktail trident, with a long conical base rising above the skull and supporting the flaming sword-shaped central prong. Three chain-links hang from each of the two side prongs, symbolising the six perfections.

The third full-length trident or trident-pike to the right, has a head formed from the combined weapons of an axe-head, a sword and an iron hook, and is similar to the pikes described in Plate 124. A long triangular flag is knotted around the trident's staff and billows upwards towards the right. Above this flag is the ornate head of a skull-marked trident, with intricate and delicate prongs. Two jewelled chain-links hang from each of the lower curves of the side prongs, and a tongue of flame coils around the slender waist of the central prong. In the upper right corner is another ornate trident-head, with leaf-shaped decorations on its side prongs.

Below the triangular flag are two small drawings of stylised trident-heads; the one on the left has five prongs symbolising the Five Buddha wisdoms as the transmutation of the five poisons of ignorance, desire, hatred, jealousy, and pride. To the right of this is a long trident with stylised prongs, and mounted above a skull and small yaktail pennant with a long billowing silk ribbon hanging below. To the upper right of this drawing is another skull-marked trident with single chain-links hanging from its side prongs.

In the lower right corner are three further drawings of trident-heads. The first drawing on the left depicts an intricate trident similar to the drawing in the upper right, and with a pair of hanging jewelled earrings symbolising renunciation. The second drawing depicts a sturdy iron trident with a pennant red yaktail. The third drawing in the lower right corner shows yet another variation of the many stylised methods of depicting the trident.

THE CLUB
(Skt. *danda, gada*; Tib. *dbyug to, dbyug pa, beng*)

The club or cudgel was man's earliest weapon. A tapering stone, a bog-preserved or petrified tree root, or a simple heavy branch could serve both as a tool for breaking or hammering, and as a hand-held weapon. In ancient Indian warfare the heavy club was a chosen weapon of the physically strong and robust – a tradition which still finds expression in the training techniques of Indian wrestlers, who use a pair of wooden clubs for strengthening exercises. Hanuman, the powerful monkey god who wields the *gada* or mace, is commonly the patron deity of Indian Vaishnavite wrestlers. Street-jugglers also wield the wooden clubs with great dexterity. Indian warfare employed four distinct methods of fighting with the club: *vikshepa*, or paired combat; *abhishepa*, or single-club combat; *parishepa*, or circling of the club amidst the throng of enemies; and *prakshepa*, or the throwing of the club. A large number of Hindu deities bear the heavy club or mace: Vishnu's mace was named Kaumodaki, Balarama's mace was named Saunanda, and Shiva's club was the *khatvanga*. The stone club of epic warfare was known as a *lakutha* or *lagudha*, the iron mace was known as a *sthuna*, and the heavy wooden club as a *danda, gada, bhusundhi, musala* or *mudgara*.

The staff or stick carried by sadhus and mendicants of the various Hindu sects is commonly known as a *danda* (staff) or *shakta* (stick). The Shaivite Kanphatas may bear a cloth-bound *danda* made of straw and known as a *sudarshan*, or a bamboo staff, or a metal trident, or a staff of *timur* wood. One sub-sect of the Shaivite Pashupatis are known as the Lakulishas or 'club-bearers'.

In the iconography of Vajrayana Buddhism the club, baton, cudgel, or mace is represented in a large variety of different forms. As a hand-held weapon it is most commonly depicted as a long tapering wooden staff, crowned by a half-*vajra* or flaming jewel. In its most complex symbolic form it appears as the *khatvanga* or 'tantric staff' of the Danda-kapalins or 'bearers of the staff and skull – as described in Plates 115 and 116 – where the basic form of the *khatva* or 'bed-leg' evolved as a club. The skull-club (see Plates 127 and 129), and the trident (see Plate 126), are derived as variations of the *khatvanga*.

Of the Tibetan terms for the club (Tib. *dbyug to, dbyug pa, be chon, gan di, gan ti, beng*) the most common is *yugpa* (Tib. *dbyug pa*), meaning stick, baton, cudgel or club. The thick wooden club (Tib. *gan ti*) that is held horizontally across the forearms by certain forms of Mahakala, derives from the wooden plank (*gandi*), which is struck with a mallet as a monastic gong. The majority of the clubs held by Buddhist deities are described as being fashioned of red sandalwood, and marked with a *vajra*, a trident, or a jewel. The notched baton or 'tally stick' of the wrathful goddess Palden Lhamo, is similarly fashioned of red sandalwood. Red sandalwood is perhaps the most sacred of Indian woods, and symbolises by its colour and fragrance the activity of subjugation. Certain deities, such as Hayagriva, bear a club fashioned from acacia or *khadira* wood; certain other deities are described as bearing a club made of Chinese briar (Tib. *shal ma li*); and many minor deities in the retinues of *dharmapalas* may brandish clubs made of iron, copper, silver, gold, crystal, coral, turquoise, lapis lazuli, bone, and Chinese oak. The skull-clubs, skeleton-clubs, and corpse-clubs carried by certain wrathful deities, such as Yama, Yamari, Yamantaka, Chitipati, Mahakala, and Ekajati, are commonly fashioned from human bone; mummified, fresh, or flayed corpses; or the skeletons and corpses of spirits such as *rakshasas*.

The club or mace is usually depicted as a hand-held weapon in the right or method hands of multiple-armed deities, such as Yamantaka, Yamari, or Kalachakra. As a weapon that breaks and pulverises, the club symbolises the pounding or annihilation of the veil of defilements created by karma. The club may also be held with both hands, as in the case of the triple manifestation of Mahakala as 'Three Excellent Brothers of Virtue' (Tib. mGon po legs ldan mched gsum). Here the club represents both the retribution exacted upon demons, enemies, and the breakers of tantric oaths, and the destruction of the pride of the gods and *asuras*.

Plates 127–129 depict various examples of tally sticks, batons, clubs, maces and skeletal-clubs.

Plate 127

This drawing shows various examples of tally sticks, clubs and skull-clubs. The first drawing on the upper left depicts the long red sandalwood 'tally stick' or 'scored magical stick' (Tib. *khram shing*), also known as a 'crossed stick of the *bdud* demons' (Tib. *bdud kyi khram bam*). The complexity ascribed to the notched stick is evident in its etymology. The Tibetan term '*khram*' has a variety of meanings, one of which refers to a speaker of falsehoods, an oath breaker, or a cunning person. It also refers to a magical diagram used in witchcraft or necromancy; to the crossed lines or marks scored in a piece of wood; and to notches. The term *khram shing* also refers to the wooden board onto which a criminal was chained for flogging. As a club the *khram shing* is defined as a wooden baton, carved with crossed squares containing mystical signs or seals that have the power to nullify curses and render witchcraft ineffectual. The term '*bam*' which appears in the expression *bdud kyi khram bam* or 'crossed stick of the *bdud* demons', also possesses a variety of meanings. Its literal meaning is 'gathered together as a series', which refers to the *khram bam* as a tally stick. But the term *bam* also means stale or decaying; the term *bam ril* refers to a fresh and undamaged human corpse; and the term *bam ro* refers to the constructed effigy of a slain enemy of Buddhism.

The red sandalwood baton forms one of the 'five magical weapons' of the goddess Palden Lhamo (Skt. Shri Devi), who is also known as Remati, and is either represented tucked into the girdle of serpents at her waist, or wielded in her right hand as a club. It is depicted as a tapering red sandalwood baton, often with a pyramidical top. The notched designs upon its shaft may be depicted as crossed or hatched designs in gold or dark red, or as mystical insignia composed of geometric or intersecting lines.

The notched tally stick appears in many cultures as a seal of agreement or pledged transaction made between two parties; just as a chiselled inscription, a knotted rope, or a hammered nail have evolved such figures of speech as 'written in stone', 'bound by oath', or bought and sold 'on the

nail'. Palden Lhamo's scored cross-stick records the tally of the punishment due to oath-breakers and the spirit enemies of the dharma; upon whom she casts spells of retribution, and counteracts the curses and witchcraft inflicted upon the faithful who are under her protection. As one of the five magical weapons of Palden Lhamo, the tally stick is also illustrated and described on Plate 134.

The second drawing from the left depicts the long sandalwood club (Tib. *tsan dan beng chen*) held by certain forms of Club Mahakala (Skt. Danda Mahakala; Tib. mGon po beng). This heavy sandalwood club has a triangular iron *phurba* blade at its base, surmounted by a knurled handle, a long hollow shaft, and a flaming jewel or triple gem at its top. The hollow sandalwood shaft of the club is described as a fortress (Tib. *dzong*) in which the entire army of the gods and *asuras* are engaged in battle, or in which their combined forces are prepared to be unleashed for war. Four half-open gates or wooden doorways are depicted along the shaft, and on very fine thangkas the small images of hordes of armoured gods and *asura* warriors may be visible behind the fortified panels of the doors. Held by its knurled handle in the right hand of Dandadhara Mahakala, this club is described as jewel-studded, with a mass of fire blazing from its top and a torrent of water gushing from its base. Its effectiveness as a 'weapon of mass destruction' is clearly revealed from its description.

The third drawing depicts a variation of Club Mahakala's sandalwood club, with flames emanating from its *phurba* blade, and three fortress gates upon its knurled and embellished gold shaft. A lotus-mounted flaming triple gem is at its top. Below the tip of its *phurba* blade and across to the left are two small drawings of the notched stick (Tib. *khram shing*) of Palden Lhamo.

The fourth drawing depicts a long *phurba*-tipped sandalwood club with a single flaming jewel at its top. The long shaft is divided into twelve sections which bear gateways or insignias shaped as the four elements, four activities or *karmas*, and the four cardinal continents surrounding Mt Meru. The circular gateways represent water and the activity of pacifying, the square gateways represent earth and the activity of enriching, the bow-shaped gateways represent air as magnetising or subduing, and the triangular gateways represent fire as destructive activity.

At the upper centre of the page is the conventional tapering *vajra*-marked club (Tib. *rdo rje dbyug*), which is wielded by a host of Vajrayana deities, including Palden Lhamo, Mahakala, and Hayagriva, and occurs as a hand-held implement of many multiple-armed deities. The shaft is usually fashioned of red sandalwood, with a large golden half-*vajra* at its top, and a smaller half-*vajra* or jewel at its base. The silk ribbon tied around its shaft may be specifically coloured according to the activity the deity performs, or the Buddha Family to which the deity belongs. Certain deities, such as Niladanda and Mahabala, carry a club with a full *vajra* at the top, whilst other deities may bear a *vishvavajra*-topped club. On the lower left side of this central club is a seven-doored tapering sandalwood club containing the armies of gods and *asuras*. On the lower right

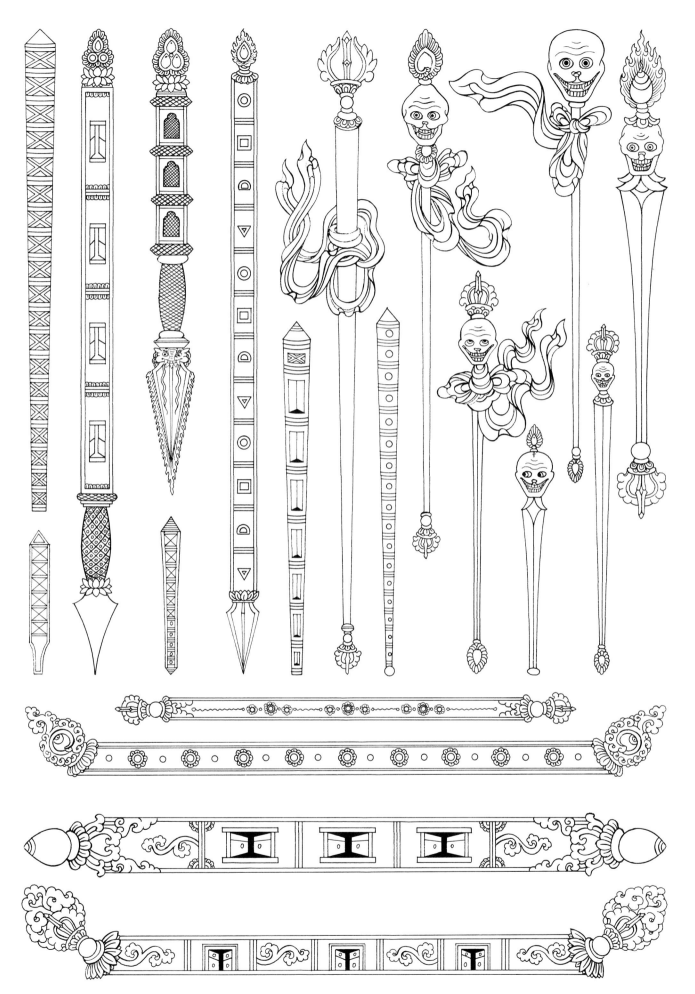

Plate 127: Tally-sticks, clubs, skull-topped clubs and transverse clubs

side is a tapering sandalwood club marked with circles and lines, and known as a 'pledge-stick' (Tib. *dam shing*), which bears the record of the tantric oaths made by practitioners.

Across the upper right side of the drawing are six examples of the skull-club (Skt. *kapala danda*; Tib. *thod dbyug*) which is wielded or held by many deities. The skull-club derives from the Kapalikas' skull-topped staff or *khatvanga*, and is usually crowned by a jewel or half-*vajra*. The slender tapering shaft of the skull-club is commonly fashioned of either red sandalwood or white bone, and is often sealed with a jewel or half-*vajra* at its base. A white or coloured silk ribbon may be tied around the upper part of the shaft. The skull-club is particularly an attribute of Yama Dharmaraja, and of the skeleton 'brother and sister of the charnel grounds' (Tib. Dur khrod bdag po lcam dral), known as Chitipati or Shmashana-adhipati. These two skeleton deities stand upon a white conch and cowrie shell respectively, the pointed and open forms of which symbolise the sexual organs of the brother and sister. The deity Red Yamantaka (Tib. gShin rje gshed dmar po), holds a club topped by a fresh yellow head, which like the skull-club symbolises the victory over the three realms and the realisation of the emptiness of phenomena. Skull-clubs and skeleton-clubs are also illustrated on Plate 129.

In the lower area of the drawing are four examples of the transverse wooden club held by Panjara Mahakala (Tib. Gur mgon po), and known as the 'magical wooden gong' (Tib. *'phrul gyi gan di*) or 'sorcerer's gong'. Panjara Mahakala, as the 'Lord of the Tent', is sometimes erroneously believed to be of Central Asian origin, due to his identification with the indigenous nomadic tents or yurts of Tibet and Mongolia. His form as 'the protector of the *vajra*-tent', however, derives from the Indian Buddhist *Vajra Panjara Tantra*. Panjara Mahakala is depicted in the form of a 'fleshy dwarf' (Tib. *mi'u thung gel ba*), who squats upon a corpse, bears a curved knife and skull-cup before his heart, and carries the long wooden 'magical gong' horizontally across his forearms. In the light of the highly sophisticated and innovative military tactics developed in Indian warfare, it is quite possible that this method of wielding the parallel club as a horizontal battering-beam was assigned to dwarfs. With his muscular body and short sturdy legs, the dwarf was a symbol of great strength, stability, and endurance, and was identified with the Indian *yaksha* (Tib. *gnod sbyin*) or 'dwarf-spirit'. In battle, the dwarf warrior may have undermined the stability of the enemy by swinging the beam-club back and forth, or by charging the legs of the enemy.

The 'wooden gong' (*gandi*) is a thick wooden plank which is struck with a mallet as a monastic gong. It usually measures around six feet in length, with a width of around twelve inches, and is commonly fashioned from white sandalwood or deodar. As a monastic gong the *gandi* was struck to summon the sangha to a religious discourse, and was employed during the lifetime of Shakyamuni Buddha, where its sound is described as 'terrifying the hosts of Mara'. With the later evolution of Vajrayana Buddhism the *gandi* became an attribute of Panjara Mahakala, who was the protector deity of the great monastic academy of Nalanda.

Panjara Mahakala's 'magical wooden gong' (Tib. *'phrul gyi gan di*), is commonly depicted as a red sandalwood beam, with gold ornamentation and ornate jewel or *vajra* bosses at either end. The first upper drawing of the *gandi* shows a horizontal red beam embellished with gold decorations and a half-*vajra* at each end. The second horizontal drawing depicts a larger example, ornamented with gold roundels and with jewels encased in golden *makara*-tail scrolls at either end. The third drawing depicts the *gandi* as a square-sectioned fortress, with three doorways enclosing the armies of the gods and *asuras*, elaborate gold decorations upon its shaft, and large jewels at either end. The bottom drawing depicts a similar *gandi*, with three half-open gateways and *makara*-scrolled *vajras* at each end.

Plate 128

This drawing illustrates various examples of the club, mace, pledge-stick, tally stick, forked stick, and plough. The first drawing on the upper left shows a variation of Club Mahakala's long red sandalwood club (Tib. *tsan dan beng chen*), as described in Plate 127. This flaming jewel-topped club has two fortress gateways on its upper shaft containing the massed armies of the gods above, and of the *asuras* below. Its long tapering sandalwood shaft is sealed by a half-*vajra* at its base. The 'Three Excellent Brothers of Virtue' (Tib. mGon po legs ldan mched gsum), comprising the identical trinity of Ajita, Bhagavan, and Narayana Mahakala, hold a similar club which is usually sealed with a jewel at its base.

The second and third drawings from the left depict two examples of the bladed Indian mace (Skt. *gada*, *musala*, or *parigha*). This heavy weapon has a large iron bulb at its top, from which radiate a circle of sharp iron blades or spikes that are capable of pulverising armour. The first mace is topped by a jewel, and has crested or inward curving blades. The second mace is topped by a *vajra*, and has radiating crescent-shaped blades.

The fourth, fifth, and sixth drawings depict examples of Mahakala's 'treasure club' (Tib. *beng gter ma*), with a flaming three or eight-faceted jewel at its top. The first of these three treasure clubs is sealed with a small *vajra*-spike at its base, and has seven fortress doorways ascending along its sandalwood shaft. The second drawing depicts a large square-sectioned sandalwood club that may typically be wielded by many deities besides Mahakala, and which may be crowned by a flaming jewel, a *vajra*, or a trident. The third drawing shows another example of the *phurba*-tipped sandalwood club held by Danda Mahakala (see Plate 127), but with a shaft that is not adorned with fortress gateways.

The seventh drawing depicts a sandalwood 'pledge-stick' (Tib. *dam shing*), which is marked with the seals of the tantric vows (Skt. *samaya*; Tib. *dam tshig*), or 'oath-bound words', of the Vajrayana practitioner. The breaking of these vows or commitments may cause serious obstacles to arise in the practitioner's path, and if broken must be reinstated. A practitioner of the *Vajrayogini Tantra*, for example, must never denigrate women.

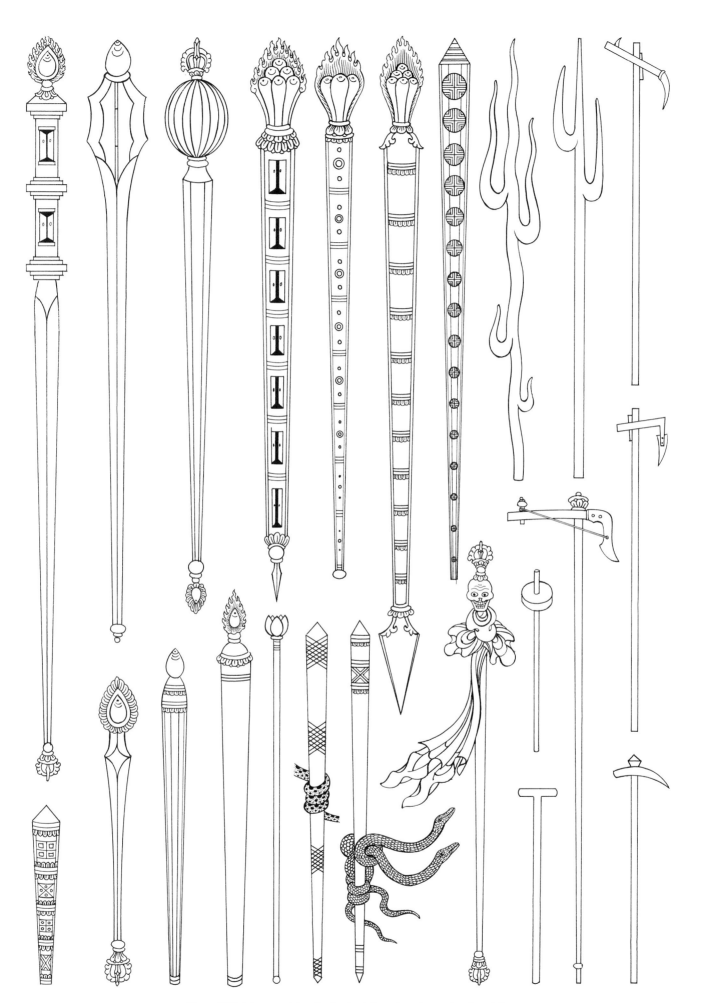

Plate 128: Maces, clubs, forked sticks, ploughs and tally-sticks

The eighth and ninth drawings from the left illustrate two examples of the forked stick (Tib. *ldem shing*). As a hand-held implement this weapon is more commonly found in the hands of Bonpo deities, or in examples of early Buddhist art, although its iconographic form is frequently painted in the complex array of weapons presented to the wrathful deities as an 'assembly of offerings' (Tib. *rgyan thogs*). The forked stick was probably a rudimentary weapon fashioned from a sharpened or fire-hardened hardwood branch, or perhaps also from the shaft-mounted antlers of a deer. As a weapon a three or five-pointed forked stick is most commonly illustrated. Nebesky-Wojkowitz mentions a three-pointed forked stick (Tib. *srid pa'i ldem shing*) as being held in the right hand of the earth-spirit (Tib. *sa bdag*), Khyim nang lha, the 'god of the interior of the house'. Gega Lama describes the forked stick as a wooden spear (Tib. *gsal shing*) made of dry, poisonous wood with sharp tips. The forked branch of a tree was also used by Tibetan disciplinary monks (Tib. *ldab ldob*) to control crowds at religious gatherings.

The tenth drawing in the upper right corner depicts a hand-held plough (Skt. *langala, hala*; Tib. *thong*), as the weapon which 'overturns the world beneath the earth'. The plough is held in one of the left or wisdom hands of the *yidam* deity Yamari, and when coupled with the sickle (Tib. *dgra zor*) – which is also held in one of Yamari's left hands – symbolises control over karma, as the activities of sowing and reaping. The pictorial activities of sowing and reaping are illustrated in the 'wheel of life' painting as symbols of the generation and fruition of karma as cause and effect. The plough or ploughshare (Tib. *thong gshol*) is also held as a left-hand implement by several of the wrathful Heruka deities of the Bardo Thodol cycle. Two other ploughs are depicted below and to the lower left of the upper plough, the second of which has a more complex iron blade (Tib. *thong lcags*), the angle of which may be adjusted by a pegged rope.

In the bottom right corner is a pickaxe (Tib. *sta gri*), which also symbolises the overturning of the world beneath the earth. Across to the left of this is a T-shaped wooden crutch, which is used as a support for the chin or arms by yogins practicing prolonged seated meditation. In Sanskrit this crutch is known as an 'immovable staff' (*achala danda*), and in Tibetan as a 'meditation stick' (Tib. *sgom shing*). Certain mahasiddhas or yogins may be depicted with this meditational crutch. The 'meditation belt' (Tib. *sgom thag*) – which is worn by yogins (Tib. *rnal 'byor pa*) such as Milarepa – serves a similar function to the meditation stick by holding the body in an immovable yoga posture. The meditation belt is commonly depicted as a sash, and usually worn across the right shoulder in the manner of a *brahmin*'s sacred thread, or it may be bound around the shins when the yogin sits with his knees raised. The small drawing above the meditation stick depicts an obscure weapon made from a millstone (Tib. *lag 'khor*) on a wooden axle-pole. This weapon is sometimes depicted in the 'conquest of Mara' painting (see Plate 131).

The first drawing in the lower left corner depicts a short 'scored magic stick' (Tib. *khram shing*), which may be represented tucked into the serpent-belt of deities such as Yama

and Palden Lhamo, and is described in Plate 127. To the right of this are three examples of the jewel-club (Skt. *ratna danda*; Tib. *nor bu be con*), held by many deities – and particularly those associated with wealth such as Jambhala and Vaishravana. The crowning jewel may sometimes be specifically identified as the wish-fulfilling gem.

The fifth drawing from the bottom left depicts a lotus-topped club representing the Padma Buddha Family. The implements of each of the Five Buddha Families may bear their specific 'seal' as an emblem.

The sixth and seventh drawings depict two further examples of Palden Lhamo's scored stick, which are both shown with a part of the serpent-girdle worn as a waist-belt by this goddess. The eighth and last drawing depicts another example of the *vajra*-sealed skull-club, as described in Plate 127.

Plate 129

This drawing illustrates examples of the skeleton-club, corpse-club, and the impaled corpse of a criminal. Across the top row are seven examples of the skeleton-club (Tib. *keng rus dbyug*), which iconographically often appears as a more wrathful form of the skull-club held in the right hand of deities such as Yama, Yamantaka, or Chitipati. The skull-club held by Yama, as the 'Lord of the Dead' (Tib. gShin rje), is sometimes described as having a shaft composed of thirteen spinal vertebrae, which brings to mind the thirteen umbrella-wheels of the stupa's axle-pole, as the 'spine' of Mt Meru.

The seven drawings of the skeleton club are depicted without arms: the shoulder-bones, rib-cage, and pelvic-bones form the central bulb of the club; the parallel leg-bones or extended spinal column form the lower handle. The 'grinning' or 'haughty skull' (Tib. *gying ba thod*) at the top may be crowned by a gold-encased jewel or a half-*vajra*. The rib-cage of the human skeleton consists of twelve pairs of ribs, which may symbolise the karmic release from the twelve links of dependent origination (see page 240). The skull-club or skeleton-club essentially symbolises the destruction or 'death' of karma, and the ultimate emptiness of all phenomena. In the hands of wrathful deities such as Yama, this weapon terrifies all demons, and subjugates all of the vicious spirits of the three realms. In its most wrathful form as a weapon, the dry skull may be described as emanating flames from its mouth, smoke from its nostrils, and trickles of blood from its eye sockets.

The first and third drawings from the left of the top row depict the skeleton-club without a crowning ornament; the second and sixth drawings show a jewel-seal above the skull's crown; and the fourth, fifth, and seventh drawings depict a half-*vajra* seal – which is typical of the club wielded by Yama. The sixth drawing depicts a flayed human skin adorning the club as a scarf, symbolising both the death of desire and the insubstantiality of outer and inner phenomena.

On the left of the centre row is a skull mounted upon a staff of seven vertebrae, with a knotted human skin and scalp

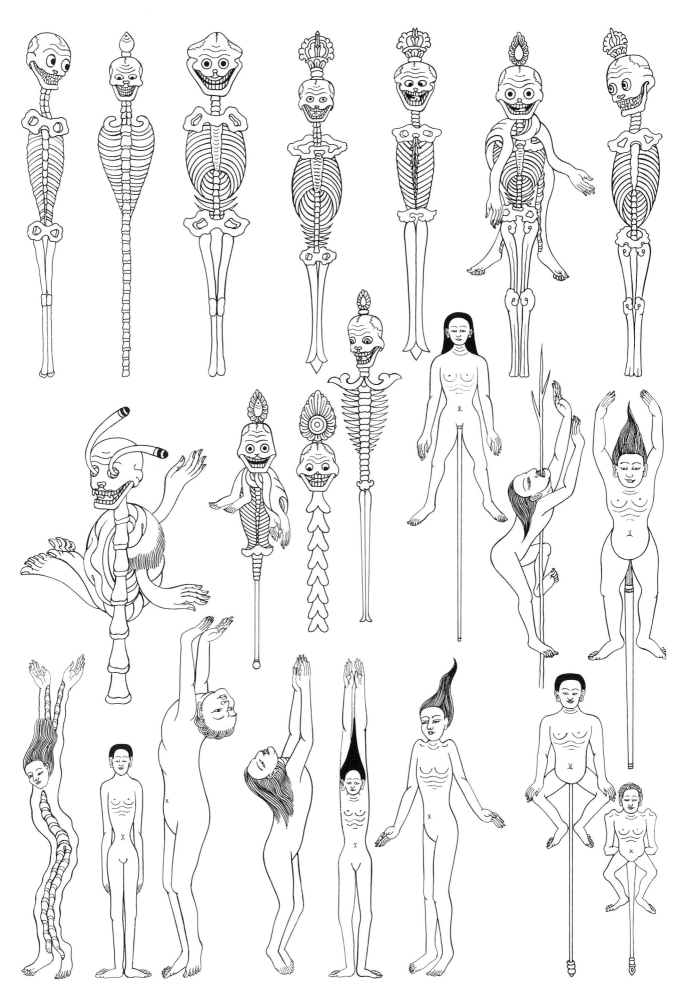

Plate 129: Skeletons and skeleton-clubs, corpses and corpse-clubs

behind, and with its eyes pulled out of their sockets. The second drawing shows a jewel-topped skeleton-club adorned with a human skin, and its lower shaft formed from a single bone handle. The third drawing shows a jewel-topped skull-club with a shaft made of eight stylised vertebrae. The fourth drawing depicts an elegant jewel-topped skeleton-club, with leaf-shaped shoulder blades, twenty-four spiked ribs, sixteen spinal vertebrae, and a lower handle formed from the joined leg-bones of the skeleton.

The highly stylised representation of skeletons in Tibetan art often reveals the creative genius of an individual artist's expression and innovation. This is especially apparent in certain black-background thangkas (Tib. *nag thang*) depicting the assemblies of offerings (Tib. *rgyan tshogs*) to wrathful deities, where gracefully dancing skeletons may bear the attributes of a particular deity; or in charnel-ground scenes, where a retinue of skeleton-spirits delight in the necromantic activities of dismembering, disembowelling, and devouring human corpses; or in the depictions of the skeleton mandala palaces of wrathful deities, such as Palden Lhamo, Chitipati, and Yama. These skeleton palaces are constructed of human skeletons in various stylised and exaggerated postures forming the walls, pillars, and arches. Rows of skulls form the horizontal beams; rib-cages or thighbones form the tiled roofs; and crossed thighbones, shin-bones and shoulder blades form the decorative friezes. The delicate embellishments of the palace – projecting eaves, water spouts, crowning roof finials, and banners – are constructed of skulls, small skeletal bones, and gracefully curving limb, foot, and hand bones. These thangkas, which date from the late seventeenth century, represent some of the most refined imagery found within the pictorial history of Vajrayana art. The more macabre – and fashionable – aspects of Western art, which probably find their greatest expression in the 'charnel ground imagery' of the modern tattoo parlour, are very stiff and crude in comparison to the subliminal grace of the skeletal forms expressed in Tibetan art.

On the right of the central row and in the lower right corner are five drawings of corpses impaled upon stakes. The 'corpse-club' (Tib. *zhing dbyug, ro dbyug*), is a hand-held implement of certain wrathful deities, such as Yamantaka, who holds it in one of his left hands. It is also borne as a weapon by many of the spirits that form the retinues of major wrathful deities. In this form the corpse-club consists of the body of a criminal, impaled upon a wooden stake (Tib. *gsal shing*) through his anus. This horrific form of execution was probably a common method of retribution after a war, where the victors would humiliate the vanquished. Western parallels can be found in the activities of figures such as 'Vlad the Impaler'. The impaled corpse was also known as a *dhvaja*, the term for a victory banner erected upon an Indian battlefield. In Yamantaka's possession this implement symbolises the intuitive realisation that all phenomena are empty or deprived of substance. On an inner level the stake symbolises the central channel, which arises in the 'secret place', and ascends to the crown of the head.

The first drawing of the impaled corpse, on the left of

the middle row, shows a woman with her legs apart and the stake implanted in her vagina. The second drawing depicts a triple-forked poisonous stake impaled through the mouth of a criminal and exiting through his heart. The third drawing depicts a male criminal, with his arms upright and hair standing on end in terror as the stake is impaled through his anus. The last two drawings in the lower right corner depict male corpses with their legs open and the stake again impaled through the anus. The smaller drawing in the right corner depicts a criminal bound in 'corpse posture' (Skt. *shavasana*; Tib. *ro 'dug stangs*) as a sacrificial victim (Skt. *bali*; Tib. *nya bo, ling ga*), with his arms bound behind his back.

On the left of the bottom row are six drawings of the dead human body as a 'corpse-club' (Tib. *zhing dbyug*), which is held by deities such as Ekajati, and Remati as the 'plague goddess'. Wielding the corpse-club in their right hands, these goddesses destroy the lives of all enemies and demons harmful to the Buddhist teachings. Their corpse-clubs also symbolise their control over various classes of spirits, such as the disease-causing demons (Tib. *ma mo*).

The first drawing on the left depicts a flayed human skin which is wielded as a club. The second drawing depicts a hard corpse-club made from a mummified human body; this club may be wielded by the feet or the neck. The third drawing shows a fresh male corpse. The fourth drawing depicts a corpse-club fashioned from the body of a seven or eight-year-old child, born from the incestuous union of a father and daughter, or a mother and son. Such corpses were believed to possess magical qualities in the left-hand tantric tradition. The fifth corpse is of a mummified human body, which may be wielded as a club, or may form one of the beams or pillars in the mandala palaces of wrathful deities. The sixth and final drawing depicts another fresh human corpse.

THE SNARE, NOOSE OR LASSO
(Skt. *pasha*; Tib. *zhags pa*)

The rope noose or snare is a hand-held implement or weapon of a large number of Vajrayana deities. It is usually held in the left 'wisdom' hand, and is frequently paired with the *ankusha* or iron hook, which is held in the right 'method' hand. This pairing is shown in Plate 60, where the monk holds the lasso in his left hand symbolising mindfulness or clear recollection, and the hooked elephant goad in his right hand symbolising mental alertness or clear understanding (see also Plate 132).

As a weapon the snare or noose represents the activity of catching or binding. In its more peaceful aspect it represents the 'binding' of wisdom or true awareness into the minds of sentient beings, or the binding of the highest wisdom into the mind of the tantric practitioner. In its more wrathful aspect it is a snare to bind and destroy all harmful spirits or demonic enemies of the teachings. The rope snare is invariably adorned with an iron ring at one end and an iron hook at the other; its more benign symbolism represents the pulling or hooking of all beings towards liberation, and its more wrathful symbolism the snaring of the 'life-veins' (Tib. *srog rtsa*) or vital energies of hindering demons.

The *vajra*-snare or noose – which may be sealed at its ends by a hook and *vajra*, or a hook and ring – is commonly fashioned of twisted twine and painted in the green colour of hemp rope. Certain deities may, however, bear a rope of a specific colour. Hayagriva, for example, may wield a golden noose, whilst in certain forms Mahakala brandishes the black noose of the *bdud* demons (Tib. *bdud zhags pa nag po*), or the red noose of the *btsan* demons (Tib. *btsan zhags pa dmar po*). The wrathful aspect of the noose is usually emphasised by the hand of the deity making the threatening *tarjani* gesture (Tib. *sdigs mdzub*), with the forefinger raised in menace and the noose coiled around the finger.

In its more benign aspect the rope may be coloured white as the 'noose of the gods' (Tib. *lha'i zhags pa dkar po*). The noose may also be described as a poisonous black serpent, as the great serpent Vasuki, as a noose of fire, wind, lightning or pestilence, as a noose of flowers, lotuses or *utpala* root, or as a noose of intestines, leather or woven corpse-hair. The flower noose of the goddess Kurukulla is illustrated in Plate 122.

Metaphorically the noose may be used for 'snaring' the ego, symbolising discipline; for 'binding' the ego, symbolising meditation; and for 'hanging' or strangling the ego, symbolising wisdom.

THE IRON CHAIN
(Skt. *shrinkhala*; Tib. *lcags sgrog*)

The iron or *vajra*-chain is a hand-held attribute of only a few major Vajrayana deities, although it may appear within the hands of the various classes of spirits who form the retinues of protective deities. As a weapon of subjugation or imprisonment the *vajra*-shackles are held in one of the left wisdom hands of Kalachakra and his protector Vajravega. They appear as an iron chain adorned with a *vajra*-hook and ring. Kalachakra also holds the rope noose in one of his other left hands as a separate implement: here the iron chain represents the sun, and the rope noose the attribute of form. In Kalachakra's astronomical symbolism, the sun – with its twelve zodiacal houses and interlocking 'wind-wheels', created from the equinoctial orbit of the sun in each of the twelve months of the year (see page 106–107) – may represent the twelve links in the chain of dependent origination (see page 240). This symbolic interpretation is revealed in the iconography of Palden Lhamo, who wears the broken black iron shackles around her ankles, signifying that she has broken the karmic fetters of the twelve links of dependent origination, and abandoned the extremes of samsara and nirvana in her absolute and unconditioned freedom.

In rituals of subjugation and destructive activity the iron shackles bind the arms and ankles of the imprisoned or captive effigy (Tib. *ling ga*) of the subjugated spirit or demon. Although eight classes of spirits are commonly listed in the Tibetan Buddhist tradition (see page 284), and nine classes

are listed in the Bonpo tradition, there are many subsidiary classes of spirits which are not included in these listings; these include local spirits of mountains, lakes, earth, sky and the underworld, and the various hybrid spirits drawn from foreign cultures. Nebesky-Wojkowitz's *Oracles and Demons of Tibet* reveals the incredible complexity of these spirit realms. Nebesky-Wojkowitz was killed in an automobile accident shortly after completing this monumental work in 1956, and some accredit his untimely death to the sectarian retribution of one of the wrathful protective deities described in his text.

In rituals of subjugation the iconographical images of the four attributes of an iron hook, a rope noose, an iron chain, and a ritual bell or *ghanta*, are often represented. These four attributes are held by the four guardian goddesses of the gateways of Vaishravana's mandala, in his form as 'Vaishravana with a red spear and blue horse' (Tib. rNam sras mdung dmar rta sngon can).

The iron chain is also an attribute of 'Avalokiteshvara who protects from the eight fears', where his chain represents protection from the fear of captivity or imprisonment. Tara, who similarly protects from the eight great fears – of lions (pride), elephants (ignorance), fire (anger), serpents (jealousy), robbers (false views), captivity (greed), shipwrecks (attachment), and demons (doubt) – may also be depicted in her form as 'Tara who releases from captivity', releasing beings from the chains of bondage. The goddess Dombhini who accompanies the manifestation of 'Four-faced Mahakala with the cruel face', also bears the attributes of a rope snare and a small tethering-chain (Tib. *lu gu rgyud*).

Although only a few major Vajrayana deities bear the iron chain as a ritual implement, it is nevertheless prominently represented as a weapon of subjugation amongst the array of weapons contained in protector chapels. It is also commonly depicted upon paintings of the assembly of offerings (Tib. *rgyan tshogs*) to wrathful deities, particularly in those dedicated to Palden Lhamo and Yama, or those displaying the wrathful weapons of subjugation and destructive activity – which sometimes combine the attributes of Palden Lhamo and Yama.

An iron chain is also held in the right hand of the Tibetan siddha Thangton Gyalpo (1385–1464), who was also known as the 'iron bridge builder' (Tib. *lcags zam pa*). Thangtong Gyalpo was one of Tibet's great 'renaissance men': as a scholar he developed his own doctrinal system, as a poet he introduced the Tibetan opera, as an architect he established the great stupa of Riwoche which almost rivals the Gyantse Kumbum in its architectural splendour, and as a bridge-builder he established many iron suspension bridges, some of which still exist in Bhutan and Tibet. His attribute of an iron chain marks this aspect of his multifaceted versatility.

Plate 130

This drawing shows examples of the various forms of snares and iron chains. In the upper left corner is a rope or leather snare, folded within a sheath of rhinoceros hide (Tib. *bse ko*), the tough armoured plates of the Indian rhinoceros being the most appropriate material for defensive armour such as the shield, sheath, and cuirass. The ends of this lasso or snare are sealed with an iron hook and a small curved knife. To the lower right of the leather snare is a long rope snare, sealed with an iron hook and ring; and to the right of this a shorter looped rope snare, with an iron hook at its extremity and its ring threaded as a noose.

The next drawing to the right shows a captive spirit being snared and pulled along by a protective deity, such as Tsiu Marpo (Tib. Tsi'u dmar po). The deity's left hand makes the threatening *tarjani* gesture, with the index finger raised and the thumb extended. The rope snare is coiled twice around the lower phalanx of the deity's index finger, as described in Tsiu Marpo's *sadhana*. Such precise iconographical details are often given in the descriptions of specific deities; White Achala, for example, is described as wielding a noose which twists three times around his raised index finger. The upper end of the snare depicted is sealed with a small half-*vajra*, and its lower hook-end is knotted around the throat and hands of the bound spirit. To the right of this is another drawing of a captive spirit which has been snared around the neck, with the parallel ropes of the snare extending upwards. This spirit has been manacled in sacrificial posture, with its ankles and arms shackled by an iron chain behind its back.

Above this spirit is a long rope snare that has been looped twice and coiled around its centre like a noose. The ends of this snare are marked by a *vajra* and an iron hook. Above this is a drawing of a large hook in an ornate design. To the right of this hook is a long coiled rope snare, sealed with an iron ring and a hooked knife. In the upper right corner are details of a ring and hook that are mounted upon lotus bases.

To the left of the page's centre is a left hand making the *tarjani* gesture and trailing a rope snare adorned with a ring and a hooked, iron blade. The snare in this illustration is not coiled around the raised index finger, as described above. To the left of this hand is a detailed drawing of a snare's iron ring.

Descending from the central left edge of the page are three drawings of the red *utpala* flower noose held by the goddess Kurukulla, whose flower attributes are illustrated and described in Plate 122. The first of these three drawings shows a long noose made entirely of red *utpala* blossoms, which are threaded upon a string like a flower garland. The ring of this noose is formed from small red *utpala* flowers, and the hook from curling leaves. The second drawing shows a noose of red *utpalas* and leaves, threaded upon a long stalk with a flower ring and curved-leaf hook. The third drawing on the lower left shows the two noose ends as *utpala* stalks, leaves, and flowers, and with both the ring and hook fashioned from leaves. Below this drawing is the end of a noose formed from interlocking hooks of fire (Tib. *me zhags*); and below again, the end of a noose of lightning (Tib. *glog zhags*).

Below and to the right are three drawings of serpent-nooses (Tib. *sbrul zhags*). The serpent-noose is invariably depicted in the form of a coiling green or black snake, and is often brandished from a deity's left hand in *tarjani* or threatening gesture. The first two upper drawings of coiled serpent-nooses are held by deities such as Rahula, Garuda, Palden Lhamo, and Virupaksha – the great guardian king of the west. Rahula usually holds a poisonous green snake in his left hand, which is held in *tarjani* gesture. Rahula's serpent-noose is described as having the head of a *makara* and binding the body of an enemy, symbolising the binding of the five 'enemies' or poisons of ignorance, desire, hatred, pride and jealousy. In pictorial representations of Rahula, however, neither the *makara* head, nor the enemy, is usually depicted, and his serpent-noose is commonly illustrated as a coiled green snake with the conventional 'ox-shaped head' of a python. Palden Lhamo, in her four-armed form as the 'Self-arisen Queen' (Tib. Rang 'byung rgyal mo), is described as wielding a black serpent-noose that trails for a length of 990 fathoms, and binds all enemies and vow-breakers; this symbolises the extent of her control over beings afflicted with hatred and malevolence. The third drawing of a long snake at the bottom of the page depicts the great serpent Vasuki (see pages 71 and 109), which is held by the twelve-armed form of Vajragaruda Samvara (Tib. bDe mchog rdo rje mkha' lding). Below this drawing are two further details of the iron ring and hook.

Above Vasuki's tail is a coiling noose of intestines (Tib. *rgyu ma zhags*), which is held as a left-hand attribute of a six-armed form of Red Hayagriva. The intestine-noose appears as a coiled length of human entrails without a hook or ring. It is identical in form to the entrails held in one of Yamantaka's left hands, symbolising his realisation of the empiness of inherent existence within all phenomena.

Above the entrails is a noose formed from the root of the red *utpala* flower (Tib. *ut pa la zhags dmar*), such as is held in the left hands of the goddesses Kurukulla and Red Tara. Although Kurukulla's *utpala*-noose is described as a root, it is usually represented as a noose of flowers. Red Tara holds the stem of a red *utpala* at the level of her heart, which blossoms at the level of her left ear, whilst its root forms a small noose within the fingers of her left hand (see Plate 122). Above the bifurcated *utpala* root are four details of the snare's hook and ring, with a *vajra*, two hooks, and a ring depicted from left to right.

Above these are several drawings of the iron chain of subjugation. The large iron chain at the top is sealed with a *vajra* and hook at its right and left ends. The smaller *vajra*-chain within and below, is sealed with *vajras* at both ends. Within this chain is drawn a snare formed from the body segments of a black iron scorpion (Tib. *lcags sdig pa zhags nag po*), with the lower half of its body and sting forming the hook, and the upper half of its body and pincers forming the ring. Across on the lower right of the page are two more drawings of iron chain sections; the upper with eliptical links, and the lower with circular links depicted in an alternating plan and elevation sequence. The upper drawing is typical of the iron chain held in the right hand of the iron bridge builder Thangtong Gyalpo.

Plate 130: Snares and iron chains

THE SHIELD (Skt. *khetaka*; Tib. *phub*)

The sword and shield are commonly paired as weapons of attack and defence: the penetrating sword is held in the right male or method hand, and the defensive shield in the left female or wisdom hand.

In Tibetan art the iron shield is represented in a small circular form and is usually decorated with lotus-petal designs, or as an eight-spoked wheel, perhaps emphasising the wisdom aspect of the shield. Concentric radial rings may also be depicted behind the eight spokes of its hub, giving it the appearance of the rattan shield which is still commonly used by the riot-police of India and South East Asia. The Indian warrior's shield was usually fashioned from rhinoceros hide that was riveted onto a circular iron frame, and often adorned with four central iron or bronze bosses.

Kalachakra and his protector Vajravega both hold the sword and shield in their paired second right and left hands, where the sword represents the element of wind and the shield the torso of the body. The shield basically symbolises both protection and the conquering of one's enemies. Yamantaka's shield represents the Buddha's triumph over the attack of Mara, victory over his enemies, and his protection towards all sentient beings.

THE DISCUS (Skt. *chakra*; Tib. *'khor lo, be rdo*)

The deployment of the hurled iron discus or *chakra* as an ancient Indian weapon dates back to the Rig Veda, where it is first mentioned as a weapon of Vishnu. Vishnu's discus was named Sudarshana, and is described as a revolving iron disc with sharp edges which could cut through anything it hit. Krishna, as the eighth of Vishnu's incarnations, inherited Vishnu's Sudarshana *chakra* from the fire god Agni, and in Krishna's hands it was known as Vajranabha, meaning 'the indestructible destroyer'.

In sculptural form Vishnu's *chakra* is commonly represented as a six or eight-spoked wheel, often with four tongues of flame emanating to the cardinal directions. In pictorial representations it is more commonly represented as a flaming or radiant ring of light – known as a *brahmachakra* – which encircles the upraised first finger of many multiple-armed Hindu deities. In this form it appears as a quoit, or a flattened ring of sharp-edged iron which is hurled in the manner of a modern frisbee or boomerang. The game of quoits, wherein a sharp iron ring is skilfully thrown to encircle a metal peg, probably originated from the discus in this form. The Greek discus, still used in the Olympic games, was originally a heavy disc of sharp iron which was thrown as a weapon.

The six-pointed *chakra*, formed by two intersecting triangles, is one of the prime symbols of Hindu tantra. It represents the union of the goddess as the downwards-pointing female pubic triangle, with the upward-pointing male triangle of the god, formed by the testicles and erect penis. In Hindu tantra the *yantra* formed from the intersection of these triangles is also known as a *chakra*, the most famous being the *shrichakra* of the goddess Tripura Sundari or Shri. The

shriyantra is composed of five downward-pointing Shakti triangles and four upward-pointing Shiva triangles, creating a perfect pattern of forty-three interlocking triangles (see illustration on page 136).

The eight-pointed *chakra* was absorbed into Buddhism as the *dharmachakra* – the absolute emblem of *ahimsa* or non-violence – where its eight spokes symbolise the proclamation of the Buddha's sovereignty throughout the eight directions, and his teachings upon the Noble Eightfold Path. The *dharmachakra* combines the elements of the ring of the discus or quoit, with the eight *vajra*-spokes of the *chakra* as a weapon. Even as a wrathful weapon, held by such deities as Yamantaka, the eight-sided fire-*chakra* peacefully symbolises the turning of the 'wheel of dharma' and the setting in motion of the Noble Eightfold Path. The *dharmachakra* appears as a divine mark on Buddha's palms and soles, and as an emblem of the *chakravartin*. In Hinduism this symbol corresponds to the Vaishnavite ideal of the *mahapurusha* or 'great man', who is said to be born with the marks of Vishnu's Sudarshana *chakra* on his palms and soles (see Plate 76 and page 160).

The *chakra* or wrathful-wheel (Tib. *drag po'i 'khor lo*) is also used as a symbolic weapon or device (*yantra*) to subjugate, imprison or destroy malevolent demons. The illustrated manuscript of *The Secret Visions of the Fifth Dalai Lama* depicts some extremely fine examples of these *chakras*, which imprison the effigies (Tib. *ling ga*) of hindering spirits with iron shackles. When a spirit is successfully 'captured' in a triangular receptacle or 'iron prison', a *chakra* is symbolically used to seal the prison gate and subdue or destroy the spirit. In certain rituals of spirit subjugation an open triangular box, decorated with ritual weapons and insignia, is buried in the ground. The spirit is then enticed with specific offerings to enter the box, which is then sealed with an iron *chakra* or a bolt of lightning which is conjured forth from the sky.

As a six or eight-pointed iron weapon the Buddhist *chakra* has in recent years become well known as the *shurokan* or 'throwing-star' of Hong Kong's 'Kung Fu' movie spectaculars. Until recently these small weapons were available from martial-art shops, but as they had a nasty habit of falling into the wrong hands and lodging into the skulls or cheekbones of opposing football supporters, they were subsequently withdrawn from sale as lethal weapons.

Plate 131

This illustration shows examples of the shield, the *chakra*, and several of the various weapons that are depicted in the Tibetan 'conquest of Mara' painting.

Across the top row are four examples of the circular iron shield. The first drawing shows Kalachakra's shield, which appears here as an eight-spoked wheel fashioned from concentric rings, and with an inner handle adorned with a silk ribbon. Kalachakra's shield in this form was depicted in both the large appliqué and painted thangkas displayed in the recent Kalachakra initiations given by His Holiness the Dalai Lama, but was deemed to be iconographically incorrect as the protective shield faced inwards rather than outwards.

Plate 131: The shield, discus or *chakra*, and other circular weapons

The second drawing shows the front view of a concentric-ringed shield as an eight-spoked wheel, with a fur edge and a silk ribbon behind. The third drawing shows a tigerskin shield with a golden central hub and outer ring. The fourth drawing shows a shield with a clockwise-turning 'joy wheel' (Tib. *dga' 'khyil*) at its central hub, and with a twelve-petalled lotus design surrounding it. Shields and armour designs are also illustrated on Plate 161.

On the left of the second row is a drawing in Hindu style of Vishnu's discus radiating as a circular metal ring positioned above the raised index finger of the deity. The second drawing shows the Indian *chakra* as a circular disc of iron, with a raised central hub and many sharp points around its circumference like a circular saw. The third drawing depicts a Buddhist eight-pointed *chakra*, geometrically formed from the intersection of two squares, with an open circular centre and small open circles where the edges of the blades meet. This form of *chakra* is drawn as a 'wrathful wheel' (Tib. *drag po'i 'khor lo*), and used to imprison the effigies of malignant spirits. The fourth drawing shows the iron *chakra* as a star-shaped weapon with eight triangular points. The fifth drawing on the right shows another eight-pointed *chakra*, with projecting triangular blades and an open centre.

Below in the third row are three small drawings of the open-centred *chakra* in the form of the Chinese or Japanese *shurokan* or 'throwing-star'. The first appears as an eight-bladed *chakra* formed from two intersecting squares, and the second and third as six-bladed *chakras*, formed as *yantras* from the geometrical intersection of two equilateral triangles.

The fourth row depicts four variations of the *chakra* as a 'wheel of sharp weapons'. The first drawing on the left is of a *chakra* fashioned from eight sword-blades with sharpened triangular points. The second drawing shows another eight-sided *chakra* with sharpened edges. The third depicts eight sword-blades emanating from eight triangular points, and is known as a 'wheel of swords' (Tib. *ral gri'i mtshon 'khor*). The fourth drawing on the right shows a wrathful eight-bladed *vajra-chakra* (Tib. *rdo rje 'khor lo*), with eight sharp *vajra* points.

Across the fifth row are five drawings of the *chakra* mounted upon a staff as a hand-held weapon. The first drawing shows an eight-pointed iron *chakra* mounted upon a spear or *shula*, with a sword-tip, a skull, and a bloodstained yaktail pennant. The second drawing depicts an eight-bladed *chakra* impaled upon a lance with a sword-tip. The third drawing shows a wheel of eight sharp swords mounted upon a jewel-topped staff. The fourth drawing shows a wheel of eight swords surmounted by a *vajra*. A flat wheel of either five or six swords, surmounted by an upright central sword, is visualised in the generation of wisdom deities, such as Manjushri or Yamantaka, who arise from the syllable *Dhih*. The fifth drawing on the right shows a wheel of eight flaming wisdom-swords radiating from a jewel-topped staff.

In the lower area of the drawing are several illustrations from the 'conquest of Mara' painting, which depicts Shakyamuni Buddha seated in meditation beneath the bodhi tree and encircled by the armies of Mara, who assail him with a variety of weapons. As each weapon or missile pen-etrates the serenity of Buddha's aura, it miraculously transforms into a flower through the power and resolve of the Buddha's wisdom and compassion.

The drawing in the lower left corner depicts a fire-wheel machine, with thirteen rotating blades that are driven by a pulley from the chassis of its carriage. As the blades rotate they draw up burning tar from a resevoir on the carriage, which is mounted upon an axle with *dharmachakra* wheels. Mt Meru and its surrounding universe is illustrated at the bottom centre of the page, and this disc of the entire universe is hurled as a weapon towards the Buddha by one of Mara's demons. Above Mt Meru is a drawing of a metal tray of boiling oil, which another demon pours down upon the meditating Buddha. The pouring of boiling oil, burning coal, or molten lead was used extensively as a defensive tactic in Indian warfare, as a visit to the fourteenth-century fortified hill fortress of Daulatabad in Maharashtra will reveal. Here the most ingenious configuration of defensive walls and juxtaposed gates eventually lead into a hill citadel, which may only be approached through a winding tunnel carved into the hillside. At strategic turns in this lightless and ascending tunnel are apertures where boiling or burning liquids could be poured down upon invaders. In spite of the most elaborate defensive devices – which reveal the explicit genius of Indian warfare – Daulatabad was eventually conquered by the bloodless Indian technique of 'baksheesh', through bribing the guards at its doorways.

The drawing in the lower right corner shows a flaming thirteen-bladed *chakra*, with an eight-spoked wheel at its centre and mounted upon a *vajra*-handle. The small drawing in the corner shows a rimless eight-spoked *dharmachakra* as a hand-held weapon.

THE AXE (Skt. *parashu*; Tib. *dgra sta, sta re*)

The function of the axe or hatchet is twofold: it may be used as a tool for cutting timber, or as a weapon of war. The Tibetan term (Tib. *dgra sta*) means 'enemy axe' or battleaxe, and symbolises the severing of all negative notions from the mind; it cuts through birth and death, root and trunk.

In ancient Indian warfare the battleaxe (Skt. *parashu, parashvada*) formed one of the main weapons of assault. Its heavy semi-circular blade was fashioned from cast iron and honed to a sharp cutting edge, capable of decapitating the head of an enemy. Its hardwood shaft – symbolically hewn by its blade – was joined to the axe-head through an aperture in the style of a woodcutter's axe, and probably secured by a wooden or iron wedge hammered into a split at the shaft's top.

The Tibetan representation of the battleaxe reveals it as a far more docile weapon than its Indian prototype. The sickle-shaped blade of the Tibetan axe is small and delicate, coloured in the dark blue tone of iron, and embellished with a leaf-shaped golden mount that attaches it to a central hub at the top of the shaft. At the top and back of this central hub are usually two golden half-*vajras*, which bestow

Plate 132: Axes, iron hooks and elephant goads

on weapons such as the elephant goad and hammer the qualities of the *vishvavajra*, representing the Buddha's four activities or *karmas*, with destructive activity as the blade's cutting-edge of expression. The shaft of the *vajra*-axe (Skt. *vajraparashu*; Tib. *rdo rje dgra sta*) is often depicted in the red colour of sandalwood, tipped at its base with a jewel or smaller half-*vajra*, and often adorned with a tied silk-ribbon coloured to represent one of the Five Buddha Families.

The axe and saw are also depicted in the hands of the demonic denizens of one of the eight hot-hell realms. This is the 'Black Thread Hell' (Skt. *kalasutra*; Tib. *thig nag*), where victims are continually chopped or sawn along the lines that a black thread has marked upon their bodies.

THE ELEPHANT GOAD OR IRON HOOK
(Skt. *ankusha*; Tib. *lcags kyu*)

The elephant goad or *ankusha* is known in Tibetan as the 'iron hook' (Tib. *lcags kyu*), and is used by an elephant driver or mahout to control and steer his elephant. Its symbolism as an instrument of control – as wisdom or clear understanding – is revealed in Plate 52 on elephants, and in Plate 60 on *shamatha* meditation where it is coupled with the lasso, representing mindfulness or recollection. As a hand-held weapon the elephant goad symbolises both the hooking of negativities or evil beings, and the pulling or driving of all beings out of samsara and towards liberation.

The hooked blade of the elephant goad is shaped like the blade of the curved knife (Tib. *gri gug*), as described in Plate 118, with a sickle-shaped blue iron blade which terminates at its upper extremity in a sharp hook. Like the axe and hammer the elephant goad is commonly ornamented with a pair of half-*vajras* or jewels at its top; with a *vajra* or jewel-sealed red sandalwood, hardwood, bone, or metal shaft; and often adorned with a coloured silk ribbon tied around its shaft.

The wrathful activity of the iron hook perhaps realises its most potent expression in the form of Black Hayagriva (Tib. *rTa mgrin nag po*), who is described as wielding an iron hook in his left hand that blazes with fire. This left hand makes the threatening *tarjani* gesture, with a black, iron scorpion poised to sting on the tip of Hayagriva's raised index finger. The simulacra of the raised and curved index finger, the raised and curved sting of a scorpion, and the curved point of the iron hook, reveal the wrathful malice replicated within this forceful gesture.

Plate 132

In the upper half of this illustration are seven examples of the axe (*parashu*), and in the lower half are seven examples of the elephant goad (*ankusha*).

The four large axes depicted across the top of the illustration all have coloured silk ribbons tied around their shafts. Three of the axes are sealed with golden half-*vajras* at the bases of their shafts, and with double half-*vajras* or half-*vishvavajras* at their tops. The third drawing from the left is

ornamented with jewel insignia. Each of these axe blades are painted in the dark-blue colour of iron, and reveal some of the variations in the crescent-shaped blade of the Tibetan axe. The first three drawings on the left show variations of the thin leaf-shaped golden mounts that embellish the two sides of the axe-head, whilst the fourth drawing depicts a golden *makara*-head mount, symbolising the tenacious power of the crocodile's *vajra*-grip.

Below are three smaller axes, which are more simply adorned. The first axe on the left depicts a mason's axe or pickaxe (Skt. *tanka*; Tib. *sta gri*). The second drawing shows a pointed battleaxe, with two heavy lotus-shaped iron bulbs (Skt. *kanda*) embellishing the central hub. The third drawing shows a hand-axe, with its jewel-topped shaft secured into the aperture of its rectangular hub.

Four large elephant goads are similarly depicted across the lower half of the page, with three small stylised goads below. The second large drawing from the left displays a *makara*-headed goad with jewelled insignia, whilst the other three are ornamented with half-*vajras*, representing the adamantine qualities of the goad's wrathful activities. The stylised and slender hooks of the two lower goads on the left resemble more closely the true shape of the traditional iron-hooked Indian elephant goad, than its common Tibetan depiction in the form of a curved knife.

MISCELLANEOUS RITUAL IMPLEMENTS AND WEAPONS

Plate 133

This composition depicts an assembly of miscellaneous ritual implements and weapons, including animal-banners, whips, slings, hammers, and objects associated with fire or the ritual fire offerings of *homa*.

On the left of the top row are two drawings of the fire-brand (Skt. *agnidanda, jvaladanda*; Tib. *me mgal*), which may be wielded by attendant or minor deities as a hand-held weapon. The first drawing depicts the firebrand as a burning juniper branch, and the second as a burning pole that has been tipped with tar. The Vedic sacred fire was kindled from the friction-heat produced by rubbing together two wooden sticks – known as *arani* sticks. These sticks were obtained from the *ashvattha* or *pippala* tree, better known as the bodhi tree (*Ficus religiosa*). The motif of two crossed *arani* sticks creating fire is believed to be one possible origin for the swastika symbol.

The third drawing to the right of the firebrands shows a wolf-banner (Skt. *vrikadhvaja*; Tib. *spyang ki rgyal mtshan*), which is carried as a battle-standard by minor deities or spirits. The fourth drawing depicts a bull-banner (Skt. *vrishabhadhvaja*; Tib. *khyu mchog gyi rgyal mtshan*), which is carried by the lion-mounted deity Ganapati Mahakala, and also appears as a battle-standard of attendant spirit retinues. Both the wolf and bull-banner are depicted as the head and flayed skins of these animals draped over a silk victory banner. The standard poles of these banners are sealed with *vajras* at their lower extemities.

The next four drawings on the right show four examples of the *makara*-banner (Skt. *makaradhvaja*; Tib. *chu srin gyi rgyal mtshan*), held by the deity Rahula. The *makaradhvaja* as a crocodile, water-spirit, or sea-monster (Tib. *chu srin*) banner, is fashioned from the combined elements of the *makara*'s skin and the silk aprons of the victory banner. The first two drawings on the left show the banner mounted upon a wooden pole as a battle-standard. The third and fourth drawings show the *makaradhvaja* impaled upon a sword, which is sealed at its pommel with a five-pronged *vajra*. The *makaradhvaja* in this form is held aloft in Rahula's upper right hand, and symbolises his severing of the five poisons with the *makara*-banner sword of the Five Buddha wisdoms. The *makaradhvaja* was originally an emblem of Kamadeva, the Vedic god of love, who is also known as Makaraketu (see Plate 122). The *makara* is described in Plate 45; its symbolism as a stupa embellishment, representing the Buddha's victory over the four Maras, is referred to on page 135.

Below, and in between the shafts of the four *makaradhvajas*, are two drawings of clubs and a bamboo staff. The first drawing shows a jewel-topped club, with a silk ribbon on its shaft forming two folded wing-shapes. The second drawing shows a staff surmounted by a lotus and flaming triple gem, with a triple valance descending from the lotus. The third drawing depicts the simple bamboo staff (Skt. *danda*) carried by a mendicant.

On the left centre of the page are two drawings of the horse-whip (Tib. *rta lcag*), which is wielded in the right hands of many horse-mounted warriors or protective deities, such as Gesar, Vaishravana, and Nyenchen Thanglha. The horse-whip of these divinities is fashioned from gold (Tib. *gser kyi rta lcag*), and is usually crowned at the end of its staff with a jewel or *vajra*, from which emanate the long rope strands of the whip in the form of a curving rainbow.

To the right of the horse-whips are two drawings of the Tibetan sling (Tib. *'ur rdo*), which is used both as a physical weapon for casting stones, and as a metaphysical weapon for the hurling of ritual substances, or offering cakes (Tib. *gtor ma*), against ghosts or demons. The Tibetan sling is woven from yak-hair, with a central diamond-shaped cradle and narrow braided ends. Its extremities are woven into looped ends, with a smaller loop for the thumb and a larger loop for the fingers. In the hands of a nomadic Tibetan herdsman a small stone can be cast from the sling with great accuracy, often hitting a herded yak precisely on its right or left horn. Geometric *gzi*-stone or folk designs are commonly woven into the Tibetan sling, which bear almost identical patterns to the Peruvian Indian slings used in the Andes.

To the right of the slings is a male figure, bound with foot and arm shackles in the sacrificial corpse-posture of a captive spirit. An effigy (Tib. *ling ga*) of a hindering spirit is often depicted in this form, and may be drawn within a wrathful *chakra* as an imprisoning destructive device or *yantra*. Scorpions, or an array of sharp weapons, may be depicted within the blades of the *chakra*, penetrating the effigy at the psychic centres of head, throat, heart, gut, and

genitals; or at the shoulders, elbows, thighs and knees. These manacled effigies are constructed for rituals of slaying, subjugating, and exorcising or casting out.

Below this drawing is the inverted effigy (Tib. *ling ga*) of a captive spirit, with his arms and legs outstretched within a burning triangular 'iron prison' or a triangular fire-pit. An effigy in this posture is usually specified for the destructive *homa* or fire activity of 'burning' (see the wrathful *homa* ritual described in Plate 144).

Beneath this downward-pointing fire triangle are three drawings of sacrificial triangular fire-pits (Tib. *'brub khung*), as iron receptacles or prisons. The first two drawings on the left depict a mass of flames emanating from the iron receptacles as the wrathful substances are burned. The third drawing shows a wrathful triangular lamp, fuelled by burning human fat instead of clarified butter, and with a wick made from the twisted hair of a corpse or a widow.

To the right of this lamp is a triangular clay or stone fire hearth (Tib. *me thab*), mounted upon a *vajra*-sealed handle. This hand-held brazier is held in one of Yamantaka's left or wisdom hands, and symbolises that the essence of all phenomena is 'clear light' (Tib. *'od gsal*), as whatever substances are offered into the *homa* fire-pit, they burn with the same flame and are reduced to the same ashes. Yamantaka's triangular brazier is described as having a door on one of its sides – in the manner of a conventional furnace – through which fuel was added. In one of his lower left hands Yamantaka holds human entrails, which along with the brazier, symbolise the attainment of the 'illusory body' and 'clear light' respectively. The drawing above shows a variation of the triangular hearth, with the triangular brazier mounted upon a jewel-topped staff with a single tongue of flame emanating from its centre.

The group of five vertical drawings to the right of the triangular hearths depict the two forms of ladles used in *homa* or fire rituals. The first and third of these drawings show the smaller circular ladle (Skt. *shruva*; Tib. *blug gzar*), which is used to pour melted ghee or clarified butter directly onto the *homa* fire, or into the ritual funnel. This circular ladle is fashioned as a small bronze bowl, mounted upon an ornate metal handle sealed with a *vajra* at its base. The interior of the bowl is engraved with a five-pointed *vajra*, and is commonly ornamented with a *vajra*-boss at its top. The first drawing of the circular ladle has a full *vajra* at the base of its handle and an ornamental coiling snake at the handle's top; the inscribed *vajra* is drawn within the circle of the bowl. The third drawing shows a half-*vajra* ornamenting the top and bottom of the ladle's handle, with the inscribed *vajra* depicted within the bowl. The second, fourth, and fifth drawings depict the pouring-funnel (Skt. *patri*; Tib. *dgang gzar*). The pouring-funnel has a square receptacle at its top, with an upper cavity or channel which extends into a pouring-spout, so that the melted ghee which is poured into it by the ladle will drain through this upper spout. The square interior of the funnel is usually inscribed with a central *vajra*, enclosed by the inscribed shapes of a triangle, semi-circle, square, and circle, representing the four *homa* activities of wrath, magnetism, enrichment, and peace

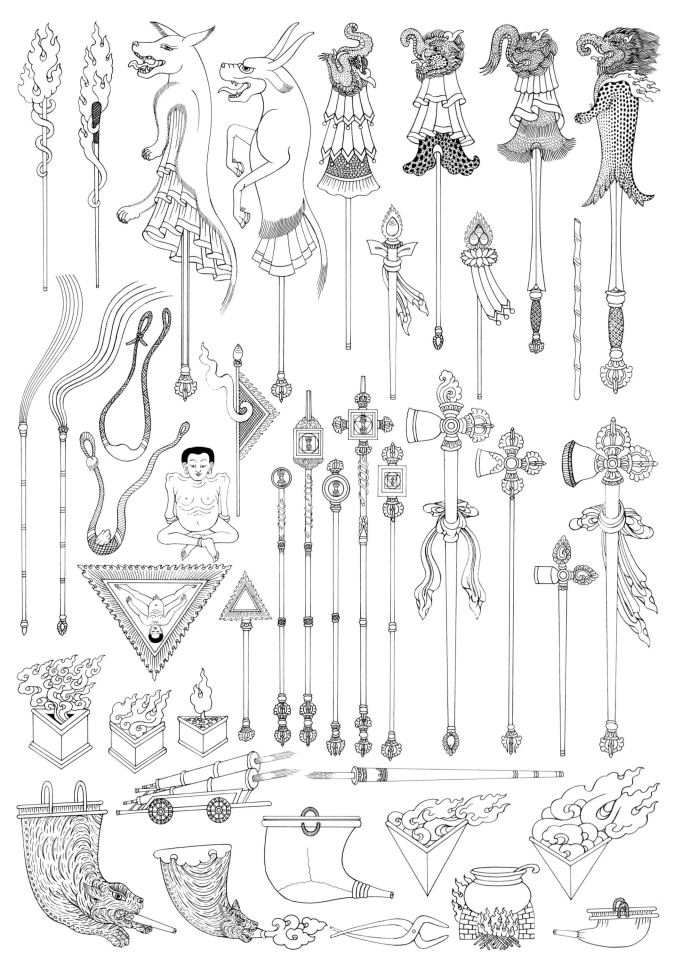

Plate 133: Miscellaneous ritual implements and weapons

(see Plates 143–145). Alternatively only the square and circle may be represented as engraved designs or ledged recesses, as enrichment and peace are the two main auspicious functions of the *homa* ritual. The second drawing shows the funnel forming a matching pair with the first drawing of the ladle. A full *vajra* seals its lower handle, two snakes are entwined around its upper handle, and the pouring-funnel of the square receptacle extends from its top. The fourth drawing shows an ornate funnel, with a full *vajra* at the base of the handle and an entwined snake at the top. The square receptacle of this funnel is ornamented as a *vishvavajra*, with its tubular funnel extending at the top. The fifth drawing depicts a *vajra*-sealed funnel, with a hollow central prong on the crowning *vajra* that serves as a pouring spout.

To the right of the ladles and funnels are four drawings of the hammer (Skt. *mudgara*; Tib. *tho ba*). The hammer or *vajra*-hammer (Skt. *vajramudgara*; Tib. *rdo rje tho ba*), is a right-hand or method weapon of many deities, and essentially symbolises the smashing or pounding of evil dispositions, especially avarice, covetousness, and miserliness. In the raised right hand of the deity Damchan Dorje Legpa, in his form as the 'dark blacksmith' (Tib. *mgar ba nag po*), the hammer is described as a foundry hammer (Tib. *khro chu'i tho ba*) made of solid cast iron with a jewelled-handle decorated with a *vajra*. As an 'oath-bound' (Tib. *dam can*) protective deity, Dorje Legpa's hammer symbolises the pulverising of vow-breakers and the 'enemies' of emotional defilements. The head of the hand-held hammer is usually depicted in the dark-blue colour of cast or meteorite iron, although bronze or gold hammers may be specified in certain deity descriptions. The first drawing shows a hammer ornamented with a scrolling jewel-insignia and *vajra* at its top, and with a tapering shaft decorated with a silk cloth and sealed with a jewel. The second drawing depicts a *vishvavajra*-crowned hammer with a *vajra* seal at the shaft's base. The third drawing depicts a small jewel-ornamented hammer. The fourth drawing depicts the *vajra*-hammer in its most common form, with two half-*vajras* surmounting its crowning hub, a silk cloth tied around its shaft, and a half-*vajra* at the base of the shaft.

Below the braziers, ladles, funnels, and hammers are two horizontal drawings of the cannon. The long-barrelled cannon on the right is a primitive form of the shoulder-held gun or mortar, used to launch missiles or fire-arrows (the fire-arrow is described in Plate 121). The second drawing on the left shows a carriage-mounted double-barrelled cannon, which may appear in thangkas depicting the great battle between the 'barbarians' or Muslims and the Buddhists, which in the *Kalachakra Tantra* is prophesised to occur in the year AD 2327. At this decisive battle Rudra Chakrin, the last of the twenty-five *chakravartin* kings of the Kingdom of Shambhala, defeats the barbarians and establishes a new golden age of the Buddhist teachings. The *Kalachakra Tantra* describes in some detail the great vehicles and weapons that will be employed in this battle – chariots, seige towers, *vajra*-tents, catapults, fire-arrows, and the 'cutting machines' of cleaver, sword, harpoon, and wind. Some of these war engines bear a striking resemblance to the military machines devised by Leonardo da Vinci, and which he drew more than four centuries after the introduction of the *Kalachakra Tantra* into Tibet.

In the recorded history of fire warfare, the Byzantine Greeks first employed a 'fireball-weapon', made from a petroleum-jelly compound of naphthenate palmitate (napalm), which was projected from a large catapult or flame-thrower as an inflammable missile known as 'Greek-fire'. With this weapon the Byzantines succeeded in destroying the wooden ships of the Muslim Arabs, who beseiged Constantinople between AD 716–18, thereby halting the advance of the Muslim invaders into Eastern Europe. The use of the giant catapult and crossbow by the ancient Greeks is believed to date back to the fifth century BC.

Gunpowder was probably first produced in China during the seventh century, and initially used in the manufacture of firecrackers, rockets, fire-wheels and other fireworks, by packing the gunpowder into rolled paper and bamboo tubes. The first recorded use of the Chinese gun dates from AD 1162, and the use of the cannon by the Mongolian warlords dates from AD 1232. The Western discovery of gunpowder is attributed to the thirteenth-century monk and alchemist, Roger Bacon, and the first recorded deployment of the European cannon dates from 1326, and the first European gun to 1354.

On the left of the bottom row are three drawings of the skin bellows (Skt. *bhastra*; Tib. *sbud pa*), which are held in the left hand of the blacksmith deity, Dorje Legpa (Skt. Vajrasadhu). The first drawing shows a tigerskin bellows with a long metal nozzle protruding from the tiger's mouth, and the upper part of the wind-bellows formed from two strapped wooden struts. The second drawing shows another tigerskin bellows with a short nozzle, and with wind gushing from its end. The third drawing shows a leather bellows, with handled upper struts and an attached nozzle (Tib. *zham cha*). With this 'black weapon' Dorje Legpa blows all enemies into dust. Below the leather bellows is a pair of foundry tongs (Tib. *me len*), and across to the right a fire-hearth (Tib. *me thab*) with a cooking pot being fanned by bellows. Above are two drawings of the wrathful triangular fire-hearth, in the form of three-sided pyramids as the *dharmodaya* or 'reality source' (see page 348).

Plate 134

The upper area of this illustration depicts the 'five magical weapons' of Palden Lhamo. The lower area depicts an assortment of ritual implements: the needle and thread, the pestle, the emblems of wind and fire, sun and moon, the head of Brahma, feathers, horns, and Mt Meru. The five magical weapons of Palden Lhamo are:

The 'crossed stick of the demons' (Tib. *bdud kyi khram bam*)
The 'bundle of red curses' (Tib. *byad dmar gyi khres po*)
The 'black and white spotted dice' (Tib. *sho rde'u dkar nag*)
The 'bag of diseases' (Tib. *nad kyi rkyal pa*)
The 'ball of thread weapon' (Tib. *mtshon kyi gru gu*)

These five magical weapons are common to many of the forms of Palden Lhamo or Remati, and to many of the retinue of spirits or 'demonesses of diseases' (Tib. *ma mo*) who accompany her.

The first drawing on the upper left depicts the short notched or 'crossed stick' (Tib. *khram bam, khram shing*), as described in Plate 127. A longer version of this tally stick is drawn horizontally in the upper right corner of this illustration.

Nebesky-Wojkowitz mentions that the notched stick was used in Tibet before the introduction of the Tibetan alphabet to record details of trade agreements. As the magical weapon of various spirit deities (Tib. *gshin rje, srin po, ma mo, btsan*), he mentions two important varieties, the one black (Tib. *bdud kyi khram shing*), and the other yellow (Tib. *srin po'i khram shing*), both of which have red notches, often numbering seven, nine or thirteen. When it is used to slay an enemy, the number of notches should correspond to the age in years of the intended victim.

The four drawings to the right of the short tally stick depict Palden Lhamo's 'bundle of red curses', with which she casts binding spells and inflicts deadly curses upon the enemies of the *buddhadharma*. The bundle of red curses is usually depicted as a red-covered text, bound with red cloth, or serpents, to the bag of diseases and the pair of dice that hang from the front of her saddle. Three of these four drawings depict the red curses as texts, whilst the fourth drawing shows them as a pair of red cylindrical scrolls.

To the right of the bundles of red curses are the two black and white spotted dice, which usually hang from a serpent-thread on Palden Lhamo's saddle. According to one of the legends of Palden Lhamo – as recorded in Ladrang Kalsang's *The Guardian Deities of Tibet* – these two dice were obtained from her human consort, who was a dice player. In Palden Lhamo's possession the dice are a divination device, whereby she can determine the karmic outcome of any situation. In the system of dice divination (Tib. *mo*) ascribed to Palden Lhamo, three dice are used, which gives numerical prognostications between three and eighteen. According to the nature of the question posed the combination of numbers thrown is interpreted through a divination text, in a manner which bears a resemblance to the Chinese *I Ching*. Palden Lhamo's two dice are usually depicted with the white dice above and the black dice below, and often with the two extremes of the highest 'six' on the white dice and the lowest 'one' on the black dice, symbolising the scope of her karmic judgement and retribution.

Many varieties of stone and bone dice have been unearthed at the ancient site of Mohenjo-Daro, 'the city of the dead', in the Indus valley. In Vedic times dice were traditionally made from camel-bone, and in later times black and white dice were commonly fashioned from ebony and ivory.

Interestingly, the black and white dice bear a strong resemblance to the two black and white divinatory stones worn within the golden breastplate of the high priest of the Temple, as mentioned in the Old Testament. These stones, named Urim and Thummim, were of Babylonian origin, and

formed the only permissible oracular medium for the revelation of the will of God to his people. The golden breastplate, as a syllable-inscribed divination mirror, is also worn by the many oracles of Tibet.

To the right of the two dice are three drawings of the bag of diseases (Tib. *nad rkyal*), which also hangs from Palden Lhamo's mule-saddle, as the fourth of her five magical weapons. According to a legend, the bag of diseases and the notched stick were the two weapons which Palden Lhamo took from her mother in order to subdue the gods and *nagas*. Along with the poisonous mist which emanates from this goddess's mouth, the bag of diseases forms an early example of 'germ warfare'. The sack or bag of diseases was probably an early Indian siege weapon, which could rapidly spread pestilence through a besieged city, especially if it could be secretly cast into a well or source of drinking water. The bag itself is described as being made of diseased human skin – probably of a leprosy, plague, or smallpox victim – and containing the raw body-tissue or vital organs of those who have died from the most virulent of contagious diseases, such as the plague, typhoid, cholera, hepatitis, leprosy, smallpox, and dysentery. Dropsy, leprosy, bile disease, blood fever, insanity, jaundice, and dysentery are some of the diseases inflicted by disease-causing spirits (Tib. *ma mo*). Nebesky-Wojkowitz mentions that several of these may carry the bag of diseases as the 'germs of leprosy' (Tib. *mdze nad kyi rkyal pa*), and that other goddesses may carry a sack full of blood, a water sack, or a sack full of lightning and hail. The three upper drawings of the bag of diseases are depicted as tied bags of green human skin.

The next row of illustrations begins on the left with two drawings of Palden Lhamo's dice threaded upon venomous serpents. The next drawing shows a human being as a skin bag full of contagious diseases, and bound at the wrists and ankles as a sacrificial victim. Around this flayed corpse's neck hangs a serpent-noose threaded with three divination dice. The next drawing shows the disease-packed skin of a cannibal-demon (Tib. *srin po*), or a disease-causing demoness (Tib. *ma mo*), with its arms and legs knotted around its neck and a pair of small dice hanging from a serpent-noose. The next drawing shows the disease-filled skin of a woman, knotted as a sack by her limbs and a dice-laden serpent-noose. The next two drawings show the skin as a plain sack tied by a serpent. The last drawing on the right shows the sack of diseases, the bundle of red curses, and the pair of divination dice bound together with serpents. These three magical weapons of Palden Lhamo are represented in this compound form, hanging by a serpent from the *rakshasa*'s skull at the front of her mule's saddle.

The next row of drawings depicts eight examples of Palden Lhamo's fifth magical weapon, the ball of thread (Tib. *gru gu*). This ball of thread is plaited or twisted as a string made from five-coloured threads (Tib. *gzungs thag*), that are said to embody the essence of all wrathful weapons. A similar thread is used in the more peaceful rituals of Vajrayana empowerment, where the thread is wound around the ritual master's *vajra*, and the wisdom-deities are invoked along its length. The Tibetan term for the coloured thread

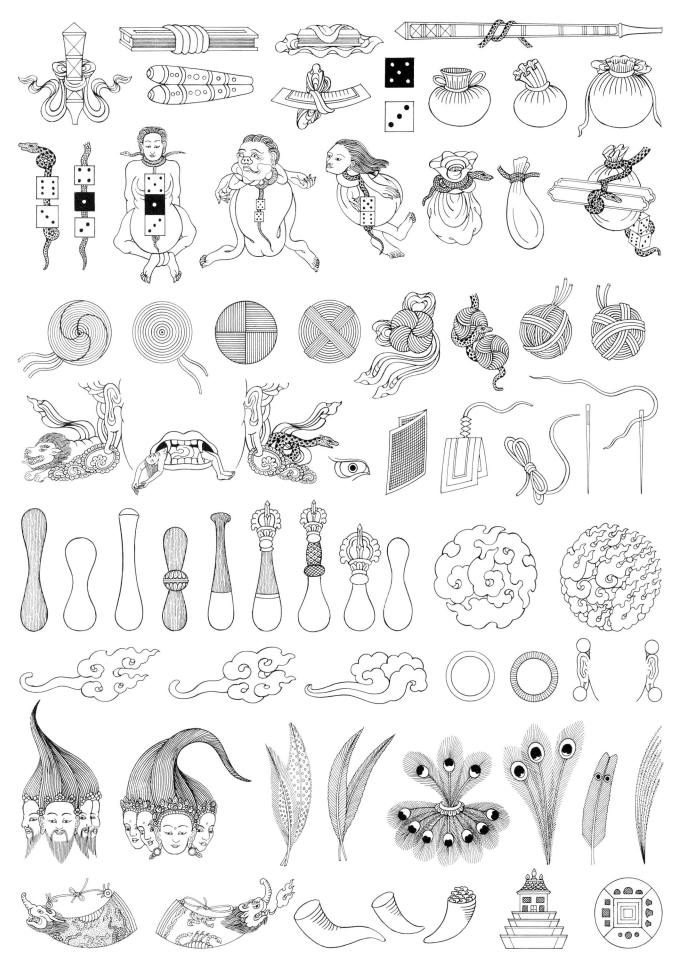

Plate 134: The five magical weapons of Palden Lhamo and the ritual implements of specific deities

(Tib. *gzungs thag*), also refers to a string that holds mystical powers or spells, and as Palden Lhamo's magical weapon it is used to bind enemy-demons or the forms of malignant spirits with invoked curses of subjugation and destruction. This ball of thread hangs from a serpent's tail at the back of Palden Lhamo's saddle, and may be represented in a variety of styles as illustrated in the drawings.

The first drawing on the left depicts the ball of thread as a three-coloured 'wheel of joy' (Tib. *dga' 'khyil*), which may be coloured red, green, and yellow, or blue-black. The second drawing shows a green or red ball formed from concentric circles. The third drawing depicts the ball coloured in the four directional quadrants of blue, yellow, red, and green. The fourth drawing shows a cross of red thread wound around a green ball, or vice versa. The fifth drawing shows a plaited ball of blue, yellow, red, and green threads adorned with a black silk ribbon. The sixth drawing depicts two small balls of variegated thread, entwined with a serpent. The seventh and eighth drawings show two wound balls of variegated thread, which are commonly depicted in the five colours or in an alternating sequence of red and green.

In India the variegated ball of thread is still used in certain religious festivals known as *rakshabandha* or 'thread binding'. The most popular of these festivals is held before the rainy season in the month of Savan, when sisters traditionally tie protective threads around their brothers' wrists in return for small gifts of money. Another festival is Guru Purnima, held at the first full moon (*purnima*) of the rainy season, when the guru is honoured and protective threads are given to the guru's disciples. Traditionally, white, red, yellow, or black threads are given, which originally corresponded to the fourfold Hindu caste system. Another group of lunar festivals are known as *panchami*, meaning 'the fifth', and fall on the fifth day of certain months. The spring *panchami* is known as *ayudhapuja*, meaning 'worship of weapons', when ritual implements, weapons, and tools are made the objects of worship. Traditionally a five-coloured ball of variegated thread is used in this *panchami* ritual to protect the weapons from possession by evil spirits. In Hinduism the number five (*panch*) is especially sacred to Shiva and the mother goddesses. The term *raksha* means protection, especially from evil spirits, and is a Sanskrit prefix for all manner of talismans and charms that protect against demons. The sacred ash (*vibhuti*) made from burned cow dung, for example, is derived from five colours of cow; and *raksha vibhuti*, from the dung of a variegated cow, specifically protects from evil spirits. The Indian ball of variegated thread is wound from extremely long strands of cotton which are dyed white, yellow, red, green, and blue, at handspan intervals along its length.

Tibetan protection cords, worn around the neck or wrist, are most commonly made from red thread with a single knot at the centre. Five-coloured threads are often plaited for specific protective purposes or woven around an astrological amulet to protect from malevolent planetary influences.

On the left of the next row is a drawing showing a detail of Palden Lhamo's face, with a human corpse in her mouth and a lion and snake rising from her right and left earrings. Her mouth is described as an open hearth for destructive burnt offerings (Tib. *drag po'i hom khung*), which conflagrates the enemies or *rudras* who pervert or destroy the teachings. Tongues of fire blaze within her mouth, which symbolically dries up the ocean of cyclic existence. A poisonous mist billows on the wind of her breath, spreading pestilence to the *rudras* and demons. Her red tongue twists like lightning as she experiences the divine taste of the food of nectar, symbolised by the human corpse which represents the consumption of desire, and the emptiness of inherent self-existence. Her four sharp canine teeth symbolise her channelling of emotional energy, which bites through the four Maras of emotional defilements, passion, divine pride and lust, and death. The roaring white lion which rises from her right 'method' earring, symbolises the lion's roar of the Buddhas proclaiming the sound of emptiness, which controls the emotion of pride. The green and black snake which rises above her left 'wisdom' earring, conquers the poisonous emotional energies of anger and hatred.

To the right of the snake earring is the single eye that appears on the left rump of Palden Lhamo's mule. According to a legend, this eye spontaneously appeared when the goddess pulled out an arrow, fired by her cannibal husband as she was fleeing from his kingdom of Lanka. The three eyes of Palden Lhamo's mule represent her victory over the three realms and the three times, with the eye on the rump gazing backwards over the underworlds and into times past.

To the right of the mule's eye are two drawings of ritual cloth implements which I have copied from the illustrations to *The Secret Visions of the Fifth Dalai Lama*. The first drawing shows a piece of woven yak-hair that may be used as a cover for the effigy (Tib. *ling ga*) of a demon, to be burned or destroyed in rituals of destructive activity; or which may be used in the *homa* rite as a fan (Skt. *dhavitra*; Tib. *rlung g.yab*) to energise the sacred fire with wind. The second drawing shows a folded rectangle of overlapping coloured cloth inscribed on its inner surface with mantras, and identified as a 'crown' (Tib. *cod pan*).

To the right of these cloth implements are two drawings of the needle (Skt. *suchi*; Tib. *khab*) and thread (Skt. *sutra*; Tib. *skud pa*). The needle and thread are attributes of the goddess Marichi (Tib. *'Od zer can ma*), who along with Ekajata (Tib. *Ral gcig ma*) is one of the two attendant goddesses of Khadiravani Tara. Marichi holds the needle and thread (Tib. *khab skud can*) in her right and left hands respectively, symbolising the union of method and wisdom, and sews up the mouths and eyes of harmful spirits and binds their limbs. The threaded needle illustrated in the second drawing occurs in one of the ritual cycles of Palden Lhamo, as illustrated in *The Secret Visions of the Fifth Dalai Lama*, where they are described as a copper needle and a red thread.

On the left of the next row are nine drawings of the wooden pestle (Skt. *musala*; Tib. *gtun shing*), which is an attribute of a number of Shaivite Hindu deities, and is similarly found in the right hands of Vajrayana deities with an affinity to Shiva, such as Vajrabhairava, Krishna-Yamari, and Ganapati. In one of Yamantaka's right or method hands, the bone-shaped wooden pestle symbolises the revitalisation of memory as the concentration of intuitive perception or knowledge, through the grinding of a compound to a paste 'of one taste' (Skt. *ekarasa*). This symbolism highlights the relationship between the sense of smell and rekindled memory, or 'the destruction of the decline of memory', as of all the sense organs, the nasal nerves of the olfactory bulb travel directly to the limbic area of the brain, which controls the unconscious intuition of memory and sexuality. Three of the nine wooden pestles illustrated are marked with a *vajra*-top, whilst the other six are drawn in the shape of a bone.

To the right of the pestles are two drawings of a wind-wheel (Tib. *rlung 'khor*) on the left, and a fire-wheel (Tib. *me 'khor*) on the right. These destructive 'wheels' may be unleashed from wrathful weapons such as the *vajra* or trident, to blow into dust or conflagrate the hindering demons of the five poisons – ignorance, desire, anger, jealousy, and pride. A blazing wind-wheel emanates in this destructive form from the left hand of the wrathful deity, Red Karma Yama, annihilating the poisons of the five emotional defilements. In the symbolically war-like rituals of destroying an enemy's fortress or stronghold, seven kinds of magical-wheels (Tib. *'phrul 'khor*) are described: a circle of stone missiles, of boats, fire, swords, wind, *vajras*, and arrows. The blazing fireball or 'army of wisdom-fire' (Tib. *ye shes me dpung*) that emanates from the left wisdom hand of Vajrakilaya is illustrated in Plate 135.

On the left of the next row are three drawings of red fire, green wind, and a white cloud, which occur as hand-held symbols of the elements, as held by deities such as Yamari. To the right of these are the two discs of a white full-moon and a red or golden sun, which also occur as hand-held emblems of Yamari, or rest above the right and left shoulders of Vaishravana. On the far right are small discs of the moon and sun – worn as earrings or upper ear adornments – which symbolise the unity of compassion and wisdom as the lunar and solar channels of white and red *bodhichitta*.

On the left of the second row from the bottom are two drawings of the severed four-faced head of Brahma (Skt. *brahmashiras*; Tib. *tshangs pa'i ngo bo*). The yellow head of Brahma is one of the attributes of Shiva, and in his hand represents the Four Vedas, the four aeons or *yugas*, the four Hindu castes, and the four directions. In Vajrayana iconography it is held in the left hands of Shaivite-related deities, such as Chakrasamvara, Kalachakra and Vajrabhairava, where it symbolises both the severence of all conceptualisations and the development of altruistic love through the 'four immeasurables' or 'abodes of the divine' (*brahmaviharas*: 'temples of Brahma') of compassion, loving-kindness, sympathetic-joy and equanimity (Skt. *maitri; mudita; karuna; upeksha*). The drawing on the left shows the yellow four-faced head of Brahma in its more correct iconographical form, with beards and flowers adorning his hairline. The drawing on the right shows the later Tibetan stylisation of Brahma's head, without beards and wearing the jewelled tiara of a bodhisattva.

To the right of the heads of Brahma are several drawings of specific bird feathers that are used as ritual objects in the cycles of certain protective deities to remove obstacles or subdue harmful spirits. The first drawing shows the speckled feathers of an owl (Skt. *uluka*; Tib. *'ug pa*); and the second drawing shows a pair of vulture (Skt. *gridhra*: Tib. *bya rgod*), or raven (Skt. *kaka*; Tib. *bya rog*) feathers. The third drawing depicts the peacock-feathered parasol (Skt. *mayura chattra*; Tib. *rma bya'i gdugs*) which crowns Palden Lhamo's head, and is illustrated and described in Plate 84. The next drawing shows a group of three peacock feathers (Tib. *rma bya'i mdongs*), which symbolises the transmutation of the three poisons of ignorance, desire, and aversion. The next drawing shows the feather of an owl, with painted eyes. The owl is an important 'messenger' of the protective warrior deity Begtse; and as a prophetic bird of ill omen, its nocturnal hoot – like the baying of dogs – often portends an inauspicious event, such as the death of a Dalai Lama, or the invasion of the Chinese army. In Hinduism the owl is one of the mounts of the wealth-goddess Lakshmi, and as a 'ghost or spirit bird', the medium of an owl's body is used to invoke prophetic spirits in the left-hand tantric practice of the 'owl ritual' (Skt. *uluka sadhana*). The eyes are painted on the feather to represent the peculiarity of the owl, as the only species of bird with forward-facing eyes. The last drawing on the right shows a bundle of *kusha* grass, which is combined with a bundle of peacock feathers to create the sprinkler (Tib. *kha rgyan*) for consecrated water.

The feathers of certain birds are used in the construction of thread-crosses (Tib. *mdos*) or 'spirit-catchers' to subdue harmful spirits, and in the steering-feathers of magical arrows (Tib. *thun mda'*) which are used to destroy spirits. Each of the various classes of spirits are accorded the feathers of specific birds, such as the peacock, goose, white-hen, owl, raven, and vulture. Birds of ill omen, such as the raven and crow, are the messengers of Mahakala; the 'iron falcon' is the messenger of Ekajati; and other birds of prey – the garuda, vulture, eagle, hawk, and owl are associated with other deities. The eight birds which are trampled under the left feet of Yamantaka – the vulture, owl, raven, parrot, hawk, garuda, myna bird, and swan – are the vehicles of the eight forms of Yama (Tib. *gShin rje*). The eight mammals under Yamantaka's right feet – a man, buffalo, bull, donkey, camel, dog, sheep, and wolf – are the eight messengers of Yama.

On the left of the bottom row are two drawings of the sorcerer's horn (Tib. *thun rwa*), employed in destructive rituals of exorcism or black magic. It is carved in relief from the horn of an ox or yak with the images of poisonous creatures, such as snakes, frogs, scorpions and other venomous insects. The tip of the horn is carved into the form of a *makara*-head, and its open end is usually sealed with a wooden stopper decorated with skulls, a crossed *vajra* or *chakra*, and a surmounting knot. In rituals of exorcism the horn may be filled with magical substances (Tib. *thun*) – such as empowered minerals, or grains of barley, sesame or mustard seed – which may be cast or hurled towards hindering spirits or obstructive ghosts. The mouth of the *makara* at the horn's tip may have a small orifice through which the magical substances may be scattered or expelled. Nebesky-Wojkowitz describes in some detail how a necromantic death-bringing horn (Tib. *ngan gtad*) may be used in its most destructive form to cause the death of an enemy.

To the right of these two carved horns are three drawings of a plain ox horn (Tib. *glang ru*) or yak horn (Tib. *g.yag rwa*), which are filled with magical ingredients (Tib. *thun*) and used in rituals of exorcism or subjugation. The first two drawings show the horn filled with the 'dry' *thun* of empowered grains or seeds, and the third drawing shows a horn filled with the 'wet' *thun* of blood.

Across from the horns in the bottom right corner are two drawings of Mt Meru, which arise as the hand-held attributes of certain deities. The first drawing shows Mt Meru in the form of a four-tiered base with Indra's palace above, and the second drawing shows the plan of Mt Meru as a disc. Mt Meru is illustrated and described in Plate 61.

Chapter Eleven
Wrathful Offerings, Tormas, and Ritual Fire Hearths

This chapter illustrates and describes various symbols and offerings which I have provisionally grouped together as follows: wrathful attributes and adornments; skulls and bone ornaments; thread crosses and *tormas*; the wrathful offering of the five senses; the 'inner offering'; an assembly of wrathful offerings and weapons; and a concluding section on the various hearth designs employed in the sacred fire offering of the *homa* ritual.

The offerings presented to wrathful deities essentially fulfil the same functions as the benign offerings presented to peaceful deities described in some of the earlier chapters, that is, 'to please' the deity with its favoured offerings, and to represent the sacrifices made by the practitioner to both appease and gain the allegiance of the deity. Many of these sacrificial objects and substances are derived from the blood sacrifices and necromantic rituals performed in the extreme left-hand practices of the early Indian tantric traditions, and in the ritual magic traditions of pre-Buddhist Tibet. However, in Vajrayana Buddhism – which evolved within the advanced altruistic context of the Mahayana's bodhisattva path – these sacrificial objects and substances are offered on a purely symbolic level, usually as sacrificial cakes or *tormas*, sculpted from barley flour, butter and dyes, and mixed with symbolic substances that substitute for the actual sacrificial substances described in these ancient rituals.

DISMEMBERED BODY PARTS AND OTHER WRATHFUL ATTRIBUTES

The drawing on Plate 135 illustrates the dismembered body parts – heart, lungs, intestines, skull, hair, and limbs, along with examples of the cotton fan, funeral shroud, *tarjani* gesture, fire emanations, and scorpions – that occur as

hand-held attributes of particular wrathful deities such as Mahakala, Yamantaka, and Vajrakilaya.

Plate 135
The heart is usually depicted like a red lotus bud or mango fruit, with a red bulb at the top, a serrated white sheath of muscle below, and a lower sheath of green petals. A single, double or triple stem of channels or veins hangs down from its base. Here the red heart and white muscle sheath represent the indestructible drop at the heart centre, the lotus of green petals represents the eight *nadi* that emanate from it, and the three veins represent the three main *nadis*.

In the upper area of the drawing are nineteen examples of the heart (Tib. *snying*), three of which are depicted with a pair of plucked-out eyes. The torn-out and blood-dripping heart of a human (Tib. *mi snying*), or the heart of an enemy (Tib. *dgra snying*), or the heart of Mara (Tib. *bdud snying*), are clutched in the left hands of wrathful deities such as Yama, Ekajati, Begtse, and Trakshad Mahakala. Begtse and several of the forms of Trakshad Mahakala are described as 'feeding the steaming heart and life veins of an enemy into his mouth'; and the wrathful deity, Black Servant-demon Yama, holds the blood-dripping heart of an enemy with two venomous black serpents sucking upon it. The warm heart, or heart and lungs (Tib. *glo snying*), of an enemy or evildoer are also held within the skull-cups of deities such as Mahakala, and paired with the chopper held above in the right hand. The cutting and consuming of the heart symbolises the severing of the roots of the five delusions, and their transmutation – through eating – into the Five Buddha wisdoms of the deity. The severence and consuming of the heart, life channels, and lungs in the 'generation stage' (Tib. *bskyed rim*) of

Plate 135: Dismembered body parts, charnel ground and fire symbols

visualisation, symbolises the activation of the drops, channels, and winds in the 'completion stage' practice (Tib. *rdzogs rim*).

On the left below the hearts are four drawings, the first and third of which illustrate the kidneys, and the second and fourth the lungs. In the Tibetan medical tradition the heart is compared to an enthroned king; the diaphragm to a silk curtain; the liver to a senior queen; the spleen to a junior queen; the lobes of the lungs to the home ministers and royal offspring; and the kidneys to the foreign ministers.

To the right are four drawings of a fresh or moist skull (Tib. *thod rlon*) with the hair and scalp attached. This form of skull-cup is known as a 'piece of skull' (Tib. *thod tshal*), and as a left-hand attribute of Yamantaka symbolises that he is full of the nectar of great compassion.

Below these skull pieces are three locks of hair from a corpse or a widow. The hair of a corpse (Tib. *shi skra*), which continues to grow after death, is employed in various left-hand tantric rituals of subjugating or destructive activity – as for example when a plug of hair from a corpse is used to seal the 'death horn' (Tib. *ngon gtad*), as illustrated on Plate 134. The *Hevajra Tantra* allegorically describes how an image of the deity may be painted, using a brush of corpse's hair and a skull-pallette containing five colours obtained from the charnel ground. To become a widow in traditional Indian society has always carried a cruel stigma of social ostracism. The main cremation ghats of Benares are surrounded by hostels full of pious and abandoned widows, who uncomplainingly await their moment of liberation on the funeral pyre. With the death of her husband the widow is considered 'unclean', and may easily be branded as a witch. The strict social rules of orthodox Hinduism prescribed that a widow should wear a white cotton sari, and that her hair should be cut short. If she were suspected of witchcraft her head would be shaved in order to remove her power. The hair of a widow (Tib. *yugs skra*) is used in many left-hand tantric rituals; in the destructive fire ritual of *homa*, for example, the hair of a widow may be used to bind the firewood, and the flame used to light the fire may be taken from a widow's house. The upright lock of hair depicted below shows the single iron hair-lock of the wrathful goddess Ekajati, whose name means 'one (*eka*) hair-lock (*jata*)'. Ekajati's single hair-lock symbolises the indestructible certainty of her resolve to protect the teachings; in contrast to a witch the iron-lock of her personal power cannot be severed.

On the left centre of the page is a drawing of one of Yamantaka's left 'wisdom' hands holding a length of human intestines (Tib. *rgyu ma*), symbolising his realisation of the insubstantiality of the inherent existence of all phenomena. This symbolism relates to the intestines' activity of digesting the most delicious and appealing of foodstuffs and transforming it into excrement. At the centre of the page are three drawings of coiling entrails, which as a noose, hanging ornaments, or a necklace, symbolise the emptiness of all phenomena (see Plates 130, 136 and 137).

Across the centre of the page are four drawings of severed arms and one drawing of a severed leg. Dismembered limbs and severed body parts are commonly depicted within the imagery of the eight great charnel grounds, and may be wielded by many of the legions of spirits who accompany wrathful deities, such as Begtse, Yama, and Mahakala. Yamantaka holds the attributes of a human leg and two severed arms in three of his left wisdom hands. Here the leg (Tib. *rkang pa*) symbolises the practitioner's rapid 'walking' or progress along the path to enlightenment. The right hand (Tib. *lag pa*) symbolises his dexterity at performing the four powerful activities of pacifying, increasing, subjugating, and destroying. And the left hand, with index finger raised in the threatening *tarjani* gesture, symbolises the dominance and terror he evokes over all obstructing demons.

Below the severed limbs are three drawings of the white or green cotton fan (Tib. *rlung ras*), held in the lower left wisdom hand of Yamantaka. This cotton cloth is mounted upon a jewel-topped staff or Kapalika trident, and symbolises by its changeable form the illusory nature of all phenomena. On an inner level this fan symbolises the nine 'transference of consciousness yogas' (Tib. *'pho ba*) of the *Guhyasamaja Tantra*. Across to the right of these three fans is a drawing of the white cotton cemetery shroud or 'corpse cloth' (Tib. *ro ras*) that is held in one of the upper left wisdom hands of Yamantaka. This white shroud symbolises Yamantaka's triumph over death: Yamantaka is the 'Slayer of Yama' (Skt. *Yama-antaka*; Tib. *gShin rje gshed*); and Yama (Tib. *gShin rje*) is the 'Lord of the Dead'. As the taking away of the cemetery shroud reveals the reality of the naked corpse, the shroud also symbolises the elimination of the veil that obstructs the realisation of emptiness, or the removal of the veil of ignorance that perceives all phenomena as being independently self-existing.

In the lower area of the illustration are images of a rope snare, two drawings of flame-emanating left hands in *tarjani* gesture, tongues of fire, the horns of Yamantaka, and scorpions. The symbiotic relationship between the snare, iron hook, scorpion, and the raised index finger of the *tarjani* gesture, have already been discussed (see Plates 130 and 132). Here the two hands in *tarjani* gesture (Tib. *sdigs mdzub*) depict examples of Vajrakilaya's upper left wisdom hand, which unleashes a blazing ball of wisdom-fire (Tib. *ye shes me dpung*). This 'host or army' (Tib. *dpung*) of wisdom-fire either emanates from Vajrakilaya's palm, or coils from the root of his index finger, and symbolises his total incineration of the five delusions or obscuring emotions. To the right of these two hands are three drawings of a blazing mass of wisdom-fire, then two drawings of the right horn of Yamantaka's central buffalo head. Yamantaka's two long horns are sky-blue in colour and tipped with wisdom-fire; their sharp points symbolise the realisation of the relative truth (left horn), and absolute truth (right horn). To the right of these horns are two scorpions and another mass of wisdom-fire.

FLAYED SKIN FRIEZES OF WRATHFUL OFFERING ASSEMBLIES

The illustrations on Plate 136 depict three drawings of the upper frieze or canopy of flayed human and animal skins that crown wall paintings or thangkas of the assembly of

Plate 136: Flayed skin friezes, carrion birds, corpses and corpse seats

wrathful offerings (Tib. *rgyan tshogs*). As thangkas the assembly of wrathful offerings are most commonly painted on a black background and often take the form of long horizontal banners, with red brocade borders on the upper three sides and hanging silk valances along the bottom. In this form they are hung upon, or represent, the walls of protective deity chapels (Tib. *mgon khang*), and are used in sacrificial ceremonies (Tib. *bskang rdzas*) to appease the wrathful deities. These skin, gut, blood, and bone friezes essentially represent the mandala environments of extremely wrathful deities; where the slain enemies are offered as a quivering mound of skin and flesh, representing ignorance; a shimmering ocean of blood, representing desire; and a glistening pile of broken and dry bones, representing hatred.

The central images of these black thangkas depict only the attributes of the deities and not their bodily forms. Several deities may be represented on a single horizontal painting, with only their mounts, hand-held implements, ornaments and attire depicted against the subtle shading of the deities' wisdom flames. A host of animal offerings – black horses, mules, yaks, buffaloes, dogs, goats, bears, camels, lions and tigers – with silk ribbons adorning their backs may stampede around the deities' invisible forms, showing that they have been ransomed from the butchers' knives and presented to the deities as a sacrificial offering. Above are depicted a flock of black birds of ill omen with human organs in their beaks. In the foreground are the wrathful outer offerings in skull-cups, along with sacrificial offering cakes (Tib. *gtor ma*) and an array of specific offerings. At the sides are assemblies of weapons, and the musical instruments used during the ritual invocations to the protective deities. Across the top of the wrathful assembly of offerings – as an appliqué banner, painted thangka, or wall mural – is depicted the canopy of flayed human and animal skins. This canopy represents the upper wall and ceiling of the protector chapel, which is commonly hung with iron weapons, and stuffed animals and birds.

Plate 136
The upper drawing shows a wrathful canopy with a flayed elephant skin on the left, and flayed human skins and skulls across the rest of the frieze. All of the sacrificial animals and humans are male. Twisting and hanging garlands of human entrails entwine amongst the skins, supporting flayed limbs, plucked-out eyes, and dripping human hearts. Hearts dangle from the jaws of the two skulls, pulled out through their throats; the right skull has its eyes pulled out also. The severed human head on the right has intestines both stuffed into its mouth and pulled out of its throat.

The second drawing shows a canopy of flayed animal skins with a single human skull and heart at the centre. The skins of a horse, leopard, tiger, and elephant are depicted across this frieze, festooned with hanging garlands of human entrails. These animals represent jealousy, pride, anger, and ignorance, and along with the human skull, representing desire, symbolise the death and ultimate emptiness of the five

delusions. The third drawing depicts a canopy made entirely of human skins, limbs, hearts, lungs, eyes, and intestines.

Below to the left are three drawings of black crows or vultures, with a human heart, intestines, and eyes in their beaks and talons. These scavenger birds are partaking of the 'feast offering' (Tib. *tshogs*) of the 'great meat' of human flesh. Below in the left corner are several drawings of the flayed arms and legs of a human corpse. Wrathful deities commonly wear a human skin as an upper garment, with the hands and feet either knotted over their shoulders or hanging freely from behind their backs.

The two drawings to the right of the birds show the cadaver of the 'corpse seat' (Skt. *shavasana*; Tib. *bam gdan*) on which many semi-wrathful and wrathful deities sit or stand. The corpse seat symbolises the emptiness of inherent self-essence from which the deity arises as pure light. The form and posture of this corpse is often specified within the deity description. Vajravarahi, for example, stands upon a corpse that lies upon its chest, whilst the goddess Nairatma tramples upon a corpse lying on its back. The forms of the two corpses depicted illustrates these examples. The third drawing in the lower right corner shows a disembowelled female corpse. Such a corpse may be depicted in charnel ground imagery, being devoured by vultures and animals.

The use of a corpse or a flayed human skin as a meditation seat is specifically mentioned in many of the tantras. The biographies of many of the mahasiddhas explicitly describe how they used such corpses to both gain and manifest their accomplishments or *siddhis*. A flayed human skin may also be stuffed with cotton, or wool, as a cushion, the prime function of which is to serve as a reminder of impermanence, suffering, death, and the ultimate emptiness of samsaric existence. The drawn effigy of a corpse may also be used as a meditation seat. But tantric practices which specify the use of a corpse are most commonly performed through the visualisation of a corpse seat. This visualised corpse is that of an enemy of the dharma who fulfils ten conditions. He or she is someone who has destroyed the dharma; abused the Three Jewels; stolen from the sangha; vilified the Mahayana teachings; harmed a teacher or guru; caused a schism in the sangha; hindered others' practices; who has no love or compassion; holds no pledges or vows; and holds wrong views about karma.

THE EIGHT ATTIRES OF THE CHARNEL GROUNDS

Wrathful deities, and many of the semi-wrathful *yidam* deities, wear as ornaments the 'eight attires of the charnel grounds' (Tib. *dur khrod kyi chas brgyad*). These consist of three facial ornaments – marks of cremation ash, blood, and human fat, applied to the 'bulges' of the face like war paint; three body ornaments – the flayed male skins of an elephant, human, and tiger; and two 'head' and 'snake' ornaments – a crown of five dry skulls and a garland of skulls or severed heads, and the 'revolting ornaments' of coiling snakes. These eight attires are said to have been torn from the slain body of the destructive Vedic god, Rudra, and worn as the 'spoils of war' by the wrathful and victorious Buddhist deities. Two further adornments are sometimes added to this list to create the 'ten magnificent attires' of the most wrathful Heruka deities, corresponding to the Herukas of the ten directions who dwell within the yogin's inner body mandala. These two adornments are a blazing mass of *kalagni* wisdom-fire, and the *vajra*-wings of Garuda.

The first facial ornament is a mark of human bone ash applied as a dot to the forehead (Tib. *thal chen gyi tshom bu*). It symbolises the ultimate conflagration of all changeable emotional defilements reduced to the same unchangeable ashes. On a more esoteric level it represents the 'seat' of the white *bodhichitta* in the crown *chakra*. Sometimes human ashes are described as being smeared all over the deity's body, symbolising the blissful spreading of white *bodhichitta* drops throughout all the channels of the subtle body.

The second facial ornament consists of drops of fresh blood (Tib. *khrag gi thig le*) applied to the 'three bulges' of the nose and cheeks, symbolising the overcoming of desire, the transmutation of self-centred passion into boundless compassion, the cultivation of great bliss as the essence of the red *bodhichitta* drops, and the realisation of the stage of 'clear light'.

The third facial ornament consists of smears of human fat (Tib. *shag gi zo ris*) applied to the bulge of the chin or neck, symbolising the emptiness of phenomena, the empowerment of the absolute truth of no self, and the realisation of the 'illusory body'. Collectively the war paint of human fat, blood, and cemetery ash also symbolise the destruction of the three poisons of aggression, desire, and ignorance; the deity's power over the three times of past, present, and future; and control over the three realms of *kamaloka* (blood; the desire realms), *rupaloka* (fat; the form realms), and *arupaloka* (ash; the formless realms).

The three bodily attires consist of the freshly-flayed and bloody skin of an elephant stretched behind the deity's back, a freshly-flayed human skin worn as a shawl, and a lower loincloth or dhoti made from a tigerskin. The stretched elephant skin (Tib. *glan po che'i pags pa*) represents the deity's 'expanse of reality' as the *dharmadhatu*, and the overcoming of ignorance, which is described as the deity's 'having torn the elephant of ignorance assunder'. The bloody interior of this elephant skin is frequently held by its two flayed right feet in the outstretched upper arms of the wrathful deity, with its head and front left foot appearing at the deity's right side, and its tail and rear left foot at the deity's left.

The flayed male human skin of an enemy of the dharma (Tib. *shin lpags kyi yang gzi*), symbolises the removal of the 'veil' of the five aggregates or *skandhas*, the deity's power to eliminate the darkness of delusion, and the overcoming of desire. This human skin is frequently draped around the shoulders of the deity with its right arm and leg knotted at the breast, its head and left arm appearing to the deity's right, and its left foot hanging to the left.

The tigerskin loincloth or dhoti (Tib. *stag lpags kyi sham thabs*) provokes terror in all enemies of the dharma, and symbolises the overcoming of anger or hatred. This loincloth is usually bound about the waist of wrathful deities, with its tail towards the front, its paws to either side, and occasionally with its head depicted over the right or left thigh. Deities in *yab yum* have loosened their tigerskin loincloths for sexual intercourse, and this loosening symbolises the casting aside of the dualistic belief in phenomena as outer object, and conceptual thought as the inner subject. The loosened tigerskin represents the deity's courage in having overcome the four Maras, and his rejection or 'casting aside' of the conceptual notion of subject and object.

Essentially the skins of the elephant, human, and tiger, symbolise the destruction of the three root poisons of ignorance, desire and hatred. Wrathful male deities wear a 'male' tigerskin, which symbolises by its phallic stripes the male emanation of *vajra*-wrath. The female consorts of these wrathful Heruka or protective deities wear loincloths of 'female' leopardskin, symbolising by its womb-shaped ovals or spots the female aspect of *vajra*-wrath and pride. However, many goddesses or *dakinis*, such as Vajravarahi, Nairatma, Kurukulla, and Simhamukha, also wear the tigerskin loincloth, though the consorts of wrathful Heruka forms such as Vajrakilaya, Yamantaka, Chemchog Heruka, Hayagriva, and Mahakala, wear the leopardskin loincloth.

The seventh attire of the charnel grounds comprises the 'revolting snake ornaments', and the eighth comprises the five-skull crown and the long necklace of fifty or fifty-one severed heads. The seventh and eighth attires are described in detail below.

Plate 137

This drawing illustrates the necklaces of skulls, severed heads, flowers, and snakes worn by wrathful deities, and the lower parts of the tiger and leopardskin loincloths worn by these wrathful gods and goddesses.

At the centres of the two drawings are shown the tail of a male deity's tigerskin to the left, and the female consort's leopardskin to the right. Surrounding the tigerskin on the left is a garland of small flowers. Certain deities wear these flower rosaries (Skt. *pushpamala*; Tib. *me tog 'phreng*), which are derived from the Indian custom of honouring a guru or respected person with a flower garland. The goddess Vajravarahi, for example, wears a long rosary of red *karavira* (Oleander) flowers, which in ancient India were presented to the corpse of a person killed by a king, and here symbolise the overcoming of concepts, or the 'death' of conceptual thought.

Surrounding the tail of the leopardskin on the right is the seventh of the 'eight great attires of the charnel grounds', the 'revolting ornaments' of *nagas* or serpents. The iconography and placement of these serpent ornaments are described on Plate 47, where the castes, colours, and names of the eight great *nagas* are listed. The long green, or blue-black, serpent depicted here as a neck garland or sacred thread is the *naga* king Vasuki, who formed the rope in the Vedic 'churning of the ocean' legend, and whom Shiva later took as his girdle.

Plate 137: Tiger and leopardskin *dhotis*, the garlands of severed heads and skulls

The eighth of the 'eight attires' are the 'head ornaments' of the five-skull crown or tiara (see Plate 138), and the long necklace of fifty or fifty-one skulls or severed heads. The necklaces of skulls and severed heads are depicted in the outer arcs of Plate 137, with the individual head of an enemy at the lower centre.

The necklace or garland of severed heads (Skt. *chinna-munda mala*; Tib. *dbu bcad ma 'phreng ba*) essentially represents the masculine principle of form; and the necklace of skulls (Skt. *munda mala*; Tib. *mi mgo skam po'i phreng ba*), the feminine principle of emptiness. Although there is no definitive rule governing whether these attributes should be worn by gods and goddesses respectively, the garland of severed heads is predominantly assigned to male deities, and the garland of skulls to female deities. The description given in a particular deity's *sadhana* always specifies which of these garlands are worn. Certain deities are also described as wearing both the severed-head garland and the garland of skulls.

The garland of skulls may be described as dry, moist, or dripping, although no visual distinction is made between these three categories in their artistic representation. The grinning or 'haughty' skulls are painted white, and may either appear in an upright sequence as depicted on the left of Plate 137, or in a continuous cranium-to-jawbone sequence as shown on the right. The eye-dots within the skulls' sockets may gaze penetratingly forwards, or glance towards the five directions – up, down, left, right, and centre. The skull's four canine teeth may also be sharply bared, symbolising the biting through of the four Maras.

The garland's severed heads are described as freshly severed and dripping with blood. The heads are male, as are all sacrificial victims, and may be individually characterised with beards, stubble, moustaches, wrinkles, long hair, short hair, shaved hair, or a balding head. Their startled eyes are wide open, and may occasionally be pulled from their sockets. In certain traditions the heads may be sequentially coloured pale red, green, and yellow, paralleling the symbolism of the *khatvanga*'s severed heads (see Plates 115 and

116). Although the heads are described as dripping with blood, this blood is rarely depicted in Tibetan art. It is however explicitly illustrated in Hindu tantric art, especially in the forms of the wrathful *mahavidya* and *matri* goddesses, such as Kali, Tara, Chinnamasta, Chamunda, and Durga. Here a garland of eight, blood-dripping, severed heads is commonly depicted, representing the eight mundane obsessions or 'worldly dharmas' of praise and blame, pleasure and pain, loss and gain, infamy and fame.

The two garlands of severed heads shown in Plate 137 are strung upon a thread made from twisting human intestines, which symbolise the illusory nature of all phenomena, with the heads representing phenomena as form. The main symbolism of the garland of fifty severed heads or skulls is the purification of speech, since the garland hangs from the neck or throat *chakra*. The purification of body is represented by the five-skull tiara at the deity's crown, which symbolises the drying up, exhaustion, or death of the five aggregates (Skt. *skandhas*) of the personality. The purification of mind is represented by the eight-spoked bone wheel at the deity's heart, symbolising the eight channels or *nadis* emanating from the heart centre.

The garland of fifty skulls or severed heads representing purification of speech, is derived from the combination of the sixteen vowels and thirty-four consonants of the Sanskrit alphabet. As a complete rosary or *mantra-mala* encompassing the whole spectrum of phonetic sound, the severed heads and skulls have a double meaning. They may represent the vowel and consonant sounds as utterances made by each individual head, which are then decapitated or 'sacrificially purified'; or in the case of skulls, purified from the 'flesh' of conventional sound. Alternatively they hang, as 'characters', from their unifying thread in the same manner that the Sanskrit characters 'hang' from a horizontal upper stave.

Mantra is the most subtle form of the deity, and every form generated or visualised arises from its own specifically coloured seed-syllable or *bija*. The numerology and

317

symbolism of the Sanskrit vowels and consonants is profound and complex in Vajrayana or 'Mantrayana' (Skt. *mantranaya*) Buddhism, especially in the *anuttarayoga tantras*. The rosaries of white vowels and red consonants may also correspond to the white and red *bodhichitta* drops, and their melting and movement through the subtle channels or *nadis* of the body.

The sixteen white vowel sounds (Skt. *ali*, *svara*; Tib. *dbyangs can*) commonly form a fixed list in both the Sanskrit and Tibetan alphabets, but the thirty-four fixed consonants (Skt. *kali*, *vyanjana*; Tib. *gsal byed*) may sometimes be extended to include a listing of forty consanants in the Tibetan alphabet. When these sixteen vowels and forty consonants are doubled, as clockwise and anticlockwise 'rosaries' of thirty-two white vowels and eighty red consonants, they correspond to the thirty-two major and eighty minor marks of a Buddha or enlightened being.

When a long necklace (Tib. *do shal*) of fifty-one severed heads or skulls are described, they symbolise the purification of the fifty-one mental factors or thought processes. These mental factors (Skt. *chaitasika*; Tib. *sems byung*), or mental events, are listed and described in the early Buddhist *abhidharma* texts, and occur as the fifty-one ways in which awareness as 'primary mind' (Skt. *chitta*; Tib. *sems*) relates to perceived objects. The philosophical nuances that differentiate these fifty-one mental factors appear as a rather obscure list in English translation, yet their metaphysical importance in *abhidharma* psychology is extremely profound. The *Abhidharmasamuchaya*, compiled by the fourth-century Indian Buddhist master Asanga, explains in great detail the philosophy of the Chittamatra, or 'Mind Only' school, on the division of primary mind and the fifty-one secondary mental events. The *Abhidharmakosha*, compiled by the fourth-century Indian philosopher Vasubandhu, presents the Vaibhashika school's philosophical division of primary mind, and only forty-six secondary mental factors are listed. However, the Chittamatra listing of fifty-one mental factors or defiled thought processes prevails in the descriptive symbolism of the long rosary of fifty-one severed heads or dry skulls.

Thus a necklace of fifty or 'half a hundred' freshly severed heads or dry skulls symbolises purification of speech as the sixteen vowels and thirty-four consonants of the Sanskrit alphabet; and a necklace of fifty-one heads or skulls symbolises purification of mind as the severance of the fifty-one defiled thought processes.

THE SIX BONE ORNAMENTS AND THE FIVE-SKULL CROWN

Wrathful male deities, and semi-wrathful *yidam* deities, wear six different bone ornaments, representing the essence of the six transcendental perfections or *paramitas*. The deity's bone earrings represent the perfection of patience or fortitude; the bone necklaces represent the perfection of generosity or charity; the bone bracelets, armlets, and anklets represent the perfection of discipline or morality; the bone belt represents the

perfection of effort or energy; the bone wheel, worn upon the crown of the deity's head, represents the perfection of meditation; and cemetery or bone ash, either smeared over the body, or marking the forehead, represents the perfection of wisdom. The first five perfections are classified into the male 'accumulation of method', and the sixth perfection is classified alone as the female 'accumulation of wisdom'. The perfection of wisdom is represented by cemetery ash, as undifferentiated ash is the one substance that remains when the whole of phenomenal reality has been conflagrated in the fire of wisdom. Female wrathful deities or *dakinis* only wear the first five of these bone ornaments, as their bodily form itself represents the perfection of wisdom.

In the highly symbolic iconography of the major *yidam* deities of *the anuttarayoga tantras*, such as Chakrasamvara, Hevajra, Guhyasamaja, Kalachakra, a profound numerological interpretation is applied to the six bone ornaments in relationship to the channel wheels and *nadis*. This numerological symbolism is described on page 146.

The six bone ornaments of male *yidam* deities, and the five bone ornaments of female *dakinis*, are worn as part of the elaborate ritual costumes used in Tibetan sacred dances. These dances are performed during major sacred festivals which have often been revealed in 'visionary transmissions' by great Tibetan masters. In general these dances are classified into the highly symbolic and slow dance movements (Tib. *gar*) of the *yidams* and *dakinis*, and the more forceful and dynamic masked dances (Tib. *cham*) of the wrathful deities. The bone ornaments worn in these ritual dances are exquisitely carved – especially the netted bone apron and belt, which are commonly adorned with intricately carved images of *dakinis*.

The six perfections are also symbolised in the jewel ornaments worn by peaceful deities or bodhisattvas. Collectively these jewel ornaments are known as the 'eight precious ornaments', and with the 'five divine silk garments' create the 'thirteen *sambhogakaya* ornaments' of peaceful deities – symbolically corresponding to the thirteen umbrella emblems of the *chakravartin* (see page 128). The eight jewel ornaments are the tiara, earrings, short necklace around the neck, medium necklace hanging to the level of the heart, long necklace hanging four finger-widths below the navel, bracelets, anklets, and jewelled belt. The five divine silks are an upper white silk bodice embroidered with gold, a multicoloured silk dhoti or loincloth, a yellow scarf worn as a sash, a multicoloured ribbon under the tiara, and a long blue or green scarf draped over the shoulders.

The five-skull crown of wrathful and *yidam* deities (Tib. *thod skam gyi dbu rgyan*), represents the undifferentiated union of the Five Buddha wisdoms. Each of the five skulls is commonly surmounted by a black iron *vajra* (Tib. *rdo rje nag po'i rtse phran*), or a precious gold-encased jewel (Tib. *rin po che'i rtse phran*). These five jewel finials are often coloured to correspond to the Five Buddhas; the central jewel represents the Lord of the Buddha Family to which the deity belongs. In the case of a deity belonging to Akshobhya's Vajra Family, for example, a blue jewel is depicted above the central skull of Akshobhya, with the yellow and white

Plate 138: Skulls and skull offerings

jewels of Ratnasambhava and Vairochana to the left, and the red and green jewels of Amitabha and Amoghasiddhi to the right. This mandala sequence is also represented on the jewel tiaras (Tib. *cod pan*) worn by peaceful deities, although more commonly these jewels are simply depicted in an alternating red and blue sequence.

Plate 138

This illustration depicts examples of the stylistic variations of skulls and skull offerings.

At the upper centre are two drawings of groups of three skulls, which form the central motif of the five-skull crown worn by wrathful deities. The diadem of five dry white skulls symbolises the qualities of the Five Buddhas as the 'death' of the five poisons and the five aggregates of the personality. These five skulls are usually joined by a chain of golden or black five-pronged *vajras*, and usually rest upon small red lotus flowers. Esoterically the white skull and red lotus represent the male and female *bodhichitta* drops; the white skull and *vajra*-chain symbolises the arising of the 'illusory body' from the state of 'clear light'.

The upper drawing of the three central skulls of the five-skull crown shows the central skull mounted upon a large open lotus, and the two side skulls mounted upon flowers. Emanating on either side and behind the central skull are two golden *makara*-tail jewel ornaments. The lower drawing of the three skulls depicts the delicate jewel-chains, which hang below the skulls and adorn the forehead of the deity wearing the skull crown. The eyes of these skulls all gaze downwards, although as a stylistic innovation the eyes may also glance towards the five mandala directions – forwards (centre), downwards (east), to the left (south), upwards (west), and to the right (north).

Below these three skulls is a single skull with its eyes gazing forwards and flames emanating from the corners of its jawbone. To the upper left is a skull with a human heart in its mouth. To the left again are two drawings of freshly-skinned and inverted blood-filled skulls, with their scalps and hair intact. Below and to the left of the lower of these two fresh skulls is a skull-lamp full of human fat, with its tongue burning as a wick. This symbolises the purification (flames) of the body (skull), speech (tongue), and mind (fat), and derives from the Hindu cremation ritual and the necromantic 'corpse practice' of *shavasadhana*. In the rest of the upper half of this illustrated page are other stylised drawings of the skull, with a skeleton-club (Tib. *keng rus dbyug*) on the right of the page.

Just below the centre of the page is a large drawing of a skull-cup full of boiling blood upon a flaming skull tripod, with the two inverted skulls on either side also full of boiling blood. An offering of a skull-cup full of blood or alcohol is said to boil in the presence of a wrathful deity. For female *dakinis* this symbolises the blazing, melting, and dripping caused by the increase of the inner heat (Tib. *gtum mo*). To the left and right of this central skull-cup are two drawings of skull-lamps (Tib. *mar me thod*) fuelled by melted

human fat, and with wicks twisted from the hair of a corpse or a widow. The lamp on the left appears as an inverted skull with three blazing twisted-hair wicks; this symbolises the three psychic channels or *nadis*, and the transmutation into wisdom-light of the three primary poisons of ignorance, desire, and aversion. The lamp on the right appears as a skull-cup mounted upon three skulls and four vertebrae, with a thick twisted-hair wick terminating in three flaming points.

Surrounding these drawings in the lower half of the page are various examples of inverted skulls, full of hot and swirling blood. Six of the drawings in the bottom area are depicted as 'fresh skulls' (Tib. *thod rlon*), adorned with hair and partially peeled scalps. The remaining four drawings depict inverted 'dry skulls' (Tib. *thod skam*).

As a 'swirling offering' the blood or *amrita* within a skull-cup circles in a clockwise motion in the symbolism of the father tantras, and in an anticlockwise direction for the mother tantras. In the three activities of pacifying, increasing, and subjugating the liquid also swirls in a clockwise direction, whilst in the fourth activity of wrath it circles in an anticlockwise direction.

RITUAL OFFERING CAKES (Tib. *gtor ma*) AND THREAD CROSSES (Tib. *mdos*)

In ancient India the offerings presented to the deities were known as *bali*, meaning a sacrificial offering or a gift. As food offerings the *bali* usually consisted of fruit, medicinal herbs, grains, sweets, rice cakes, and various auspicious ritual substances. In certain rituals the prescribed sacrificial offering consisted of meat, blood, or alcohol; animal sacrifice often constituted the ritual *bali*. The left-hand Hindu tantric ritual of *panchamakara* – meaning the five 'M's – prescribed offerings of wine (*madya*), meat (*mamsa*), fish (*matsya*), parched grain (*mudra*), and sexual union (*maithuna*).

Several legends are recounted of how during the lifetime of the Buddha his disciples were advised to present sacrificial food offerings to the hungry ghosts in order to placate their hindering influences. One early legend describes how an ogress with five hundred children took to stealing human children in order to feed her offspring. Shakyamuni Buddha took one of the ogressess's children and hid it in his alms bowl, and with increasing grief, having searched everywhere for her child, the ogress approached the Buddha for help. Shakyamuni revealed to her the extent of the suffering that she had caused by pointing out to that she had only lost one of her five hundred children, whilst many of her victims had lost their only child. The ogress vowed that she would stop killing children if her own child was found, and taking the child from his alms bowl the Buddha gave her a piece of kneaded dough that he held in his hand, promising that every day his disciples would present a similar cake of dough from their midday meal. This tradition of presenting a portion of the meal as a food offering to the spirits and hungry ghosts has been maintained in many monastic traditions since the time of the Buddha.

As the early Indian Mahayana and later Vajrayana traditions evolved, the *bali* offering composed of the pleasing substances of grains, fruit, the 'three whites' of milk, curds, and ghee, the 'three sweets' of honey, sugar, and molasses, medicinal herbs, flowers, water, and incense, became an indispensable preliminary offering for all ritual practices.

With the advent of the Indian Buddhist traditions into Tibet, and the scarcity of many of the prescribed substances as freshly or freely available products, the Indian *bali* took on the form of the Tibetan sacrificial cake or *torma*, made primarily from the indigenous ingredients of barley flour and yak butter. According to Bonpo histories the practice of making sacrificial cakes from a dough of moulded barley flour was already well established in Tibet before the introduction of Buddhism. Both of these Tibetan traditions have many written texts which specify the designs and ingredients for a multitude of *torma* offerings.

The Tibetan term *torma* (Tib. *gtor ma*), meaning a sacrifical object or offering, is derived from the verb (Tib. *gtor ba*) meaning to cast, throw, scatter, or break up. The term '*gtor*' also implies the act of giving without attachment as an expression of pure motivation; the suffix '*ma*' means mother, and implies the selfless unconditional love that a mother bestows upon her children.

There are three main types of *torma*. The first is the offering *torma* that is presented in mundane rituals such as pacifying, increasing, and eliminating hindrances. This form of *torma* is broken into pieces after the ritual and scattered as food for birds, wild animals, spirits and hungry ghosts. The second type of *torma* is the conical food *torma* (Tib. *tshogs gtor*), which is distributed and eaten by the participants after a ritual as a medicinal or spiritual substance. The third and largest category of *tormas* are the deity *tormas*, which are usually uniquely constructed to represent the symbolic form or mandala of a particular deity.

Although there are a limited number of basic shapes for *torma* designs, there are a vast number of decorative designs and embellishments that occur within the different schools and lineages of Tibetan Buddhism. Some *tormas* are extremely simple, consisting only of a small unadorned tapering cone or triangular pyramid, whilst others are extremely elaborate and may measure more than a man's height.

The colour and shape of a *torma* is related to the form of the meditational deity being propitiated, or to the activity being performed. Peaceful *tormas* for deities such as White Tara and Avalokiteshvara are commonly white with a rounded conical form. The *tormas* for semi-wrathful *yidam* deities, such as Chakrasamvara or Vajrayogini, are commonly red with a circular base, a heart-shaped body with shoulders, and a '*vajra*-tip' shaped like Mt Meru. The *tormas* for wrathful deities, such as Mahakala, Yamantaka, or Vajrakilaya, are commonly red with an upper triangular flame embellishment, and often with the main attributes of the deity modelled as butter sculptures. For directional protectors the *torma* is round and coloured according to the direction of the deity. *Tormas* used for destructive rituals are commonly triangular in shape and coloured red or black. White, yellow, red, and black *tormas* may also be employed to correspond to the four activites or *karmas*. But in general the body of a *torma* is usually coloured white (Tib. *dkar gtor*) or red (Tib. *dmar gtor*), representing the peaceful and wrathful deities as compassionate activity and blood sacrifice.

Various ingredients are mixed with the dough – which is moulded like plasticine from barley flour, butter or water. These include the twenty-five substances (see Plate 103), black tea, alcohol, or meat, to accord with the 'tastes' of the meditational deity. For the wrathful and semi-wrathful *anuttarayoga tantra* deities the ingredients prescribed may include grains, pulses, meat, fish, alcohol, garlic, sweets, milk, and water.

The body of the *torma* is usually heart-shaped with three sides and represents the body, speech, and mind of the deity. The heart-shaped centre also represents the central channel, and the 'wings' which are placed upon the two outer sides, represent the lunar and solar channels. This symbolism is often repeated at the finial of the *torma*, where the emblems of a crescent moon, sun, and dissolving point or *nada*, are displayed. The pointed tip or *nada* of the *torma* represents wisdom, and the round lower base represents the activity of pacification. The triangular base of red or black *tormas* which are employed as symbolic weapons to exorcise evil spirits, and which are caste away at a crossroads after the ritual, represent destructive activity. A four-tiered square base represents Mt Meru, and the four elements of earth, water, fire, and air. A five-tiered base represents the five mental and physicial constituents, and the five elements which are to be purified.

A single, coloured, or multicoloured sculpted lotus, which commonly has eight petals and often supports the base of the *torma*, represents both the lotus throne of deity *tormas* and the eight petals of the heart centre. The heart-shaped body of the *torma* which arises from the lotus represents the ascent of the central channel embodying the indestructible drop as the most subtle consciousness of the deity.

The front faces of many *tormas* are commonly decorated with a series of flat butter-sculpted discs which either ascend vertically or are arranged in a cross formation in the cardinal directions. These discs represent the petals of flowers, and are commonly coloured white with variably coloured central dots or seed-syllables. A cross of four petals, with a central fifth petal, is usually orientated with the eastern petal at the bottom, and either represents the mandala directions in deity *tormas*, or the five aggregates of form, feeling, perception, motivation, and consciousness, which form the bases to be purified in offering *tormas*. Often four small auxiliary *tormas* are placed in front of, and below, the main *torma*, representing the four directional guardians positioned in the east, south, west and north, from left to right. The top petal of many *tormas* is often extended into a pointed *nada* at its circular tip. Multicoloured and multi-petalled flower and lotus designs are meticulously sculpted on the most elaborate *tormas*. Circular jewels – fashioned from flat discs of coloured butter of decreasing size creating a series of ascending crescents – often adorn the bases and sides of such highly decorated *tormas*.

The red or black *tormas* offered to wrathful deities are usually embellished with decorations of white, red, and black. Elaborate wrathful *tormas* may be decorated on their red or black bodies with meticulous designs in a large palette of colours. The emblems of the deity, such as the skull-cup and chopper in the case of Mahakala, may be sculpted within the upper triangle of fire at the *torma*'s summit. The outer flames of these wrathful *tormas* are most commony coloured in the five-colour sequence of the mandala's 'mountain of fire' (Tib. *me ri*). On the *tormas* of semi-wrathful *yidam* deities this five-coloured flame band represents the 'rosary of light' (Tib. *'od phreng*) which encircles the deity's aureole as the Five Buddha wisdoms. Wrathful *tormas* may also be decorated with the face of the deity at its centre, and the wrathful ornaments of skulls, flames, hearts, and friezes of dots and threads in its surrounding areas. Wooden moulding boards (Tib. *zan par*) are used to impress the small forms of animals, spirits, humans, effigies, weapons, and magical symbols, which form the retinues or assemblies of the most complex *tormas* used in rituals of ransoming and exorcism (Tib. *glud tshab*), or where complex mandalas are constructed with *tormas* representing the deities of the mandala and a thread cross (Tib. *mdos*) representing the mandala palace itself.

Deity *tormas* may also be classified into female *tormas* (Tib. *gtor mo*) with a slender form, and male *tormas* (Tib. *gtor po*) with a more substantial or angular shouldered form. Some of the main classes of *tormas* are: the main deity *torma*; the *yidam, dakini,* lama, and protector *tormas*; the initiation *torma*; the red *torma* (Tib. *dmar gtor*) and the white *torma* (Tib. *dkar gtor*); the long-life *torma*; the *torma* for the wrathful offering of the five senses (see Plate 140); the *tormas* for worldly guests, hindering forces, local deities, earth lords, spirits, *nagas*, and the fire god Agni; the *tormas* of the four activities which are cast into the sacred fire in the *homa* rituals; the feast offering *torma* (Tib. *tshogs gtor*); the *tormas* of the great prayer festival, the end of year, and new year festivals; and the multitude of auxiliary *tormas* that are specifically constructed for a vast number of ritual purposes.

Four levels of *tormas* are esoterically described in the Highest Yoga Tantra systems. The first is the 'outer offering *torma*', which either takes the form of the main deity *torma* or the form of eight skull-cups containing drinking water, water for washing the deity's feet, flowers, incense, light, perfume, food, and musical instruments, representing the substances which are pleasing to the deity being propitiated. The second is the 'inner offering *torma*' as described on Plate 141. The third is the 'secret offering *torma*', which arises as the visualisation of the merged white and red *bodhichitta* drops in the lotus of the heart centre. The fourth is the 'excellent offering *torma*' which arises as the coincidence of great bliss and emptiness, or as the direct and spontaneous realisation of Mahamudra – with no distinction between offerer, offering, and deity. In the realisation of Mahamudra there is no meditator, no meditation, and no object of meditation.

Plate 139

In the upper area of this illustration are examples of thread-crosses (Tib. *mdos; nam mkha'*) which, like *tormas*, are constructed to function as a temporary abode of a deity during the performance of a ritual, or serve as 'spirit-catchers' to ensnare harmful spirits. The employment of the thread-cross in magical rituals is common to both the Bon and Buddhist traditions, and is believed by the Buddhists to have been introduced into Tibet by Padmasambhava. Similar traditions of constructing crosses of coloured thread for the magical purposes of exorcism, healing and the worship of ancestral spirits are found throughout many indigenous cultures and folk traditions around the world.

The ceremonial construction of a Tibetan thread-cross is often an extremely elaborate procedure, involving much preparation of *tormas*, offerings and substitute images as ransom offerings. Nebesky-Wojkowitz devotes a whole chapter to this subject in *Oracles and Demons of Tibet*, and Stephan Bayer includes a section on the employment of the thread-cross in his book *The Cult of Tara*.

In its simplest form the thread-cross is constructed of two pieces of wood tied into the shape of a cross, around which is strung a diamond-shaped arrangement of coloured threads creating the appearance of a spider's web. The threads are arranged in a specific colour sequence depending upon the ritual being performed, and up to six colours – black, white, red, yellow, green and blue – may be used. More complex thread-crosses are constructed in a large variety of geometrical forms. These include a diamond with four smaller directional crosses, a knot-shaped form, an inverted kite-shaped form, a hexagonal form, or a combination of various geometrical forms. The most elaborate thread-crosses are often constructed in three-dimensional form, with a foundation of horizontal hexagonal discs representing the element bases, a four-walled mandala palace with a triangular roof, and a complex two-dimensional thread-cross construction arising above the roof. The lower base of the thread-cross is usually constructed on a four-tiered representation of Mt Meru, with directional lamps, food offerings, dough stamped images of animals and weapons, and representations of a host of ransom offerings and effigies placed upon the tiers. The ends of the supporting sticks may be decorated with feathers or white cotton tufts representing the sky and clouds. A small image (Tib. *tsak li*) of the propitiated deity may be placed at the top of the thread-cross and the symbolic face of a man or woman may be drawn or modelled at the centre of the cross.

In rituals of subjugation and destructive activity the thread-cross functions as a web into which evil spirits are enticed by specific offerings and become ensnared within the maze of the threads. These thread-crosses are then destroyed by breaking, burning, or casting away at a crossroads, and serve a similar function to the wrathful *tormas* that are specifically molded to ensnare different classes of spirits. As a protective device a thread-cross is often erected upon the roofs of dwellings or monasteries to ensnare the

Plate 139: Thread crosses, *tormas*, ransom offerings

wandering spirits and ghosts that may afflict these establishments.

Across the top of the illustration are three sections of diamond-shaped and hexagonal-shaped crosses, with balls of coloured thread in the upper right corner. In the upper left is a knot-shaped cross formed from eight sticks creating a pattern of five diamonds. In the upper centre is the most common form of a thread-cross arranged as a large central diamond with four surrounding smaller diamonds. To the the upper left of this cross are two small drawings of crossed sticks with the syllables of the four elements (*Lam, Yam, Ram, Vam*) represented by small circles. These crossed sticks are used for pinning down and enclosing evil spirits. To the right of the upper central cross are two six-pointed stars forming a *dharmodaya* or 'reality source'. The lower interwoven *dharmodaya* is commonly represented upon the *torma* of Vajrayogini. In the upper right corner is an inverted kite-shaped thread-cross, and below on the right edge is a section of a complex thread-cross formed from several geometric shapes. Across to the left of this is a thread-cross shaped in the form of an interwoven endless knot. Across again to the left of the centre is an interwoven knot of nine crossed swords which is held in the left hand by the Bon protective deity 'Red Razor Takla' (Tib. sTag la spu gri dmar po).

Across from the swords on the left edge of the illustration is a drawing of the shouldered base of a male protector *torma* with a squared '*vajra*-tip'. The curved front of this triangular *torma* and its two straight sides are decorated with circular discs, jewels, emblems and embellishments which correspond to the particular deity being evoked. Below this is a long-life *torma* (Tib. *tshe gtor*), molded in the form of a longevity vase with a lotus base and a conical lotus-mounted tip. Below again is the *torma* ornament of a jewel fashioned from overlaid discs of coloured butter sculpture. To the right of this is a heart-shaped 'feast offering' *torma* (Tib. *tshogs gtor*) placed at the centre of a bowl of fruit. This *torma* is made of barley flour mixed with ingredients such as barley beer (Tib. *chang*), the three 'sweet substances' and the three 'white substances', and meat in certain rituals. The front of this *torma* is decorated with a butter-sculpted lotus, an eight-spoked wheel, and with the emblems of a crescent moon, sun and *nada* at its tip. At the end of a feast offering ritual (Tib. *tshogs puja*) the *torma* is broken into pieces and distributed as a medicinal food offering to the ritual participants. Above this food *torma* is a bell-shaped *torma* with a triangular front used in rituals of spirit subjugation. To the right of this is a stupa-shaped *torma* with a four-tiered Mt Meru base, and below this a group of three flame-topped *tormas*.

To the right of the lower handle of the crossed-swords is a conical *torma* with two discs and three 'fingers' (Tib. *mtheb kyu*) or buttons of dough at its base. This form of *torma* is offered as a group of three *tormas* to a specific category of goddesses (Tib. *btsan ma*). These three *tormas* are depicted below in a tray, and are coloured red, white and black respectively, with triangular, round and square-shaped bases. To the right of this conical *torma* is a larger drawing of the

front of a red *torma* (Tib. *dmar gtor*) offered to a protective deity. This *torma* has two discs on its front and is ornamented with triangular friezes of black and white. Across to the right is a drawing of the back of this red *torma* showing its ornamental triangular sides and rounded conical top. Between and above these two drawings of the red *torma* is a conical white *torma* (Tib. *dkar gtor*) which is presented to the 'lords of the earth' (Tib. *sa bdag*) as a preliminary offering, requesting these spirits to allow the ritual to be successfully performed. Across to the right of the back of the red *torma* is a small drawing of two 'fingers' (Tib. *mtheb kyu*) of barley dough topped by a round pill (Tib. *ril bu*), commonly placed around *tormas* as an additional food offering to the deities or spirits.

To the right of the handle of the endless-knot thread-cross are three conical triangular *tormas* in offering bowls. The first *torma* with an enclosing bud or vaginal-shaped base is the black *torma* for another group of goddesses (Tib. *sman mo*). The second is a general red *torma* offered to female demons. The third is a black *torma* presented to the four Maras. Above these three *tormas* are two drawings of triangular receptacles or 'iron prisons' containing crossed sticks and grasses which are thrown as magical weapons (Tib. *thun*) or hurled offerings (Tib. *zor rdzas*).

Across from left to right in a row beginning beneath the *vajra*-handle of the crossed-swords are nine *tormas*. The first is a triangular red *torma* enhaloed in flames, used for dispelling hindering forces (Tib. *bgegs gtor*). The second, third and fourth drawings show the basic shapes of three auxiliary *tormas* which are employed for general purposes. The fifth drawing depicts the shape of the red triangular *torma* which is common to many classes of spirits. The sixth drawing depicts the principal *torma* (Tib. *rtsa ba'i gtor*) of the goddess Palden Lhamo, with a triangular receptacle at its base and a triangular flame-enhaloed body decorated with flowers, discs and jewels. The seventh and eighth drawings depict the shapes of several offering *tormas* (Tib. *mchod gtor*) which are presented to the main deity. The ninth drawing depicts the shape of the presentational food *torma* (Tib. *gsol gtor*) which is employed for concluding rituals.

In between the seventh, eight and ninth *tormas* are two drawings of *tormas* formed by the simple procedure of squeezing a piece of rolled dough in the fist to create wave-like indentations. This 'fist *torma*' (Tib. *chang bu*) occurs in two forms: when it is pressed at one end by the thumb it represents an abundance of food; when it is pressed at both ends it forms a specific offering for the *nagas*.

In the row below are another group of nine *torma* offerings. The first drawing on the left depicts a bowl containing the three (Tib. *bstan ma*) goddess *tormas* described previously. The second bowl contains three triangular fire *tormas* which are coloured black, white and red, and function as a wrathful variation of the former The third drawing shows a triangular *torma* decorated with a human heart, which is presented to the *ma mo* goddesses. The fourth smaller triangular *torma* is pierced with poisonous thorns, and is used in a ritual of destroying malignant spirits imprisoned within the *torma* by symbolically hacking them to pieces with weapons or burning them in fire. The next two conical *tormas* depicted in bowls are the red *tormas* presented to Rahula. The first is decorated with the slanting rows of wrathful eyes that cover Rahula's bodily form. The second is decorated with slanting bands of colour. In between these two *tormas* is the black *torma* for the *maras* (Tib. *bdud gtor*). To the right of this is a triangular *naga torma* (Tib. *klu gtor*) encircled by a snake. The last *torma* on the right depicts the form of the red or black auxiliary *torma* employed in the ritual cycles of many wrathful deities, such as Palden Lhamo and Vajrakilaya.

Below the *tormas* of the human heart and Rahula's eyes are two *tormas* specifically dedicated to Shiva as Mahadeva, 'the great god'. The upper drawing depicts Mahadeva's erect penis encircled by a rosary of smaller penises and with three vulture feathers inserted into the tip, symbolising the trinities of Shiva's trident and the three main psychic channels. The lower drawing depicts a triangular *torma* with Mahadeva's penis and testicles at its apex, again crowned with three feathers, and his consort Parvati's vagina discharging menstrual blood below.

Across to the right is a large heart-shaped deity *torma* (Tib. *mchod gtor*), resting upon a lotus base and embellished with flowers. Below this is a magical weapon (Tib. *thun*) which is cast and broken as a 'hurled offering' (Tib. *zor rdzas*). To the right of this is a heart-shaped black *torma* with five discs, mounted upon a lotus above a square four-tiered Mt Meru base. In the lower right corner is an offering *torma* to a principal deity, such as Chakrasmvara, with three small entourage *tormas* placed in front of it. Above is a drawing of the main *torma* for Chakrasamvara and Vajravarahi, and above to the left is a small entourage *torma* for the retinue of these two principal deities.

Across the bottom right corner is a drawing of a wooden molding board (Tib. *zan par*) which is used to stamp out the dough impressions of the multitude of animals, weapons, diagrams, and ransom offerings employed in both thread-cross and *torma* rituals.

In the bottom left corner are two drawings of the 'ransom offerings' (Tib. *glud tshabs*) which are used as substitutes or decoys to divert the malignant influences of spirits away from human beings, their property and possessions. The wooden tablet on the left depicts the image of a man above, with the male symbol of an arrow in his right 'method' hand. His property is depicted in the lower half of the tablet and the symbol of the male *vajra* crowns this triangular plaque. The tablet on the right depicts the image of a woman holding the female symbol of a spindle in her left 'wisdom' hand, and the woman's property and livestock depicted below, with the symbol of the female lotus at the plaque's top. To the right of these two tablets are two smaller plaques bearing the images of the male arrow crowned by a *vajra*, and the female spindle crowned by a lotus. To the right again are three drawing of spindles (Tib. *'phang*). The first depicts the long elegant Central Asian spindle. The second shows a typical Tibetan spindle, consisting of a wooden rod weighed down with a drilled-stone or a clay or wooden weight. The third drawing shows a conical Tibetan wooden

spindle. As a magical weapon the spindle is wound with multicoloured thread and is known as a 'variegated spindle' (Tib. *'phang bkra*).

Ransom effigies are commonly made from dough in the likeness of the person afflicted by evil spirits, and includes amongst its ingredients the nail clippings, hair, and a piece of clothing from the afflicted victim.

THE WRATHFUL OFFERING OF THE FIVE SENSES

The 'wrathful offering of the five senses' (Tib. *khro bo'i dbang po lnga tshogs*) is also known as the 'garland of the five senses' (Tib. *dbang po lnga yi me tog*), or the 'flower of the senses' (Tib. *me tog dbang po*).

This offering is commonly depicted as a *torma* presented to wrathful deities, and corresponds to the peaceful offerings of the senses which are presented before peaceful deities (see Plates 92–95). Here, however, instead of the beautiful objects of the senses – a mirror, a musical instrument, perfume, fruit, and silk – the actual sense organs themselves are represented. The base of the wrathful sense offering consists of a skull or skull-cup – which may be mounted upon a tripod of three small skulls or severed heads – containing the five sense organs. These are the heart (Tib. *snying*) or body (Tib. *lus*), representing touch; the eyes (Tib. *mig*), representing sight; the ears (Tib. *rna wa*), representing sound; the nose (Tib. *sna*), representing smell; and the tongue (Tib. *lce*), representing taste.

As a *torma* this offering is hand-moulded from a dough made from parched barley flour and water, and colourfully glazed as a butter sculpture with mineral pigments or vegetable dyes. Specific ingredients are mixed with the dough in order to please the deity being propitiated (see *tormas* on Plate 139).

As an outer offering *torma* the wrathful offering of the five senses is commonly depicted on thangkas of wrathful deities, and is usually positioned in front of the centre of the deity's lotus throne, or it may be placed to one side of the deity's throne with a blood-filled skull-cup on the other side. Symbolically the presentation of this offering of the five sense organs represents the most subtle level of consciousness.

When the wrathful offering of the five senses is pictorially depicted on a thangka, the five sense organs of the heart, eyes, ears, nose, and tongue are represented as having been torn or ripped from the body, and assembled as a 'flower offering' (Tib. *me tog tshogs*). The sixth sense faculty of consciousness is represented by a silken arrow penetrating the heart. This silk arrow symbolises the body, speech, and mind of the deity as empowering the organs of the five senses. The arrow's shaft represents the central channel or body of the deity; the arrow's flight and silk banner, the *mantra* or speech of the deity; and the arrow's tip penetrating into the heart represents the mind of the deity, manifesting as the most subtle consciousness of the 'indestructible drop' at the heart centre (in ritual use the arrow is removed from the *torma* before it is cast away).

Plate 140: The wrathful offering of the five senses

Plate 140

The drawing illustrates nineteen different examples in which the 'flower of the sense organs' may be depicted. The central heart is coloured red, and is commonly painted like a lotus bud, with a lower sheath of muscle from which the naked 'bud' of the heart arises. The ears and nose are painted in flesh tone, with the ears attached to the sides of the heart, and the nose tilted back to reveal the nostrils in front. The tongue is painted pink or red, and usually lolls over the front of the skull-cup. The eyes and optic nerves are painted as long white stalks, which usually arise behind the heart and gaze towards either side. The eyeballs are usually coloured yellow and brown or blue-black on their pupils, with a red tint on the white of the eyes to show that they are bloodshot. The red bloodshot eyes of wrathful deities symbolise their vigilance, wrathful compassion, and *vajra*-anger. The silken arrow (Tib. *mda' dar*) that penetrates the centre of the heart, is usually adorned with a red or black silk canopy, banner or ribbon, symbolising the subjugating or destructive activity of the wrathful deity. Fresh red blood usually fills the edges and centre of the skull-cup, and flames may emanate from around the skull.

Seven of the skull-cups depicted in this illustration rest upon tripods of skulls or severed heads. Three of the drawings in the lower right corner include an arm and a leg within the skull, symbolising the body and the sense of touch. Two of these arms make the threatening *tarjani* gesture. The drawing in the bottom left corner shows two smaller skull-cups of blood and *amrita* placed before the central offering, symbolising the union of the mother's fecund blood and the father's semen with the sense faculties of a being seeking rebirth. Three fresh skulls are shown in the lower area with their hair and scalps still intact.

THE INNER OFFERING (Tib. *nang chod*)

Specific and common to all of the *anuttarayoga tantra* practices or *sadhanas* is the 'inner offering' – so named because it consists of the visualised offering of the inner substances derived from the bodies of humans and animals. These substances are the 'five nectars' of human faeces, marrow, semen, blood, and urine; and the 'five meats' of a cow or bull, a dog, an elephant, a horse and a human being. These ten 'impure' substances are visualised as boiling and melting within a skull-cup to create a pure elixir of consecrated nectar or *amrita*, which is then used to bless the outer offerings and *tormas*, and to transform the five impure aggregates and elements of the practitioner into the wisdoms of the Five Buddhas and their consorts, the Five Mothers.

In actual practice the symbolic material representation of the inner offering takes the form of a skull-cup, or similarly shaped vessel, containing black tea or alcohol, into which is mixed a nectar pill (Tib. *bdud rtsi ril bu*) compounded from the 'synthesised essence' of the 'five nectars' and 'five meats', and blessed by the lineage guru. Black

tea is generally employed as the liquid for a monastically ordained practitioner, whereas alcohol – as a symbolic substitute for *amrita* – may be used by the lay practitioner. During the consecration of the inner offering the ring fingers of both hands are placed together and circled three times within the liquid of the skull-cup – in a clockwise direction for father tantra practices, and in an anticlockwise direction for the mother tantras. The left and right ring fingers symbolise the sexual organs of the mother and father as wisdom and method, which when 'churned' produce the red and white *bodhichitta* drops. The skull-cup or vessel of the inner offering is placed upon the left side of the practitioner's altar table, and accompanied by the practitioner's *vajra*, bell, *damaru*, action vase, and rosary, respectively placed to the right.

There are four stages of consecration of the inner offering: the elimination of hindrances; the purification of appearances and conceptualisations; the generation of the visualised offering; and the transformation and increase of the offering substances into divine nectar.

On account of its symbolic and ritual importance within the Highest Yoga Tantras this complex and highly esoteric visualisation practice is described in full below. This visual description is based upon the *Heruka Chakrasamvara sadhana* according to the system of the Mahasiddha Ghantapa, and I have compiled the visualisation description mainly from a commentary on this practice given by Lati Rinpoche. My reasons for including this *sadhana* are twofold: the first is that it reveals the deep inner symbolism of a Vajrayana *sadhana* and is far more concise than the visualisation practice of deity generation; the second is that it reveals the incredible beauty and sophistication of the Vajrayana's many visualisation practices. The inclusion of several passages from David Snellgrove's *Hevajra Tantra* that pertain to the inner offering also reveals a little of the enigmatic and symbolic 'twilight language' (Skt. *sandhabhasha*) in which the Tantras are written.

Following on from the visualised description are mentioned some of the variations which occur within other tantras such as the *Vajrayogini, Kalachakra, Guhyasamaja* and *Yamantaka Tantras*. Next is presented the symbolism of the inner offering, as explained in both the generation and completion stages of *anuttarayoga tantra* practices. Finally the possible origins of the enigmatic symbolism of the five meats are discussed.

The Visualised Generation of the Inner Offering According to the *Chakrasamvara Tantra*

Out of the blissful expanse of wisdom and emptiness arises the blue syllable *Yam* of the wind element, lying flat with its head towards the practitioner in the east. The *Yam* dissolves into light and transforms into a vast bow-shaped blue wind mandala, with its semi-circular expanse lying flat and its straight base facing forwards. At each edge of the wind mandala are two white vases filled with nectar, from which rise red sandalwood poles crowned with a golden *vajra* and a yaktail pennon. A victory banner is attached to each pole in the form of a triangular flag adorned with three strips, and decorated with the symbols of the 'four supernatural animals' and the 'three harmonious creatures' (see Plates 42 and 48). The billowing of these banners activates the wind mandala, causing a powerful wind to arise.

Above the centre of the wind mandala arises the red syllable *Ram* of the fire element. The *Ram* dissolves into light and transforms into a blazing red triangular fire mandala, with its lower point touching the centre of the wind mandala's straight base. The convection of the wind below the fire mandala causes the flames to blaze.

At each of the fire mandala's three corners arise the three syllables *Om A Hum* coloured white, red, and blue respectively. The white *Om* arises on the right northern corner, the red *A* arises on the left southern corner, and the blue *Hum* arises on the eastern corner to the front. These three syllables dissolve into light, then transform and converge into a tripod of three freshly severed and moist human heads. These heads are coloured to correspond to the syllables they arise from. The heads face forwards, with their eyes wide open and their long hair hanging down to their eyebrows.

Above this tripod of human heads there next arises a large white *A* syllable, which dissolves into light and transforms into a vast 'unified' skull-cup with a single red cranial fissure at its centre. This vast skull-cup is large enough to contain the three realms. The skull-cup is white on its outside and red on its interior, and rests upon the tripod of three moist heads.

Within the skull-cup the ten syllables *Om Kham Am Tram Hum Lam Mam Pam Tam Bam*, spontaneously arise. The white *Om* syllable of Vairochana's mirror-like wisdom arises at the eastern front of the skull-cup, and transforms into yellow human faeces marked with the white syllable *Om*. The green *Kham* syllable of Amoghasiddhi's all-accomplishing wisdom arises in the north (right), and transforms into flesh-coloured marrow or 'great meat' (Skt. *mamsa*) marked with the green syllable *Kham*. The red *A* syllable of Amitabha's discriminating wisdom arises in the west (back), and transforms into white *bodhichitta* or semen marked with the red syllable *A*. The yellow *Tram* syllable of Ratnasambhava's wisdom of equanimity arises in the south (left), and transforms into red blood marked with the yellow syllable *Tram*. The blue *Hum* syllable of Akshobhya's all-pervasive wisdom arises in the centre of the skull-cup, and transforms into blue urine marked with the blue syllable *Hum*. The syllables that mark these 'five nectars' are half-submerged in their respective substances, and drip with the nectar of blessings.

The white syllable *Lam* of Vairochana's consort, Lochana, arises in the south-east (left front) as the nature of Heruka's loving-kindness, and transforms into the corpse meat of a black bull marked by the white syllable *Lam*. The blue syllable *Mam* of Akshobhya's consort, Mamaki, arises in the south-west (left rear) as the nature of Heruka's compassion, and transforms into the corpse meat of a red or blue dog marked by the blue syllable *Mam*. The red syllable *Pam* of Amitabha's consort, Pandara, arises in the north-west (right rear) as the nature of Heruka's joy, and transforms into the

corpse meat of a white elephant marked by the red syllable *Pam*. The green syllable *Tam* of Amoghasiddhi's consort, Tara, arises in the north-east (right front) as the nature of Heruka's equanimity, and transforms into the corpse meat of a green horse marked by the green syllable *Tam*. Finally the red syllable *Bam* of Heruka's consort, Vajravarahi, arises at the centre of the skull-cup as the union of Heruka's great bliss and emptiness, and transforms into the red corpse meat of a human being marked by the red syllable *Bam*.

The five nectars are visualised in an anticlockwise formation, and the five meats in a clockwise sequence. The corpses of the five animals are visualised lying upon their right sides with their heads positioned towards the centre of the skull-cup. The human corpse at the centre lies above the blue urine with its head pointing backwards towards the west. The upright syllables of these five meats penetrate into the left shoulders of their corpses, and drip with nectar. Although these five animals appear as recognisable corpses from the outside, their interiors are boneless and full of small chopped pieces of their respective meats – packed together as pellets the size of a thumb-joint, so that they will 'melt' easily.

On the lotus and moon disc at the practitioner's heart there next arises the syllable *Hum* (*Bam*, in the case of Vajrayogini), which radiates light rays that converge upon and activate the wind mandala. This causes the fire mandala to blaze ferociously, melting and boiling the five meats and the five nectars into an orange coloured liquid resembling the rising sun.

Above this melted liquid arises the white syllable *Hum*, which dissolves into light and transforms into an inverted white *khatvanga* made from the pure white *bodhichitta*, which is the essence of Heruka's mind. The steaming heat from the molten liquid causes the white *khatvanga* to melt and drip into the skull-cup. With its full melting, the white liquid of the *khatvanga* swirls three times in an anticlockwise direction and then completely merges with the boiling liquid, cooling and sweetening the elixir into the colour of liquid mercury.

Above the elixir there now arise three horizontal rows of the sixteen Sanskrit vowels and thirty-four consonants, beginning with the additional syllable *Om*, and ending with the syllables *Hum Hum Phat*. These fifty-four syllables are arranged in three horizontal rows. Those in the first row above the liquid are coloured white, the second red, and the third blue. Then the syllables at either end of each row simultaneously merge towards the centre, and finally resolve into three inverted syllables above the skull-cup's elixir, with an inverted white *Om* at the bottom, red *A* in the middle, and blue *Hum* at the top. Light rays emanate from these three radiant syllables towards the ten directions, touching and transforming all beings into Heruka and Vajravarahi. Throughout the universe these countless manifestations of Heruka and Vajravarahi enter into sexual union, and from their blissful fire of passion they melt into pure *bodhichitta*. Again as light rays this infinite *bodhichitta* returns and dissolves back into the three syllables, empowering them with the pure essence of great bliss and emptiness. These three syllables then descend one after the other and melt into

Plate 141: The inner offering

the nectar within the skull-cup, transforming the elixir into the three *vajras* of *vajra* body, *vajra* speech, and *vajra* mind; they manifest as the deities of Heruka's body, speech and mind mandala wheels. These three syllables purify, transform and increase the nectar into an inexhaustible panacea of alchemical medicine bestowing bliss, vitality, immortality and wisdom.

The triple repetition of the syllables *Om A Hum* concludes the visualised generation of Heruka Chakrasamvara's inner offering.

Certain variations arise in the inner offering visualisations of different *anuttarayoga tantra* deities – or even of the same deity within the various lineages of transmission. In the *Vajrayogini Tantra*, for example, the three severed heads arise from three coloured *A* syllables, and transform into a tripod of heads with a red, blue, and white sequence from left to right. The *Kalachakra Tantra*, with its unique cosmology, contains many variations in the colours and placements of the ten syllables, which here arise upon an eight-petalled red lotus within the skull-cup. The *Guhyasamaja Tantra* gives a colour sequence of a white cow, a yellow dog, a red elephant, a green horse, and a blue man, and again changes the sequence of the severed heads and reverses the order of the *Om A Hum* syllables. In many of the tantras the human meat at the centre, representing the element of space , is not mentioned, though it tends to be included in most visualisation practices. In general, the colour of the human corpse at the centre corresponds to the colour of the principal goddess or the deity's consort.

In the *Guhyasamaja*, *Hevajra*, and *Yamantaka Tantras* the syllables of the five nectars and five meats are derived from their Sanskrit names. These are as follows: *Vi* for faeces (*vit*); *Ma* for marrow or 'meat' (*mamsa*); *Shu* for semen (*shukra*) or white *bodhichitta*; *Ra* for blood (*rakta*); and *Mu* for urine (*mutra*). The five great meats are similarly marked: *Go* or *Ga* for the cow (*go*); *Ku* or *Shva* for the dog (*kukkura, shvan*); *Ha* for the elephant (*hastin*); *Shva* for the horse (*ashva*); and *Na* for the man (*nara*).

These few variations reveal a little of the levels of complexity contained within the esoteric symbolism of the inner offering.

Plate 141

This drawing depicts the iconographical representation in which the inner offering is drawn and painted. The drawing is based upon a very fine wall painting at Likhir Gompa in Ladakh.

On either side of the inner offering and at the two corners of the blue bow-shaped wind mandala are the two vases filled with nectar. These vases are painted white in the Heruka and Vajrayogini tantric systems, and gold in certain other tantric systems. The red sandalwood poles are crowned with red yaktail pennants and golden half-vajras. The billowing victory banners are represented by triangular flags which blow towards the inner offering. These flags are painted white in the Vajrayogini systems, or blue with a red edging in the Guhyasamaja system.

The red triangular fire mandala points downwards with its lower apex just touching the central base of the blue, bow-shaped wind mandala. The three freshly-severed heads that support the skull-cup are coloured red, blue, and white, from left to right in the Heruka and Vajrayogini systems, and red, white, and blue in the Guhyasamaja system. The eyes of these three heads are wide open and their hair hangs down to their eyebrows.

The vast white skull-cup arises above the three heads as a 'unified' skull, that is, a single bone structure not divided into segments by the five red cranial fissures. A single central fissure rises from the 'aperture of Brahma' at the base of the skull and terminates at the skull's centre. The rim of the skull-cup is embellished with a golden leaf-shaped edging, and its interior is coloured blood red. The five great meats are depicted in their directional positions with their heads facing outwards – unlike their description which specifies that their heads face inwards. The five nectars are positioned between the five meats, with three lumps of yellow faeces to the left of the cow at the front, four curved ovals of marrow to the right of the cow, blue urine behind the central man, red blood to the left of the elephant's head, and white semen to the right of the elephant's rump.

The Symbolism of the Inner Offering

The visualised consecration of the inner offering symbolically encompasses both the generation and completion stages of Highest Yoga Tantra. Thus whilst an accomplished practitioner is visualising the progression of the inner offering in the generation stage of practice, he or she may be simultaneously experiencing the blessings of the inner offering within the completion stage of practice.

Within the generation stage symbolism the wind mandala, fire mandala, skull-cup, and the contained substances which melt and liquify, symbolise the four elements of wind, fire, earth, and water. The three severed heads – coloured white, red, and blue, and which arise from the three syllables *Om A Hum* – symbolise the practitioner's body, speech, and mind as the three bases to be purified, and their transformation into the three *vajras* of an empty body, pure speech, and an unchangeably blissful mind. The white syllable *A* from which the skull-cup is generated symbolises emptiness, and the skull-cup itself symbolises great bliss. The white exterior of the skull-cup represents the white *bodhichitta* of the father, and its red interior the red *bodhichitta* of the mother. The single fissure of the unified skull-cup symbolises the inseparability of method and wisdom, compassion and tranquility, form and emptiness. The generation of the five nectars and the five meats from the seed-syllables that form the first letter of their Sanskrit names, symbolises that all of these substances exist by designation and arise through conceptual thought.

The five nectars symbolise the Five Buddhas, the five senses, and the five aggregates (Skt. *skandhas*) to be purified. Human excrement represents Vairochana, sight, and the aggregate of form; marrow or 'flesh' (Skt. *mamsa*) represents Amoghasiddhi, touch, and the aggregate of motivation or volition; semen represents Amitabha, taste, and the aggregate of perception or discrimination; blood represents Ratnasambhava, smell, and the aggregate of feeling; and urine represents Akshobhya, sound, and the aggregate of consciousness.

The five meats symbolise the Five Mothers or consorts of the Five Buddhas, the five elements, and the five delusions or poisons. The cow or bull meat represents Lochana, the element of earth, and the delusion of ignorance; the dog meat represents Mamaki, the element of water, and the delusion of aggression; the elephant meat represents Pandara, the element of fire, and the delusion of passion or desire; the horse meat represents Tara, the element of wind, and the delusion of jealousy; and the human meat at the centre represents either the consort of the meditational deity or the goddess Vajradhatvishvari, the element of space, and the delusion of pride. More commonly only four of the Five Mothers are symbolised by the four directional meats, representing the elements of earth, water, fire and air – with space as the fifth element, placed at the centre, permeating all of the other elements.

In the completion stage symbolism the wind mandala symbolises the downward-voiding wind, located below the navel *chakra*. The fire mandala symbolises the inner fire, located at the navel *chakra*. The three severed heads, coloured white, red, and blue, symbolise the three signs of white appearance, red increase, and black near-attainment, which arise as the fifth, sixth, and seventh signs occurring in the death process as the winds dissolve into the central channel (see page 141). The fluttering of the banners on either side of the wind mandala symbolises the concentration of the downward-voiding wind, which causes the fire mandala of *tummo* to blaze upwards, dissolving the winds within the central channel and giving rise to the three signs of white appearance, red increase, and black near-attainment. The white skull-cup that arises above the three severed heads symbolises the mind of clear light, which arises as the eighth and final stage of the death process after the winds have completely dissolved within the central channel.

The five nectars and five meats represent the five impure aggregates and elements, which are transformed into the Five Buddhas and the Five Mothers through meditation upon the clear light. Their melting and transformation into nectar symbolises the distillation of these ten substances, as purified wisdoms, into an elixir of 'one taste' (Skt. *ekarasa*). The four surrounding nectars of faeces, marrow, semen, and blood – which circle in an anticlockwise direction around the central urine – symbolise the four serial joys experienced as the *bodhichitta* drops descend from the crown to the throat, heart, and navel *chakras*. The four surrounding meats of cow, dog, elephant, and horse – which circle in a clockwise direction around the central human – symbolise the reversal of the four joys as they ascend from the navel to the heart, throat and crown *chakras*.

Within the Highest Yoga Tantras the 'four joys' (Skt. *chaturananda*) are accorded a metaphorical sexual symbolism.

The first of the four joys is known as 'joy' (Skt. *ananda*) and symbolises the contact of the *vajra* and lotus as the entry of the penis into the vagina. The second 'perfect joy' (Skt. *paramananda*) represents the duration of sexual intercourse and the arising of the desire for more joy or passionate pleasure. The third 'cessation of joy' (Skt. *viramananda*) represents orgasm and the cessation of the increased passionate urge. And the fourth 'innate joy' (Skt. *sahajananda*) represents the blissful transcendental experience which arises as the 'afterglow' of orgasm and springs forth from the preceding joy.

The four joys are also identified with the 'four moments' and the 'four *mudras*', which also possess a sexual symbolism. The four moments are: variation (Skt. *vichitra*); development (Skt. *vipaka*); consummation (Skt. *vimardha*); and signlessness (Skt. *vilakshana*). The four *mudras* are: the 'action symbol' (Skt. *karmamudra*) symbolising joy as the consort; the 'commitment symbol' (Skt. *samayamudra*) symbolising perfect joy as meditation upon the union of the deity and his consort; the 'truth symbol' (Skt. *dharmamudra*) symbolising the cessation of joy as the realisation of the absolute truth of emptiness; and the 'great symbol' (Skt. *mahamudra*) as the attainment of Buddhahood.

The alchemical transformation of the boiling orange liquid into a cool and sweet elixir, coloured like mercury, and caused by the descent and melting of the inverted white *khatvanga*, symbolises the purification (heating) and transformation (cooling) produced by the melting and spreading of the *bodhichitta* drops through all of the channels or *nadis*. The arising of the white vowels and red consonants, as the white and red *bodhichitta* drops which dissolve into and increase the nectar, symbolises the attainment of the four 'bodies' or *kayas* – the *nirmanakaya*, *sambhoghakaya*, *dharmakaya*, and the *svabhavikakaya* or *vajrakaya* – as the indivisible essence of the previous three *kayas*.

The Possible Origins of the Inner Offering Substances

In the *Hevajra Tantra* it is written:

> *For the sake of perfection in Hevajra he should consume the fivefold sacrament of initial* Na, *initial* Ga, *initial* Ha, *final* Shva *and initial* Shva. *So five ambrosias one should consume for the sake of perfection in Hevajra.*
>
> *Those who keep to the convention of Hevajra should eat according to the external interpretation and be watchful according to the internal.*
>
> *As for this the first letter of the name man* (nara) *is* Na, *the first letter of the name cow* (go) *is* Ga, *the first letter of the name elephant* (hastin) *is* Ha, *the last letter of the name horse* (ashva) *is* Shva, *and the first letter of the name dog* (shvan) *is* Shva. *Putting these materials together, one should make them into pellets the size of a thumb-joint, then purify them, mix them together and burn them, make them into an elixir and eat them; by this means one gains external perfection. Likewise by saying that these are the five faculties of sense, the eye and so on, with the name of cow* (go), *etc., which are turned away from their spheres and kept so, there is produced the*

extreme state of watchfulness. Likewise the five ambrosias, Mu (mutra), Ma (mamsa), Vi (vit), Ra (rakta), *and* Shu (shukra) *are to be treated with the distinction of exoteric and esoteric significance, such is the teaching of the Tathagata.*

(*Hevajra Tantra*, trans. Snellgrove, Part 1 p. 86)

Here the five nectars and five meats of the sacrament are literally described as substances, which when purified, burned, compounded and eaten, bestow miraculous powers or *siddhis* upon the tantric practitioner. Human meat is specifically described as the flesh of a 'seven-timer' (Skt. *saptavarta*), or one who has been reborn seven consecutive times in human form. Consuming the flesh of such a perfectly endowed human being is said to bestow the *siddhi* of a *vidyadhara* or 'knowledge holder', who possesses a knowledge 'as vast as the sky'. Symbolically a seven-timer also refers to the seven embryonic stages of conception, and the sequential formation of blood, flesh, skin, veins, bones, and marrow.

The five nectars (Skt. *panchamrita*) form the liquid substances, and the five meats (Skt. *panchamamsa*) form the solid substances. The incorporation of the five bodily 'nectars' – excrement, marrow or flesh, semen, blood, and urine – are easily explained, as they form the impure 'left-hand' tantric equivalents of the orthodox Hindu 'right-hand' nectars of the *panchamrita* or 'five nectars'. These 'pure nectars' are milk, curds, ghee, honey, and molasses, which are mixed together in a vase and used as a divine nectar to bathe and quench the thirst of sacred images or statues.

The five meats, or the 'five great meats' (Skt. *mahapanchamamsa*), are not so easily explained and have presented themselves as an enigma to Buddhist scholars. Their placement within a vast fivefold 'ocean of nectar' immediately calls to mind the Vedic legend of the churning of the ocean (see page 109), where Airavata the elephant, Surabhi the cow, and Uchaishravas the horse, emerge from the cosmic ocean as three of the great meats. Vishnu, who presses down on the central churning stick of Mt Mandara, represents the human meat at the centre of the skull-cup, and Halahala, as 'poison incarnate', symbolically arises in the form of a rabid dog.

The five meats of a man, an elephant, a horse, a cow or bull, and a dog, can also form a symbolic equivalent for the fivefold Hindu caste system. The man represents the *brahmin* or 'twice-born' priestly caste; the elephant, the *kshatriya* or warrior caste; the horse, the *vaishya* or merchant caste; the cow or bull, the *shudra* or labourer caste; and the dog, the 'untouchable' outcastes, referred to as *shvapakas* or 'dog-eaters', literally 'the cookers of dogs'.

The sacrament of the five meats is also specifically referred to in the early Buddhist tantras as the *gonahashva* or *gokunahashva* ritual, and this points towards a deeper esoteric meaning. The term itself is compounded from the initial syllables of the Sanskrit names for these five creatures – cow (*go*), dog (*kukkura*), man (*nara*), elephant (*hastin*), and horse (*ashva*).

The sacrament of the *gokunahashva* rite forms a strong parallel to the Indian tantric practice of *panchamunda* or 'five

heads'. Here the corpses of five animals are used to create a raised platform as a meditation seat (*asana*) or an altar. Many of the sacred shrines of ancient India – and certainly many of the Buddhist and Hindu temples of the Kathmandu valley – have been erected over pits where the corpses of five animals have been ritually buried. This seemingly bizarre practice has certain parallels with other cultures, where the bodies of young children, for example, may be interred within the foundation of a building, or even the European tradition of burying a faithful dog or a trusted stallion with its lordly master, within the sanctity of a church or cathedral.

The five animals of the *panchamunda* ritual are usually listed as a man, a dog, a horse, a jackal, and a monkey. The first three occur in the Buddhist inner offering, and the last two replace the cow and elephant. The term *panchamunda*, meaning 'five heads', refers to the arrangement of a buried human corpse at the centre which is surrounded by the corpses of four directional animals with their heads pointing towards the centre.

In the extreme left-hand Indian tantric practice of *mundasiddhi*, the corpses, heads or skulls of five animals are used as an *asana* or corpse seat upon which to perform the *shavasadhana* or corpse ritual (see page 249). The purpose of this necromantic practice is to gain the *siddhis* of certain spirits, who are 'conjured forth' through the medium of these corpses. Different human and animal corpses are used within the various practices of *mundasiddhi*.

The tantric performance of the *panchamunda* rite has its origins in the Vedic ritual of *panchamunda*. Here the corpses of a human and four animals, which had either died simultaneously from 'natural causes', in battle, or had been ritually sacrificed, were buried together in a clay pit. When these corpses had decomposed, the sanctified clay obtained from the pit was used to fashion the sacred pot (*kumbha*) or vase (*kalasha*), employed as the ablution vessel in Vedic rituals. The clean decomposition of these corpses into clay might also suggest that the bones were removed, so that the chopped meats of the carcasses would decompose more rapidly. The tantric skull-cup essentially replaced the earlier Vedic clay pot, which is referred to in the Vedas as a 'piece of pottery'. Male goats, fowl, oxen and bulls were the common animals of sacrifice, and are still ritually beheaded at certain temple festivals in India and Nepal. The sacrifice of dogs and elephants was not religiously prescribed, and the sacrifice of horses was only performed for the most sovereign or sacred of reasons. The main pilgrimage thoroughfare of Benares city leads down to the central ghat of Dasashvamedh on the River Ganges, and Dasashvamedh Ghat means 'the place of the ten horse sacrifice'. Human sacrifice was certainly performed in many Indian left-hand tantric rituals, and with the later debasement of Hindu tantra into material rather than spiritual acquisition, such murderous sects as the 'thugees' or 'thugs' proliferated. The thugees strangled many thousands of innocent people with a knotted handkerchief in honour of their wrathful goddess, Kali. Between 1830 and 1840 the British Raj took stringent measures to suppress the 'thugees', whose name derives from the Sanskrit *sthaga*, meaning a deceiver or robber.

The Vedic preparation of sacred clay, as described above, is still used in many traditional Vedic and tantric rituals, and the broken fragments of the sacred clay vessels are returned to their site of origin, which are known as a *pithas* or 'sacred sites'. Interestingly, the sacred sites of many excavated stone circles or neolithic burial mounds invariably reveal the consistent debris of broken pieces of pottery and various charred animal bones.

The *Hevajra Tantra* further states that the bones of certain animals and certain 'nectars' may be used for various tantric activities:

"The bone of a human causes hatred; the bone of a dog is used for driving away; the bone of a *brahmin* is used for conjuring forth [see Plate 117]; the bone of an elephant causes rain; and the bone of a buffalo is used for slaying. The nectar of milk is drunk for petrifying; blood is drunk for slaying; excrement is used for conjuring forth; human flesh causes hatred; and urine is used for bewitching. Or one may use the flesh of a horse, a dog, a man, a cow and an elephant."

AN ASSEMBLY OF WEAPONS AND WRATHFUL OFFERINGS

Plate 142

The last drawing in this section illustrates an improvised assembly of weapons and wrathful offerings.

In the upper left corner is a *torma* or sacrificial offering of the five senses, consisting of a skull-cup containing the sense organs of eyes, ears, nose, tongue, and a heart pierced by a silk arrow. Two further drawings of this wrathful offering are depicted at the centre and to the upper right of the page. The wrathful offering of the five senses is illustrated and described on Plate 140.

Across the top edge of the drawing are a curved knife, two *phurbas*, a crescent-shaped chopper, a *damaru*, and a small skull with a *vajra*-snare threaded through its eye sockets. Below this skull is the four-tiered base of Mt Meru, and below this a triangular receptacle full of swirling blood. Below again is a metal tripod, upon which is mounted a *vajra*-lidded skull-cup containing the melted substances of the 'inner offering', as described on Plate 141. The three legs of this tripod represent the three *vajras* of body, speech and mind.

At the upper centre is a large drawing of a *vajra*-sealed skull surrounded by a rosary of small skulls; outside these are drawn four further skulls, the lower two of which are crowned with jewels. Below these are two triangular receptacles; the left one contains fresh blood, and the right one is depicted as an inverted pyramid or hearth containing fire. To the left and right of these are two skull-cups filled with blood and mustard seed; above these are two details of the 'ocean of blood' through which Palden Lhamo's mule gallops. Across to the left is a skull-cup of blood mounted upon a square receptacle full of *amrita*.

To the left and right of the wrathful offering of the five senses at the upper centre are two skull-cups full of blood and alcohol, representing the menstrual blood and semen of the mother and father as red and white *bodhichitta*. This trinity of skull-cup offerings symbolises the three primary causes for human conception as the conjunction of the fertile drops of the mother and father merging with the five sense faculties of the being seeking rebirth. The tripod of three severed heads supporting the blood-filled skull-cup on the left represents the three *vajras* of body, speech, and mind as the bases to be purified, and the arising of the 'clear light' of the mother. The tripod of three dry skulls supporting the *amrita* or alcohol-filled skull on the right represents the purification of body, speech and mind, and the arising of the 'illusory body' of the father.

To the left and right of the protruding eyes of the central offering are two small drawings of the iron rings and *vajra*-hooks of the rope snare. Across to the left of the rings is a human heart drawn in the shape of a lotus bud, with two further drawings of hearts depicted below the central offering. Drawn in line with the two lower hearts are three small jewel-ornament chains, and on either side of these jewel-chains are two sacrificial offering cakes or *tormas*. The one on the left is a food offering *torma* (Tib. *tshogs gtor*), the rounded conical shape of which represents the heart of a male deity or the breast of a female deity. The tetrahedron-shaped *torma* on the right stands upon a flat metal tray, with decorative flames emanating from its sides and three smaller *tormas* arranged in front. The upper pyramid of this *torma* is ornamented with a butter-sculpted image of a skull-cup and curved knife. To the right is a drawing of a thighbone trumpet.

Below the central offering is another blood-filled skull-cup supported upon a tripod of three skulls, with four divination dice depicted below. To the right of this skull-cup is an inverted human skull, blazing with fire and with tongues of flame emanating from its eye sockets. To the right of this is a flame-enhaloed divination mirror, which stands within a metal bowl with a silk ribbon tied around its base and three small conical *tormas* positioned in front. Below this tray are two small drawings of thread crosses (Tib. *mdos*), as illustrated and described on Plate 139. To the left of the thread crosses are a 'sack of diseases', and a butter lamp with a wrathfully twisting flame.

To the left of the divination dice is a triangular flaming *torma*, held within a skull-cup mounted upon a lotus pedestal; above and to the left again are three red triangular 'Mt Meru' *tormas*, held within a skull-cup full of *amrita*. Across to the left is a skull-cup of *amrita* placed upon a lotus-mounted vase, as described and illustrated on Plate 119. Below this vase and to the right is a small triangular hearth or brazier (Tib. *me thab*), as described on Plate 133. Descending from the centre at the left edge of the illustration are three drawings of a rope snare coiled into a noose; the magical crossed-stick (Tib. *khram shing*) of Palden Lhamo; and the point of a spear.

Across the bottom row of this page are four drawings of *tormas*. The first drawing on the left depicts a wrathful triangular *torma* sculpted with the face of Mahakala, and with

Plate 142: An assembly of weapons and wrathful offerings

flames emanating from its mouth. The tip of this black *torma* is embellished with flames and surmounted by a silk victory banner. Positioned to the right of the main *torma* is a smaller red triangular *torma* symbolising the consort of Mahakala.

The drawing at the bottom centre depicts a lotus-based *torma*, supported within a metal tray with three small heart or jewel-shaped *tormas* positioned in front. The circular centre of this *torma* is designed as a small thread cross known as the 'mouth of the sky' (Tib. *gnam kha'*), with five coloured butter-sculpted discs at its centre representing the five constituent elements and aggregates to be purified. To the left and right of this central tray are two small drawings of conical *tormas*.

In the lower right corner are two drawings of groups of three triangular *tormas*, with their main central points ornamented with the motif of the crescent moon, sun and dissolving point or *nada*. The first of these *tormas* rests within a metal tray, and the second in a skull-cup. Between the lower row of *tormas* are small drawings of 'iron-mountain' peaks. Scattered around the page are small drawings of flame motifs.

THE RITUAL FIRE OFFERING
(Skt. *homa*; Tib. *sbyin sreg*)

At the end of a long Vajrayana retreat it is traditional for the practitioner to perform a ritual fire or *homa* ceremony in order to purify any faults or transgressions that may have arisen during the course of the retreat.

The worship of the sacred fire and its presiding deity, Agni, dates back to the origin of the first and foremost of the four Vedas, the Rig Veda (*circa* 1500 BC), which begins with the written name of the fire god, Agni. Throughout Indian history the complex ritual worship of the Vedic sacrificial *homa* fire, or *yajna*, has remained unchanged.

Of all the elements fire was most readily worshipped, as it provided the swiftest and most effective conduit between the worshipper and the deity. Agni, as the god of the sacrificial fire, acted as the mediator who delivered the offerings of men directly to the gods. The Vedic *yajna* or *homa* site was constructed as a raised platform or pavilion that was specifically dedicated to the worship of fire.

One of the most important early Vedic rituals was the *soma* sacrifice (Skt. *somayajna*) in which a sacred beverage was extracted from the pulp of a vine (*Sarcostema viminalis* or *Asclepia acida*) and consumed by the presiding *brahmin* priests before being offered to the gods as a libation. In 1996 a group of *brahmin* priests from the *soma-veda* tradition of south India came to London to perform the *somayajna* ritual over a three-day period. This was the first time that this ancient ritual had ever been performed outside of India. During the course of this ritual when the sky god Indra was invoked to make his presence known to the 'king of the realm', a bolt of lightening struck and caused minor damage in the gardens of Buckingham Palace!

The performance of the Vajrayana Buddhist *homa* ritual can be just as complex as its Vedic prototype, and follows many similar procedures. Extensive *homa* rituals may take several weeks to perform, and involve great expense for the donors. The Chinese business community in Hong Kong, for example, frequently employ Tibetan lamas and monks for lavish rituals of enrichment and prosperity. But traditionally a *homa* ritual is more commonly performed at the end of a practitioner's meditation retreat, in order to purify the faults commited and increase the merits gained. Here the practitioner becomes the ritual master, and self-identifying with the meditational deity, brings to completion the fruits of his or her long retreat practice.

Plates 143–145 illustrate six designs for the sacred hearth (Skt. *homakunda*; Tib. *sbyin sreg me thab*) used in the *homa* or ritual fire offering. Plates 143 and 144 show the hearth designs employed in the four activities (Skt. *chaturkriya*; Tib. *las bzhi*) of tantra, with the circular hearth for pacification (Tib. *zhi ba*), and the square hearth for enrichment (Tib. *rgyas pa*) illustrated on Plate 143, and the bow-shaped hearth for subjugation or influence (Tib. *dbang*), and the triangular hearth of wrathful or destructive activity (Tib. *drag po*) illustrated on Plate 144. The upper drawing on Plate 145 depicts a variation in the square hearth design employed for enrichment or increase, and the lower drawing depicts the hearth design employed in the Vajrayogini *homa* ritual.

The designs for the fire hearths of the four activities, illustrated on Plates 143 and 144, occur in the same shapes, and order, as the four continents surrounding Mt Meru: circular, square, semi-circular or bow-shaped, and triangular or trapezoid. These shapes also correspond to the four elements: the pacifying circle of water, the square of the element earth, the bow-shape of the wind element, and the triangle of fire. Water cools and calms, earth enriches, wind subjugates, and fire destroys.

"For pacifying the fire hearth should be round, for enriching square, and for slaying it should be triangular and used only for others. For pacifying the fire pit should be one cubit across and half a cubit deep; for increase two cubits across and one deep; and for slaying twenty fingerwidths or *angulas* across and ten deep. For pacifying the colour is white, for increasing it is yellow, for slaying black, and for subjugating red. Conjuring forth is the same as for subduing, and causing hatred is the same as slaying. For pacifying one uses sesame oil, for increase curds, for slaying and causing hatred one uses thorns, and for subduing and conjuring forth one uses a blue lotus." (*Hevajra Tantra*)

Originally there were six activities within the tantras, as indeed are still prescribed within many of the Hindu tantras. But in Vajrayana Buddhism the two activities of conjuring forth and causing hatred were absorbed into the latter two categories of subjugation and wrath.

Most commonly the *homa* rituals of pacifying and enriching are performed, either for oneself or others. The pacifying activity removes faults, defilements, and illnesses, and clears away obstructions in one's future path. The enriching activity increases one's merit, wisdom, wealth, prosperity, and longevity. The rituals of subjugation and forceful activity are only performed in adverse or extreme circumstances, and may only be performed for the altruistic benefit of others. Subjugation is employed to control harmful forces that affect other beings, such as the activities of malignant spirits or the virulent 'possession' of human beings by the five poisons. Destructive activity is only employed when subjugation fails, such as for the conflict caused by extremely malignant spirits, the persecution of the dharma, or the invasion of hostile forces.

Unlike the established Vedic *homa* site, the Buddhist hearth is temporarily constructed either near the place of retreat, or in a secluded open area – such as a garden, courtyard or rooftop. The *kunda* or fire pit is built as a low square structure of brick plastered with cow dung, and aligned along an east–west axis. A stepped wall, about a metre in height, is constructed in front of the throne of the ritual master to protect him from the fire. This wall is coloured according to the ritual activity being performed (white, yellow, red or black), and marked at its centre with the syllable *Bam* or *Vam* of the water element. On a brocade-covered altar to the left of the master's throne are the four 'purifying waters', three waterbowls, and three conch-shell receptacles. On a separate altar to the right may be the ritual implements of the master, including the inner offering, the action vase and *kusha* grass sprinkler, and a bowl of consecrated rice. On a large table to the right of the throne are arranged the substances to be offered to the sacred fire. Several accomplished attendants usually assist the ritual master with the elaborate procedures of the ritual, such as tending to the fire, presenting the offerings, handling the ritual ladles, playing the ritual music and reciting prayers. Throughout the performance of the *homa* ritual the master holds the *vajra* and bell in his right and left hands.

The colours used and worn for the *homa* ritual correspond to the activity being performed. For pacifying, the master wears white clothing, the ritual implements are marked with white silks, and the ritual offerings are predominantly coloured white. For enriching, yellow clothing is worn, and the offerings are predominantly yellow. For subjugating red is worn and offered; and for destructive activity black is the colour. If the practitioner is a monk or lama, brocade robes and a crown of the Five Buddhas are traditionally worn, representing the attire of the meditational deity.

The firewood (Skt. *samidh*; Tib. *yam shing*) used for pacifying and enriching is described as 'milk-wood' – a white sappy wood that symbolises the bodhi tree of enlightenment, although *sirisa* wood may be prescribed for rituals of increase. *Khadira* (acacia), rosewood or sandalwood are employed in rituals of subjugation. Thorny black woods or poisonous woods are used for wrathful activity. These thorn branches may sometimes be tied together with the hair of a corpse or a widow. The flame used to ignite the fire for pacification may be kindled from the friction of two sticks, or taken from a previous *homa* fire, or from the hearth of a virtuous householder. The flame for enrichment may be kindled by a jewel or crystal magnifying glass, or taken from a monastic kitchen, or from the hearth of a king. In certain rituals of subjugation or bewitching the flame may be taken from the hearth of a notorious prostitute, and in destructive rituals the flame is usually taken from a blacksmith's furnace, from

a funeral pyre, or from the hearth of a widow. Since the rituals for subjugation and wrath are only rarely performed in extreme circumstances, the particular offering substances are kept secret and not openly described. Red flowers, red cloth, copper filings, and red substances are employed in rituals of subjugation. For wrathful rituals the liquid offerings may consist of alcohol, animal fat and blood, with meat, iron filings, earth from a cemetery or crossroads, black cloth, and black substances forming the solid offerings.

The two ritual ladles illustrated on Plate 133 are used in all of the four activities of *homa*. The circular ladle (Skt. *shrava*; Tib. *blug gzar*) is used to pour the melted ghee and liquid substances into the square pouring-funnel (Skt. *patri*; Tib. *dgan gzar*), and a bowl or scoop is used to pour the grains and solid substances into the fire.

The substances used in the pacifying and enriching *homa* rituals are as follows:

The firewood (Skt. *samidh*; Tib. *yam shing*) used to fuel the sacred fire should be as thick as the circle formed from the joined thumb and ring finger. The firewood represents strength and courage.

The milk-wood offering sticks are twelve finger-widths long and as thick as the little finger. These sticks are cut from the barked ends of branches, and are fresh, straight and unblemished. The ends of the sticks are dipped into ghee and honey, and their burning symbolises the perfect illumination of the bodhi tree. The sticks are presented in pairs and eliminate all transgressions and broken vows.

The clarified butter or ghee (Skt. *ghrita*; Tib. *shun mar*) used to combust the sacred fire, symbolises the removal of all obstacles to prosperity and the increase of wealth.

Sesame seeds (Skt. *tila*; Tib. *til*) symbolise the elimination of all misdeeds and impure actions.

Durva grass stalks (see Plates 90 and 91) are presented in pairs with their tips dipped into ghee and honey. *Durva* grass is offered to increase the lifespan.

Unbroken rice (Tib. *'bras*) is offered to increase the merit.

A sweet of barley flour mixed with curds (Tib. *zho zan*) is offered, representing the increase of wisdom and supreme bliss.

Kusha grass stalks (see Plates 90 and 91) are presented in pairs with their tips dipped into ghee and honey. *Kusha* grass is offered for purification and protection.

White mustard seeds (Skt. *sarshapa*; Tib. *yungs dkar*) pacify all hindrances and eliminate all obstructive spirits.

Unhusked barley (Tib. *nas*) removes all obstacles to prosperity and brings abundant harvests to fruition.

Husked barley increases the development of the mental powers.

Lentils or peas (Skt. *vartuli*; Tib. *sran ma*) increase the vitality and physical strength.

Wheat (Skt. *godhuma*; Tib. *gro*) helps to remove illnesses.

All of these offering substances are rubbed with honey and ghee to enrich their qualities, as honey and ghee are considered the most nourishing of foods in the Indian Ayurvedic

Plate 143: Designs for the *homa* fire hearths employed in rituals of pacification and increase

medical tradition. Additional offerings may include boiled rice; puffed rice and wheat; the 'three whites' of milk, curd and ghee; the 'three sweets' of honey, crystal sugar and molasses; fragrant flowers; cloth; perfume and incense. White flowers and cloth are offered in pacifying rituals, and yellow flowers and cloth in rituals of increase. Two pieces of silk cloth are offered as representations of the deity's upper and lower garments. A specific offering to please the deity's sense of taste is the Indian paan offering, which is symbolically made of three substances mixed with ghee. Paan – consisting of chopped betel nut or supari, mixed with powdered lime and tobacco in a folded leaf – is traditionally chewed in India as a mild stimulant and digestive tonic.

Sacrificial cakes or *tormas* – coloured white, yellow, red or black, depending upon the activity being performed – are offered to the local spirits, the 'mundane' fire god Agni, and the 'supermundane' *yidam* deity or protector to whom the *homa* ritual is propitiated. The offerings of water to bathe the face and feet of the deity, perfumed water to anoint the breast, flowers, incense and a lamp are also offered into the sacred flame.

In the performance of the *homa* ritual the hearth becomes firstly the seat of the fire god Agni. Agni rides upon a gelded goat and appears in different forms according to the ritual being performed. Agni, as a 'mundane' deity, is invoked to intercede between the practitioner and his 'supermundane' *yidam* deity, and to ensure that the offerings are consumed through the divine fire of the *yidam* deity rather than in the flames of the conventional fire. To attract Agni to the hearth, a proportion of the offerings (usually one tenth) are first mixed together and offered to the fire simultaneously. The blazing core of the fire represents the open mouth of Agni. After Agni has been propitiated the main offering to the *yidam* or protector deity is performed, with the individual offering substances being presented in the order listed above.

Plate 143

The upper drawing shows the design for the fire hearth employed in the *homa* ritual of pacification. The square base of the hearth, which theoretically measures forty-four finger-widths across, is firstly evenly sprinkled with white earth, sand or powder pigment. Traditionally a string line is used to create the axial *brahma* lines and diagonal lines of the design. This string is streched taut across these lines, and snapped from its centre to leave an impression in the white earth base. The string is also used as a compass to inscribe the circles of the design. The large central circle enclosing the eight-petalled lotus measures one cubit (Tib. *khru*) in diameter, or twenty-four finger-widths or *angulas*. At the centre is a small circle measuring eight finger-widths in diameter, within which is drawn an upright yellow *vajra*. A card stencil is usually used as a template for the sprinkled powder designs of the *vajras* and the crescent-moon and *vajra* motifs at the corners. Light blue powder is usually used to outline the basic design, and five coloured powders are used to fill in the coloured sections. These powders may either

be applied by hand or more meticulously drawn with a serrated conical powder sprinkler (Tib. *chag pu*).

Outside of the lotus circle is drawn a surrounding circle four *angulas* wide, and measuring thirty-two *angulas* in diameter. This is the inner circle (Tib. *mu ren*) upon which the firewood is placed. Outside again is drawn an outer circle (Tib. *kha khyer*), upon which are stencil-sprinkled eight yellow *vajras* in the eight directions. Between the *vajras* are placed five or seven small circles of coloured powder. Two *angulas* outside of this outer circle are drawn the square 'root lines' that form the boundary of the fire hearth design. In each of the four corners are drawn the emblems of a white crescent moon surmounted by a yellow half-*vajra*. Originally these emblems were placed upon the four corners of an established and tiered fire pit, and were represented three-dimensionally by a white hemispherical moon crowned by a half-*vajra*.

The lower drawing depicts the design for the hearth used in *homa* rituals of enrichment or increase. Here the flat earthbase of the hearth is coloured yellow. At the centre of the hearth is an eight or nine-faceted coloured jewel, measuring either six or eight *angulas* in height. Surrounding this jewel circle is an eight-spoked yellow wheel, inscribed within a square measuring one cubit across. Outside of this is drawn the square (Tib. *mu ren*) upon which the firewood is stacked. Outside again is the square (Tib. *kha khyer*), embellished with the emblems of coloured jewels or white wheels (see Plate 145). These two outer squares usually measure eight *angulas* in width, but on the drawings illustrated they are drawn in a four *angula* width. The square root-lines marking the boundary are drawn two *angulas* beyond the lines of the outer square, and are marked with the emblems of a white crescent moon and yellow half-*vajra*.

The white hearth for peace is sprinkled with white nectar and white perfume, and fragrant white flowers are scattered around the perimeter of the hearth. Similarly the yellow hearth for increase is sprinkled with yellow nectar, perfume and flowers.

Plate 144

The upper drawing depicts the most common hearth design for the *homa* activity of subjugation. The base of this hearth is coloured red, with a bow-shaped centre. The central area of the design is fashioned as an eight-petalled lotus, with a *vajra*, flower or hook at its central hub. Outside of the central hearth is the bow-shaped inner surround (Tib. *mu ren*), and beyond this is an outer bow shape (Tib. *kha khyer*), which is commonly decorated with flower or hook designs. In each of the four corners are the emblems of a crescent moon and half-*vajra*.

The lower drawing depicts the hearth design for the *homa* activity of wrath or destruction. At the black triangular centre of this hearth is an eight-bladed iron *chakra*, with a wrathful *vajra* at its centre. The triangular surround (Tib. *mu ren*) encompasses this, and is usually decorated with red flames. The outer triangle (Tib. *kha khyer*) is either decorated with wrathful three-pronged *vajras*, or an array of wrathful

Plate 144: Designs for the *homa* fire hearths employed in rituals of subjugation and wrathful activity

Plate 145: A variation of the square hearth design for
rituals of increase, and the Vajayogini hearth design

weapons. Again the emblems of a crescent moon and half-*vajra* are placed in the four corners.

No dimensions are given for the two fire pits illustrated in this drawing. The width of the triangular hearth is sometimes described as an arrow's length, and the wrathful fire pit usually consists of three tiered ledges, coloured black, red and white.

Plate 145

The upper drawing depicts a variation of the fire hearth for increase, as described on Plate 143. Here the outer square surround (Tib. *kha khyer*) is decorated with eight-spoked yellow wheels instead of jewels.

The lower drawing depicts the specific hearth design for the Vajrayogini *homa* ritual. The outer circular design and measurement of this hearth is the same as for the hearth for peaceful activity, as described on Plate 143. The two overlapping triangles at the hearth's centre form the 'reality source' or *dharmodaya* (Tib. *chos 'byung*) of the Vajrayogini mandala, as described on Plate 154. The triangles are geometrically measured by inscribing twelve *angula* arcs from the upper and lower points where the central axis intersects the enclosing circle. When these four arc-points are joined with their two axial tips, a double intersecting triangle is created. An inner line of one *angula* thickness is drawn within both triangles, and the upward pointing triangle is drawn on top of the downward pointing triangle. At the centre of the hearth is a circle measuring eight *angulas* in diameter, within which is drawn either a white *vajra* or the red seed-syllable *Bam* of Vajrayogini. In each of the four left and right corners of the *dharmodaya* are drawn four 'joy wheels' (Tib. *dga' 'khyil*). The *dharmodaya* and joy wheels are coloured white against a red background. The rest of the hearth is coloured white, and within the inner circle may be drawn flames or curved knives. The outer circle is decorated with a rosary of eight white *vajras*.

Plate 146: Composite Chinese pictograph symbolising longevity, destiny and happiness

Chapter Twelve
Geometric Borders, Patterns, Designs, and Motifs

The chapter illustrates a variety of the geometric borders and patterns that commonly occur as ornamental designs in both Tibetan and Chinese art. Many of these designs are derived from the swastika, key, knot, wave and scroll patterns of Chinese art and architecture.

Like the swastika, the geometric key, knot, wave and scroll designs that occur in many of these drawings are common to many cultures. The eternal or endless knot, for example, appears in an infinite variety of Celtic knot designs, especially in manuscript illumination. The mathematical precision of Islamic designs, which are often based on complex combinations of centred and repeating grids, reveal both the scientific genius of their discovery and the artistic genius of their creation.

All of the geometric designs depicted are drawn on two basic grids of intersecting squares bisected by diagonals, and equilateral triangles forming composite hexagrams. The majority of these designs either create infinite repeat patterns, or infinite linear borders. Many of these geometrical repeat designs are quite difficult to draw. However all of the drawings illustrated here have been created with a pen and brush, and, with the exception of the last four drawings (Plates 166–169) which I drew as 'half-drop' repeat patterns for Tharpa Publications, none have been mechanically or computer generated. The double outer lines of all these lattice drawings have been drawn with a fine rapidograph pen, and then filled in with a paintbrush to create the required thickness of line. Some of these designs are based upon the work of my friend, David Wade, who has spent many years collecting, collating, analysing and reconstructing geometric patterns from all over the world, and is undoubtedly one of the greatest living exponents of this subject.

Following the geometrical drawings, Plate 158 illustrates Tibetan syllables and motifs. Plates 159 and 160 illustrate

Chinese *shou* or longevity designs, and other Chinese auspicious symbols which are commonly found as silk brocade designs. Plate 161 illustrates Tibetan armour designs and the repeat patterns of oriental armour. Plates 162 and 163 depict a variety of curvilinear and geometric border designs. Plate 164 shows examples of brocade designs, and Plate 165 depicts examples of *makara*-tail scrolls. This section concludes with four endlessly repeating motifs of the lotus; lotus and *vajra*; lotus, *vajra* and bell; and lotus, book and sword (Plates 166–169).

THE SWASTIKA

The swastika (Skt. *svastika*) is a common symbol found in many cultures and civilisations. It occurs in Egyptian, Trojan, Roman, Teutonic and Celtic stone carvings; as a symbolic motif of the American Indians, throughout North, Central and South America; and in Persian, Central Asian, Indian, Chinese, Japanese and South East Asian art. In ancient Greece the swastika was known as a 'Greek Cross', or a *gammadion*, formed from four clockwise-rotating Greek *gamma* letters. In early Christianity the Greek letter *gamma* symbolised a cornerstone, and the *gammadion* or swastika became a symbol for Christ as the 'cornerstone of the Temple or Church'. A similar symbolism is found in Buddhist art, where the swastika represents the stability of the element earth. In later Christian art the *gammadion* became known as a 'flyfot', which occurs as a geometric design on the lower areas of stained glass cathedral and church windows.

The Indian symbol of the swastika first appears amongst artifacts unearthed from the ancient Harappan city of Mohenjo-Daro in the Indus valley (*circa* 2500 BC). The swastika was first indentified with Vishnu, as a solar or fire symbol of his *chakra*, or as the auspicious mark which adorns Vishnu's breast – known as the *shrivatsa* – meaning 'beloved of good fortune'. In Indian art Buddha, as the ninth of Vishnu's ten incarnations, is also commonly depicted with the swastika or *shrivatsa* adorning his breast. Later the swastika was also identified with Shiva and the snake cults of the Naga civilisation, originating possibly from the markings on a cobra's hood or the entwined knotting of serpents.

The Sanskrit word *svastika* derives from the root *sv-asti*, meaning well-being, good fortune, success or prosperity. The precise origins of the Indian swastika symbol are unknown, and various theories have been postulated regarding its derivation. The most commonly held view is that the swastika is a sun symbol, derived from the clockwise motion of the sun in the four quarters and seasons. As a fire symbol it is also thought to have originated from the Vedic fire-sticks, known as *arani*, which are rubbed together to kindle the flame for the sacred fire. Another theory ascribes the motif to the interlocking of the syllables of the root *sv-asti*, written in the characters of the Ashokan alphabet to form the monogram of the swastika; or to the Pali syllables *su* and *ti*, which together form the shape of a swastika, and are derived from the Sanskrit *sv* – meaning 'well', and *asti* – meaning 'it is'.

In the Tibetan Bon tradition the swastika (Tib. *g.yung drung*), meaning eternal or unchanging, essentially corresponds to the Buddhist *vajra*, and likewise gives its name to the Bonpo tradition (*g.yung drung bon*). The Bon swastika rotates in an anticlockwise direction, unlike the Hindu, Jain and Buddhist swastika, whose sacred motion is clockwise. For this reason practitioners of the Bonpo tradition circumambulate sacred buildings or pilgrimage sites in an anticlockwise direction. In Indian symbolism the right (Skt. *dakshina*) or clockwise-rotating swastika is identified with the male principle of the god, and the left (Skt. *vama*) or anticlockwise swastika (Skt. *sauvastika*) with the feminine principle of the goddess.

In China the swastika (Ch. *wan*) was originally a Taoist symbol of eternity and divinity, and as the *wan tzu*, or 'ten thousand character sign', it represents the Taoist principle of the 'ten thousand things under heaven'.

Whatever its origin the swastika was essentially an ancient and widespread auspicious symbol of good fortune, though its adoption by the German Nazi Party as the symbol of the Third Reich has recently bestowed the most sinister impression of nationalism upon it.

Plate 146

This complex Chinese pictograph combines the *shou* symbol of longevity, the *ming* symbol of destiny, and the double *fu* symbol of happiness. The circle represents heaven, the square at the centre earth, and the eight outer divisions the eight directions. The nine divisions of the circle represent the nine *mewas* or numbers, and the nine provinces of China. The central square also represents earth surrounded by the eight *parkhas* or trigrams. The symbolism of 'the square of

earth within the circle of heaven' is also found in the traditional design of Chinese coins.

Plate 147

The repeating pattern of the endless knots at the centre of the upper design is based upon a hexagonal grid formed from equilateral triangles, and creates a three-dimensional illusion of cubes. The repetitive meander pattern in the circle surrounding the central hexagram is drawn in a T-shaped wave or fret pattern. The outer square surrounding this circle has endless knot designs on its lower corners, and a meandering upper border enclosing two earth squares. Below the upper square are four repeat border patterns – the first as a T-shaped wave or fret design, and the lower three as endless scroll designs. In Chinese art the auspicious endless knot is known as the 'fish entrail' design, and the continuous wave or fret line is known as the 'thunder-scroll' or 'cloud-band' designs. The term 'meander' derives from the Greek Maiandros – the name given to a winding river in Phrygia, Greece.

Plate 148

The upper area of this drawing shows five endless border designs based upon T-shaped, S-shaped and U-shaped cloud-bank and thunder-scroll designs. These fret or key patterns are also commonly found as decorative motifs in classical Greek art and architecture. The lower area of the

Plate 148: Geometric border designs

Plate 147: Meander and endless knot designs.

drawing depicts a fourfold swastika motif at the centre, producing two *fu* symbols of double happiness or secular power. The continuous arms of the swastikas lead into small knots which then form cross-shapes, with crosses and intersecting lozenges at their centres.

Plate 149

On the left side of the page are various examples of interlocking chains and knots – with chains produced from two meandering lines in the top three drawings, from three interweaving lines in the fourth drawing, and from four interweaving lines in the fifth drawing. The sixth drawing depicts a chain of interlocking squares. The seventh, eighth and ninth drawings show knots made from a continuous single line, an interlocking double line, and a chain of endless knots which are united by their diagonal corners. The two scroll borders in the lower left corner are formed from single black folding lines, which create the illusion of overlapping diagonals against their white surrounds.

Across to the right are three vertical swastika motifs, composed of alternating swastikas; a T-shaped wave border is drawn vertically on the far right. In the bottom right corner are a T-shaped wave or thunder-scroll design, and an alternating swastika border.

Plate 150

At the top left is a repeat pattern formed from alternating right and left-facing swastikas within a grid of diagonal squares. Below this are two endless knot patterns, the upper with white knots on a black background and the lower reversed. Below this is a continuous frieze of endless knots, and at the bottom two cloud-band or thunder-scroll designs.

On the upper right are six small swastika borders on black backgrounds. The first is composed of a cloud-band of right-facing swastikas; the second of alternating swastikas with U-shaped keys; and the third of alternating swastikas with M-shaped keys. The fourth border shows an intricate design of left-facing swastikas creating a frieze of S-shapes, with outer bridging-lines creating T-shaped patterns. The fifth drawing shows a frieze of left-facing swastikas with alternating square windows; and the sixth drawing shows a similar frieze with alternating knots. Below these are three vertical swastika borders with offset designs. In the bottom right corner are two more meandering wave or thunder-scroll borders.

Plate 151

In the upper left corner is a *vishvavajra* within a square of cloud-band border designs. Below are six different swastika borders, the first of which is formed from the spiralling arms of right-facing swastikas. The second, third and sixth

are reversed images of three of the borders on Plate 150. In the bottom left corner are two small sections of continuous swastika patterns.

In the upper right corner is a continuous pattern of alternating swastikas within slightly offset squares. Below are two drawings of perhaps the most classical of Chinese swastika designs; the upper drawing appearing as a white pattern on a black background, and the lower reversed. In the bottom right corner are two continuous patterns formed from right-facing swastikas, the first of which is constructed within a square grid.

Plate 152

In the upper area are eight repeating swastika patterns drawn upon square grids, which create secondary shapes of swastikas, double-barred crosses or *fu* symbols of happiness, and irregular key patterns. On the left of the third row is an asymmetrically repeating swastika pattern, composed of regular components that move upwards one grid-square in their repetition. On the right of the third row is a symmetrical swastika design within repeating squares. On the left and right of the fourth row are two identical swastika patterns; the drawing on the left is outlined in white upon a black background, and the drawing on the right is reversed with a black outline on a white background.

At the centre of the third row is an off-axis repeating swastika pattern that creates a secondary pattern of interlocking horizontal and vertical lines. Below this and at the centre of the fourth row is the same design, filled in with alternating black and white sections that create the illusion of an interlocking basket-weave design.

On the bottom left is a diagonal swastika pattern formed from four T-shapes within a square; this pattern also moves asymmetrically by one grid-square in each repeat. At the bottom centre is an endless swastika pattern that creates secondary shapes of interlocking crosses. The drawing in the bottom right corner shows the same design drawn diagonally and off-axis.

Plate 153

On the left side of this illustration are five examples of repeating swastika patterns, which are drawn upon the grid of horizontal and vertical squares shown at the top. On the right side are five diagonally repeating swastika patterns, which are drawn on the grid of diagonal squares shown at the top.

Plate 154

This drawing illustrates examples of knots and borders. In the upper area are four entwined-knot corner designs, with a simple cross-shaped knot at the centre. Corner designs such as these may be depicted upon Tibetan book covers,

Plate 149: Borders of interlocking chains, knots, squares, and swastikas

Plate 150: Repeating knot and swastika patterns and borders

Plate 151: Repeating swastika borders and patterns

Plate 152: Endlessly repeating swastika patterns

Plate 153: Repeating swastika patterns constructed upon squared horizontal and diagonal grid

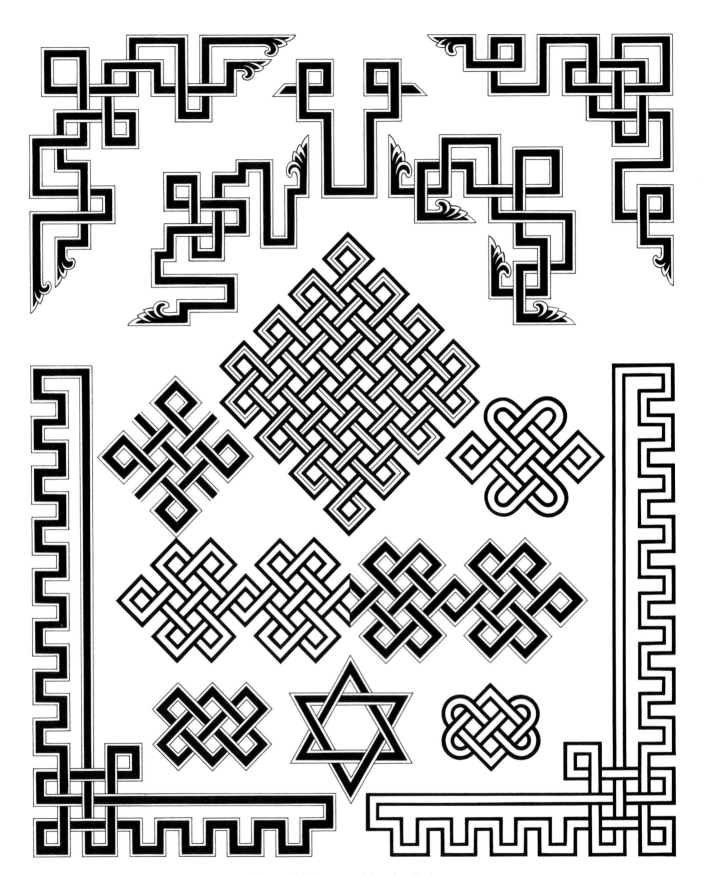

Plate 154: Knots and border designs

stitched tent designs, or upon carpet and furniture designs. The ends of these knot designs terminate in leaf-shaped decorations. In the lower left and right corners are two endless-knot borders, depicted in bold black on the left and black outline on the right.

At the centre of the page is a large eternal knot formed from the interweaving of nine crossing lines. To the left and right of this are two smaller knot designs. Below is a frieze of four entwined eternal knots, outlined in black on the left and bold black on the right.

At the bottom centre is a six-pointed star formed from the interlocking of two equilateral triangles, like the Jewish 'Star of David'. In Hindu tantra this design appears as one of the main *yantras* or 'devices' representing the union of the god and goddess, with the upward-pointing 'male' triangle representing the sexual organ or *lingam* of the god, and the downward-pointing 'female' triangle the sexual organ or *yoni* of the goddess. In Buddhist tantra this *yantra* appears as a six-pointed *chakra*, which may be depicted at the centre of certain mandalas or form the lower seats of deities such as Vajravarahi, Simhamukha, and certain forms of Mahakala. In this form the triangle (or intersecting triangles) is known as a 'reality source' (Skt. *dharmodaya*; Tib. *chos 'byung*). In visualisation practices the *dharmodaya* always arises from the syllable *E* (*evam*), which in early Indian script was written in the form of a triangular letter. The word *evam* forms the opening term for early Buddhist scriptures, which usually begin: "*Evam*, [thus] have I heard". The visualised *dharmodaya* may be coloured blue, red or white, or may be described as white on the outside and red within. In certain visualisation practices, such as Vajrayogini, the *dharmodaya* arises as the intersection of two three-sided pyramids or tetrahedrons made from light, which appear as a six-pointed star when viewed from above. The *dharmodaya* appears at the centre of the fire-hearth used in the Vajrayogini *homa* ritual, which is illustrated on Plate 145. To the left and right of the six-pointed star are two further drawings of endless knots.

Plate 155
This illustration depicts examples of meandering-line and endless-knot borders. At the top and bottom corners are two designs of endless-knot borders, with swastika designs inside the upper border and meandering cloud-band designs within the lower border. Within the upper swastika band is a double-line border with complex eternal knots at its corners. Within this is a meandering fret or key design, with three small key designs above and an earth-base square below. Within the lower cloud-band frieze is another complex eternal knot border formed from a double line. Within this again is another meandering fret or key design, with a small eternal knot above.

Across the centre is a rectangular swastika border composed of double lines; this design is taken from an early Tibetan wooden book cover. Within this rectangle are two eternal-knot corners, and a triple key-shaped design.

Plate 156
Within the endless-knot border of this illustration are nine drawings of knots. At the top left is a knot formed from five interweaving lines, and on the top right is a knot formed from seven horizental and eight vertical lines. On the left of the second row is an unusual knot formed from a square and four interweaving loops. At the centre is a knot formed from five vertical lines interwoven with eight horizontal lines. On the right of the second row is a knot formed from four interlocking loops. Across the third row is a frieze of four joined endless knots. In the bottom left is a knot formed from a four-cornered square intersected by a cross formed from two long rectangles. At the bottom centre is a large knot formed from nine interweaving horizontal and vertical lines. And in the bottom right corner is an endless knot with curved corners.

Plate 157
This illustration depicts fourteen examples of the endless knot, or 'fish entrail' design. Across the top row are three drawings of circles interwoven within a simple 'five square' knot composed of four interweaving horizontal and vertical lines. The five squares of this knot represent the centre and four directions of earth, and the circle represents heaven.

Across the second row are three drawings of the most common Tibetan form of the endless or 'glorious knot' (Skt. *shrivatsa*; Tib. *dpal be'u*). The first drawing on the left shows a symmetrical knot formed from the interweaving of seven horizontal and vertical lines. The second drawing shows a knot composed of five broad horizontal and vertical lines against a black background; and the third drawing shows the same knot in its most common Tibetan form.

At the left and right of the centre are two drawings of a complex knot formed from the combination of a simple five-lined knot with a secondary knot formed from four intersecting rectangles. This design is drawn in black on the left side, and as a white interwoven knot against a black background on the right side. Centred below these two drawings is a three-dimensional knot, drawn like a raised enclosure or a maze. Below to the left and right are two five-lined knots which are drawn upon a grid of equilateral triangles. At the bottom centre is a seven-lined knot with black interior squares. In the left and right corners are two innovative variations of the *shrivatsa* or glorious-knot.

Plate 158
Within the repeating endless-knot border of this illustration are symmetrically arranged motifs and syllables. At the top centre is an endless-knot with extending leaf-shaped scrolls, and below a pair of angular corner designs enclosing two endless-knots and a swastika. These designs are commonly used as applique motifs on Tibetan tents and door-hangings (Tib. *sgo ras*).

Plate 155: Swastika and endless knot borders

Plate 156: Endless knots

Plate 157: Endless knots

Plate 158: Knots, *jui'i* symbols and syllables

Descending from the upper right and left corners are five symmetrical variations of the trefoil cloud-scroll or *jui'i* design. Below these are the three Tibetan syllables *Om A Hum,* representing body, speech and mind. These syllables, which are visualised in a white, red and blue sequence, are commonly inscribed on the back of a consecrated thangka at the positions of the forehead, throat and heart *chakra* of the main deity. Between the two lower *Hum* syllables are two drawings of the rotating 'wheel of joy' (Tib. *dga ' 'khyil*) or 'jewel-wheel' (Tib. *nor bu dga ' 'khyil*) symbolising the Three Jewels. Above are the wisdom emblems of a flaming-sword and the text of the Prajnaparamita Sutra, with a *vajra* and bell positioned to the left and right. Across the bottom is a continuous frieze of clockwise rotating swastikas.

Plate 159

This illustration depicts ten circular examples and three upright examples of the Chinese *shou* symbol of the Chinese god of longevity, Shou-lao (see page 96). This Taoist design is created from the stylisation of the Chinese written character *shou*, denoting longevity, and its representation in a circular form symbolises the immortality of the Taoist heavens. There are believed to be more than a hundred stylistic variations of this symbol, and it is commonly found on Chinese porcelain and seals, Tibetan tent decorations, carpets, and as a motif on implements and furniture. But its most common application is found on the designs of Chinese silk brocade, which is extensively used by Tibetan tailors to create silk banners and hangings, secular and religious costumes, and to frame brocaded *thangkas*.

Three of the circular *shou* designs depicted incorporate the auspicious motif of the swastika. The double upright Chinese pictograph at the top centre shows a form of the Chinese *fu* character of 'double-happiness'. The upright or 'long' *shou* character at the centre of the page is copied from a brocade design of a Chinese Emperor's 'dragon robe' of the eighteenth century Qing dynasty. The shape of this symbol represents the 'mountain of heaven'. The two symmetrical *shou* characters depicted at the bottom corners are described in Plate 160.

Plate 160

This page depicts examples of Chinese symbols that are drawn in a bold black line. Across the top row are five variations of the *shou* character drawn in the form of a bat or a butterfly. The butterfly is a favoured symbol in Chinese art, and recalls the dream of the Taoist philosopher, Chuang Tzu, who having dreamed that he was a joyously flitting butterfly, posed the question, "Did Chuang Tzu dream he was a butterfly? Or is the butterfly still dreaming that he is Chuang Tzu?" The caterpillar, chrysalis and butterfly, as unified symbols of transmutation, resurrection and immortality, are perhaps best described in the aphorism, "What the caterpillar perceives of as the end of all things, the rest of the world

perceives as the beginning of the butterfly". The horizontal central bar of this design represents the body of the butterfly, the two concave sides represent its wings, and the central axis represents the wing markings.

On the left and right ends of the second row are two drawings of the stylised *fu* character representing double happiness – the material and spiritual happinesses of earth and heaven – with the squares and horizontal bars representing earth, and the vertical bars representing heaven. On the inner left and right of the *fu* characters are four drawings of the Chinese *ya* character, created from two back-to-back *chi* or 'self' characters. The *ya* symbol represents the ability to discern between good and evil – and along with the sun, moon, stars, mountain, dragon, phoenix, libation cups, pond weed, fire, rice, and axe-head – formed one of the 'twelve ornaments' of the Chinese Emperor's silk brocade robe. Here the sun, containing the three-legged bird; the moon, containing the hare; the three stars; and the heavenly mountain, represent the four annual sacrifices of the Emperor. The dragon and 'flowery bird' (pheasant or phoenix) represent dominion over heaven and earth, through the powers of inspiration and virtue. The pond weed, libation cups, flame, rice and earthly mountain symbolise the five elements of water, metal, fire, wood and earth, and the five qualities of purity, piety, effort, abundance and stability. The double *fu* or *ya* symbol represents the Emperor's justice, and the axe-head his punishment. Two drawings of the axe-head are depicted to the inner left and right of the *ya* symbols.

In the upper centre is a circular drawing of the eight trigrams or *parkas* (Ch. *pa kua*; Tib. *spar kha*), as illustrated and described on Plates 64 and 65. The origin of the eight trigrams, which consist of continuous or unbroken *yang* lines, and divided or broken *yin* lines, is believed to have been realised from observations made on the markings of a tortoise-shell by the legendary Chinese Emperor Fu Hsi (*circa* 2850 BC). The arrangement of the trigrams depicted in this drawing follows the Chinese 'Fu Hsi' system, as follows:

the 'creative' trigram (*ch'ien*) of heaven at the top;
the 'joyous' trigram (*tui*) of the lake anticlockwise at the upper left;
the 'clinging' trigram (*li*) of fire at the centre left;
the 'arousing' trigram (*chen*) of thunder to the lower left;
the 'gentle' trigram (*sun*) of wind clockwise from the top on the upper right;
the 'abysmal' trigram (*k'an*) of water is on the centre right;
the 'keeping-still' trigram (*ken*) of the mountain is on the lower right;
the 'receptive' trigram (*k'un*) of earth is at the bottom

The arrangement of these trigrams around a central *yin-yang* symbol is used as a protective plaque or talisman against harmful influences in the Chinese geomantic system of *feng shui*. This plaque or 'mirror' is often hung above a doorway to repel and divert evil spirits from entering a building. The *yin-yang* symbol is composed of two comma-shaped sections

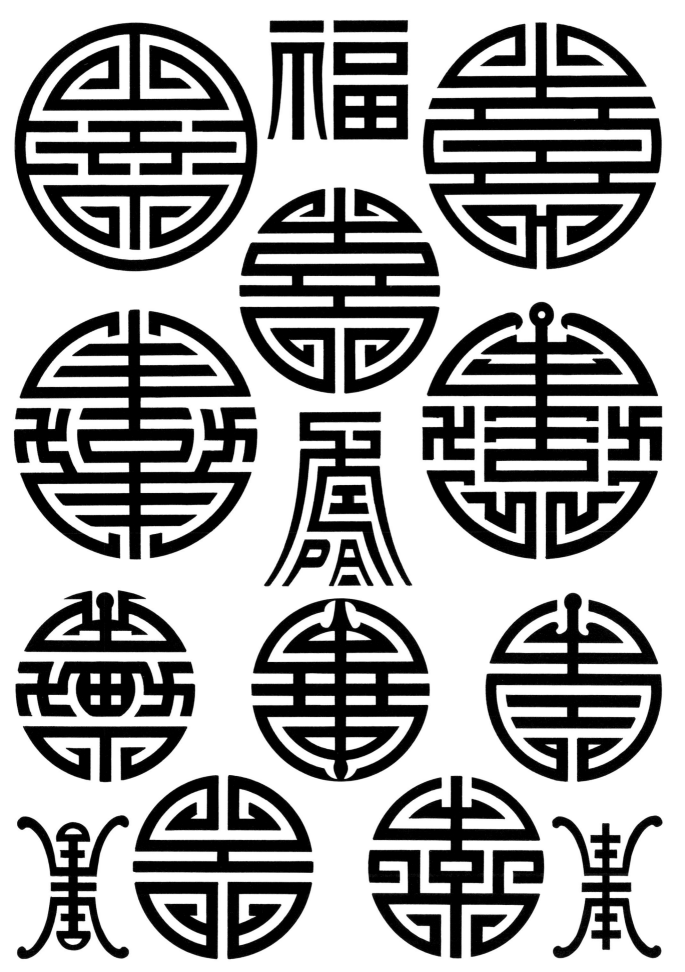

Plate 159: Chinese *shou* or longevitiy symbols

Plate 160: Various Chinese symbols and trigrams

of a black *yin* and a white *yang*, which are derived from the 'first cause' (Ch. *t'ai chi*) of creation, represented by the yolk and white of an egg. The terms *yin* and *yang* originally referred to the shaded and sunlit slopes of a mountain or valley. The black comma of the *yin* symbol represents the dark feminine principle of the earth, the moon, passivity, the north, shadow, even numbers, and the symbol of the tiger. The white comma of the *yang* symbol represents the light masculine principle of heaven, the sun, creativity, the south, light, odd numbers, and the symbol of the dragon. Alchemically each of these two polarity symbols contains the seed of its opposite at its strongest point, represented by the white and black circular seeds within the centre of the *yin-yang* commas. Below this upper drawing is a hexagonal plaque containing the *yin-yang* symbol, surrounded by the eight trigrams arranged in the 'King Wen' sequence of the 'I Ching', as described below and on Plate 64.

Surrounding the upper drawing of the eight trigrams are the silhouettes of five bats. The bat (Ch. *pien fu*) is a Chinese auspicious symbol of happiness and longevity. The second character (*fu*) of its name is synonomous with the *fu* character of happiness. The symbolism of the five bats represents the 'five blessings' of a long life, health, wealth, virtue, and a natural death. The five bats are found as decorative motifs on Chinese porcelain, carpets, silk brocade and furnishings. They are commonly painted in the auspicious colour of vermilion red, and often represented with curved 'embracing wings' (Ch. *fu'i*) that form the shape of a Chinese sceptre (Ch. *jui'i*). The sceptre is described as a 'short blunt sword', but is commonly fashioned as a triple-eyed gem, a triple cloud-scroll, a lotus, or a fungus of immortality.

On the left and right of the third and fourth rows, beneath the *fu* and *ya* pictographs, are twelve variations of the swastika design, with six clockwise or right-turning swastikas on the left and six left-turning swastikas on the right.

Across the fifth and seventh rows, which are divided by a frieze of spiralling and alternating thunder-scroll patterns to the left and right, are block drawings of the eight trigrams. The upper fifth row displays the 'Fu Hsi' sequence of: heaven (*ch'ien*), wind or wood (*sun*), water (*k'an*), and mountain (*ken*) on the left; and earth (*k'un*), thunder (*chen*), fire (*li*), and lake (*t'ui*) on the right. The lower seventh row displays the 'King Wen' sequence of; thunder (*chen*), wind or wood (*sun*), fire (*li*), and earth (*k'un*) on the left; and lake (*t'ui*), heaven (*ch'ien*), water (*k'an*), and mountain (*ken*) on the right.

In the bottom left corner is a rectangle containing the eight trigrams arranged in the 'King Wen' sequence described above, and following the clockwise sequence of the trigrams displayed in the hexagonal *parka* plaque above. In the bottom right corner is a swastika design forming key patterns within a square, and representing the four directions and stability of the element earth.

Not illustrated in this drawing are the two Chinese collectives of the 'eight treasures', and the 'eight symbols of the Taoist immortals'. The 'eight treasures' are most commonly listed as: a lozenge or painting, a stone chime or gong, two golden coins, a mirror, a pearl, two books, a pair of rhinoceros horns, and an artemisia leaf. The 'eight Taoist symbols'

are; a flower basket, a lotus, a sword, a fan, a flute, a gourd, bamboo castanets, and a musical bamboo tube. A third collective of 'antique treasures' may include: a chess or *go* board, a flaming pearl, a triple-eyed gem or *jui'i* sceptre, a coral branch, a peach, a bat, musical instruments, rhinoceros horns, elephant tusks, a pair of scroll paintings, *fu, ya* and *shou* characters, and interlocking jewels or earrings. These symbols may also be found on all manner of Chinese artifacts, including porcelain, brocade, carpets, jade and wood carvings.

Plate 161

This illustration depicts examples of armour (Tib. *go khrab, go cha*) and chain-mail designs, and interwoven lattice or basketwork patterns. In the upper left and right corners are four details of armour designs as depicted on the forearms of warrior-deities, such as Begtse, Vaishravana, Gesar, or the four guardian kings of the four directions. The literal meaning of the name Begtse is 'hidden coat of mail'. The armour of warrior-deities is commonly fashioned of small rectangular or tongue-shaped iron plates, which have small holes at their overlapping ends enabling them to be bound together with a leather thong. The most vulnerable parts of the body, such as the shoulders, breast, upper forearms, wrists and thighs are usually protected by separately shaped metal plates that provide additional cover to these areas.

The upper left drawing shows a forearm covered in rectangular plates of chain-mail. The wrist is protected by a cuff of lotus-shaped iron plates that serves to deflect sword blows. The upper forearm is covered by a curved iron plate with a leaf-shaped upper bar. The lower forearm is protected by a similar bar with a decorative jewel at the elbow. Just visible on the upper arm is a circlet made of rhinoceros hide that again serves to protect against sword blows. The drawing below depicts a forearm with its armour patterned in a 'fish-scale' design, and with the same protective elements as described above. The third drawing from the upper left shows a section of 'fish-scale' armour, with a base fringe made of rhinoceros hide.

The forearm drawing in the upper right corner is again fashioned from overlapping rectangular iron plates, and the drawing below depicts a variation of armour in a 'fish-scale' design. The third drawing from the upper right is fashioned from rectangular iron plates that are threaded onto a leather cuirass in separate rows. The frieze at the bottom may be made of sword-shaped iron plates or of coloured silk valances. Although the armour of deities is commonly fashioned of iron and leather, it may be described and coloured as a precious substance, such as gold, silver, copper, crystal, lapis lazuli, ruby, coral, emerald or conch shell. The armour of wrathful deities may include black silk robes adorned with the designs of magical weapons, or armour made of copper, foundry iron, meteorite iron, black rhinoceros skin, or the scales of a black iron-scorpion.

At the top centre are five examples of breastplate designs that are drawn against a background of elongated

Plate 161: Armour and chain-mail designs

honeycomb-patterned armour. The breastplate on the up-per right is fashioned from concentric circles enclosing two sixteen-petalled lotuses. Below this is a *kirtimukha*-faced breastplate, with garlands of jewels hanging from its mouth. The small breastplate in the centre has an outer ring of lotus petals, and an inner hub of a four-petalled lotus enclosing a three-spoked 'triskele' (Tib. *dga' 'khyil*) or 'wheel of joy'. The breastplate on the upper right has a lotus hub surrounded by a radial wheel of overlapping lotus petals. The last breast-plate on the lower right has a lotus hub with six leaf-shaped ornamental bars curving inwards towards the centre.

The lower half of this page shows chain-mail and lat-tice-weave designs. Across the top row are three chain-mail designs drawn against a black background. The first draw-ing on the left shows the interlocking rings of the Chinese 'coin design' chain-mail. The second drawing shows iron rings interlaced with a double Y-shaped lattice of iron strips. The Y-shaped strips interweave from the top and bottom with the iron rings to create a complex pattern of triangles and hexagons. The third drawing shows chain-mail fash-ioned from interlocking squares.

The first drawing on the left of the lower second row shows a basket-weave of horizontal and vertical strips, with two layers of diagonal strips behind. This pattern is often used to depict woven straw mats, or the palm-leaf huts in which yogins or mendicants live. The two drawings at the centre show two variations of the Y-shaped designs of leather or metal armour. This design of chain-mail is quite difficult to draw, and thus is usually only found on the finest *thangkas*. The Y-shaped design of interlocking sections, which pro-vides flexibility in six directions, proved to be a popular model for Chinese and Japanese armour. The drawing on the right of the second row depicts X-shaped armour plates interwoven by overlapping squares. This complex armour pattern is only rarely depicted in Tibetan art. On the left and right of the bottom row are blacked-in links of ring and square chain-mail. At the bottom centre are two separate designs of Y-shaped plates that converge into a triangular formation from the top and bottom.

Plate 162
This illustration shows examples of geometric border de-signs and linear brocade patterns. At the top left and right are two border designs based upon the triangular grids at the top, with a simple design of parallel lines on the left and alternating floral motifs on the right. Below these are two groups of three floral and cloud designs, which are based upon the meandering wave grids above. Next are two di-agonal swastika patterns to the left, and a composite cloud motif to the right. Next are two triangular patterns to the left, and two diagonal patterns to the right. The two wide diagonal bands below show friezes of auspicious symbols decorated with silk ribbons and separated by geometric borders on the left, and cloud motifs with 'fish-egg' decora-tions on the right. In the bottom left corner is a common interlocking swastika pattern, and in the bottom right corner

is a three-coloured sequence for painting this pattern, with the three separate colours depicted as white, cross-hatched, and black sections.

Plate 163
This illustration depicts examples of geometrical border designs that are based mainly on swastika, meandering key or thunder-scroll designs, and repeating squares. The fourth and fifth drawings from the top of the left hand column show lotus petal designs, and the seventh drawing across all three columns shows examples of concentric semi-circular pat-terns. The fifth drawing from the top of the middle column shows a 'pine tree' pattern, such as may be used on the deco-ration of monastic ceiling beams. The eighth drawing in the central column shows a border of triangular-tipped silk val-ances, with small silver bells at their ends. A 'herring-bone' pattern is shown in the fourth drawing from the top of the right column, and the eighth drawing shows a hexagonal 'honeycomb' pattern.

Plate 164
This page shows thirty-six various brocade pattern designs drawn within separate ovals. These brocade designs are painted in gold outline on the silk clothes and robes worn by Buddhas, deities, human gurus and lineage lamas. The finest of these gold patterns are often underpainted with a gradated gold wash, which gives a radiant depth and lumi-nosity to the patterns final gold outline. Each Tibetan artist had his own repertoire of favoured brocade designs, the sim-plest consisting of groups of dots as 'fish-egg' patterns, and the most complex being intricate swastika patterns or the cloud-enhanced motifs of the dragon and phoenix. Early Tibetan paintings often display the most meticulous and innovative of brocade designs, which may consist of grace-fully dancing goddesses, subtle floral motifs, or creatures such as lions, deer, swans and mythological animals. These miniature designs were usually painted in full colour, and often with several hundred different designs in a single com-position. It was through such details that the artist was able to express his conception of the 'heavenly silks' worn by deities. But the most common brocade motifs in later Ti-betan art consisted of stylised flower and leaf compositions, with their alternating spaces filled in with groups of dots or fish-egg motifs.

Between the ovals depicted here are individual patterns of circular brocade designs. Between the ovals in the three bottom rows are three square designs and three examples of the Chinese *shou* character of longevity.

Plate 165
This illustration depicts thirty-four drawings of the *makara*-tail scrolls and jewel-finials that commonly adorn the thrones

Plate 162: Border designs and linear brocade patterns

Plate 163: Geometric border designs

Plate 164: Brocade pattern designs

Plate 165: *Makara*-tail scrolls and crests

or throne-backs of seated gurus and lamas. These thrones usually consist of a cushioned seat upon which the figure sits, with an oval or aura-shaped back support (Tib. *rgyab yol*) behind, draped with silk cloth. The cushioned base of the throne may rest upon an ornate throne-base with four short legs, rather like a low table or raised plinth. The arched top of the back support is commonly fashioned from a sandalwood and gold crest-bar, which terminates at either end in an encased-jewel or golden *makara*-tail scroll.

At the bottom centre of the page are two examples of these golden crest-bars. The upper drawing shows two phoenix or peacock heads at the ends of the bar, with a silk cloth draped over its centre. At the bases of the bar are two lotus and moon disc pedestals, which form the capitals to the two vertical pillars that support the crest-bar. The heads of lions, dragons, *garudas*, or other mythological creatures may alternatively be depicted at the ends of the bar, often with a jewel-chain or tapering silk valance hanging from their mouths. Surrounding these these two drawings are various examples of golden *makara*-tail scrolls, many of which are inset with precious gems.

Above the heads of the birds are three jewel-finials that may crown the top of the bar, but more commonly the six or eight-faceted jewel, as illustrated on Plate 98, forms the crowning jewel. Across the top row are five intricate examples of *makara*-tail scrolls with floral and leaf-shaped decorations. Across the second row are two symmetrical pairs of scrolling crest-bar ends, and across the third row and below are further examples of *makara*-tail finials.

Plates 166–169

The four 'half-drop' repeat patterns depicted on these four plates were drawn as book cover designs for Tharpa Publications, London. Half-drop patterns are commonly designed as repeating patterns for fabric or wallpaper designs. Here only one central motif and its connecting surrounds are initially drawn; then this image is mechanically duplicated and connected to create an endless repeat pattern. These four drawings are the only images in this book that have entailed the use of computer scanning technology.

Plate 166 shows a repeating peony-style flower in a circular scrolling-vine surround. Plate 167 depicts a *vajra* and lotus in an oval scrolling-vine surround. Plate 168 depicts a *vajra* and bell upon a lotus, which again is contained within an oval scrolling-vine surround. Plate 169 depicts the emblem of Manjushri, as a sword and book upon a lotus, contained within a diamond-shaped vine surround.

Plate 166: Repeating lotus or peony flower designs

Plate 167: Repeating *vajra* and lotus designs

Plate 168: Repeating *vajra* and bell upon lotus designs

Plate 169: Repeating sword and book upon a lotus, as the emblem of Manjushri

Select Bibliography

The main reference material consulted in my writing of this text is drawn mainly from unpublished or restricted manuscripts, and from a compilation of tangential notes that I have accumulated over the years from a large variety of oral and descriptive sources. I have not listed the restricted manuscripts in this bibliography, but the translators and editors of these commentaries are listed in my acknowledgements.

Anonymous, various authors articles in *Cho Yang - The Voice of Tibetan Religion and Culture*. No 2 (1987); No 3 (undated); No 6 (1994); No 7 (1996). New Delhi. Norbulingka Institute.

Auboyer, J. & Beguin, G. 1977. *Dieux et Demons de l'Himalaya*. Catalogue of Exhibition at the Grand Palais. Paris. Editions des Musees Nationaux.

Bayer, S. 1978. *The Cult of Tara - Magic and Ritual in Tibet*. Berkley. University of California.

Brauen, M. 1997. *The Mandala: Sacred Circle in Tibetan Buddhism*. London. Serindia.

Boord, M. 1993. *The Cult of the Deity Vajrakila in the Northern Treasures Tradition of Tibet*. Tring. Institute of Buddhist Studies.

Chatterjee, G. 1996. *Sacred Hindu Symbols*. New Delhi. Abhinav.

Cozort, D. 1986. *Highest Yoga Tantra*. Ithaca. Snow Lion.

Dagthon, J. G. Kalsang, J. & Choezom, T. 1995. *Tibetan Astronomy and Astrology: A Brief Introduction*. Dharamsala. Astro. Dept. T.M.A.I.

Dagyab, L.S. 1995. *Buddhist Symbols in Tibetan Culture*. Boston. Wisdom.

Dhargyey, Geshe N. 1985. *Kalachakra Tantra*. Dharamsala. L.T.W.A.

Dorjee, P. 1996. *Stupa and its Technology*. Delhi. Motilal Banarsidass.

Dowson, J. 1982. *A Classic Dictionary of Hindu Mythology and Religion*. Calcutta. Rupa & Co.

Das, S. C. 1970. *A Tibetan-English Dictionary*. Delhi. Motilal Banarsidass.

Essen, G.W. and Thingo, T.T. 1987. *Die Gotter des Himalaya*. (2 vols.). Munchen. Prestel-Verlag.

Evans-Wentz, W. Y. 1969. *Tibet's Great Yogi Milarepa*. London. O.U.P.

Evans-Wentz, W. Y. 1969. *The Tibetan Book of the Great Liberation*. London. O.U.P.

Evans-Wentz, W. Y. 1968. *The Tibetan Book of the Dead*. London. O.U.P.

Feuerstein, G. 1990. *Encyclopedic Dictionary of Yoga*. London. Unwin Hyman Ltd.

Gega Lama. 1983. *Principles of Tibetan Art*. (2 vols.). Darjeeling.

Gyatsho, T. L. (trans. Jackson, D.P.)1979. *Gateway to the Temple*. Kathmandu. Ratna Pustak Bhandar.

Gyatso, Geshe K. 1982. *Clear Light of Bliss*. London. Tharpa.

Gyatso, Geshe K. 1991. *Guide to Dakini Land*. London. Tharpa.

Gyatso, Geshe K. 1994. *Tantric Grounds and Paths*. London. Tharpa.

Jackson, D. P. and Jackson. J.A. Illustrated by Robert Beer. 1998. *Tibetan Thangka Painting: Methods & Materials*. London. Serindia.

Jinpa, T. & Dorje, G. (eds. Coleman, G). 1993. *A Handbook of Tibetan Culture: Glossary of Key Tibetan, Buddhist and Sanskrit Terms*. London. Rider

Kakar, S. 1984. *Shamans, Mystics and Doctors*. Mandala Books/Unwin.

Karmay, S. G. 1988. *Secret Visions of the Fifth Dalai Lama*. London. Serindia.

Liebert, G. 1986. *Iconographic Dictionary of the Indian Religions*. Delhi. Sri Satguru.

Monier-Williams, Sir M. 1993. *A Sanskrit-English Dictionary*. Delhi. Motilal Banarsidass.

Nebesky-Wojkowitz, R. 1975. *Oracles and Demons of Tibet*. Graz. Akademische Druck-u. Verlagsanstalt.

Norbu, J. and Turnbull, C. N. 1969. *Tibet: Its History, Religion and People*. London. Chatto and Windus.

Parfionovitch, Y. Dorje, G. & Meyer, F. 1992. *Tibetan Medical Paintings*. (2 vols). London. Serindia.

Sharpa Tulku & Perrott, M. 1987. *A Manual of Ritual Fire Offerings*. Dharamsala. L.T.W.A.

Singh, S.D. 1989. *Ancient Indian Warfare*. Delhi. Motilal Banarsidass.

Snellgrove, D. L. 1980. *The Hevajra Tantra - A Critical Study*. (2 vols.). London. Oxford University Press.

Snellgrove, D.L. 1987. *Indo-Tibetan Buddhism: Indian Buddhists and their Tibetan Successors*. London. Serindia

Svoboda, R. E. 1986. *Aghora: At the Left Hand of God*. Albuquerque. Brotherhood of Life.

Svoboda, R. E. 1993. *Aghora II - Kundalini*. Albuquerque. Brotherhood of Life.

Wade, D. 1982. *Geometric Patterns and Borders*. New York. Van Nostrand Reinhold Co.

Wayman, A. 1990. *The Buddhist Tantras - Light on Indo-Tibetan Esotericism*. Delhi. Motilal Banarsidass.

Williams, C. A. S. 1976. *Outlines of Chinese Symbolism and Art Motives*. New York. Dover.